NORTH-FRANCE
BELGIUM
LORRAINE AND ALSACE

C. B. BLACK

L $^{30}_{176}$

NORTH FRANCE,
BELGIUM, LORRAINE AND ALSACE

CONTINENTAL GUIDES

NORMANDY, BRITTANY, AND TOURAINE, their CELTIC MONUMENTS, ANCIENT CHURCHES, and PLEASANT WATERING PLACES. With a TOUR IN THE CHANNEL ISLANDS. Maps, Plans, and Views. 5s.

NORTH FRANCE, BELGIUM, LORRAINE AND ALSACE. Containing the BATHING STATIONS on the NORTH SEA from DUNKIRK in FRANCE to DOMBURG in HOLLAND, the MINERAL SPRINGS of SPA and AIX-LA-CHAPELLE and those in the VOSGES. Illustrated by 14 Maps and 10 Plans. 5s. This, and the GUIDE to NORMANDY, embrace the territory between NANTES and BREST on the BAY of BISCAY to BASEL and STRASSBURG on the RHINE and form together the

North Half of France.

SOUTH FRANCE—West Half—SUMMER RESORTS. Including the WINTER STATIONS of AMELIE-LES-BAINS, VERNET-LES-BAINS, PAU and MALAGA; the invigorating SEA-BATHING QUARTERS on the BAY of BISCAY, the HEALTH RESTORING SPAS of VICHY and of the PYRENEES and the CLARET WINE VINEYARDS of MEDOC. Illustrated by 8 Maps and 7 Plans. 2s. 6d.

SOUTH FRANCE—East Half—THE RIVIERA. Including CORSICA, the WINTER STATIONS on the MEDITERRANEAN and the cities of TURIN, BOLOGNA, FLORENCE, LUCCA, GENOA, CARRARA, LEGHORN and PISA. Illustrated by 9 Maps and 14 Plans. 5s. These two guides embrace the territory to the south of the LOIRE, from the BAY of BISCAY to TURIN, LUCCA, FLORENCE and LEGHORN, and form together the

South Half of France.

FRANCE—South Half, from the LOIRE to the MEDITERRANEAN, including CORSICA, part of ITALY, and part of SPAIN. Illustrated by 13 Maps and 19 Plans. 7s. 6d.

SWITZERLAND AND THE ITALIAN LAKES, including MILAN, VERONA, and VENICE. Illustrated with numerous Maps. 2s. 6d.

THE RHINE AND ITS BATHS, with a Map of the River. 1s. 6d.

TOURISTS' ROAD AND RAILWAY MAP OF BRITTANY. 1s.

SPAIN AND PORTUGAL, by H. O'SHEA. 15s.

NORTH FRANCE

BELGIUM

LORRAINE AND ALSACE

INCLUDING

THE BATHING STATIONS ON THE NORTH SEA

THE MINERAL WATERS IN THE VOSGES

SPA AND AIX-LA-CHAPELLE

Illustrated by Fourteen Maps and Ten Plans

C. B. BLACK

SECOND EDITION

EDINBURGH
ADAM AND CHARLES BLACK

Printed by R. & R. CLARK, Edinburgh.

PRELIMINARY INFORMATION.

THE LANDING PLACES ON THE FRENCH SIDE OF THE CHANNEL.

THE six principal ports on the French side of the English Channel connected by railroad with Paris are :—

DIEPPE—distant from Paris 125 miles ; passing Clères Junction, 100 m. ; Rouen, 85 m. ; Gaillon, 58 m. ; Mantes Junction, 36 m. ; and Poissy, 17 m. from Paris. Arrives at the station of the Chemins de Fer de l'Ouest, Saint Lazare. Time, 4½ hours. Fares—1st class, 25 fr. ; 2d cl. 19 fr. ; 3d cl. 14 fr.

London to Paris *via* Newhaven and Dieppe (240 miles) :—tidal ; daily, except Sunday, from Victoria Station and London Bridge Station. Fare —1st class, 31s. ; 2d cl. 23s. ; 3d cl. 16s. 6d. Sea journey, 60 miles ; time, 8 hours. Time for entire journey, 16 hours. For tickets, etc., in Paris apply to Chemin de Fer de l'Ouest, Gare St. Lazare, Rue St. Lazare 110, ancien 124. Bureau spécial, agent, M. Marcillet, Rue de la Paix, 7. A. Collin et Cie., 20 Boulevard Saint Denis.

From Dieppe another line goes to Paris by Arques, Neufchatel, Serqueux, Forges-les-Eaux, Gournay, Gisors, and Pontoise. Distance, 105 miles. Time by ordinary trains, 5 hours 10 minutes. Fares—1st class, 21 fr. ; 2d, 15½ fr. ; 3d, 11¼ fr. Arrives at the St. Lazare station of the Chemins de Fer de l'Ouest.

From Tréport a railway extends to Paris by Eu, Gamaches, Aumale, Abancourt, Beauvais, and Creil. Distances, 119¼ miles. Time, 8 hours 40 minutes. Fares—1st class, 24 fr. ; 2d, 18 fr. ; 3d, 13 fr. Arrives at the station of the Chemin de Fer du Nord. There are few through trains by this line.

BOULOGNE—distant 158 miles from Paris ; passing Montreuil, 134 m. ; Abbeville, 109 m. ; Amiens, 82 m. ; Clermont, 41 m. ; and Creil, 32 m. from Paris. Arrives at the station of the Chemin de Fer du Nord, No. 18 Place Roubaix. Time by express, 4½ hours. Fares—1st class, 31 fr. 25 c. ; 2d cl. 23 fr. 45 c. ; 3d cl. 17 fr. 20 c.

London to Paris, *via* Folkestone and Boulogne (255 miles) :—tidal route ; from Charing Cross, Cannon Street, or London Bridge. Express trains daily to Folkestone, and from Boulogne, first and second class. Sea journey, 27 miles ; time of crossing, 1 hour 40 minutes. Fares from London to Paris by Boulogne—1st class, 56s. ; 2d cl. 42s. Time for the entire journey, 10 hours. For tickets, etc., in Paris apply to the railway station of the Chemin de Fer du Nord.

CALAIS—185 miles from Paris; by Boulogne, 158 m.; Montreuil, 134 m; Abbeville, 109 m.; Amiens, 82 m. Clermont, 41 m.; and Creil, 32 m. from Paris. Arrives at the station of the Chemin de Fer du Nord, No. 18 Place Roubaix. Time by express, 5¼ hours. Fares—1st class, 36 fr. 55 c.; 2d cl. 27 fr. 40 c.

London to Paris, *via* Dover and Calais (mail route, distance 283 miles):—departing from Charing Cross, Cannon Street, or London Bridge. Sea journey, 21 miles; time about 80 minutes. First and second class, express. Fares—60s.; 2d cl. 45s. Total time, London to Paris, 10 hours. Luggage is registered throughout from London, and examined in Paris. Only 60 lbs. free. For tickets, etc., in Paris, apply at the railway station of the Chemins de Fer du Nord.

CALAIS—204 miles from Paris; by Saint Omer, 177 m.; Hazebrouck, 165 m.; Arras, 119 m.; Amiens, 82 m.; Clermont, 41 m.; and Creil, 32. Arrives at the station, No. 18 Place Roubaix. Time, 7 hours, 40 minutes. Fares—1st class, 36 fr. 55 c.; 2d cl. 27 fr. 40 c.; 3d cl. 20 fr. 10 c.

DUNKERQUE—190 miles from Paris; by Bergues, 185 miles; Hazebrouck, 165 m., where it joins the line from Calais; Arras, 119 m.; Amiens, 81 m.; Clermont, 41 m.; and Creil, 32 m. Arrives at the station, No. 18 Place Roubaix. Time, 10½ hours. Fares—1st class, 37 fr. 55 c.; 2d cl. 28 fr. 15 c.

England and Channel, *via* Thames and Dunkirk (screw):—tidal; three times a week from Fenning's Wharf. Also from Leith, in 48 to 54 hours.

LE HAVRE—142 miles from Paris; by Harfleur, 138 m.; Beuzeville Junction, 126 miles; Bolbec-Nointot, 123 m.; Yvetot, 111 m.; Rouen, 87 m.; Gaillan, 58 m.; Mantes (Junction), 36 m.; and Poissy, 17 m. from Paris. Arrives, as from Dieppe and Cherbourg, at the station of the Chemin de Fer de l'Ouest, No. 124 Rue St. Lazare. Fares—1st class, 28 fr. 10 c.; 2d cl. 21 fr. 5 c.; 3d cl. 15 fr. 45 c. Time by express, 4 hours 50 minutes, and nearly 3 hours longer by the ordinary trains.

England and Channel, *via* Southampton and le Havre:—Monday, Wednesday, and Friday, 9 p.m. from Waterloo, leaving Southampton 11.45 p.m. Sea journey, 80 m.; time, 8 hours.

CHERBOURG—231 miles from Paris; by Lison, 184 m.; Bayeux, 167 m.; Caen, 149 m.; Mezidon Junction, 134 m.; Lisieux, 119 m.; Serquigny Junction, 93 m.; Evreux, 67 m.; Mantes Junction, 36 m.; and Poissy, 17 m. from Paris. Time by express, 8½ hours; slow trains, nearly 13 hours.

FRENCH, BELGIAN, AND GERMAN RAILWAYS.

On these railways the rate of travelling is slower than in England, but the time is more accurately kept.

To each passenger is allowed 30 kilogrammes, or 66 lbs. weight of luggage free.

PRELIMINARY INFORMATION.

Railway Time-Tables.

Time-tables or Indicateurs. For France the most useful and only official time-tables are those published by Chaix and Cie, and sold at all the railway stations. Of these excellent publications there are various kinds. The most complete and most expensive is the "Livret-Chaix Continental," which, besides the time-tables of the French railways, gives those also of the whole Continent, and is furnished with a complete index; size 18mo, with about 800 pages. The index makes it very easy to consult. The "Livret-Chaix Continental" is sold at the bookstalls. Price 2 fr.

Next in importance is the "Indicateur des Chemins de Fer Français," sold at every station; size, 80 small folio pages, price 60 c.

The great French lines of the "Chemins de Fer de l'Ouest," of the "Chemins de Fer d'Orleans," of the "Chemins de Fer de Paris à Lyon et à la Méditerranée," of the "Chemins de Fer du Nord," and of the "Chemins de Fer de l'Est," have each time-tables of their own, sold at all their stations—Price 40 c. Size 18me. With good index.

For Belgium, the best time-tables are in the "Guide Officiel sur tous les Chemins de Fer de Belgique." Sold at the Belgian railway stations. Size 18me. Price 30 c. It contains a good railway map of Belgium.

For Italy, use L'Indicatore Ufficiale delle Strade Ferrate d'Italia. Containing excellent maps illustrating their circular tours. Price 1 fr. Sold at all the stations. There is also a smaller edition. Price 25 c.

For the Rhine, use Hendschel's Telegraph. Published at Frankfurt am Main. Price 12 groschen. Size, square 12me., 444 pages. This publication is especially adapted for the Rhine and all the S.W. of Germany, and is met with in the booksellers' shops and railway stations of that quarter.

In England consult the Continental Time-tables of the London, Chatham, and Dover Railway, sold at the Victoria Station, Pimlico, price 3d., for Dover to Calais and Queenboro' to Flushing. The Continental Time-tables of the South-Eastern Railway, 1d., for Folkestone or Dover to Boulogne and Ostende. The Continental Time-book of the Great Eastern Railway, 1d., for London and Harwich to Rotterdam and Antwerp. In all are ample instructions about through tickets to distant towns and management of luggage.

In the Railway Station.

Before going to the station it is a good plan to turn up in the index of the "Livret-Chaix Continental" the place required, to ascertain the fare and the time of starting, which stations are supplied with refreshment rooms (marked B), and the time the train halts at each on its way.

On arriving at the station join the single file (queue) of people before the small window (guichet), where the tickets (billets) are sold. Your turn having arrived, and having procured your ticket, proceed to the luggage department, where deposit your baggage and deliver your ticket to be stamped.

After your articles have been weighed, your ticket, along with a luggage receipt, is handed you from the "guichet" of the luggage office, where, if your baggage is not overweight, you pay 10 c. or 2 sous. Before pocketing the luggage ticket, just run your eye down the column headed "Nombre de Colis," and see that the exact number of your articles has been given. The French have a strange way of making their 3s. 5s. and 7s. Whatever is overweight is paid for at this office; but remember, when two or more are travelling together, to present the tickets of the whole party at the luggage department, otherwise the luggage will be treated as belonging to one person, and thus it will probably be overweight. Another advantage of having the entire number of the party on the "Billet de Bagage" is, that in case of one or other losing their carriage tickets, this will prove the accident to the stationmaster (chef-de-Gare), and satisfy him. If, after having purchased a ticket, the train is missed, that ticket, to be available for the next train, must be presented again to the ticket office, to be re-stamped (être visé).

The traveller, on arriving at his destination, will frequently find it more convenient not to take his luggage away with him; in which case, having seen it brought from the train to the station, he should tell the porter that he wished it left there. He retains, however, his luggage ticket, which he only presents when he desires his luggage again.

On the Railway.

In the carriage cast the eye over the line as given in our railway map, and note the junctions; for at many of these—such as Amiens, Rouen, Culoz, Macon, etc. etc.—the passengers are frequently discharged from the carriages and sent into the waiting-rooms to await other trains. On such occasions great attention must be paid to the names the porter calls out, when he opens the door of the waiting-room, otherwise the wrong train may be taken. To avoid this, observe on our railway map what are the principal towns along the line in the direction required to go; so that when, for example, he calls out, "Voyageurs du Coté de Lyon!" and we be going to Marseilles from Macon, we may, with confidence, enter the train, because, by reference to the map, we see we must pass Lyon to reach Marseilles. The little railway map will be found very useful, and ought always to be kept in readiness for reference.

Buffet means refreshment-room, and Salle d'Attente, waiting-room.
There are separate first, second, and third class carriages for ladies.
French express trains have seldom second and third class carriages.

Railway Omnibuses.

At the stations of the largest and wealthiest towns three kinds of omnibuses await the arrival of passengers. They may be distinguished by the names of the General Omnibus, the Hotel Omnibus, and the Private Omnibus. The general omnibus takes passengers to all parts of the town for a fixed sum, rarely above half-a-franc; so that, should the omnibus be full, it is some time till the last passenger gets put down at his destination. The hotel omnibus takes passengers only to the hotel or hotels whose name or names it bears.

CONTENTS.

RAILWAY TABLES.—Mode of procedure in the railway station and on the railway. Railway omnibuses. See beginning of volume.

	PAGE
DOVER AND CALAIS TO PARIS	1

For through tickets by this route to the principal towns on the Continent and for the conveyance and registration of luggage, see the Continental Time-tables of the London, Chatham and Dover Railway.

FOLKSTONE AND BOULOGNE TO PARIS 3

This, the continuation of the above route, passes by and near many places of great interest. The branch line from Etaples passes the castle of Beaurainville, p. 9, where Harold was confined. From Noyelles a short branch line extends to St. Valery, p. 10; whence the fleet of William the Conqueror sailed to England. Fourteen miles from Abbeville is Crecy, p. 11, where the Black Prince "won his spurs." At Amiens, p. 11, is the magnificent cathedral, and 'at Chantilly, p. 15, the famous racecourse. For London and Folkstone to Boulogne consult the Time-tables of the South-Eastern Railway, 1d.; full of useful information.

CALAIS TO PARIS by Hazebrouck and Arras . . . 18
LILLE TO PARIS by Arras and Amiens 21
CALAIS TO BRUSSELS by Lille 22
DUNKERQUE TO PARIS by Hazebrouck and Amiens . . 26
DUNKERQUE TO BRUGES by Dixmude and Cortemarck . . 30
DUNKERQUE TO BRUSSELS by Cortemarck, Roulers, Iseghem, Waereghem, Audenarde and Alost 30
PARIS TO BRUSSELS 31

The direct route, passing by the important junction of Creil; the interesting town of Compiègne with the beautiful castle of Pierrefonds; Noyon with a splendid cathedral and the birthplace of Calvin; Chauny the station for the glassworks of St. Gobain and for the vast ruins of the castle of Coucy-le-Chateau; the important junction of Tergnier, 13 m. from Ham, where Napoleon III. was confined; the manufacturing town of Saint Quentin near which is Peronne, where Louis XI. was confined; Busigny junction whence a branch line extends to Cambrai, where cambric was first manufactured, and Aulnoye the station for the manufacturing town of Valenciennes, the birthplace of Froissart and 7¼ m. N. from the famous mud baths of St. Amand. At Feignies is the French and at Quevy the Belgian custom-house. The most important town passed through in Belgium is Mons, with valuable coal-mines.

CONTENTS.

PAGE

PARIS TO AIX-LA-CHAPELLE AND COLOGNE by Crépy, Soissons, Laon, Hirson, Anor, Chimay, Mariembourg, Hastière, Dinant, Namur, Huy, Liège and Verviers 43

The French portion is of historical and architectural interest; while the Belgian part contains beautiful scenery. Plessis-Belleville is the station at which to alight to visit Ermenonville where J. J. Rousseau spent the last days of his life; Villers-Cotterets is the birthplace of Alexander Dumas père and from it a branch line extends southward to Ferté-Milon where Racine was born; Soissons, the ancient capital of France, contains among many other interesting structures the remains of the once famous abbey of St. Jean-des-Vignes; a little farther is the curious town of Laon on an isolated hill. Belgium is entered at Momignies, whence the picturesque portion of the route commences with the village of Hastière. From Hastière to Liège the rail extends between cliffs by the side of the Meuse, passing Dinant and Namur. A steamer sails between these two towns, but the journey is rather tedious.

PARIS TO AIX-LA-CHAPELLE AND COLOGNE—the direct route . 54

PARIS TO MEZIÈRES-CHARLEVILLE by Chelles, where
Chilperic was assassinated; Meaux containing the tomb of Bossuet; Chateau-Thierry the birthplace of Lafontaine; Epernay one of the great champagne towns; Reims another great champagne town with a splendid cathedral; and Amagne the station for Attigny. . . 55

CHARLEVILLE TO METZ by Sedan 65
From this line ramify roads from Sedan, Carignan, Montmédy and Longwy into some of the most beautiful parts of Belgium.

PARIS TO METZ by Verdun. 72
This is the most direct road to Metz from Paris.

METZ TO STRASSBURG by Falquemont, St. Avold, Saarbrücken, Sarreguemines, Niederbronn and Reichshofen . . . 76
This is the rail to take to visit the battlefields of 1870.

NANCY TO METZ by Frouard and Pont-à-Mousson . . 78

PARIS TO STRASSBURG, LORRAINE AND ALSACE . . . 80
This route after having passed Bar-le-Duc with its currant jam, Commercy with its cheesecakes, Pagny-sur-Meuse near the birthplace of Jeanne d'Arc and Toul with its handsome church, arrives at **Nancy**, the principal town in French Lorraine; whence railways ramify southwards to the baths of Vittel, Contrexéville, Martigny, Bourbonne, Plombières and Luxeuil: and south-east, to the lovely valleys of Alsace in the Vosges mountains. Good beer is sold at nearly all the stations between Nancy and Strassburg. On entering Germany luggage is examined at Deutsch-Avricourt.

PARIS TO BASEL by Troyes, Chaumont, Langres, Vesoul, Belfort and Mülhausen 94
From Chalindrey (p. 96) a line extends N.E. passing the mineral water establishments of Martigny, Contrexeville and Vittel with springs having a reputation for the cure of stone. From Vitry (p. 97) a short branch line extends to Bourbonne with intensely saline springs. From Port d'Atelier (p. 99) a line extends to the baths of Plombières and the hot salt-water baths of Luxeuil. From Belfort a railway (106) extends to Basel by Porentruy without traversing German territory.

BELFORT TO BASEL by Delle and Porentruy . . . 105

PAGNY-SUR-MEUSE TO NEUFCHATEAU, or a visit to the country of Jeanne d'Arc; where she spent her early days . . . 106

CONTENTS.

NORTH ALSACE.

	PAGE
EXCURSIONS FROM STRASSBURG	93
SAINT DIÉ TO SAINTE MARIE-AUX-MINES or Markirch by coach, and thence to Schlettstadt and Strassburg by rail	110
SAINT DIÉ TO ROTHAU by coach, and thence to Schirmeck, Mutzig, Molsheim and Strassburg by rail	110

All the above routes lead through the charming wooded valleys of the Vosges mountains. From Schlettstadt the Hohen-Königsburg is visited.

SOUTH ALSACE.

REMIREMONT TO CORNIMONT by rail 111
    Thence by coach to La Bresse, whence Gérardmer is 7½ m. North.

EPINAL TO GÉRARDMER by rail 112
    From Gerardmer by private conveyance over the Schlucht Pass to Münster 20 m. E. From Munster descend by rail through the "smiling" valley of the Fecht to Colmar 12 m. E. Colmar is 42 m. S. by rail from Strassburg. Between Munster and Colmar are Sulzbach with its refreshing chalybeate springs; Türkheim with its good wine; and the Trois-Epis, a pleasant mountain village in a pine forest, with pine-wood vapour baths.

REMIREMONT TO SAINT MAURICE by rail 114
    From St. Maurice diligence to Wesserling 11 m. E., passing Bussang with its sparkling tonic waters and the Source of the Moselle. From St. Maurice the ascent is made of the Ballon d'Alsace. From Wesserling rail to Mülhausen 21 m. E. by the valley of the Thur, passing Weiler, the best place whence to commence the ascent of the Ballon Gebweiler, the highest of the Vosges mountains; and Thann, the principal town in the valley.

CERNAY TO SENTHEIM, 9 m. S. by rail 115
    Whence 4 m. by omnibus up the Dollerthal to the quaint town of Masmünster. 4 m. farther up by omnibus is Oberbrück, another of the villages whence the Ballon d'Alsace is ascended. From the Dollerthal ramify many beautiful smaller valleys.

BOLLWEILER TO GEBWEILER, 4½ m. N.W. by rail . . 116
    Nearly 4 m. N. by the ruins of the castle of Hugstein (built in 1216) and the valley of the Rothbach, is Murbach, whence the ascent and descent of the Ballon Gebweiler may be made in 7 hours.

ROUTES THROUGH ALSACE INTO SWITZERLAND.

STRASSBURG TO BASEL 116
    This railway, extending between the west bank of the Rhine and the Vosges mountains, has several branch lines into Alsace.

PARIS TO BASEL by Dijon and Besançon 120
    From Besançon a new railway extends 11 m. E. to Locle, within a few miles by rail of Neuchatel.

PARIS TO NEUCHATEL by Dijon, Mouchard and Pontarlier . 126

POLIGNY TO NYON on Lake Geneva 127
    By diligences, passing Champagnole, Morillon, St. Laurent and Morez.

PARIS TO GENEVA by Dijon, Bourg and Culoz . . . 129

BELLEGARDE TO BOURG by Lake Nantua 130
    At Bellegarde the Rhone disappears. At Bourg, in the church of Brou, are mausoleums of rare beauty. Bourg is 27 m. N.E. from Lyons.

MAPS AND PLANS.

MAPS AND PLANS OF NORTH FRANCE, LORRAINE AND ALSACE.

	PAGE
AMIENS	12
BOULOGNE	4
COLOGNE	54
METZ	70
NANCY	83
NORTH ALSACE. From Strassburg to Colmar	85
SOUTH ALSACE. From Colmar to Porentruy	104

These two maps show the roads from France across Alsace and the Vosges mountains to the railway in the valley of the Rhine.

NORTH FRANCE AND BELGIUM, showing the connection by railway between the two countries	1
PARIS TO LORRAINE, ALSACE AND SWITZERLAND, showing all the entrances from France into Lorraine, Alsace and Switzerland	76
REGION OF THE MINERAL WATERS IN THE VOSGES, showing the relative position between the baths of Bains, Bourbonne, Contrexéville, Luxeuil, Martigny, Plombières and Vittel	97
REIMS	60
STRASSBURG	89

APPROACHES TO BELGIUM.

                                                                                      PAGE

LONDON TO OSTENDE *via* DOVER 133
    By the London, Chatham and Dover Railway or the South Eastern Railway; whose trains run in connection with the Dover and Ostende boats. Passengers at Ostende step from the steamer into the railway carriage. The General Steam Navigation Co. steamers sail from London to Ostende. This is a cheaper way, but not so convenient.

LONDON TO ANTWERP *via* HARWICH 266
    By the Great Eastern Railway (see their Time-tables, 1d.) or by the London, Leith and Hull steamers.

LONDON TO FLUSHING *via* QUEENBORO' 293
    By the London, Chatham and Dover Railway. From Flushing trains to Rotterdam, Antwerp and Brussels.

LONDON TO ROTTERDAM *via* HARWICH 296
    By the Great Eastern Railway. By the arrangements of this Company, travellers can pass through Rotterdam without further expense.

BRUGES TO OSTENDE, BLANKENBERG, HEYST AND GHENT . 135
    The pleasant quiet town of Bruges is within an easy visiting distance of the three great sea-bathing stations of Belgium and also of the historical and art-city of Ghent.

BRUGES TO DUNKERQUE 153
    By some quaint Flemish towns and the newer bathing stations of Nieuport and La Panne.

GHENT 155
    Occupying a central point between Brussels, Antwerp, Ostende and Courtrai.

BRUSSELS 169
    Situated at the convergent point of the Belgian railway system.

BRUSSELS TO THE VILLAGE OF WATERLOO . . . 201
    To visit the Field of the Battle of Waterloo it is much better to continue in the train to the station of Braine l'Alleud, as at Waterloo there is very little to see; and, if on foot, a great deal of time is lost on the hard and often dusty road from Waterloo to the Lion-Mound. A coach leaves Brussels every morning for the field and is back in time for dinner.

BRUSSELS TO BRAINE L'ALLEUD by train 204
    Those unable to walk can at this station take the omnibus to the hotel at the Lion-Mound; whence the whole field may be surveyed. The better way is, from the station to walk to Hougoumont, then across the fields to La Belle-Alliance and thence to the Lion-Mound by the Haye-Sainte.

CONTENTS.

	PAGE
SKETCH OF THE BATTLES OF LIGNY AND QUATRE-BRAS	211
BRUSSELS TO ANTWERP by Vilvorde and Malines	216

From Vilvorde station it is easy to visit the chateau of the Three Towers near Perck; where Teniers the younger painted so many of his landscapes. To visit the country residence of Rubens, the chateau Steen, it is necessary to alight at the next station, Epeghem. Those who come to Antwerp merely for the day, should, on arriving, take the tram opposite the station, whence it runs down the long Boulevard, and alight at the Place Verte, between the Post-Office and the Cathedral. If the object, however, be to visit the London, Hull or Leith steamers, remain in the tram to its terminus, whence walk down by the river-side.

BRUSSELS TO PARIS by Hal, Jurbise, Mons, Aulnoye, Busigny and Tergnier—the direct road 221

BRUSSELS TO LILLE and thence to Calais by Hal, Ath and Tournay 224
 At Baisieux is the French custom-house.

BRUSSELS TO LUXEMBOURG by Louvain, Liège, Pepinster and Spa 229
 This is not the direct road to Luxembourg.

PEPINSTER TO SPA 241

SPA TO LUXEMBOURG 245
 Through a beautiful country, partly by the valleys of the Woltz and Alzette.

LIÈGE TO MARLOIE 247
 By the picturesque banks of the Ourthe.

GIVET TO NAMUR by Dinant 248
 Either the rail or the steamer may be taken between Dinant and Namur. The boat goes slowly.

NAMUR TO LIÈGE by Huy 251
 The line follows the course of the Meuse.

BRUSSELS TO LUXEMBOURG, the direct line, by Ottignies, Namur, Marloie, Marbehan and Arlon, with entrances into France . 252

LUXEMBOURG TO TRÈVES 260

TRÈVES TO COBLENCE 262
 Either by rail or by the Moselle steamer.

CHARLEROI 264
 The centre of the most industrial part of Belgium.

TAMINES TO METTET 265

CHARLEROI TO CHARLEVILLE by the Sambre and the Meuse . 265
 A most picturesque route.

CHARLEROI TO BRUSSELS 266

ANTWERP 266

ANTWERP TO AIX-LA-CHAPELLE by Lierre, Hasselt and Maestricht 291

ANTWERP TO DÜSSELDORF by Herenthals and Gladbach . 292

ROTTERDAM 296
 A pleasant short trip may be taken to Schiedam.

ROTTERDAM TO ANTWERP AND BRUSSELS . . . 302

MAPS AND PLANS OF BELGIUM.

	PAGE
ANTWERP	268
BATHING STATIONS ON THE NORTH SEA	154

Extending from Dunkerque in France to Domburg in Holland. The most frequented are those in Belgium.

BRUGES 138

Well situated for frequenting the bathing stations.

BRUSSELS 170

CENTRAL BELGIUM AND WATERLOO-TOWNS . . 212

Showing the relative position of the most industrious towns and a portion of picturesque Belgium. Also all the towns connected with the Battle of Waterloo.

FLUSHING TO ROTTERDAM AND THE HAGUE. Brussels and Antwerp are easily approached by way of Flushing . . 295

Ghent 156
Liège 235
Ostende 133
Rotterdam 297
Spa, environs of 242
Waterloo, Field of 204

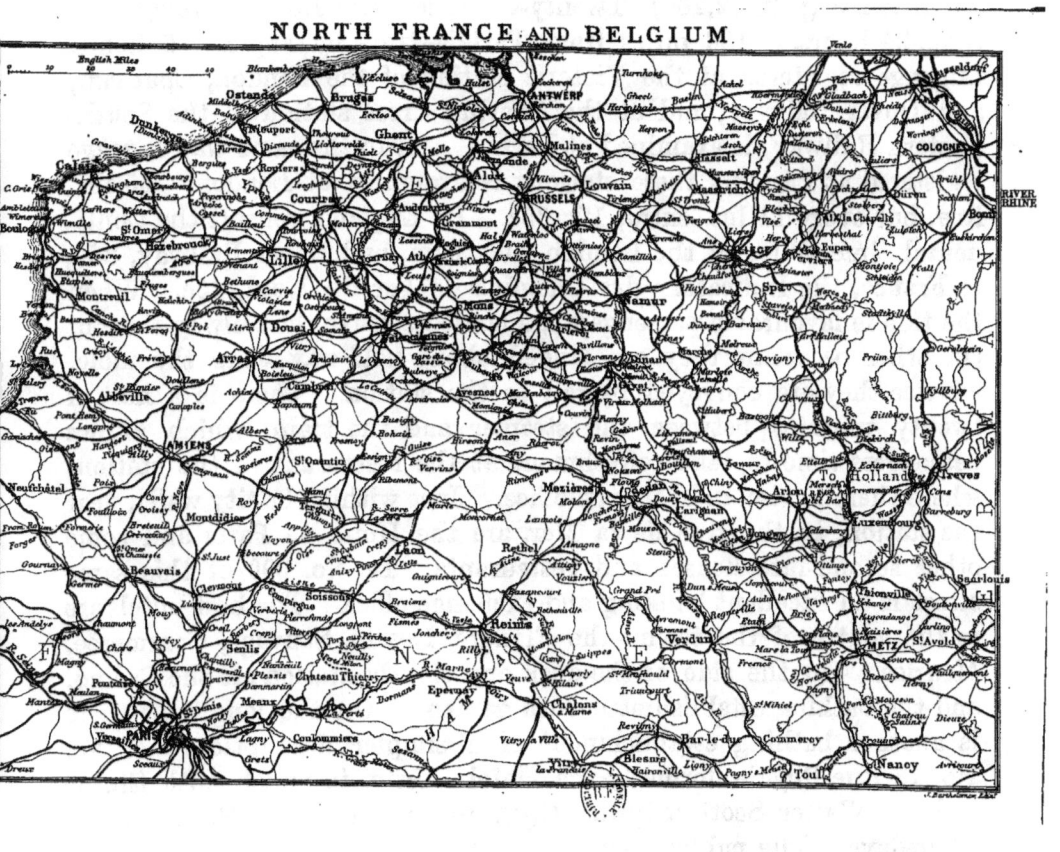

Dover and Calais to Paris.
Folkestone and Boulogne to Paris.

See accompanying Map.

CALAIS MILES FROM   **Dover and Calais to Paris.**   PARIS MILES TO 186

CALAIS (pop. 12,160). Twenty-one miles from Dover—average time, 2¼ hours. 186 miles from Paris — time by express, 5 hours. Luggage registered at the Victoria station of the London, Chatham, and Dover Railway, and at the Charing Cross station of the South-Eastern Railway, is examined at Paris. And in the same way luggage registered at Paris for these stations is examined at London. 55 lbs. free, but every 11 lbs. extra, 1fr. 65c. In England consult the Continental time-tables of the London, Chatham, and Dover Railway, 3d.; in France, the Indicateur des Chemins de Fer du Nord, 40c. When the tide is favourable passengers are landed close to the railway station. On other occasions they are landed about half way along the mole, whence they are conveyed by rail to the station. There is a halt of twenty minutes between the steamer and the train, which allows passengers time to take refreshment at the restaurant of the station, where there is also an exchange-office. Just within the city walls, near the station, in the Rue de la Mer, are the Hotel de Paris and some other second-rate houses and restaurants. In No. 390 of this same street is an excellent banking and exchange office. The best hotels are in the centre of the town—the Flandre, Dessin, Sauvage, Commerce, Meurice. On the side of the dock opposite the station are the Casino, and the bathing establishment with gardens. On the long mole there is another bathing establishment of a simpler description. *Musée*, No. 18 Rue Royale, formerly the Hotel Dessin, in which both Sterne and Sir Walter Scott lodged. Open to the public on Sundays and Thursdays. The public library is in the Hotel de Ville.

As the traveller approaches Calais from the sea the principal objects which present themselves to his view are—the lighthouse, rising in front of the Courgain or fishermen's suburb to the height of 180 feet, ascended by 253 steps; the tower of the parish church Notre Dame; the Tour de Guet, an old watch-tower built in the 14th century; and close to it the fine belfry of the Hotel de Ville. On the mole, not far from the station, stands a column commemorating the return of the Bourbons and the landing of Louis Philippe at this spot in 1844. In the Place d'Armes is the Hotel de Ville, built in the 18th century, but the belfry

| CALAIS MILES FROM | CALAIS. ARDRES. BALINGHEM. | PARIS MILES TO |

was built in 1609. On the balcony in front is a bust of Eustache St. Pierre Standing by themselves on pedestals are busts of Cardinal Richelieu, the founder of the citadel and arsenal of Calais, and of the Duc de Guise (Le Balafré), who, as a large picture in the north transept of the church of Notre Dame relates, "Sous le règne de Henri II., le VII. Janvier MDLVIII., les troupes françaises commandées par Fr. de Lorraine, Duc de Guise, reprennent Calais sur les Anglais et conservent la ville au Catholicisme." This church of Notre Dame is directly southeast from the Hotel de Ville by the Rue des Boucheries, and was built in the 14th century. The high altar is of marble, with ornaments of alabaster. The painting on the reredos is by Seghers. To the right of the principal entrance is rather a curious Entombment. The best dwelling-houses are situated along the pleasant promenade called the Cours du Sud, sheltered by the ramparts, on which are walks commanding views of the sea.

A few yards south from the church are the Public Gardens, where the band plays on Sundays and Thursdays. Walking along these gardens westwards, and passing through the fortifications by the first gate, we find ourselves on the high road to St. Pierre. Here, on a rectangular piece of ground planted with trees, just beyond the outworks of the fortifications, was interred Emma Harte (Lady Hamilton), whom Lord Nelson so touchingly recommended to the care of Captain Hardy in his last moments. She died in extreme destitution, and was buried, through the kindness of an English lady, in this piece of ground, at that time her garden. Lady Hamilton lived in the Rue Française.

12 CAFFIERS, with coal pits in the neighbourhood. Three miles 174 distant in the forest a pyramid marks the spot where the aëronauts Blanchard and Jeffreys arrived from England in 1785. From the station a coach runs to Guines, 2½ miles distant. Guines (pop. 4400). *Inn:* Ville de Calais. Famous for draught horses. Two and a half miles distant on the road to Ardres is Balinghem. Also approached by the Calais and Hazebrouck Railway, where stop at the Ardres station, 7 miles from Calais; then other 3 miles in omnibus to the town of Ardres (pop. 2200). *Inns:* Debruyne; Lion d'Argent. From Ardres, Balinghem is 2¼ miles by the road to Guines, the length of the third kilometre stone; whence take the first road to the right. If approached from Guines, take the road to Ardres the length of the fourth kilometre stone; whence take the first road to the left.

The famous interview between Francis I. and Henry VIII. in 1520 took place at Balinghem. The pavilions of the monarchs were draped

| CALAIS MILES FROM | AMBLETEUSE. WISSANT. | PARIS MILES TO |

with cloth of golden tissue, which gave the well-known designation to this place. Cardinal Wolsey was master of the ceremonies, and Queen Catherine was present with all her ladies. Two fountains ran with claret and malmsey wine. Nearly 6000 persons and 4325 horses were assembled at this interview between the two "loving brothers," for which, almost a year beforehand, 2000 English workmen were sent over to make preparations in scaffolding, towers, and pageants.

17 RINXENT MARQUISE, the station for Marquise (pop. 4090; *Inn:* Grand Cerf), with marble quarries. From Marquise a road leads N.W. by Bazinghen to Cape Gris-Nez, 19 miles from Dover pier, crowned with a lighthouse 164 feet high. Directly W. from Marquise, or on the coast road between Gris-Nez and Wimereux, is Ambleteuse (pop. 900), where James II., disguised as a coachman, landed on January 5, 1689. The village of Wissant, 4 miles N. from Gris-Nez, is supposed by some to be the Portus Itius of the Romans, where Cæsar embarked for the conquest of Britain on Saturday the 26th of August, 55 B.C.; but Mr. T. Lewin, in his "Invasion of Britain by Julius Cæsar," gives Boulogne (Gesoriacus) as the site of his embarkment; and Napoleon III., in the "Histoire de Jules César," vol. ii. p. 201, *et seq.*, after deep research and mature consideration, arrives at the same conclusion. Cæsar left Britain on the 18th September, 55 B.C., and arrived at Gesoriacus next day. The following year Cæsar again sailed for Britain, and having subjugated the island returned to Gesoriacus. 169

25 WIMEREUX. Station for the Boulogne race-course, and 3 miles N. from Boulogne. The steeple-chases are run in the valley between Wimereux and Wimille. N. from Wimereux, at the Pointe aux Oies, opposite the race-course, Prince Louis Napoleon landed on 6th August 1840. 161

26 WIMILLE, pop. 2400. The village, on the Wimereux, is nearly a mile inland from the station. In the cemetery are buried the aeronauts Romain and Pilatre de Rosier, whose balloon, when at an elevation of 3600 feet, while attempting to cross the Channel on the 15th of June 1785, caught fire, and they were precipitated to the ground. An obelisk marks the spot where the bodies were found. 160

Boulogne to Paris.

28 BOULOGNE-SUR-MER, pop. 3970. Thirty miles from Folkestone—average time, a little over 2 hours. 158 miles from Paris —time by express, 4 hours 10 min. Luggage registered at Charing 158

BOULOGNE—LANDING REGULATIONS—HOTELS.

Cross is examined at Paris; 55 lbs. free. The day mail steamers between Folkestone and Boulogne of the South-Eastern Railway Company arrive at and sail from the extremity of the Quai Bonaparte on the west side of the port, where railway carriages await passengers and convey them and their luggage (if registered) directly to Paris. Opposite the landing place is a good restaurant, and by the side of one of the doors a post-office letter-box. Adjoining is a branch custom-house, chiefly for luggage. The *night mails* of the same company and the London and Thames boats start from the opposite quay, the Quai des Paquebots, on the eastern side of the port. An omnibus conveys the passengers and luggage, at the expense of the company, from the train to the boats and *vice versa*. For London, Folkestone, and Boulogne, see the Continental Time-tables of the South-Eastern Railway, 1d.

Hotels.—On the beach fronting the sea, *H. du Pavillon, and the H. Imperial des Bains de Mer. Fronting the Casino gardens, the custom-house and the Quai des Paquebots, the *Brighton and Marine Hotel in a capital situation. More towards the custom-house, Berry's Family Hotel, and the Bedford. Then follow in succession the Folkestone; Globe; Paris, Boulogne, and Albion; Windsor; and L'Europe. Farther up, opposite the statue of Jenner and the Fishmarket, is the large Hotel des Bains, and behind it, in the Rue de l'Ecu, the Angleterre. Most conveniently situated in the Place Frederic Sauvage, at the town end of the bridge, is the *H. Christol. On the other side of the bridge, close to the station, the Louvre; Castiglione; Gare. In the Rue de l'Ecu, the first street parallel to the port, are the Univers; Londres; Meurice; Nord; and the bank of Adam et Cie. In this street are also the best money-changers. The rate of exchange is displayed in their windows. In the Rue Neuve Chaussée, the street above the Ecu and parallel to it, are the Commerce; the Lion d'Argent; and the best cafés. About the middle of the Grande Rue, opposite the museum, the H. Dervaux. In the high town, No. 11 Rue de Lille, the H. de Bourgogne, a small family hotel. Near the mole, the Casino and the Etablissement des Bains, with a long row of bathing machines. There are besides numerous boarding houses (pensions).

Public Library, Museum and Picture Gallery in the Grande Rue. The Library is closed only on Fridays and during the vacation. Merridew, bookseller and publisher, 60 Rue de l'Ecu, has an excellent local guide and a circulating library containing a well-assorted collection of British and foreign publications.

English Churches.—Trinity Church, Rue de la Lampe; British

BOULOGNE

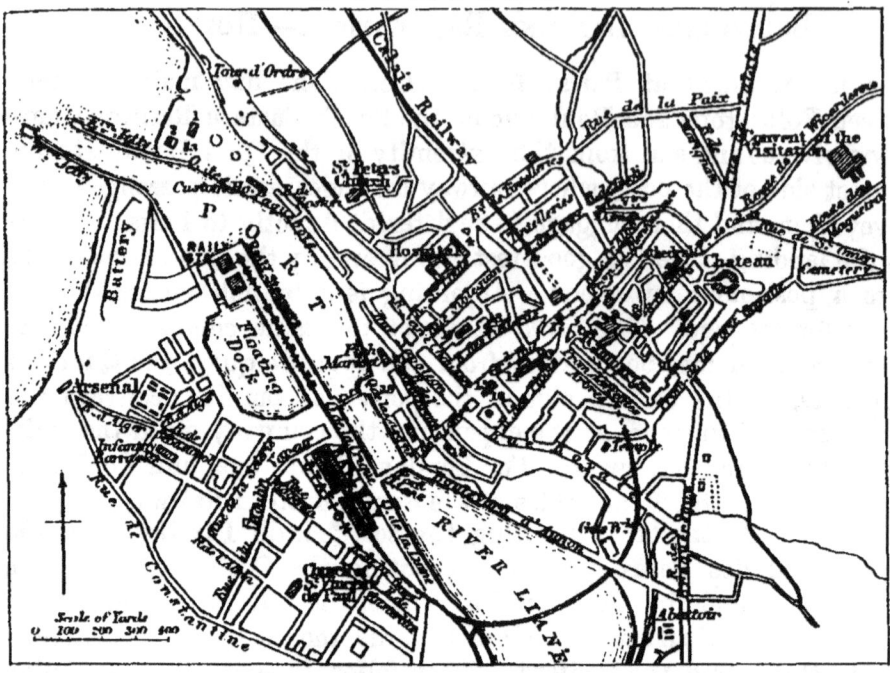

EXPLANATION OF PLATE.

FROM the wharf on the west side of the Port, marked "Railway Steamers," the Folkestone day steamers arrive and sail. The small branch railway conveys passengers and their luggage to and from the railway station. One of the houses opposite the landing-place contains the waiting and refreshment rooms. The other contains a custom-house, principally for luggage, and the office of the London and South-Eastern Railway Company.

The Folkestone night-boats and the Thames and London boats leave from the opposite wharf, the Quai des Paquebots, near the custom-house and the principal hotels. The Hotel du Pavillon is quite close, but the Hotel Christol is up at No. 19, fronting the first bridge. From the Pont Liane, the bridge higher up, a steep street, the Grande Rue, leads up to the Hauteville, surrounded with ramparts. Half-way up, right hand, No. 14, is the Museum. On the highest parts of the Hauteville are the Cathedral and the Chateau.

On the eminence rising from the vicinity of the eastern jetty Nos. 1, 2 and 3 indicate the Etablissement, including Baths, Aquarium, and Skating Rink ; 4 Place Navarin ; 5 Rue Wissocq ; 7 Palais de Justice ; 8 Mairie ; 9 Convent : 10 Place Godefroi ; 11 Porte Gayolle ; 12 Sous Prefecture ; 13 College ; 15 St. Nicholas ; 16 Market Place ; 17 Theatre ; 18 English Churches ; 19 The Place Frédéric Sauvage.

LUGGAGE—CAB FARES.   GESORIACUS.

Episcopal, No. 9 Rue du Temple; St. John's, No. 137 Rue Royale; Upper-town Church, Rue St. Martin; Wesleyan Church, Rue de l'Ancienne Comedie; English Roman Catholic service held in St. Nicholas in the Grande Rue.

Luggage for Boulogne must be examined at the custom-house. Commissionaires charge for passing articles through ½ fr. for one; above that number, 25 c. each; hat-boxes, bags, and haps free. The women who act as porters have to give a printed receipt. Landing baggage and conveying to residence any package under 24 lbs. weight, 60 c.; above that weight, each 1 fr. The delivery of the baggage *at the street door* is the accomplishment of *the porterage*. Porterage upstairs is subject to a small gratuity.

Cabs.—From 6 A.M. to midnight, for the course, 1 horse, 1 fr. 50 c.; per hour, 1 horse, 2 fr.; per hour, two horses, 2 fr. 50 c. From midnight to 6 A.M., for the course, 2 fr. 50 c.; per hour, 2 fr. 50 c. In the country, by the hour, 2 fr. 50c.

Passengers from Boulogne to Dunkerque, or *vice versa*, must change at the St. Pierre station of Calais. At Dunkerque, in the town, are the Hotels Chapeau Rouge and Flandre. Opposite the station the Belle Vue. Steamers for Hull, London, and Leith.

Boulogne, at the mouth of the river Liane, is one of the most pleasant towns in France. The Rue de la Lampe, and its continuation the Grande Rue, lead from the E. end of the station bridge up to the Promenade de la Bienfaisance. To the right of this Promenade is the Porte des Dunes, the entrance into the Haute Ville, containing the Hotel de Ville, the Cathedral, and the Château. The Haute Ville, on an eminence, occupies the site of the town founded B.C. 50 by Quintius Pedius, whom Cæsar on his departure for Rome had left in charge of this division of Belgic Gaul called Morinia, covered at that time with swamps and forests. The little Roman settlement designated at first Gesoriacus took afterwards the name of the new city, which Quintius Pedius called Bononia after his native town. The French Bononia has now become Boulogne and the Italian Bologna.

In the Grande Rue, about half way up to the Haute Ville, is the building containing the Museum and Public Library. The latter contains 41,000 vols. and some 300 MSS., of which the most valuable are the Missal used formerly by the Bishops of Boulogne at Rome, a ninth cent. Gospel of St. Matthew, a tenth cent. Psalter, and the oldest copy known of Bede's Homilies. Open from 10 to 4. The Museum, open from 10 to 4 every day (except Tuesday) from 1st June to 1st Nov., and on Sundays and Thursdays from 2d Nov. to 31st May. In the Natural History section the fossils of the neighbourhood are well represented. Among them are a magnificent Plesiosaurus dolichoderus and a rare Spathobathia named Bononia by the discoverer. In the Egyptian department is one of the finest mummies in Europe, the dried body of Nes-month, who, 3500 years ago, was the keeper of the sacred bark of the god Ammon. "The brilliant colouring and the forcible variety of scenes painted on the double wooden case in which this high personage is enclosed, make it a most perfect specimen of Egyptian art and archæology. Notice the rich assemblage of emblems, sacred beetles, mortuary statuettes, the linen bands in which he was swathed after embalmment, also the mummy of a cat, and the emblematic representation of the god Anubis under the figure of a dog. There are also a valuable series of Merovingian jewellery in gold, enamel, glass, and precious stones found in the district; several oak and ivory carvings, and a low relief oak carving of the Last Judgment, containing upwards of fifty figures; a very rare earthen '*couvrefeu;*' a rich collection of coins and medals, and more particularly a large set of *monnaies obsidionales,* or tokens struck in besieged towns."— *Merridew.* Among the latter is the medal struck by Napoleon in 1804, which he intended for London. It bears the inscription "Frappé á Londres, 1804," "Descente en Angleterre," with the device of a man being carried off. The picture gallery contains 200 paintings, of which the most interesting are those illustrative of the visit paid by Queen Victoria in August 1855 to Napoleon III., when she was accompanied by Prince Albert, the Prince of Wales, and the Princess-Royal.

At the top of the Grande Rue is the Sous-Prefecture, and in the garden before it a bust by David of Henri II., who in 1550 ransomed Boulogne from the English. Then follow the delightful Promenade de la Bienfaisance and the no less pleasant retreat called the Tintelleries. Through the Porte des Dunes, built in 1231, is the *Haute Ville,* within lofty ramparts 440 yards from east to west and 335 from north to south. The large edifice in the Place Godefroi de Bouillon is the Hotel de Ville, 1784, supposed to occupy the site of the palace in which Godfrey of Bouillon was born 1066. Attached to it is the belfry, 13 cent., a massive square tower becoming octagonal, 104 feet high. At the S.E. angle of the ramparts is the Chateau, now barracks. It is an ugly circular building (13th cent.), supported by six attached towers, in which Napoleon III. was shut up (6th Aug. 1840), after attempting in vain to raise an insurrection in his favour. Near the Hotel de

CAMPBELL. CATHEDRAL. CRYPT—CEMETERY.

Ville, in the House No. 5 Rue St. Jean, died the poet Campbell on the 15th of June 1844. He was buried in Westminster Abbey. Le Sage died on the 17th Nov. 1747, aged 80 years, in a house which stood upon the site occupied by No. 3 Rue du Chateau.

On the highest part of the Haute Ville stands the Cathedral, built in 1869 on the foundations of the church erected in 1104 by Ida, mother of Godfrey of Bouillon, and of another erected in 1624, which was destroyed in 1791, and the remains sold seven years afterwards for £20,420. The present church owes its existence to the Abbé Haffreingue, who died in 1871, and now reposes in the crypt he himself discovered in 1827. Part of this crypt may belong to the first church, but by far the greater portion is probably due to Ida, Countess of Boulogne. The first church was built in the 7th cent. for a miracle-working image, which continued to display itself in the principal church of Boulogne till 1587, when the Huguenots, after trying in vain to burn it, hid it under a heap of manure. After sundry other mishaps the image was restored to the cathedral in 1630, but in 1791 the revolutionists got hold of it and threw it into a bonfire, where it was entirely consumed excepting one of the hands, which Cazin de Caumartin had managed to cut off and thus saved. This hand is now enclosed in a silver-gilt heart suspended on the new image of the Virgin in the highly-decorated apsidal chapel of the choir. The church is in the form of a Latin cross 320 feet long, extending from S.W. to N.E. The ceiling is throughout double, the lower one being open and the upper painted in fresco. Over the choir rises the great dome to the height of 300 feet, ascended by 325 steps, and surmounted by a colossal image of the Virgin by Bonnassieux, seen from a great distance.

From the top is a good view of the Colonne de la Grand Armée now called La Colonne Napoleon, nearly two miles distant (see page 110). The altar below the dome is of most costly marbles, and was made in Rome, and presented to the church by Prince Torlonia. The twelve figures on the panels are exquisite mosaics, and the twenty surrounding colonnettes are of malachite.

Below is the crypt, 315 feet long by 140 wide. It contains some mural paintings, a group of statues representing our Lord and his Apostles on the Mount of Olives, and a few antiquarian curiosities. Fee to visit the crypt, 1 franc; and 1 franc to ascend to the top of the dome. The respective entrances are on the opposite sides of the church.

Beyond the cathedral, by the Porte de Calais and the St. Omer road, is the large Cemetery, in which are interred a considerable num-

BOULOGNE. JETTIES. COLONNE NAPOLEON.

ber of English; among others are Catherine, Countess of Dundonald, wife of Admiral Cochrane; and Captain W. Tune, who for many years commanded the first steamer between London and Boulogne.

From the Quai Bonaparte, on the W. side of the Port, the western jetty extends 2196 feet, with a small lighthouse at the extremity. On the western side are the smooth sands of Capécure. From the Quai des Paquebots, on the E. side of the Port, the eastern jetty extends 1938 feet (a delightful promenade), with a small lighthouse at the extremity; while at the land end are the handsome Casino, having on one side a large bathing-establishment and on the other an aquarium amidst an artistic group of rocks. A pleasant road (the Boulevard Ste. Beuve) extends northwards between the cliffs and the sea. Opposite the Casino gardens a steep road leads up to the fishermen's quarter, where the most conspicuous object is the Church of St. Pierre des Marins, with a "much reverenced" Calvary; while northwards are the crumbling brick walls of the lighthouse, Turris ardens (corrupted to Tour d'Ordre), built A.D. 40 by Caligula, when encamped on this plain at the head of 100,000 men to invade Britain. From 1798 to 1804 this same plain, the Camp de Droite, was again occupied by an army of 120,000 under Napoleon, with the same intention. During Napoleon's visits to the camp he occupied a small hut which was erected near the Tour d'Ordre. During one of these visits Napoleon, seated on the throne of Dagobert, made the first distribution of the decorations of the Legion of Honour. An obelisk marks the spot. Near this is the Colonne Napoleon, of which the foundation stone was laid in 1804 by Marshal Soult, but the monument was not completed till August 1841. It cost £61,120, is 166 feet high, is built of marble from the quarries near Marquise, and is surmounted by a bronze statue of the Emperor in his robes, by Bossio. Fee to ascend, ½ fr. The view extends into the county of Kent.

In 1865, on the quay near the Hotel Christol, the French erected a statue in honour of the great philanthropist Dr. Jenner, who in 1796 introduced vaccination into England. Into France it was introduced by Drs. Woodville and Nowell, who on the 18th of June 1800 performed the first operation on a family in the Rue des Pipots of this city.

HESDIGNEUL, branch to St. Omer, 35 miles east.

ETAPLES (pop. 2900). *Inns*: H. Lion d'Or; Chemin de Fer. Rather a pleasant little port at the mouth of the Canche, here crossed by a viaduct 320 yards long. The Church of St. Michel was

| CALAIS | BEAURAIN. | PARIS |
| MILES FROM | | MILES TO |

built in 1004, but the chancel was rebuilt in 1701. The town cemetery occupies the site of the castle built in 1172. Henry VII. signed in this castle the treaty of peace of 1492 with Charles VII. The twin lighthouses of Etaples are each 173 feet high, and their light is seen within a radius of 20 miles.

Junction with branch line to St. Pol-sur-Ternoise, 38½ m. east. The two most interesting places on this branch line are:—

Montreuil-sur-Mer (pop. 4000). *Hotels:* de France et de l'Europe; Londres et Lion d'Argent; Renard d'Or; Cornet d'Or. 7 miles E. from Montreuil and 14 miles E. from Etaples is Beaurain. Those pressed for time should make the Lion d'Or at Etaples their headquarters. The pleasant little town Montreuil, the ancient stronghold of Ponthieu, occupies an eminence which was fortified by Hugues Capet in 981, to which period belongs the Tour du Guet. In the upper town is the church of St. Saulve, almost entirely rebuilt. The Hotel Dieu (1857) contains a beautifully decorated chapel.

Beaurainville (pop. 800). Some small cafés. Along the line, a short way east from the station, is all that remains of the castle in which Count Guy de Ponthieu imprisoned the unfortunate Harold on his arrival from England in 1065. To reach it walk from the station down through the village of Beaurainville to the church (16th cent.), where take the road leading to the right, and on arriving at the railway take the path leading by the side of it past the chateau to the village BEAURAIN. All that remains of the castle are two sides of a tower (fast falling to decay) 20 feet square by 50 high. This tower most probably stood over one of the gateways. The village of Beaurain-chateau is on the Canche, and on both sides of the railway. The church was founded about the same time as the castle. See Black's *Normandy*, page 76.

Twelve and a-half miles east from Beaurain is HESDIN (pop. 3400.) *Inn:* H. de France. A busy manufacturing town on the Canche.

St. Pol-sur-Ternoise (pop. 3800). *Hotels:* Commerce; Angleterre, near the station, situated on a wooded slope rising from the river. It is an important railway junction. Those going into Normandy should take the line to Amiens by Frévent, Doullens, and Canaples. Owing to difference of ownership on this branch line, carriages have to be changed at each of these places. At Frévent the hotel is the Amiens.

Doullens (pop. 4800. *Hotels:* Quatre Frères; Bons Enfants) is the best resting-place. It is situated on the Authie, from which rises the citadel commenced by Francis I., now a prison for females. The church St. Martin, 15th cent., contains elegantly formed vaulting shafts.

52 / 134 — VERTON. Omnibus to Berck, 3 miles S.W. on the sea (pop. 4400). *Hotels:* Berck; Plage. Good sea-bathing. There are two hospitals here for scrofulous children; one belongs to the municipality of Paris, with accommodation for 500, and the other to the Rothschilds.

62 / 124 — RUE (pop. 2460). *Inns:* Voyageurs; Chemin de Fer.

| CALAIS MILES FROM | SAINT VALERY. ABBEVILLE. | PARIS MILES TO |

Church of St. Esprit, 13th, 15th, and 16th cents. ; restored belfry. Coach in summer to Le Crotay (pop. 1800). *Inns:* St. Pierre ; Marine. Good sea-bathing. A small port on the Somme opposite St. Valery, and 5 m. S. from Rue.

69 NOYELLES-SUR-MER. **117** In the neighbourhood of this station the army of Edward III. forded the Somme on Friday the 25th August 1346 on their way to Crecy. A branch line from this station goes to St. Valery-sur-Somme, 4 m. distant, seen distinctly from this station. Coach from Noyelles to Le Crotay.

Saint Valery (pop. 3620), at the mouth of the Somme. Hotel de France ; Etablissement des Bains. Numerous furnished lodgings in the new town and fronting the sea. The new town is about ½ m. from the station, and a little beyond it on a hill is the old town, partially surrounded by its old fortifications, built in the 12th cent. The Tour Harold, however, on the side of the hill, belongs to the 11th cent. On it is a summer-house. The present church, standing on a terrace, dates only from the 13th cent. Both towns are clean and full of pretty cottages. It is a good bathing-station, but offers especially great facilities for boating and fishing. Miles of embanked walks (supplied with seats) stretch along the side of the estuary, and even extend out into the sea. There are also pleasant walks into the country. An inscription at the entrance into the new town states—"De ce port en 1066 Guillaume de Normandie partit à la tête d' une flotte de 400 voiles pour la conquête de l' Angleterre."

77 ABBEVILLE, pop. 18,000. **109** *Hotels:* France, Commerce, Tete de Bœuf. Diligence awaits passengers at this station for Eu on the Bresle, 20½ m. W., fare 4 frs. Coach to Crecy 14 m. N., fare 1½ fr. Rail to Bethune 58½ m. N., passing Saint Riquier 8 m. N. from Abbeville. Coach with two horses to Tréport, 29 frs.

Abbeville is a modernised old town on the Somme, with some good streets, such as the Rue St. Gilles and the Rue des Lingers. In the third street, up the latter—the Rue Minimes or Rue Boucher-de-Perthes—is the Museum of Antiquities, containing Gallo-Roman articles and flint hatchets found in the vale of the Somme.

The Cathedral, St. Vulfran or Wlfran, belongs to the 15-17th cents. The façade, in the florid Gothic style, is flanked by two square buttressed and mullioned towers 170 feet high, rising over the side doorways. To the left, at the transept, is a leaning tower, surmounted by a mitre. The interior does not correspond with the exterior in decoration. The chapels are separated from the aisles by bare walls, with plain window openings. The best walks are on the ramparts.

12 m. from Abbeville, or 10 m. from Noyelles, is the village of

| PARIS MILES TO | CRECY. ST. RIQUIER. | CALAIS MILES FROM |

Crecy (pop. 1630). *Inns:* Canon d'Or; Commerce. On these plains Edward III. encamped his army on the afternoon of Friday the 25th of August 1346, saying: "Let us post ourselves here, for we will not go farther till we have seen our enemies. I have good reason to wait for them on this spot, as I am now upon the lawful inheritance of my lady mother, which was given her as her marriage-portion, and I am resolved to defend it against my adversary, Philippe de Valois." The two armies met on Saturday the 26th of August 1346. The old windmill, from which Edward III. viewed the English army led on by his son, the Black Prince, stands on the eminence just behind the village. It is easily distinguished from the other mills by its massiveness and being of stone. 2 m. from Crecy, by the Fontaine and Noyelles road, a cross indicates the spot where the King of Bohemia was slain.

"There lay upon the field of Crecy two kings, eleven high princes, eighty bannerets, one thousand two hundred knights, and more than thirty thousand private soldiers. The meeting of Edward and his son took place by torchlight after the battle was over. 'Well have you won your spurs!' said the brave king; 'persevere in the career which you have opened, and you will become the brightest honour of the noble kingdom of which you are the worthy heir.' The battle of Crecy was one of the greatest victories ever gained by a King of England, and Edward prepared to avail himself of it in a manner which should produce some permanent advantage."—Sir Walter Scott's *Tales of a Grandfather.*

Eight miles from Abbeville by railway, or 9 m. from Crecy, is St. Riquier, pop. 1000. *Inn:* Ange Gabriel. In this small village is the Church of St. Riquier, built in the 15th and 16th cents. The fine crucifix over the high altar is a *chef-d'œuvre* of Girardon. The frescoes are of the 16th cent., the belfry of the 14th cent.

$87\frac{3}{4}$ LONGPRÉ, pop. 2000, an important junction (see Map, page 1), $98\frac{1}{4}$ $22\frac{1}{2}$ m. S. W. from Doullens, and 36 m. E. from Tréport. The village contains the crypt and portal of the collegiate church founded in 1190.

96 PICQUIGNY (pop. 1400), with a church of the 13th to the 90 15th cents. Ruins of a fortress of the 16th cent. Large turf beds in neighbourhood. 2 m. distant the Roman camp of Tirancourt.

103 AMIENS (pop. 62,000), 76 m. from Boulogne. A large and 83 important station, with good refreshment-rooms. *Post-office*—No. 37 Rue Dumeril, second street south from the Hotel de Ville.

Hotels: The Hotel de *France et d'Angleterre in the Rue des Rabuissons. Pleasantly situated in the Place St. Denis are the Univers and Rhin. Opposite the Univers in the Rue Noyon the Hotel Saisset-Dubois. Near the Hotel de France is the Commerce, frequented

AMIENS. CATHEDRAL—DIMENSIONS.

chiefly by commercial men. Fronting the station are the Hotel de Londres et du Nord, and the Hotel Restaurant de l'Est.

Cabs.—The course, 1 fr.; the hour, 1½ fr. There is a stand just outside the station.

The most important place to visit is the **Cathedral of Notre Dame.** The first stone of this majestic edifice, towering above the whole town, was laid by Evrard de Fouilloy, forty-fifth Bishop of Amiens, in 1220, and was completed during the occupation of Picardy by the English, in the reign of Henry V. of England. It occupies an area of 26,250 square feet. Its greatest length is, from the western to the eastern extremity 469 ft., and 220 ft. at the transept. The nave is 230 ft. long, and the roof 140 ft. above the pavement. One hundred and twenty-six pillars sustain the massive yet graceful arches which carry the triforium gallery, so justly famed for its elegance and beauty. Over the beautifully sculptured portal of the great façade is a brilliant rose window 100 ft. in circumference, flanked by square towers 210 and 180 ft. high, and linked together by richly sculptured galleries. The portal of the south transept is also elaborately ornamented. From the point of intersection of the nave with the transept, rises to the height of 422 ft. the central spire constructed in 1529. To visit the triforium, towers, and spire, apply to the Suisse in the small house by the side of the main entrance. Fee, 1 fr. For a party, ½ fr. each. For the interior no guide is necessary; yet those who desire to have the places shown them should join the party that follows the beadle. Fee, ½ fr. When on the top of the tower, request the man to point out the Promenade de la Hotoire and the fertile market-gardens of the Hortillonnages; when descending, the turret from which Henry IV. watched the Spaniards during the siege in 1597; and when in the triforium, the chain of Spanish iron (14th cent.) to give support to this part of the edifice. 315 steps lead to the top of the tower.

The Interior.—Above main entrance, organ commenced in 1425. 1st chapel *right* St. Christopher's. 2d, chapel of the Annunciation. The relief in marble on the altar is by Blasset. 3d, chapel of the Incarnation. Over the altar is a Madonna in white marble by Blasset. 4th, chapel of St. Etienne. On reredos, painting representing the Assumption At the right side, statue of St. Etienne, and at the left, of St. Augustin, by Blasset. 5th, chapel of St. Marguerite, with statue by Vimeu. (In the nave, fronting the 2d chapel, is the mausoleum of Evrard de Fouilloy; and, on the other side of the nave, that of Gaudefroy d'Eu, who continued the work his predecessor had commenced).

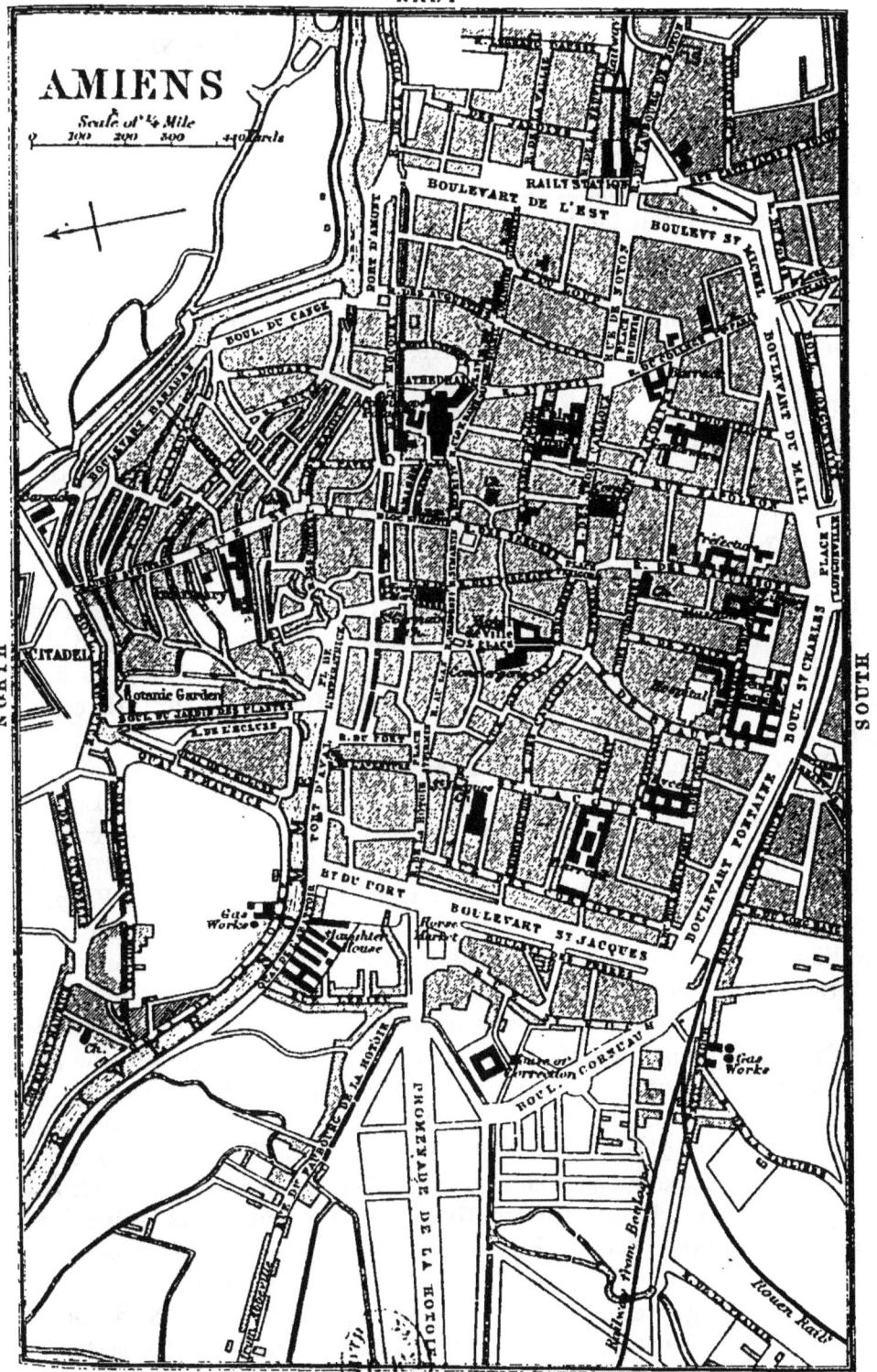

ROSE WINDOWS.   ENFANT PLEUREUR.   SHRINE.

From the 5th chapel enter the south transept, lighted by a splendid rose window of 24 leaves, and 92 ft. in circumference, glowing with 14th cent. glass, of which the predominating hue is red, and represents fire. Opposite in the north transept is a similar rose of 32 leaves of 13th cent. glass, of which the predominating colour is green, and represents air and water. These two and the rose over the main entrance are of great value. The reliefs on the wall of the south transept represent scenes in the history of St. James. On the column in front is the monument to the Canon Claude Pierre, by Blasset; and near it, standing against another column, is the chapel of Notre Dame du Puy, entirely by Blasset. The reredos, painting representing the "Assumption," is by Franken, 1628.

Now enter the choir, south side. 1st chapel right, Chapel of St. Peter and Paul, with statues by Dupuis. Opposite, on screen of sanctuary, admirably sculptured figures in relievo (15th cent.) representing incidents in the lives of St. Firmin and St. Salve. 2d, nothing remarkable. 3d, door to sacristy. Over this door are two busts in stone, the portraits of the couple who gave the ground on which the church is built. 4th chapel, St. François d'Assise. 5th chapel, the Sacré Cœur. 6th, the Virgin's Chapel, with 14th cent. glass. Altar, by Violet le Duc.

Here at the back of the high altar, and fronting the Chapel of the Virgin or "Our Lady's" Chapel, is the mausoleum of the Canon Lucas, with the *"Enfant pleureur" by Blasset, in 1636, his chef-d'œuvre. The 7th, 8th, and 9th chapels are of no importance. The 10th is to Notre Dame de la Pitié, with a large marble statue of the Virgin. The 11th, the chapel of St. John the Baptist is enclosed in an iron railing. The reredos was carved by Carpentier in 1780, and the statues of St. Firmin and St. François de Sales by Poultier in 1710. On the screen of the sanctuary opposite this chapel are admirably sculptured figures in relief, representing the principal scenes in the life of St. John, executed like those on the other side in the 15th cent.

North transept. On the west wall of the N. transept are scenes in the life of David connected with the temple of Jerusalem. Nearly under them is a stone baptismal front (11 cent.), 6 ft. long, which belonged to the original church, built in the 7th cent. The pedestal is of the 13th cent. The Gothic shrine of wood standing apart by itself is said to contain a piece of the skull of John the Baptist.

Similarly situated in the north transept as the chapel of Notre Dame du Puy in the southern, is the chapel of St. Sebastian, with a statue of

CALAIS   AMIENS. SANCTUARY. MUSÉE.   PARIS
MILES FROM   MILES TO

the saint by Blasset. Then leaving the N. transept and walking towards the main entrance—First chapel contains nothing remarkable, but opposite is the beautiful pulpit resting on the statues of Faith, Hope, and Charity, designed by Christophe and executed by Dupuis. Second chapel, Notre Dame de Bon Secours, with a lovely statue of the Virgin by Blasset in white marble. Third, nothing particular. Fourth chapel, on reredos of altar a curious Byzantine crucifix. Fifth and sixth chapels, nothing remarkable.

The sanctuary or choir contains 110 elaborately carved stalls under lace-like canopies by Boullin, Huet, and Turpin in 1528. The reredos of the altar is of stone gilt. On it is a delicately wrought shrine containing bones of saints. The cathedral has been recently completely restored by Violet le Duc. Amiens is the native town of Peter the Hermit, who persuaded the faithful to undertake the first crusade. His statue is beside the Cathedral. He was born in 1048, and died 8th July 1115, in the Abbey of Neufmoustier, at Huy.

A short way west from the cathedral by the Rue Basse Notre Dame is the church of St. Germain, built in the 15th cent. St. Leu was built at various periods; it has an elegant tower. St. Remy belongs to the 14th and 15th cents.

Beyond the Hotel de France, at the top of the Rue Rabuissons, are the Bibliotheque and the Musée. The museum is a very handsome building. On the ground floor are antiquities and statues, and upstairs a collection of works of modern painters—among others, Horace Vernet, Muller, and Gue. Amiens makes a pleasant residence; the expense of living is moderate, provisions of all kinds are good, especially vegetables, and the promenades and walks are very enjoyable. It is besides within 2½ hrs. of Paris, 2¼ hrs. of Boulogne, 2 hrs. 40 min. of Lille, and 4 hrs. of Rouen by the direct line passing Poix, Abancourt, Serqueux, and Montérolier.

107   LONGUEAU. Junction of the Calais and Arras line.   79

137   BRETEUIL. Junction, whence a branch line extends 4¼ m.   49
west to the town of Breteuil (pop. 3000). *Hotel:* St. Nicolas. A quiet town. Church partly of the 12th cent. Remains of abbey founded in the 11th cent. 4 m. distant is Folleville, with ruins of castle, 16th cent. In church, tomb of Raoul de Lannoy and his spouse.

145   CLERMONT DE L'OISE (pop. 6000). *Hotels:* Deux Epées;   41
Mouton-Blanc. This is a nice, breezy, healthy, clean town, overlooking the railway, with a comfortable inn and pleasant promenade, but

the pavement of most of the streets is rough. It makes a good retreat from Paris, and is situated on the top of a hill bordered by the fine promenade Chatellier. The Chateau is now a penitentiary for females, of whom it contains generally about 800. The square tower, 82 feet high, was built in the 10th cent. The church, St. Samson, built in the 14th and 15th cents. and recently restored, contains a great deal of fine glass. Between this church and the promenade is the Porte Nointel, 14th cent. In the street leading from the H. Deux Epées to the church is the Mairie, fronting a fountain, a legacy from Mme. Massé.

150 — LIANCOURT (pop. 4000). *Hotels:* Nord; Renaissance; Chemin de Fer. — 36 — A pretty and a flourishing town, in which shoemaking is an important industry. In the principal square is a statue of the Duc de la Rochefoucauld, the philanthropist and founder of the town hospital, 1830. In the church (1578) is a monumental tomb with two kneeling figures by Coustou.

154 — CREIL ON THE OISE (pop. 5000). *Hotels:* H. Du Chemin — 32 — de Fer; H. du Commerce, both at the end of the short Boulevard in front of the station. A town owing its importance to being situated at the junction of five important railways, but not a nice place to stop at. The parish church, built on a somewhat peculiar plan, belongs to the 13th and 16th cents. On an island in the river are the ruins of a royal castle, 14th and 15th cents.; and near it the ruins of the church of St. Evremont, 12th cent. One mile from Creil is the straggling village of Nogent-les-Vierges, containing an old Gothic church.

160½ — CHANTILLY (pop. 2500). 47 minutes from Paris. *Hotels:* — 25½ — At station the H. de la Gare. The best is the Angleterre in the 'Place,' at commencement of the long street of Chantilly. Adjoining church the Cygne; and near it the Bains. Wesleyan church near station. One-horse cab to the Chateau de la Reine Blanche and back, 8 fr.

Chantilly, formerly the seat *par excellence* of the Princes of Condé, has now, on account of its splendid race-course, become the Newmarket and the Goodwood of France, and the abode of a multitude of English grooms. The races are held in May, September, and October. The village consists of one long street, having at the farther end from the station the palatial stables, constructed during 1719 to 1735, by Louis Henri de Bourbon. They contain accommodation for 175 horses, with, besides, suites of apartments for carriages, saddles, harnesses, and grooms. Adjoining is the church finished in 1692, containing pic-

Chantilly Lace. Senlis.

tures by Bonouville and Leneveu. The painting on the window to the left of the altar represents the founding of the church by Louis de Bourbon, Prince of Condé (d. 1686), and his wife, Clémence de Maillé. To the right of the altar, in a shrine on Ionic columns, are the hearts of the Princes of Condé; while in the two shrines before the altar are ashes of saints. Beyond the stables, in the midst of a small lake, is the chateau built by Anne de Montmorency in 1545, and recently repaired and greatly enlarged by the Duc d'Aumale. It is adorned with sculptures and frescoes; among which are some choice pictures by Watteau, and large paintings representing the battles of Louis de Bourbon. In the absence of the family the public are admitted into the chateau and grounds on Sundays and Thursdays from 11 to 5. The rectangular building to the right is the Chateau d'Enghien.

Near the 'Place' is the hospital, founded by the last of the Princes of Condé, and behind the long street is the racecourse.

The best drive through the Forest of Chantilly is by a road leaving the racecourse at the S.E. angle, and following southwards almost in a straight line to the "Table Ronde," a large stone table, where twelve roads meet, and where "Le Grand Condé," on the occasion of a royal hunt, gave a breakfast to Louis XIV. About a mile farther are the "Étangs de Commelle," and the diminutive Château de la Reine Blanche, flanked with turrets. From this point it is not necessary to return to Chantilly, as a little farther is the station of *Orry-Coye*, four miles nearer Paris than Chantilly. Chantilly is also famous for silk lace, wrought by the lacemakers in their own homes, and then brought to the merchants, who pay them for their work. At Chantilly, junction with branch to Crepy, pop. 3000. *Inn:* Banniere, 19 m. E.; passing at 8 m. E.

Senlis (pronounced Senlisse), pop. 6200, situated to the north of the forest of Halatte and to the south of the forests of Ermenonville and Chantilly. Coach to Nanteuil passing by Pont L'Eveque. *Hotels:* Near the station the Nord; a little farther off, the Grand Cerf. The ancient town of Senlis, formerly occupied by the Romans, was in their time surrounded by a wall 920 yards in circumference and garnished with 16 towers. The present streets and houses have a modern aspect. The principal edifice is the church of Notre Dame, built in 990 by Bishop Eudes; but reconstructed in 1153 by Bishop Thibault. The western façade displays considerable originality of design. Of the 2 towers only the southern is finished, a charming structure 256 ft. high with elegant lancet windows. The lower stage is square and the upper octagonal, covered with a peaked crocketed roof, from which project 8 long narrow canopied dormer windows. The central portal is within a soffit, covered with 4 rows of sculpture. On the tympanum a low relief represents the death of Mary, and, next it, another represents angels preparing to carry her body to heaven. Above, in bold relief, she is represented sitting in conversation with Christ in heaven. The profusely sculptured south façade was built by Bishop Parvi in the 16th cent. The portal is under a shallow recess between decorated towers and canopied buttresses. From the soffit hang pendants, and over them extend an elegant arcaded gallery, and a large wheel window with a carved axle in the midst of flamboyant tracery. The north side, bearing the arms of François I., is similar, only not so richly decorated. The interior is 210 ft. from W. to E. and 30 ft. wide at the transept. A gallery the breadth of the aisles, with a stone vaulted 4 partite roof, extends round the church. Several windows have painted glass, those in the chancel are the best. Under this church, as well as under all the abbey churches, are great excavations cut through the thick seams of soft sandstone; by which it is said, the inmates of the different convents could communicate with each other.

In the large garden in front of the western entrance are the ruins of the chateau built by the kings of the Merovingian dynasty, on the site of the castle of the Roman pretor. Immediately behind Notre Dame is the abandoned, but still elegant abbey church of St. Pierre, built in the 14th and 15th cents., and reduced, like the others, to its present condition by the ruthless hordes of 1793. It can readily be distinguished by the somewhat heavy square tower, with a sentry-box-like erection on the top. The chancel, which is very short, deflects towards the north-east. A little to the south is another abandoned church, St. Frambourg, now a storehouse, founded by Adelaïde wife of Hugues Capet and rebuilt by Louis-le-Jeune in 1177. Over the elegant portal is a large circular moulding enclosing 3 lancet windows.

Beyond the Place de la Halle is St. Aignan, 16th cent., now the theatre. The first street left from the H. Grand Cerf leads to the abbey church of St. Vincent, founded in 1060 by Anne of Russia, wife of Henri I. From the western side of the N. transept rises a neat square belfry. The church is 154 feet long, 26 wide and 46 high. On the N. side is an aisle, and on the S. the cloister of the monastery built in 1660. It consists of a colonnade 29 yards wide and 44 long, under the upper story of the buildings. A few yards distant is the nunnery. Both are now a school under the direction of the clergy.

About a mile S.E. from Senlis are the ruins of the Abbey de la Victoire built by Philip Augustus. They are hidden among trees and stand close to the house of a M. Colombier. Visitors admitted only in the absence of the family. To go to it, take the road which runs nearly parallel to the railway from the H. du Nord, the length of an iron crucifix on a low square column; where take the road right hand by the side of the wall. On arriving at the mill turn to the left and ascend by the right-hand road. Before the entrance is a great iron gateway with twisted iron spikes.

The excavations below Senlis are very remarkable. They exist almost under every house in the town, and are always in two stages. The first

| CALAIS | BETHUNE. ARRAS. | PARIS |
| MILES FROM | | MILES TO |

stage is from 12 to 15 feet deep, and the stage below generally a little more, and always furnished with a draw well. One of the best specimens is seen under the grocer's shop No. 25 Place de la Halle. Seventeen steps cut in the rock lead down to the first stage, which has a groined roof, 12 feet high. Twenty-three more steps descend to the lower stage, which in execution is much ruder than the one above. They formed part of the excavations of the suppressed convent of St. Frambourg.

4¼ m. eastward by rail is Barbery, the station to alight at to visit the ruins of the fortress of Montépilloy, 12th cent., a short way S. from the station. The keep is 147 ft. high.

48 m. from Paris and 22½ m. E. from Senlis is Crepy-en-Valois, close to station, pop. 3000. Change carriages for Soissons, page 45.

185 PARIS. Arrive at the station of the Chemin de Fer du Nord, No. 18 Place Roubaix, where the registered luggage is examined. Immediately outside are small omnibuses, and a little beyond cabs. See Black's "Paris."

Calais to Paris, by Hazebrouck and Arras.

CALAIS	Distance 204 miles. Time 7 hours 40 minutes. For Timetables see under "Calais et Dunkerque à Paris," in the "Indicateur des Chemins de Fer du Nord."	PARIS
MILES FROM		MILES TO
		204

CALAIS. For the first 38 miles southwards, between Calais and Hazebrouck, see p. 22. Between Hazebrouck and Arras are the stations of Aire-sur-la-Lys, Lillers, Bethune, and Lens. Of these the most important is Bethune, pop. 8500. *Inns:* Nord, Lion d'Or; a fortified town on the river Brette, and the Lawe and Bassée canals. In the principal square is a handsome embrasured belfry erected in 1388; near it the church of St. Vaast, 16th cent. (restored), visited by pilgrims. A native of Bethune is said to have invented Artesian wells. Of the celebrated family of the Lords of Bethune, a branch, in the 12th cent., was established in Scotland; to whom belonged Cardinal Beaton, born in 1494, and assassinated under circumstances of horrible mockery and atrocity on the 29th of May 1546. Junction by rail with St. Pol, p. 9, 24¼ m. S., by Fouquereuil and Brias.

84 ARRAS, pop. 22,000. On the Scarpe Junction, with rail to **120** Douai 16 m. N.E. *Hotels:* L'Univers, in the Place de la Croix Rouge, the best but most expensive; the Petit-Saint-Pol, in the Place du Theatre; the Commerce, just within the Porte Ronville—din. 3½ frs. with wine; room 2 frs. The omnibuses of the hotels await passengers. Fare ½ fr. Temple Protestant. Arras is fortified by a citadel built by Vauban in 1670, and surrounded by two strong ramparts, cased with

ARRAS. HOUSE OF ROBESPIERRE.

brick. In different parts of the town are large and extensive barracks, generally fully occupied. In nearly the centre of Arras is the Cathedral of St. Vaast (1755-1833), approached from the Rue des Teinturiers by a flight of 47 steps. Behind the high altar in the Chapelle de la Vierge is a Madonna in white marble by Cortot. To her left is the mausoleum and colossal marble statue of Cardinal Charles de la Tour d'Auvergne Lauraguais, died 1851. Opposite is the mausoleum of P. Ludovicus Parisis, died 1866. To the left of the high altar, N. side, is a "descent from the cross," attributed to Rubens. In the S. transept is "Christ rising from the grave," attributed to Van Dyck. In the transepts are colossal statues of the four evangelists. Adjoining the cathedral are the former abbey buildings; which now contain the bishop's palace, entered from the S., or Place de la Madeleine end; the Musée, entered by the horseshoe staircase from the gardens, and the Depot of the Archives, entered from the end next the cathedral. Near the Archives is the Public Library, with 40,000 volumes and 1100 manuscripts. The Rue St. Aubert leads N.W. from the gardens to the Prefecture, passing by the entrance to the Hospital of St. Jean, founded in 1178; and nearly opposite it, at No. 87, is a handsome house with a great deal of mullion work, built in 1866. A little farther, at the end of the street, is a monumental fountain, erected in 1864. Near the Prefecture are very large barracks, and a seminary. The church near the Prefecture is called St. Nicolas, built in 1846. It contains some curious pictures and the reliquary of Ste. Manne. South from it, at the west end of the Rue d'Amiens, is the church of the Saint-Sacrement, built in 1846 of fine-grained white sandstone. Within and without, even to the top of the spire, 193 feet high, it is one mass of sculpture. The elegantly mullioned building adjoining is the residence of the Benedictine nuns to whom the church belongs. Behind are great barracks, the principal arsenals, the promenade, the Botanic garden, and the citadel.

Opposite the theatre, the Rue des Rapparteurs joins the Place du Theatre at right angles. In the house No. 3 of this street was born Robespierre, a plain one storied building, the upper consisting of six windows, and the ground floor of five, with a door. Below are cellars.

Occupying one of the small ends of the Petite Place is the Hotel de Ville, a very beautiful structure, built in 1510. In some parts it is one story, and at other two stories high; consisting of handsome square transomed windows, separated from each other by banded, or fluted, or otherwise richly wrought columns in couples. The tiers of richly decorated dormer windows projecting from the steep roof and the elegantly sculptured chimney stalks rising above it, add considerably to the charming beauty of the edifice. Above the entrance rises, 238 feet high, a handsome tower, at first square, then round, surmounted by a crown, over which stands a lion with a flag. It contains a good chime of bells. The Petite Place is a large parallelogram, bordered on three sides by houses with rounded gables. Adjoining is the Grande Place, surrounded by similar houses and enclosing a space of $7\frac{4}{10}$ acres. Near the eastern end of the Petite Place is the church of St. Jean-Baptiste, 16th cent. Over the high altar is a cleverly painted window representing the baptism of our Lord. To the left of the altar is an ascension of Mary into heaven by Champaigne, and to the right a "descent from the cross," a copy of the picture in the S. transept attributed to Rubens. The carving of the pulpit, as well as of the wainscoting behind the high altar, is delicate and elaborate. Near the Hotel du Commerce is the church of the Ursuline nuns, with some good glass, and a tower, at first square, then round. From the corners peer forth statues of animals and birds.

Arras has a preparatory school of medicine and pharmacy, a College communal, an Ecole communale de musique, and two seminaries. Its tapestry manufactures have been long extinct; but it still manufactures pipes, pottery, lace, sugar, and oil.

92. BOISLEUX, a hamlet on an affluent of the Cojeul. Junction 112 here with branch to Marquion on the Agache, pop. 910, with quarries and potteries, 17 m. E. from Boisleux, and 6 m. W. from Cambrai. This branch passes Boyelles, pop. 400, on the Cojeul; St. Leger, pop. 719, on the Sensée; Ecoust, pop. 906, with a handsome parish church and the crumbling ruins of a castle, and Inchy, pop. 1090, on the Agache. The baptismal fonts in the church date from 1555.

95¾. ACHIET, pop. 780. *Inn:* Trévaux. Junction with branch 108¼ line to Cambrai, 26 m. E. passing Bapaume, 4½ m. E., pop. 3060. *Inns:* Pas-de-Calais; de la Fleur. A pleasant town with manufactures of fine wool, calicoes and cambric. The Hotel de Ville was built in the 16th cent., and the belfry in 1610. The church of St. Nicolas, 16th cent., contains an image visited by pilgrims.

107. ALBERT, pop. 4260. *Inns:* Tete de Bœuf; Gare. An industrious town with distilleries, saw, cotton, and paper mills, printworks and bleachfields. In the neighbourhood is a cave 1100 feet long by 6 broad, containing a great variety of petrifactions.

| CALAIS MILES FROM | CORBIE. DOUAI. | PARIS MILES TO |

117 CORBIE, pop. 4060. *Inns:* at the corner of the large Place, **87** the H. de France, the best; near the church, the H. du Commerce, and the Corbie. The parish church St. Pierre, 16th cent., has two low square towers over the façade, and is supported by heavy buttresses. In the interior is the miracle-working image of St. Collette. Three reliquaries are on each side of the high altar. Under the northern aisle is a very large monumental slab, with a great part of the inscription defaced. The lofty portal in the "Place," out of all proportion to the diminutive size of the Hotel de Ville, was originally the entrance to the abbey buildings, of which little remains. The staple employments of the villagers are agriculture and the weaving of woollen petticoats. The best walk is by the side of the canal of the Somme, passing a large manufactory of silk and wool thread.

125 LONGUEAU, where the train goes 1¼ m. W. to enter Amiens, **79** see p. 11. Longueau is a small village ¼ m. from the station. The train then returns to Longueau station, and proceeds to Paris by Breteuil, p. 14; Clermont, p. 14; Creil, p. 15; Chantilly, p. 15; and then arrives at the station of the Chemin de Fer du Nord of Paris.

Lille to Paris, by Arras and Amiens.

| LILLE MILES FROM | Distance 156 miles. Time by express train, 5¼ hours. See Map, p. 1. | PARIS MILES TO |

LILLE, pop. 165,700, 66½ miles from Calais (see p. 23). **156**

14 CARVIN, pop. 7020, with coal-mines. **142**

21 DOUAI, pop. 27,000. *Hotels:* Europe, Flanders, Commerce, **135** Chapeau-Rouge. Temple Protestant. A prosperous town in the great northern coal-fields of France, possessing important manufactories and foundries. The finest, and indeed the only remarkable building in Douai, is the **Hotel de Ville**, a profusely sculptured edifice of the 15th century. From the centre of the façade, in the Rue de la Mairie, rises a square buttressed tower to the height of 130 feet, adorned with turrets on each corner, and surmounted by a curiously-wrought spire, 48 feet higher, ornamented with numerous gilded vanes. Along each side of this tower extend five windows, each with one mullion, a transom, quatrefoil tracery, and crocketed finials. The first and fifth window on each side are under the level of the others. The other façade is much larger, but is of brick, dressed with stone. Opposite this façade is the Rue de l'Universite, leading to the Academie. Syllabus on the door. Northwards from the Hotel de Ville, by the

LILLE — DOUAI BIBLE. ST. OMER. — PARIS

Place d'Armes, is St. Pierre, built in the 18th century, easily recognised by its massive square tower. The church of Notre Dame has a curious reredos, painted on nine panels, by Bellegambe. The Museum is near the Place St. Jacques. Public on Sundays; other days 1 fr. It contains some paintings by Velasquez, Rubens, Teniers, etc. Westward, on the other side of the river, in the Rue Benoit, is the Benedictine Convent for the training of English youths for the Romish Church. The course lasts seven years. There is accommodation for 100 pupils, but generally the number does not exceed 90. Daniel O'Connell studied here. Douai gives its name to an edition of the Bible by Roman Catholic divines, printed in this city.

36 ARRAS. See p. 18. — 120

59 ALBERT. See p. 20. Amiens, p. 11. Clermont, p. 14. — 97

124 CREIL JUNCTION. See p. 15. — 32

156 PARIS. Arrive at the station of the Chemins de Fer du Nord.

Calais to Brussels.

By St. Omer, Hazebrouck, Lille, Tournai, Leuze, Ath, Enghien, and Hal, 133 m. east. Time by quickest train 4 hrs. 40 min. The slowest 8 hrs. 27 min. See Map of Paris, Brussels, and the Rhine. For Time-tables, see under "London to Brussels and Back *viâ* Calais," in the Continental Time-tables of the London, Chatham, and Dover Railway; sold at the Victoria station, Pimlico, price 3d.; or by letter to the manager of the station, enclosing 4½d. in stamps.

CALAIS — See Map, p. 1. — BRUSSELS
MILES FROM — MILES TO
— — 133

CALAIS, p. 1. Seven m. from Calais is Ardres, p. 2. Twenty-six m. S.E. from Calais is **Saint Omer**, pop. 22,000, a fortified town of the first class on the small river Aa. *Hotels:* Porte d'Or et d'Angleterre; Commerce. English church in Rue du Bon Pasteur. Coach daily to Fruges, where it corresponds with coach to Hesdin, Montreuil, and Abbeville.

The principal objects of interest in St. Omer are—the Church of Notre Dame, built during the 11th–14th centuries, at the western extremity of the town; and the ruins of the Abbey of St. Bertin, built about the same time, at the eastern extremity near the arsenal and the railway station. The massive square tower of St. Bertin is 190 feet high and is ascended by 294 steps. From the top eastwards are seen Cassel, and an extensive tract of flat marshy land, where large quantities of vegetables are cultivated, the cultivators inhabiting chiefly the small adjoining villages of Haut Pont and Lyzel. To the west are seen the graceful steeple of St. Sepulcre; and on the left the broad dome of the Hotel de Ville, commenced in 1834 and finished in 1841. In the same square in which it is situate is the Museum, open to the public on Sundays and Thursdays. Farther to the left we have St. Denis, Notre Dame, and the church of the Jesuits, now forming part of the Lycée. Of these buildings Notre Dame is the most important. Walking up the nave of this church, we have on the left the tomb of St. Omer, a work of the 13th cent.; at the north transept below the bright-coloured rose-window, is a curious clock; and in the southern transcept is the chapel containing the wooden image of Our Lady of Miracles, venerated and visited by numerous pilgrims. The wonders which have been performed by her are carefully recorded in large letters on the walls and pillars. St. Louis and his mother visited this image in 1231. In a chapel in the south aisle is a curious Entombment. The figures, as usual, are painted. On this side, below the organ, is a "Descent from the Cross," after Rubens, and an ancient uncouth stone figure of the god Therouanne with his 2 attendants. The chief manufactures are white clay pipes and linen. Thomas Becket, when on his way from Gravelines to Pontigny in 1164, stayed some days in the Abbey of St. Bertin; where 60 years before Anselm of Canterbury had taken refuge, when driven from England.

38 **HAZEBROUCK**, pop. 9450. *Inns:* Trois Chevaux; St. **95** George. Junction with line from Dunkerque, 25½ m. N., and junction also with line from Dunkerque to Brussels by Ypres and Courtrei.

16 m. E. from Hazebrouck is *Armentières*, on the Lys, pop. 20,900. *Hotels:* Nord; Paris. French custom-house station and junction with a line to Courtrai, 22¼ m. N., by Le Touquet, the Belgian custom-house station, Warneton and Comines. Situated as Armentières is on the frontier, its annals are full of instances of military occupation and pillage from the 14th cent. downwards. It manufactures large quantities of linen, table-cloths, and lace. It has also important foundries.

66 **LILLE**, pop. 165,700. Junction with line to Antwerp, 76 m. **67** N. by Courtrai, 23¼ m. N., Ypres, 22¼ m., and Ghent, 45 m. N., see index. *Hotels:* In the centre of the town, near the Grande Place, the Europe; Villeroy; France. In the Grande Place the hotels Gand, and Commerce. In the Place du Theatre the Singe d'Or. In the railway station the Buffet-hotel. Opposite the station the hotels Paris; Flandre et Angleterre; Normandie.

All the tram-cars either start from or traverse the "Place" in front of the station and the Grande Place. Temple Protestant, in the Rue

LILLE. HOTELS. PICTURE GALLERY.

Josephine fronting the Prefecture. On the other side of this broad boulevard, in the Rue Watteau, is the Anglican chapel.

Lille, on the Deule, is a fortified town of the first class. The old ramparts have been converted into handsome streets, boulevards, and parks, and the new fortifications have been built at such a distance from the centre as not to interfere, as formerly, with the traffic. From the railway station the broad street, the Rue de la Gare, lined with elegant houses, leads directly to the Grande Place and the Place du Theatre. In the Grande Place is a column with a statue by Bra commemorative of the valour displayed by the inhabitants when the city was besieged by the Austrians in 1792. The principal building here is the Bourse, profusely ornamented with caryatides, commenced during the dominion of the Spaniards. In the court is a statue of Napoleon I. by Lemaire in 1854. At the end of the narrow street opposite the Bourse is the Hotel de Ville, containing an excellent **Picture Gallery,** open, excepting on the Mondays, from 9 to 4. Entrance by the stair to the left. The door to the right at the top of the stair leads into the Moillet and Leleux collections; and the door to the left, into the Public Picture Gallery; where all the pictures are distinctly labelled. The first room is occupied nearly entirely with pictures of the Italian school, both originals and copies. Among the former are works by Fra Bartolommeo, 1517; G. Bassano, 1592, his genuine works are very scarce; L. Bassano, 1629; S. Botticelli, 1510, one of the most fascinating painters of the Florentine school; M. A. Caravaggio, 1609, whose best works are in the Vatican; Domenichino, one of the most celebrated painters of the school of Bologna; B. Gentile da Urbino; B. Grillandajo (Ghirlandajo), 1497; G. Lanfranco, 1647, famous for his bold paintings in fresco; C. Maratta, 1713, a most industrious painter; Guido Reni, 1642; Andrea del Sarto, 1531, who in this room has a lovely Madonna; Tiziano (Vicelli), 1576; P. Veronese (Caliari), 1588. The second and third rooms contain pictures chiefly of the Flemish school. Among other artists are:—Philippe de Champaigne, 1674, who painted an immense number of pictures, now distributed all over Europe; Gaspard Crayer, 1669, whose pictures abound in the churches and museums of Brussels and Ghent; besides there is scarcely a church in Flanders that cannot boast of one or more of his canvases; A. Van Dyck, the miracle of St. Anthony, a starving ass preferring to kneel before a communion wafer blessed by the saint, than to satisfy its hunger on the oats offered to it; H. Flandrin, 1864, the painter of the beautiful frescoes in the church of St. Germain des Près, Paris; Jakob Jordaens, 1678, one of the most notable and most productive of the Flemish painters; F. Hals, 1666, one of the great masters of portrait painting, of which the best collection is at Haarlem; G. Honthorst, 1680; C. Lorrain, 1682; N. Poussin, 1665; P. P. Rubens, 1640; F. Snyders, 1657, famous for the vigour of his colouring and the lightness of his touch; F. Stuerbout of Haarlem, 1475; D. Teniers, 1694; G. Tilborgh, 1678. From the third room is the entrance into the very valuable collection of 1437 drawings, chiefly by the celebrated masters of the Italian school, bequeathed by the painter J. B. Wicar to this his native town. He made the greater part of the collection in Rome, where he died in 1834. Among the gems of this collection is a wax bust of the Virgin by Raphael, under a glass case, in the small centre room. This gallery joins again the Public Museum at the fourth room, opposite a large painting by Wicar, the "Restoration to life of the widow's son." In rooms five and six are modern paintings. From room seven, the door to the left leads down to the Musées Ceramique and Archéologique, and the door to the right to the Industrial Museum and the Ethnological Museum bequeathed by Moillet, and the collection of pictures bequeathed by Leleux in 1873. At the northern end of the town are the churches of St. Catherine, Notre Dame de la Treille, and the Madeleine. St. Catherine's was begun in the 12th cent.; the nave is of the 14th, and the choir of the 17th cent. The picture over the high altar represents the "Martyrdom of St. Catherine" by Rubens. To the left under the aisle is a figure of Notre Dame de Lourdes. A short way W. from St. Catherine's by the Rue des Fossées Neufs, is the beautiful promenade, by the side of the Deule, 765 yards long, and planted with trees. On the other side of the Deule, adjoining the citadel, is the Jardin Vauban.

East from St. Catherine's, on the site of the castle of Buc, constructed by Julius Cæsar B.C. 50, is **Notre-Dame-de-la-Treille et Saint Pierre**, commenced in 1855, but as yet only part of the choir is finished and covered in with a temporary roof. It is much frequented on account of an image of Notre Dame de la Treille, which has been revered by the citizens since the 11th cent. Near the General Hospital is, on the other side of the Deule, by the Pont Neuf, the Madeleine, built in 1675, in the form of a Greek cross, with a handsome dome in the centre. Over the altars are: an "Adoration," by Rubens, and a "Crucifixion," by Van Dyck. In the chancel are pictures by Van Oost. At the head of the Rue Royale, and at the north end of the town, is

St. André, 18th cent. The sounding-board of the pulpit is carved in imitation of drapery suspended from the adjoining pillar. The best pictures are by Otto Venius, Jacob Van Oost, and Arnould de Vuez. Near the railway station is the modern church of St. Maurice, easily recognised by its tall spire formed of open work.

Lille has numerous foundries, cloth, ribbon, and sugar manufactories, dye and chemical works, and breweries, the Lille beer enjoying considerable celebrity. 22½ m. S. is St. Amand and its mud baths, p. 41.

Thirty minutes N. from Lille, 53 miles' E. from Dunkerque, and 67 miles W. from Brussels, is French Comines, and five minutes beyond, Belgian Comines, 9 miles E. from Ypres, and 13 miles W. from Courtray. French Comines, pop. 4000, on the south side of the Lys, at the foot of the stately ruins of the castle in which was born, in 1445, Philippe de Comines, the father of modern history. In 1468 Charles le Temeraire appointed him his councillor and chamberlain, and consequently when in the same year Louis XI. was entrapped at Peronne, Comines was able to soften the passion of the duke, and to give useful advice to the king, whose life he did much to save.

BAISIEUX. French custom-house and time.

BLANDAIN. Belgian custom-house and time. 4½ miles beyond Blandain is Tournai, see Index. After Tournai the train passes Leuze, Ath, Enghien, and Hal, and arrives at the Station du Midi of Brussels, where cabs and tram-cars await passengers.

Dunkerque to Paris.

By Hazebrouck, Bethune, Arras, Amiens, Clermont, and Creil. See map, p. 1. For Time-tables, the "Indicateur des Chemins de Fer du Nord," sold at the stations, 6 sous. Distance 190 miles south. Time 9½ hours.

DUNKERQUE, pop. 33,600. *Hotels:* Flandre, and Chapeau Rouges, adjoining each other in the Rue des Capucins, near the principal square, the Place Jean Bart, and the Parc de la Marine. Opposite the Flandre is the H. de la Ville de Lille, a second-class house. English chapel in the Rue des Arbres, at the north end of the town, near the Fishermen's chapel, in the Rue de la Grille. Post-Office in the Rue du Chateau. Every quarter hour, during the bathing season, trams start from railway station and the Place Jean Bart to the Casino. Fare, 30 c. The London steamers moor close to the custom-house, but at some distance from the railway station. The wharf of the Leith boats is within 8 minutes' walk of the station. Dunkerque is 29 miles east by rail from Calais, and 26 miles more by rail from Boulogne. Passengers from Dunkerque to Boulogne have to change carriages at St. Pierre-Les-Calais, 1¾ m. south from Calais, and 28 m. west from

Dunkerque. Bourbourg. Gravelines.

Dunkerque. On this line the two most important stations are **Bourbourg**, pop. 2500, on the Aa canal. The church, which is adorned with paintings of the Flemish school, is of the 13th cent., but the choir was rebuilt in the 16th and 17th cents. **Gravelines**, pop. 7800, *Inn :* H. des Messageries. A fortified town on the Aa, 1¼ m. from the sea, and 195 m. N. by rail from Paris, which it supplies with fish. To London it sends fruit, eggs, and butter. When Thomas Becket fled from Henry II. he embarked (Nov. 2, 1164) at Sandwich in a little boat managed by two priests, and reached the opposite coast in the evening near Gravelines. From Gravelines he went to St. Omer, and lodged in the great abbey of St. Bertin.

DUNKERQUE, said to have originated in a chapel built by St. Eloi in the 7th cent., is a fortified seaport on the Northern Ocean, at the junction of 5 important canals, whose traffic, however, has been considerably diminished by the railways. It is an excellent station from which to enter Belgium, especially for visiting Bruges and the sea-bathing stations of La Panne, Nieuport-les-Bains, Ostende, Blankenberg, and Heyst. Dunkerque is 120 m. W. from Brussels; 50¼ m. S.W. from Bruges; and 110 m. W. from Antwerp by rail, passing Ghent. See Index.

The port is provided with a first-class lighthouse, 170 ft. high, and 100 acres of docks. The entrance is rather narrow, between two jetties, of which the eastern is 2556 ft. long. After the lighthouse, the most conspicuous object is the belfry of St. Eloi, a square tower 300 ft. high, commanding a prospect of 30 miles round. From the top, Cassini, Biot, and Arago made many of their most important observations. Opposite is the church, reconstructed in 1560. A little beyond is the great square, having in the centre a statue, by David of Angers, to the memory of Jean Bart, a fisherman of Dunkerque, who rose to the rank of admiral, and is celebrated in the annals of France for his valour and naval exploits. He died in 1702.

West from St. Eloi, by the Rue Vierge, towards the Arrière Port, is the church of St. Jean-Baptiste, built in the last century. On both sides of the nave are some very good paintings by Crayer and others. On the left side of the altar is a painting by Van Dyck, 1599—1641, of "Jesus being mocked," and near it a "Magdalene," by F. Solemena, 1657—1747. On the right side of the high altar is a "Holy Family," by Guido Reni, 1575—1642, and "Portrait by Lanfrancs, 1581—1647.

From the north side of St. Eloi, the Rue Chaudron and its continuation, the Rue St. Gilles, lead to the Theatre, and to the handsome

CASINO OF DUNKERQUE. BERGUES.

building next it, containing on the ground floor a small museum of natural history and a picture gallery—open on Sundays and Thursdays. Upstairs is the Public Library, containing about 10,000 vols.—open from Monday to Friday, inclusive. Behind is a little garden.

A little less than 2 miles from the "Place" is the *Casino*, a great brick building on the beach, to the east of Dunkerque. It contains within itself a large and comfortable hotel, with reading, concert, and ball rooms. "Pension," including everything, from 12 to 20 frs. Residents in the hotel pay half price for admission to the concerts and theatricals. The surroundings are mere sand in undulating eminences, with, in front, a flat beach of immense length and breadth. A few yards from the Casino are the Dunkerque tramway station, the houses in which the bathing tickets are sold, and a very large concert and ball room. Bathing tickets cost 1 fr. each; six for 4½ frs. Scattered up and down are villas and furnished lodgings. Behind, or on the south side of the Casino, is the village of Tente-Verte, with, at the most distant end, a railway station. 5 miles from Dunkerque by rail is

BERGUES, pop. 5780, at the junction of the Colme canal with the canals Dunkerque and Furnes. *Inns:* In the "Place" the Tête d'Or, and the Ange. Near them the H. Sauvage. Situated on an eminence surrounded by ramparts, and defended by four forts. The principal edifice is the church of St. Martin, with a large square tower constructed in the 17th cent. In the interior, over the western entrance, is a handsome organ. In the second chapel, right hand, is a representation of Our Lord in the tomb. In the next, or third chapel, are 14 pictures, painted on copper, by R. Van Oucke, representing the death of our Lord, and of each of the apostles. The reredos, representing the martyrdom of Saint Barbara, is by Janssens.

In the "Place" near St. Martin rises to the height of 164 feet an elegant square belfry, constructed in 1456, and consisting of 8 stories of blind arches, of which 7 or 10 are on each side. On the summit is an octagonal tower with a balloon-shaped spire and gilt vane, representing a lion holding a spear. To each corner of the tower is attached a projecting octagonal turret, after the manner of an oriel window, descending about ¼ of the height of the square part of the tower, and rising only a few feet above it. Opposite is the Mairie (1665) containing the public library and picture gallery, both of them supplied almost entirely from the Abbey of St. Winoc. The picture gallery has 150 paintings and water-colours, chiefly by masters of the Flemish school; such as Abraham Janssens, d. 1632; Beekmans of Bergues, d.

BERGUES. PICTURE GALLERY. CASSEL.

1770; Bockhorst, d. 1671; Breughel, d. 1569; Bril, b. 1556; P. de Champaigne, 1674; J. G. Cuyp, b. 1575; A. Van Dyck; M. Elias, 1558; A. and F. Franck; J. Van Oost, father and son; G. Poussin; J. Reyn of Dunkerque, d. 1678, pupil of Van Dyck; G. Thys, d. 1677; Pieter Verbruggen, d. 1686; C. Vos, d. 1651; M. Vos, d. 1603; S. Vos, d. 1676; and Wauters, d. 1659, pupil of Rubens. There are a few belonging to the Italian and Spanish school, such as Barocci, d. 1612, Ribera, and Salvator Rosa. An excellent descriptive and critical catalogue sold by the concierge, 1 fr.

From the Mairie a street leads up to an eminence on which the early inhabitants worshipped an idol called Malbrancq, till converted to Christianity by St. Winoc in 685: when the zealous missionary founded here the abbey, which soon became rich and powerful. In the 13th cent. it was rebuilt, and in 1793 it was pillaged and destroyed by the French themselves. All that remains are the "Tour Blanche," or the square tower, and the "Tour Bleue," or the octagonal tower, with a lofty tapering slated steeple. The grounds of the abbey have been converted into the Promenade. In the centre stand two excellent archers' poles, "Perches," both 110 ft.

Many may find it more agreeable and more profitable to await the departure of a steamer in Bergues than in Dunkerque. Besides the rail, an omnibus leaves every morning for Dunkerque. Bergues carries on a considerable trade in cattle, grain, cheese, and butter. After Bergues, the train having passed Esquelbecq, a straggling hamlet, and Arneke, a small village close to the station, *Inn*: H. Belle Vue, reaches **Cassel**, 19 miles from Dunkerque, and 171 from Paris. At the station an omnibus awaits passengers for the town, nearly 2 miles distant on an eminence. Fare ½ franc. *Hotels:* Sauvage, with a fine view from the back windows, and the Lion d'Or, both in the "Place." At the other end of the "Place" is the ancient residence of the Counts of Halluin, now the Hotel de Ville. From the Hotel de Ville a narrow street leads up to the gardens and terrace on the top of the hill, occupying the site of a former Roman Castellum. The view here is so very extensive, that in clear weather 30 towns and 100 villages, some nearly hidden in clumps of trees, may be distinguished. 25½ miles farther is **Hazebrouck**, 164½ m. from Paris. At station are bedrooms 2 frs. the night. Here the Dunkerque passengers, both for Paris and Lille, change carriages. From Hazebrouck, see route from Calais to Paris by Hazebrouck and Arras, page 18.

In **PARIS** the train stops at the station of the Chemins de Fer du Nord, 18 Place Roubaix.

ROOSENDAEL.   ZUYDCOTE.   GHYVELDE.

Dunkerque to Bruges.

By Furnes, Dixmude, Cortemarck, where sometimes carriages are changed; but oftener at the next station—Lichtervelde. See Map, p. 1.

From Dunkerque the first place passed is Tente-Verte, a suburb of Dunkerque, extending to the Casino. Then follow Roosendael and Zuydcote, with vegetable gardens like little oases in the midst of the surrounding undulating plains of sand. Eight miles from Dunkerque is the little village of *Ghyvelde*, the French custom-house station. Four miles farther is *Adinkerke*, the Belgian custom-house station, with, in the neighbourhood, the little sea-bathing village of La Panne. The train now passes by Furnes, Nieuport, Lichtervelde, and Thourout, and arrives at Bruges, 50¼ miles from Dunkerque. For the above places, and for Bruges to Dunkerque, see Index. Bruges is 28 miles west from Ghent, and Ghent is 35½ miles west from Brussels.

Dunkerque to Brussels.—112 miles east, by Furnes, Dixmude, Cortemarck, Lichtervelde, Roulers, Ingelmunster, Waereghem, Anseghem, and Audenarde or Oudenaerde. For Dixmude, 24½ m. from Dunkerque, and Lichtervelde, 36 m.; see Bruges to Dunkerque. 17½ miles farther is Ingelmunster, a small town with extensive carpet manufactories and a handsome chateau. 15¼ miles E. is Anseghem. 5 miles E. from Anseghem and 38 miles E. from Brussels is Audenarde, on the Escaut, pop. 6300. *Hotels:* Saumon; Pomme d'Or; Lion d'Or, and numerous Cafe-Restaurants. In the Place de Tacambaro, at the entrance into the town from the station, is a monument to the memory of the natives of Audenarde, who died in the Mexican expedition in 1864. South from the "Place" is the church of Sainte-Valburge, of which the choir belongs to the 12th cent.—the remainder was rebuilt in the 14th. The tower, one of the finest in Belgium, is 321 feet high. On the other side of the Escaut is the very handsome church of Notre Dame de Pamele, built in 1239. In the interior are two interesting tombs, 16th and 17th cents., with statues in a recumbent posture.

But the glory of Audenarde is its Hotel de Ville, built in 1535 by Van Peede and de Ronde. When they drew their plans they were commissioned to include all the recognised beautiful parts of existing Belgian edifices which would harmonise with each other. The façade is 79 feet wide, the larger side 69 feet, and the smaller 39 feet. From the centre rises an elegant 5 storied belfry, terminating with a gilt statue, which serves also as a vane. Fee to visit interior ½ fr.

Adjoining the Hotel are the old "Halles," now the theatre. Here

AUDENARDE.   MARGARET OF PARMA.

the Duke of Marlborough defeated the French on 7th July 1708. And here was born in 1522 Margaret of Parma, Regent of the Netherlands under Philip II., daughter of Charles V. and Johanna van der Gheenst.

From this the train passes several small towns and arrives in 2 hours from Audenarde at the Station du Nord, Brussels.

Paris to Brussels.

The direct route by Creil, Compiegne, Noyon, Tergnier Junction, St. Quentin, Busigny, Mons, Jurbise, Braine, and Hal. Arrive at the Station du Sud. Distance 193 m. N.E. 7 hours 40 minutes by express train.   Fares 36 frs., 27 frs., 18¾ frs. See Map, p. 1. For London to Brussels, viâ Dover and Calais, or Dover and Ostende, see the Continental Time-table of the London, Chatham, and Dover Railway, Victoria Station, Pimlico, price 3d.; or by letter to the manager of the station, enclosing 4½d. in stamps. In Brussels, Messrs. Cook, 22 Galerie du Roi.

PARIS	BRUSSELS
MILES FROM	MILES TO

PARIS, start from the station of the Chemins de Fer du Nord. **193**

32 CREIL Junction. *Inns:* H. du Chemin de Fer; H. du Com- **161** merce; both at the end of the short boulevard in front of the stat.

52¼ COMPIÈGNE, pop. 1150. *Hotels:* Cloche; France; Soleil **140¾** d'Or. English chapel. Omnibus at station for Pierrefonds, 8 m. S.E. Fare 1 fr. Palace open from 10 to 4. Doorkeeper's room, first in left wing. Rail or steamer from Compiègne to Soissons, 28 m. E.

Compiègne is a pleasant town on the left bank of the Oise, in a vast plain, at the northern extremity of a large forest. Among the public buildings deserving notice are—the Hotel de Ville, built in the Gothic style. At each corner of the façade is an octagonal tower with conical roofs, and between them the great clock-tower flanked with turrets. Above the clock are the three little figures of men, called the "Picantins," which strike the quarters. The museum contains a painting of St. Veronica, by Annibal Carracci, and another of two boys, by Murillo. Among the relics is a spur which belonged to Jeanne d'Arc. The church of St. Antoine has a fine portal, nave, choir, pulpit, and a beautiful font consisting of one stone. On the way up to the chateau from the "Place" is the church of St. Jacques, commenced in the 12th century, with a heavy but not unpleasing tower of the 15th century. In the south transept is a painting representing the vow of Anne of Austria to the Virgin. In this church, on the morning of the 24th of May 1430, Jeanne d'Arc heard mass; and then at the head of 500 soldiers sallied forth from the town and drove the army of the

COMPIÈGNE. JEANNE D'ARC. CHATEAU.

Duke of Burgundy from their entrenchments, who, however, having been joined by the English, rallied and forced her to retreat. On arriving at the gate, she found the drawbridge up, and the portcullis closed, by order of the Governor Guillaume de Flavi, so that she was taken prisoner by Lyonnel, the bastard of Vendôme, who gave her up to Jean de Luxembourg, by whom she was sold to the English. This happened at the Porte de Pont, which adjoined what is now called the Tour de Jeanne d'Arc, entered from the doorway No. 5 of the Rue de Jeanne d'Arc, at the end near the river.

The Castle of Compiègne was built by Louis XV. and XVI., and restored and enlarged by Napoleon I. and Louis Philippe I., and altered and improved by Napoleon III. The principal entrance is by the façade fronting the town; through a spacious court called the Cour d'Honneur, enclosed by a row of Doric columns, extending from the extremities of the two wings of the palace. The grand entrance, in the centre of this court, is surmounted by four Ionic columns, supporting a bas-relief, representing a hunting scene, by Beauvalet. The visitor enters by the Galerie des Colonnes or vestibule, at the foot of the Escalier d'Honneur, ornamented with the marble statues of Hospital and Daguessau. Ascending this staircase, the first rooms shown are the Salle des Gardes and the Salon des Huissiers, and then through some rooms of minor importance into Saloons Nos. 1 and 2, and the bedroom of the princes, all hung with beautiful tapestry. Then follow the private rooms and the Salle de Recepcion, hung with tapestry, and the Salon de Conseil, a splendid room. The bedroom adjoining the library was occupied by Napoleon III. before he left for Sedan. Beyond is the bedroom of the Empress. The ceilings of these three rooms were painted by Girodet. Then follow the theatre and the Galerie de Don Quichotte, with 31 paintings by Coypel; of which there is a continuation by Natoire in the Galerie Neuve. In the antechamber of the Ball-room is a stuffed bear, shot by the Emperor of Russia, and presented to Napoleon III. The Ball-room is 100 feet long by 42 feet wide, lighted by 22 windows, supported by 20 columns, and ornamented with 12 allegorical paintings by Girodet. At one end is the statue of Napoleon I. attired as a Roman Emperor, and at the other, one of Lætitia, his mother. The façade of the chateau overlooking the forest measures 633 feet, and stands on a handsome elevated terrace, adorned with white marble statues. A wide road, covered with green sward, and perfectly straight, extends as far as the eye can reach from the palace into the forest. This forest is pierced by

CASTLE OF PIERREFONDS. NOYON.

340 excellent roads, contains 36,168 acres, and yields an annual revenue of £26,000.

Omnibuses leave the Compiègne railway station and the Hotel de la Cloche for **Pierrefonds**, pop. 2000. Hotel des Bains, in a beautiful park, with a lake. Behind the hotel is a bathing establishment supplied by cold sulphurous springs, and possessing all the usual apparatus. Overlooking the town is the noble and imposing **Castle**, built by Louis d'Orleans in 1390, and restored by Napoleon III. This castle is the most perfect of its kind in Europe, and as it is so easily approached from Compiègne, a visit to it should not be omitted. Fee ½ fr. each. 7½ miles west from Pierrefonds is the poor hamlet of **Champlieu**, with the ruins of a small Roman amphitheatre. In front are the ruins of a temple to Apollo. The shafts of the exterior columns are sculptured with acanthus leaves, or simply with intersecting straight lines. A broad trough or gutter surrounds the building, and steps lead up to it. Drive to Champlieu by the villages of Palesne, Morienvale, and Orrouy. Return to Pierrefonds by the Poste des Gardes, St. Nicholas, and St. Jean in the Forest. One-horse coach there and back, 12 fr. The stables are nearly opposite the hotel.

10¼ m. beyond Compiègne and 5 m. from Noyon is Ourscamps, on the east side of the railway, with a cotton mill established in an abbey founded in the 13th century, to which date belongs the curious chamber, the Salle des Morts. On the other side of the railway is Chiry, with, on the crest of the hills behind the village, a great Babel-like tower, which, although recently built, is composed of such bad stone that it has already begun to crumble.

NOYON, pop. 6100. Hotel du Nord opposite cathedral. In the Place du Marché au Blé is a house, partly a hotel and partly a café, built in 1683, in which John Calvin is said to have been born, although the date of the great Reformer's birth is the 10th of July 1509. Front of station, the H. du Chemin de Fer.

Noyon is a quaint, quiet, and interesting town, full of curiously built 17th cent. houses, of which a very large proportion is occupied by "rentiers," or gentry living on their income. The cathedral, well seen from the railway, is a grand yet peculiar edifice, built in the 12th, 13th, and 14th cents., on the foundations of an earlier church erected by Pepin le Bref and Charlemagne. The main entrance is bold, pleasing, and severe. Beyond the three recessed portals projects a broad porch (14th cent.) resting on three arches springing from clustered columns, strengthened by two neat flying gabled buttresses. Along the edge of the porch runs a carefully chiselled balustrade, and a delicate frieze similar to those in bands on the towers. Over the portals rise two massive square towers, covered with pyramid roofs, terminating with balustrades. The transepts and the apse have spherical terminations.

NOYON. CATHEDRAL. CALVIN.

The portals of the transepts are on the sides next the choir. The choir or chancel is short, but of great breadth, and rises in three nearly equal stages. The lowest stage consists of 9 radiating chapels with cylindrical roofs.

The interior of the edifice is 330 ft. long, upheld by 36 columns in two rows, of which 14 are plain, and the others clustered. From the columns in the nave spring early pointed arches, and from those in the choir and transepts, semicircular. Two triforium galleries extend round the church; the lower of the two is of great height and width and faced with open mullion-work, in most cases divided by an impost column. The roof groining at the extremities of the choir and transepts is gathered together with great elegance.

The chapels contain some good statues and paintings, but no valuable old glass. The most richly adorned is the chapel in front of the pulpit. The columns are encrusted with canopy work, and the roof covered with groining hung with pendants. The centre window illustrates the genealogy of our Lord; the other two, incidents in the life of Mary. The organ case and pulpit display great beauty in form and workmanship. The first door left from the main entrance opens into the cloisters, 13th cent., of which only one side still remains. Three deeply set arches with crocketed soffits and imposts of short clustered columns each with a statue under a Gothic column, separate the cloister from the Salle Capitulaire, 13th cent., which is lighted on the other side by 5 nearly lancet windows, corresponding in form with the three arches, and also with the mullion-work of the nave, only they have six instead of three foil decorations. At one end is the great chimney and chimney-piece. Four slender columns standing in the centre support the profuse groining of the roof. A door from this beautiful hall opens into the street near the main entrance. Adjoining the church and fronting the H. du Nord, is the Bibliothèque des Chanoines, 14th cent., generally closed.

Near the cathedral is the Hotel de Ville, 16th cent., of which the façade is loaded with elaborate sculpture. Opposite is a beautiful fountain 1770, on which are the words, that in Noyon "Chilperic ii. fut inhumé l'an 721. Charlemagne sacré 768. Hugues Capet elu roi 987." In the park, between the railway station and the town, is a statue to the memory of Jacques Sarrazin, a sculptor, born at Noyon in 1592; but to John Calvin there is nothing. Theodore Beza, in whose arms Calvin expired on the 27th of May 1564, says—"I have been a witness of him for 16 years, and I think I am fully entitled to say, that in this man there was exhibited the life and death of the Christian, such as it will not be easy to depreciate, such as it will be difficult to emulate." His memory was prodigious, but he used it only as the servant of his higher faculties. As a reasoner he has seldom been equalled, while as a theologian he stands on an eminence which only Augustine has surpassed.

77 CHAUNY, pop. 9020, on the Oise, with large bleachfields and **116** cotton mills. The best hotel is the Pot d'Etain in the Rue du Pont Royal, in which street, No. 13, is also a curious small timber house. The Boulevard de la Gare leads straight up from the station, parallel with the Rue du Pont Royal, to the town park. At the foot of the road leading up to the park there are to the left, the "Place," with the Palais de Justice, and a little farther the parish church.

Branch line to Saint Gobain, pop. 2100, $9\frac{1}{2}$ m. east. H. du Soleil d'Or. In this village is the most extensive manufactory of mirrors in France, founded in 1860. Below the parish church is a curious crypt.

Coach from Chauny station to **Coucy-le-Chateau**, pop. 740, $8\frac{3}{4}$ m. S. passing the villages of Pierremaude and Follembray. From Coucy another coach runs to Anizy-Pinon on the line between Laon and Soissons, which enables the tourist to visit those towns, or to proceed to Paris or Belgium without returning to Chauny. *Inns:* Pomme d'Or; Trois Empereurs; both at the Porte de Laon. Coucy is a clean walled village on an eminence adjoining the magnificent ruins of the castle founded in the 9th cent., and reconstructed in the 13th by Enguerrand III., Sire de Coucy. This fortress, considered by the celebrated French architect, Violet le Duc, the most beautiful military structure of the Middle Ages, occupies a vast area of four unequal sides, with massive round towers at each corner. Nearly in the centre of the longest side is the great dungeon tower, 206 feet high, and 110 in diameter (outside measure); ascended by 221 steps, cut within the wall, 26 feet thick. At one side is a well 236 feet deep. Above the ground floor are 4 stories, each with 12 pointed arches, from which sprang the groining of the roofs, now destroyed. The fifth, or highest tier, has 24 arches.

Of the four towers, the most interesting is the Tour du Roi, 115 feet high, and 59 in diameter. The walls, $16\frac{1}{2}$ feet thick, have still remains of mural paintings. In the centre is a deep oubliette. From this tower the visitors are generally conducted to what was formerly the Salle des Preuses (lady knights), the Salle des Gardes, with an oubliette and beautifully groined roof, and the Salle des Preux (gentlemen knights), retaining still some of the canopied niches, and lastly, to the Tour de la Poterne, where the knights had their escutcheons.

Near the Tour de la Poterne is one of the staircases leading down to the spacious underground vaulted chambers. It was here that the Empress with her suite had a dance, when she visited Coucy with Napoleon

III. in the summer of 1858. In the Tour de la Bibliotheque is a collection of spearheads, statues, and fragments of sculpture, found among the ruins.

One of the best walks is to leave the village by the Porte Soissons, near the church (also interesting), and then take the first narrow path left, round by the foot of the walls to the Porte Laon, where re-enter the village. Some pleasant views are had on the way, while the fortifications of the Porte Laon look as imposing as those of Metz.

81 TERGNIER JUNCTION, pop. 3080. Refreshment-room in 112 the station. Opposite, the Inns, Chemin de Fer; Voyageurs; France; Europe. 50 miles S.E. by rail is Reims, p. 60, passing Laon 16½ m. E. 49 m. N.W. by rail is Amiens, p. 11, passing Ham 12 m. W.

Tergnier, although a most important railway junction, is a most uninteresting village, and a most unfortunate place to be detained at. Those who cannot remain quietly in the waiting or refreshment rooms may stroll through the village to the canal, and perhaps see a barge passing the locks. Thence walk down to Tergnier, and visit the poor old church and churchyard. Round the chancel, between the painted glass windows, are curious ancient canopies bedaubed with whitewash. The railway company have large works here for the making and repairing of their rolling stock.

13 miles W. from Tergnier by the branch line to Amiens is **Ham**, pop. 2800, on the Somme. *Inns:* France; Nord. Ham is a quiet little town in the midst of marshes, with a church in part belonging to the 12th century. The interior walls are ornamented with panelled reliefs, mostly of stone. . At the opposite extremity of the town, by the Grande Rue, on the road to the railway station, is the once formidable fortress of Ham, now abandoned. Here it was Napoleon III. was imprisoned in 1840, after having been for a short time detained in the Conciergerie jail, on the Seine, in Paris. The first two rooms on the ground floor were occupied by General Montholon, then followed the guard-room, adjoining the Emperor's bath-room at the foot of the stair. Upstairs were his bedroom and library. On the other side of the passage two small rooms, exactly similar, were occupied by his doctor and servant. The doctor's room served afterwards as a prison for General. Cavaignac. Along the passage to the left, in a line with the servant's room, are the dining-room and the laboratory. On the esplanade, to the west of the Tour de Connetable (now a powder store), is his garden, with a cypress planted by him.

"On the 25th the Prince rose early, cut off his moustaches and imperial, and put on the prepared disguise—a labourer's dress, consisting of blue linen blouse and trousers, a dilapidated cap, rough wooden shoes, and dirty apron. The costume was completed by blackened eyebrows, a rough black wig hanging about his ears, a painted face, and a

HAM. THE ESCAPE OF NAPOLEON III.

short clay pipe. In spite of the risk of keeping about him papers which might betray his identity, he would not part with a couple of letters, one from his mother, the other from the Emperor. He might especially value the latter, from its containing the sentence : ' I hope that Louis Napoleon, as he grows up, will make himself worthy of the destinies which await him.'

"At seven in the morning the masons entered the fortress to resume their work. Thélin offered them something to drink, and having got them together round the table in the vestibule, ran to tell his master that the moment was come. The Prince, shouldering a plank procured beforehand, walked down the stairs, avoiding the vestibule where the men were drinking. Thélin, dressed as for a journey, also stepped into the courtyard leading his dog by a string, and walking a few paces before the Prince. As he had obtained permission the previous evening to go to St. Quentin, the keepers wished him a pleasant journey; at which he stopped to chat with them, to divert their attention from the Prince, who was gravely advancing with the plank on his shoulder, held in such a way as to screen his face. So impossible was it to guess who he was, that a labourer, taking him for one of his comrades, went up to him to speak to him; but Thélin, with great address, directed his attention to something else. A little farther on he met an officer, who, luckily, was busy reading a letter. Then he had to pass through a group of thirty soldiers assembled in front of the guard-house. Finally, having passed through all the courts, he came to the outer lodge. The porter, fearing a blow from the plank, quickly drew back his head. A few paces beyond the last sentinel, who followed him with his eyes, the Prince dropped his pipe and picked it up again. This movement served to hide his face, already half-concealed by the plank. At last, crossing the two drawbridges he was free!"

In 1815 Marshal Moncey was imprisoned in this fortress for refusing to sit in judgment on his colleague Marshal Ney; and in 1830 Prince Polignac, the minister of Charles X. But the most extraordinary case was that of Generals Lamorcière and Cavaignac, whom Napoleon III. himself shut up here after the *coup d'état* in December 1851. Ham has manufactures of cotton stuffs and clogs (sabots).

SAINT QUENTIN, pop. 37,400. *Hotels:* Cygne; France; Nord; Angleterre. This, the ancient Augusta Veromanduorum, is a strongly fortified town on a hill, on the banks of the Somme, here connected with the Scheldt by the canal St. Quentin, by which are brought the principal supplies of coal from the pits in Hainault, necessary for the important manufactures of linen and cotton carried on in this city as well as in the neighbouring towns of Cambrai and Valenciennes. The collegiate church of St. Quentin, which from a distance is a most conspicuous object, is in the town itself, concealed by houses. It is a beautiful Gothic edifice, of which the greater part was rebuilt in the 12th and 13th cents. In the crypt, 9th and 13th

St. Quentin. Ribémont. Guise. Peronne.

cents., is the tomb of Saints Quentin, Victorie, and Gentien. Some of the glass is of the 13th cent. In the principal square is the Hotel de Ville, a handsome building of the 15th cent., completely restored. Some of the walls of the halls are hung with beautifully embossed leather, and the beams of the roofs are adorned with strange-looking painted heads, made by the Spaniards. The Rue St. André leads directly from the Hotel de Ville to the church. Just behind the Hotel de Ville is the Palais de Justice, containing the ball-room of the town; and the Musée, possessing some paintings and water-colours of merit.

Branch line from St. Quentin to Guise 25 m. N. by the Sambre canal. On this line the most important towns are Ribemont (Ribodi-Mons), 10 m. from St. Quentin, pop. 3050. *Inn:* H. de l'Etoile. A small manufacturing town on an eminence rising from the Sambre canal, with walls of the 12th cent., and the parish church, in part, of the same date. Like the other places in this neighbourhood, it has manufactures of linen and calico. In this town was born M. J. A. N. C. Condorcet in September 1743. He died, bleeding and hungry, on the cold floor of a damp cell in the prison of Bourg-la-Reine, near Paris, on the 7th of April 1794. His philosophical fame is chiefly associated with the work which he wrote, when lying concealed from the emissaries of Robespierre, and with the vision of the guillotine before him.

Guise, pop. 6000. *Inn:* Couronne. A fortified manufacturing town on the Oise, and traversed by the Sambre canal. It contains a set of workmen's houses, or Familistère, with accommodation for 400 families, a castle of the 16th cent., two churches, and an hospital. Coaches to Vervins, 15 m. E., fare 3 frs., on the line from Laon to Soissons; and to Hirson on the same line by La Capelle, $12\frac{1}{2}$ m. N.E., Villers-lès-Guise and the forests of Regnaval, and Nouvion.

27 m. north-west from Saint Quentin by rail is **Peronne**, on the Somme, pop. 3880. *Hotel:* St. Claude. A fortified town in the midst of marshes and surrounded by a deep fosse. The church of St. Jean, built in 1509, and recently restored after the bombardment by the Prussians, has still some good old glass, mural paintings, and sculpture. In the Grande Place is the Hotel de Ville, 17th cent.

The Chateau, now used as barracks, has been completely restored. At the entrance are four great towers, and under them dungeons and casements, of which one is said to extend 3 miles below ground. The first tower to the right of the entrance is the Tour de Louis XI. The second tower, left hand, is the Tour Herbert, in which Charles the Simple died on the 7th October 929, after a long imprisonment. His bed occupied the triangular recess in the wall. This also is the tower in which Charles the Bold confined Louis XI., or Louis de Valois, in 1468, thus noticed by Sir Walter Scott:—

"As he entered within its darksome and gloomy strength, it seemed as if a voice screamed in his ear that warning which the Florentine has inscribed over the portal of the infernal regions, 'Leave all hope behind.'

PERONNE.　IMPRISONMENT OF LOUIS DE VALOIS.

"The broad glare of the torches outfacing the pale moon, which was more obscured on this than on the former night, and the red smoky light which they dispersed around the ancient buildings, gave a darker shade to that huge donjon, called the Earl Herbert's Tower. It was the same that Louis had viewed with misgiving presentiment on the preceding evening, and of which he was now doomed to become an inhabitant, under the terror of what violence soever the wrathful temper of his overgrown vassal might tempt him to exercise in those secret recesses of despotism. To aggravate the King's painful feelings, he saw, as he crossed the courtyard, one or two bodies, over each of which had been hastily flung a military cloak. He was not long of discerning that they were corpses of slain archers of the Scottish Guard, who having disputed, as the Count Crèvecœur informed him, the command given them to quit the post near the King's apartments, a brawl had ensued between them and the Duke's Walloon body-guards, and before it could be composed by the officers on either side, several lives had been lost.

"Meanwhile, the Seneschal, hastily summoned, was turning with laborious effort the ponderous key which opened the reluctant gate of the huge Gothic keep, and was at last fain to call for the assistance of one of Crèvecœur's attendants. When they had succeeded, six men entered with torches, and showed the way through a narrow and winding passage, commanded at different points by shot-holes from vaults and casements constructed behind, and in the thickness of the massive walls. At the end of this passage arose a stair of corresponding rudeness, consisting of huge blocks of stone, roughly dressed with the hammer, and of unequal height. Having mounted this ascent, a strong iron-clenched door admitted them to what had been the great hall of the donjon, lighted but very faintly even during the day-time (for the apertures, diminished in appearance by the excessive thickness of the walls, resembled slits rather than windows), and now, but for the blaze of the torches, almost perfectly dark. Two or three bats, and other birds of evil presage, roused by the unusual glare, flew against the lights, and threatened to extinguish them; while the Seneschal formally apologised to the King that the State-hall had not been put in order, such was the hurry of the notice sent to him; and adding, that, in truth, the apartment had not been in use for twenty years, and rarely before that time, so far as ever he had heard, since the time of King Charles the Simple.

"'King Charles the Simple!' echoed Louis; 'I know the history of the Tower now.—He was here murdered by his treacherous vassal, Herbert, Earl of Vermandois—So say our annals. I knew there was something concerning the Castle of Peronne which dwelt on my mind, though I could not recall the circumstance.—*Here*, then, my predecessor was slain!'

"'Not here, not exactly here, and please your Majesty,' said the old Seneschal, stepping with the eager haste of a cicerone, who shows the curiosities of such a place—'Not *here*, but in the side chamber a little onward, which opens from your Majesty's bedchamber.'

"He hastily opened a wicket at the upper end of the hall, which led into a bedchamber, small, as is usual in those old buildings; but, even for that

| PARIS. | BUSIGNY. CAMBRAI. FÉNELON. | BRUSSELS |
| MILES FROM | | MILES TO |

reason, rather more comfortable than the waste hall through which they had passed. Some hasty preparations had been here made for the King's accommodation. Arras had been tacked up, a fire lighted in the rusty grate, which had been long unused, and a pallet laid down for those gentlemen who were to pass the night in his chamber, as was then usual.

"'We will get beds in the hall for the rest of your attendants,' said the garrulous old man; 'but we have had such brief notice, if it please your Majesty—And if it please your Majesty to look upon this little wicket behind the arras, it opens into the little old cabinet in the thickness of the wall, where Charles was slain; and there is a secret passage from below, which admitted the men who were to deal with him. And your Majesty, whose eyesight I hope is better than mine, may see the blood still on the oak-floor, though the thing was done five hundred years ago.'

"While he thus spoke, he kept fumbling to open the postern of which he spoke, until the King said, 'Forbear, old man—forbear but a little while, when thou mayest have a newer tale to tell, and fresher blood to show.'"

Fee to Concierge 1 fr. From Peronne a line extends 10½ m. S. to Chaulnes, pop. 2000, with large modern church: an important junction, 13 m. W. from Ham, and 24 m. W. from Amiens.

114 BUSIGNY, pop. 3250, on the Riot, at the foot of wooded **79** hills. It has manufactories of merinoes and cashmere shawls. Junction with line to Cambrai, 15½ m. north.

Cambrai, pop. 19,050. *Hotels:* France; Commerce; Messageries. A fortified town of the second class on the Escaut, the original seat of the manufacture of cambric (batiste), for which it is still famous. The citadel and the castle of Selles, with its 5 gates, date from the 16th cent. Just outside the gate Notre Dame are two menhirs called the twin stones. The cathedral, lately rebuilt, was commenced in the 12th cent., finished in the 15th, and burned down in 1859. Among the works of art saved, are: water-colours by Geeraert of Antwerp, and the monuments of Fénelon and Belmas by David of Angers. The tomb of Fénelon was violated in 1793, and his coffin melted into bullets. It was from the pulpit of this church that he poured forth those splendid discourses which have now become classic. When the misfortunes of the war which chastised the ambition of Louis brought the allied army into the diocese, Fénelon, by his firmness, wisdom, and eloquence, inspired the hostile commanders, Marlborough and Eugene, with pity and respect for the unfortunate province of Flanders.

Of the former archiepiscopal palace nothing but a portal remains, the present palace being, in what was a Benedictine convent, founded in the 13th cent., but repaired and restored in the 17th. The church of St. Gery, 18th cent., has a Christ being laid in the tomb, by Rubens.

Besides these buildings there are, the hospital of St. Julien, restored; the Tour des Arquets, 14th cent.; the Hotel de Ville, 14th cent., and altered and repaired in 1861, and the Belfry, commenced in the 15th cent. In what was formerly the church of the hospital of St. John, is the public library, containing upwards of 35,500 vols., and 1230 manuscripts.

PARIS — VALENCIENNES. ANTOINE WATTEAU. — BRUSSELS
MILES FROM / MILES TO

5½ miles beyond Busigny is Le Cateau-Cambresis, pop. 10,000, on the Selle. *Hotels:* France; Mouton Blanc. An important manufacturing town. The parish church, 16th cent., formed part of the abbey of St. André, founded in 1021. In the church, the "via crucis" is represented on large pictures.

134¼ AULNOYE. Bedrooms and refreshment rooms at station. 58¾ The village, pop. 1000, is about a mile from the station. Junction with line to **Valenciennes**, 21¼ m. N.W., pop. 23,850. *Hotels:* Commerce; Princes; Poste; Restaurant du Chemin de Fer. 20 m. from Mons, 20 from Douai, 30 from Lille, and 59 from Brussels. Valenciennes is a fortified and manufacturing town on the Escaut, in the centre of a great coal basin covering an area of 148,270 acres. It has a very large square, some wide streets, and many agreeable walks. The Picture Gallery is in the Hotel de Ville, built in 1612. The best picture is a triptych by Rubens, in the last room, representing the martyrdom of Stephen. Enter by the gate nearest the end of the Place, and ascend to the right. North from the Grande Place, by the Rue de Lormerie, is the Place de St. Gery, with a garden, containing a statue to the memory of Jean Froissart, the author of the celebrated chronicles, born at Valenciennes about the year 1337, and for some time the private secretary of Philippa of Hainault, wife of Edward III., and mother of the Black Prince. No historian has ever drawn so many and such vivid portraits as are to be found in his graphic account of the things done in the 14th cent. 'Most of them are, however, portraits of men as they seemed to the writer, not of men as they were. His design was to give delight and pleasure. "Before I commence this book," he says, "I pray the Saviour of all the world, who created everything out of nothing, that he will also create and put in me sense and understanding of so much worth, that this book, which I have begun, I may continue and persevere in, so that all those who shall read, see, and hear it may find in it delight and pleasure." Another of the children of Valenciennes is Antoine Watteau, born in 1684, died on July 18, 1721. His fêtes elegantes, pastoral pieces, and genre pictures, are remarkable for grace and originality, as well as his landscapes; which inaugurated a more unconventional method of painting.

A great deal of lace and cambric is manufactured at Valenciennes.

22½ m. S. from Lille, and 7½ m. N. from Valenciennes by rail, is **St. Amand-les-Eaux**, pop. 10,500. *Hotels:* Mouton Blanc; Nord. In the principal square is a remarkable façade, all that remains of a Benedictine Abbey, built in the 17th century, consisting of three square towers adorned with circular and rectangular niches, and supported by five tiers of columns, of which the upper four are banded and fascicled. Over the towers are crocketed and perforated domes on drums similar to the towers. Two miles from St. Amand is a large bathing establishment, with cold sulphurous springs and deep mud baths. The course lasts three weeks. Pension in the establishment per day, 20 frs.

In a hundred parts of mud, 90 are silica, and the remaining ten consist of carbonate of lime, peroxide of iron, alumina, carbonate of magnesia, and oxide of manganese. It is strongly impregnated with carbonic acid and sulphuretted hydrogen gases. The space, 750 square yards, containing the semi-liquid earth, is divided into baths, the contents of which are constantly renewed by the unceasing flow of the mineral springs that liquefy the substance. The natural temperature is 75° Fahr., but it is raised by artificial means. These baths are recommended for atrophy of the limbs, muscular contractions, stiffness of the joints, and sprains.

142 MAUBEUGE, pop. 13,400. *Hotels:* Grand Cerf; Nord. A 51 first-class fortified town on the Sambre, by which it exports large quantities of coal, marble, and slate. It has important manufactories of firearms, and of articles of beaten and rolled iron. The parish church contains a curious reliquary. On the right bank of the river is the fountain de la Falize visited by pilgrims. Coach to Solre-le-Chateau. *Inns:* Croix de Bourgogne; Lion d'Or, 11¼ m. S., fare 1¾ frs., pop. 2780. The parish church, 15th cent., has some beautiful glass painted in 1532. The Hotel de Ville is of the 16th cent. In the neighbourhood are 2 menhirs, called the Pierres de St. Martin.

143½ FEIGNIES, pop. 2660. Refreshment-room at station. Hotel 49½ du Nord. French custom-house and time. 2 m. W. is the village of Malplaquet, the scene of the victory gained by the Duke of Marlborough and Prince Eugene over the French under Marshals Villars and Boufflers, 11th Sept. 1709. It was here also, where, after the battle of Waterloo, the Duke of Wellington entered France (June 21), and whence, on the 22d of June 1815, he issued his friendly proclamation to the French nation, assuring them, "that nothing should be taken, either by officers or soldiers, for which payment be not made." No proclamation of a similar nature was issued by Blücher, hence his troops in their advance to Paris committed great excesses, and imposed severe exactions along their whole line of march.

146 QUEVY. Belgian custom-house and time, 9 minutes before 47 French time. From Quevy the train passes Frameries and Cuesmes, and then halts at Mons, 9 m. from Quevy, 155 from Paris, and 38 from Brussels. From Mons the train moves northward by Ghlin, Jurbise, Soignies, Braine-le-Comte, and Hal, and arrives at the Station du Sud of Brussels, 193 m. N.E. from Paris.

Paris to Aix la Chapelle and Cologne.

By Soissons, Laon, Vervins, Hirson, Anor, Momignies, Chimay, Mariembourg, Bomerée, Doische, Hastière (beautifully situated on the banks of the Meuse), Dinant, Namur, Huy, Liege, Pepinster, Verviers, and Herbesthal 310 m. N.E.

The more direct route is to approach Namur by Tergnier, p. 36; **Busigny**, p. 40; Aulnoye, p. 41; Jeumont, French frontier town and custom-house; Erquelines, Belgian frontier town and custom-house; and Charleroi. Although only 8¼ miles shorter, it is considerably more rapid, but not so picturesque. Namur is from Paris, by Charleroi, 191¼ m., or 8 hours 45 minutes. See page 54.

PARIS	See Map, p. 1.	COLOGNE
MILES FROM		MILES TO

PARIS, start from the station of the Chemins de Fer du Nord. **310** If it be desired to take the long route, consult the table "Paris, Soissons, Laon, Vervins et Hastière." But for the other, the table on the second leaf back, "Paris, Liège et Cologne."

21 miles N.E. from Paris is **Dammartin**, pop. 1900. *Inn:* St. Anne. Omnibus at station. A pleasant town on an eminence 460 ft. high. St. Jean, the parish church, was built in the 13th, 15th, and 16th cents. Farther from the station is Notre Dame, built in the 13th and 14th cents. It contains the tomb of a famous political adventurer, Antoine de Chabannes, who enriched himself by exactions, and from the spoil of Jacques Cœur, when he fell into disgrace. According to the words on the monument, he died on the Christmas of 1488. Of the magnificent castle, blown up by Richelieu, there remain only a few pieces of the walls. The site is now occupied by a park.

27 miles from Paris, and 38 miles S.W. from Soissons, is **Le Plessis-Belleville**, a village of 400 inhabitants. 3¾ m. N.W. from Plessis, by coach 1 fr., is **Ermenonville**, pop. 500, on the **Launette**. *Inn:* H. de la Providence. Jean-Jacques Rousseau, in his 66th year, distressed in mind and body, accepted the hospitality offered him by M. Gerardin in his chateau of Ermenonville, in April 1778. To testify his gratitude, he assisted in the education of the children. Six weeks afterwards, on the 3d of July 1778, he terminated his existence, and was buried in the Ile des Peupliers, whence his remains were removed to the Pantheon of Paris, in 1794. On a hill overlooking the castle and this lake, a temple has been erected to his memory, of which each column bears an inscription. No. 1. Newton, lucem; 2. Descartes, nil rebus inane; 3. Voltaire, ridiculum; 4. Penn, humanitatem; 5. Montesquieu, justitiam; 6. Rousseau, naturam.

About 1¾ mile from the Chateau is Chalis, with the ruins of an abbey, founded in 1136 by Louis Le Gros. Near it is a charming little chapel of the 13th cent.

PARIS MILES FROM **Alexander Dumas. Racine. Soissons.** COLOGNE MILES TO

30½ miles from Paris, and 3½ from Le Plessis, is **Nanteuil-le-Haudouin**, pop. 2000, in the valley of the Nonette. *Inns:* Croix d'Or; Ville de Nanteuil. Coach daily to Senlis (p. 16), passing Pont l'Eveque. Nanteuil has large beds of cresses, and manufactories of trimmings and gloves.

38 miles from Paris is **Crepy**, pop. 3500. *Inn:* H. de la Bannière. Junction with branch to Chantilly, 19 m. W., passing Senlis, 11½ m. W., p. 16. Crepy is a very pleasant little town, with large excavations, some of them not unlike those of Senlis. 7 m. N. from Crepy, on the border of the forest of Compiegne, is Marienval, with a beautiful abbey, 11th cent., restored

43½ miles from Paris is Villers-Cotterets, pop. 3500, on the border of a forest, and on a small tributary of the Oise. *Inns:* Dauphin; Epée. This is the birthplace of Alexander Dumas, père, 1802, in the Rue Lormet. Junction with branch to Port aux Perches, 5½ m. S., on the Ourcq. A little farther up the Ourcq is Ferté-Milon, with a castle and church dating from the 15th cent. In the town is a statue by David of Racine, who was born here, and died in Paris, on the 22d April 1699, in No. 21 Rue Visconti, where he had lived 40 years. He is the poet of the heart and the affections, and yields to none in the truth, the beauty, and the force of his delineations; while such is his perfection of purity and harmony of diction, that in all his pieces there is not a single verse which could be replaced by another. All is just and true; all is full of that poetry of imagery and sentiments, and that continued elegance, which, since the time of the Greeks, Virgil and Racine have almost alone possessed.

7½ miles beyond Villers-Cotterets station is Longport, pop. 300, with the interesting ruins of a Cistercian abbey, founded in 1131 by Raoul IV., Count of Crepy. Adjoining is a chateau, built in the 17th cent., containing a collection of the art treasures found in the abbey. Catalogue, 1½ fr., sold by the concierge.

65¼ **SOISSONS**, pop. 12,000, on the river Aisne. *Hotels:* Nearest 244¾ the railway station is the Hotel Soleil d'Or; farther up the main street the Lion Rouge, the best; a little beyond is the Couronne. Between these two hotels are the post and telegraph offices, and opposite, the large barracks of Notre Dame. The fortified town of Soissons was an important place even before the arrival of the Romans. Cæsar says, B.C. 58, that the territory of the Suessiones was fertile and extensive, and governed by King Galba, one of the most powerful chiefs of Gaul. When Clovis, by the defeat of Syagrius in 486, had put an end to the

Soissons. St. Jean-des-Vignes. St. Médard.

Roman rule in France, Soissons was chosen as the capital of his dominions, and for some time afterwards, the Kings of France were called the Kings of Soissons. Christianity was brought to Soissons by Saints Crepin and Crepinien, who suffered martyrdom in 297. Not to be chargeable to their converts, they preached through the day, and laboured at night, working with their own hands at shoemaking. On this account they have been considered ever since the patrons of the guild of the shoemakers.

But although the town dates from such an early period, it has been so often destroyed and rebuilt that it has a modern aspect. From the railway station, an avenue nearly a mile long leads to the town. Just within the gate is the Hotel Soleil d'Or, on the right; and to the left, the road which leads round by the ramparts to the truly magnificent façade (13th cent.), of what was the abbey of St. Jean des Vignes. It is within a large enclosure just without the arsenal. At the large iron gate is the house of the concierge, where permission to ascend is obtained. The greater of the 2 towers is 246 feet high, and is ascended the length of the high window in the spire by 308 excellent stone steps. The other tower is $229\frac{1}{2}$ ft. high, and is of a different form, which is most certainly a defect, but a defect atoned by their transcendent elegance, and the beauty of the portals, and the other parts they enclose. Adjoining the lower of the two towers, is the refectory, now converted into a storehouse. On the other side of it, in the arsenal, is part of the cloister (1230-1241), of which the piece at right angles to it is seen distinctly from the tower; but those wishing to inspect the cloisters more minutely must go round to the concierge of the arsenal.

When up the great tower the height of the base of the wheel window, a passage in front leads across the façade to the smaller tower, whence there is a good view of the cloister. From this part the small tower may be ascended to the balustrade at the foot of the spire; but the steps are considerably worn and encumbered with the small sticks from the jackdaws' nests. This noble church, with its palatial buildings, surrounded by a mighty buttressed wall of hewn stone, was, with the exception of the few remaining fragments, levelled to the ground by the French themselves in 1794. Fee to concierge $\frac{1}{2}$ fr.

Now walk back to the main street, and continue it till past the H. Lion Rouge, the barracks, and the post-office, to the Place St. Pierre, on the right, with the decorated church of St. Pierre, 12th cent.

To visit St. Médard and the remains of the royal castle, descend by the steep street leading from St. Pierre to the bridge across the Aisne.

Asylum for the Deaf and Dumb. Cathedral.

On the other side of the river take the first narrow road right, which, after ascending a short way by the right bank, crosses the fields to the avenue leading up to the church.

The concierge conducts visitors, first to the chapel, which is a piece of the old cloister, dating from about the 13th cent.; then to the crypt, which was formerly under the church of St. Médard, but now it is under some modern class-rooms. Part of the crypt was constructed by Clotaire, and dates from the 6th cent., and the rest from the 11th. A lobby 22 yards long extends down the centre, from north to south. From the eastern side ramify chapels, 16 feet long and 10 feet wide; while from the western ramify similar excavations, in which the stone sarcophagi were deposited. At the entrance are shown the stone coffins of Clotaire and St. Médard. From the crypt visitors are taken to the remains of the castle of the early kings, where exists still the cell in which Clothaire perfidiously confined his father, Louis le Debonnaire, son of Charlemagne, in 833. In the same cell is an inscription scratched on the wall by some unhappy prisoner of the 15th cent. In the tower near the terrace, Abelarde is said to have been imprisoned.

Within the grounds are 2 large houses, one for blind, deaf, and dumb boys, and the other for girls. The boys are taught trades, and the girls occupations connected with a household. Besides communication by signs, they are taught to speak with the lips, an extremely difficult kind of instruction, requiring the exercise of great patience.

Now return to St. Pierre and walk up the street, to the **Cathedral**, seen on the left. It was commenced in 1130, and left as it now is in 1212. The façade is plain and chaste, but incomplete. Only the S.W. tower, 216 feet high, is finished. It is ascended by 354 steps, and commands an excellent view. The concierge lives at the foot. It is difficult to see the outside of the church properly on account of the surrounding houses and walls. The interior presents an admirable assemblage of well-proportioned parts, all harmonising with each other. Thirty-four columns, including the large piers, surround the nave and choir. On them rest the early pointed arches, which bear the arcaded triforium, and the clerestory windows; and from them spring the clustered shafts which support the vaulting of the roof. In the apse, just behind the altar, are 9 tall windows of richly coloured, 13th cent., glass. Above them are 5 more in the clerestory. The glass in the rose, and skilfully-designed double mullioned windows of the north transept is also brilliant and valuable. In the N. transept is a Visitation of the Shepherds attributed to Rubens, and a piece of old tapestry. The south transept has a semicircular termination surrounded by arches on slender and graceful shafts. At the right and left of the main entrance are statues of Henriette Lorraine d'Elbœuf, abbess of Notre Dame from 1660 to 1669, and Gabrielle Marie de la Rochefoucauld, abbess of Notre Dame from 1683 to 1693. Originally they stood in the abbey church of Notre Dame.

A little farther down the main street is the Hotel de Ville, 18th cent., with, in the court, the statue of Paillet. In the building are the library and museum. At the end of the street is the church of Saint Léger, dating from the 13th cent., but the most of the church is much later. The apse is seven-sided over a crypt of the 11th cent. The door on the left, or north side of the choir, opens into the cloister, 13th cent., of the conventual buildings, now a seminary. From the cloister a stair descends to the crypt. At Soissons junction with line to Reims, 33 m. S.E., p. 59, and to Compiègne, p. 31, 23 m. W.

76½ m. from Paris is the station for Anizy and Pinon. Anizy, pop. 1200. *Inns*: at station Alsace et Lorraine; in village Lion d'Or. Coach to Coucy-le-Chateau, p. 35. This pleasant little town on the Ailette, nearly a mile from the station, produces large quantities of asparagus. Pinon, pop. 700, is south from Anizy, near a beautiful castle built in 1730, in the midst of grounds containing some fine pine-trees; hence the name.

LAON (pronounced Lang), pop. 9250. *Hotels*: fronting the stat. at the foot of the hill are some good second-class houses; Hotel du *Commerce, clean and moderate; carriages hired out. H. and Café de la Gare. By the side of it are the steps leading up to the town. The carriage-road is more circuitous. An omnibus awaits passengers. At the top of the road, immediately after passing the town gate, are the hotels Ecu de France and Bannière. Farther up, this street joins another at right angles, of which the extension towards the left is called the Rue du Bourg, and towards the right the Rue de St. Jean. In No. 9 Rue du Bourg are the Library and Museum, and opposite the *Hotel de la Hure, the best. At No. 38 Rue Saint Jean is the Post-Office. Diligences from the station to Liesse and Montcornet. Liesse is 10 m. distant and is visited by pilgrims. The hotels St. Martin and the Lion d'Or of Liesse send their omnibuses to the Laon.

In a general way it may be said that the main street of Laon extends with a curve from east to west, having at the west end the cathedral and at the other termination the church of St. Martin. From the main street, numerous short streets ramify to the left and

LAON. PUBLIC LIBRARY. CATHEDRAL.

right, leading to the beautiful walks round by the ramparts commanding extensive views of the plain below and shaded by rows of elms. Ascending by the Rue du Bourg, we reach on the right at No. 9, the Public Library, open daily excepting Sunday, from 1 to 3. It contains 2000 autographs of the kings of France, from those of Lothaire, grandson of Charlemagne, to those of the latest date; along with autographs of most of the distinguished men born in France. There are also 30,000 vols. and a valuable collection of miniatures and paintings. The Museum contains Roman and Celtic antiquities. A little higher up this street is the Hotel de Ville, a modern building, with, in front, a bronze statue of Maréchal Serurier, who died in 1819.

On the highest part of the town stands the **Cathedral**. The façade, 12th and 13th cent., consists of 3 recessed doorways, each having about one-fourth of the soffit of the arch covered with sculpture, and each enclosed in a triangular canopy with figures in bold relief at the apex. Over the centre and largest portal is a very beautiful rose window, glowing between two open square towers, each 186 ft. high, supported by pillared buttresses attached diagonally. Through the mullion-work at the top of the towers, peer colossal figures of horses and horned cattle, cut in stone. At the centre and over the transepts are similar towers, each 196 ft. high, but with less ornament.

The interior presents a splendid pile of masonry lighted by 3 magnificent circular and 4 oblong windows of valuable 13th cent. glass, and sustained by 58 detached columns, of which 10 are great massive piers, ascending to the vaulting of the roof. Fifty-six arches spring from the capitals of the columns. Over these arches run 2 triforium galleries. The lower triforium is of great dimensions, the arches too are equal in span to those resting on the columns, only, as in Noyon, they have in the centre an impost column. Behind the outside row of columns, piers, and arches, runs an equal number of arches on strong attached piers, each arch, excepting the three first on each side of the main portal, covering the entrance into a chapel, shut off from the aisles by a balustrade of 12 stone colonnettes, in no way interfering with the area of the building nor with the harmony of all the different parts composing the vast and lofty interior, of which the length, inside measure, is 120 yards by 22 wide. The length of the transepts is 58 yards by about 20 wide. The height of the roof is 79 ft. and of the cupola 128 ft. On one side of the church is the former Palais Episcopal with a cloister, now the Palais de Justice. On the other side is the Salle Capitulaire, with a frieze below the eaves of the roof.

St. Martin. Anor. Momignies. Chimay. Mariembourg.

Returning to where we started, and taking the street to the right, the Rue Saint Jean, at No. 38, right hand, we pass the Post-Office ; and a good way beyond, at the extremity of the town, arrive at the church of St. Martin, rebuilt in the 13th century. Here, to the left, on the main entrance, is a white marble monument of an abbess, 14th century ; and to the right the monument of the Sire de Coucy, killed at the battle of Mansourah in Egypt, fighting by the side of St. Louis.

Adjoining St. Martin's is the Hotel Dieu, in an old monastery.

From St. Martin's descend again to the avenue outside the ramparts, and walk southwards to a large building on the point of the hill. It was a Benedictine monastery, but is now a seminary. Under the gardens are enormous cellars. 32 m. S. by rail is Reims, p. 59.

The railway between Laon and Hirson, 35½ m. N., traverses a well-cultivated undulating country. A little more than halfway between these 2 towns, it passes Vervins, pop. 2860. *Inns:* Epée ; Grand Cerf. A small manufacturing town built on an eminence. Coach to Guise, 15 m. W. Hirson, pop. 4400, on the Oise. H. de la Gare, junction here with line to Mezières-Charleville, 35 m. S.E., see p. 64.

Anor, 127¼ m. N.E. from Paris, 5 m. from Hirson, and 40½ m. from Laon, is a small French frontier town and custom-house station. Five m. E. is Momignies, Belgian frontier town and custom-house station. Belgian time 9 minutes in advance of French. 8 m. beyond is Chimay, pop. 3000, a manufacturing town with a castle in the centre of an extensive park intersected by the river Blanche. The church Ste. Monegunde claims the honour of holding the bones of the great chronicler Jean Froissart, of which he was a canon. Tradition assigns 1410 as the date of his death. 10 m. beyond Chimay, or 22½ m. from Anor, is Mariembourg, pop. 1000. H. du Commerce, built in 1542 by Mary of Hungary, sister of Charles V. 18½ m. from Mariembourg, 41 from Anor, and 168½ m. N.E. from Paris, by Soissons, Laon, and Anor, is Hastière on the Meuse, whence the road becomes very picturesque. For Hastière, see under Givet to Liege.

177 m. N.E. from Paris and 14¼ from Givet is Dinant, 17½ m. S. from Namur. 194 m. from Paris is Namur. Liege 232 m. from Paris by Dinant, 62¼ m. S.E. from Brussels, and 78 from Cologne. 5 m. from Liege is Chaudfontaine. 12½ m. E. from Liege is Pepinster, 240 m. from Paris, 22 m. W. from Aix-la-Chapelle, and 65¼ from Cologne. For the above, see Index.

243 m. from Paris and 63 from Cologne is **Verviers** (*Hotels:* at the station the H. du Chemin de Fer ; H. Allemagne ; in the town

the Pays Bas), pop. 42,000, on the Vesdre or Vesder, of which the water is favourable for dyeing. The Belgian army receives its cloth from the extensive manufactories in this town. 3¼ m. beyond Verviers, is Dolhain station, where carriages can be had for visiting (half-hour) the gigantic reservoir formed by damming up the little river Gileppe, capable of containing nearly 14 millions of cubic yards of water. The wall is 154 ft. high, 689 ft. long, 197 ft. thick at the base, and 83 ft. thick at the top. The reservoir is about 150 ft. deep, and covers an area of 200 acres. The lion by Bourre, on the top of the embankment, is 39 ft. long and 43 ft. high. This reservoir was necessary to maintain in dry summers a sufficient supply of water for the manufactories of Verviers; with which it is connected by an aqueduct 5½ m. long. Dolhain is prettily situated in the valley of the Vesdre. It has supplanted the ancient town of Limburg, destroyed by Louis XIV. in 1675. Above the town is the castle of Limburg, the seat of the ancient noble family of that name. In the neighbourhood are important coal and zinc mines. A great deal of very good cheese is made here.

5 m. from Dolhain, and 253 from Paris, is Herbesthal, Prussian custom-house. Then after passing Astenet station and crossing the Göhl valley by a viaduct, 125 ft. high, and traversing a tunnel in a sandhill, 2220 ft. long, it reaches Ronheide station, whence the train descends to

Aix-la-Chapelle, or Aachen, 9 m. from Herbesthal, 262 from Paris, and 44 from Cologne. Pop. 80,000. For London to Aix-la-Chapelle *viâ* Calais or Ostend, see the Continental Time-tables of the London, Chatham, and Dover Railway, 3d., or by post 4½d. German custom-house at station.

In the Friedrich Wilhelm Platz is the drinking fountain called the Elisenbrunnen, under a handsome colonnade of fluted Doric columns. Opposite is the Hotel Nuellens, and a little farther off the Hotel Belle Vue. In the Büchel is the Hotel du Grand Monarque; then the hotel and bath-house of the Grand Bain Neuf; and at the head of the street the principal bath-house and hotel, called the Kaiserbad, a very large establishment. The Kurhaus is in the Komphausbadstrasse, opposite the hotel and bath-house of Cornelius; almost adjoining is the hotel and bath-house of the Rose. On the other side of the Kurhaus are the Imperial Crown Hotel and the Hotel Dragon. All the above are first-class hotels. Near the stations at the Marschierthor is the *Union Hotel; and the Stadt Duren in the Bahnhofs Platz; the Nord in the Römer Strasse, which are less expensive.

Aix-la-Chapelle. German Money. Cathedral.

English chapel in the Anna Strasse.

Cab-fares. The course.—1 person 60 pf., each additional person 20 pf. Each trunk 30 pf. From 10 p.m. to 6 a.m. double fares.

The money used here is now the silver mark equivalent to our shilling, divided into 100 small copper coins called pfennings. The gold coins are in pieces 10 and 20 marks; whose intrinsic value is under that of the sovereign and half-sovereign, as the Prussian coins have a larger amount of alloy. The old thaler still exists in the form of a silver piece of 3 marks, and the old silber groschen in the form of a nickel coin worth 10 pfennings. A 10-mark gold piece is called a krone, and a piece of 20 marks a doppelkrone, worth respectively 9s. 10d. and 19s. 8d. The Deutsche Reichsbank issue notes of 100, 500, and 1000 marks.

The waters of Aix-la-Chapelle are sulphurous, temperature 136° Fahr., and are recommended for rheumatic and arthritic pains.

Aix-la-Chapelle lies in a valley surrounded by hills. The handsome streets and houses are all in the neighbourhood of the Elisenbrunnen. In the centre of the town is the **Cathedral**, built by Charlemagne in 796, as a chapel for his place of sepulture, and consecrated by Pope Leo III. in 804. The choir, by Gerhard Chorus in 1353, is lighted by nine small and four large modern painted windows. The exterior is supported by richly ornamented buttresses. The central part, or octagon, built by Charlemagne, is of rough masonry, 48 ft. in diameter and 104 high. Two tiers of semicircular arches surround the interior; the arches of the upper tier being divided by columns, of which the capitals were presented to the church by Pio Nono. The roof of the octagon is in the form of a dome, with eight triangular divisions like the keels of ships, and ornamented with a mosaic of Jesus Christ, surrounded by saints, on a gold ground. The gilded candelabrum was presented to the church by Frederick Barbarossa in 1165. In the vault, under the large slab in the centre of the floor of the octagon, with the words "Carolo Magno" inscribed on it, Otho III., in the year 1000, discovered the body of the emperor arrayed in imperial robes, seated on a white marble throne covered with plates of gold. His feet were resting on a beautifully sculptured sarcophagus. On his head was the crown he had worn during life, a sceptre was in his right hand, and a jewelled mantle of state over his shoulders; a sword was buckled to his side, and a copy of the gospels lay upon his knees. Otho, having removed all the valuables, closed the vault, which, however, was again opened, in 1266, by Frederick Barbarossa. This time the body on

Relics. Hotel de Ville. Springs or Quellen.

being touched crumbled into dust, excepting the skull and some of the large bones now in the reliquary. The marble chair is now in a box in the gallery under the second tier of arches, and the sarcophagus in a kind of cupboard to the left. To see the throne and the relics, apply to the sacristan. The door of the sacristy is on the right hand of the choir, below the pulpit. To see the throne and sarcophagus costs from 1 to 1½ mark. There are 2 classes of relics, the great and the small. The former are shown every seventh year between the 10th and 24th of July. Of them, the 4 most precious are contained in a sumptuous Romanesque shrine; a gown which belonged to Mary; the swaddling clothes of the child Jesus; the linen our Lord wore round his loins on the cross; and the cloth in which the head of John the Baptist was wrapped. Within glass cases are: a gold enamelled bust of Charlemagne, 14th cent., his hunting horn; a cross presented by Lothaire to the church, 12th cent; magnificently executed reliquaries and numerous gold and silver vessels. The smaller relics embrace an immense number of less valuable articles, many very curious and requiring the exercise of a vigorous faith to be able to appreciate. Among the articles of art are shrines, monstrances, pyxes, chasubles, chalices, and crosses of gold, silver, and ivory, many set with precious stones. Fee to see the small relics for 1 to 3 persons 3 marks, each additional person 1 mark.

Near the cathedral in the Market Place is the Rathhaus or Hotel de Ville, erected in 1353 on the site of the palace of Charlemagne. The hall in the upper story is ornamented with eight modern fresco paintings illustrating the history of Charlemagne. One of them represents the opening of his vault by Otho III. Immediately below this hall is the council-chamber, which contains, among other paintings, a full-length portrait of Charlemagne, painted in the 16th century. In front of the Rathhaus is an ancient well, with a statue of Charlemagne on a pedestal rising from the centre of the basin. To visit the Rathhaus, apply to the doorkeeper. His bell is on the left hand of the vestibule.

The springs of Aix-la-Chapelle are divided into upper and lower, temperature being the only real difference between them, according to their position with respect to their common source. The upper or Obere Quellen being the nearer, their temperature ranges from 125° to 131° Fahr.; while that of the Untere Quellen ranges from 112° to 118° Fahr. The medicinal effects of the water depend in a great measure on the amount of sulphuretted hydrogen gas it contains, in combination with a larger amount of nitrogen, than in any other sulphurous

ACTION. TEMPERATURE AND CONTENTS. BORCETTE.

spring in Europe. Although highly sulphurous, the water is seldom rejected by even the most fastidious stomach.

"The action of the water is that of a stimulant, operating principally on the kidneys and skin. This determination to the surface and renal organs explains the efficacy of the water in many cutaneous diseases, glandular enlargements, biliary obstructions, atonic dyspepsia, renal complaints, uterine derangements, impaired health from metallic poisoning by mercury or lead, and in cases of lurking constitutional syphilis. The mineral waters of Aix-la-Chapelle are also prescribed in cases of chronic rheumatism-arthritis, rheumatism, and sciatica; and Dr. Velten informs me that he has seen benefit derived from their use in some forms of chronic bronchitis and catarrh. The course of the *Aachen* baths and waters is usually six weeks, and few can continue it longer, as the effect is so debilitating that most patients can only use the douche twice a week, and at the end of a course, even when cured of their original complaint, generally require a short course of some chalybeate water," such as Spa, p. 242.—Dr. Madden's *Health Resorts*.

All the springs contain a little iron, but there are others which contain about ½ a grain to the pint, and which are cold and rise from the clay slate; while the hot springs rise from fissures in the limestone rock. These feeble chalybeate springs are of little therapeutic importance.

About 1½ m. from Aix, by the Marschier Thor, is the **Lousberg**, 200 feet above it, laid out as a park with shady walks commanding good views. On the top are an obelisk and a café.

To the S.E. of Aix, is what now may be called its suburb, Borcette or Burtscheid, pop. 10,500. *Hotels:* Rosenbad; Carlsbad; Schwertbad.

"The mineral springs of this quarter are divided into sulphurous and saline. The sources in the upper part of the town are distinguished from the lower springs, as well as from those of Aachen, by not containing either sulphate of soda or sulphuretted hydrogen gas. Of the sulphurous waters of Borcette, the most important is the Trinkquelle. The temperature of this spring is 150°, and it contains 30 grains of saline ingredients to the pint, 20 grains of which is chloride of sodium, 2 grains sulphate of soda, and 6 grains carbonate of soda.

"Amongst the non-sulphurous sources that most generally used is the Kochbrunnen, the temperature of which is 156°, and its chief saline constituents carbonate and sulphate of soda, and chloride of sodium.

"The waters of Borcette, which are warmer than any of those of Aix, are employed internally and externally, and are prescribed in cutaneous diseases—in dyspepsia and hepatic complaints, and in calculous affections."
—Dr. Madden's *Health Resorts*.

44 miles from Aix-la-Chapelle, or from 1½ to 2 hours, through a very picturesque and interesting country, is Cologne.

COLOGNE. HOTELS.

Nearly half-way, or 27 m. from Aix, and 17 from Cologne, is the busy manufacturing town of Düren, pop. 15,000. *Hotels:* Mommer; *Windhäuser: containing large asylums for the blind and insane, and the church of St. Anne, with a lofty tower.

At Düren, junction with rail to Treves, 108 miles south, by the beautiful valley of Kylthal.

Cologne: a fortified town of the first class, on the Rhine, 115 ft. above the sea. Pop. 136,000. The streets leading to the Rhine have their names painted red. Those parallel to the Rhine have their names painted black. *Hotels:* on the Rhine, at the side of the railway bridge to Deutz, and near the cathedral, the Hotel du Nord; in the centre of the town, in the Brücken Strasse, the Disch, Vienne, and Mayence; in the Heumarkt, the Victoria; opposite the Museum, the H. de Paris; between the station and the cathedral are H. Ernst, and near it the Dom hotel (not the Domhof). All the above are good. On the wharf of the Cologne and Mayence steamers, the hotels Holland, Cologne, and Royal; in the Hoch Trasse, the Weber hotel, also good; in Deutz, the hotels Belle Vue, Prinz Carl.

Post-office in the Glocken Gasse, near the Hotel Disch. At No. 4711 of this same street is one of the shops for the sale of J. M. Farina's Eau de Cologne. *English Chapel*, No. 3 Bischofsgarten Strasse. Steamers leave for Bonn, Coblence, Mainz, and Mannheim, every three hours.

Cab-fares.—(Droschken.) Between any two points within the walls, or to Deutz, for 1 or 2 persons, 75 pfennings; for 3 persons, 1 mark; for 4 persons, 1 mark, 25 p. Per hour, for 1 or 2 persons, 2 marks; for 3 or 4 persons, 3 marks.

The iron bridge between Cologne and Deutz is 1332 feet long, and 51 broad. One half is used by the railway, and the other by foot passengers and carriages. It cost £600,000.

J. M. Farina's Eau de Cologne is sold at No. 129 Hochstrasse; at J. M. Farina's, No. 4 Jülichsplatz; and in most of the hotels.

The nave of the Cathedral is open the whole day. Fees: to visit choir and chapels 1½ mark each. To the top of the tower, 1 mark. See Black's Holland and the Rhine.

Paris to Cologne.

306 miles N.E. by Creil, Compiègne, Busigny, Maubeuge, Thuin, Charleroi, Namur, Liege, and Aix-la-Chapelle.

PARIS. Start from the station of the Chemins de Fer du Nord, and follow the route Paris to Brussels, by Compiègne and Tergnier junction as far as Maubeuge, 142 m. from Paris, and 51 from Brussels.

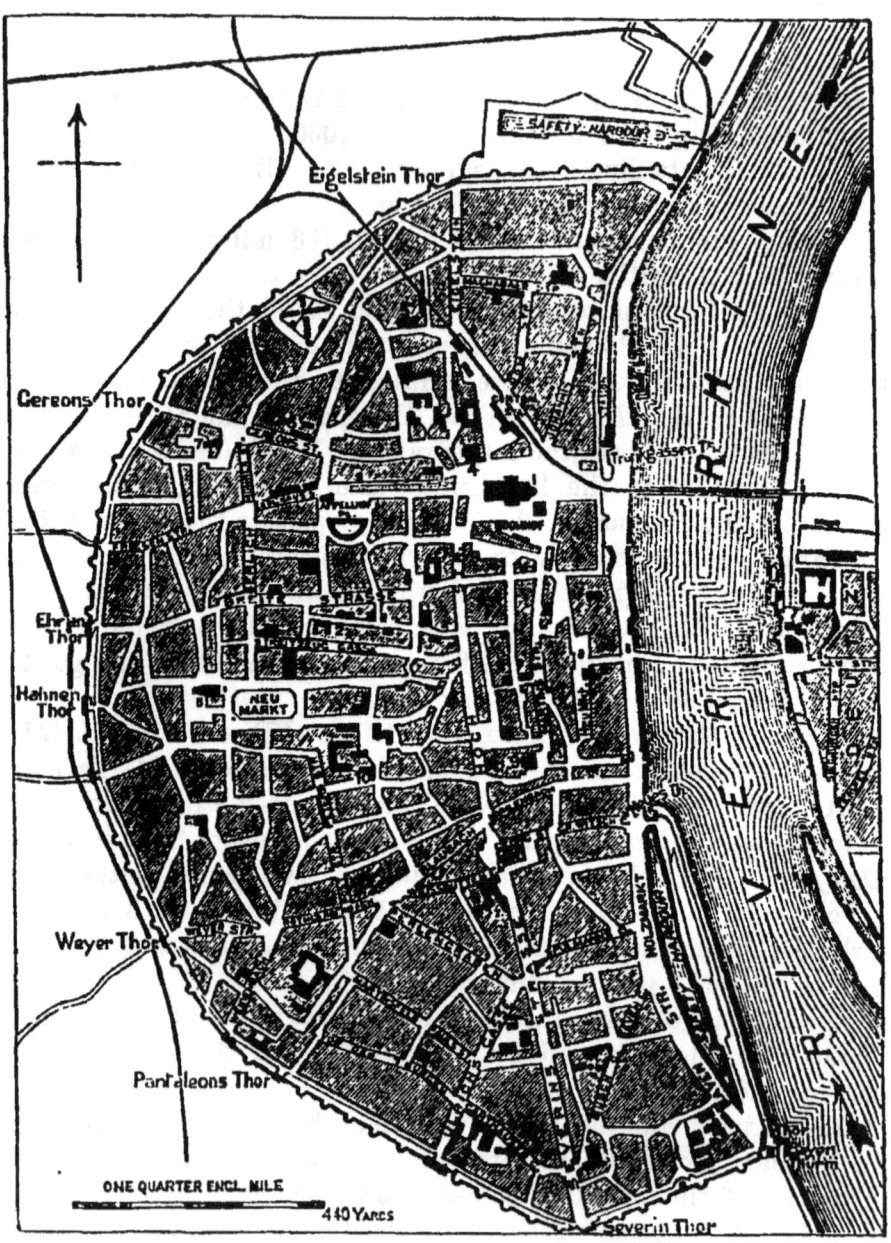

Plan of Cologne.

1. Cathedral.
2. Post-Office.
3. Diorama.
4. Jesuits' Church.
5. St. Ursula's Church.
6. Archbishop's Palace.
7. St. Gereon's Church.
8. Church of the Apostles.
9. St. Maria's Church.
10. St. Peter's Church.

CHELLES. LAGNY.

5½ m. from Maubeuge is Jeumont, French custom-house. The village, pop. 2300, has a mirror manufactory and some marble works.

149¾ m. from Paris, 156¼ from Cologne, 18¾ from Charleroi, 41¾ from Namur, and 79 from Liege, is Erquelines, Belgian custom-house. 8 m. E. from Erquelines is Lobbes, and 1¼ m. farther, Thuin, pop. 4100. On the 15th of June the French attacked the Prussian posts at Thuin and Lobbes, on the Sambre, at daylight in the morning. Seven miles from Thuin is Marchiennes, almost a suburb of **Charleroi**, which is 164 m. from Paris, 142 from Cologne, 76½ m. S. from Antwerp, by Louvain, 22½ S. from Brussels, by Ottignies, 29¼ m. N. from Mariembourg, and 22½ m. W. from Namur, one of the most industrial centres in Belgium. 2½ m. E. from Charleroi is Chatelineau, on the N. bank of the Sambre, and on the S. bank Chatelet, a busy manufacturing town of 11,000 inhabitants. 5½ m. E. from Charleroi is Tamines, 10 m. W. from Namur. For all the above towns, see Index.

191¼ m. N.E. from Paris by this route, 35 m. S. from Brussels, 37½ m. S.W. from Liege, and 16¾ m. N.E. from Dinant, is Namur. From Namur the train passes several minor stations, and halts for some time at Liege, 2 hours and 48 minutes from Aix-la-Chapelle. For Aix-la-Chapelle, see p. 51, and Cologne.

Paris to Mezières-Charleville.

162 m. N.E. by Meaux, Chateau-Thierry, Epernay, Reims, and Rethel.

PARIS   See Map, p. 1.   MEZIÈRES
MILES FROM   MILES TO

PARIS. Start from the station of the Chemins de Fer de l'Est, 162 with one of their time-tables. 5½ m. from Paris the train passes Noisy-le-Sec, and then arrives at

12 CHELLES, pop. 3000, nearly a mile from the station. *Inn:* 150 in the village, the H. de France. 298 paces from below the railway bridge towards the village, is, in a garden to the right hand, part of the shaft of the Croix St. Bauteur; which indicates the spot where Chilpéric I. was murdered in 584 by order of Frédégonde. The parish church is on the highest part of the town. In the chancel, 13th cent., are 10 shrines with relics of saints, and on the left hand of the main entrance a wooden crucifix of considerable merit.

17½ LAGNY, on the Marne, pop. 4100. *Inns:* at the station, the H. Joannés; across the bridge in the town, the H. du Pont-de-Fer. On the high part of the town is the parish church, built from the 12th to the 15th cent. The interior resembles a very handsome choir, surrounded by 14 tall fascicled columns, on which rest the pointed arches which bear the triforium and clerestory, and from which spring the clusters of vault shafts which ramify in groining on the roof. The painted glass, which is modern, is so resplendent with red that it makes the columns look as if they were built of red sandstone. The façade is modern. Originally the church was to have been much larger.

28 MEAUX, pop. 12,000, on the Marne and the Ourcq canal. **134** *Hotels:* The Sirène, Trois Rois. Meaux in the Theodosian table is called Jatinum, the capital of the Meldi; but after the Roman conquest it got the name of Meldæ, which was gradually corrupted into Meaux. It is a silent town, with narrow crooked streets, and still retaining portions of its old walls flanked with towers. Broad avenues encircle the town, and ramify also in various directions.

Meaux was the theatre of seven councils, and from 1681 to 1704 the see of Bossuet, one of the glories of the Gallican church, and of the reign of Louis XIV. The principal edifice is the cathedral, dedicated to St. Stephen (founded in the 9th century), though the more ancient parts of the present building are not older than the end of the 12th. Most of the statues on the doorways have been sadly mutilated. The tower is 220 feet high, ornamented on the ground story, and commanding a view of the hills surrounding Paris. The length of the building is 276 feet, height 101, and width 134. Flying buttresses and long eel-looking gargoyles project round the exterior. The south windows are very beautiful, and the arcade supporting the organ-loft, as well as its flamboyant leafy balustrade, are remarkable for elegance. The pulpit contains panels belonging to the older one, in which Bossuet delivered his eloquent harangues. A large black marble slab to the right of the high altar covers his tomb. He died on the 12th of April 1704, aged 76 years, 6 months, and 16 days. Farther to the right, in the south aisle, is a marble statue of him in a sitting posture.

The large building on the northern side of the church is the episcopal palace. At the entrance into the court to the left is the house of the concierge (doorkeeper), who shows the garden and study of Bossuet—both behind the palace. The garden, planned by Le Notre, is small and unimportant. At the end of it a stair leads up to the top of the ramparts, on which are the study built by Bossuet, and continuous with it a beautiful walk between two high yew hedges planted in the reign of Louis XIII. The study is 42 feet long by 16½ broad, divided into three rooms, of which the centre one is the largest. The inner-

PARIS	ROSE GARDENS. LAFONTAINE.	MEZIÈRES
MILES FROM		MILES TO

most room was his bedroom. The only remaining relics are a sofa and a chair, both very hard.

In the flower-gardens is cultivated the rose de Meaux, so well known as one of the smallest of roses; but the most diminutive of all is the petite rose Pompon, not larger than a very small double violet. The famous cream cheese, called Fromage de Brie, is made in the neighbourhood of Meaux.

41 LA FERTÉ-SOUS-JOUARRE, pop. 5000. *Hotels:* At the **121** station, the Paris; in the town, the Porc-Epic, Epée. Charmingly situated on both sides of the Marne. In the neighbourhood are important quarries of Burr stone, of which millstones are made. Above 1300 pairs are made annually; few, however, of one piece, the most consisting of wedge-shaped parts bound together by iron hoops.

2 m. distant, on the height opposite, is Jouarre, pop. 2500. *Inn:* Plat d'Etain; containing a church of the 15th cent., with glass of the 16th, and several rich reliquaries, of which the most remarkable, dating from the 13th cent., contains the bones of St. Jules. Under the church is a crypt, 11th or 12th cent., with sarcophagi of the 12th and 13th cents. Behind the church is a cross, 13th cent.

59 CHATEAU-THIERRY, pop. 6800. *Hotels:* Elephant, on the **103** promenade, the best; the Sirene, behind the Elephant; the Angleterre, between the bridge and the station. Chateau-Thierry is a very pleasant little town on the Marne, at the foot of a fortress, founded in the 8th cent., in which Charles the Simple was imprisoned by the Count of Vermandois. It is now converted into an agreable park, commanding varied and extensive views. The direct way up is by the stair from the Place du Marché, fronting the bridge. The large house seen from the castle is the town hospital. Near it is the belfry, consisting of a spired tower with pepper-box turrets. To the west is the Madeleine, 15th cent., with a lofty square tower and gabled chapels, with plain, slightly receding, buttresses between them. The windows are glazed partly with beautiful 16th cent. glass. Between the church and the foot of the hill is the house, built in 1559, in which Lafontaine was born. It consists of 2 stories. On the ground floor is a large window on each side of the door; while the 2 upper stories have each 3 windows. The room to the right of the entrance was the drawing-room, 20 ft. square, now the picture gallery, including a white marble bust of Lafontaine, by Claude Vignon. In the room to the left is the public library. Upstairs, over this room, are the kitchen, with a window to the street, and the chamber in which Lafontaine was born, with a window to the garden. The garden is small. At the end, in a projecting semicircle, still lives the hawthorn under which he is said to have written many of his fables. Attached to Lafontaine's house, which was formerly isolated, is the town grammar school. A few yards from the house commences the best road up to the castle.

Coach starts from the H. Elephant for Fère, *Inn:* Pot d'Etain, 17 m. N. on the Ourcq; and Coincy, *Inn:* Lion Noir, 10 m. S.E.

72¾ DORMANS, pop. 2300. *Inn:* H. de France. Parish Church 89¼ with central tower, 13th cent. On an eminence the picturesque ruins of the Chateau Chatillon, the birthplace of Pope Urban II. Eleven miles farther east is Damery-Boursault. To the right, or south, is the chateau of Boursault, built in the Renaissance style by Madame Cliquot, the champagne wine grower.

88 EPERNAY, pop. 13,000, on the left bank of the Marne. 74 Champagne at station 50 c. per glass. Good refreshment-rooms. *Hotels:* Europe; Sirene. This is the great centre of the champagne wines, known as the Vin de la Riviere. The great champagne-growers Perrier, Moët, Pipre, etc., have their handsome houses and establishments in the suburb de la Folie; in whose soft chalky strata are excavated their vast cellars, which always contain several millions of bottles of champagne. It is estimated that annually 5 million bottles of the wine are put into them, of which 800,000 are the produce of the vineyards around Epernay.

The nature of the manufacture of champagne wine renders great equability of temperature, with capacity of cellarage, indispensable. At the beginning the wine is allowed to ferment in the ordinary way, in barrels, till June, when it is put into bottles, which are laid with their necks inclining slightly downwards. They are then gradually turned round, and the degree of the angle of the neck of the bottle increased till it reaches a right angle, or, in plain terms, till the bottle is turned upside down, with the wine clear and a black sediment on the cork. Up to this stage the wine has a disagreeable taste. The string is now cut, and with the cork flies off the sediment, altogether about a glassful, which is replaced by a liqueur composed of sugar-candy and some generous wine, more or less alcoholic, according to the taste of the market for which it is destined. In the fermenting process a great number of bottles burst. Still champagne is made in the ordinary way, and is a properly fermented wine.

From Epernay, a line 52¼ m. S. to Romilly, passing several towns, all more or less engaged in the production of champagne. Of these the most famous are Oiry, but especially Avize, 4½ m. S. from Epernay (*Inn:* St. Nicholas, pop. 3000), where an excellent sparkling wine is produced.

Six miles farther south is Vertus, pop. 6000. *Inn*: Croix d'Or. A quiet town with a handsome church of the 11th cent., under which is a crypt. The interior of both the church and the crypt has been so thoroughly restored, that were it not for the venerable appearance of the exterior, the edifice might be taken for a modern imitation of an ancient church. The belfry, which rises from the extremity of the S. transept, is the most characteristic part of the structure.

21 m. S. from Epernay is Fère-Champenoise. *Inn*: Phenix, about a mile from the station at the foot of some hills. 16½ m. farther is Sezanne. *Inn*: H. de France. Romilly, on the Seine, is 52½ m. S. from Epernay, and 74 S.E. from Paris. Pop. 7000.

At Epernay the Reims and Mezières line separates from the line to Nancy, and goes northward to Ay, 90 m. from Paris, and 17 from Reims, pop. 4300, at the foot of a hill on which is one of the most famous of the champagne vineyards. After Ay the train passes by Avenay, pop. 1050, and Germaine, where it traverses the tunnel, 3595 yards, through the mountain of Reims, 900 ft. high. Then passing Rilly-la-Montagne, and crossing the river Vesle, and the Aisne and Marne canal, arrives at

107 REIMS, pop. 74,000. *Hotels*: around the cathedral, the *Lion d'Or; the *Maison Rouge, formerly called the Ane Rayé, where, it is alleged, the father and mother of Jeanne d'Arc were lodged in 1439, during the consecration of Charles VII. Their illustrious daughter had apartments in the precincts of the palace. Hotel du Commerce. A few yards down from the entrance into the cathedral is the *Grand Hotel in the Rue St. Catherine. Near the station, the Nord, more moderate.

There is a cab stand just before the station, and another in front of the Hotel de Ville. Fares: Cab for two and one horse, the course 1 fr.; the hour 2 frs. Cab for four, with 1 or 2 horses, the course 1 fr. 25 c.; the hour 2½ frs.

The best champagne cellars to visit are those of Pommery, at the south extremity of the town, on the Chemin de la Porte Gerberte. Those of Roedderer in the Rue de la Justice, and Cliquot in the Rue du Temple. Both are at N.E. end of the town. An introduction from some wine merchant is required for the Cliquot cellars.

Reims is the metropolitan see of France, and although really an ancient city has been completely modernised. The old gates have been removed, the narrow and tortuous streets widened, straightened, and paved, and the quaint old houses have, as at Rouen and numerous other towns, been replaced by modern buildings. The hand of restora-

Reims Cathedral. Stained Glass.

tion has not even spared the magnificent cathedral, Notre Dame, commenced on the 6th of May 1210 by the Archbishop Alberic de Humbert, under the direction of the architect Robert de Coucy. The façade, 154 feet wide, was not finished till the 15th century. The elaborately sculptured portal, containing three recessed doorways with triangular canopies, is adorned with 550 figures of various sizes, and surmounted by a rose window in 24 sections, the most splendid in France, rivalling in colours those of the finest precious stones. Above it, and extending along the whole front, stand, in beautiful niches, 42 statues representing the kings of France from Clovis to Charles VI. From each side rises a square tower, 292 feet high, in open mullion-work, with turrets on the corners. The French, in expressing their beau ideal of a cathedral, say, "Take the portal of Reims, the nave of Amiens, the choir of Beauvais, and the spire of Strasburg." Over the northern entrance is some rather droll sculpture; the comical attitudes of the people rising out of their coffins, and the rueful countenances of a string of bishops in purgatory, waiting their turn to enter the cauldron, already full, are more amusing than impressive. The interior of the edifice is chaste and imposing—466 feet long, 99 wide, and 124 high. The transept is 184 feet long. Fifteen arches, carried on massive pillars of clustered columns, run round the nave and choir, and meet at the sixteenth. The apse is lighted by a brilliant rose window, which, with the beautiful clerestory windows, sheds a delightful light over the choir. But there is nothing so beautiful in the interior as the lovely stained glass of the façade (13th and 14th cents.), when the sun is in the west, for it then glows with all the brilliancy, purity, and effulgence of clusters of rubies, emeralds, and amethysts, of the first water. On the topmost step of the choir **Jeanne d'Arc** stood, holding her sacred banner, on the occasion of the coronation of Charles VII. on July 17, 1429; rejoicing in the realisation of her positive assurance that, in spite of all that threatened her and him, he would there be crowned. Before he left the church she besought him, on her knees, to permit her to return to her cottage at Domrèmi, but this was refused—a denial which, in the issue, cost her the loss of her life. Here also were crowned the whole line of French monarchs, from Philip Augustus, in 1179, to Charles X., some of whose royal gifts are displayed on great festivals.

There are only two chapels in the nave, the rest of the walls is hung with pieces of tapestry, of which the colours are faded. The figures show great expression. Fourteen of the tapestries are by Lenoncourt

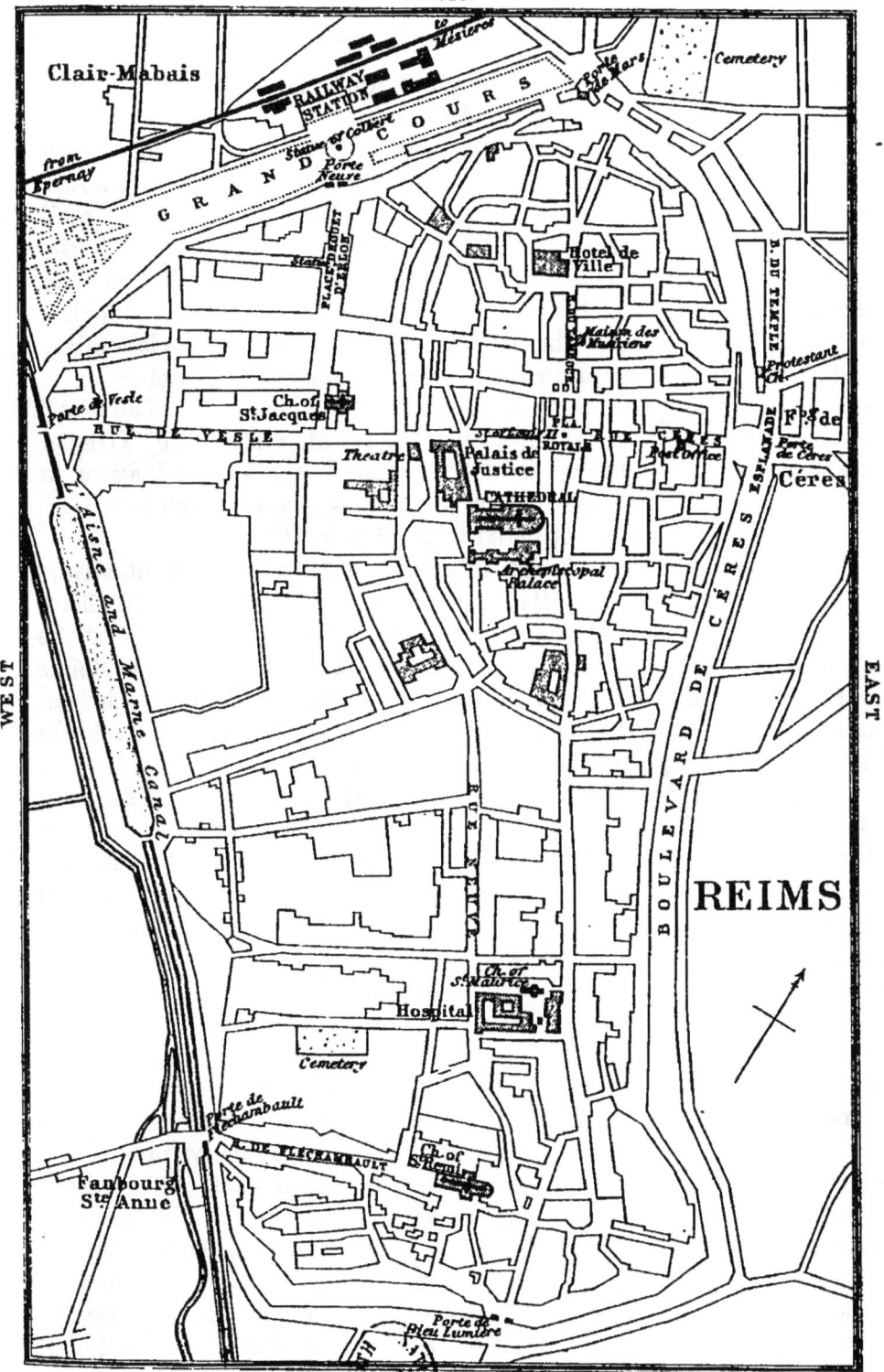

REIMS. ROYAL PALACE. ST. REMY.

in 1530, 19 by Pepersack in 1640, and 2 from the Gobelins presented in 1848. Gobelin was a native of Reims.

In the north transept, in a case, not unlike an oriel window, is a clock made in the 14th cent., considered the oldest going clock known. On the face are four pigeon holes. When the hour is struck, small figures, in single file, issue from one of the pigeon holes of each of the two pairs, and enter the next hole. Below is a "Crucifixion" by Germain de Reims. At the east corner is the "Baptism of Clovis," 496, by Abel de Pujol. The same subject is much more elaborately treated in a large painting in the picture gallery in the Hotel de Ville. In the south transept are the best pictures in the church—"A Nativity," by Tintoretto, and "Christ appearing to Mary Magdalene," by Tiziano. The organ was constructed in 1481, repaired in 1647, and again in 1849. The choir is surrounded by 7 deep chapels, of which 5 radiate. The iron railings were constructed from 1826 to 1832.

The treasury contains beautifully executed articles in gold, silver, and ivory, many of them gifts from the kings who were crowned here.

The concierge at the gate into the Archbishop's Palace shows the Royal Palace in which the kings resided when they came to Reims to be consecrated, fee 1 fr. A horseshoe staircase leads up to the entrance. The first apartment is the banqueting hall, or the Salle du Tau, 131 ft. by 52, constructed in 1138 and rebuilt in 1498. It contained portraits of all the kings consecrated at Reims, but all, excepting 14, were destroyed in 1793. From the centre a door opens into an elegant chapel of the 13th cent. Below is a crypt, founded, it is supposed, by Clovis in 496. From the N. end of the banqueting hall commences what was the suite of the royal private rooms. The farthest removed was the bedroom. The last crowned head who reposed in it was the Emperor William of Germany in 1870.

At the S.W. extremity of the town, in a straight line from the cathedral, by the Rue Neuve, stands, on the site of the chapel of St. Clotilda, the abbey church of St. Remy, commenced in 852 and consecrated in 1041. It is 361 ft. long and 79 wide. Within the sanctuary, and just behind the high altar, is the magnificent mausoleum of St. Remi, erected in the middle of the 16th cent. by Cardinal Lenoncourt, and restored in 1847. At the west end is the entrance into the vault, and at the east a group representing St. Remi baptizing Clovis. On the south side are the life-size statues of the 6 ecclesiastical peers of France, Archbishop Duc de Reims, Bishop Duc de Laon, B. Duc de Langres, B. Duc de Beauvais, B. Count de Noyon, and B. Count

PORTE BAZÉE.   HOTEL DE VILLE.   PORTE-DE-MARS.

de Chalons. On the N. side stand the statues of the 6 lay peers, the Counts of Champagne, Flandre, and Toulouse, the Dukes of Angoulême, Normandie, and Bourbogne, all of the purest white statuary Carrara marble, against slabs of dark marble supported by 18 rose-coloured veined marble columns, decorated in the Renaissance style. In the apse is some valuable 14th cent. glass. The side aisles have no chapels.

On the road from the cathedral to St. Remi, at No. 23 Rue de l'Université, is on each side of the street a massive sculptured jamb, or side support of what was the Porte Bazée, a Roman triumphal arch, supposed to have been erected in the 4th or 5th century.

The churches of St. Jacques (transition Gothic of the 12th century) and of St. Maurice (of the 10th century) claim also the attention of the ecclesiologist.

The large building near the N.W. corner of the cathedral is the Palais de Justice. Further N., towards the railway, is the Hotel de Ville, commenced in 1627, and only lately finished. It contains the Public Library, the Picture Gallery, and the Museum of Antiquities. The paintings are chiefly modern works of the French school. Among the antiquities, the most interesting is a beautiful alto-relievo in white marble from the cenotaph of Flavius Jovinus, converted to Christianity in 366. It is of one block of marble, 9 ft. long by 4 wide. The sculpture represents Jovinus on horseback, engaged in a lion hunt. Still nearer the railway station is the Porte de Mars, 4th cent., 102 ft. wide, 37 ft. high, and 20 thick, supposed to have been erected by Agrippa. It consists of 3 nearly equal arches, the centre one being the highest. The sculpture on both sides is similar, but that on the northern is less defaced. The soffits are covered with panel sculpture. Opposite, on the other side of the railway, is the church of St. Thomas, built in 1847 on the site of the Roman amphitheatre.

Among the houses the most noticeable are: the façade of the Douane by Pigalle, in the Place Royale, and at No. 2 the house of Jacques Callou, built in the reign of Charles VI. In the Rue Tambour is the house des Musicians, 13th cent., and in the Rue du Marc No. 4, the Maison Pluche. Opposite is a house of the 16th cent.

Reims is the great centre of French wool-spinning, being situated in that part of the country where sheep are most numerous. There are 275 establishments for spinning carded wool, and nearly 55,000 spindles, or 60 establishments, for combed wool. The number of workmen employed in this manufacture averages 52,000, and the annual value of the produce two and a half millions of pounds sterling.

PARIS   REIMS.   SHAWLS.   BISCUITS.   ATTIGNY.   MEZIÈRES
MILES FROM   MILES TO

Besides the above, Reims employs 20,000 workmen, in the town and neighbourhood, in the manufacture of shawls, veils, cloth, etc. Shawls became fashionable in France, as an indispensable article of female apparel, after the expedition of Bonaparte to Egypt. The first lady who wore one (1801) was Madame Gaudin, the beautiful Duchess of Gaeta, a Greek by birth, whose husband was then a high functionary. Many of the officers who were attached to the army brought back presents of shawls, and they were imported in great quantities from Constantinople, Moscow, Vienna, and London. These shawls, however, brought an enormous price when imported into France, which necessarily limited the consumption to the richer classes.

In the making of champagne above 2000 workmen are employed, and the annual produce averages five millions of bottles.

Sponge-cake is said to have been first made here, for which confection, under the name of "Biscuit de Reims," it is still famous. When fresh they are brittle and of a rich delicate flavour. The coffee rolls are browned in the same way, and are of the same shape (oblong), only larger. The biscuits are served at the dessert in the hotels, and are sold in the shops in small packets. The finger-shaped sponge-cakes are not the true "Biscuits de Reims."

Reims possesses also important glass staining and painting establishments. From Reims a branch line extends to Amiens, p. 11, with a beautiful cathedral, 100 m. W., passing Laon, p. 48, 33 m. N.W., and Tergnier Junction. Opposite Tergnier station are the *Inns:* Chemins de Fer; Voyageurs; France.

117½ BAZANCOURT, pop. 1400, on the Suippe, close to the stat. 44½ Junction with line to Béthéniville, 10½ m. S.E.

131 RETHEL, pop. 9000. A quiet manufacturing town. An 31 omnibus awaits passengers for the inn.

137 AMAGNE station, with a comfortable little inn. Here change 25 carriages for branch line to Vouziers, 17 m. southwards. The train, after passing the villages of Amagne and Alland'huy, arrives at Attigny, pop. 6000. *Inn:* Cheval Blanc, 6¼ m. from Amagne. Attigny on the Aisne is a pleasant quiet country town, which shared with Soissons in the favour and predilection of the early kings. Off the market-place is a remnant of the royal palace built by Clovis II. in 647, in which in 727 Chilperic II. died. The general assembly of Franks met in it, from 765 to 822; and in it in 786 Witikina and Albion were baptized. Behind is a handsome church with a square tower between the double north transept. This church was founded at an early date, but on account of frequent rebuildings

and repairs, it can hardly be classed earlier than the 12th or 13th cent., while many parts are much more recent. 11 m. S. or farther up the Aisne is Vouziers, pop. 4000, with a church partly of the 15th cent.

162 MEZIÈRES-CHARLEVILLE. The station is in Charleville on the N. side of Meuse. Before the station is a very large Place planted with trees. *Hotels* in Charleville: Lion d'Argent; Grand Hotel; Commerce; Europe. Fronting the station, the Nord. At the station a small omnibus awaits passengers for Mezières and its hotel.

Charleville, pop. 13,000, founded in the 17th cent. by Charles de Gonzague, governor of Champagne, is commercially the more important of the two towns. The parish church, 1863 (opposite the Hotel du Commerce), is a beautiful imitation of a church of the 12th century. The groining, columns, and colonnettes, are all of a dark brown sandstone, and those at the chancel are elaborately sculptured. The principal square in the town is the Place Ducale, 412 ft. long and 295 ft. broad, surrounded on all sides, excepting on that occupied by the Hotel de Ville, by arcades and high houses with peaked roofs. To the east of the fountain in the centre, at the end of the Rue St. Catherine, is a building of the 17th century, occupied by a mill on the Meuse. The bridge here across the river leads to the top of a low hill called Mont Olympe, laid out as a garden, from which there is a fine view. The road to Mezières is to the west of the fountain, by the Rue de Saint Charles, passing on the right the Hotel de Lion d'Argent, and then the monument, "Aux Ardennais morts pour la patrie 1870-1871." Among the manufactures of Charleville the most important is that of nails, in which dogs are extensively employed for blowing the bellows; a labour for which they are physically much more fitted than for dragging heavily laden barrows along the rough and often steep streets of the towns in Belgium and Holland, harnessed more or less like horses. They work and toil with more sagacity than either horses or mules.

Connected with Charleville by a bridge of 26 arches, across the Meuse and marshy land, is **Mezières**, pop. 4400. A fortified town of the first class on an eminence 355 ft. high, nearly surrounded by the Meuse. On the highest part of the town is the parish church, a very handsome edifice, commenced in 1499 and finished in 1566. The tower was built in 1626. A good deal of the painted glass belongs to the 15th and 16th cents. A black marble slab in the S. transept records that: "In this church Charles IX. was married to Elizabeth of Austria on the 27th November 1570." Opposite it another slab with an inscription records that: "On the 29th August 1521 a numerous army

Mezières. Sedan.

of Charles V. attacked the town, which was freed from them by the prowess and wisdom of Peter Jorrail, on the 27th of September 1521." On the north side of the choir an inscription on another black marble slab relates that: "En 1815 pendant la siège de Mezières par les Prussiens, ce temple assailli d'une grêle de bombes et de Boulets, à été à la veille de sa ruine." In the war of 1870 the Prussians nearly ruined it again.

The railway from Charleville to Givet, 64 m. N., follows the Meuse all the way; which here flows between fertile plains and wooded hills, whose stone and slate quarries, iron and coal mines, give ample and profitable employment to the inhabitants of the towns in this picturesque quarter. For Givet and Givet to Dinant and Namur, see under Givet.

Mezières-Charleville to Metz, by Sedan.
162 miles south-east.

CHARLEVILLE. 8 m. E. from Charleville, or 170 from Paris, is Donchery, pop. 2000, where Henri IV. resided in 1606 during the siege of Sedan. The church, dating from the 16th cent., has some good glass. Ten miles by rail from Charleville, and 172 m. from Paris, is

Sedan, pop. 17,000, on both sides of the Meuse. *Hotels:* Croix d'Or, in the Place Turenne; Europe, in the Grand Rue. Since the disastrous war of 1870-71, the ramparts and fortifications (with the exception of the old chateau which serves as barracks) have been demolished, and in their place are large wide streets lined with handsome houses and extensive manufactories, built of a sandstone of an agreeable yellow tint. On a round tower in the chateau are the words "Ici naquit Turenne, le 11th Septembre 1611." In the Place d'Armes is the parish church, built in the 16th cent. Till the revocation of the Edict of Nantes it belonged to the Protestants, whose place of worship is now in an insignificant building in the Rue des Francs Bourgeois. During the siege Napoleon III. resided in the Sous Préfecture, a handsome building at the foot of the Avenue de Lamarck. When he went out of the city to treat with Bismarck he left by the Donchery road. During the battle he had been six hours on horseback, all the time suffering acute physical pain.

Sedan manufactures a great deal of flannel and cloth. It gave its name to the vehicles called sedans, or sedan chairs, which were first made here. They were introduced into England in 1581, and came into general use about 1649.

Chateau Belle-Vue. House of the Weaver.

Two miles from Sedan by the Donchery road on the left bank of the Meuse, is the Chateau Belle-Vue, a country house in three parts, on a wooded eminence. The way to it separates from the highroad at the third kilometre post; where, passing between the two inns, it leads directly up to the front of the chateau. Up the centre of the principal pavilion is a small octagonal tower with a clock. The room on the ground floor, with a window on each side of this tower, was the place where Napoleon III. met King William of Prussia and acknowledged himself his prisoner. Napoleon slept that night at the chateau, and left next morning, 3d September 1870, for Wilhelmshöhe by Bouillon. The capitulation of Sedan was concluded in the same room between Moltke and Wimpffen.

On each side of the principal pavilion is a smaller pavilion, each with a round tower attached diagonally to one of the corners. Near the chateau are the wooded heights of Trénois, whence the Prussians bombarded Sedan, and set it on fire in various places, causing great consternation among the terrified inhabitants. The sight of the blazing town, and of the numerous burning villages, becoming too horrid and dreadful for the good king, he suspended the firing, and despatched General Bronsart to Sedan to demand its surrender.

About a mile beyond the Chateau Belle-Vue, on the left side of the road to Donchery, is the house "du tisserand," weaver; where Napoleon III. met Bismarck on the morning of the 2d September 1870; but as the Emperor refused the conditions of peace offered by the Chancellor, he left for the chateau of Belle-Vue to have an interview with the King himself, who arrived several hours after him. The house of the tisserand has 4 windows and 2 narrow doors on the ground floor. In the upper story are 4 windows in front. The room they met in is in the N.E. corner, with a window to the north and one to the east. The stair up is round by the back. When the Emperor left he put into the wife's hand 4 napoleons, which she set in a frame.

"Notwithstanding a thick fog, the battle began at Bazeilles early in the morning (of September 1). It was eight o'clock A.M. when I reached the front before Sedan. The villages of Selg and Floing were taken, and the fiery circle drew gradually closer round Sedan. It was a grand sight from our position, on a commanding height behind the above-mentioned battery, when we looked to the front beyond St. Forey.

"In twenty minutes the town was burning in several places, which, with the numerous burning villages over the whole field, produced a terrible impression. I accordingly ordered the firing to cease, and sent Lieutenant-Colonel von Bronsart, of the general staff, with a flag of truce, to demand

King William's Account of the Taking of Sedan,

the capitulation of the army and the fortress. He was met by a Bavarian officer, who reported to me that a French parlementaire had announced himself at the gate. Colonel von Bronsart was admitted, and on his asking for the commander-in-chief he was unexpectedly introduced into the presence of the Emperor, who wished to give him a letter for myself, when the Emperor asked what his message was, and received the answer,—to demand the surrender of the army and fortress.

"He replied that on this subject he must apply to General Wimpffen, who had undertaken the command in the place of the wounded General MacMahon, and that he would now send his adjutant, General Reille, with the letter to myself.

"You may imagine the impression which this made upon all of us, but particularly on myself. Reille sprang from his horse, and gave me the letter of the Emperor, adding that he had no other orders. Before I opened the letter I said to him, 'But I demand, as the first condition, that the army lay down its arms.' The letter begins thus—

"N'ayant pas pu mourir a la tête de mes troupes, je depose mon epée a votre Majesté,' leaving all the rest to me.

"My answer was that I deplored the manner of our meeting, and begged that a plenipotentiary might be sent with whom we might conclude the capitulation.

"After I had given the letter to General Reille, I spoke a few words with him as an old acquaintance, and so this act ended.

"I gave Moltke powers to negotiate, and directed Bismarck to remain behind in case political questions should arise. I then rode to my carriage and drove here, greeted everywhere along the road with the loud hurrahs of the trains that were marching up and singing the National Hymn. It was deeply touching. Candles were lighted everywhere, so that we were driven through an improvised illumination. I arrived here at eleven o'clock, and drank with those about me to the prosperity of an army which had accomplished such feats.

"As on the morning of the 2d I had received no news from Moltke respecting negotiations for the capitulation which were to take place in Donchery, I drove to the battlefield, according to agreement, at eight o'clock, and met Moltke, who was coming to obtain my consent to the proposed capitulation. He told me, at the same time, that the Emperor had left Sedan at five o'clock in the morning, and had come to Donchery, as he wished to speak with me.

"There was a chateau and park in the neighbourhood, and I chose that place for our meeting. At ten o'clock I reached the height before Sedan. Moltke and Bismarck appeared at twelve o'clock, with the capitulation duly signed. At one o'clock I started again with Fritz, the Crown Prince; and, escorted by the cavalry and the staff, I alighted before the chateau, where the Emperor came to meet me. The visit lasted a quarter of an hour. We were both much moved at seeing each other again under such circumstances. What my feelings were—I had seen Napoleon only three years before at the summit of his power—is more than I can describe.

SEDAN AND THE CAPTURE OF NAPOLEON III. METZ
MILES FROM   **MILES TO**

"Now, farewell—a heart deeply moved at the conclusion of such a letter.—WILHELM."
(*Extracted from King William's letter to Queen Augusta, dated Vendresse, South Sedan, September 3, 1870.*)

From Sedan a coach runs to Bouillon, 12 m. E., time 2½ hours. From Bouillon another coach runs to Poix, 20½ m. E. on the line between Namur and Luxembourg, see under Poix.

58½ miles south from Sedan, by rail along the banks of the Meuse, is Verdun, see under Verdun.

Five miles from Sedan, at the entrance into the valley of the Chiers, is Bazeilles, which was literally destroyed during the siege of Sedan, not one single house having been left standing. In the Place is a monument to the memory of the brave men that fell in its defence.

79 DOUZY, pop. 1800, on the Chiers. A coach at this station **83** awaits passengers for Mouzon, 6 miles south-west, pop. 2500, with a 13th century church.

85 CARIGNAN, pop. 2400, with manufactories and mills. Coach **77** to Florenville, 9 m. N., in Belgium, see under Florenville.

99 CHAUVENCY. A coach at this station awaits passengers **63** for Stenay, 6¼ miles south-west on the Meuse. Stenay is a very ancient village with important forges and mills.

102½ MONTMÉDY, pop. 2500, on the Chiers. *Inns:* St. Nicolas; **59¼** Croix d'Or. Built on a rocky hill, and composed of a high and low town. The high town is part of the citadel, where are also the Hotel de Ville and the principal church.

From Montmédy a line extends 26 miles to Marbehan on the Brussels and Luxembourg line. 4 m. N. on this line is Avioth, pop. 450, with a beautiful church, 13th to 15th cent., containing some valuable glass. The interior is 138 ft. long and 59 wide. Outside is a pretty little chapel called La Recevresse. At Ecouviez on this line is the French custom-house, and at Lamorteau the Belgian. See under Marbehan.

115 LONGUYON, pop. 2000. *Inn:* Lion d'Or. Junction with **47** line to Arlon, 103 m. N. On this line, 10 m. N. from Longuyon, is Longwy, pop. 35,000, on an eminence rising from the Chiers, and consisting of a high and low town. In the high town is the H. Croix d'Or, a very comfortable house. In the low town the Europe. The fortifications belong to the second class.

| SEDAN MILES FROM | AUDUN-LE-ROMAN. FONTOY. METZ. | METZ MILES TO |

2 m. N. from Longwy is Athus, the Belgian custom-house. See under Arlon.

From Longuyon a line extends 26 m. S. to Conflans Jarny, on the line between Verdun and Metz.

121 PIERREPONT, pop. 1000. With cloth manufactories. Well **41** seen from the station.

130 AUDUN-LE-ROMAN. French Custom-house station. **32**

135½ FONTOY. German Custom-house station. **26½**

141 HAYINGEN or HAYANGE, pop. 4000. With great forges. **21**

145 THIONVILLE or DIEDENHOFEN, pop. 8000. *Hotels:* **17** St. Hubert. A fortified town at some distance from the station, on the Moselle, taken by the Germans in 1870. The parish church belongs to the 18th century. The old clock-tower is partly 14th and partly 17th century. From Thionville a railway extends 23 miles north to Luxemburg, whence a line extends 34 miles eastwards to Treves or Trier. For page see index.

160½ DEVANT-LES-PONTS. The line describes here a long curve **1½** towards Metz, which is seen in the distance with its spires and barracks.

162 METZ, pop. 45,500, capital of German Lorraine, is on an eminence 581 feet above the sea, at the confluence of the Seille with the Moselle, 34 miles N. from Nancy, 40 S. from Luxembourg, 125 N.W. from Strasburg, and 262 from Paris by Mezières and 215 by Verdun.

Hotels: The Europe; the Metz, opposite each other, in the Rue des Clercs, both expensive. The Londres et du Commerce, comfortable, and moderate charges, situated in the Rue du Blé, near the cathedral. The France; and the Paris, at the N. side of the cathedral, in the Kammerplatz; the H. Poste, in the Rue des Clercs, close to the Esplanade; the H. Luxembourg, in the Römer Strasse, near the Bahnhofthor.

The most remarkable sights in Metz are the gates and the fortifications; but these in a conquered city, taken by the Germans on the 27th October 1870, can be only imperfectly visited. Besides the mighty walls and ramparts, with their deep wide fosses, and steep sloping glaces, a circle of forts, 15 miles in circumference, surrounds the city, of which St. Quentin, 1 mile distant, is the nearest, and Fort Alvensleben, 4 miles distant, the farthest. The other sights are the small Cathedral, on a high part of the city and the Esplanade.

Metz. Cathedral. Tower. Windows. Hotel de Ville.

The **Cathedral**, commenced in 1014, and finished in 1516, seems to have been built for the display of window architecture, to which every part has been made subservient, even the two square towers, each consisting of 2 tiers of great mullioned and traceried windows, crowned with slender pinnacles. The walls also are composed of windows, excepting the narrow space between them occupied on the outside by the slim flying arches of the buttresses, and in the interior, by the elegant vaulting shafts. The façade, 1765, is faulty, and by no means an ornament to the edifice. The other sides are occupied with detached, narrow, elaborately sculptured buttresses, terminating in short crocketed pinnacles. A beautiful octagonal buttress, one of the supports of the choir, contains a staircase up to the roof. The stair by which the public are admitted to the roof and the great tower is at the south doorway. This tower, 12th cent., built in three stages, crowned with a most elegant spire, 1427, is 387 feet high, and is ascended to the topmost platform by 293 steps, whence there is a splendid panoramic view.

The interior of the church is 397 ft. long, 75 ft. wide, and 142 high above the floor. Clusters of vaulting shafts, like bundles of ropes, rise from 30 short columns, up between the triforium and clerestory windows, to roof, where they expand in profuse groining over the vault. The clerestory windows are immense, but glazed with plain glass. Round by the sill runs a deep foliated frieze partly overhung by an admirably carved piece of sculptured drapery. Under the choir, but not under the level of the ground, is a crypt. By the side of the altar adjoining the sacristy is a kneeling figure of the architect of the church, Pierre Perrat, died 1400. To the left of the main entrance, in the chapel of Notre Dame du Bon Sécours, is an ancient baptismal vat or bath of porphyry 8 ft. long by 5 wide.

But the most lovely objects in the interior are the windows, and of them the most superb are those rising tier above tier in the choir glowing with vivid and splendid colours, painted by Valentin Bousch, at the commencement of the 16th cent. The greatest surface of glass is in the windows, 14th cent., of the S. and N. transepts, provided with double mullions to give them extra strength. The glass in the façade window, as well as that in the small window over the organ on the N. side, is also of the 14th cent.

Fronting the cathedral is the Stadt Haus, Hotel de Ville. The narrow street called the Haut Poirier, Hoch Birn Baum Gasse, leads to the edifice containing the Public Library, the Archæological and

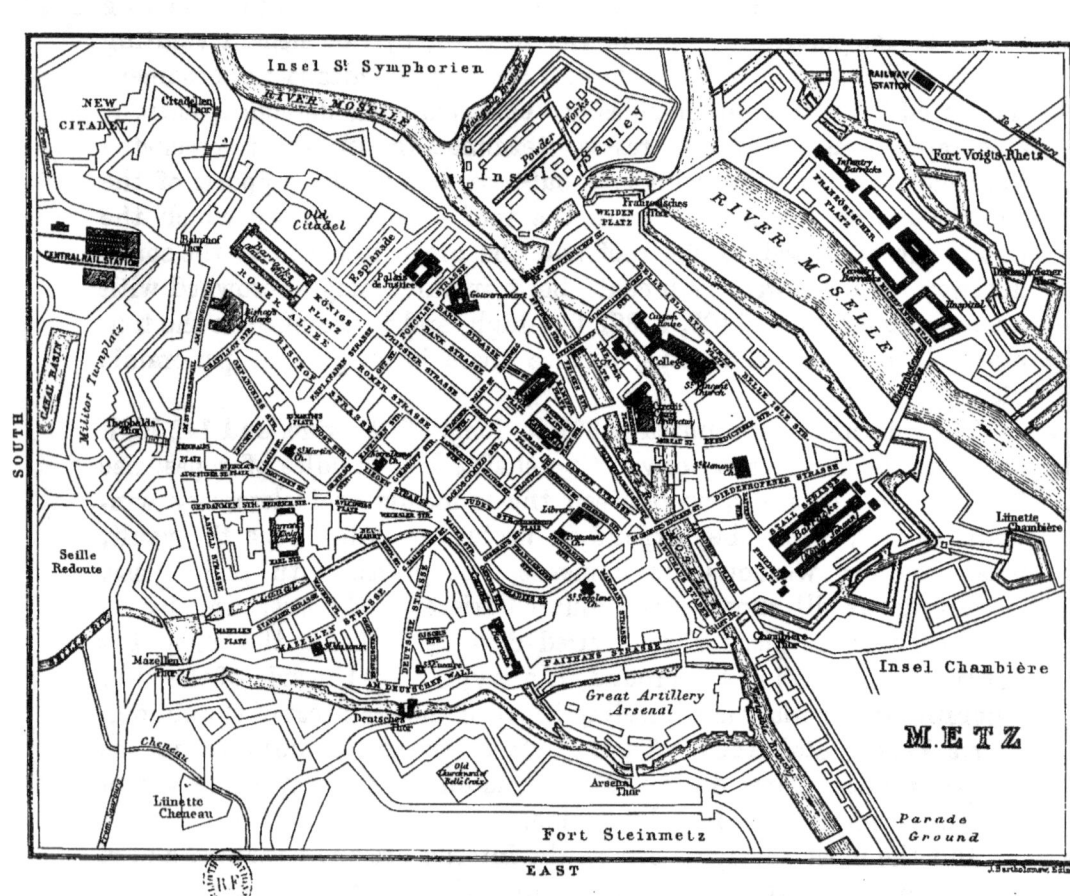

METZ. ESPLANADE. GATES.

Natural History Museum, and the Picture Gallery. The Library contains 50,000 volumes, and is open every day except Sunday. The Picture Gallery, open on Sunday, Thursday, and Friday, contains some very excellent paintings chiefly by French artists. The gem is a portrait in enamel of Charles IX. Behind is the Protestant church, and a little way farther by the Rue des Trinitaires is St. Ségolène, 13th and 14th cents., with good modern glass and wood figures in the same style as those in St. Martin's.

Any of the streets extending from the front of the cathedral lead to the Esplanade, with its beautiful walks and still more beautiful views, from the terrace at the west end, overlooking the Mosel-Arm, and a little beyond the Moselle itself. One side of the Wechsel Strasse and Ludwigs Platz is lined by a long arcade of elliptic arches; approached from the S.E. corner of the cathedral by the Goldschmied Strasse.

From the Esplanade a walk may be taken round by the Bahnhofthor, the Theobaldsthor, the Mazellenthor, and the Deutsches Thor. The Seille flows with great rapidity past the two last gates. In the neighbourhood of the Theobaldsthor is the church of St. Martin, 13th cent. with glass of the 15th. In the transept left of altar is a curious nativity in carved wood under three frescoes. Eastward by the Oelstrasse are the Ludwigs Platz and the Wechselstrasse lined with an arcade; while the part of the Gerber Strasse fronting the Ober Saalstaden Canal exhibits many curious old houses. Between the Mazellen Thor and the Deutsches Thor is a pleasant public promenade on the ramparts. Near the Deutsches Thor is the church of St. Eucaire, 13th cent., with a beautiful organ case from the church of St. Paulin in Treves. In the choir are frescoes and figures carved in wood. In the neighbourhood are the villages of Gravelotte, St. Marie, and St. Privas, the scenes of the great battles fought on August 17th and 18th of 1870. On these battlefields all that remains are here and there square mounds of earth, covered with turf. Fare of a two-horse carriage to make the tour of the battlefield, 30 francs, and 3 francs to the driver.

In the time of Cæsar Metz was called Divodurum, and was the capital of the Gallic tribes of the Mediomatrici, from whom, in the 5th cent., it took the name of Mettis, whence its modern appellation. At the death of Clovis in 510, it fell to his son Thierry I., and remained the capital of his dominions, Austrasia, till annexed to the empire of Charlemagne. Under Otho II. it was made a free city, and in 1552 formed again a portion of France, until taken by the Germans on the 20th of August 1870, after a siege of 72 days. At the capitulation

CAPITULATION OF METZ.

there fell into the hands of the victors an army of 150,000 men, with besides 53 generals, 6000 officers, 53 standards, 66 mitrailleuses, 800 fortress guns, 541 field pieces, 200,000 muskets, and an immense quantity of ammunition.

For Metz and Mayence, etc., see Time-tables of the "Chemins des Fer de l'Est," under Paris à Sarrebrück, Mayence, Frankfort, Hombourg, et Wiesbaden. This line extends 228 miles east down the beautiful valley of the Nahe to Bingen on the left bank of the Rhine, opposite Rüdesheim. At Neunkirchen, 71 m. east from Metz, a branch of this same railway extends to Mannheim on the Rhine, 143 m. east from Metz. Another ramification of this line from Beningen extends to Hagenau and Strassburg.

PARIS TO METZ, by VERDUN.

PARIS MILES FROM   Distance, 215 miles. See Map, p. 1.   METZ MILES TO

PARIS. Start from the railway station of the Chemins de Fer de l'Est, in the Place de Strasbourg. For Time-tables, see under "Paris, Epernay, Chalons, Reims et St. Hilaire-au-Temple, à Verdun," in the Indicateur des Chemins de Fer de l'Est. — 217

2¾ NOISY-LE-SEC, pop. 3000, page 56. — 214¼

28 MEAUX, pop. 1150, page 56. — 189

59 CHATEAU-THIERRY, pop. 6600, page 57. — 158

88 EPERNAY, page 58. Good refreshment-room. — 129

107 CHALONS-SUR-MARNE, pop. 18,000. Good refreshment-rooms at the station of the Chemins de Fer de l'Est. Meat breakfast, 3 frs.; dinner, 4 frs.; both with wine. Champagne, ½ fr. the glass. Passengers for Troyes 58 m. S., Sens other 41½ m. W., Montargis 38½ m. farther W., and Orleans 185 m. S.W. from Chalons, start from the station of the Chemins de Fer de l'Etat. *Hotels:* in the Marché au Blé, the Haute-Mère-Dieu; next it, the Rénard, plainer and cheaper; in the Rue St. Jacques, the Cloche. Their omnibuses await passengers. Behind the H. Rénard are the Post and Telegraph Offices. Temple Protestant. Champagne cellars. — 110

Chalons, one of the three champagne towns, has some pretty avenues and a good park, by the side of the Marne canal, near the cathedral. Between the H. Mère-Dieu and the Paris station is the Cathedral of St. Etienne, a very handsome building, constructed in the 13th cent.

CHALONS—CHURCHES.

on the site of a chapel of the 5th cent., built on the spot formerly occupied by a Temple to Apollo. The north tower dates from the 12th cent., part of the choir from the 14th, and the western façade from the 17th. The interior is extremely light and elegant, large gracefully-traceried windows occupying nearly the whole side walls, strengthened between each window by a massive yet handsome buttress. The stained glass in the transept windows, as well as that of most of those in the chancel, dates from the 16th cent. The high altar consists of a large gilt baldachin on six rose-coloured marble columns with gilt capitals and pedestals. Below the choir is a crypt. There are no chapels in the aisles of the nave. The organ-case is very handsome. Almost opposite the H. Mère-Dieu is the Church of St. Alpin, principally of the 13th cent. The choir and the low square tower are of a little later. The stained glass in the windows of the chancel and of the S. aisle dates from the 16th cent. Among the numerous tombstones one great black marble slab, opposite the pulpit, $12\frac{1}{2}$ ft. long by 6 ft. 3 in. wide, covers the remains of St. Alpin. An "Ecce Homo," on a gold ground, near the entrance, is attributed by some to Albert Durer.

In the centre of the town, near the H. de la Cloche, are the Hotel de Ville and the Church of Notre Dame.

The Hotel de Ville, built in 1771, contains the Public Library with 33,000 vols., the Picture Gallery, and the Natural History Museum.

Notre Dame, constructed of wood in the 5th cent., was rebuilt during 1158 and 1322, excepting the S. portal, which was not finished till 1469. Over the principal entrance are two tapering square towers, each terminating in a lofty 4-sided needle-shaped spire, with a break near the top, occupied by neat small dormer windows. At the base of each of the 2 spires are 4 small spires, roofed like the centre one with shingle, lead, and slates. Needle-shaped slated spires are very common in the centre of France. Towards the east they assume the balloon shape, while towards the west they disappear altogether. No chapels are in the aisles of the nave, and only four radiate from the choir. A spacious gallery extends round the entire interior, and over it runs a narrow triforium in exactly the same style, pointed arches resting on an impost column. Splendid 16th cent. windows light the aisles of the nave and choir; the two best being the second from the entrance, north aisle, representing the "Miraculous Victory over the Moors" near Tolosa; and the next "the Death and Ascension of Mary."

East from Notre Dame, by the Rue Grande Etape, is St. Loup, 15th cent., restored, and all the windows filled with modern stained glass.

CHAMPAGNE. SILLERY.

The 9 windows in the chancel have a fine effect; they are in threes, 3 at each of the two sides, and 3 at the end, each 3 being of a different predominating hue. No chapels in aisles of nave. Under second window, right hand, is a small triptych on wood, of which the centre piece represents an "Adoration of the Magi," ascribed to Primaticcio. In the S. transept is a statue in wood of St. Christopher, 15th cent.

The most curious place to visit is, a little beyond the Paris railway station, the *Champagne cellars of M. Jacquesson*, where the general stock amounts to 4 million bottles, stored in 6½ miles of galleries excavated in the chalk rock, served by 2185 yards of tramway.

5 m. N.E. from Chalons, on the coach road to St. Menehould, is a poor hamlet with a very elegant church in the florid Gothic style; Notre Dame de l'Epine, built in the 15th cent., partly at the expense of Charles V., and restored in 1860. The façade consists of a profusely decorated triple portal, surmounted by windows with glowing 16th cent. stained glass, and an elegant open spire.

117½ ST. HILAIRE AU TEMPLE. Refreshment-rooms. Junction 99¼ with rail to Reims, 25 m. N.W., passing Mourmelon-le-Petit 6 m. W., and Sillery other 10 m. Mourmelon-le-Petit is the station for the Camp of Chalons, occupying 2965 acres. 3 m. N.E. from Mourmelon-le-Petit is Mourmelon-le-Grand, pop. 7000. 27 m. from Chalons and 9 m. E. from Reims is Sillery. An omnibus at the station awaits passengers for the town and inn, a little south from the station, among vineyards of the "Premier Cru," producing the first-class champagne bearing its name. The train now crosses the Vesle and arrives at

121¾ CUPERLY, with a church partly of the 12th cent. On the 95¼ rt. bank of the Noblette, near the village of La Cheppe on the Roman road, is the site of the Camp of Attila, where he fortified himself after having been repulsed in 451, on these plains, by the combined armies of Rome and Theodoric, which checked the advance of his innumerable host of Scythian barbarians. According to some accounts 162,000, and according to others 300,000, were left dead on the field.

6¼ m. farther is Suippes, pop. 2200. *Inn*: H. Ville de Reims.

140 VALMY, pop. 500. On the heights of Orbeval is a monument 77 to the memory of General Kellermann and the soldiers who fell at the battle of September 20, 1792, when the Prussians were defeated.

| PARIS MILES FROM | CLERMONT. VERDUN. | METZ MILES TO |

147½ STE. MENEHOULD, pop. 5000. *Hotels:* Metz, Nicolas. 69½ Situated on the Aisne, in a beautiful valley. The parish church, built between 1280 and 1350, contains the relics of Ste. Menehould, a curious picture of the 17th cent., and a group of statuary representing the death of Mary. It was while driving through the "Place" of this town, 21st June 1791, that the unfortunate Louis XVI. and his family were recognised, which led to their being arrested at Clermont. The country around produces excellent asparagus. The pork ham and pork sausages are held also in high repute.

From Ste. Menehould the train passes through a tunnel of 859 yds. below the forest of the Argonne, and after crossing the river Biesme arrives at the station of Les Islettes, 151 m. from Paris, a village of poor houses, nearly all of wood, of which material most of the houses in the neighbourhood are built. 34 m. farther is Clermont-en-Argonne, pop. 1600, on the side of a hill bordering the railway. 9 m. N., on the Aire, is Varennes-en-Argonne—*Inn:* Grand Monarque—where Louis XVI. and family, while on their way to Germany, were seized by the Procureur of the Commune and sent back prisoners to Paris, where they were guillotined.

174 VERDUN, pop. 13,200. *Inns:* The Trois Maures, the best, 53 in the low town near the statue of Chevert, and next the Hotel de Ville; in the high town, in the Rue du Saint-Esprit, the H. St. Martin and H. Coq-Hardi; near the post-office, and fronting the Palais de Justice, the H. Cloche. Verdun is a strongly-fortified town of the first class, situated on the Meuse, which here divides into five branches, the largest almost encircling the high town. Near the summit is the Cathedral, commenced in the 11th cent., but altered in the 17th. Over the high altar is a baldachin supported on 4 large spiral monolith columns of marble. In the transepts are some statues and shrines, with bones of defunct saints. Adjoining are the seminary and the bishop's palace. Beyond the Cathedral, by the Porte Chatel, is the promenade De la Roche, within the fortifications, commanding an extensive view. It was at Verdun that Charlemagne, in 843, partitioned his vast empire among his 3 sons, Louis, Charles, and Lothaire. Here also the first English prisoners taken in the war against Napoleon I. were confined from 1803 to 1814. On the 25th August 1870 it was invested by a German army of 10,000 men, under the Prince of Saxe; and at last, after a great deal of hard fighting on both sides, the garrison found itself compelled to surrender on the 8th November 1870.

| PARIS MILES FROM | BRIEY. BATILLY. LORRAINE. | METZ MILES TO |

Junction with rail to Sedan, 59 m. N. by the valley of the Meuse, passing Dun-sur-Meuse 25 m. N. from Verdun, pop. 1000, with the ruins of a castle and an underground way extending from the high town to a neighbouring mountain. 8 m. farther is Stenay, pop. 3000, *Inn:* Chariot d'Or, with forges, sawmills, and limestone quarries. 13 m. farther Mouzon, 13 m. S. from Sedan, pop. 2100, with a handsome parish church, 13th-15th cents., an ancient Benedictine abbey, and the castle of Gévaudan. See Map, p. 1.

199½ CONFLANS-JARNY. Junction with line to Longuyon, 26 **17¼** m. N., whence rail into Belgium by Arlon. See Arlon in Index.

7 m. N.E., by branch line from Conflans, is the very prettily situated town of Briey, pop. 2000, *Inns:* Croix Blanche, Lion d'Or, Croix d'Or, situated on an eminence rising from the Woigot, nearly surrounded by a wood containing charming walks. The parish church dates from the 15th cent. Vestiges of fortifications of the 12th cent. The famous Mathilda, the devoted friend of Pope Gregory VII., was Countess of Briey. Junction with line to Pagny, 20 m. S.

204½ BATILLY. French custom-house stat. The country between **12½** Batilly and Verdun is flat and undulating.

208½ AMANWEILER (AMANVILLERS). German custom-house, **8½** and time 25 min. before French time. The country between Amanweiler and Metz is very beautiful.

217 METZ, page 69. Capital of German Lorraine.

Metz to Saarburg, 51½ m. S.E., through a hilly wooded country. None of the stations are important. About half-way is Mörchingen.

LORRAINE.

METZ TO STRASSBURG,

By FORBACH, SAARBRUCKEN, SAARGEMUND, NIEDERBRONN, REICHSHOFEN, and HAGENAU.

| METZ MILES FROM | Distance 126 m. Map, p. 76. | STRASSBURG MILES TO |

METZ, see p. 69. **126**

22 FALQUEMONT or Falkenstein, pop. 2500, on the Nied. **104**

29 ST. AVOLD, on the Roselle, at foot of Bleyberg, 922 ft. high. **97**

34 HOMBURG L'EVEQUE, ironworks, ruins of castle, 16th cent. **92**

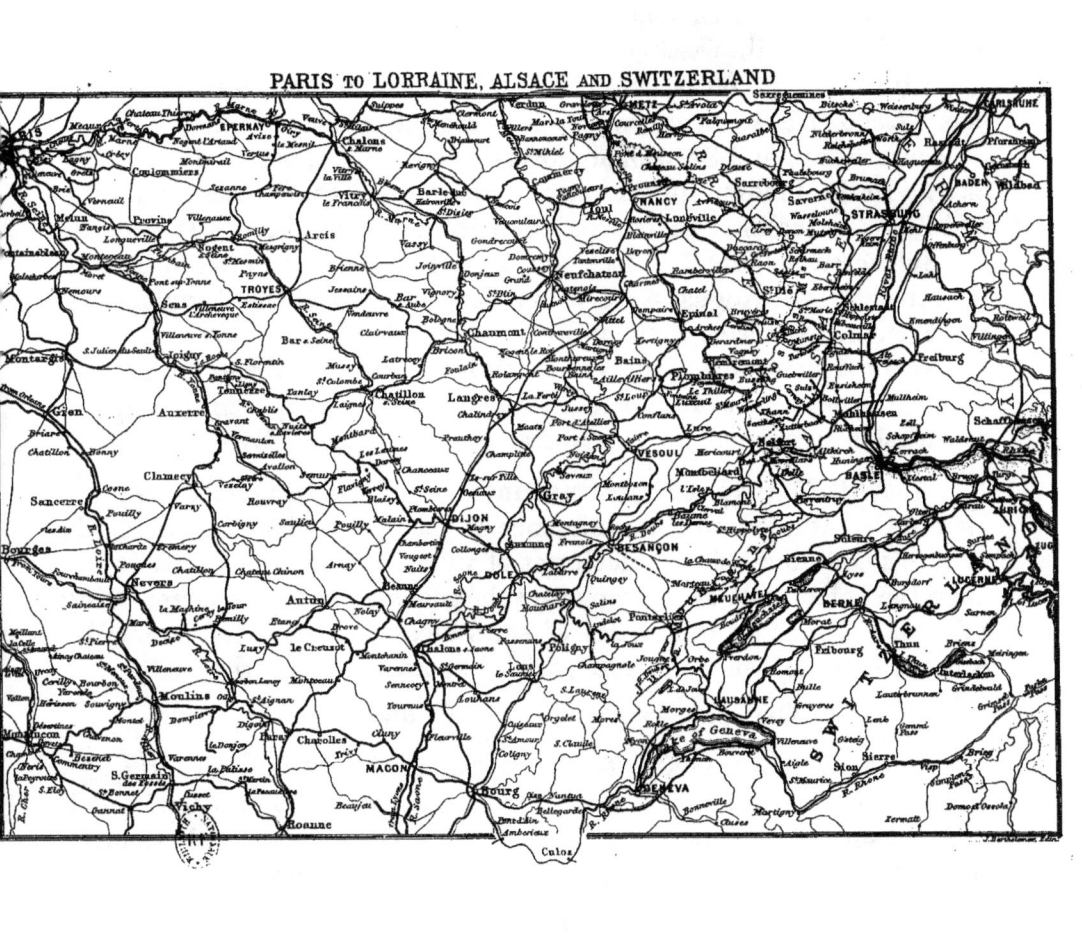
PARIS TO LORRAINE, ALSACE AND SWITZERLAND

| METZ MILES FROM | SPICHEREN. NIEDERBRONN. | STRASSBURG MILES TO |

36 BENINGEN-MERLENBACH Junction. Passengers who do **90** not go round by Forbach and Saarbrücken save nine miles by going directly to Saargemünd.

41 FORBACH, pop. 6100, Chariot d'Or, at foot of the Schlossberg. **85**

48 SAARBRÜCKEN, pop. 10,000, on the Saar; 91 m. W. from **78** Mannheim by rail, passing Kaiserslautern and Neustadt. Junction also with line to Treves, 55 m. N., see under Treves. Kaiserlautern, pop. 17,000, *Hotel:* Schwan, is a busy manufacturing town.

Saarbrücken and St. Johann are two towns on opposite sides of the Saar. In St. Johann are the railway station and the Hotels Guepratte and Zur Eisenbahn. In Saarbrücken is the Hotel Post. It was on the Spicheren heights, 875 feet, and 3 m. to the south of Saarbrücken, that the battle of August 6, 1870, was fought between the Germans and the French. Carriage there and back 12 mark.

Nearly a mile south-east from Saarbrücken are the village and church of St. Arnual, a most interesting edifice, built in 1315, containing 21 remarkable tombstones of the Nassau-Saarbrücken family.

59 SAARGEMUND or Sarreguemines, pop. 7000, *Hotels:* Paris; **67** Lion d'Or, situated on the confluence of the Blies with the Saar. It contains considerable manufactories of velvet and crockery, and is besides the great depot of the papier maché goods made in the surrounding villages. Immense quantities of snuff-boxes are exported annually. 9 m. S. is Saaralben, pop. 4000, with important salt-works.

71 ROHRBACH, pop. 2000, and 1105 ft. above the sea-level. **55**

79 BITSCH, pop. 3500. *Inns:* Metz; Croix d'Or. Both the **47** town and the fortress are well seen from the station. The latter, which suffered severely during the war of 1870-71, stands on a rock 1386 ft. above the sea-level. The country now becomes picturesque.

92 NIEDERBRONN, pop. 4000. *Hotels:* Goldene Kette; Vaux **34** Hall; Arbre Vert. Abundance of cold mineral water, impregnated with the chloride of soda, used both in baths and for drinking.

Niederbronn is a large village on the Falkenstein stream, at the foot of the Vosges mountains, much frequented on account of its mineral waters and the beautiful excursions around it. Among these may be mentioned to Weissenburg and Wörth, which, however, are best visited from the next station, Reichshofen.

95½ REICHSHOFEN, pop. 1500. *Hotels:* Belle Vue, close to **30½**

METZ	GEISBERG. HAGENAU.	STRASSBURG
MILES FROM		MILES TO

the station; Engel, in the town. Charge for carriage to Weissenburg, passing Fröschweiler, Wörth, and Lembach, 15 to 20 francs. Distance 20 miles across the Vosges mountains, through a beautifully wooded country. The battle of Wörth took place on the 6th, and of Weissenburg on the 4th of August 1870.

Reichshofen is the best station to alight at, to visit the ground on which the above battles were fought, which extended from this village to Weissenburg, 20 miles eastwards on the railway between Winden and Hagenau. Weissenburg, pop. 6000. *Hotels:* Engel; Löwe. A fortified town on the Lauter, 10 miles from Wörth and 20 from Reichshofen. It has some ancient houses, a parish church of the 13th century, and a Protestant church with bust of Luther. The battle of Weissenburg took place on the heights of Geisberg, about 2 miles S.

107½ HAGENAU, pop. 12,000, on the Moder, refreshment-room at 18½ the station. Good red wine. *Hotels:* Post; Wilder Mann; Europe.

Hagenau, fortified by Frederick Barbarossa in 1164, contains one fine edifice, the church of St. George, built in the 12th century. Observe the window over the façade, the octagonal tower over the transepts, and the turrets of the choir; and in the interior, the high altar, the stone pulpit, the windows, and the large wooden figure of Christ, carved in 1488. The church of St. Nicolas, although built in the 13th century, was enlarged and altered in the 15th century.

120½ VENDENHEIM. Junction with line from Nancy, p. 82. 5½

126 STRASSBURG. See p. 87.

LORRAINE.

NANCY TO METZ.

NANCY	33 miles north by Frouard, Pont-à-Mousson, and	METZ
MILES FROM	Pagny. See Map, page 76.	MILES TO

NANCY, page 82. Five m. N. from Nancy is Frouard 33 junction, 214 m. E. from Paris, where change carriages for Metz. 2½ m. beyond is the village of Marbach, among picturesque limestone cliffs crowned with trees. 4¼ m. farther Dieulouard, pop. 1500. Church 15th cent., subterranean chapel 11th cent. On this plain, where Jovinus in 366 defeated the Allemanni, stood the Gallo-Roman town of Scarpone.

16 PONT-A-MOUSSON, pop. 8500, on the Moselle, crossed by a 17 bridge built in 1580. *Inns:* The Poste, near the station and at the commencement of the beautiful avenue of horse-chestnut trees; in the "Place,"

NANCY	PAGNY-SUR-MOSELLE. NOVÉANT.	METZ
MILES FROM		MILES TO

surrounded by an arcade of elliptic arches, the France; and the Cygne. Between the France and the post and telegraph offices, the Charue d'Or. To the left of the "Place" is the church of St. Laurent, with, in the north aisle, near the altar, a triptych, 17th cent. Great variety of tracery in windows. At the other end of the bridge is St. Martin, commenced in the 13th cent. In the south aisle is an entombment, and opposite a mausoleum of some unknown knight and his wife. A little way up the river is an old convent of the Jesuits, now occupied by a seminary. The edifice is spacious and commodious and in excellent repair. The most remarkable parts are, the two splendid staircases, the library hall containing 10,000 vols., the cloisters, and the façade fronting the play-ground. From the church of St. Martin, the Rue des Frontières leads straight up, by the cemetery, to the top of the hill, on which are situated the ruins of the chateau de Mousson.

21¾ PAGNY-SUR-MOSELLE, pop. 1400. French custom-house, 11¾ and time 25 min. behind German time. On the hill overlooking the town are the ruins of the chateau Preny, which belonged to the Counts of Lorraine. 2 m. S. from the chateau are the ruins of the abbey of Ste. Marie aux Bois. Around Pagny are extensive vineyards, producing a pleasant light wine.

25½ NOVÉANT, pop. 1300, on the Moselle, crossed here by a chain bridge connecting Novéant with Corny. German custom-house and time. At the station omnibuses await passengers for Thirion. *Inn:* Lion d'Or; and for Gorze, 4 m. dis. *Inn:* Croix d'Or, situated at the head of a picturesque valley. Parish church 11th cent. Castle 17th cent., formerly the residence of the abbots of Gorze, whose abbey was secularised in 1752. From the Novéant station to the next, are seen at intervals parts of the aqueduct constructed by Drusus to convey water from Gorze to Metz. The train then passes by Ancy, pop. 1300, with a plantation of fir-trees and five lofty piers. On the other side of the Moselle is Jouy, with 17 more arches.

28½ ARS-SUR-MOSELLE, pop. 6000. Large and important 4½ forges. This is one of the best places to alight to inspect the aqueduct, which was 3420 ft. long, and contained 118 arches 57 ft. high.

33 METZ, p. 69. 244 m. E. from Paris; 40 m. S. from Luxembourg; and 125 N.W. from Strassbourg.

PARIS TO STRASSBURG, LORRAINE, AND ALSACE.

By MEAUX, EPERNAY, CHALONS, TOUL, and NANCY.

For Time-tables from London, see under "London to 'Bale, *via* Calais and Paris," in the Continental Time-tables of the London, Chatham, and Dover Railway. And from Paris, under "Relations entre les stations de la ligne de Paris à Avricourt; et celles de la ligne d'Avricourt à Strasbourg et Kehl," in the Indicateur des Chemins de Fer de l'Est, sold at the station. For Strassburg to Basel, p. 115.

PARIS
MILES FROM
312 miles east, see Map, page 76.
STRASSBURG
MILES TO

PARIS. Start from the station of the Chemins de Fer de l'Est, 312 where request a "billet" for Strasburg by Nancy and Avricourt. Buy also one of their time-tables, 40 centimes or 8 sous.

5¼ NOISY-LE-SEC. Junction with line to Basel, by Belfort, p. 103; 306¾ Chelles, p. 55; Lagny, p. 55; Meaux, p. 56; La Ferté sous Jouarre, p. 57; Chateau Thierry, p. 57; Epernay, p. 58; Chalons sur Marne, p. 72.

116¾ VITRY-LA-VILLE, with chateau, 17th cent., in grounds 195¼ planned by Le Notre.

127 VITRY-LE-FRANÇOIS, pop. 8500, on the Marne, founded 185 by François I., a fortified town of the third class, surrounded by ramparts and a broad deep moat. From this town commences the canal, which connects the Marne with the Rhine. It extends a long way by the side of the railway. *Inns:* opposite the station, the H. de la Gare; just outside the ramparts, the Commerce; within the town, near the Place d'Armes, the Cloche, the best hotel. From the station a wide street leads to this clean, well-paved town, something in the style of Nancy. In the centre is the spacious Place d'Armes, with its ornamental fountain, handsome houses, and the church of Notre-Dame, 17th cent., constructed in the Italian style. By the S. side of the church is a bronze statue by Marochetti of Royer Collard. From the W. corner of the "Place" a short street leads into the large covered market-place, while three other broad straight streets diverge from the "Place" to the principal gateways of the town.

135½ BLESME. Hotel and café in front of station. Junction with 176¾ branch to Boulogne, 47¼ m. S., the station for the line to Neufchateau, in the centre of the mineral-water district of Alsace and the Vosges mountains. See p. 105.

158 BAR-LE-DUC, pop. 18,000, on the Ornain. At station, H. 154 de la Gare. In the refreshment-room are sold boxes containing 12

small glass pots full of *currant jam*, at from 9 to 10 francs the box. Although the berries are entire, the seeds have been removed by means of a quill. *Inns:* Lion d'Or (where the jam is made); Commerce; Grand Cerf; Temple Protestant, in the Rue de l'Evêché. Bar-le-Duc consists of a high and low town; the latter is modern, and in it are all the best streets, houses, and shops. The other, occupying the top and sides of a hill, consists of houses belonging to the poorer classes, yet it contains also the only building of note in the place, the church of St. Pierre, 14th cent., on the summit of the hill. It has some good painted glass, and in the chapel to the right of the main entrance a large marble font. In the chapel to the right of the high altar is a most singular white marble statue, representing a half-decomposed body. According to the card on the wall, it formed originally part of the mausoleum of René of Chalons, Prince of Orange, killed in 1544 at the siege of St. Dizier, erected to his memory by Louise de Lorraine his spouse, and sister of Francis I. In front of the church is the Musée. At Salvanges, near Bar-le-Duc, is a large establishment for the manufacture of stained glass, open to visitors. The Pretender, Charles Edward, resided three years at Bar-le-Duc.

7 m. farther or E. by rail is Nançois, whence a branch line extends to Neufchateau, 43 m. S., passing Gondrécourt.

183 COMMERCY, pop. 5300. Opposite the station, to the right, **129** is a "Fabrique de Madeleines et Macarons;" behind, in the garden, is the H. de Paris; in the town, the Hotel de la Cloche. At the station are sold cheesecakes called *Madeleines*, made in the form of scallop shells. They are in boxes costing from 22 to 44 sous; a single Madeleine costs 4 sous. They will keep for a long time without spoiling, but before being eaten should be warmed. The town and station are 765 ft. above the sea. By the side of the station is the castle of Stanislas Leckzynski (now barracks), in which Voltaire in 1747 wrote "Semiramis" and "Nanine;" and in which Cardinal de Retz spent the last years of his life, and wrote a large part of his memoirs. There are some pleasant walks in the woods around the town.

191 PAGNY-SUR-MEUSE, 842 ft. above the sea. Direct branch **121** line to Neufchateau, 29¼ m. S., passing Vaucouleurs, 3½ m., and Domremy 11¾ m. See pp. 105 and 106. From Neufchateau train to Mirecourt, 28½ m. E.; whence trains to the baths of Vittel, 15 m. from Mirecourt, Contrexéville, 3¼ m. farther, and Martigny other 6¼ m. See Index and Map, page 76.

| PARIS | NANCY. | STRASSBURG |
| MILES FROM | | MILES TO |

199 TOUL, pop. 8000. *Inns:* Europe; Metz; Cloche. Toul, on **113** the Moselle, the ancient Tullum, the capital of the Leuci in the time of Cæsar, offered to the Prussians in the campaign of '70-71 a more determined resistance than any other of the French fortified towns. It possesses a handsome church, **St. Etienne,** which ecclesiologists should not pass by. The façade is in the rich Gothic style of the first-class cathedrals, covered with sculpture, and surmounted by 2 beautiful towers 246 ft. high, a *chef-d'œuvre* in architecture, by Jacquemin of Commercy, in 1447. The nave is 289 ft. long, 88½ ft. wide, and 118 ft. high. The transepts are short, and there is no triforium. The arch which sustains the organ-loft is nearly flat. There is some good stained glass of the 16th cent., but the most effective is the modern. In the sacristy there is a nail, said to be of the true cross, which Constantine used as a bit for his horse. In the chapel nearest the north transept is the stone chair, 13th cent., of St. Gerard; while opposite, at the south transept, is the door that opens into the beautiful cloister, 610 ft. long by 437 ft. broad. The present edifice belongs to the 13th, 14th, and 15th cents.; while St. Gengoult, at the other end of the town, belongs to the 13th cent. It has also a fine cloister, entrance by north aisle.

207 LIVERDUN, on a hill, with its old towers and walls. **105**

214½ FROUARD, 19 m. S. from Pagny and 11 more from Metz. **97½**

219 NANCY, pop. 55,000, is 37 m. N. from Mirecourt, pp. 96 and **93** 107, whence rail to Vittel, Contrexéville, and Martigny. 46 m. N. from Epinal, p. 107, whence the railways to the East lead into the finest parts of the Vosges mountains; and those to the South and West to the baths of Bains, p. 103; Plombières, 79½ m. S., p. 99; Luxeuil, 83½ m. S., p. 102; and Bourbonne-les-Bains, p. 96, not to be confounded with Bourbon-les-Bains, west from Moulins. Nancy is also 113 m. N. from the famous fortress of Belfort, p. 103; while only 60 m. farther is the other strong fortress of Besançon, p. 120.

Hotels: First-class—in the Rue Poissonnerie, the *France; and near it the Europe; Commerce; Paris. Second-class—near the station, the H. Metz; a little farther, near the Porte Stanislas, the H. Angleterre, and the H. *Meuse; No. 70 Rue Stanislas the H. Lorraine; below the France in the Rue Poissonnerie, the Nord. *Cabs.*—The course, 1½ fr. The hour, 3 frs. Post-office, between the Place Stanislas and the Cathedral.

Nancy, on the Meurth, the most handsome city in France, is the

NANCY

NANCY. STANISLAS. MAUSOLEUMS.

ancient capital of Lorraine and the former seat of the ex-King of Poland, Stanislas Leckzynski, who, on being appointed to this dukedom in 1736, through the interest of his son-in-law Louis XV., took the title of Duc de Bar et de Lorraine. He was beloved by his new subjects, and among them he at last tasted the pleasure he had so long desired—the pleasure of making men happy. He embellished Nancy and Lunéville, and created in both of them useful public institutions. He died in 1766, when his duchy became a part of France. From the Porte Stanislas, near the railway station, the Rue Stanislas leads in a straight line to the pride of Nancy, the Place Stanislas with its 5 gilded gates, 8 gilded lamp posts, 4 artistic rocky fountains shaded by elms and horsechestnut trees, and a statue of its Polish benefactor in the centre. The entire side of the square behind the statue is occupied by the Hotel de Ville ; while facing the statue is the triumphal arch, called the Porte Royale erected by Stanislas in honour of his son-in-law Louis XV. Beyond the Porte Royale, by a well-kept avenue, is the semicircular "Place Clarrière," containing the Palais du Gouvernment. To the left of the Palais is the beautiful church of St. Epvre. Behind are the Palais Ducal and the church of the Cordeliers, both in the Grande Rue ; while to the right is the lovely park called the Pépinière or nursery. These form the principal sights in Nancy. On the way to the Place Stanislas, in the Place Dombasle is a statue by David of Dombasle the agriculturist, and in the Cours Léopold, another by the same sculptor of General Drouot.

The most beautiful of the churches is St. Epvre, finished in 1874, easily recognised by its elegant spire 285 ft. high. The interior, 276 ft. long and 79 ft. high, is remarkably elegant in design and decoration, having a large space occupied with 74 rectangular and 3 circular stained glass windows of great size and beauty, presented to the church by Napoleon III., the Emperor of Austria, church dignitaries and some of the best families belonging to Nancy. Behind the Hotel du Gouvernment is the Palais Ducal, of which all that remains, is the façade and the hall containing the Musée Historique-Lorraine. Adjoining is the church of the Cordeliers, built in the 15th cent. It contains several Mausoleums, of which the best are those of the wife of René II., in the second chapel to the left of the entrance, consisting of a reclining figure in white, black, and gray marble; and the second to the right of the high altar, the mausoleum of René II. Opposite is the mausoleum of Leopold, Duc de Lorraine, and next the altar that of Charles de Lorraine. A passage to the left of

Chapelle-Ronde—Museum. Charles the Bold.

the altar leads to the **Chapelle-Ronde**, with a cupola of sculptured stone, 98 feet high. Under it, on the high altar, is a very fine marble statue of the Virgin Mary. Round the walls are 7 black marble sarcophagi, and under them the names of the 77 princes and princesses buried in this chapel. It is copied from the mortuary chapel of the Medicis family at Florence. The **Museum-Lorraine** contains in the gallery on the ground floor, Celtic and Roman monuments and tombstones, and sculptures of the middle ages. In the "Galerie des Cerfs" are medals, coins, and portraits of the Princes of Lorraine. The most interesting object, however, is the embroidered tapestry, 82 ft. long and 13 ft. wide, found in the tent of Charles the Bold after the battle of Nancy. It represents two subjects, the "Revocation of the edict of Ahasuerus," and an allegory showing the evils of revelry and intemperance.

In the corner behind the right side of the Stanislas statue is the Rue de la Constitucion, which leads to the **Cathedral**, built in 1700 in the composite style. The three paintings in the chapel, at the end of the right or south aisle, are by Girardet; and the two behind the high altar, by Claude Charles. The cupola is painted by Claude Jacquart. The four statues at the altars, in the opposite ends of the transepts, are by Nicolas Drouin.

In the first story of the Hotel de Ville is the Picture Gallery (Musée de Peinture), open on Sundays and Thursdays from 11 till 4. The roofs of the staircase and of the ball-room are painted in fresco, by Girardet. In the picture gallery most of the Italian paintings are of little value; while of the Flemish, the best are second-rate works by De Crayer and Jordaens. The French school is much better represented.

From the railway station, walk up the Rue St. Jean, the first street right, the Rue de la Commanderie, which continue to the Rue Jeanne, where keep to the left the length of the short street, de Bourgogne, in which is the cross erected by René, duc de Lorraine, to mark the spot, where after the battle of Nancy, 5th January 1477, the body of Charles the Bold was found in a ditch stripped naked, horribly mangled and the cheeks eaten away by famished dogs. The body was buried in front of the high altar of the church of St. George, whence it was removed to Bruges in 1550. See under Bruges.

Since the Franco-German war, many manufactories and industrial establishments from Alsace have settled in and around Nancy. Nancy is famous for macaroons and other sweetmeats, for the manufacture of artificial flowers, and embroidery on cambric pocket-handkerchiefs.

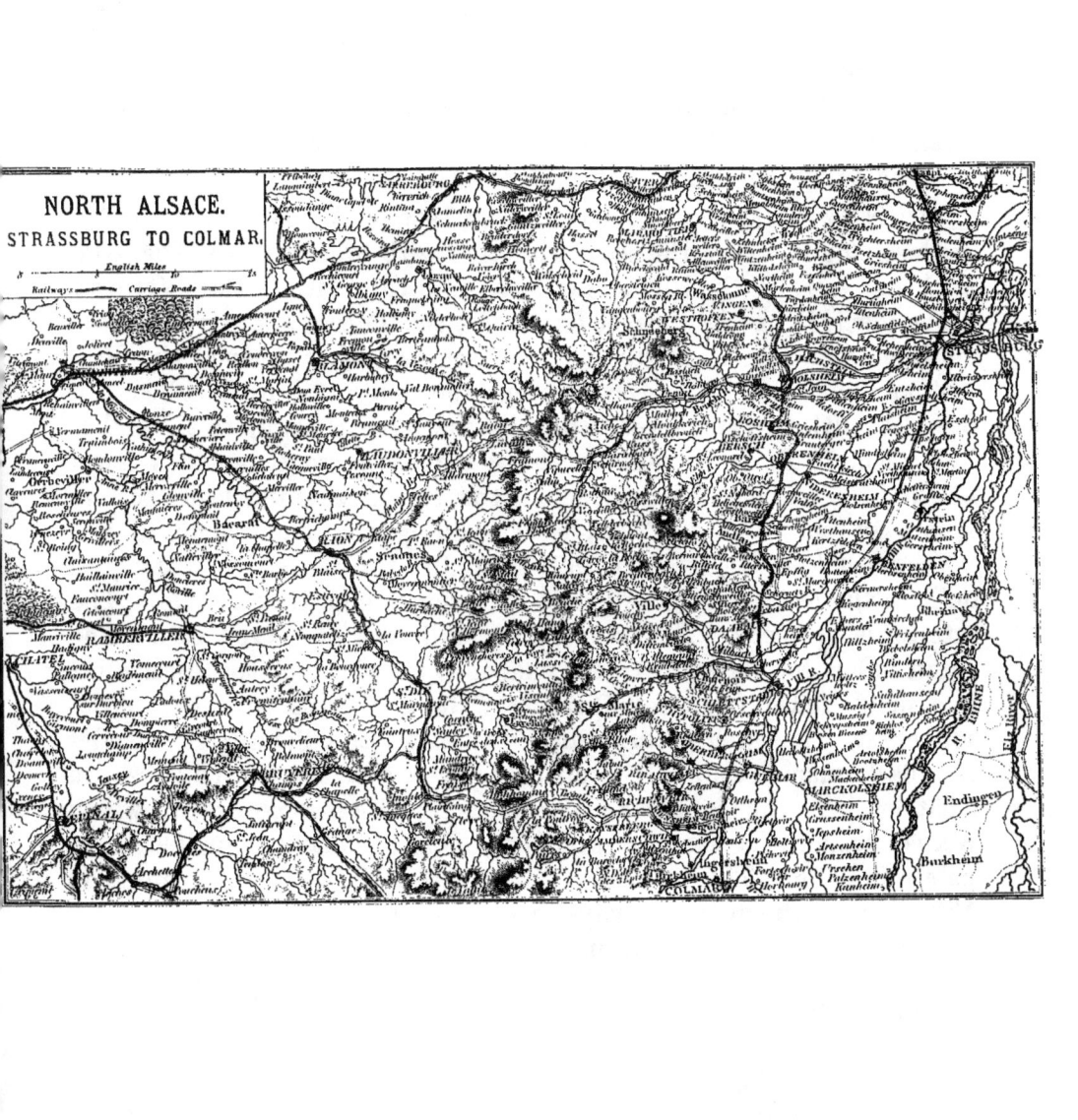

| PARIS MILES FROM | BACCARAT. AVRICOURT. DIEUZE. | STRASSBURG MILES TO |

233 BLAINVILLE, pop. 11,000, junction with branch to Epinal, **79** 31¾ m. S., one of the best head-quarters to commence the exploration of the beautiful Vosges mountains. From the station Charmes, half-way between Blainville and Epinal, a branch line extends 17½ m. E. to **Rambervilliers**, pop. 6000. *Inns:* Poste; Cerf, on the Mortagne, in a vast plain famous for the quantity and quality of the hops it produces. It makes a pleasant residence, and is within an easy distance by coach or by foot of many important places in the Vosges.

239 LUNÉVILLE, pop. 14,000, situated between the Meurthe and **73** Vezouze, 758 ft. above the sea. Junction with branch to St. Dié, 31¾ m. S. *Hotels:* in the Rue de la Gare, near the station, the *Vosges; in the town, in the best street for shops, the Faisan. From the stat. the Rue de la Gare leads up to the Place Léopold; whence the Rue des Capucins leads to the Chateau and the delightful park called the Bosquet, with two entrances, either by the large gateway to the right, facing No. 10 R. de Lorraine, or by a narrow passage, facing a large sun-dial. From the Place Léopold, the Rue Bernardon leads to the square in the Rue du Temple, containing the monument to the "Victimes de la Guerre 1870-1871;" and to the church of St. Jacques built in the last cent. The façade is in the Roman-Greek style. The interior is spacious. The pulpit and stalls are of carved oak. The organ loft is too showy. In the chapel to the right of the high altar is a much faded fresco by Girardet, "St. Catherine with the philosophers." The other pictures are by Girardet and Schuppen. Under the black marble slab at the entrance is buried the Marchioness du Châtelet. To the right in the corner, is a white marble urn, in which were deposited the viscera of Stanislas, King of Poland, who died in the palace in 1766. This palace, built by Leopold, Duke of Lorraine in 1702, is now one of the principal cavalry barracks.

16 m. S. from Lunéville, and 15 N. from Saint Dié is Baccarat on the Meurthe, pop. 6000. *Inn:* H. du Pont, with glass and crystal works on a magnificent scale, founded by Montmorency-Laval, bishop of Metz, in 1760, employing about 1700 persons. Admission is not readily granted.

254¾ AVRICOURT or Igney-Avricourt, 932 ft. above the sea. **57¼** French custom-house and time. 11¼ m. S.E. by rail is Cirey, pop. 3000, *Inns:* Sauvage; Sapeur, a picturesquely situated little town with a large manufactory of mirrors. Four minutes farther is Deutsch-Avricourt. German custom-house and time, 25 minutes before Paris time. Large waiting and refreshment rooms. Branch line to Dieuze, 14 m. N., pop. 2700. *Inn:* Lion d'Or. This, the Decem-Pagi of the

PARIS   ZABERN.   HOH-BARR.   STRASSBURG
MILES FROM   MILES TO

Romans, possesses important saline strata, from which salt has been extracted for the last 800 years.

268 SAARBURG, pop. 3500, on the Saar. Good draught ale sold **44** at the station. *Inn:* Hotel de l'Abondance. This insignificant village occupies one of the most important entrances into the Vosges. Junction with line to Metz, 2 hours or 51 m. N.W. Between Saarburg and Zabern, the line traverses the Vosges by tunnels and lovely valleys. Among the most prettily situated towns passed is

278 LUTZELBURG, pop. 1000. *Inn:* Cigogne. Situated in the **34** midst of rocks and trees. The ruins of its castle overlook the station. This is the stat. for Pfalzburg, 3 m. north by coach, 1035 ft. above the sea, pop. 6000. *Inns:* Ville de Bale; Cheval Noir. A formerly fortified town, renowned for its liqueur de Noyau and Kirschwasser.

285 ZABERN or Saverne. This, the Tres Tabernae of the Romans, **27** 670 ft. above the sea, pop. 6000, situated on the Zorn and the Rhine and Marne canal, was formerly the capital of Wasgau. Good beer sold at station. *Inns:* close to the station, the Gasthof zur Eisenbahn; at the end of the street, the H. du Boeuf Noir; in the Haupt Strasse, at the corner of the Schloss Platz, and opposite the telegraph and post-office is the *Gasthof zur Sonne. At the head of the Schloss Platz is the Chateau, the ancient palace of the Bishops of Strassburg, rebuilt in 1780 by the Cardinal de Rohan, and restored by Napoleon III., by whom it was converted into a retreat for the widows of high civil and military functionaries. By the Germans it has been made into barracks. The principal façade is on the side fronting the gardens. In the centre of the "Platz" is a small obelisk, recording the distances of important and remarkable places in the world from Zabern. Facing the obelisk is the abbey church, 15th cent., with a curious figure of Christ on the right-hand wall, and an ascension of Mary on the left. Higher than the Chateau is the parish church, 12th to 15th cent., containing paintings on wood by H. Wohlgemuth, and pulpit by Hammerer, 15th cent. Behind it is the museum, with numerous Gallo-Roman antiquities. The town contains many old gabled timber houses with oriel windows. Omnibus to Pfalzburg, 6½ m. N.E., see above.

    The principal excursions from Zabern are to the Haut or Hoh-Barr and to the Greiffenstein, castles on the tops of two mountains. The former on the left, and the other on the right side of the canal. For the Haut-Barr follow the railway side of the canal the length of the high bridge, and thence by a number of cross roads to the first house on the hill; where turn to the right, and ascend the hill to the left. There a sign-post will

| PARIS MILES FROM | GREIFFENSTEIN. MOLSHEIM. | STRASSBURG MILES TO |

be found, indicating in French and German the rest of the way to the Haut-Baar. Among the ruins, is a house where beer, deliciously cool, is sold. At about 25 minutes' walk behind Haut-Barr are the ruins of Gross-Geroldseck, 1578 ft.; and nearly the same distance beyond it, the Klein Geroldseck. All that is seen there, is seen best from the Haut-Barr.

For Greiffenstein follow the *railway* side of the canal for about a mile, where some stone steps on the bank lead down to the road opposite a bridge over the Zorn. Cross this bridge and the railway also, and take the path behind the house to the left. In about half an hour Greiffenstein is reached. When at Greiffenstein the road in front leads in about 40 minutes' walk to the Grotte de St. Vite, 1280 ft.

Zabern to Strassburg, 33 m. S.E. by Wasselnheim or Wasselonne and Molsheim, see map, p. 76. The country passed through is very beautiful, especially during the hop season. 11 m. S. is Wasselnheim, *Inn*: Pomme d'Or, prettily situated on the Mossig, at the entrance into the valley of Kronthal. It contains the ruins of a castle and stocking manufactories. 7½ m. S. is Wangenburg, Hotel Weyer, 1476 ft. above the sea, beautifully situated in a pine forest: visited on account of the pleasant air from the pines, and for the ascent of the Schneeberg, 3160 ft. in about 2 hrs., by footpath constructed by the Vosges Club.

19¾ m. S. from Zabern, 13 m. W. from Strassburg, and 16¼ m. E. from Rothau, is Molsheim, famous for its Finkenbergwein, pop. 3080, about ½ m. from the station. *Inns*: Charrue d'Or, just within the gate of the Dungeon tower, 13th cent.; the Deux Clefs in the Markt-Platz. An interesting town on the Breusch, in the midst of hop gardens and vineyards. It has still part of its old walls and many houses of the 15th and 16th cent., some very artistic. In the Markt-Platz is the old Hotel de Ville, a very beautiful gabled building. A double staircase leads up to the portico, having on each side a heavy but handsome stone balcony. Over the portico is a curious clock. The parish church, 15th cent., is a substantial building. Near it is a small monument to the memory of the "enfants de la ville morts pour la patrie 1870-1871." Junction with rail to Rothau by Mutzig and Schirmeck, whence the Donon is ascended by a good road in about 3 hrs. Coach from Rothau to St. Dié, 22½ m. S., see under St. Dié, p. 110; 13 m. E. from Molsheim is Strassburg.

306¾ VENDENHEIM. Junction with branch from Hagenau, 13 5¼ m. N.; whence to Metz, Carlsruhe, and Stuttgart.

312 STRASSBURG, or Strasbourg, pop. 100,000. Arrive at the Central Railway Station, on the western side of the town. *Hotels*: near station, in the Alte Weinmarkt Strasse, the *Angleterre; fronting station, adjoining the Angleterre, the H. Ville de Vienne, and near it the H. de l'Esprit; in the Meissengasse and the Promenade Broglie, the *Ville de Paris. Episcopalian service held in the hotel. The *Maison Rouge in the Kleber Platz. In the centre of this square is the monument to General Kleber, over his tomb. He was born in Strassburg on March 6, 1753, and poisoned at Cairo on June 14, 1800. The *Europe, near the Promenade,

Goose-Liver Pasties. Beer. Trams.

in the Blau-Wolken Gasse; near it, the France; the Ville de Lyon, in the Kinderspiel Gasse; the Charrue d'Or, in Stein Strasse. The asterisk indicates first-class hotels with first-class prices. Cab-fares, 1 to 2 persons the course within the city, 60 pfennig. Per half-hour 1 mark. Per hour 1 m. 60 pf. Request to see tariff.

The best places to buy the Strassburg goose-liver pasties (Patés de foie gras) are at the large establishments of L. Henry, 5 Rue du Dome, or the Münster Gasse. Also in same street, Doyen, No. 13, and Schneegans-Reeb, No. 27. A. Henry, Grosse Kirch-Grasse and Hummel, Lange Strasse. The poor geese, when about to be fattened, are confined in stalls so narrow that they cannot turn round, and maize is crammed down their throats three or four times daily for at least three weeks. These stalls are frequently ranged in cellars. Strassburg was at one time famous for snuff. It is needless to say that the *Beer* brewed here is held in high repute. Among the best beer-houses (Estaminets) are the Taverne Alsacienne and the Estaminet Pilon situated in the Gewerbslauben, the arcaded street between the Kleber Platz and the Gutenberg Platz; and the Felsenkeller in 139 Lange Strasse.

Post and Telegraph offices opposite façade of cathedral.

Sights.—Cathedral, closed between 11 and 2. Tickets for the spire sold throughout the whole day at the entrance into the south tower, 15 pfennig to the platform, 40 pf. to the turrets, 1 mark 20 pf. to the top. For the last apply at the Rathhaus. A walk over the town, and a few drives in the trams, starting from the Kleber Platz; especially to Hœnheim and the Rheinbrücke.

Trams.—From the Kleber Platz start the omnibus for Robertsau, and trams for Hœnheim and for the Rheinbrücke. At Hœnheim there are only breweries, beer-houses, and beer-gardens, with excellent beer, much frequented on feast-days. The omnibus to Robertsau or Ruprechtsau traverses the Münstergasse, Bruder Hof's Gasse, and St. Stephan's Gasse, where it crosses the Ill, and leaves the town by the Fischer-Thor. Before entering the village of Robertsau, the omnibus passes through a wooded park, much frequented on feast days, and stops nearly in front of the neat Protestant church. The tram to the **Rhein-Brucke** traverses the arcaded street the Gewerbslauben, the Gutenberg Platz, and the Alter Fischmarkt, where it crosses the Ill, and leaves the town by the Metzger-Thor. It stops at the bridge of boats, a little above the very handsome railway bridge across the Rhine. On the other side is the pleasant town of **Kehl**, with a large and commodious railway station. Opposite this station is the Hotel Saumon, then follow in the long street of Kehl several minor yet comfortable inns. Omnibus from Kehl to the village of Lichtenau. Kehl is situated on the east side of the Rhine, on a branch line between Strassburg, 7½ m. W., and Appenweier, 8½ m. E.

Strassburg is a strongly fortified town, with a circle of outworks and forts extending beyond the Rhine, 1½ m. distant. The Ill flows through the town in two semicircular branches, which unite at the bridge, where the river leaves the city. It was besieged by the

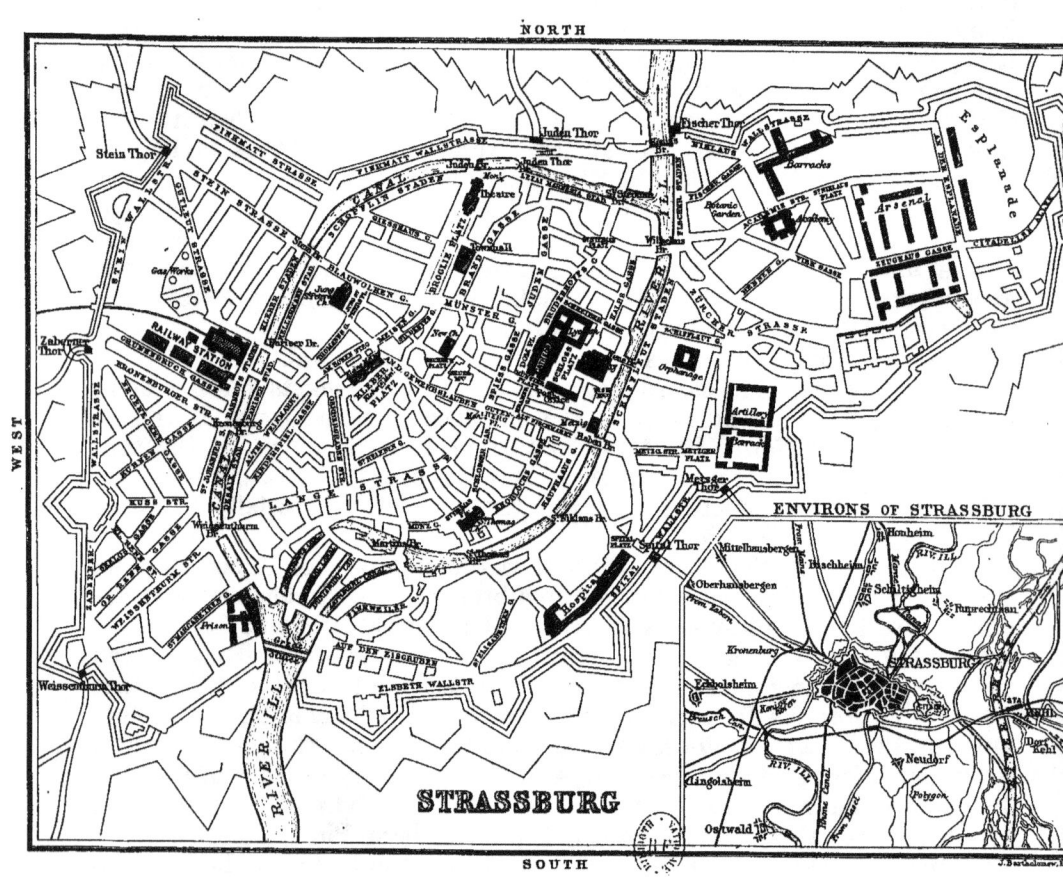

Spire. Dimensions. Windows.

generally the only door left open. Of the two towers, the northern alone has a spire, finished in 1439 by John Hültz of Cologne. It is 466 ft. high, ascended by 633 steps, and is 16 ft. higher than the Great Pyramid; 18 ft. higher than St. Peter's at Rome; 31 ft. higher than the chimney of St. Rollox of Glasgow; 128 ft. higher than St. Paul's of London; but 32 ft. lower than the spire of the Cathedral of Rouen, and 5 ft. lower than the spire of the Nicolaikirche at Hamburg.

On the top of the southern tower, 230 feet above the street, are a spacious platform, provided with telescopes, and the house of the watchman, where a glass of beer can be had. Below is the town, or rather the roofs of the houses; to the east is the Black Forest; to the west and north the Vosges mountains; and to the south the Kaiserstuhl, with the Jura mountains in the background. Among the names scratched on the wall are Voltaire's and Goethe's. Thus far the visitor is allowed to ascend alone; from the platform he is accompanied to the top of the northern tower by a watchman, which, for most people, will be found high enough. From the top of this tower a very narrow, and not in the least dangerous, staircase leads up through the open mullion-work of the spire to the roof of the couronne of the pinnacle. Higher up is the summit, which is reached by means of iron steps outside fastened into the wall. As this last part is attended with danger, the tickets for the summit are sold at the Rathaus or Hotel de Ville, and granted only to those judged capable of climbing up the ladder.

The **Interior** is 525 feet long, 195 feet wide, and 95 feet high, supported by 4 attached and 16 unattached massive clustered columns. The nave, a beautiful example of German 13th cent. Gothic, is 13 steps lower than the chancel, which, in the interior, is semicircular, but, in the exterior, rectangular. Under the chancel is a crypt. To visit the chancel and crypt, ticket 35 pf.

The most remarkable objects in the interior are: the clock; the three tiers of beautifully stained windows, of which the best are of the 14th cent. by Kirchheim, "the very glory of colour;" the organ built by Silbermann in 1704; and the fine stone pulpit erected by John Hammerer in 1486, adorned with nearly 50 statuettes. The sound-board was put up in 1824. At the eastern extremity of the south side of the nave is the chapel of St. Catherine, built in 1349 and revaulted in 1547. It contains the tomb of Conrad Bock, who died in 1480. This work is remarkable for the manner in which the figures surrounding the bed of the dying man are grouped. A door to the right leads out to the workshop (Steinhütte) of the masons and stone-

Strassburg Cathedral. Clock. Chapels.

cutters of the cathedral, who form a corporation of themselves. In the south aisle of the nave, fronting the clock, is the statue of Bishop Wernher, meditating on the plans for the erection of the church. Just before the statue is the beautiful column called the Angel's Pillar or Erwinspfeiler, adorned with figures of angels and other sculptures.

In the south transept, or to the right of the high altar, standing with the face towards it, is the **Astronomical Clock**, constructed by Schwilgué, a watch and clock maker of Strassburg, who commenced it in June 1838, and finished it at the end of 1842. It occupies the place of a less perfect one, completed in 1574, by the brothers Isaac and Josiah Habrecht, which ceased to go in 1789, and which is now, along with many other architectural curiosities connected with the cathedral, in that old gabled house called the Œuvre-Notre-Dame, on the south or chateau side of the cathedral. The earliest astronomical clock of Strassburg was begun in 1352, and finished two years afterwards.

The present clock is set to Strassburg time, 22 minutes before Paris time, and the crowing of the famous cock takes place at 12 midday. A crowd is always waiting to hear and see the performance. Get, if possible, a place well back close to the wall, and do not be induced to go forward by any beckoning of the beadle. While waiting for the hour to strike, observe the position of the cock, perched high up by himself to your left. Also that above the clock stands the figure of Death, with a bell on each side, and above him that of our Lord. Around Death are figures representing boyhood, youth, manhood, and old age, each of which in succession strikes the quarters, old age striking the last. Just before the hour strikes a man cautions spectators to beware of their purses. In due time a tiny figure, old age, enters the compartment where Death stands, and strikes the quarters on the smaller bell. While Death strikes the hour on the large bell, a genius turns over the hour-glass he holds in his hand, and the Twelve Apostles pass in single file in procession before our Lord, each in turn gravely making Him a bow, which He acknowledges by giving each His blessing. During this performance the cock, after vigorously flapping his wings, gives three times a joyous crow, with a considerable pause between each.

In the south aisle of the chancel is the oldest of the chapels, Saint Andrews, 12th cent., with additions in the 13th, remarkable for the style of its columns and decoration. In it are the tombs of several bishops, the oldest being that of Heinrich von Hasenburg, d. 1190.

On the other or N. side of the chancel, and similarly situated as

CRYPT. JOHN OF GUTENBERG. ST. THOMAS.

the chapel of St. Andrew, is the chapel of **St. John the Baptist**, 13th cent. Within is the mausoleum of Bishop Conrad of Lichtenberg, d. 1290, executed by Erwin of Steinbach the architect of the present cathedral; whose own tomb, with those of his wife Husa and son John, is in the small adjoining court. Near the entrance to this chapel, surrounded by an elegant railing, is the baptismal font of sculptured stone, the masterpiece of Josse Dotzinger of Worms, d. 1449.

At the east end of the N. aisle is the chapel of St. Lawrence, completed in 1505, containing the entrance into the vaults, in which the mortal remains of the bishops of the cathedral are deposited.

The **Crypt** below the chancel is considered to be part of the church erected by Bishop Wernher at the beginning of the 11th cent. The arches are round, the capitals of the columns cushioned or cubical, and stone seats run along the side of the walls. It contains a group representing " Our Lord and his Disciples on the Mount of Olives," placed here in 1683, from the church of the Augustines, built in 1378.

Facing the south portal of the cathedral is the formerly Bishop's palace, built in 1741, now one of the University buildings, containing lecture-rooms, and a library with 490,100 vols. The principal university building is outside the Fischer Thor. In the S.W. corner of the Münster Platz is the Frauenhaus, or the Maison-de-l'œuvre-Notre-Dame, built in 1581 in the Renaissance style. The winding staircase is light and elegant. In this house are preserved parts of the astronomical clock made in 1354, as well as of the second, designed by Conrad Dasypodius in 1570, and executed in 1574 by Tobias Stimmer and the two brothers Habrecht. Working drawings on parchment of the cathedral, a model of the spire, and several pieces of sculpture, are among the other curiosities.

Straight from the façade of the cathedral is the Gutenbergs Platz, with, in the centre, the fine bronze statue by David in 1840 of **John Gutenberg**, whose first experiments in printing were made in this town about the year 1436. He is represented as having just pulled a proof, on which are the words " Et la lumière fut." The continuation, in the same direction, by the Schlosser Gasse, leads to the church of **St. Thomas**, on the left bank of the Ill, built between 1270 and 1330. When the church is shut, as it generally is, apply to the sacristan, No. 5 Thomas-Platz, from whom tickets, 40 pf. each, are obtained. It is visited on account of the Mausoleum of Marshal Saxe, d. 1750, son of Augustus I. of Poland, erected to his memory by Louis XV., and executed by the sculptor Pigalle, who finished it in 1776,

STRASSBURG. STORKS. ROSHEIM.

after twenty years of incessant labour. Death is raising the lid of a coffin, into which the Marshal is descending, while weeping France tries to retain him. There are also a curious sarcophagus of Bishop Adeloch, with the date DCCCXXX., and monuments to the memory of the historians Schœpflin and Kock, and the erudite Jérémie-Jacques Oberlin.

The north-east portion of the town is occupied with buildings connected with science and war, although, unfortunately, the former has a very small share of the space. On the right bank, and a short way inwards from the second lowermost bridge, are the Botanic Gardens, small and crowded; and a little beyond, the Académie, containing the Natural History Museum. The medical department is in the Rue d'Or, near the town hospital. The Lycée and Seminary are in large buildings adjoining the cathedral. All the other wide-spreading buildings are barracks, hospitals, arsenals, or stables, etc., extending to the esplanade; and beyond it the citadel, through which is the road to Kehl.

Among the peculiarities of Strassburg must not be omitted the storks, which in April commence to build their nests on the tops of the chimneys, or rather on the bricks over the mouths of the chimneys. There used to be about fifty nests every year. As, however, coal instead of wood is being now more generally used, they seem to have deserted Strassburg, and to have remained only in some of the small neighbouring villages. Strassburg has two parks, both outside the fortifications.

A great variety of easy and agreeable excursions are afforded by that small branch line westwards from Strassburg. At Molsheim it divides into two branches, one going southwards and the other northwards. Of these the former leads to the more interesting places. The northern branch goes to Wasselonne, 21 miles distant, passing numerous small villages; and from Wasselonne to Saverne, see p. 87. $2\frac{1}{2}$ miles from Molsheim is Soultz les Bains, with a bathing establishment supplied by cold mineral springs, containing bromine, iodine, etc. From Mutzig the train goes to Shirmeck, 14 miles westwards, and Rothau, other 2 m.; whence diligence to St. Dié station, 24 m. southwest. From Schirmeck, Mount Donon, 3315 feet high, is ascended.

By the south branch, $3\frac{1}{4}$ m. from Molsheim, or 16 from Strassburg, is the village of Rosheim. *Inns:* Pflug; Sonne. Pop. 4100, with mineral waters containing lithine. Church 12th cent. Old picturesque houses. Here those alight who wish to visit the castle of Gir-

Paris to Bale.

baden, 1870 ft. and 7 miles westwards by the village of Mollkirch, 5¾ m. from Rosheim. Continuing the line 3¼ m. S. from Rosheim is Obernai or Ober-Ehnheim, pop. 5000. *Inns:* Dubs; Zwei Schlüssel. A little manufacturing town, with some picturesque houses and a town hall built in 1523. Diligence for Odilienberg, 9 m. W. On the E. side of the rocky ridge is a Franciscan convent 2470 ft. above the sea, on the site of the one founded in the 7th cent. by Ste. Odilie, the patroness of Alsace. Adjoining is a comfortable inn. Southwards from the nunnery is the Mennelstein, the highest point (2673 ft.) of the ridge, ¼ hour from the inn, commanding a glorious view. Around the hill is what is called the Heidenmauer, a thick wall from 6 to 10 ft. high, composed of roughly hewn superimposed blocks of sandstone without cement, erected in all probability posterior to the 4th cent.

Paris to Bale.

BY VESOUL, BELFORT, and MULHAUSEN, traversing LORRAINE and ALSACE. Distance 326 miles.

Time by quick trains, 13 hours. For Time-table, see under "Paris à Belfort," in "Indicateur des Chemins de Fer de l'Est." This is the route to take for the famous baths of Vittel, Contrexéville, and Martigny.

See Map, page 76.

PARIS 'BALE'
MILES FROM   MILES TO

PARIS. Start from the station of the Chemins de Fer de l'Est. 326

5¼ NOISY-LE-SEC, pop. 3000. Here the line separates from the route to Bale by Epernay, Nancy, and Strassburg. 320¾

24 GRETZ-ARMANVILLIERS. Junction to Coulommiers, 24 m. E. 302

55 LONGUEVILLE. Junction with branch to Provins, 4 m. N.E. 271

60 FLAMBOIN. Junction to Montereau, 16 m. W. 266

69 NOGENT-SUR-SEINE, pop. 4000. H. Clef d'Argent. 257

Five miles south, in the village of St. Aubin, pop. 700, are the ruins of the "Abbaye du Paraclet," where the mausoleum of Heloïse and Abeilard, now in the cemetery of Père la Chaise, originally stood. Nogent is also the station for Villenauxe, pop. 300, 8 miles northwards, with a fine 15th century church and some picturesque timber houses.

74 PONT-SUR-SEINE, pop. 1000. "Dolmens" in neighbourhood. 252

80 ROMILLY-SUR-SEINE, pop. 5000, with manufactories of 246

hosiery. 1¼ m. from Romilly is Scellières, where Voltaire was buried, and where his body remained 13 years, till it was transported to the Pantheon of Paris.

104 TROYES, pop. 37,000. See Black's *France, West Half.* **222**

Junction with branch line 20 m. S.E. to **Bar**-sur-Seine, pop. 3000. *Inns:* Fontaine; Ecu. With some houses of the 16th cent., and church, 16th and 17th cent. 22 m. beyond is **Chatillon-sur-Seine**, pop. 5000. *Inns:* Poste; Cote d'Or. Parish church, St. Vorle, rebuilt in 991; St. Nicolas, 12th cent.; St. Jean, 16th cent. The tower, all that remains of the chatelet, is in the midst of a beautiful park, with a terrace commanding a good view. 22 m. S.W. from Chatillon is **Nuits**-sous-Ravières, pop. 500, on the Armançon, with a handsome Gothic chapel, 12th cent., and church, 12th to 15th cents.

124 VENDEUVRE, pop. 3000, on the Barse, with crockery and **202** linen manufactories, an ancient cemetery, a castle of the 12th cent. repaired in the 17th, and the church of St. Pierre, in the Renaissance, with fine pulpit and altar.

131 JESSAINS. Station for Brienne-Napoleon 10 m. north. **195**

BRIENNE, pop. 3000. *Hotel:* Des Voyageurs. Possesses a fine chateau built in 1780. In the square is a statue of Napoleon I., in the uniform of the military college, which formerly stood here, and which he attended from April 1779 to October 1784.

137 BAR-SUR-AUBE, pop. 3000. *Inns:* Poste; Pomme d'Or. A **189** pretty town at the foot of Mount St. Germaine. The parish church, St. Maclou, is from the 12th to the 14th cent.; and St. Pierre, from the 12th to the 13th cent. Remains of fortifications, 13th cent.

145 CLAIRVAUX-SUR-AUBE, pop. 1300, about a mile from **181** station. The village contains ironworks, a large monastery, founded in 1115, now a prison, and ruins of ancient castle.

155 BRICON, junction with Chatillon-sur-Seine, 27 m. S.W. **171**

163 CHAUMONT, pop. 9000. *Hotels:* Ecu; Poste; Commerce. **163**

Junction with Paris and Strassburg line by a branch to Blesme, 56 miles northward. From this branch another from Boulogne extends to Neufchateau, 31 miles north-east, or 38 from Chaumont; and another from St. Dizier to Vassey, 15 m. south-west. The quiet town of Chaumont possesses a church, St. Jean Baptiste, commenced in the 13th cent., of which, however, the spire, in the flamboyant style, was rebuilt in the 16th cent. The tower, Hautefeuille, built in the 10th cent., is all that remains of the palace of the Counts of Champagne.

185 LANGRES, pop. 9000. *Hotels:* Poste ; Europe. **141**

The omnibus requires 40 minutes to go from the station to the town, which is perched on the top of a hill. The principal street runs from north-west to south-east. At the north-west end are avenues of elms and the fine gateway called the Porte des Moulins. From the Porte we pass first the College and then the Cathedral St. **Mammes**, 309 ft. long, and height of roof 90 ft. The façade, in the Roman style, was finished in 1761, but the greater part of the rest of the church belongs to the 12th cent. It contains some good pictures and statues; and in the chapel to the left on entering, a baptismal font of the 13th cent. The street in front of the cathedral leads to the Museum and Picture Gallery, only a few yards distant. South-east from the Cathedral is a "Porte," reconstructed in 1851. This is the best part from which to commence a walk round the ramparts, 1094 yards in circuit, and commanding extensive views.

To the right of the gateway, on descending from the town to the station, is an arch built in the wall, which dates from the middle of the 3d century. It is close to the gateway leading up by the Rue aux Chevres to the Hotel de Ville. Langres is famous for cutlery, but the best is made in the neighbouring town of Nogent-le-Roi.

The *Post-Office* is in No. 16 Rue Neuve, and near it the Church of St. Martin, partly of the 13th cent., with a tower 170 ft. high. The crucifix over the altar was sculptured by Gentil in the 16th cent.

Three miles east from Langres are "les sources" of the river Marne and a large cave ; carriage there and back, 6 fr.

Denis Diderot, the philosopher and encyclopædist, was born here in 1713. He was one of that group of the last century who, unable to distinguish between superstition and religion, vainly strove to extinguish religion itself.

191 CHALINDREY, an uncomfortable station ; village on opposite side of hill. Junction with line to Mirecourt, $60\frac{1}{2}$ m. N.E., passing Martigny, Contrexéville, and Vittel, p. 98; also with line to Belfort, $40\frac{1}{2}$ m. S.E., p. 103 ; and to Dijon, $43\frac{1}{4}$ m. S., passing Is-sur-Tille, 20 m. N. from Dijon. The village of Is, pop. 2300, is situated in the midst of an undulating wheat-growing country. *Inn :* at station H. de la Gare, comfortable. Behind the station is the hamlet of Marcilly-sur-Tille, with a small church, 11th cent. At station omnibus awaits passengers for Is-sur-Tille, $\frac{1}{2}$ m. dist. *Inn :* H. du Lion d'Or, comfortable. Pension, $8\frac{1}{4}$ fr. Church belongs to the 11th cent. Many old but plain houses. **135**

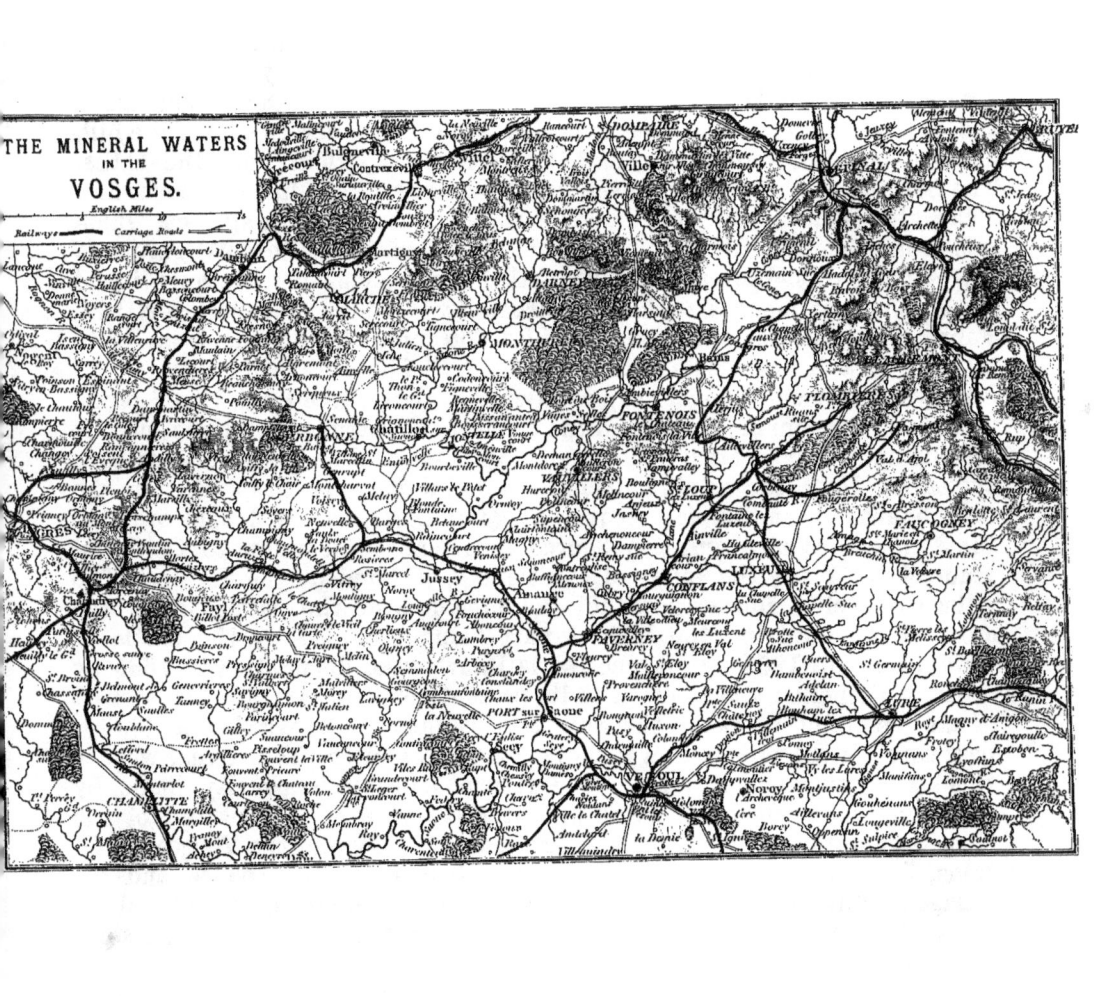

| PARIS MILES FROM | CHATILLON-SUR-SAONE. SERQUEUX. | BALE MILES TO |

208¾ VITRY, junction with branch line to Bourbonne-les-Bains, 117¼ 11¼ m. N. Bourbonne, pop. 4275. *Hotels:* near the bathing establishment, the Maison Beaurain, a private house and dear, 10 to 15 frs. ; the G. H. des Bains, 7½ to 9½ frs. ; Maison Lucette Gaillard ; Maison Berthe Gaillard 4 Place des Bains ; in the main street H. du Commerce and the H. du Bœuf Gras. Temple Protestant, Rue de Montletang. Bourbonne is situated on the confluence of the Borne with the Apance, on a hill 755 ft. above the sea. The town is clean and many of the streets are very steep. The church, near the highest part of the town, belongs to the 12th cent. There are 2 promenades, each on a different side of the hill, the Promenade Montmorency and the Promenade Orfeuil near the baths. The bathing establishment is well constructed and kept in excellent order. The water is employed more in douches than in baths. The springs, which rise from the Muschelkalk formation, are intensely saline, 47 grains of the chloride of sodium to the pint, with besides a considerable quantity of the sulphate of magnesia and the carbonate of lime. Temperature 140° Fahr. The bath is continued from 30 to 60 min., the douche from 15 to 30 min. Each bath costs with linen 1¼ fr. The cure lasts from 21 to 30 days, but even a longer stay is advised. Daily dose from 1 to 2 pints. The water acts upon the skin in the manner of astringent lotions, and is recommended for sciatica and other complaints of the nervous and osseous systems. Near the establishment is a large military hospital. In the neighbourhood, at the picturesque village of Larivière are 2 cold springs, the Source Maynard and the Source Larivière. Excursion to Coiffy-le-Haut, 4 m. W. by the valley of Montletang, watered by the Borne. The village of Coiffy, formerly within the precincts of the castle, is on the crest of a mountain ; the highest part being occupied by the castle of Coiffy, built in 1255 by Marguerite de Bourbonne, dismantled in 1635 by order of Richelieu and reduced to its present condition in 1660. The best of the remaining parts are the walls and bastions. On arriving at Coiffy, pass through the village to a little beyond the church, 11th cent., whence there is a magnificent view. The return journey is usually made by Montecharvot ; whence there is an extensive view of Alsace and of the Vosges mountains. To Chatillon-sur-Saone, a village in the Vosges mountains, 7 m. E. from Bourbonne, by the banks of the Apance and the village of Villars-St.-Marcellin, with a church of the 11th cent. Chatillon, situated on the confluence of the Apance with the Saone contains some old houses and a modern castle.

2½ m. N. from Bourbonne is Serqueux, pop. 1500, with a forest granted to it by letters patent from Charles VI. and VII. Beyond the forest, on the top of a hill is the village of Aigremont, fortified in 1080 by Foulques d'Aigremont. The castle was besieged and destroyed in 1630. Many of the ancient lords of Aigremont belonging to the families of Choiseul and Montmorency were buried in the church ; but in 1793 the mob rifled and partly destroyed their tombs. At the end of the valley, at the foot of Aigremont hill, is the village of Larivière, with a cold chalybeate spring. North from Aigremont hedr Fresnoy, or 10 m. N.W. from

VITTEL. BATHS. CONTREXÉVILLE. BATHS.

Bourbonne, are the ruins of the Abbey of Morimond (mori mundo), founded by Odolric, Lord of Aigremont, and his wife Adeline in 1115, and destroyed in 1793. 19 m. northward from Bourbonne, near the Abbey of Vacheresse, is the oak called the Chêne des Partisans, 43 ft. in circumference at the base and 108 ft. high. Under this tree the robbers of Lorraine used to meet to arrange their raids into France. Near this is the old town of La Mothe, with the interesting ruins of its castle, impregnable before the discovery of gunpowder; but taken and destroyed 1634.

To the N. of Bourbonne, or on the railway between Mirecourt and Chalindrey, are the three famous mineral water stations of Vittel, Contrexéville, and Martigny, with similar springs, differing principally in their degree of efficacy. See Map, page 76.

15 m. S.W. from Mirecourt, $45\frac{1}{2}$ m. N.E. from Chalindrey, and 52 m. S. by rail from Nancy is **Vittel**. On the S. side of the railway station is the village of Vittel, pop. 1400, on the Vair. *Inns:* Commerce, pension 7 to 8 frs.; H. de la Source. Those requiring to take the waters of Vittel and at the same time unable to bear the expense of the hotel at the establishment, will find either of these houses sufficiently comfortable. The inn opposite the station is still cheaper.

On the other side of the railway, and standing in its own grounds, is the Hotel of the establishment, consisting of 2 large comfortably furnished houses. The pension is from $10\frac{1}{2}$ to 15 frs. per day, which includes room, service, and 2 meals, both with wine. A complete tea or café au lait in the morning, 1 fr. extra. The water, which is taken principally inwardly, is cold, limpid and nearly tasteless, and, like that of Martigny and Contrexéville, used on account of its solvent properties, in the cure of gravel, of affections of the bladder, and of gout. The chief ingredients in the Grande Source of the establishment are, in 1000 grammes or 36 oz., 0·680 parts of the sulphate of lime, 0·246 of the sulphate of soda, 0·202 of the bicarbonate of lime, and 0·182 of the sulphate of magnesia. Of the chloruret of soda, potash, and magnesia, it contains 0·090. Of the silicate of soda, 0·039. Of the bicarbonate of lithia, 0·0014. The "Source Marie" is an aperient, and is used especially for stubborn constipation. The "Source Salée" is cathartic and is used for diseases of the liver. In the grounds is also a chalybeate spring. The cure lasts 21 days. For drinking the water, 20 frs. the season. The wine grown in the neighbourhood of Vittel is thin, and has a slightly bitter flavour; yet in warm weather it is very palatable. The beer brewed in Vittel is considered among the best in France.

237 m. S.E. from Paris by Mirecourt, 55 m. S. from Nancy, $3\frac{1}{4}$ m. S.W. from Vittel, and $6\frac{1}{4}$ m. N.E. from Martigny is **Contrexéville**, pop. 1300. The "Etablissement," with its large hotel, casino, bath-house, fountains, and galleries, all within a garden; are close to the station. The pension in the hotel of the Etablissement, as well as in the other first-class hotels near it, viz. the Paris and Providence, is from 14 to 25 frs. per day, including only two meals, wine, service, and everything else, which, considering the style of the furniture and food, is rather dear. The less pretentious hotels, such as the *H. des XII. Apôtres; Parisot; Mansuy;

Vosges; Harmand; Pavillon; charge only from 7½ to 10½ frs. per day, including everything, and they are quite as comfortable. The cure lasts 21 days, and the season from June to October. The charge for drinking the water during the whole season is 20 frs. A first-class mineral water bath 3 frs. Second-class 1½ fr. The waters of Contrexéville owe their reputation to the solvent power they possess, of deleterious matter in the blood and the bladder, through the influence of lithia and sundry silicates. The Source du Pavillon contains in 36 oz. or 1000 grammes, 1·165 parts of the sulphate of lime, 0·402 of the bicarbonate of lime, 0·236 of the sulphate of magnesia, 0·035 of the bicarbonate of magnesia, 0·30 of the sulphate of soda, 0·015 of silica, and 0·004 of the bicarbonate of lithia. The tower of the parish church dates from the 11th cent. The picture forming the reredos of the high altar represents one of the visits of Jesus Christ to Marguerite Alacoque.

Among the drives are, to the Haut-des-Salins, 3¼ m., with view of the Vosges and the Jura mountains. 5 m. into the forest of St. Ouen, with the large oak called, of the "Partisans." 9 m. to the ruins of the Castle de la Mothe. Coach from Contrexéville to Aulnois 9½ m. N., fare 2½ frs., whence rail to Neufchateau, 10 m. N.W.

Martigny-les-Bains, 6¼ m. by rail S. from Contrexéville, and 9½ m. from Vittel, and 243 from Paris. The least known of the three stations, although possessing the greatest quantity of the ingredients, to which the water owes its power of eliminating the virulent matter from the blood; which causes gout, and its dissolving power of calculi composed of layers of uric acid and of oxalate of lime. The "Source No. 1," contains in 36 oz. or 1000 grammes, 1·424 parts of the sulphate of lime, 0·330 of the sulphate of magnesia, 0·229 of the sulphate of soda, 0·198 of the bicarbonate of magnesia, 0·170 of the bicarbonate of lime, 0·053 *of the silicate of soda*, 0·065 of the chloruret of sodium, and 0·030 *of the chloruret of lithium*. The pension per day in the Hotel de l'Etablissement is from 8 to 15 frs. The hotel and all the other buildings are situated close to the station in a large domain belonging to the company. The village is dirty and fortunately small. The parish church, in part belonging to the 13th cent. but repaired, has at the west end a low square tower surmounted by an octagonal slated spire. The apsidal termination is pentagonal, with a receding buttress attached diagonally to each angle.

JUSSEY, 730 ft. above the sea, pop. 3050. *Inns:* in the town the Aigle Noir; at the station the Commerce. Remains of a fortress.

PORT D'ATELIER, 722 ft. above the sea, pop. 200. *Inn:* H. de la Gare. Junction with branch line to **Aillevilliers,** 18½ m. E., by Conflans and St. Loup. *Inn:* H. de la Gare. From Aillevilliers branch line up the beautiful valley of the Augromme to Plombières, 6½ m. N.E. Also up the parallel valley of the Combeauté to Faymont, 12½ m. N.E., passing Val d'Ajol. 10 m. S. from Aille-

PLOMBIÈRES. BATHS AND EXCURSIONS.

villiers, on the main line to Belfort, is Luxeuil, p. 102. 8¾ m. N. from Aillevilliers is Bains, see p. 103, and Map, page 76.

299 m. S.E. from Paris, and 79½ m. S. from Nancy, is **Plombières** (formerly Plumières), pop. 2500, situated in the narrow valley of the Augromme, 1320 ft. above the sea. The greater part of the town consists of large houses with furnished lodgings. *Hotels:* the *Grand Hotel des Thermes in a large park at the west end. Pension 9½ to 13½ frs. per day, not including wine. Room 74 was the bedroom of Napoleon III., and No. 72 his study. Adjoining the hotel is the first-class bathing establishment, the Grand Bain des Nouveaux Thermes. The other two hotels are not recommended; the Tete d'Or, 8½ to 10½ frs., including wine and service; and H. de l'Ours, 8 frs. 15 sous to 9 frs. 15 sous per day, dear for quality. The best lodging-houses are, *Resal-Cornuot, opposite the Bain des Dames, from 7½ to 12 frs. per day, including service but not wine, which none of the following furnished houses give. A little farther down the street, opposite the Bain Romain, is the *Maison Augustin-Parisot, 8 frs. 10 c. to 12 frs. 10 c. Opposite the Bain Romain the Maison Resal-Duroch, 8 to 11 frs., principally apartments are let in this house. Maison Fournie, close to the Bains des Dames, 8½ frs. to 12 frs. Maison Laplace, 9½ frs. Opposite Bain Romain, Maison Véhrlé, 9½ to 12½ frs. Opposite Bain National, Maison Cholé, 7½ to 9½ frs. Opposite the Casino, the Maison Deschaiseaux, 7½ to 10½ frs. There are many more besides, all charging about the same. Post-office, Rue Luxeuil.

In the "Place" is the parish church built in 1861. E. from the church is the Promenade des Dames, having in the centre a chalybeate spring, the source Bourdeille. From the western corner of the "Place" commences the R. Stanislas, containing the best private hotels and all the bathing establishments, excepting the "Grand Bain des Nouveaux-Thermes." At the head of the Rue Stanislas is the second-class establishment of the "Bains de Dames (entered also from the Rue de Luxeuil), with 14 bath cabinets, 1 fr. 80 c. each. In the great vaults (partly built by the Romans) under the street, are the vapour baths, the "Etuves Romaines" 1½ fr.; but with douche, manipulation, and bed, 3½ frs. Farther on, in a low building in the centre of the street, is the "Bain Romain" with 24 bath cabinets, 2 frs. 30 c. each. Almost adjoining, is the third-class bath establishment, the "Bain Tempéré," containing under a great vaulted chamber a piscina in 4 compartments, 80 c. each, and baths 90 c., on each of the two opposite sides. In the gallery above are 13 bath cabinets, 1 fr. 20 c. each. Attached, is the Bain des Capucins, consisting of a very large piscina under a spacious vaulted hall. Opposite, is the second-class establishment, the "Bain National," with on the ground floor, round the sides, 15 bath cabinets, 1 fr. 80 c. each; and in the centre a piscina in 4 compartments, 1 fr. 55 c. Upstairs are 25 bath cabinets.

At the W. end of the town, near the railway station, are the handsome Casino standing by itself, and a little beyond, the first-class hotel, the Grand Hotel des Thermes, and first-class bath establishment, forming a large palatial edifice. This bathing establishment contains 52 bath

PLOMBIÈRES. BATHS. FEUILLÉ DOROTHÉE.

cabinets 2 frs. 30 c., and 4 small piscinæ. All the baths of all the establishments are copper-tinned, and none are sunk into the floor. The duration of the bath is 1 hr., and of the vapour baths 30 min. The cure lasts 21 days, and depends principally on the bathing. There are 4 drinking springs: the Source des Dames, 124°, at the head of the Rue Stanislas; the Source de Crucifix, 107°, and the Source Savonneuse, both situated in a recess under the arcade of the Rue Stanislas. The fourth is the cold chalybeate spring, the "Source Bourdeille" in the Promenade des Dames. The hot springs are all slightly saline, and feebly mineralised, the principal ingredients being: a glutinous or saponaceous substance like Baregeine, the silicates of soda, lime and magnesia, the sulphate of soda and silicic acid, together with minute traces of alumina, iron and arsenic. The hottest of the springs, the "Source Bassompierre," 158° Fahr., supplies the vapour baths. Excepting in temperature, there is little difference between the springs; some too are a little more saponaceous than others. All are easily borne by the stomach and are considered efficacious in the cure or alleviation of gout, rheumatism, neuralgia (especially tic), diseases of the intestines and chronic catarrh of the stomach.

Opposite the railway station, on wooded hills rising from the Augromme, is the Parc of the Grand Hotel des Thermes, intersected with paths and carriage drives, one of the most frequented being the road leading 2 m. down by the Augromme to the Fontaine Stanislas, a tiny stream of water gurgling forth from below an overhanging rock under a clump of trees. On the rock are verses recounting the virtues of the King of Poland, "Stanislas le Bienfaisant." For the view, ascend the path behind the fountain. The sunniest and driest road is the "Route de Luxeuil," which begins to ascend near the post-office. On the opposite side of the valley is the Epinal road, bordered at the commencement by a row of houses. It leads up to a statue of the Virgin, and the chapel of St. Joseph. From the chapel a path leads up to a fir plantation, whence there is a good view of the country below.

At the E. end of the Promenade des Dames are large iron-works, where tools and utensils of various kinds are manufactured. On the top of the hill on the other side of the road is a calvary. A path at the foot of this hill leads up to the "Fontaine du Renard," a clear limpid spring. The best of the walks and drives are to the Feuillée Dorothée or Ancienne and the Feuillée Nouvelle, both 2½ m. S., and to the town of Ajol, 4½ m. S. on the river Combeauté, and on the branch line from Aillevilliers, from which it is 5½ m. N.E. The nearest way to the Feuillée Dorothée is by the first path, diverging to the S. from the Fougerolles road. It leads through woods and fields, but is here and there a little intricate. By the Fougerolles road it is hardly possible to go wrong. Follow it to the first fingerpost, bearing on one pointer Luxeuil 17·5 kil. and on the other Val d'Ajol 5·3 kil.; take the latter. A little way beyond this, and the 3d kil. stone from Plombières, is a large inn called the Auberge Enfoncée; from it a straight broad road leads down to the Val-d'Ajol; the narrow road to the right, between the trees, leads to the Feuillée Nouvelle, with a restaurant; while the road to the left leads to the **Feuillée Dorothée**, with a little inn, where a bedroom, with a small window commanding a splendid view,

FOUGEROLLES. LUXEUIL. BATHS.

costs 1½ fr., and breakfast, dinner, and service 6½ frs. The Feuillée Dorothée is a terrace on the brow of a mountain rising from the Ajol valley, parallel to the Augromme valley, but separated by a range of mountains. On the brow of the next mountain, to the right, is the Feuillée Nouvelle; but the view is not so good. Down in the valley is the town of Ajol, 10 m. by rail from Aillevilliers and 2½ from Faymont, pop. 7050, on the Combeauté, an affluent of the Saône. From Ajol the road ascends to **Faymont,** 12½ m. N.E. by rail from Aillevilliers, and 5 m. from Plombières by the road, following the course of the Combeauté and passing Bouchatel and Les Chênes, 4¼ m. S.W. Down the Combeauté on the rail to Aillevilliers is Fougerolles, a pretty village famous for cherries, from which a great deal of Kirschwasser is made. From Faymont a path leads up eastwards to the hamlet of Moulin, passing about half-way two mountain tarns. Near Moulin, a little way down the stream, are the falls of Géhard, and farther down on the left bank an enormous block of granite called the Pierre du Tonnerre. From this a path leads down the narrow wooded vale of the Géhard to its junction with the Combeauté in the valley of Hérival. From Faymont the highway ascends by the course of the Combeauté, through a narrow wooded valley, to the Val d'Hérival, which it crosses at the hamlet of Bas d'Hérival, and joins the Plombières road 8 m. from Plombières. Hérival is about 9 m. from Plombières, at the head of a valley near two small lakes, surrounded by mountains covered with pine forests.

Coach from Plombières to Remiremont, 8 m. E.; fare, 1½ fr. The road, after passing down the Promenade des Dames, ascends to the left between the river Augromme and the pine forest of Humont, full of splendid trees. At the small inn 5¾ m. from Plombières, the road attains its culminating point, and then descends into the watershed of the affluents of the Moselle, and enters Remiremont by the foot of Mont Parmont, 2012 ft. For Remiremont, see p. 111.

10 m. S. from Aillevilliers, 83¼ m. S. from Nancy and 303 m. S.E. from Paris, is **Luxeuil,** pop. 4200, on the Breuchin, 1625 ft. above the sea. *Hotels:* in the main street, the *Grand Hotel des Thermes; with also another house opposite the Bathing Establishment; pension 8½ to 12½ frs.; behind the H. des Thermes is the Maison Ganeval 8½ to 14½ frs. per day; the *Lion Vert 9½ to 12½ frs.—a comfortable house. This price includes, besides service and the two meals with wine, café au lait in the morning.

Luxeuil consists of a very long street, with short streets ramifying from it. At the north end, in its own grounds, is the handsome hospital built in 1879 and presented as a gift to the town by M. Grammont. Near it, down one of the branch streets, is the "Etablissement Thermal," a good and well-arranged establishment in a small park.

The alkaline springs, which are the most abundant, contain of the chloride of sodium about 12 grains to the pint, and a lesser quantity of the sulphate of soda and of alkaline carbonates. Temp. from 67° to 122° Fahr. They are employed in chronic rheumatism, sciatica, and in certain forms of dyspepsia and of uterine derangement. The ferruginous spring yields traces of the oxide, phosphate and arseniate of iron. It is not easily digested. The establishment contains 84 cabinet baths and 4 piscinæ. Though none of the latter are large, yet both sexes may bathe in them at the same time. A bath with linen costs 1¼ fr. Season, from May 15 to September 15. Napoleon III. visited this establishment on 7th July 1856. A great quantity of Gallo-Roman coins, trinkets, tools, and pottery, have been dug up under and around the establishment.

On the main street, beyond the Hotel des Thermes, is the old Hotel de Ville, now the seat of the Juge-de-Paix, built in the 16th cent. and crowned with a tower commanding an excellent view of the town. A beautiful oriel window projects from the building. Opposite is the house of Cardinal Joufroy, 16th cent., also with an oriel window, but not so elaborate. Farther down the street, and on the same side, is the Maison des Arcades, 16th cent., adorned with columns set into the walls. The next house to it is said to be the oldest in Luxeuil. Opposite, in the Place de Baille, is the beautiful abbey, now the parish church, built in 1340 and recently restored. In the interior the most remarkable objects are the massive and carefully carved organ-loft, 17th cent., and the statue of St. Peter, 13th cent., in the north transept. Adjoining are the cloisters, 15th cent., and the extensive abbey buildings, now occupied by the Hotel de Ville, the post-office, and the Lycée or Grammar School.

8¾ m. N. from Aillevilliers, on the direct line to Epinal, Nancy and Metz, is **Bains**, 1330 ft. above the sea, 252 m. S.E. from Paris, and 20 m. N. from Epinal. Omnibuses at the station await passengers for the town, about 3 m. west. *Hotels:* Clef d'Or; Poste; Commerce. Bains, pop. 3000, on the Baignerot, contains 11 sulphurous soda springs 180° Fahr., similar to those of Plombières, utilised by two establishments, the Bain Neuf and the "Bain Vieux." Season, June to October.

The parish church dates from the 18th cent. About a mile from Bains, on the Epinal road, is Notre-Dame-de-la-Brosse, visited by pilgrims. In the neighbourhood are large iron-works and millstone quarries. Among the excursions the best are—to the Moulin au Bois, 2 hrs. there and back; to the hill of Noirmont 1880 ft. above the sea; the Fontaines Chaudes, 7½ m.; Thunimont, by the valley of Cony, 9¼ m. 7 m. N. from Bains, on the railway to Epinal, is **Xertigny** station, 1419 ft. above the sea. Omnibus to village 2 m. distant, pop. 3900. Church 12th cent. Falls of the Gué-du-Saut. For the above baths see Map, p. 97.

Here we resume the route of Paris to Basel.

234¼ VAIVRE, junction with line to Gray, 36 m. S.W. 91¾

237 VESOUL, pop. 8000; junction with line to Besançon, 40 m. S. 89

Vesoul is a well-built town, situated on the junction of the rivers Durgeon and Colombine, at the foot of a hill covered with vineyards, and reaching the elevation of 1452 ft. above the level of the sea. The parish church was built in 1745, the Palais de Justice in 1765, and the barracks in 1777. *Inns:* Europe; Madeleine; Aigle Noir; Commerce.

PARIS	BELFORT.	BALE
MILES FROM		MILES TO

255 LURE, pop. 4000. Containing an old abbey founded in the 71 7th century. *Inns:* H. de la Cigogne; Colné. Junction with branch to Aillevilliers 21¼ m. N., passing Luxeuil 11 m. N., page 102.

276 BELFORT, 1176 ft. above the sea, pop. 12,000, on both sides 50 of the Savoureux, 59 m. N. from Besançon, 11 N. from Montbeliard, 8¾ m. N. from Morvillars, 7½ m. N. from Petit-Croix, 31 m. W. from Mülhausen, 38½ m. E. from Vesoul, 67 m. N. from Epinal, and 113 m. N. from Nancy. Omnibuses for the hotels at station. Cabs 2 frs. per hour. In front of station the H. Thann, a second-class house.

To visit Belfort, which can be done in a very short time in a cab, turn to the left from the station and then take the last broad street or road to the right, the "Faubourg de France." A little way down, right hand, is the H. Lapostolest; farther on, left hand, the H. des Messageries, a smaller but a good house; and at the foot of the street fronting the bridge, the H. Ancienne Poste, a first-class house. Across the bridge, and between the Savoureuse and the ramparts, is the town promenade. A little beyond is the citadel, about 400 ft. above the river, erected by Vauban in 1687, but greatly strengthened and enlarged since 1871. On the face of the sandstone cliff on which it stands is a *Lion* sculptured in bold relief, 82 ft. long by 39 high. From the promenade we pass through the Porte de France, built in 1687, and enter the Place d'Armes. To the left are the best hotel in Belfort, the "Tonneau d'Or," and the Telegraph Office. Fronting the gate is the parish church of St. Denis, built in 1750 of the red sandstone of the place. To the right are the Hotel de Ville and the Post-Office. In the Hotel de Ville are the Library and the Picture Gallery.

The street, Rue de la Grande Fontaine, between the church and the Hotel de Ville, leads up to the Porte de Brisach, built of red sandstone in 1687. Outside this gate take the centre road, having on the right the Fort de Justice, 1515 ft. above the sea and 339 ft. above the river; and on the left the Fort de la Miotte, 1316 ft. above the sea, easily recognised by its square look-out tower, seen from a great distance. In the hollow on the left are large military buildings, and an intrenched camp capable of holding 20,000 men. A little way up on the right hand is the cemetery, indicated by an obelisk, where the "defenseurs morts pendant le siege" from the 2d November 1870 to the 15th February 1871, were buried. Continue the road to the guard-house at the top of the hill, where take the road, left, leading up to the entrance of Fort de la Miotte. When at the gate, pass on to the raised terrace, left hand, at the foot of the Tower de la Miotte. The view from here

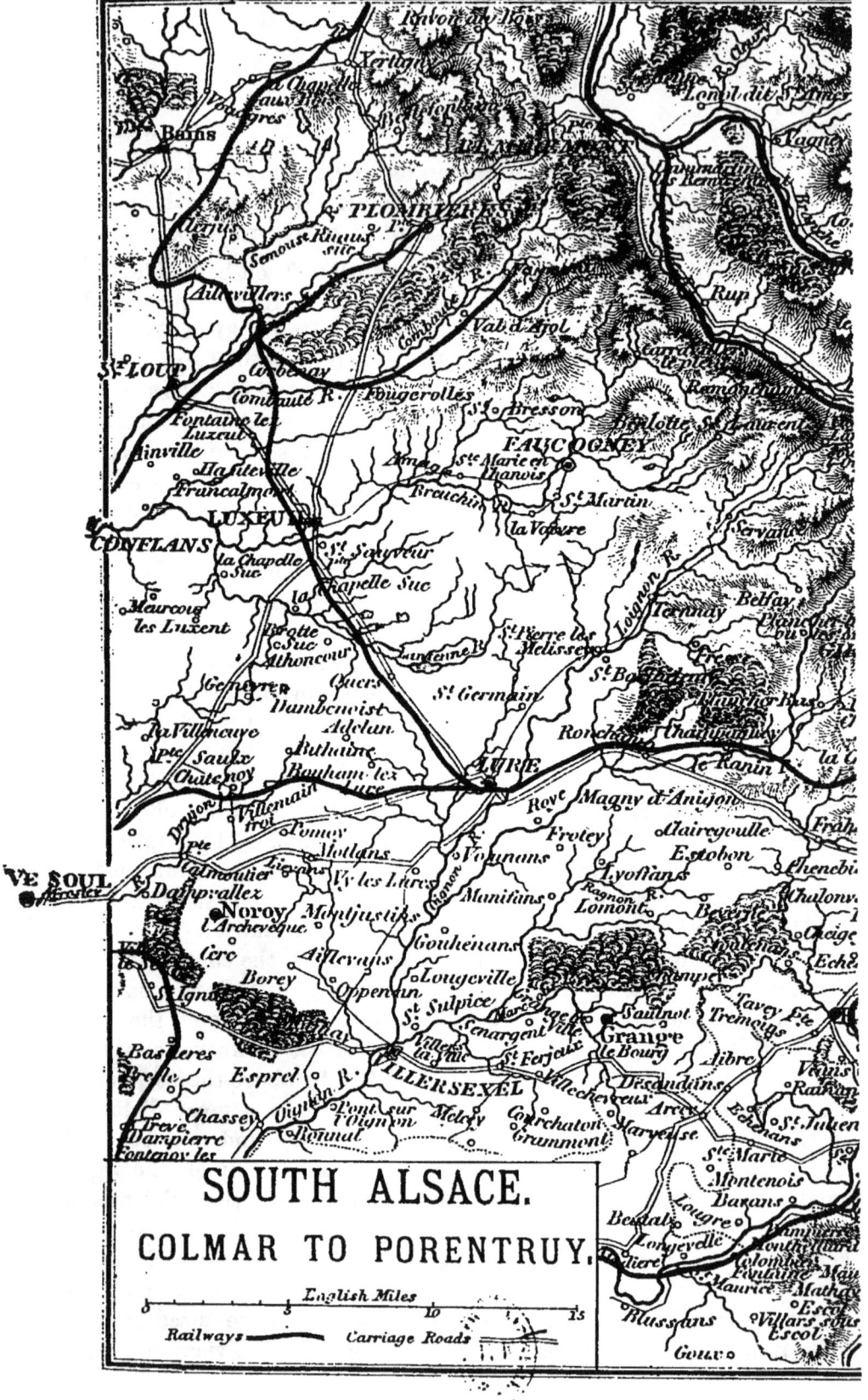

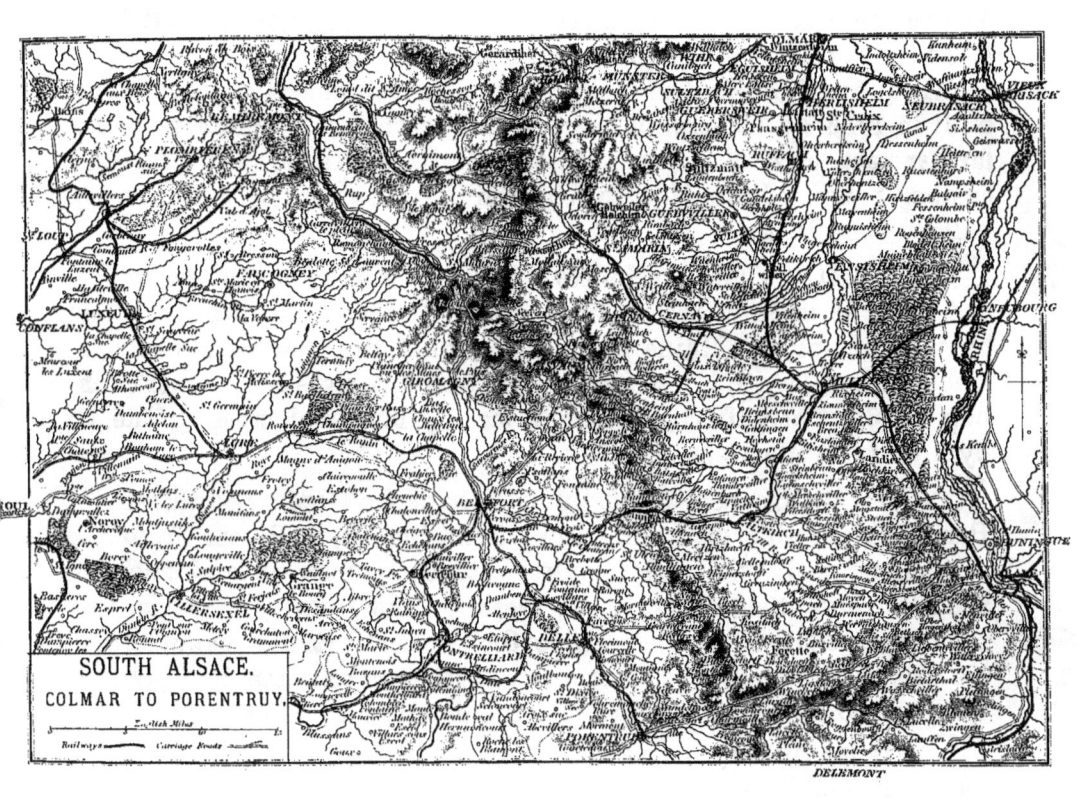

of the citadel and its defences, the Hautes and Basses Perches, is excellent. On the other side of the river are the Forts des Barres and Bellevue; while in the distance are the Vosges and Black Forest. If on foot, it is better not to descend to the town the same way, but rather by the walk between the trees alongside the ramparts.

The railway between Belfort and Epinal, 67 m. North, and Nancy other 46 m. N., runs along a high level, on the wooded slopes of the Vosges mountains. At Bas-Evette, 4½ m. N. from Belfort, and 1300 ft. above the sea, are 2 large tarns on the plateau.

3¾ m. east from Belfort is Chevremont or Geisenberg, with a church built in 1783 by General Kleber, who was then an architect. 4 m. farther east, or 283¾ m. from Paris, is **Petit-Croix**, French time and custom-house. From this to Altkirch the railway ascends the pretty valley of the Ill to

284 **ALT-MÜNSTEROL** (Montreux-Vieux). German custom-house 42 and time, 25 minutes before Paris time. The train having run along by the side of the Rhine and Rhone canal and crossed 2 viaducts, whose united length is 965 yards on 71 arches, arrives at Dammerkirch, pop. 1200. Then after traversing a marshy land and crossing the Ill by 2 viaducts it arrives at

295 **ALTKIRCH**, pop. 3300. *Inns:* Goldener Kopf; Schwarzer 31 Bär. On the side of a hill rising from the Ill, well seen from the station, especially the parish church, standing upon an eminence, on the site where stood formerly the castle of the Dukes of Austria. In the town are large potteries, where the especial articles manufactured are glazed tiles and those earthenware stoves so common in Germany. Omnibus to Pfirt 12 m. S. in the Jura mountains. *Inn:* New York.

316 **MÜLHAUSEN**, p. 118. Junction with rail from Strassburg 10 68 m. N., and with line to Wesserling 21 m. N.W., p. 114.

322 **ST. LOUIS**, pop. 2000. Where passengers from Switzerland 4 alight to have their luggage examined at the German custom-house.

326 **BASEL** or BALE 401 miles from Paris by Strassburg, see p. 120.

Belfort to Basel.

Through the openings in the Jura Mountains by the Jura railway, passing Delle, Porentruy and Delemont, a most picturesque route, which leads directly from France into Switzerland. From Belfort the line passes by Meroux 4¼ m. S.E. from Belfort, Bourogne 7½ m., and Morvillars 8¾ m. S., where it joins the line to Basel from Mont-

Domrémy. Jeanne d'Arc.

beliard 12½ m. W. After Morvillars is Grandvillars, 10½ from Belfort, with large forges. The train now crosses the Cavatte and arrives at Delle or Dettenried 13¾ m. from Belfort, pop. 1400, on the Allaine, Swiss custom-house and time. Porentruy 21 m. from Belfort, pop. 5400, on the Allaine 1479 ft. above the sea. Ruins of the castle of the prince-bishops of Basel. Three hours and a quarter from Porentruy, passing Delemont or Delsberg, is Basel.

THE COUNTRY OF JEANNE D'ARC AND ALSACE.

Pagny sur Meuse 191 miles east from Paris and 28 miles west from Nancy, see p. 82, and Map, page 76.

29¼ m. south from Pagny by rail is **Neufchateau**, passing Vaucouleurs, 3½ m. from Pagny, and Domrémy, 11¾ m. from Pagny. Neufchateau is 28⅓ m. E. from Mirecourt, whence the baths of Vittel are 15 m. S.W. by rail, Contrexéville 3⅓ m. farther, and Martigny 6¼ m. more, p. 99, Map, p. 76. 3½ m. from Pagny, and 194½ m. from Paris, is *Vaucouleurs*, pop. 3000. *Inn:* Jeanne d'Arc. To this little country town Jeanne d'Arc repaired, by the advice of her uncle, to communicate her designs to Robert de Baudricourt, captain of the troops stationed in this district, and to request his aid. She was received with scorn, till certain of her friends, especially the chevaliers Jean de Novelonpont and Bertrand de Poulengy, expressed themselves so strongly in her favour, that Baudricourt, unwilling to take upon himself the responsibility of a refusal, furnished her with letters to facilitate for her an interview with Charles VII.

203 miles from Paris, 12 S. from Pagny, and 17¼ N. from Neufchateau, is the station Domrémy-Maxey. From the station take the road, left hand, through the village of Maxey, with its dunghills; then the first road left, bordered by poplars, extending to the village of Greux, which pass through and walk ½ m. farther to the village of **Domrémy-la-Pucelle**, about 1¾ m. from the station by this way. At the entrance to the left is a poor inn, and farther on to the right a restaurant and the church. Over the façade, which is at the eastern end, is a low square tower, and in front an ugly kneeling statue in bronze of the maid. Behind the church is the humble cottage in which Jeanne was born 6th January 1412, a small half-gabled house with massive stone walls, the property of the State since 1820. Its original appearance has been destroyed by the addition of a school on one side and a reception room and museum on the other. Even the neat little garden in front did not exist in her time; but instead, most probably, a large dunghill. Over the door is the motto inscribed in 1480, "Vive labeur, vive le roy Louys." To the left are the blazoned arms bestowed on her family by Charles VII. In the centre the Fleurs de lis of France, and to the right the arms of Charles VII. with a dagger. Above, in a niche, is a replica of the statue of her in a kneeling position, placed by Louis XI. This door opens into the room in which she, Jeanne, the third daughter of Jacques d'Arc and Isabella Romée, was born. To this room very little has been done by way of restoration; the

JEANNE D'ARC. NEUFCHATEAU.

walls and great beam and projecting pole beside the fireplace are exactly as they were in her time; and the chimney-piece, at which she sat and planned her journeys to Reims and Orleans, has been only slightly retouched. The cross, cornices, pilasters, etc., in this room belonged to the small chapel in which she used to pray (see below). In the centre is a replica of the beautiful statue of Jeanne by the princess Marie d'Orleans, presented by her father Louis-Philippe. By the side of the wall is the original statue restored, presented by Louis XI. From this room a door opens into her bedchamber, a small low room lighted by a window about 12 inches square, which then looked into the churchyard, and from which she could see into the church. The recess on the left hand was her bedroom. Her brothers slept in the adjoining small room. Opposite the house is an execrable bust of her under a stone canopy. To visit the chapel in the wood Bois de Chêne (Chénus), where she spent whole days in prayer, leave the village by the south end, by the road Bois de Chêne, and then ascend to the right by the Chemin de la Pucelle. The chapel, being rebuilt, is on the right side of the road, about a mile from Domrémy. Vineyards now occupy a large part of the wood, in which, while herding her flock, she heard the voices of her guardian saints, St. Margaret and St. Catherine, urging her to haste to the rescue of France. The village in the distance, opposite the chapel, is Coussey on the railway, passed on the way to Neufchateau. The castle with the 3 round towers and a pavilion is the chateau Bourlémont. The nearest way back to the station is by the bridge across the Meuse, in front of the church, but this path should not be taken in wet weather.

220¼ m. E. from Paris by Pagny, 38 m. N.E. from Chaumont, and 49 m. N.W. from Epinal, is **Neufchateau**, pop. 6000, between the Meuse and the Mouzon. *Inns:* opposite station, the H. d'Europe; but a little farther down the Avenue de la Gare are the two best inns, the H. de la Providence and the H. de Paris, in the Rue de France. From the Rue de France up the first large street left is to the right the church of St. Cristophe, 11th cent., but altered and repaired in the 15th. In front of the façade, or rather projecting from the pediment, is what has been originally a narthex, but is now a continuation of the church. At the N. corner is a square tower, and under the tower the present entrance. The windows in the aisles have mullions and tracery filled mostly with plain glass, the principal exception being the 3 lancet lights of the chancel. The clerestory windows are small, round-headed, and in couples, with a small impost column on each of the outside jambs. The exterior of the apse is pentagonal. Higher up in the town, in the Place Jeanne d'Arc, is a statue of her on foot in bronze; in her right hand she holds her banner. Higher up still, on the most elevated part of the town, is the church of St. Nicolas, and in a garden behind a high wall a house built on the site of the former castle. St. Nicolas, built in 1097, but lately altered and restored, consists of an under and an upper church, both being above ground. In the main features it resembles the other churches in this neighbourhood; square tower with slated spire on N.W. corner, buttresses sloping off to the eaves and a pentagonal apse, with buttresses attached diagonally. The

Mirecourt. Epinal. Bruyères.

principal difference is in the irregularity of the windows, many displaying great beauty combined with simplicity. An immense round-headed portal forms the main entrance. The under church was necessary from the nature of the ground.

Four important lines meet at Neufchateau—to Pagny-sur-Meuse 29¼ m. N. and Nançois-le-Petit 43 m. N., both on the direct line between Paris and Strassbourg; to Mirecourt 28½ m. E. on the line between Nancy and Epinal; and to Bologne 34½ m. W. on the line between Vitry and Langres. Map, page 76.

37 m. S. from Nancy and 20½ m. W. from Epinal, is **Mirecourt**, pop. 5600. *Inns:* at station, H. de la Gare; in town, Poste; Halles. Situated on the Madon, and containing manufactories of lace and embroidery, and a very handsome market-place. Junction with line to Chalindrey, 60½ m. S.W., passing the important mineral-water towns of Vittel, 15 m. from Mirecourt, Contrexéville 3¼ m. farther, and Martigny-les-Bains 6¼ m. more.

Epinal, pop. 12,100. *Inns:* in front of station, H. des Vosges; in town, Poste; Louvre. Epinal is 247½ m. E. from Paris on the main line to Basel, 49 m. E. from Neufchateau, 49 m. N.W. from Remiremont, 46 m. S. from Nancy, and 88½ m. N.E. from Gray. The part of the town in which the hotels and railway station are situated is called the Faubourg des Bons Enfants, which extends along the east bank of the small branch of the Moselle. Across the bridge to the right (the Rue Auber), leads to the Public Library, Museum, and Picture Gallery. Here another bridge crosses the Moselle, leading from the Petite Ville into the Grand Ville. To the right is the Public Promenade, and in front the Rue du Cours. To visit the castle, follow the Cours till it joins the Rue d'Ambrail, which descend a few paces to a large doorway on the right hand; enter it, and the concierge of the castle will be found in the court. Fee ½ fr. From the court, a winding path among trees leads to the top of the hill, crowned with some scanty ruins, all that remains of the castle, but from which there is a fine view of Epinal and neighbourhood. At the top is a restaurant.

At the foot of the chateau hill, in the Place St. Goëry, is the parish church of St. Goëry, 11th cent., restored. A gallery similar to the triforium extends round the exterior. Leaving this church by the north door, we enter the Place des Vosges, with arcaded houses, and leave the Grande Ville by the Rue du Pont, and by the continuous streets and bridges reach again the Faubourg des Bons Enfants at the Hotel du Louvre.

From Epinal the line extends southwards to Port d'Atelier, 46 m. distant on the main line between Paris and Bâle. Nineteen m. south from Epinal is Bains; 8 m. farther south is Aillevillers, station for Plombières, p. 99, and Luxeuil, page 102.

From Epinal commences the Chemin de Fer de la Vologne, leading through some fine scenery to BRUYÈRES, near the forest of Mortagne, 21 N.E., to Laveline 22½ m., and to Gérardmer, 11 m. more, see p. 112.

Bruyères, 1740 ft. above the sea, pop. 3000. *Inn:* H. de l'Ange, charmingly situated amidst wooded mountains, full of picturesque walks and drives. 1½ m. farther is Laveline, whence one branch of the line

Saint Dié. Faintrux. Kamberg.

extends 11 m. S.E. to Gérardmer, and the other 15½ m. N. to St. Dié by St. Léonard. From St. Léonard branch to Fraize, 5 m. E.

31¾ m. S. from Lunéville, p. 85, is **Saint Dié** on the Meurthe, 1032 ft. above the sea, pop. 14,000. *Hotels:* Poste, in the centre of the Grande Rue, the starting-place of the coach to Ste. Marie aux Mines or Markirch ; whence rail to Schlettstadt, 13 m. E. The H. du Commerce, in the Place des Vosges, at the N. end of the Grande Rue. About half-way up the Grande Rue, to the left, is the Rue Stanislas, with the Inn Stanislas and the Hotel de Ville, containing the Post and Telegraph Offices, and the Public Library. Temple Protestant, No. 6 Grande Rue du Casino.

St. Dié is a pleasant town in front of Mounts Ormont, Madeleine, and St. Martin. From the railway station, a broad street, the Rue St. Martin, extends northwards across the bridge of the Meurthe, built in 1816, with three large elliptic arches. To the left, along the banks of the river, is the town park. Between the station and the bridge is the church of St. Martin, built in the last century. The continuation of the road at the other end of the bridge is called the Grande Rue, of which the E. or right side is the old town, and the W. or left side, the new town, built principally by King Stanislas after the fire of 1787. At the N. end of the Grande Rue, in the Place des Vosges, is the Cathedral, of which the most modern part is the heavy façade, flanked by square towers, with balloon-shaped spires, a favourite form in all this part of France. The nave dates from about the 11th cent., and the choir a little later. A door under the N. aisle opens into a vast cloister, with, on the east side of the court, a rude stone pulpit. At the other end of the cloister is the chapel built in the 9th cent., and in excellent preservation. The façade consists of a tall narrow gable, with two blind round-headed arches running up the wall. In each arch is a slit window with two tiny impost colonnettes. The roof of the nave and aisles is quadripartite, borne by semicircular arches resting on piers with attached columns, with carved and cushioned capitals. Above the arches runs a kind of dental cornice. The windows in the aisles are small, those in the clerestory seem to have been altered. The nave of the cathedral is almost a counterpart of this church, only more ornamented. Between the Cathedral and the Place des Vosges, a narrow street, the Rue St. Charles, leads to the Promenade Gratin. On arriving at a small bridge, take the middle road which ascends. On the top of the hill, the Chemin Dijon separates from the Promenade Gratin to the right. The walks below the fir trees are very agreeable, disclosing from time to time beautiful views of the valley of the Meurthe. The best view, however, is from Mount St. Martin, 1365 ft. above St. Dié. It is that mountain behind the railway station, with great isolated rocks on the summit, resembling the ruins of a castle. A good road leads up to the top. From the steep side of its neighbour, Mount Ormont, projects an immense mass of conglomerate, composed of glittering pebbles.

5¾ m. S. from St. Dié is the village of Faintrux, near the base of the ridge of the Montagne de Kamberg, with curious peaks. To the east of the Kamberg is the remarkable cliff called the Roche d'Anozel, another great mass of conglomerate pierced with large caverns. To the N.E. is

MARKIRCH. ROTHAU. SCHIRMECK.

a similar cliff, "La pierre l'Aitre," 2089 ft.; to the N. the "Grand Jambe," an enormous rock, resting on three slender columns; to the W. is La pierre de la Roche," 2146 ft., overlooking the valleys of Faintrux and of the Rouges-Eaux. From the platform, from which these cliffs rise, there are splendid views. All are easily accessible; but a guide is useful.

Coach from St. Dié to St. Marie aux Mines or Markirch, 15½ m. E., whence rail to Schlettstadt, 14 m. E. and 28½ m. from Strassburg. The mountain road from St. Dié to Markirch is exceedingly beautiful. Having passed the pretty villages of Gemaingoutte and Wisembach, it gradually ascends the pass by numerous windings, disclosing an ever-extending view over the smiling valleys, bounded by mountains covered with pine forests. On the summit of the pass, 2546 ft., 3¾ m. E. from St. Dié, and 13¾ W. from Markirch, is the boundary-line between France and Germany. On the French side, at a large house with stables, the horses are changed. The road, down to Markirch, is perhaps more picturesque than on the other side. Shortly before entering the town, the coach stops at the custom-house.

Markirch on the Leber, 1250 ft. above the sea, pop. 12,000. *Inns:* near the station, the Commerce; at the other end of the town, the Grand Cerf. Markirch consists principally of a long street parallel to the Leber, utilised by the numerous dyeworks and cotton-mills. One of the most interesting excursions is to the summit of Mount Brezouard, 2760 ft. above Markirch, by the valley of the Leber, and the hamlet of Echery, and then across an alpine region, with farms owned by Anabaptists.

Rail from Markirch to Strassburg, 42 m. N.E. by Schlettstadt, 14 m. E. from Markirch. At Schlettstadt, change carriages for Strassburg, 28 m. N., and for Basel, 61 m. S. From Markirch, the country is very picturesque, till within a short distance of Schlettstadt. The best of the villages to alight at on the way is Leberau, pop. 2620. *Inn:* Zum Grünen Baum, situated on the Leber, at the entrance into a most picturesque valley.

Saint Dié by coach to Rothau, 22¼ m. N., whence rail to Strassburg, 29 m. E. The culminating part of this mountain road is shortly before arriving at Saalés, 11¼ m., where it attains the height of 1830 ft. At Saalés there is an *Inn:* the Commerce; and at Rothau, the Deux Clefs situated in the beautiful valley of the Breusch, flowing between lofty wooded heights mingled with rocks and cliffs of red porphyry. Rail from Rothau to Strassburg, 29 m. E., by Schirmeck, Mutzig, and Molsheim.

2 m. from Rothau by rail, and 27 m. from Strassburg, is **Schirmeck**, pop. 1600, at the junction of the valleys of the Breusch and the Grandfontaine. *Inns:* France; Croix d'Or. 2½ m. up the valley of the Grandfontaine is the village of the same name, *Inn:* Grand Cerf. From it the ascent is made of the **Grand Donon**, 3314 ft. On the plateau of the Donon, about 3 m. from the village of Grandfontaine, is an Inn, whence the summit, indicated by a pile of stones, is about 1 hour distant.

15 m. W. from Strassburg, and 14 E. from Rothau, by rail, is **Mutzig**, pop. 3700. *Inn:* Post; Couronne on the Breusch, at the foot of a mountain 1280 ft. high. On the south side of the Breusch is the Dreispitz mountain, 1315 ft. high. After Mutzig the valley of the Breusch widens before reaching **Molsheim**, pop. 3080. *Inns:* Charrue d'Or; Deux Clefs.

REMIREMONT. CORNIMONT. LA BRESSE.

A quaint town with houses of the 16th and 17th cent. and fortifications and church of the 15th and 16th cents. Junction with line to Zabern, 19¼ m. N., page 86.

Remiremont, 1338 ft. above the sea, pop. 7300. 8 m. E. by coach from Plombières. 13¾ m. N. by rail from Le Thillot. 63½ m. S. by rail from Nancy, passing Epinal, 17½ m. N., see Map, p. 76. *Hotels:* *La Poste; under the arcade, the Cheval de Bronze; near the station the Nord: down the main street, the Mulhouse. Remiremont is famous for a round flat cake called Quiche, about a foot in diameter, and composed of flour, butter, and eggs, with a shade of an onion. They are baked in an oven, and are eaten hot. Cost 3 frs. each. Also for trout pies. They require to be ordered, as they are not kept ready made. In the neighbourhood, good potatoes are grown. Remiremont is a pleasant little town on the Moselle, surrounded by mountains, and plentifully supplied with pure water, flowing even in the gutters of the streets. The parish church, though founded in the 10th cent., has had, on account of fires, to be so often reconstructed, that its style more resembles now something between the first and second periods of pointed Gothic. The five Noah-ark-like boxes over the high altar contain relics of saints.

The hill rising opposite the main entrance into the church is the Fort Parmont. The road to the left of the main entrance on leaving the church passes first by the Mairie, in the ancient abbey buildings; and then ascends to a Golgotha (Calvaire), commanding a view of the town. Around the calvary is the town park, with pleasant shady walks, and a good road up to the hill behind, through the plantation.

From Remiremont, rail to Cornimont, 13 m. S.E. passing Vagney, Thiéfosse and Saulxures. From Cornimont, coach to La Bresse, 4½ m. N. by the valley of the Moselotte. Also to Le Thillot, 8¾ m. South by the beautiful valley of the Menil, see Map, page 76. Rail also from Remiremont to St. Maurice 17 m. S.E., passing by Rupt and Le Thillot. The making of paper, the weaving of cotton, and the sawing of timber, are the principal industries in the towns, and the making of cheese and butter in the mountains. The first important station between Remiremont and Cornimont is **Vagney**, 7 m. E. from Remiremont, pop. 3190. *Inn:* H. de la Poste. Coach to Gérardmer, 12 m. N.E. The train then passes the manufacturing town of Zainvillers, pop. 1300, and the hamlets of Thiéfosse and Les Graviers, and arrives at **Saulxures**, on the Moselotte, 12¼ m. from Remiremont, and 1368 ft. above the sea. *Inn:* Cheval Blanc. 2½ m. N.E. is the Haut du Roc, 3333 ft. above the sea, commanding extensive views. **Cornimont**, pop. 4050. *Inns:* Moselotte; Cheval de Bronze; Vosges. A manufacturing town on the Moselotte. From Cornimont, a road leads up the valley of the Ventron, by the pretty village of Ventron, to the village of Oderen, 12 m. E., pop. 2000. *Inn:* Canon d'Or, at the foot of Mount d'Oderen, 2905 ft., on the border between France and Germany. Coach also from Cornimont to **La Bresse**. *Inn:* Soleil, 4½ m. N., 2065 ft. above the sea, pop. 3850, on the Moselotte. Around the town are numerous lakes and remains of glaciers. A delightful road leads from La Bresse to Gérardmer, 7½ m. N. From La Bresse, road to Wildenstein, 7. m. E., p. 114.

GÉRARDMER. SCHLUCHT. HOHENECK.

79 m. S. from Nancy by rail, or 33½ m. E. from **Epinal** by rail, and 26¾ m. S. from St. Dié by rail, and 12 m. by coach from Vagney, by the valley of the Rochesson, is **Gérardmer**, pop. 7000. *Hotels:* The Poste, a large comfortable house, 9 to 11 frs. per day, including everything, service, lights, café au lait, and wine at both meals. Carriages with one horse, 15 frs. per day, 2 horses, 25 frs. Pourboire for both, 2½ frs. Boat on the lake, 1½ fr. per hour, without a man.

This pleasant little place is an excellent station from which to explore the Vosges mountains. It is situated on the eastern extremity of Lake Gérardmer 2186 ft. above the level of the sea, surrounded by high mountains; surface 296 acres; depth 42 to 140 ft. The outlet is the stream Jamagne, which flows into the Vologne. Fishing with the rod always allowed. At the south end, near Ramberchamp, is a good echo. Famous botanising ground. The chief occupation of the villagers is the weaving and bleaching of linen; while higher up among the mountains, it is the felling of timber and sawing it into boards, and cheese-making.

Excursions to Lake Longemer, 4 m. E. from Gérardmer by the road to the Schlucht and Münster. Lake Longemer, in the midst of wooded mountains is 2448 ft. above the sea 115 ft. deep and contains an area of 185 acres. 3 m. S.E. from this lake is Lac Lispach, gradually drying up. From the southern end of Lake Longemer, a road through a narrow glen leads to Lake Retournemer, a beautiful little lake of 15 acres, 2822 ft. above the sea, and so closed in between steep wooded hills, that the only exit from its basin seems to be the road by which the traveller approaches it, hence the name, Retournemer. On the road between the two lakes, nearly under the Roche du Diable, is a cascade. From Retournemer the Chemin des Dames leads up to the Schlucht, 1 hour distant.

Gérardmer to **Munster** by the Schlucht, 19½ m. E. by a good carriage-road. 2 m. from Gérardmer, at the bridge across the Volognes, the road to St. Dié separates to the left from the road to Münster. Here the river makes a small cascade, called the Saut des Cuves. The road now ascends the mountain covered by tall pines, and after passing Lake Longemer, arrives at a tunnel near which there is an isolated rock called la Roche du Diable, commanding an excellent view of the country below. 10 m. from Gérardmer, the road attains its culminating point, called the **Schlucht**, with a good Inn, 4100 ft. above the sea, on the boundary-line between France and Germany. ½ m. beyond is an excellent view of Münster and the surrounding country. From the Inn, a good road leads up to the top of the **Hoheneck**, 4480 ft. above the sea, or 380 above the pass, in the centre of the Vosges mountain chain, of which it is one of the culminating points. Grand view from the top; to the E., Alsace and the silvery Rhine, bounded by the chain of the Black Forest mountains. To the S., the Ballon Soultz or Gebweiler, 4680 ft., and the Rothenbach, 4328 ft. To the N., the Donon, 3317 ft., with its double peak. And to the W., towards France, the gradually diminishing offshoots of the Vosges.

From the Schlucht Inn are also conveniently visited the lakes Vert, Noir, and Blanc. Lake Blanc is seen from the hotel. Lake Vert has a surface of 10 acres and is 3117 ft. above the sea. Lake Noir has a sur-

MÜNSTER. TÜRKHEIM. TROIS-EPIS.

face of 35 acres and is 3130 ft. above the sea. Lake Blanc has a surface of 79 acres, is 3471 ft. above the sea and derives its name from the white quartz at the bottom. A pleasant walk may be taken along the crest of the mountains, from the Lac Blanc to Hoheneck by the Schlucht, without encountering any fatiguing descent.

16¼ m. from Gérardmer, or 7½ E. from the Schlucht, is the village of **Sulzeren**, pop. 1570, at the entrance into the valley which leads to Lake Vert, 3¾ m. Lake Noir, 1¼ m. farther, and Lake Blanc another 1¼ m.

From Sulzeren, the road to Münster descends by the valley of the Kleinthal to Stossweier, 1¼ m. farther E., pop. 1830. Two miles farther is **Münster**, 1181 ft. above the sea, pop. 5000, at the base of the Mönchsberg, and at the junction of the valley of the Fecht with the Kleinthal. *Inns:* Cigogne; Stadt Strassburg. An ancient village, owing its origin to a Benedictine convent, founded at the commencement of the 7th cent. by King Childeric and called originally the "monasterium confluentis." The town contains a handsome modern Protestant church, Hotel de Ville, 16th cent., a hospital founded by H. Löwel and a very excellent grammar school founded by F. Hartmann, Peer of France, died 1861. The principal spinning-mill belongs to the Hartmann family. Visitors are allowed to enter their pleasure grounds of the Schlosswald, 1¼ m. E. from the town. On an eminence are the ruins of the Schwarzenburg, built in 1261 by the Lord of Géroldseck. To the S. of Münster is the Solberg, 1493 ft. above Münster. There and back, 2½ hours. 2 m. from Münster, up the valley of the Fecht, is Lüttenbach, pop. 1000, with paper-mills. Voltaire spent the year 1754 in the house of the paper-mill now belonging to M. Kiener; where he wrote the "Orphelin de la Chine" and part of his "Annales de l'Empire."

From Münster the railway extends 12 m. E. to Colmar by the Fecht in the most beautiful and most highly cultivated valley in the Vosges mountains. The inhabitants are chiefly Protestants. 4 m. from Münster is Weier im Thal. At Station-Nouvelle, 1 m. S. or 3 m. E. from Münster, is **Sulzbach**, pop. 1000, with a bathing establishment supplied by sparkling acidulate chalybeate springs, 3 hrs. from Sulzmatt by a road across the hills.

3¾ m. from Colmar and 8¼ from Münster is **Türkheim**, on the Fecht, pop. 2600. *Inn:* Petitdemange, situated amidst vineyards producing one of the best wines of Alsace, called the Tokay of Alsace. It is still surrounded by its old walls pierced by fortified gates. Between the Fecht and the Logelbach is the town promenade. 500 steps lead up to the top of the Letzenberg with chapel on top.

Omnibus at station for Notre-Dame-des-Trois-Epis, or the Drei Aehren, about 900 ft. above Türkheim, by a winding road of 6 m. It consists of a church, hotels, and cottages, situated in a pine forest, much resorted to in summer on account of the salubrity of the pine and mountain air. The hotels are both cheap and comfortable. In the Hotel des Trois Epis, the pension, including everything, is 30 marks the week. The establishment has also turpentine and pine-wood vapour baths, which are very efficacious in the cure of many diseases. Other hotels, the Trois Rois and Notre Dame.

On the other side of the valley, 1¼ m. S.E. from Türkheim, is

St. Maurice. Source of the Moselle. Wesserling.

Winzenheim, pop. 3400. *Inn:* Cigogne, in the Münster valley, 725 ft. above the sea. A narrow road commencing opposite the parish church leads up to the ruins of the castle of Hohenlandsberg, 1345 ft. above the village. It was taken by Othon of Ochsentein in 1281, occupied by the Swedes in 1633 and dismantled by the French in 1635. From Hohenlandsberg it is usual to descend to the dungeon tower of Plixburg, 12th cent., on a conical hill 1486 ft. above the sea. Finger-posts indicate the way.

3¾ m. E. from Türkheim is **Colmar**, p. 118, 42 m. S. from Strassburg, and 47 m. N. from Basel, page 120.

Remiremont to Mulhausen.

Remiremont to St. Maurice, 17 m. S.E. by rail. From St. Maurice to Wesserling 11 m. E. by coach, and from Wesserling to Mülhausen, 20½ m. E. by rail. The principal places passed are: **Maxonchamp**, 6¼ m. from Remiremont. 1¼ m. S.W. is the lake of Fondromaix, 560 feet above the valley. 2 m. beyond Maxonchamp, the rail passes **Rupt**, pop. 4130, with a petrifying and chalybeate spring. To the S. is the fort of Roche-la-Haie, 2535 ft., commanding the road to the Col Mont de Fourches. 13¾ m. from Remiremont is **Le Thillot**, pop. 2190. *Inn:* Cheval Blanc. Coach to Cornimont, 8¾ m. N. To the S. is the fort Tête-de-l'Ours, 2487 ft., commanding the Col de Chateau Lambert. 17 m. **St. Maurice**, pop. 2190. H. de la Poste, 1685 ft. above the sea, at the foot of the Ballons d'Alsace and Servance. The Ballon d'Alsace, 2419 ft. above St. Maurice, is easily ascended by a good winding road. Inn near top. On the summit there is an image of Mary and a very extensive view, page 116. The ascent of the Ballon de Servance, 2215 ft. above St. Maurice, is not nearly so easy, and requires a guide, 4 frs. The view is not so extensive but the scenery is wilder.

Coach from St. Maurice to Wesserling, 11 m. E. 2½ m. from St. Maurice is **Bussang**, 2047 ft., pop. 2120. *Inn:* Deux Clefs. This picturesquely-situated village possesses 5 springs of alkaline chalybeate water, containing a little free carbonic acid gas, which improves the taste of the sour wines drunk in the hotels of the Vosges, and is recommended for dyspepsia. About 4 m. farther, and just before arriving at the tunnel of the pass, is the **Source of the Moselle**, 2408 ft. above the sea. Within the tunnel, 152 ft. long, is the boundary-stone between France and Germany. The road now commences to descend to the charmingly-situated village of **Urbès**, 8½ m. from St. Maurice, and 2½ from Wesserling, pop. 1100. *Inn:* H. Couronne. In the many streams in this neighbourhood is capital fishing, and on the hills and valleys good botanising ground. After crossing the Thur the coach arrives at **Wesserling**, 28 m. E. from Remiremont, and 20½ W. from Colmar. *Inn:* H. de Wesserling. A little town among mountains, with important cotton and spinning mills, situated in one of the most prosperous districts of Alsace; where cleanliness and comfort prevail. Most of the inhabitants are Protestants. Omnibus, partly by the picturesque valley of the Thur, to **Wildenstein**.

St. Amarin.   Weiler.   Thann.

H. du Soleil, 8 m. N., bounded on 3 sides by steep rocky mountains. On an eminence about 2 m. from Wildenstein are the ruins of the chateau, 14th cent., and behind this castle, the remains of a moraine composed of large blocks of erratic rocks. Between Wesserling and Wildenstein are the villages of Felleringen, ½ m., pop. 2000; Odéren, 3 m. pop. 1900. *Inn:* Canon d'Or; and Krüth, 3½ m., pop. 2000. *Inn:* Cerf d'Or.

From Wildenstein a road extends 7 m. W. to La Bresse by the Col de Bramont, 2920 ft. above the sea, commanding a view of the upper valley of the Thur. To the N. is the Rothenbach 4330 ft. the source of the Thur, to the S. the Grand Ventron 3664 ft., and towards the extremity of the valley the Ballon de Gebweiler 4677 ft., the culminating peak of the Vosges. The road then descends to La Bresse by a beautiful forest.

From Wesserling the railway descends the valley of the Thur, passing the manufacturing village of **St. Amarin**. *Inn:* Lion d'Or, pop. 2200, with cotton-mills. From St. Amarin the Gebweiler can be ascended by Geishausen, a village of 900 inhabitants, 3¾ m. dis., and 2535 ft. above the sea. 5 m. from Wesserling is the manufacturing and wood-cutting village of **Weiler**, pop. 2600; considered the best station from which to make the ascent of the Gebweiler, 6¼ m. distant, by Goldbach 2953 ft., pop. 700, and 3¼ m. dis. Guide necessary. 1 m. farther is the next station **Bitschweiler**, pop. 3000. Mills, felt and cloth manufactories.

36½ m. E. from Remiremont, 8¼ m. E. from Wesserling, and 12 m. W. from Mülhausen, is **Thann**, 1148 ft. above the sea, on the great plain of Alsace, at the mouth of the narrow valley of the Thur, pop. 8000. *Hotels:* Kaiser; Zwei Schlüssel. A manufacturing town with cotton and silk mills, and one of the most beautiful churches in Alsace, St. Theobald, commenced in the 14th cent., and completed in the 17th, representing the finest expression of the best style of these epochs. The handsome double portal, forming the main entrance, and dating from the beginning of the 14th cent., is set between 2 buttresses, most tastefully ornamented. The square tower in 3 stories, the last being octagonal, is surmounted by a most elegant open spire 220 ft. high, begun in 1430 and completed in 1516. The Campanile dates from 1428. The choir exhibits great beauty, combined with elegance and fine proportion. In the interior the roof is ornamented with arabesques among the sculptured groining. Stained glass of the 16th cent. Pulpit 15th cent., and carved stalls of the 16th. The Hotel de Ville is modern. There are a few old houses; among the best, is the one in front of the main entrance to the church.

A road laid out as a promenade leads up to the ruins of the castle of Engelburg, 492 ft. above the town, built in the 12th cent., and destroyed in 1674 by Turenne with gunpowder. The upper part of one of the towers has by the explosion separated from the base, on which one end rests and the other on the ground, representing the appearance of a gigantic cask, called by the inhabitants the eye of the witch. From Thann the train arrives at **Cernay** or Sennheim, *Inn:* Zwei Schlüssel, 8¾ m. from Mülhausen, where a branch line diverges to Gewenheim, 7 m. S., and **Sentheim**, 9 m. S. From Sentheim omnibus to **Masmünster**, pop. 3500. *Inn:* Adler, situated in the highly-picturesque Dollerthal; whence numerous

GEBWEILER. MURBACH. EBERSHEIM.

lovely glens ramify containing little villages possessing comfortable inns. 4. m. up the valley by omnibus is Oberbrück, whence the ascent is made of the Ballon d'Alsace. See also page 114.

From Cernay the rail having reached Lutterbach junction, passes on to Mülhausen, 3½ m. farther, p. 119.

Bollweiler to Gebweiler, 4½ m. N.W., Bollweiler, p. 119, 3 m. N.W. is Sulz, pop. 5000. *Inn:* Deux Clefs. Houses, 16th cent., with turrets. Silk and saw mills and breweries. Gebweiler, at the entrance of the beautiful valley of the Lauch, pop. 11,400. *Inns:* Ange; Canon d'Or. An important manufacturing town, with tanneries, breweries, and printing establishments. The wines grown around Gebweiler are considered among the best of Alsace, and of them the most famous is called the Kitterlé.

The most important edifice in the town is the old parish church of Saint Léger, built in the 12th cent., with 3 grand towers of unequal height in 4 stages. The Romanesque porch, with 3 entrances, extends the whole breadth of the W. end, and forms a kind of narthex. 4 m. N. from Gebweiler is Murbach, pop. 400, in a very beautiful situation at the head of a valley among wild scenery. This village was the seat of one of the most wealthy and illustrious monasteries of Alsace, till destroyed in the fatal year of 1793. It was founded at the commencement of the 8th cent. From Murbach to the top of the Ballon Gebweiler and back, 7 hours. 1590 ft. from the top is a lake of 185 acres, 90 ft. deep, surrounded by cliffs 650 ft. high.

Strassburg to Basel.

Distance, 89 miles.—Time, 3½ hours.

This line passes between the Rhine and the Vosges mountains. Map, p. 76.

STRASSBURG   BALE
MILES FROM   MILES TO.

STRASSBURG. French money taken at the station. — 89

6 — GEISPOLSHEIM, pop. 3000. Church 1771. — 83

8 — FEGERSHEIM. Stat. for ruins of Guirbaden, above Rosheim. — 81

17½ BENFELD, pop. 3200, on the site of the Roman Elcebus, destroyed by the barbarians in the 5th cent. A coach from this station runs to Barr, on the small branch line from Strassburg. — 71½

23 EBERSHEIM, pop. 2000. 2 m. distant is Ebermünster, where Duke Athic founded, in 667, the monastery of the Sanglier. Beyond Ebersheim and above Dambach (pop. 3000, *Inn:* Krone) are the ruins of the castle of Berstein, 11th cent.; and farther south, the ruins of the castles of Ortenburg, 13th cent. above Scherweiler (pop. 3000) and Ramstein above Chatenois or Kestenholz (pop. 4000) with saline springs rising from the Hahnenberg, and utilised by the bathing establishment of the hotel Bronn. Fifteen minutes dist. is the village of Kinzheim charmingly situated. Other 15 minutes are required for — 66

the ascent to the ruins of the castle, built in the 14th cent. From Chatenois are also easily visited the ruins of the castles of Ramstein and Ortenburg dating probably from the 11th cent.

$28\frac{1}{2}$ SCHLETTSTADT, pop. 11,000. *Inns:* Bouc; Aigle. The $60\frac{1}{4}$ 2 castles seen from this station are Hohenkönigsburg and Kinzheim.

Schlettstadt is an interesting though poor town, formerly surrounded by strong fortifications. The streets are narrow and crooked, and many of the houses curiously gabled. The churches of Sainte Foi and of St. George are so near each other that, standing between them, it is easy to distinguish the difference of their styles of architecture. St. George, although commenced in the 13th cent., was not finished till the 16th, to which period the beautiful glass of the windows belongs. Sainte Foi was built nearly entirely in the 11th cent. The church of the Recollets is at some distance and abandoned. The clock tower, with four small turrets, is in the Chemin Neuf. Within little more than a mile is the castle of Kinzheim. But the grand excursion is to the massive and imposing ruins of the castle of Hohenkönigsburg. Carriage there and back 18 frs.; time 8 hrs. Reached, however, more easily from the neighbouring station of Saint Hippolyte or Pilt, 2 m. S. A picturesque road leads from Schlettstadt to Hohenkönigsburg by Kinzheim, and from Hohenkönigsburg to Sainte Odile. For Sainte Odile and the Heidenmauer, see page 94. Branch line from Schlettstadt to Markirch, $15\frac{1}{2}$ m. W. (p. 110), passing Val-de-Villé or Weilerthal, $3\frac{3}{4}$ m. W. from Schlettstadt, the station to alight at to visit the Hohenkönigsburg. An excellent carriage-road ascends through a wood to the forester's house with an inn, 8 miles distant; whence the castle is about 30 minutes farther by a path. The forest and castle now belong to the town of Schlettstadt. The principal entrance is near the great S.W. tower. The castle was reconstructed between 1469 and 1480 by Count Oswald of Thierstein, and was garrisoned till 1633, when it was taken and destroyed by the Swedes in the Thirty Years' War.

30 SAINT PILT, pop. 2000, three miles from its station, situ- 59 ated at the foot of a conical hill 1679 ft. above the sea, crowned with the ruins of the Hohenkönigsburg (2 hrs. distant), the largest and most imposing of the ancient fortresses of Alsace.

34 RIBEAUVILLE or Rappoltsweiler (small), pop. 8000. *Inn:* 55 Agneau, $2\frac{1}{4}$ m. from the station. Temple, Protestant. This little town, hemmed in between vine-clad mountains, has some 15th and 16th cent. houses, and a parish church belonging to the 14th cent.

Up the valley, at the extremity of the town, are important cloth manufactories. The ruins of 3 castles—Saint Ulrich, Girsberg, and Hoch-Rappoltstein—occupy the summits of hills immediately behind the town, the first and the last being distinctly seen from the station. To reach them, walk straight up the town from the Inn Mouton, and take the first steep path to the right by the old wall, then the first path left. The lowest and largest castle is Saint Ulrich; then, at a little distance, Girsberg; and about 210 ft. above both, Hoch-Rappoltstein, whose round keep, of the 14th cent., resembles a telegraph tower.

39 BENNWEIER, pop. 1200. Station for Kaysersberg, pop. **50** 3500, and Kinzheim, pop. 1300, 1¼ m. farther. The old town of Kaysersberg—*Inn*: Krone—with its modern cotton-mills, is situated in the narrow part of the Weissthal, under the ruins of the Kaiserburg. The church, principally 12th cent., including the Romanesque portal and the piers of the nave, has a handsome reredos, 16th cent., over high altar. In chapel of St. Michael, colossal figures, 15th cent., of Christ, Mary and John. The town-hall was constructed in 1604. There remain considerable portions of the walls, dating from the time of the castle, and quaint houses of the 15th and 16th cent. Good wine and beer made in the neighbourhood. A little way S. from Kaysersberg, on the road to Colmar, is **Ammerschweier**, pop. 2000, *Inn*: Grüner Baum, with remains of its walls, 15th and 16th cent., garnished with towers, of which the most interesting is the Schelmenthurm, bearing the date 1535. Of the church, the belfry is of the 14th cent., the nave and choir the 15th, the ramp of the organ-loft the 16th, and the iron font and statues in wood the 16th. The Kaufhaus and Rathhaus are also of the 16th cent., as well as many of the houses. Omnibus runs from Colmar to Kaysersberg, passing through Ammerschweier.

42 COLMAR, pop. 24,000. *Hotels*: Deux Clefs; Trois Rois— **47** both near each other in the Grande Rue. An ancient and curious town on the Lauch, 10 m. from the Rhine. From the railway station by the Rue Bruat we pass the Promenade, called the Champ de Mars, having at the railway end the Prefecture and gardens, and in the centre the statue of Bruat. At the head of the Champ de Mars is the semicircular street called the Rue des Clefs, which, with the Grand Rue, form the principal thoroughfares. Numerous narrow streets from the Grande Rue lead to the Cathedral (13th and 14th cents.) The façade, supported by four strong projecting buttresses, has a tower only on the south corner. The pulpit is elegant, and the glass of the windows behind the altar glows with beautiful colours. In the sacristy is a painting with figures life size on a gold ground by Martin Schöngauer, d. 1488, representing Mary and Child in a bower of roses.

By taking the street in front of the corner of the façade, we pass first, on the right, a church built in the 13th cent., now the corn market; and afterwards a large building, the military hospital. Here turn to the right. The first building is the theatre, and adjoining the Dominican convent, 13th cent., now containing the Museum, the Picture Gallery, and Library, with above 40,000 volumes and 500 MSS., and the first Bible printed in German in 1466, by Eggenstein of Strassburg. The Picture Gallery (open Sundays and Thursdays 2-6 free, other days ½ mark) contains a few paintings of the early German school from the monastery of Isenheim. In this square, called the Place des Unterlinden, are the statues of Schoengauer and Pfeffel. From Colmar branch line to Münster, p. 113, by the lovely valley of the Fecht.

45 EGISHEIM, pop. 2000. First station south from Colmar. 44 Those 3 towers on the mountain, 2 m. west from the village, belonged to a castle built in the 11th cent., called Dreien-Egisheim.

50 RUFACH, pop. 4200. *Inn:* Ours: the Rubeacum of the 39 Romans, on the Lauch. The church of St. Arbogast is of the 11th, 12th, and 13th cents. The Hotel de Ville contains a bust by David, of Maréchal Lefèvre, a native of this town. On the neighbouring hill is the castle of Isenburg. Omnibus, 2 daily, to Sulzmatt, 5 m. W., with mineral water resembling that of Selters.

58 BOLLWEILER, pop. 1200, with important nurseries. Omni- 31 bus to Ensisheim 5 m. E. on the Ill, pop. 3000. *Inn:* Krone. In the Hotel de Ville, 16th cent., with handsome octagonal tower, is an aerolite which fell on the 7th November 1492. Houses of the 15th and 16th cents. Branch line from Bollweiler to Gebweiler 4½ m. W., by Sulz 3 m. See p. 116. The Ballon is 10 m. distant.

65 LUTTERBACH. Junction with branch line to Wesserling 24 20½ m. W., in the heart of the Vosges mountains. From Wesserling there is a beautiful road among pine trees and lakes to Gérardmer, whence rail to Remiremont. For Gérardmer, see p. 112; and Remiremont, p. 111.

68½ MÜLHAUSEN, pop. 60,000. Junction with line from Troyes. 20½ *Hotels:* fronting the station, La Paix, and near it the Pfeister; in the town, in the Place du Nouveau Quartier, Les Etrangers; and a little way up the Rue Sauvage, the Hotels Romann; Wagner.

From the station enter the town by first stone bridge to the right, and pass up by the Rue Riedesheim to the Place du Nouveau Quartier. Behind it is an arcaded triangle, at the base of which is a

| STRASSBURG | BASEL. | BALE |
| MILES FROM | | MILES TO |

large building containing the Bourse, the Société Industrielle, and the Industrial Museum. Beyond the Place du Nouveau Quartier is the principal street, the Rue du Sauvage, extending under various names to the other extremity of the town.

The beautifully crocketed spire and pinnacles seen from this street and the station belong to the Protestant church of St. Stephen, a most elegant and graceful edifice, built in the florid Gothic style, and finished in 1860. It stands on the site of a former church which belonged to the Catholics. In this same place is rather a curious building, the Halle au Blé (corn market); and following the street in front of St. Stephen, we come to a very large covered market, where vegetables, cheese, fruit, shoes, etc., are sold. In this neighbourhood is the Parish Catholic church, also recently built, but in the simpler and more chaste style of the early perpendicular. Mülhausen manufactures muslins and cotton prints.

72 RIXHEIM, pop. 4000. With paper-mills. 17

85 ST. LOUIS or LUDWIG, pop. 2000. German custom-house 4 station. Coach awaits passengers for Hüningen, 3½ m. N., with piscicultural tanks, established in 1850, which have been of immense service in replenishing with salmon and trout the Rhine, the Moselle, and many of the smaller rivers of Alsace.

89 BASEL or BALE, pop. 32,000. *Hotels:* Trois Rois; Tête d'Or; Cigogne.

Railway Stations.—Passengers who reach Basel by the railway on the east side of the Rhine arrive at the Baden Railway station on the northern side of the town, or on the Little Basel side. The railway from this station runs eastwards to Neuhausen, the station for the falls of the Rhine, Shaffhausen, and Constance on Lake Constance or the Bodensee. Passengers who arrive at this station with the intention of proceeding direct to Bern, Luzern, or any of the towns in the interior of Switzerland, must drive over to the Central Railway station, situated at the southeast corner of Basel, by the Post omnibus, which awaits passengers outside the station; fare, 1 franc each. There are also cabs and omnibuses for the hotels. Passengers reaching Basel by the railways on the west side of the Rhine arrive at the Central Railway or Swiss Railway station, situated in the new part of Basel. On the façade of this station are two clocks, one with Swiss, and the other with French time—the former being 22 minutes before the latter. At this station the Post omnibus awaits passengers who require to go to the Basel station. Omnibuses from the hotels also await passengers. At both stations sovereigns are taken for 25 francs.

Paris to Basel by Dijon and Besancon.

Start from the railway station of the "Chemins de Fer de Lyon," where request a ticket for Besançon, and from Besançon proceed to Basel.

| PARIS | | BALE |
| MILES FROM | Distance 364 miles. Map, p. 76. | MILES TO |

PARIS. This is the direct route to Marseilles and the Riviera, 364 by Fontainebleau, Sens, Joigny, Dijon, Macon, and Lyons. Also the direct road to Italy, by Dijon, Bourg, Culoz, Aix-les-Bains, Chambery, and Mont Cenis tunnel, see "Black's South of France," Both of these routes are the same as far as Dijon. Fontainebleau, Sens and Dijon are the best resting-places on the line.

196 DIJON, 810 ft. above the sea. Among the cheap hotels near 168 the station is the Hotel-Restaurant du Chemin de Fer; opposite is a shop in which are sold mustard, gingerbread, and cassis, the "spécialités" of Dijon. *Hotels:* near the station, the Jura; in the town the Cloche; the Bourgogne. Junction to Chalindrey 43½ m. N., p. 96.

216 AUXONNE, pop. 6000. *Hotel:* Cerf. A fortified town on 148 the left bank of the Saone, containing an arsenal, large barracks, and a church—Notre Dame—of the 14th cent. In the neighbourhood is Mount Roland, whose summit, 1116 ft. high, is covered with the ruins of a monastery, which belonged to the black monks. The church was built by the Jesuits in 1843. From Auxonne a branch goes 23 m. N.E. to Gray junction, and thence other 31 m. in the same direction to Vesoul, on the Paris and Troyes Route to Bâle. From Gray a branch rail extends 14 m. N.E. to Bucey-les-Gy, a pleasant town, situated in an agricultural district. At Gray, pop. 7000, the Paris and Lyons and the Eastern Railway systems meet. The town is situate on the Saone, at some little distance from the station. *Hotels:* Parc; Paris.

226 DOLE, pop. 12,000. An important junction and station, with 138 a good refreshment-room, 89 m. from Neuchatel. All generally change carriages here. *Hotels:* Ville de Lyon; Ville de Geneva. Dole is a well-built town, pleasantly situated on the Doubs, and on the canal between the Rhine and the Rhone. From the esplanade St. Maurice there is a fine view of the large forest of Chaux and of the Jura mountains. The church of Notre Dame is of the 16th cent., and the Hotel-Dieu of the 17th.

237 LABARRE. Junction with branch line to Gray 24½ m. north. 127 This is another of the points where the system of the Lyons Railways joins that of the Eastern Company's Railways.

254 BESANÇON, 116 m. N. from Bourg, pop. 49,000. *Hotels:* all 110 near each other, and near the Grande Place. The Paris; the Nord; the Europe. The Jura and the Centre are smaller and cheaper. Money-changer opposite the Paris. Temple Protestant up the Doubs, near the Musée. Besançon, the ancient Vesuntio, is divided into two unequal parts by the river Doubs, which almost encompasses the

BESANÇON.   WATCHMAKING SCHOOL.

larger by a curve resembling, according to Cæsar's expression, "the form of a horseshoe." The town occupies a hollow surrounded by high hills crowned with forts. On the northern hill are Fort Griffon and the railway station; and on the southern the citadel, having on the hills to the east of it Forts Beauregard and Bregille, and to the west Fort Chaudane 1378 ft. above the sea. Three long parallel streets intersect the part of the town forming the horseshoe. Of them, the most important now, as well as in the time of the Romans, is the Grande Rue, which extends, in nearly a straight line from the Pont de Battant, to the foot of the citadel, passing through the triumphal arch. In the Roman period it was paved throughout with large flat stones, and was 7 ft. below its present level. All the important places are near the Grande Rue. At the westerly end is the Pont de Battant, on the foundations of the Roman bridge. At the west end of the bridge is the church of Ste. Madeleine, the best of the modern ecclesiastical edifices. At the east end, at the foot of the parallel street, the Rue des Granges, are—the market-place, the Ecole Municipale d'Horlogerie, the Archæological Museum and Picture Gallery, and the Temple Protestant (13th cent.), served by 3 clergymen. The *Watchmaking School* is a most useful institution, which has conferred great benefits on the community. Boys, natives of Besançon, are taught the profession gratis. All others, as well as foreigners, have to pay £8 the year. The age at which they are admitted varies from 12 to 15. As a general rule 3 or even 4 years are required to attain the necessary proficiency in the art—that is, to be able to make a good going watch from small plates of brass, steel, and nickel. The mainsprings they receive from the forges of Montbeliard and other places. They are taught also mechanical drawing, geometry, chemistry, and natural philosophy, especially as applied to the science of watchmaking. Pupils can board in the town or in the Lycée for 780 frs. the year or 65 frs. the quarter. The town contributes annually £1200 towards the expenses of the institution.

The Archæological Museum and Picture Gallery are open on Sundays and Thursdays. As the paintings have not the artists' names attached, I note here a few of the best. At the entrance is 120 a large painting representing the Death of Leonardo da Vinci by Gigoun; 92 Crucifixion by A. Dürer; 94 A Dutchman by Van Dyck; 71 Portrait of himself by Coypel; 287 St. Francis by Zurbaran; 268 Galilee by Velasquez; 262 Portrait of Granvelle (Minister of Charles V.), by Titian (his empty stone coffin is downstairs before the entrance); 259 Temptation of St. Antony, Teniers; 241 Forest Scene,

Hotel de Ville.   Porte Noire.   Cathedral.

Ruysdael; 240 Being led to the Cross, Rubens; 218 Triumph of Venus, Paul Veronese; 51 and 52 Canaletto. A very interesting part of the Museum is the room containing the "Collection Paris," in which are preserved the best of the specimens found in the neighbourhood belonging to the stone, iron, and Roman periods.

From the Pont de Battant, passing up the Grande Rue, we reach on the left the church of St. Pierre, and opposite, on the right, a large edifice, 16th cent., containing the Hotel de Ville and the Palais de Justice. At the foot of the H. de l'Orme, behind the Hotel de Ville, is the Arsenal, on the site formerly occupied by the Roman Colosseum destroyed in the 5th cent. Opposite is the hospital built in 1703, considered one of the best constructed and best managed in France. Next it is the Promenade de Chamars (Campus Martis of the Romans), on one of the bends of the Doubs.

Ascending the Grande Rue from the Hotel de Ville, we come to, on the right, the Palais Granvelle, built by Cardinal Granvelle, minister of Charles V. and of Philip II., in 1540, now occupied by the Post and Telegraph Offices. The façade consists of 2 stories, with 3 stages of attached banded pillars. Within is a large arcaded court, with 6 elliptic arches on the two smaller sides, and 7 on the two larger. Over them is a row of 34 plain transomed windows. A little farther up the street, on the left, is the Rue de la Bibliotheque, leading to the Public Library, containing a large and valuable collection of books and manuscripts managed by obliging librarians. Beyond, to the left, are the remains of the Roman theatre, consisting of 8 isolated Corinthian columns, some pedestals, and subterranean masonry. At the head of the street is the Roman Triumphal arch, the Porte de Mars, but called ever since the 7th cent. the Porte Noire, on account of its blackened appearance. It is covered with nearly effaced bas-reliefs, is 32 ft. high and 18 wide, was erected in honour of Crispus Cæsar, son of Constantine, and at present forms a kind of portico to the cathedral. The **Cathedral**, of which the oldest parts date from the 11th to the 13th cent., is 216 ft. long, 82 wide, and 85 high, inside measure. The entrance is on the N. side, near the eastern apsidal termination, rebuilt in the 18th cent., and occupied by the chapel of the Holy Shroud (Sueur),. called thus because the linen sheet was kept in it, in which our Lord was wrapt, and which bore, in a faint yellow tint, the impression of his body. Over the altar is the Resurrection of Christ, by C. Vanloo. The chapel to the left of the altar, just at the entrance, contains the mausoleum of Cardinal Carondelet,

Besançon. Porte Taillée. Locle.

ambassador of Charles V. at Rome. In the upper part he is represented in full sacerdotal costume; in the under, divested of clothing, and the prey of the ministers of death. Over it is the death of Ananias and Sapphira by Sebastiano del Piombo; and over the altar, the martyrdom of St. Sebastian. Opposite, on the other side of the church, is one of the faces of the clock made by Verité of Beauvais. It consists of 30,000 pieces, took $2\frac{1}{2}$ years of constant labour to finish, and is in the style of the Strassburg clock; but without the figures. On the same side, just behind the chaste marble pulpit, is the chapel of N. D. du Rosaire. A painting by Passignano of Mary and child hangs over the altar. Under the floor of the second chapel beyond is a vault which J. M. A. C. Mathieu, "a fait construire," "et y a transferé les restes mortels des Comtes de Bourgogne," 1865. Their bones are in 4 coffins. The stair behind the altar leads down to the vault. On the walls of the chapel are the portraits of the 8 Counts. The high altar is in the western chancel. The triforium and clerestory are constructed in an unusual style, necessitated by the short distance of the lofty arches from the roof. A broad winding road leads up from behind the cathedral to the Citadel, 410 ft. above the river. But before ascending, it is necessary to be provided with an order procured from the Commandant de la Place, to be found at the "Direction de Genie," in the Place de l'Etat Major, east from the cathedral, at the head of the Rue des Granges.

The street below the cathedral, the Rue Rivotte, leads by the side of Doubs to the Porte Taillée; originally a tunnel cut by the Romans in the reign of Marcus Aurelius, for their aqueduct from the Arcier. In the reign of Louis XIV. it was widened, and afterwards, when the road to Switzerland came to pass through it, it assumed its present form; that of a simple gateway. The aqueduct itself, which was destroyed in 451, is now completely hidden by the embankments of the new railway from Besançon to Locle, about 11 m. E. A few miles farther by this rail is Neuchatel. This forms one of the best railway entrances from France into Switzerland. The line passes at a little more than half-way by Morteau on the Doubs, pop. 2000. *Inn:* Commerce. Church founded in 13th cent.: Hotel de Ville in 17th cent. $7\frac{1}{2}$ m. from Morteau the Doubs falls over a plateau 88 ft. high, into an abyss of unknown depth. Behind are cliffs 630 ft. high.

The drinking water for Besançon still comes from the Arcier, but it is brought by an underground aqueduct, $6\frac{1}{2}$ m. long. The neck of the peninsula of Besançon has been tunneled through, to make way for a canal, which passes right below the citadel. It leaves the Doubs about half-way between the Porte Rivotte and the Porte Taillée, and re-enters it below the Porte Notre-Dame. Down the Doubs from the forests which cover the Jura mountains, are floated rafts of larches, many 90 ft. long, by 16 in. square at the base. There is a very pleasant walk of $3\frac{1}{4}$ m. to a cliff called the Bout du Monde, over which tumbles the stream Mercurot.

Watchmaking in private houses, by former pupils of the school, forms an important industry and means of subsistence in and around Besançon. They procure the works in a rough state from the manufacturers, which they adapt, finish and put together.

The railway, 1000 ft. above the sea, from **Besançon to Montbeliard**, follows the course of the Doubs, flowing at the base of the Jura mountains, covered with splendid forests. $5\frac{1}{2}$ m. from Besançon is Roche station, opposite Arcier; whose springs supply Besançon with drinking water. After having passed through several tunnels, and the large village of Laissey, with iron mines and forges, the train arrives at

$\underset{\sim}{274}$ BAUME-LES-DAMES, pop. 3000, on the Doubs in a hollow $\underset{\sim}{90}$ on one side of the station. It possesses a large hospital, and marble quarries, and the ruins of a fortress destroyed by the Swiss in 1576. *Inn:* H. du Commerce; France. 13 m. farther N. is Clerval, pop. 1400, with a castle. The line then crosses the Rhine and Rhone Canal, and the Doubs, and having passed the towns of Isle-sur-le-Doubs, Colombier-Fontaine, and Voujaucourt, arrives at Montbeliard station, situated below the best part of the castle.

$\underset{\sim}{302\frac{1}{2}}$ MONTBELIARD, 1050 ft. above the sea, pop. 7000, on $\underset{\sim}{61\frac{1}{2}}$ the Rhine and Rhone canal. *Inns:* at station, the Mulhouse: Couronne; in centre of town, in the Place Dorian, the Inn XIII. Cantons; Lion Rouge. In the Rue Belfort, the Balance, frequented chiefly by commercial travellers. On arriving, walk straight down the street in front of the station to a small two-storied house, left hand, No. 22 Rue Cuvier, with a black marble slab bearing the inscription, "Ici naquit G. Cuvier le 23 Aout 1769." To the right, in the Place St. Martin, is a bronze statue of him by David. Facing the statue is the principal Protestant church, St. Martin, built in 1605, and behind, the Hotel de Ville, a modern edifice. Cuvier, the illustrious naturalist (died 1832), possessed a range of knowledge surpassingly great. He had all his life read much, and had ever been a constant observer, and had never forgotten anything worth remembering. He was, moreover, a good as well as a great man, combining

Paris to Neuchatel by Dijon.

with accomplishments of the first order those graces which shed the brightest lustre on the highest mental endowments.

Continuing down the principal street, we arrive at the Place d'Armes, with, on the right, the Market, 16th cent., and in front, the well-merited statue to Col. Denfert-Rochereau, the bold, prudent, and intrepid commander of the fortress of Belfort, while besieged by the Germans from the 2d November 1870 to the 15th February 1871. Beyond, in the Place St. Georges, is the Protestant church St. Georges, and above it the Catholic church, with a needle spire. On the eminence rising from the railway is the castle, rebuilt in 1751, with 3 towers, and some large plain houses used as barracks. Montbeliard contains a college for the education of Protestant clergy and teachers, and several good private schools. It manufactures clocks, watches, and tools.

Coach to St. Hippolyte, 17 m. S., passing by Pont-de-Roide, 11 m. S. Pont-de-Roide, pop. 2200, has important manufactories of cutlery and tools. St. Hippolyte, pop. 1000, is in a picturesque country at the confluence of the Doubs with the Dessoubre.

After Montbeliard the train reaches Hericourt station, 5 m. N. and 1125 ft. above the sea. The village contains foundries and forges. 6 m. farther is Belfort (page 104), $303\frac{1}{2}$ m. from Paris by this way but by Troyes, Chaumont, and Vesoul, 276 m. From Belfort enter Switzerland either by Mülhausen to Basel, 50 m. E., p. 119, or by Porentruy, p. 105, the more direct way.

Paris to Neuchatel.

By MELUN, FONTAINEBLEAU, MONTERAU, SENS, JOIGNY, DIJON, AUXONNE, DOLE, MOUCHARD, and PONTARLIER.

For the general summary, see in the Time-tables of the "Chemins de Fer de Paris à Lyon," under "Dôle à Pontarlier et Neuchatel;" and for the part between Paris and Dijon, see under "Paris à Lyon."

In purchasing the ticket, say to Neuchatel by Pontarlier. For the fares to the various places on this line, see under "Prix des places du service direct des voyages entre la France et la Suisse," in the Indicateur of the Lyons Railway.

PARIS MILES FROM   Distance, 315 miles. Map, p. 76.   NEUCHATEL MILES TO

PARIS. Start from the station of the Chemins de Fer de Paris à Lyon. This route is the same as the preceding route the length of Dole, which see, p. 121.   315

238   CHATELAY. Junction with branch to Montferrand.   77

246   MOUCHARD, pop. 500, important junction. Refreshment-rooms, and book-stall with English newspapers. The village is below   69

POLIGNY TO NYON BY CHAMPAGNOLE.

the station—descend by the steps. It has two small *Inns*: Gerard; and through the arch, the Inn *Javel. 71 m. S. from Mouchard by rail is Bourg; see Black's South France. 5 m. from Mouchard by branch line is Salins, with a bathing establishment supplied by salt-water springs, considered efficacious in giving tone to the system. *Hotels*: De l'Etablissement; Marsoudet; Messageries.

About half-way between Mouchard and Bourg is **Lons-le-Saunier**, pop. 10,200, on the Vallière. *Hotels*: Geneva; Paris; Europe; Cerf. Their omnibuses await passengers. Bathing establishment, with cold salt-water baths. In the Grande Place are the theatre, a statue to General Lecourbe over the public well, and the clock-tower. From this tower extends the Rue du Commerce, arcaded on both sides, having towards its left extremity the Hotel de Ville, with the Library and Picture Gallery, and behind, the public hospital. At the extremity towards the right is the Rue du Puits Salé, leading to the salt baths (Bains Mineraux du Puits Salé). Lons-le-Saunier is 31 m. S. from Mouchard by rail, 40 m. N. from Bourg, and 41 m. E. from Chalons-sur-Saone. $18\frac{1}{2}$ m. S. from Mouchard and $12\frac{1}{2}$ N. from Lons-le-Saunier is **Poligny**, 970 ft. above the sea, pop. 6000. *Inns*: France; Cerf. A pleasant country town. In the "Place" is a bronze statue "au brave et vertueux General Travot," and in the promenade a bust "à l'historien Chevalier." The rock, Roche du Midi, in the centre of the cliff behind the church, serves as a sort of sun-dial; because exactly at midday it is in the shade. About 1 m. to the left of the 1 kilometre stone on the Champagnole road, are the caves called the Trou de Lune and the Trou de la Baume.

Poligny and Champagnole to Nyon on Lake Geneva.—A coach starts twice daily from the H. de France to Champagnole, $14\frac{1}{4}$ m. E., fare $2\frac{1}{4}$ frs., 3 hrs., whence coaches to Nyon, passing St. Laurent and Morez, by a most picturesque road. The road from Poligny ascends for $3\frac{1}{4}$ m., disclosing beautiful views all the way, to the H. du Valon, situated on the commencement of a vast undulating plain, covered with a forest which extends to the first village, Montrond—*Inn*: Paix—10 m. from Poligny. After this the country becomes monotonous, till the road begins to descend to Champagnole. **Champagnole**, pop. 3400, on the Ain and Londaine, in a plain surrounded by the Jura mountains covered with fir-trees. Junction with branch line to Andelot, 9 m. N., p. 128. The town consists of one long wide well-paved street, from which ramify a few short narrow lanes. The best inn is the *H. Dumont, a very comfortable house; the Cheval Blanc is a smaller and humbler house. It has a great many pretty excursions in the fir-clad mountains. At Andelot, $8\frac{1}{2}$ m. S., the Champagnole branch joins the railway between Mouchard and Neuchatel, see map, p. 76.

A coach runs daily from Champagnole by St. Laurent to Morez, 21 m. S., by a picturesque road in the Jura mountains—fare, $2\frac{1}{2}$ frs.; time, $3\frac{1}{2}$ hrs. After having crossed several times the Lemme, while ascending its beautiful valley, the coach arrives at the hamlet of Morillon, between two mountains, $9\frac{1}{4}$ m. from Champagnole. The coach then enters the Val de

Grand-Vaux, a vast bleak plain between the parallel mountains of La Joux-Devant and La Joux-Derrière.

15 m. S. from Champagnole is St. Laurent, pop. 1000, *Inn:* Commerce, a poor village in a bleak region 2976 ft. above the sea, where watches and agricultural implements are manufactured. 3½ m. from the village is the Lake Abbaye, 1¼ m. long and 98 ft. deep. The road afterwards becomes picturesque at the Montée and Descente of St. Laurent to Morez, a village of 5400 inhabitants, on the Bienne, 2625 ft. above the sea, at the end of a deep gorge. *Inn:* Poste. It possesses a watchmaking school and manufactories of clocks, roasting-jacks, tools, and instruments. Near Morez-le-Haut are the source of the Doye-Gabet and the crevice of the Roche-Fendue 39 ft. wide. From Morez another diligence runs through a beautiful but little frequented country to **Nyon** on Lake Geneva.

261 **ANDELOT**, Junction with Champagnole, 9 miles South. 54

283 **PONTARLIER**, pop. 5200, on a cold high plateau. Station 32 of the French custom-house; luggage entering France examined here. Refreshment-rooms. *Hotels:* Poste; Paris. This, the ancient Pontalia, is famous for the manufacture of that deleterious liqueur called absinthe, for which large quantities of the plant *Artemisia absinthium* (wormwood) are cultivated in the neighbourhood. 2½ m. beyond Pontarlier, towards Neuchatel, are Fort Joux on the right, where Mirabeau was imprisoned, and on the left a modern fort, both on the tops of high cliffs.

291½ **SWISS VERRIERES**. Station of the Swiss custom-house. 23½ The road after this becomes very picturesque, and is, perhaps, the finest entrance into Switzerland. 315 m. from Paris is

315 **NEUCHATEL** or **NEUENBURG**, pop. 11,000. The *Railway station* is on the top of a hill overlooking the town. Opposite the station is a very good restaurant. Omnibuses from the hotels await passengers. The *Steamboat* and small boat station is on the Quay beside the Hotel Bellevue. The *Post-office* is No. 7 Rue de l'ancien Hotel de Ville.

Hotels: Belle-Vue; Alpes; Commerce—all three on the Lake. More inland, the Lac; Faucon; Post. See Black's "Switzerland."

Paris to Geneva.

By Dijon, Macon, Bourg, Ambérieux, and Culoz.

Time-table under "Paris, Macon, et Genève," in the "Indicateur des Chemins de Fer de Paris à Lyon." This Company issue during summer circular tickets, available for 1 or 2 months, for visiting Switzerland from Paris. The London, Chatham, and Dover Railway Company issue circular tickets from London to Paris and Switzerland. Apply also at No. 98 Fleet Street for Cook's Excursion Tickets.

| PARIS MILES FROM | Distance 388 m. Map, p. 76. | GENEVA MILES TO |

PARIS. Start from the station of the Chemins de Fer de Paris à Lyon in the Boulevard Mazas. Purchase at the stat. one of their Time-tables. For description of the first 196 miles of this route, from Paris to Dijon, see Black's South France. Dijon is a good resting-place. *Hotels:* Cloche; Parc; Jura. From Dijon the railway extends 28 m. by a narrow strip of land, on the sides of the lower range of the hills of the Cote d'Or, which attain the elevation of 324 feet. Behind rises a higher range reaching the height of 1315 feet, which serve as a shelter from the cold winds for the others. On the low range, between Dijon and Meursault, grow the first-class Burgundy wines; and south from Meersault follow the Macon wines. After Dijon the principal stations are Macon, 274 m. from Paris, and 114 m. to Geneva; and Bourg, 295 m. (p. 131) from Paris, and 93 m. from Geneva, see Black's South France.

347½ CULOZ, pop. 1200, a most important station, where the trains 40½ meet to and from Italy, Switzerland, and the South of France by Grenoble and Aix. There are 2 small inns about 300 yards beyond the N. side of the stat. The village is a little farther away on the Rhone.

357 SEYSSEL, pop. 3000. *Inn:* Ecu de France. Most pictur- 31 esquely situated on both sides of the Rhone, crossed by a suspension-bridge. Near this stat. the line passes through several tunnels in the Jura mountains. The longest is the tunnel of Paradis, 3362 ft. long. At Seyssel are excellent quarries of a beautiful soft white stone.

367 BELLEGARDE, 1220 ft. above the sea, pop. 800, on the Val- 21 serine. French custom-house. Passengers from Geneva alight here to have their luggage examined. *Inns:* Poste; Perte du Rhone.

This poor village, situated a short way down from the station, has within a few minutes' walk from the inn that part of the course of the Rhone where it disappears altogether, lost under the gravel and boulders which form its bed; but over which, when flooded, it rushes in tem-

K

pestuous rapids. The inn itself occupies a picturesque position, immediately above the dark ravine of the Valserine, by the side of the bridge which crosses it. To visit the **Perte du Rhone** cross this bridge and walk up the first road to the right, to the bridge over the Rhone, about a quarter of a mile distant. When the river is low, no water is seen below the bridge. The place where it begins to disappear is a few minutes' walk farther up the river. A road to the left of the inn leads down to a ravine, among high steep cliffs, where the Rhone and the Valserine unite. Here too, is a "Perte" of the Valserine; but the chief "Perte" of the Valserine is about 1¼ m. distant, by the road to Chatillon. It, however, is tame and uninteresting, and can moreover be seen well enough from the road. Near the spot there is one of the small houses belonging to the custom-house officers.

384 Before reaching Meyrin the line passes Fort de l'Ecluse on the 4 S. side. N. from Meyrin are Gex and the Col de la Faucille. We now leave the Jura mountains and have before us the Alps and Switzerland.

GENEVA, 388 m. from Paris. The station is 1286 ft. above the sea. Around the station are some less expensive hotels. Fronting it is the *Pension Fromont and Jackson, entered from the Rue Pradier, No. 1. A comfortable house from 5½ to 6½ frs. per day. In the square are also the H. et P. des Arts and H. Suisse; both large houses. A short way down the handsome street, which leads from the station to the lake, is the *Hotel et P. Genève. Behind the church is a small house, the H. et P. Fribourg, moderate charges.

At the foot of the Rue Mont Blanc are the steamboat station, and the most expensive first-class hotels: the Paix; the Beau Rivage; the Russie; and the Bergues. Across the bridge Mont Blanc, on the left side of the Rhone, are hotels not quite so expensive: the Couronne; Paris; Lac; under the Lac is the office of Messrs. Cook, and almost adjoining, in the Rue du Rhone, a good exchange office. Farther up the river is the Metropole, the largest hotel in Geneva. Near the Metropole the H. et P. Flaegel. Down the river near the post-office, the H. de la Poste, another large house. See Black's Switzerland.

Bellegarde to Bourg, 49½ m. by Nantua. See Map, p. 76. The train after passing Musinens arrives at Chatillon-de-Michaille on the Semine, 3¾ m. W. from Bellegarde, pop. 1300. The valleys between this and Nantua become narrower and the mountain sides more precipitous, of which the northern are covered with large fir-trees. The felling of these trees and the sawing them into planks, forms the principal industry of the inhabitants. Three m. farther at the E. extremity of Lake Sylant,

NANTUA. BOURG. EGLISE DE BROU.

1½ m. long, is the village of La Voulte (custom-house) between steep wooded hills. At the W. extremity is the village of Neyrolles, very picturesquely situated. 34¼ m. E. from Bourg, and 15¼ m. W. from Bellegarde, is **Nantua**, on Lake Nantua, pop. 4000. *Inns:* *Nord; Brossard. Although a very pretty place with good fishing, it is not much visited. The lake, in the midst of the Jura mountains, contains 656 acres, and is 1558 ft. above the sea. High calcareous cliffs rise round it on all sides, while pleasant walks border the margin. From Nantua to the station of Simandre, 14 m. E. from Bourg and 20 m. W. from Nantua, the train passes through a succession of tunnels, revealing occasionally glimpses of grand mountain scenery. **Bourg** is 23½ m. E. from Macon, 102 m. S. from Dijon, and 116 m. S. from Besançon, p. 121.

Bourg en Bresse, pop. 14,000, on the Reyssouze. *Hotels:* at station, H. de la Gare; in the town, in the Place de Bernard, the *H. France; fronting the promenade, the Europe. Their omnibuses await passengers. The great sight is the **Eglise de Brou**, about a mile from the station. Walk to the parish church, where take the second street right, the Rue des Marches, which continue, the length of the broad street or rather road of St. Nicolas, right hand, which take. The large building with a dome is the town hospital, the next large edifice on same side is the **Eglise de Brou**. It will probably be shut. The doorkeeper lives in the seminary, in the adjoining building. In front of the façade, on the ground, is the great sun-dial, made in the 16th cent., and restored in 1732 by Lalande. In the centre of the circle is an oblong stone divided into two parts by a straight line. On one side of the line are the letters J, F, M, A, M, J, and on the other D, N, O, S, A, J, the first letter of each month. By standing upon the proper letter, the shadow of the person points to the hour. On the way to the church several shops are passed with in their windows toy wooden shoes, sabots, a "specialité" of Bourg. The Eglise de Brou is visited on account of the superb mausoleums of Philibert-le-Beau, Marguerite-de-Bourbon, and Marguerite d'Autriche. Fee when church is shut ½ fr., or party 1 fr.

In 1480, when Philippe II. Duke of Savoy was hunting he broke his arm, which caused such a severe illness that his life was despaired of. His wife Marguerite de Bourbon vowed that if he should recover she would build a church and a monastery in the territory of Brou where the accident had happened. He did recover, but she died shortly afterwards at the chateau de Pont-d'Ain; without having had time to fulfil her vow. The prince himself died at the same chateau in 1497, and left to his son Philibert II., surnamed the Beau, the fulfilment of his mother's vow. He married Marguerite d'Autriche, daughter of the Emperor Maximilian, granddaughter of Charles le Téméraire, and aunt of Charles V. On the 10th September 1504 he died in the same chateau from having drunk, while hunting, too freely of cold water when overheated. Marguerite d'Autriche, overwhelmed with grief, determined to fulfil the vow of her mother-in-law, and for this purpose sought the aid of the most famous artists.

In 1505 Jean Perréal of Paris commenced the church, which was continued from 1512 by Loys van Boghem of Flanders, by whom it was finished in 1531

Eglise de Brou. Mausoleums.

and cost £1,600,000. Michel Coulombe of Tours made the models of the mausoleums and the 2 brothers Meyt of Dijon executed them in 7 years, in marble brought from Carrara. The bodies are in the vaults below the mausoleums. The stalls were designed by Van Boghem and executed by Flemish workmen. The church, at the revolution of 1793, was saved from total destruction by having been filled with hay for the army of the Alps. Notwithstanding in the year 2 of the Republic, the dome and spire were demolished. The edifice is cruciform, 229½ ft. long from west to east, 115 ft. from north to south at the transepts, 98 ft. wide at the nave, and 66 ft. high from the floor to the roof. The 2 angels, about 5 ft. high each, which support the pulpit, are by the Princess Marie d'Orleans.

All that is most beautiful is within the **Choir**, shut off from the nave by an elaborately sculptured rood-loft of 3 arches, 37 ft. wide and 25½ ft. high. The letters 𝔓.𝔐. interlaced, recur frequently among the friezework. Immediately within are 74 beautiful oak stalls, the sculpture of those on one side representing scenes from the Old Testament and those on the other from the new. Above on the rood-loft are 27 much plainer stalls. In front of the high altar is the mausoleum of Philibert-le-Beau, the *chef-d'œuvre*. On the top he reclines arrayed in his ducal vestments with a crouching lion at his feet and 6 winged cupids around him. Below between the 12 massive short piers, which support the upper part, he is represented as a corpse divested of clothing, on the bare shroud; which seems to yield to his weight. To his right is the mausoleum of his mother Marguerite de Bourbon, wearing her ducal mantle and a graceful greyhound at her feet. On each side of the basement, between cupids, are four most expressive mourners executed with the minutest attention to the smallest detail. On the left side of the Duke is the mausoleum of his wife Marguerite d'Autriche, the most massive and the most elaborate of the mausoleums. She reclines under a canopy on four pillars, dressed in full costume, with a coronet on her head and a profusion of lace and flowing drapery falling on the couch. The hound at her feet is not so successful. In the lower compartment is her inanimate form, attired in an embroidered chemise, stretched out on a shroud. Round the railings and along one of the upper friezes, runs her motto :—"𝔉𝔬𝔯𝔱𝔲𝔫𝔢—𝔦𝔫𝔣𝔬𝔯𝔱𝔲𝔫𝔢—𝔣𝔬𝔯𝔱𝔢 𝔲𝔫𝔢." In fortune and misfortune, one woman strong. The reredos of the altar opposite this mausoleum presents in a series of groups sculptured in stone the whole history known and supposed of the Virgin Mary. On the large window here, filled like the others with valuable glass, are represented in a kneeling posture Philibert and Marguerite with their protecting saints. On the 4 graceful lancet windows of the chancel are represented amidst glowing colours the arms of Savoy, Burgundy, France and Germany. The adjoining buildings, constructed for monks of the order of St. Benoit, are now occupied by a seminary. They contain spacious cloisters. The parish church of Bourg was commenced before the church of Brou but not finished till 1545.

Rail from Bourg to Lyon 37 miles south across a plain containing 1000 lakes, 30 of which are traversed by the line.

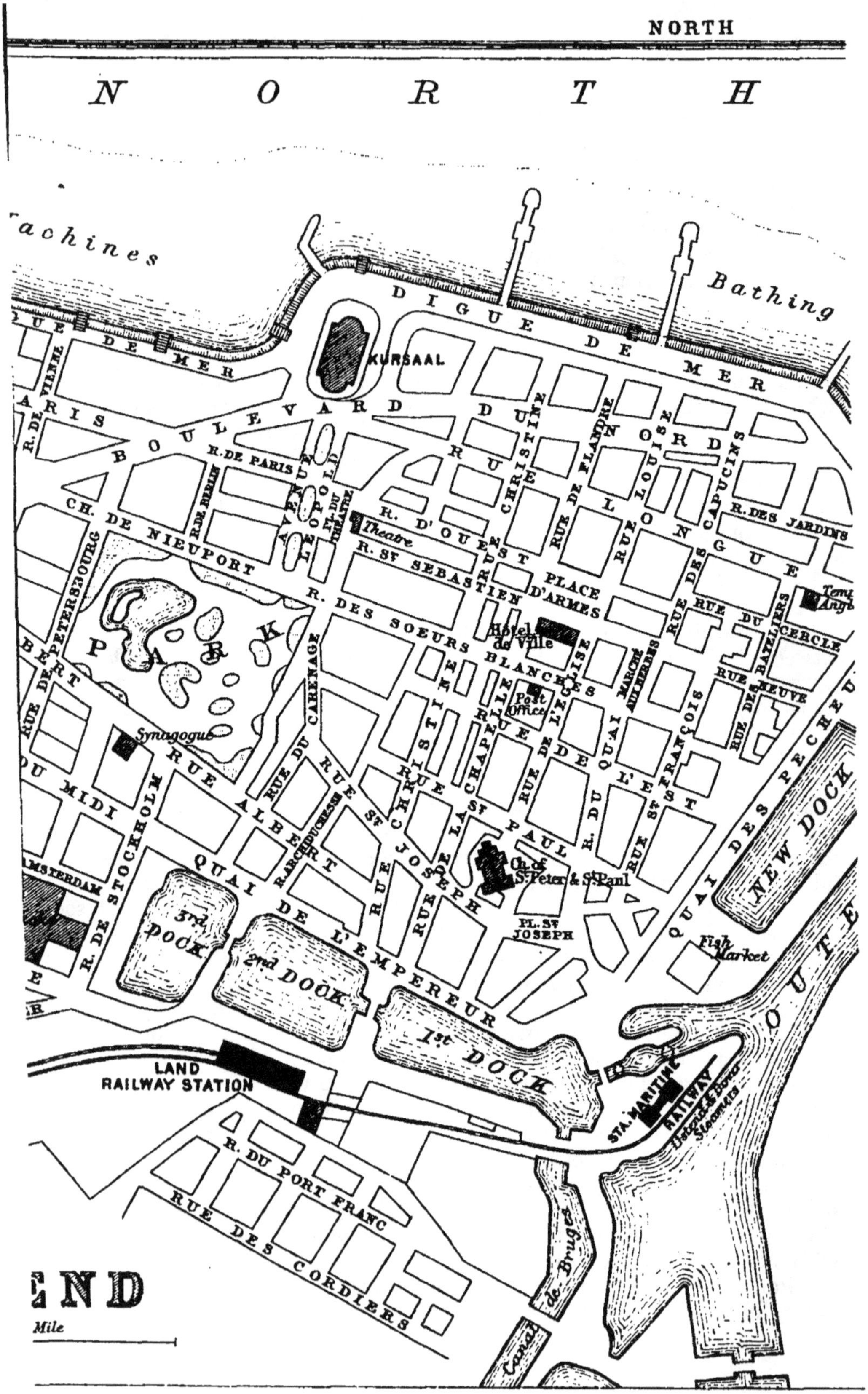
NORTH
N O R T H
Bathing
Machines
DIGUE DE MER
KURSAAL
BOULEVARD DU NORD
R. DE PARIS
R. DE VIENNE
CH. DE NIEUPORT
R. DE BERLIN
AVENUE LEOPOLD
PL. DU THEATRE
Theatre
R. D'OUEST
R. ST SEBASTIEN
RUE CHRISTINE
RUE DE FLANDRE
RUE LOUISE
RUE DES CAPUCINS
R. DES JARDINS
RUE LONGUE
PLACE D'ARMES
Hôtel de Ville
Post Office
R. DES SOEURS BLANCHES
RUE DE L'EGLISE
MARCHÉ AUX HERBES
RUE DU CERCLE
RUE DES BATELIERS
RUE NEUVE
QUAI DES PECHEURS
PARK
RUE DE PETERSBOURG
Synagogue
RUE ALBERT
RUE DU MIDI
RUE DE STOCKHOLM
R. DE STOCKHOLM
R. AMSTERDAM
RUE DU CARENAGE
RUE ST JOSEPH
R. ARCHIDUCHESSE
RUE DE LA CHAPELLE
RUE ST PAUL
RUE DE L'EST
QUAI ST FRANÇOIS
R. DU QUAI
Ch. of St. Peter & St. Paul
PL. ST JOSEPH
QUAI DE L'EMPEREUR
3rd DOCK
2nd DOCK
1st DOCK
NEW DOCK
Fish Market
OUTER
LAND RAILWAY STATION
STA. MARITIME
RAILWAY
Ostend & Dover Steamers
R. DU PORT FRANC
RUE DES CORDIERS
Canal de Bruges
END
Mile

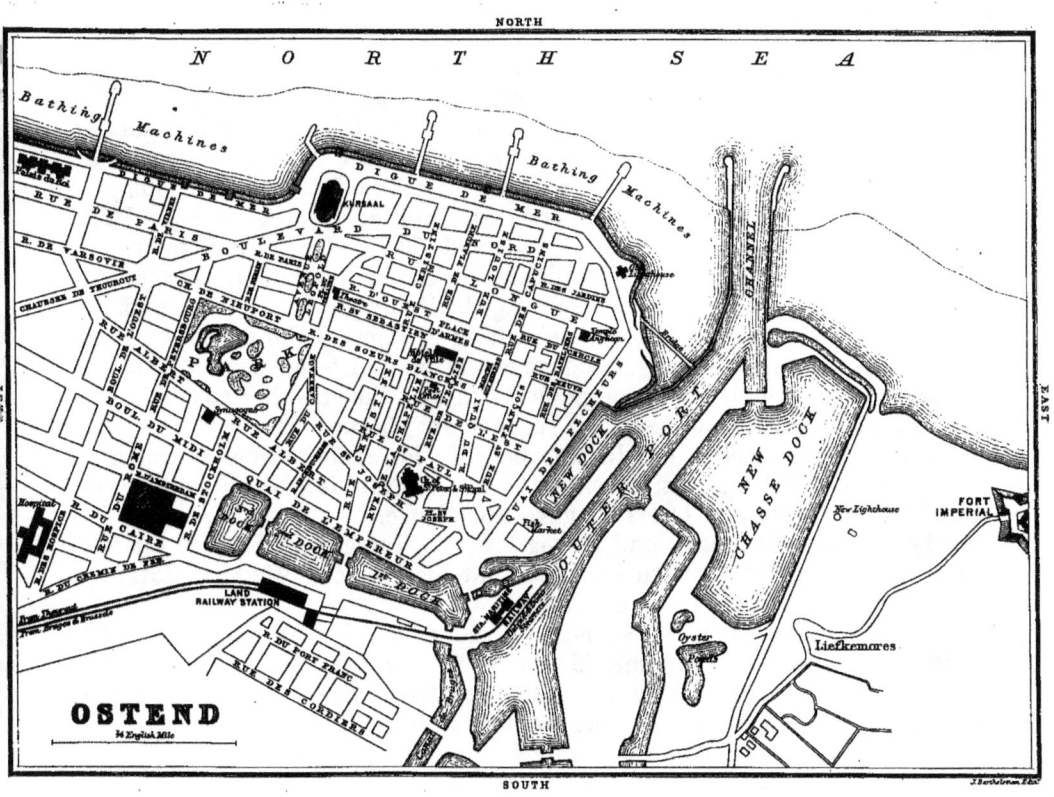

BELGIUM

Approaches by Steamer to Ostende.

Map, page 1 and p. 154.

OSTENDE, pop. 19,000, is approached from London by the boats of the General Steam Navigation Company twice weekly; or twice daily by the Belgian Government steamers sailing between Dover and Ostende (7 to 7½ hrs.) in connection with the trains of the South-Eastern Railway; and in Belgium, with those of the Belgian Government. On their arrival at Ostende, these boats correspond with the trains for Brussels, 9½ hrs. from London, 59¼ and 42½ frs., Cologne 15 hrs., and Berlin 56 hrs. Luggage can be registered *viâ* Dover and Ostende—in London, for Brussels or Cologne, at Cannon Street or Charing Cross; in Cologne, for Dover or London, to Charing Cross, Victoria and Holborn Viaduct Stations; in Brussels, for Dover or London, to same stations as from Cologne. Each passenger registering his luggage is allowed 56 lbs. free of charge on the Continental railways. For any weight over 56 lbs. he will be charged the usual rates. No charge is made for registration; and no subsequent demands for porterage, landing, or embarking of luggage should be complied with on the through journey. Baggage can be registered at every station on the route at which the through ticket allows the traveller to stop.

By South-Eastern Railway, all luggage for Cannon Street is examined at Dover. Whenever time will not permit the examination at Dover of the luggage registered for *Cannon Street Station*, it will be sent on for examination at Charing Cross luggage warehouse.

By London, Chatham, and Dover Railway, luggage registered for Victoria Station will be examined there; that for Holborn Viaduct Station *at Dover*, in the Customs room of the Company's station.

In England, see the Time-tables of the South-Eastern Railway (1d.); in Belgium, the *Guide Officiel*, 5 sous. In London, apply to the Dover and Ostende Mail Packet office, 53 Gracechurch Street; in Brussels, to John Piddington, general mail agent, 90A Montagne de la Cour.

The South-Eastern Railway Office in Brussels for tickets and time-tables to London, by either Calais or Ostende, is at 46 Montagne de la Cour, where through tickets, including steward's fee on board, are issued. On Sunday morning all registered luggage is examined at Dover. Parcels for England forwarded at moderate charges *viâ* Ostende and Dover.

The Ostende and Dover steamers arrive at and sail from the Maritime Railway station, where there are excellent refreshment-rooms and comfortable bedrooms, 2 frs., and where passengers enter the carriages from the boats, and *vice versâ*. Behind is the fishmarket.

The station for those not going nor arriving by the boats is a little way more landward, opposite the Quai de l'Empereur, with the hotels Concorde and Couronne. Ostende is within a short distance of the best Belgian bathing stations. It is 14½ m. W. from Bruges, 39¼ m. W. from Ghent, and 76 m. W. from Brussels. In Belgium the price is printed on the railway tickets.

OSTENDE. HOTELS. CABS.

Hotels: On the Digue, commencing at the western end, the Beau Rivage, 12 to 15 frs.; the next two, the Plage and the Ocean, have no fixed charge; then the Cercle des Bains. Off the Digue and behind the Kursaal are the H. de la Digue, 8 to 15 frs. and the Imperial 9 to 16 frs.; both good and comfortable. Next the Kursaal is the H. des Tourists 12 frs. G.* Hotel du Littoral, 13 to 15 frs.; the Russie, no fixed prices. Opposite the old lighthouse and near the western jetty is the Hotel Cercle du Phare, 10 to 15 frs. In this corner of the beach is one of the stations of the bathing machines. From this part, too, a wooden bridge leads across to the western jetty. Where this bridge joins the jetty is suspended the boat tariff. A boat with two men, for 1 to 2 hrs. with one to four passengers, costs 6 frs. At the extremity of this jetty many people amuse themselves fishing with handnets, which are let down and raised by pulleys. They catch shrimps, flounders, sprats, and other small fish. Each net costs 1 fr. per hour. At the land end of this jetty is the fishing-boats harbour, with the quay, at which the London steamers arrive. The Ostende and Dover steamers arrive at and sail from the **Maritime Railway**, more inland; see above. The Rue de la Chapelle and its continuation, the Rue de Flandre, lead from in front of the station bridge, in a straight line to the Digue, passing through the best part of the town and the Place d'Armes. In this street are the H. des Nations 9 to 12 frs.; H. St. Denis 9 to 11 frs.; H. de la Marine; and the Cour d'Angleterre 8 to 10 frs. Situated in the best part of the town, and near the Digue, is the *Lion d'Or in the Place d'Armes, 8 to 10 frs.; a comfortable house. In a corner of this " Place," H. du Grand-Café, 12½ frs. A little nearer the sea than the Lion d'Or is the H. de Flandre in the Rue de Flandre 9 to 11 frs. In the Rue Longue, the H. Fontaine, no fixed price; next it, the H. Frank 10 to 15 frs. In the Rue Longue, near the H. Frank, is the **English Church**. In the Boulevard du Noir, immediately behind the Digue, is the *Hotel Royal de Prusse 11 to 15 frs.; comfortable house. Near it, in the Rue Louise, H. de France, 12 to 15 frs. Parallel to the Rue de la Chapelle is the Rue de l'Eglise with the church of St. Peter and St. Paul. At the entrance is a Calvary and below the Calvary a purgatory with a petition in Flemish to the living to help to pray them out of that "place of torment." Within the church, in a small chapel under the right aisle, is the mausoleum of Queen Louise Marie, daughter of Louis Philippe, who died at Ostende on the 11th of October 1850. Her remains, along with those of her husband, Leopold I., are in the vault of the church of Laeken. The monument is of white marble, by Fraikin. The queen is in a reclining posture, looking up to an angel with extended wings, who is about to crown her. The female figure in tears represents Ostende. Near this church, in the Rue du Quai, is the H. *Allemagne, 9 to 11 frs. For those who intend to make a prolonged stay in the Ostende hotels, it is prudent to arrange the price beforehand.

Cabs.—Closed cabs, the course 1 fr., per hr. 1½ fr.; open cabs, the course 1½ fr., per hr. 3 frs. To the lighthouse and back, 2 frs.

The three attractions at Ostende are the beach, the Kursaal, and the Digue. **The beach** is smooth, but too flat till a great way out, when suddenly it sinks to the depth of 120 ft. At low tide it is 440 yards

OSTENDE. BLANKENBERGHE.

broad. Tickets costing each 80 c. are sold in the small wooden houses; they give the right to a machine, two towels, and a bath costume. When 25 tickets are taken, the price is less. When a lady and gentleman bathe together, they receive a machine with two compartments. At the N.W. end of the Digue, at the part called Le Paradis, the costume may be dispensed with. The greatest number of machines are by the west side of the Kursaal. Eastward, in front of the old lighthouse, is another but a smaller station.

The Kursaal is an immense affair decked with turrets and minarets, and containing many sources of amusement for old and young. Good music, well supplied reading-rooms, balls, and theatricals. Single entry for one day, $2\frac{1}{2}$ frs.; for four days, 9 frs.; and for eight days, 17 frs. Connected with the Kursaal is the Casino. The large building on a sandhill to the west is the palace of King Leopold, which cost £10,000. Behind the Kursaal is the Avenue Leopold, which has at its other end the "Parc."

The Digue, or Terrace, faced with stone and paved partly with bricks on their narrow sides, and partly with stone, is a noble work. It is 34 yds. wide, 2 m. long and 30 ft. above the beach, by a gentle slope, and makes a splendid promenade, though unfortunately it has no trees. At the S.W. and N.E. sides of the Digue are tanks or reservoirs in which oysters brought from England and other places are fattened.

Amidst sandhills at the N.E. end of Ostende, near the eastern jetty, is the lighthouse, built in 1859 at the cost of £9840; it is 170 ft. high, and is ascended by 273 steps. The view is very extensive; 50 c. each.

Ostende does not make a good bathing station; the beach is too flat, and the water not very pure; yet it is a curious place to visit, especially the Digue, during the height of the season. The great proportion of the strangers are Germans and Austrians, who have not had much experience of sea-bathing stations. Coach between Ostende and Nieuport, $11\frac{1}{2}$ m. S., passing the small bathing station of Middelkerk; from Ostende it starts from the post-office. See under Nieuport. See map, page 154.

Blankenberg and Heyst.

Bruges to Blankenberg or Blankenberghe, $9\frac{1}{4}$ m. northwards, and thence $5\frac{1}{2}$ m. N.E. to Heyst, by rail. The line leaves Bruges by the canal basin, and then traverses a flat well-cultivated country. See map, page 154.

Blankenberghe, pop. 3000, but variable. *Hotels:* on the "Digue," or terrace fronting the sea, commencing towards the S. end, near the little harbour of the fishing boats, and going northwards to the Kursaal:—The Univers, rooms 6 to 8 frs.; Venise, rooms 6 to 7 frs.; *Océan, board and lodging per day 7 to 15 frs., service $\frac{1}{2}$ fr., an excellent establishment in three different parts; Victoria, 8 to 15 frs., including everything; H. Saxe, 10 to 15 frs.; H. d'Hondt, same; Kursaal, same, with free entry to the fêtes and concerts; *G. Hotel Godderis, 9 to 15 frs.; *G. Hotel des Bains et des Familles, 10 to 15 frs., service $\frac{1}{2}$ fr.; a large, beautiful, and comfortable house; *Pavillon des Princes, 8 to 10 frs., service, $\frac{1}{2}$ fr.

In the main street, the Rue de l'Eglise, leading from the railway station to the terrace, are, commencing with those nearest the terrace:—*Hotel de Bruges, 8 to 10 frs.; Lion d'Or, 9 to 10 frs.; *H. de Courtrai, 7 to 9

HEYST. BRUGES.

frs. ; *Maison des Bains de Madame Marchand, 8 to 9 frs., very comfortable. ; *G. H. de la Paix, 7½ to 9 frs. ; G. H. d'Hondt, 7½ to 10 frs. ; H. *Allemagne, 7 to 8 frs. Near the station are the Flandre ; Mille Colonnes ; Chemin de Fer ; but they are more second-class restaurants.

The difference of the price per day is caused by the room. All receive the same board, which includes tea or coffee and bread and butter in the morning, dinner at 1, and supper at 6 or 7 ; but never wine.

There are also villas and furnished lodgings ; an English church. Boats are let out ; donkeys are greatly used. Bath tickets cost 75 c., and are sold at wooden houses along the terrace ; they give the right to a bathing machine, bathing dress, and towels. The machines are pushed into the sea by men. The beach is smooth, and has a very gentle inclination. Broad stairs at intervals ascend from it to the truly grand terrace, which slopes about 25 ft. upwards, is paved solidly with bricks, and is faced with stone. On the top it is from 24 to 27 yds. wide, and is about 1½ m. long. The coast, as in Holland, consists of a succession of sandhills, yet not entirely destitute of vegetation.

Between Blankenberghe and Heyst are Les Ecluses, the locks of the great canal where it enters into the sea. In the village is the H. de Flandre.

Heyst, pop. 1900. *Hotels :* as in Blankenberg, the best are on the "Digue," or Terrace. Commencing at the west end and going east, the Hotel du Phare, pension 6½ to 7½ frs. ; the Flandre, 7 to 8 frs. ; the G. Hotel de la Plage, 6 to 9 frs., service 25 c. ; the Kursaal, 8 to 12 frs. In the village, the H. Leopold II., 6 frs. for pension ; the H. du Rivage, 5½ to 6 frs., service 25 c. ; the H. de l'Océan, 4½ to 6 frs., service 25 c.

All the above prices include bedroom, breakfast, dinner, and supper. Heyst is still a cheaper but less fashionable place than Blankenberg ; but equally good, if not better, for sea-bathing. Sloping 25 ft. upwards from the beach, at a slight inclination, is the "Digue," or Terrace, firmly constructed of brick and stone, 22 yds. wide at the top, and about a mile long. Beyond, at both ends, are the low sandhills which bound the coast.

Bruges is 9¼ m. S.E. from Blankenberghe by rail and other 5½ m. from Heyst ; 14¼ m. E. from Ostende and 26 m. W. from Ghent ; which is 35½ m. N.W. from Brussels. Bruges is 33 m. N. from Courtrai.

Bruges, Flemish Brugge, bridges, pop. 48,000, is surrounded and intersected by the great canal from Ghent, is within 28 min. of Ostende, 25 min. of Blankenberg, and 45 min. of Heyst, or within a few min. of the great Belgian bathing stations, which enables the tourist to enjoy the sea-side with all its amenities, while having his headquarters at Bruges. Bruges, formerly the residence of the Counts of Flanders, and afterwards of the Dukes of Burgundy, attained its highest prosperity and splendour in the 15th cent. For their names, see p. 147, under Hotel de Ville. To be enjoyed, it must be taken leisurely. For this purpose the hotels Londres, Ours d'Or, or St. Amand, offer good lodgings at a moderate price. Those with little time at their disposal, should on arriving walk from the station down the broad street, the Rue Sud du Sablon. The large church on the right is the cathedral

BRUGES.   CATHEDRAL—ENTRANCE.

(p. 137), which enter. The high spire at the back belongs to Notre Dame (p. 140), which enter, and afterwards visit the Hospital of St. Jean, p. 143. From this go to the Grande Place, in which is the handsome **Belfry of the Halles**, whose sweet chimes are heard every quarter. Ascend it for the view, if possible, see p. 146. At the foot of the belfry is a cab-stand, where a vehicle can be hired by the hour, to run over the remaining places. Consult the coachman's tariff before starting. *Hotels:* opposite the station the *Hotel du Londres, room $2\frac{1}{2}$ frs., din. $2\frac{1}{2}$ frs., service $\frac{1}{2}$ fr.; Univers, room 2 frs., din. 3 frs., service $\frac{1}{2}$ fr.; Singe d'Or; Comte Flandre. In the Rue Nord du Sablon, near the station, the Hotel de Flandre, rooms from $2\frac{1}{2}$ to 5 frs., din. 5 frs., service 1 fr. In the Rue St. Jacques, next the church, the Commerce, room from $2\frac{1}{2}$ to 3 frs., din. 4 frs., service 1 fr. In the Rue St. Amand, close to the Grande Place, is the *Hotel St. Amand, room 2 frs., breakfast 1 fr., din. 2 frs., service $\frac{1}{2}$ fr. Near it in the Rue Courte d'Argent; the *Ours d'Or—same prices at the hotel St. Amand. Both are clean and comfortable. Post-office, No. 15 Rue Cordoue, near the Grande Place. English chapel near the church of St. Jacques. Service at 11 A.M. and 7 P.M. *Cab-fares.*—The course, in a closed cab, 1 fr., in an open cab, $1\frac{1}{2}$ fr. The hour, in a closed cab, $1\frac{1}{2}$ fr., in an open cab, 2 frs. The cabmen carry with them the authorised tariff. It is best not to take a cab till after having visited the Cathedral, Notre Dame, the Hospital of St. Jean, and the Belfry. At the foot of the belfry is a cab-stand.

Cathedral of Saint Sauveur.—From the station the Rue Sud du Sablon leads in a few min. to the cathedral; an ugly vast brick building constructed in the 13th, 14th, and 15th cents., on the site of a smaller edifice consecrated in 652 by St. Eloi. Over the western entrance rises a square tower in two stages, of which the under stage belongs to the 12th, and the upper to the 19th. The usual entrance is by the door at the N. side of the tower; but after mid-day, the general way in is by the door on the S. side of the tower, beside a kneeling figure of Christ, and the grave of Marie Anna Sonck and kin. Fee $\frac{1}{2}$ fr. each. The sacristan lives at No. 11 Place de la Cimitière.

The interior, much more beautiful than the exterior, is 110 yards from W. to E., 41 yards broad, and 30 yards high. The transept is 58 yards from N. to S.

Just under the tower at the W. end is a square room with a triptych (closed), by Pourbus (1540-1580), one of his best. The centre picture is a Last Supper. On wings, Elijah in the desert, and Abraham, and Melchisedec. Over it "Miraculous draught of fishes," by J. Van Orley.

BRUGES.   CATHEDRAL.   SALLE DE CONSEIL.   SOUTH AISLE.

On opposite wall, "Battle of Lepanto," by Minderhout, in grisaille, in 1672; so admirably executed, that one could almost fancy the sails to be fluttering, and the spray to be rising from the waves. Above, also by Orley, is "Jesus in the house of Simon the Pharisee." To the left is the "Martyrdom of Ste. Godelive," by J. Van Oost; she is being strangled. Above, is "St. Jerome in the desert," by P. Ricx, 1644.

On west end wall there is a row of pictures. Commencing at the N. corner, we have "The descent of the Holy Ghost on the Apostles" by J. Van Oost. The steps and the open book exhibit a curious perspective. Next it a Crucifixion by J. Van Hoek, 1635. On the other side of the archway, "St. Charles Borromeo administering the sacrament to the plague-stricken inhabitants of Milan," by Backereel, 1600. In corner an embossed copper plate representing the "Descent from the cross," by Wolfzanck, 16th cent. Above small door "Christ triumphing over death," J. Van Oost.

At this part of the wall a door opens into the **Salle du Conseil**, containing a Mater Dolorosa by Jan Van Eyck, 1420. Above it portrait Philippe le Beau by H. Vander Goes, 1480. Four panel pictures by Cooninxloo, 1570, representing the "Fall of Manna," "David dancing before the ark," "The paschal lamb," and the "Disciples at Emmaus."

Under the case is an ivory crozier, 6th cent. A crook, 12th cent. A piece of a rosary which belonged to Anne d'Autriche. On the wall in a frame is an "Indulgence," from the Pope, written in 1517. On the table are two missals, 13th and 14th cent.

Now begin the tour round the church, taking the S. side first. In the corner, over the S.W. door is the "Genealogical tree of St. Anne," composed of little gilt wooden figures, 15th cent. She is seated on a throne, with her ancestors ranged on each side. Over them is a genealogical tree with Mary at the top. Near it is a Holy Family by Zegers, 1620. Now follows the first chapel, with a triptych by Memling (covered) representing the Martyrdom of St. Hippolytus, painted with great skill. On left wing the donor H. Berthols and wife. Right wing—Judgment of St. Hippolytus. Above the triptych is the "Death of Mary," by J. Schoreel, 1529.

2. Second chapel. Crucifixion by Gerard Van der Meeren, 1500 (covered). 3. St. Dorothea and Rosalia offering flowers to the Virgin. J. Maes born 1660.

Now enter S. transept, lighted by a beautiful window with coloured glass (1866), representing the 12 apostles and 10 prophets. Three large pictures by J. Van Orley representing the Presentation, the Marriage Feast, and the Entrance of our Lord into Jerusalem. Below are 7 small pictures representing the 7 deeds of mercy, 4, 5, 6, and 7 by Josse Laval, 1551; and the rest by Van Oost, 1643. On the end wall is "Mary interceding with Christ," J. Van Oost, 1636; and the "Martyrdom of St. Barbara" by Cels Liranus 1809—she is about to be slain by her father. Small triptych by P. C. Claeissens 1009, representing the "Scourging of Christ," with the Donors on the wings. Now enter *Choir*.

On wall of screen of sanctuary opposite the last chapel are two pictures by E. Quellin: St. Augustine finding the child on the beach, and St.

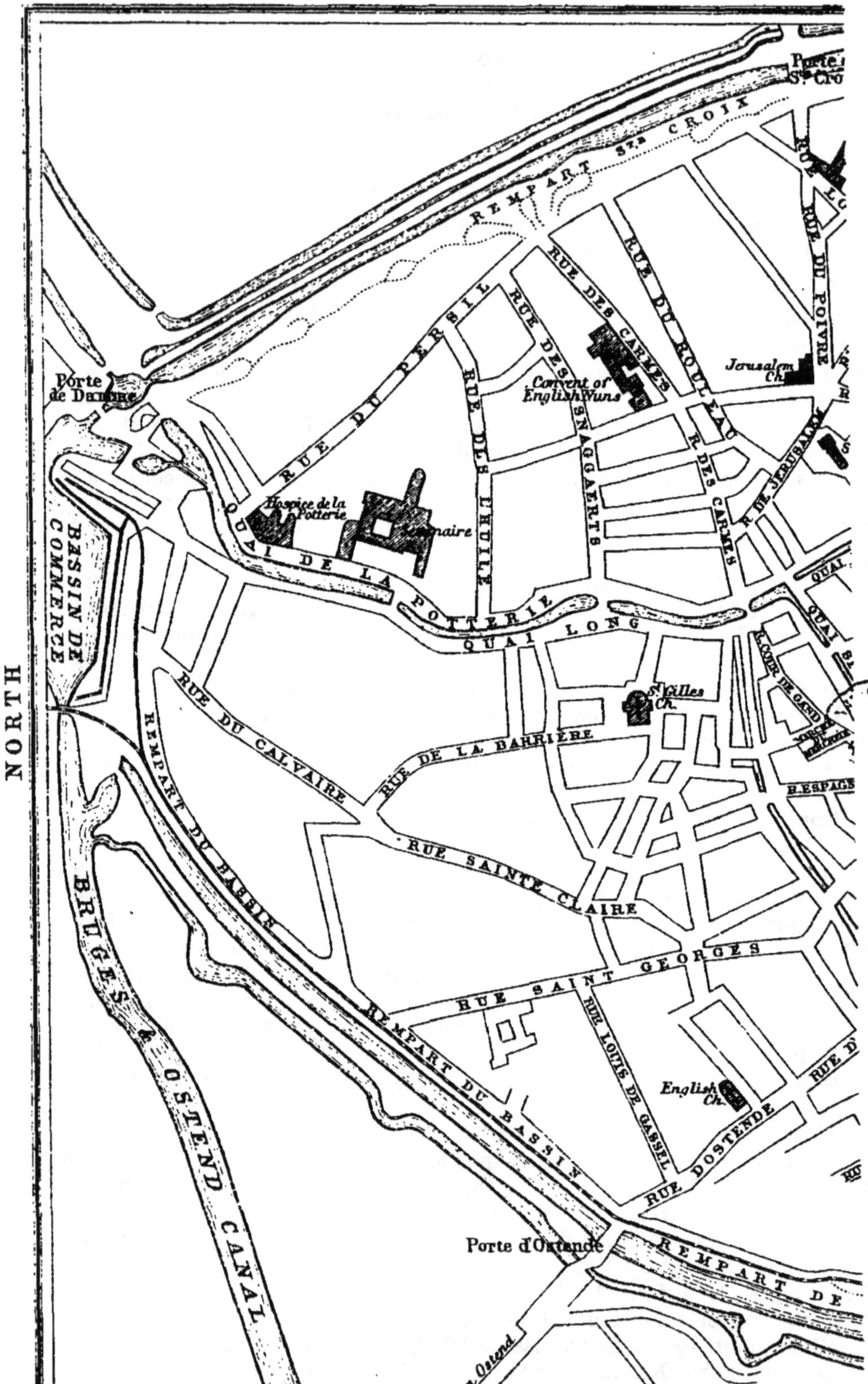
NORTH
REMPART Ste CROIX
RUE DU POIVRE
RUE DU ROULEAU
RUE DES CARMES
Jerusalem Ch.
Convent of English Nuns
RUE DES SNAGGAERTS
RUE DE L'HUILE
RUE DU PERSIL
Porte de Damme
Hospice de la Potterie
QUAI DE LA POTTERIE
QUAI LONG
R. DES CARMES
R. DE JERUSALEM
BASSIN DE COMMERCE
St Gilles Ch.
RUE DU CALVAIRE
RUE DE LA BARRIERE
REMPART DU BASSIN
RUE SAINTE CLAIRE
RUE SAINT GEORGES
BRUGES & OSTEND CANAL
RUE LOUIS DE GASSEL
English Ch.
RUE DOSTENDE
Porte d'Ostende
From Ostend

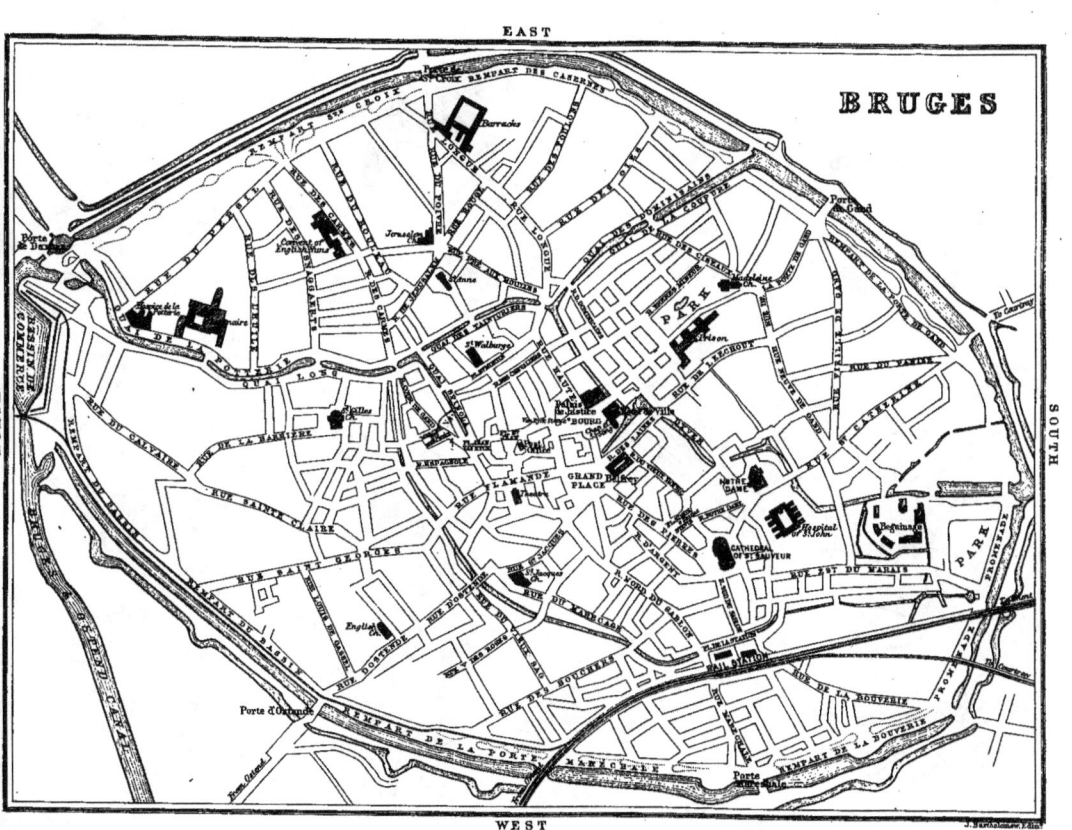

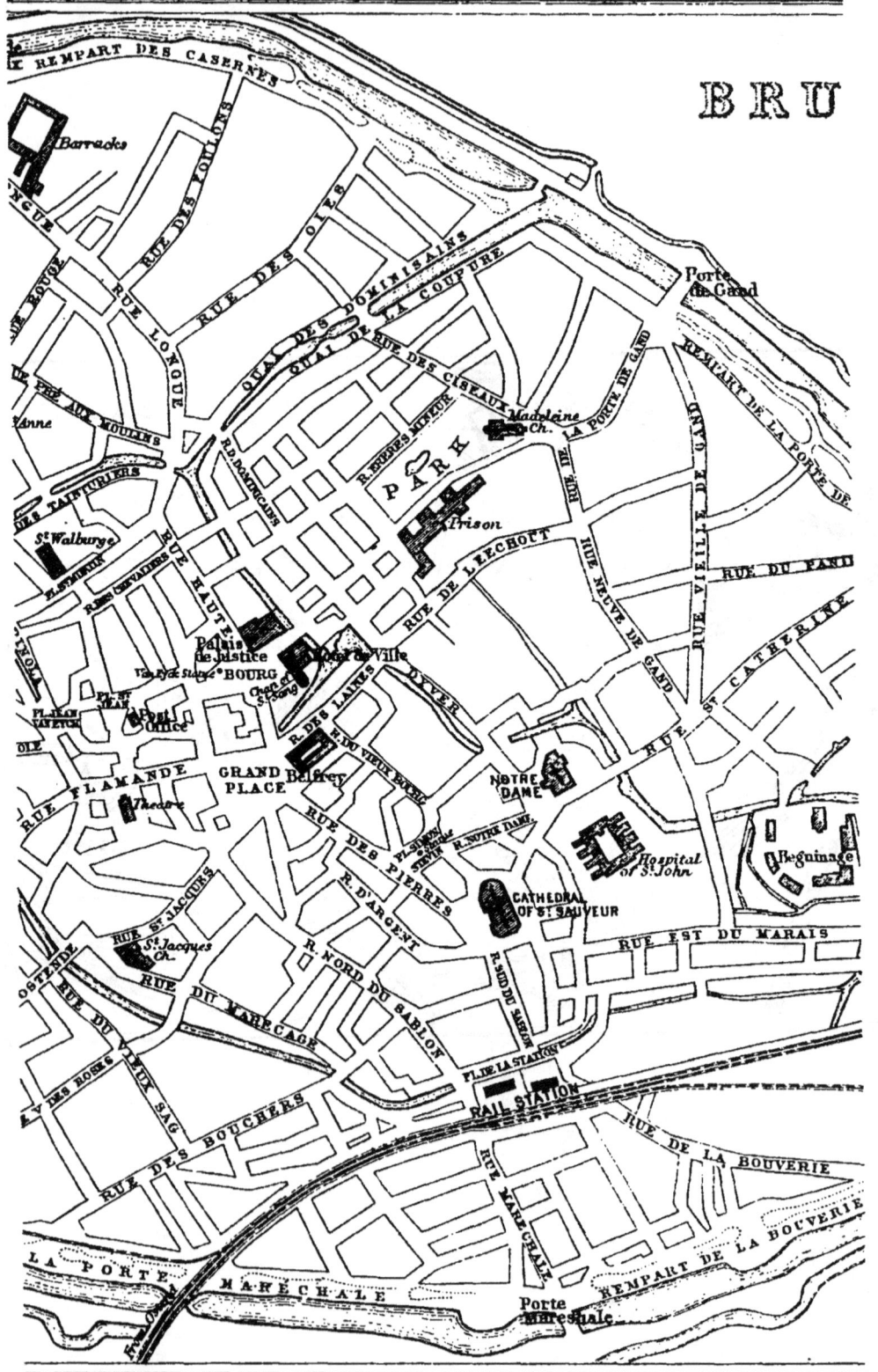

South Transept. Choir. North Transept.

Augustine washing the feet of Christ. Opposite this picture, on the chapel wall, is an "Ascension of Mary," by Baelen, 1640, the apostles regard with astonishment the flowers in the empty tomb. Next it is a large picture representing "Mary instructing St. Dominic to wear a scapulary as part of his dress," by E. Quellinus, 1687. Below in 3 divisions are the Nativity, Presentation, and Marriage of Mary, by Van der Straeten, 1618.

2. Second chapel in S. side of choir. Reredos by A. Janssens, "Adoration of the shepherds." Opposite, Consecration of St. Eloi (Eligius), unknown. By side of altar, mausoleum of Bishop Caïmo, 1775, by Pepers.

3. At foot of 2 windows, pictures by J. Van Oost, 1636. Left hand, "Jesus foretelling his crucifixion, death, and resurrection to Mary." Right hand, "Takes farewell of her." On floor, beautiful monumental tombstone inlaid with copper of Jan de Coudenbergh, 1525, secretary of Philippe le Beau. 4. Good glass by J. Bethune, 1861. Curious crucifixion and group against pier, to the memory of the Fortelboom family, 1660. 5. Chapel of Ste. Croix, behind high altar. Now enter *North Aisle* of Choir. 6. Reredos, "Child Jesus playing with shavings" by J. Van Oost. Opposite by Claeissens, 1609 (covered), "A descent from the Cross." On right wing, portraits of St. Philippe fourth bishop of Bruges and Charlemagne. Left wing, St. John the Baptist. Above this altar piece, "Flight to Egypt," a beautiful picture and the *chef-d'œuvre* of J. Van Oost, 1636. To view it properly enter corner by side of altar. In this chapel is the mausoleum with reclining statue in alabaster of Bishop Jean Carondelet, 1544. 7. Reredos, "Mary instructing St. Bernard how to found his order." Under a glass case, a piece of the woollen mantle of St. Bridget, 7th cent. 8. Chapel of Charles le Bon, 13th Count of Flanders, assassinated in the cathedral in 1127. The small shrine on the altar contains his bones, and a portrait of him. In the wall opposite is a sculptured slab of touchstone, which formed part of the reredos of the original altar.

Now enter the North Transept. The three large pictures here by Van Orley are a continuation of those in the S. transept, illustrating the life of Jesus. Below them are, Mary and St. Dominic by Roose, 1028, and a Crucifixion by Frickx, 1780.

The chapel that opens off the N. transept is the Shoemakers' Chapel, built by the corporation in 1400. On the reredos is a very fine "Miraculous" Byzantine crucifix, 12th or 13th? cent. On the wall are two richly wrought monumental plates of massive copper to the memory of W. Coopman, 1385, and M. Coppelle, 1452. On each side of the altar is a swing picture by F. Pourbus, 1608. On one side of the left swing picture is a portrait of St. Crispin, the patron of shoemakers, and on the other, those of various members of the guild of shoemakers. The other picture has on one side St. Crépinien, and on the other more portraits of shoemakers. On the altar and on the sculptured gate are represented high-heeled boots, the badge of shoemakers.

Now, to avoid confusion, return to the main entrance and walk up the N. aisle. Over door on north or left side are five groups of little figures in gilt wood, representing the sufferings of our Lord, 15th cent.

BRUGES. NORTH AISLE. ORGAN LOFT. NOTRE DAME.

First chapel N. side, P. Claeissens, a "Resurrection, 1585." 2. Apparition of Mary with the child to a bishop. 3. Baptistery. Large font of one block of white marble. On wall opposite, "Baptism of Constantine," by Maes, 1658. In a corner, within a box, is a crucifixion, painted in 1315. This is the most interesting and most ancient painting in the church, and should not be omitted. It was executed before the art of oil painting was understood, when colour was fixed by the white of eggs. The figures are not deficient in grace. Mary is in a faint at the foot of the cross; the high priest, on the other side of the cross, is exclaiming, "This is really the Son of God." The right end of the picture is filled up with St. Catherine, the "betrothed of J. C.," and the left by St. Barbara. The angels in the air have the form of fishes, and their wings resemble those of bats. In the interior of the chapel projects a curiously chiselled iron bracket. At the entrance are two handsome monumental slabs inlaid with brass; the slab on the right, the best in the church, commemorates De Munter and spouse, 1423, and the other on the left Liekerke and spouse, 1423.

From the Baptistery approach the sanctuary, separated from the transept by a very handsome organ loft on three arches, closed by a massive brass gate. The soffits of the arches are of sculptured white marble. Upon the centre is a magnificent colossal statue in white marble of the Creator, surrounded by cupid angels. The resurrection of Christ by A. Janssens forms the reredos of the high altar; below are Peter and Paul by Van Oost and the Saviour and Mary by Van Thulden.

On the right side of the altar is the superb mausoleum (1758) of H. Susteren, solaced while dying by Mary, and on the left that of J. B. Castillion (1758), solaced by John the Baptist, both by Pulinx 18th cent. Over the stalls are the escutcheons of the first 28 knights of the Order of the Golden Fleece, founded in Bruges on the 10th of January 1429. The pulpit resting on the head of St. Eligius, is by Tamine.

Near the cathedral is the Place Simon Stévin, named after the mathematician, born at Bruges in 1548, whose statue, by Simonis, stands in the centre. The fruit and vegetable market is held here.

A short way from the cathedral is the church of **Notre Dame**, built in the 13th, 14th, and 15th cents. The tower, with its modern spire 442 ft. high, was commenced in 1230. At the foot of it was built, in the 15th cent., the beautiful Gothic portal called "Het Paradys," now converted into the Baptistery chapel. In the interior are many art treasures. Fee to be shown the pictures, ½ fr. each, and the same for the mausoleums; but the services of the sacristan are necessary only for the mausoleums, as the chapel which contains them is locked and boarded.

The church is 240 ft. from W. to E., 165 wide, and 210 high. On the W. end wall, just at the entrance, is the first of four good pictures: An adoration of the shepherds by De Crayer in 1662; the lady in the rich dress is St. Helena, and near her is St. Dominic; then follows the picture of "Jesus in the house of the Pharisee" by Francken 1626; then a superbly coloured painting by G. Zegers 1630, representing an "Adoration of the Magi." The king in the red mantle and the soldiers behind

South Aisle and Transept.   Choir.

are attributed to Rubens. St. Joseph is a portrait of Rubens, and Mary of his first wife. Lastly, a triptych, of which the central painting, a "Calvary," is by Pourbus, and the wings by De Vos.

Now commence west end of South Aisle. First chapel right, a baptism. On pier opposite, "Holy Family," by J. Van Oost, 1648.

2. Reredos, "Esther before Ahasuerus," by L. Deyster, 1695. On the two piers opposite, the "Martyrdom of St. Laurent," by Kerckhove 1702, and St. Druon, by Herregouts 1717. Here also is the elaborately carved pulpit by Klauwaert, in 1739, elegantly poised on a sitting statue of Truth, and ascended by a triangular stair with a richly carved balustrade.

3. Chapel. Triptych, Madonna and donors, by Claeissens, 1584. On side wall another triptych, centre by Claeissens, wings by Pourbus 1579, with portraits of the family of Adriana de la Corona. 4. Chapel. Triptych on wall; centre, Transfiguration by Mabuse; wings by P. Pourbus in 1573, representing the family of Batz. On one wing is the father with seven sons, and on the other the mother with three daughters. The family likeness is skilfully preserved throughout. On the reredos of the altar is a picture by Maes, "Warned to flee to Egypt," an effective painting; the trustful expression of the sleeping child contrasts well with the alarm depicted in the face of Mary.

Enter South Transept. Two quaint and superbly coloured paintings on a gold ground by Bles 1520; an "Annunciation" and a "Nativity." Then on front wall, "Jesus giving up the ghost," a replica of the famous painting by Van Dyck 1626. Next it is a monumental slab inlaid with brass, commemorative of the family of Damhoudere, 1500. Nearly opposite the pictures of Bles, on a pier in the transept, is the "Betrothal of the child Jesus to St. Catherine" by Rottenhamer 1598. On the altar of this, the chapel of the Sacrament, is a most charming group in white marble, representing the Virgin and Child, attributed to Michael Angelo, but also, and with more probability, to Torrigiani, who, envious of the popularity of Michael Angelo, left Florence and sojourned in France, Flanders, and England. Mary is in an easy sitting posture, while the child is on foot leaning against his mother's knee. This valuable art treasure was presented to the church by Moscron in 1510. Above is a "Last Supper," by Pourbus. To the right of this altar is the mausoleum of Haveskerke and his two wives, one a native of Valladolid, the other of Ideghem. Above it is another "Last Supper."

Enter Choir, south side. On the left wall, the screen of the sanctuary, is the "Marriage of Christ with St. Catherine" by Quellinus 1656, an absurd picture. Next it, the "Crowning of St. Rosalia," one of the best pictures by J. Van Oost 1646; and then "St. Margaret contending with the Dragon" by J. Van Oost fils 1667. Opposite it, by Bernaerdt 1660, "King David, the Apostle Peter, and Mary Magdalene engaged in prayer." Higher up, on a group of cupids, the Virgin interceding before Christ. Near this picture is the door of the vestry, where those in search of the beadle may ring the bell over the door, provided worship is not being performed.

In the adjoining chapel, which is boarded up, are the magnificent

BRUGES.   NOTRE DAME.   MAUSOLEUM OF CHARLES THE BOLD.

Mausoleums of Charles le Temeraire or the Bold, slain at the battle of Nancy in 1477, p. 84, and of his only child, Marie, wife of the Emperor Maximilian of Austria, who died in her 25th year, in consequence of a fall from her horse when out hunting in 1482. They are both life-size statues in gilt copper, recumbent on black marble tables similarly ornamented, and of the same size—$8\frac{1}{4}$ ft. long, $4\frac{7}{8}$ wide, and $4\frac{3}{4}$ high. Mary wears the crown of Austria, her hands are folded, and over her shoulders is thrown a richly-embroidered mantle. At her feet are two small dogs, of which one is a pug. On the left side of the marble table is her genealogy, with the escutcheons of the father's side, and on the other those of her mother. Round the entire margin, in gilt scrolls, are her titles. This monument was executed by Jan de Beckere in 1495. As a work of art it is superior to her father's by the sculptor Jongelincx, erected in 1558 at the expense of Philip II., a descendant of Charles. The crumbling remains of the Duke were removed on the 20th Sept. 1550 from the church of St. George, in Nancy, and deposited here. On the mausoleum is his recumbent effigy in nearly full armour, his helmet and gauntlets lying at his feet. Round his neck is the chain of the Order of the Golden Fleece, while the figure of the lamb is worked into the embroidery of the mantle thrown over his shoulders. At his feet is the Lion of Flanders. Along the sides are rows of escutcheons emblazoned with the numerous quarterings of Duke Charles. At the head is an inscription which enumerates his glories and successive achievements. At the foot is another tablet, on which is the motto he adopted at the time of his accession, when the future was radiant with triumphs to be won :—" Je l'ay emprins ; bien en avienne !" I have undertaken it ; may good come of it !

Just outside this chapel, on the wall of the choir, is a picture representing the founding of the church of Sta. Maria Maggiore at Rome by Claeissens, 1575. The reredos of the end chapel in corner represents the " Vision of St. Antony of Padua," a very sweet picture by Berghe, 1780. The saint kisses the hand of the child. Behind the high altar is a wrought iron gate, well worthy of notice. The chapel opposite this gate has good modern glass. The reredos of the altar, containing 5 groups of little figures, is also modern, and was sculptured by Blanckaert.

A little farther, and against the choir wall, is a very beautiful **Mater Dolorosa**, by Mostaert 1534, of which however, the effect is weakened by the vignettes round the margin, representing her 7 griefs.

Near this, projecting from the wall, is a small Gothic gallery resembling a triple oriel window, in which was the church pew occupied by the Gruuthuyse family. It was connected with their palace, that beautiful

Hospital of St. Jean.

building with great peaked roofs and 5 large dormer windows, which still adjoins the great tower. Next it is the "Triumph of the Church" by J. Van Oost, 1652. Then follows, by Crayer, 1644, "Thomas Aquinas being delivered from prison." Opposite it by J. Van Oost 1640 "The tribute money." The man in the centre with his hand on his breast is Oost the father, and the youth with the red cap opposite turning round, is his son. Next it is Christ at Emmaus by M. Angelo da Caravaggio 1604. Below it are confessionals by Klauwaert and Bion. Within the chapel opposite is a triptych by Pourbus 1574—centre, an Adoration of the Shepherds—left wing, portraits of the donors the Damouders, who assisted greatly in the building of the church. On the right wing is Henry IV. Exterior of wings in grisaille, an Adoration and a Circumcision, displaying great freedom of design.

Enter N. Transept, in which is the Baptistery; and over the entrance to it the portraits of St. Francis and of St. Peter of Alcantara by Herregouts 1720. To the right is the Chapelle de la Croix with a series of pictures on the left side by Deyster representing the passion of our Lord; and on the other side pictures representing the mishaps and final storing in this church of a piece of the true cross. The door next the altar opens into the stair that leads up to the room where it is preserved.

Now go down to the W. end of N. aisle and walk up. First chapel, J. Maes, 1720, "St. Margaret on her knees before Mary and child." Second chapel, Reredos, 3 female saints by Gaeremyn, 1769. On altar marble Madonna. Opposite, by Nollet, "Elias seeing those who were pursuing him being destroyed by fire from Heaven." Third chapel, A large Madonna (1585) under a canopy. Opposite, "St. Anthony with his pig." Beyond is the N. transept with the baptistery. The sanctuary has nothing remarkable excepting the iron gate behind the altar. Opposite on pier, "Flight into Egypt," a very pleasing picture by De Laere, 1865. The armorial bearings over the stalls were put up in remembrance of the 11th chapter of the order of the Golden Fleece, held here in 1468.

Nearly opposite the entrance portal into Notre Dame is the celebrated **Hospital of St. Jean**, for the poor of both sexes. It contains a small gallery of paintings, and among them are the six choicest works of Hans Memlinck or Memling, d. 1495. Open from 9 to 12, and from 1 to 6 in summer. Fee each ½ fr., which give on leaving the room. A considerable part of the hospital, which is large and well managed, has to be traversed before arriving at the hall with the pictures. A man shows the way.

In the centre of the room is **No. 2, the Shrine of St. Ursula,** resembling a large Noah's ark, on which are depicted the principal events of the pilgrimage and martyrdom of St. Ursula, a daughter of one of the kings of the English heptarchy, and of the virgins who accompanied her. The number of them is generally believed to have been 11,000; but later writers, horrified at such a wholesale massacre, reduce the

Bruges. Shrine of Saint Ursula.

number to one, by stating that the name of the one attendant of the princess was Undecimilla, which, through a misconception of the manuscript, was read as if it were undecim millia. Others again maintain that the number was 11, and that the mistake arose from reading the abbreviation XI.M.V., as if it stood for Undecim millia virginum, instead of Undecim martyrum virginum, which is the opinion adopted by Memling, and consequently in all the pictures he represents St. Ursula with eleven virgins. The object of her pilgrimage was to get the Pope's aid, to save her from being married to a Pagan nobleman.

On one side of the roof of the ark or shrine is Mary in Heaven, being crowned by God and Jesus Christ. On the other, St. Ursula and her 11 virgins. Under the gable at one end is Mary between two kneeling nuns; at the other St. Ursula covering with her mantle her 11 virgins, but 10 only are seen; unless she herself be the eleventh.

On the side of the shrine is No. 1. The arrival at Cologne, the top of the cathedral most minutely painted is seen behind the gateway. 2d. Arrival at Bale, the spire of whose church is seen. 3d. Arrival at Rome and reception by the Pope (St. Cyriacus). In the corner is the baptism, partly by immersion, of some English knights who had accompanied them. 4th. Departure from Rome with the Pope and return to Bale, on one and the same compartment, where there is hardly room for the two boats. 5th and 6th. The return to Cologne and martyrdom. Throughout all those scenes, but especially in the 2 last, there runs an exquisite, almost ridiculous quaintness. The company seem to be awaiting with more than stoic indifference the piercing of the arrows or the slashing of the swords, while the executioners themselves perform their part in a careless, unimpassioned manner. All the faces are essentially Flemish and some of the virgins display to great advantage the pretty national feature of the slight curl in one or in both lips. The eyes are too like dolls' eyes. The execution evinces the most patient labour; indeed, even the minutest objects are finished with the careful precision of a complicate Chinese work.

At the inner end of the room is **No. 1**, a triptych painted in 1479. In the centre is the *betrothal* or *marriage* of the child Jesus with St. Catherine, who puts a ring on her finger, Mary in the meantime reading from a missal, probably a prayer; while an angel at the side chants and plays the organ, and St. John (a noble figure behind) blesses the cup. On the wings are the beheading of John; and St. John in Patmos. On the exterior, portraits of Hospitallers. **No. 3**, on the right side of the entrance door, a triptych painted in 1479, the

HOSPITAL OF ST. JEAN.

greatest of the works of Memling. The centre is an Adoration of the Magi, the dark brown face looking through the window is supposed to represent Memling himself. On the left wing is a Nativity, and on the right a Presentation, where the face of St. Anne is executed with wonderful skill. Projecting from the fourth window is **No. 4**, a diptych with Mary and Child, and portrait of a youth Newenhowen, for whom the picture was executed. Above it is No. 5, "Sibyl Sambetha," but most probably a portrait of some Flemish lady; she wears a high cap and white veil.

Projecting from the second window is **No. 6**, a triptych: centre, the body of Christ at foot of cross, John supporting the head and Mary in tears. In the distance men are seen preparing the tomb. On right wing St. Barbe; on the other Adrian Reins, the superior of the hospital for whom Memling painted the shrine of St. Ursula in 1480.

By the side of triptych No. 1, at inner end of room, are some of the best of the miscellaneous pictures. **No. 7**, Mary Magdalene at the feet of Christ. **No. 9**, The body of Christ on the knees of the Creator. **No. 10**, A holy family on a gold ground. On other side **No. 14**, A maternity. **No. 23**, Holy family. **No. 24**, Guardian angel. At left of entrance **No. 12**, a Descent from the Cross; and **No. 13**, St. Augustin, by Van Oost. Above No. 3, at right hand of entrance, **No. 11**, a Philosopher in contemplation, one of the best pictures by the elder Van Oost.

The old hospital is now unoccupied. The new buildings, in front of the entrance gate, extend round three sides of the garden. They contain 8 halls each with 24 beds. Four of the halls are allotted to females and 4 to men. Any one may walk round the wards. The patients are nursed by the nuns of the order St. Augustin.

To go to the Beguinage from St. Jean, continue to the right, and having crossed the small bridge take the 2d street right, the Rue de la Vigne. At the foot of the street is the entrance. The establishment contains on an average about 20 nuns. In the private chapel, diametrically across the square, is the finest piece of *memorial brass* in Belgium. It is to the memory of a nun, dates from 1444 and is only 18 inches long and 10 inches wide. Fee ½ fr. The church of the Beguinage, which is always open, has a handsome altar of black marble, supported on 4 spiral columns of white marble. The virgin and the fluttering angels are also of white marble.

From the hospital of St. Jean return to the cathedral and walk down the broad street the Rue Sud du Sablon to the

Bruges.   Les Halles with Belfry and Chimes.

Grande Place, with on one side the Halles and their fine Belfry. At No. 18, at the foot of the Rue St. Amand, is the tall brick house with mullioned windows, in which, it is said, Charles II. resided during part of his exile. No. 19, at the opposite corner, occupies the site of the Crænenburg, in which the Emperor Maximilian was forced to remain 12 days in 1488 by the citizens of Bruges, till he would solemnly swear to renounce all claim to the guardianship of his son Philip, heir to the crown of the Netherlands. The **Halles**, finished in 1565, form a picturesque rectangular edifice 142 ft. wide and 276 ft. long. From the centre of the façade rises a handsome square belfry 354 ft. The S. and E. sides are occupied by the meat market; the roofs are of brick, vaulted, and the halls dry and well ventilated. On the first floor is the civic reception-room, which extends the whole length of one side. The belfry should be ascended by all who are able, on account of the excellent bird's-eye view and the very interesting chimes. Having entered the court, ascend to the first story by the stair to the right, where will be found the bell-pull for the concierge of the tower; fee 10 c. each. From this 86 stone steps lead up to the first room; 108 more to the commencement of the wooden steps, and of them 132 lead up to the room of the keepers. From the small glass windows of their room are admirable views of the town and neighbourhood. Every Sunday, Wednesday, and Saturday, at ¼ past 11 A.M., there is a chime performance here; the player beats the keys with his closed fists. 19 steps below is the room with the mechanism, including a huge musical-box-like cylinder of copper weighing 19,166 lbs., and punched with 30,500 square holes, which cost 6d. each. This cylinder, which is made to revolve by a suspended weight of 4000 lbs., puts in motion the hammers of the chimes. 13 steps above the keeper's room is the open vaulted chamber in which is suspended the Bourdon or great tocsin bell, weighing 19,000 lbs., originally in the tower of Notre Dame. From this part there is another splendid view. 26 steps higher is the chamber containing the chiming bells, 48 in number, and weighing collectively 55,166 lbs. The largest of them weighs 11,589 lbs., and the smallest 12 lbs. They ring at every quarter. Three bells are wanting to complete the four octaves. These bells were cast by Jacques Dumery, and are composed of ¾ copper and ¼ tin, and were rung for the first time on the 15th August 1748. The face of the clock is 19 ft. in diameter, and the figures 3 ft. long.

From the N. corner of the Halles a narrow busy street leads directly to the **Place du Bourg**, in which is situated the Hotel de Ville. To the right of it is the Chapelle du Saint-Sang, with in the corner the

Hotel de Ville.

beautiful entrance into the crypt. To the left of the Hotel de Ville are the Maison de l'Ancien Greffe (restored) and the Palais de Justice. In the promenade under the trees is the statue of Jan van Eyck, born at Maaseyck in 1381, and died at Bruges 9th July 1440. In this promenade a flower market is held every Friday.

The first stone of the **Hotel de Ville** was laid by Louis de Male, Count of Flanders, in 1376. The façade, 85½ ft. wide and 62½ ft. high, is occupied by six elegant windows extending from nearly the ground up to the eaves of the roof. Two neat Gothic doorways encroach upon the length of each of the two windows next but one to the corner, without marring the symmetry or injuring the general effect. A closed or crenellated balustrade conceals the peaked roof behind, with its decorated spiral chimneys. From each corner, and likewise from the centre, rises a square spired tower of the same breadth and similarly ornamented as the space between each window, of which it may be considered a prolongation. In four stages, across the whole breadth of the façade, are 48 statues in niches under delicately-sculptured canopies. At the base of the first tower, left hand (towards the Palais de Justice), the statues represent Robert-le-Frison, Robert de Jerusalem, and Baudouin à la Hache. Under the centre tower Charles le Bon and William of Normandy. Under the right corner tower, Thierri, Philippe, and Marguerite d'Alsace.

In the second row are 15 statues, commencing again at the left—Baudouin and Jeanne of Constantinople; Ferrand of Portugal and Marguerite de Dampierre; Gui de Dampierre and Robert de Bethune; Louis de Crecy and Louis de Male; Philippe de Bourgogne and Margaret de Male; Jean sans Peur and Philippe le Bon; Charles le Temeraire; Maximilian and Marie de Bourgogne. The third row has also 15 statues—Philippe le Beau and Marguerite d'Autriche; Charles V. and Philippe II.; Philippe III. and Albert; Isabella and Philippe IV.; Charles II. and Philippe V.; Charles IV. and Maria Theresa; Joseph II., Leopold I., and François I. On the basement is ranged the fourth row—The Virgin of Ardenburg and Baudouin Bras de Fer, David, Solomon, Daniel, Job, Mary, Gabriel, Jeremiah, and Zachariah.

Within are some indifferent pictures. The most interesting is a painting by Dobbelaare (1857) representing the finding of the body of Charles le Temeraire after the battle of Nancy in 1477.

In the upper story, recently repaired, is the town library, containing 20,000 vols. and 600 MSS. Opposite stood the church of St. Donat, in which Van Eyck was buried. His statue marks the spot.

BRUGES.   PALAIS DE JUSTICE.   CHAPELLE DU SAINT SANG.

The handsome house next the Hotel de Ville is the **Ancien Greffe**, now the Police-Office, built in 1537 and repaired and restored in 1880.

Adjoining is the **Palais de Justice**, of which the back, the part towards the canal, belongs to the "Palais du Franc," built in 1521; the rest was constructed in 1727. In the hall where the magistrates meet, called the Chambre Collegiale, is the beautiful chimneypiece of touchstone, executed in 1529 in honour of Charles V. It was designed by L. Blondeel and G. Beaugrand and sculptured by H. Glosencamp, A. Rasch, and R. Smidt. Below the shelf are little cupids and four narrow pure white marble panels, representing in relief the history of Susanna. The wall above, from the chimneypiece to the ceiling, is panelled with carved oak. In the centre is the statue of Charles V., to the right those of Charles le Temeraire and his third wife, Margaret of England, and on the other side Maximilian and Marie de Bourgogne—the Emperor's paternal and maternal ancestors. To show the chimneypiece the concierge charges $\frac{1}{2}$ fr. each. A large picture by Gilles Thillerugghe represents a meeting of the magistrates in the olden time in this room. The tapestry is modern, but made in imitation of what formerly covered the room. Adjoining this hall, in the former magistrates' chapel, are the archives, including 10,000 charters and deeds, of which the earliest date from the 11th cent.

Behind the Hotel de Ville is the fish market, and a little farther the town park and prison, and the church of the Madeleine. The park, though small, is well laid out.

To the right of the Hotel de Ville is the elegant Gothic façade (1533) of the **Chapelle du Saint Sang**, composed of two parts—the lower chapel or crypt of St. Basil, founded by Baudouin Bras de Fer in 865 and rebuilt by Thierry of Alsace in 1150. The upper chapel was reconstructed in 1824. Open every Friday from 6 to 12, when a constant stream of people flock to the church to kiss the crystal cylinder enclosing the bottle containing about an ounce of the blood of "Jesus Christ." It is held by a priest sitting on a dais, who wipes the bottle after every kiss. Both the portal and the staircase leading up to the church are of the 15th cent. The high altar is of stone, designed by Bethune d'Ydewalle and sculptured by Abbeloos in 1858; the pulpit is in the form of a globe; the walls are adorned with mural paintings, and hung with some very good pictures of which the most important is a "Descent from the Cross" a triptych by Gerard David. The painted windows are by Pluys, Bethune, and Dobbelaere, and represent in colour the Burgundian princes, whose statues are on the Hotel de Ville.

Shrines—Saint Jacques.

Between the pulpit and the altar is the door opening into the Sacristia. Here, in the wall, are two iron safes. In the safe to the left is preserved the gold and silver shrine under a canopy of gold and silver executed by Jean Crabbe in 1617. It is a delicate and precious piece of work studded with jewels, among which is a very fine emerald. On the three pinnacles above the canopy are 4 solid gold statuettes; and under the canopy, over the shrine, a miniature crown said to have been presented by Mary of Burgundy.

In the adjoining iron safe is a solid silver shrine weighing 25 lbs., with 16 statuettes illustrative of incidents connected with the holy blood, brought in 1149 by Thierry d'Alsace, 15th Count of Flanders, from the Holy Land, of which this is the real shrine. Into the gold shrine it is put only on great occasions. The bottle containing the blood is about 5 in. long and sealed; the blood is of a lightish yellow. The crystal cylinder enclosing the bottle is about 8 in. long, and ornamented with gems (?) set in gold at each end.

In the lower chapel, entered from the square, is the miraculous image of the virgin of the blood, also visited on Fridays.

S.W. from the Grande Place, by the Rue St. Jacques, is the church of St. Jacques, consecrated in 1469; resembling a picture gallery in the interior. As nearly all the pictures are well-known Scripture subjects, with the names of the artists in gilt letters on the frames, it is unnecessary to specify them. On the right hand, S. side, there is a series of panel pictures by Nollet 1694 and above them some large pictures by Achtschelling 1694, Devisch and L. Deyster 1694. All the chapels are in the choir. First chapel right of altar, large terracotta figures representing Mary, St. Anne and child. On wall, an inlaid monumental slab. 2. Chapel. Reredos, Last Day, with the Trinity and Mary in the centre; an ancient painting. On walls paintings by Kerckhove 1707; above, ancient triptych. 3. A very small chapel. On reredos, valuable Lucca della Robbia ware, and the tomb, in two stages, of the Chevalier Ferry le Gros and his two wives, in painted stone, 16th cent. The chapel to the right of the altar contains pictures by P. Pourbus d. 1584, Coxcie d. 1692, and Bockhorst d. 1668; and on the reredos, *St. Leonard, by Macs, well executed.

Returning to the main entrance, and walking up the N. aisle, we have a continuation of the panel pictures by Nollet and over them large paintings by A. Coxcie, Vleys, Deyster and Duvenée. In the first chapel left, on reredos, a St. Antony by Duvée, and against the wall 7 handsome inlaid monumental brasses. The first two are large and

BRUGES.   PRINZENHOF.   ACADEMIE DES BEAUX ARTS.

beautiful brass plates to the memory of Pedro de Valencia d. 1615, and his companion Mlle. Marie Bailleul d. 1599. Then follow, one to the memory of Catherine "hija de Coland d'Ault," 1461 ; and another very large inlaid black marble slab to Francisco de la Puebla d. 1577, and his wife Maria de Ferry, d. 1572. Second chapel left, on reredos, a Christ crucified, surrounded with souls from Purgatory, Mary on one side interceding, by Bernaerts. Triptych by Lanceloot Blondeel (rare).

On the reredos of the chapel, immediately to the left of the high altar, is Mary entering the temple, by Van Oost, and near it the raising of Lazarus, by Grebber, 1623. On the left wall of this chapel are several pictures by Visch, Pourbus, J. Van Oost, Herregouts, and Claeissens, 1556. The reredos of the high altar is a richly-coloured Adoration of the Magi, by Hondhorst, between two spiral veined marble columns, and a border of foliage and fruits in white marble.

The sanctuary is separated from the nave by a handsome organ loft in black marble, with columns of veined marble. The pulpit, 17th cent., is a superb piece of elaborate sculpture.

The large corner house, No. 19 Rue Marécage, beyond the eastern entrance of St. Jacques, occupies the site of the Prinzenhof, the ancient palace of the Counts of Flanders, in which Charles the Bold was married to Margaret of York, sister of Edward IV., in 1468. In it also Philip le Bel, the father of Charles V., was born. Near the Hotel du Commerce is the house of Count Egmont. A little beyond St. Jacques is the English chapel, service at 11 A.M. and 7 P.M.

Leaving the Grande Place by the Rue Flamande we have on the left the theatre, whence the first street right leads to the **Academie des Beaux Arts**, in the house of what composed formerly the assembly rooms of the citizens or the Poorters Loodze, built about the 14th cent., and containing a small Picture Gallery. Free on Sundays between 11 and 1. At other times ½ fr. In the square in front is a statue of John Van Eyck, the inventor of the art of painting in oil. In the first two rooms are modern paintings and charters belonging to the Academy. In the tribune of the large room are portraits of Academicians, by Odevaere. Round the walls are hung among other pictures landscapes by Maygret, P. J. Clays, E. Pratere, C. J. Vernet, d. 1789, Achtschellinck, d. 1631, Goyen, 1656, P. Brueghel, d. 1568. Village festival, J. Van Oost, d. 1671. Portraits, etc., Minderbout, d. 1796. The canal basin of Bruges, and Mary, Jesus and John by Lombardo.

In the centre of the inner room, left side, is one of the best pictures, painted by J. Van Eyck in 1436, for the Canon Van der Paelen, who figures at the right of the picture on his knees, with an eye-glass in his hand. By his side is St. George in full armour lifting his helmet in honour of the child Jesus on the knees of Mary, whom he regards with wonder and admiration. To the left is St. Donatus, dressed as an archbishop, the best figure in the group. Near this is the portrait of the wife of Van Eyck, painted by himself. She has the pretty Flemish slightly protuberant under lip, and wears large chignons in her hair. Beside it is a head of Christ, painted by him in 1440.

To the left of Van Eyck's large picture is a triptych by Gerard David. Centre, Baptism of Christ: on one wing St. John and the donor, Trompes and his son; on the other, the wife and 4 daughters. The charm of the picture is the landscape; observe the ivy on the tree. On the opposite side is a triptych by Memling in 1484, one of his best. St. Christopher carrying the child Jesus on his shoulders across the Jordan. Right, St. Benedict; left, St. Egidius with the donors. At the farthest off end of the room are excellent portraits by Pourbus in 1551 of a man and his wife.

Ste. Walburge, St. Anne, Church of Jerusalem, and English Nuns.

From the front of the theatre by the Rue St. Jean are three churches, almost in a straight line—Ste. Walburge, St. Anne, and the Church of Jerusalem. A little to the N. of the church of Jerusalem is the church of the English Augustinian nuns. Ste. Walburge was built in 1641. The chancel is separated from the nave in its entire breadth by a sculptured white marble balustrade. A resurrection by Suvée forms the reredos of the high altar. The reredos of altar to the right represents Christ appearing to Ignacio Loyola; and of the one to the left, Mary received into heaven by the Trinity, both by E. Quellyn. There are besides pictures by Odevaere 1812, Pourbus, and Van Oost.

The church of St. Anne is easily recognised by its tall spire and tapering roof. The interior is lined with wainscoting and covered with pictures. The confessionals are by Desangher and Berger in 1677. Over the entrance is an immense picture of "The last day" by Herregouts in 1685. Commencing at the right hand we have an Ecce Homo by J. Cobrysse 1691. An angel dressing the leg of St. Roch by Heyden, 1680. Next pulpit "Holy family;" and on other side "Christ among the Doctors" by J. Clef 1692. A balustrade in carved oak and a high organ loft (1642) in black marble, supported by veined marble columns with decorations in white marble, separate the chancel from the nave.

Church of Jerusalem. English Nuns.

In this jubé are two altars, the reredos of the one is Mary regarding the child Jesus by *De Roose, and the other the Virgin and Jesus surrounded by angels by V. Oost. The reredos of the high altar is a very large "Holy Family" by Gaeremyn, by whom are also the three landscapes on each side, illustrating scenes in the Old and New Testament. To the left is a Circumcision, and St. Anne teaching Mary to read by Van Oost.

The **Church of Jerusalem** was built in 1430 by Opice Adornes, after the model of the church of the Holy Sepulchre at Jerusalem. In the centre of the church is his black marble tomb, with that of his wife Isabelle Braderick. {The reredos of the high altar is of stone, and on it are represented the different instruments connected with the passion of our Lord. Behind is another chamber, with a low opening in the corner, leading into the representation of the tomb of Jesus. The body is life size, made of wax.

To the N. of this church, in the Rue des Carmes, is the Augustinian convent of **English Nuns**, founded in Bruges in 1621. Their number is generally about 30, among whom there are 8 or 10 Belgian sisters. Their school is one of the best on the Continent for the daughters of Roman Catholic parents. They take only 50 pupils, and that number is generally nearly complete. The children are well fed, well housed, and well taught, according to Roman Catholic ideas. They speak French and English on alternate days. The annual charge is £40, which includes board and all the usual branches of education. Music, drawing, and dancing are extras. Those who remain in the school during the holidays pay no more. They have not only large courts and a large kitchen garden and orchard within their walls; but also a handsome church by Pulincx 1739, containing paintings by Murillo, Velasquez, and Andrea del Sarto. The high altar, made in Rome and composed of precious marbles, is not well placed. Neither has it the usual images, which may be out of respect to the second commandment.

At Bruges it is said the first pendulum clocks were made.

Three m. N. from Bruges on the canal leading to Sluys is the decayed village of Damme, once the port of Bruges. The church of Ste. Marie, belonging to the 13th cent., contains some inlaid monumental slabs and an old rood-loft. The Halles, built in 1468, were restored in 1860. Off Sluys, in 1340, Edward III. gained a naval victory over the French.

Bruges to Dunkerque.

By Thourout, Lichtervelde, Dixmude, Furnes, and Adinkerke.

BRUGES
MILES FROM
See Map, pages 1 and 154.
DUNKERQUE
MILES TO

BRUGES. 11¼ m. N. from Bruges is Thourout, in ancient $\overset{50\frac{1}{4}}{\sim}$ times the site of the grove of the Pagan divinity Thor. Pop. 8150. Two good inns close to station. Large institution of St. Joseph. 1½ m. W. are the ruins of the castle of Wynendaele.

$\overset{14\frac{1}{4}}{\sim}$ LICHTERVELDE, pop. 6000. Here change carriages for $\overset{36}{\sim}$ Dunkerque. The train now passes by the stations of Cortemarck (where carriages are sometimes changed), Handzaeme, Zarren, and Essen.

$\overset{25\frac{3}{4}}{\sim}$ DIXMUDE, pop. 4000, on the Yser. *Inns:* opposite station, $\overset{24\frac{1}{4}}{\sim}$ *Hotel de Dixmude. In the "Place" the Hotel de la Poste. The conspicuous building opposite is the Hotel de Ville, 1879. Behind is the handsome church of St. Nicolas 1530, with a low square tower containing a sweet-sounding chime of bells. Fronting the nave is a very beautiful jubé or organ-loft, one mass of lace-like sculpture, with 15 statuettes in niches on the side towards the nave, and 8 on the side towards the altar. On the reredos is a very beautiful, though somewhat faded, "Adoration of the Magi" by Jordaens. The composition differs considerably from the generality of the pictures of that subject. Next the altar is a lofty tabernacle in black marble, with white marble statuettes. The archery pole is in a green a little beyond. Good butter.

9½ m. north by rail from Dixmude is Nieuport-Ville, and 2 miles farther **Nieuport-Bains.**

NIEUPORT-VILLE, pop. 2500. *Inn:* H. Pelican, where the coach that runs between Ostende and Furnes changes horses. Nieuport is 11¼ m. from Ostende, and 6¼ from Furnes. Fare, 1 fr. 80 c. This coach starts from the post-office in Ostende. About half-way between Nieuport and Ostende is the clean little village of Middelkerke, with several little inns. It is also a small bathing-station with a good beach. The village church is very large. The road between Ostende and Nieuport extends along the base of the sandhills of the coast.

In the same " Place" as the Pelican, are also the *Inns* (Estaminets) A la Fortune and A l'Union. In the "Place" is also a curious and interesting building Les Halles, constructed about the middle of the 13th century, but in a state of decay. On each corner are battlemented turrets, and over the main entrance a square tower. In the Place side of the edifice are curious canopied recesses like chapels. Behind it is the church, also a large building. Nieuport being situated near the mouth of the Yser and a system of canals, has an important series of locks for regulating the water. Near the locks is the archers' pole.

Two miles by rail from Nieuport-Ville is **Nieuport-Bains**, a quiet but excellent sea-bathing station, with a long jetty, a digue 34 yards wide, and a clean smooth beach provided with machines. On the Digue there are two first-class hotels—the Grand Hotel de la Digue, pension 9 to 11, and the Grand Hotel des Bains, pension 8 to 11 francs. Behind them, but within sight of the sea, are the second-class houses, the Hotel des Arcades, pension $6\frac{1}{2}$ frs., and the H. de la Mer, pension 6 frs. These prices include service, breakfast, dinner and supper.

The bathing tickets cost 60 c., but if 25 be taken 50 c. each.

The great defect here, as well as at Ostende, Blankenberg, and Heyst, is the want of trees. This station, quite of modern date, without any old town, is situated on sandy hills at the mouth of the Yser.

$34\frac{3}{4}$ **FURNES**, pop. 4700. *Inns*: immediately opposite the station is the H. de France. In the town, at the first bridge, the H. du Nord. In the "Place" the H. Noble Rose. Coach for Ostende, $17\frac{1}{2}$ m. N., starts from the Estaminet near the H. de France. Fare 3 frs. Time 3 hrs. Furnes is a pretty little town on the ramification of the canals to Dunkerque, Bergues, and Nieuport. The greater part of the old ramparts has been converted into avenues of elms, while those portions of the ancient walls still standing, protect gardens, or have become incorporated into houses. Near the "Place" is the church of St. Nicolas (14th cent.), with a large square tower. Below the pulpit is a very pretty group, life size, in white marble, representing St. Nicolas teaching three children. In the "Place" is the Hotel de Ville. Behind it is a very handsome belfry, unfortunately not sufficiently exposed to view. Near it is Ste. Valburge, commenced on a grand scale in the 15th cent., but little more than the choir finished. The organ-loft, which shuts off the choir, has on one side a group representing the disrobing of our Lord, and on the other an entombment—both badly done. The organ case, the pulpit, and the gates and stalls of the sanctuary (all close together), are of tastefully carved oak. Under the pulpit is St. John, life size, writing the Book of Revelation.

$38\frac{1}{4}$ **ADINKERKE**, pop. 1800. Belgian custom-house station. 12 Opposite station *Inn*: Pavillon Belge. $2\frac{1}{4}$ m. N. by a pleasant road, between poplars, is the sea-bathing station of La Panne, pop. 500.

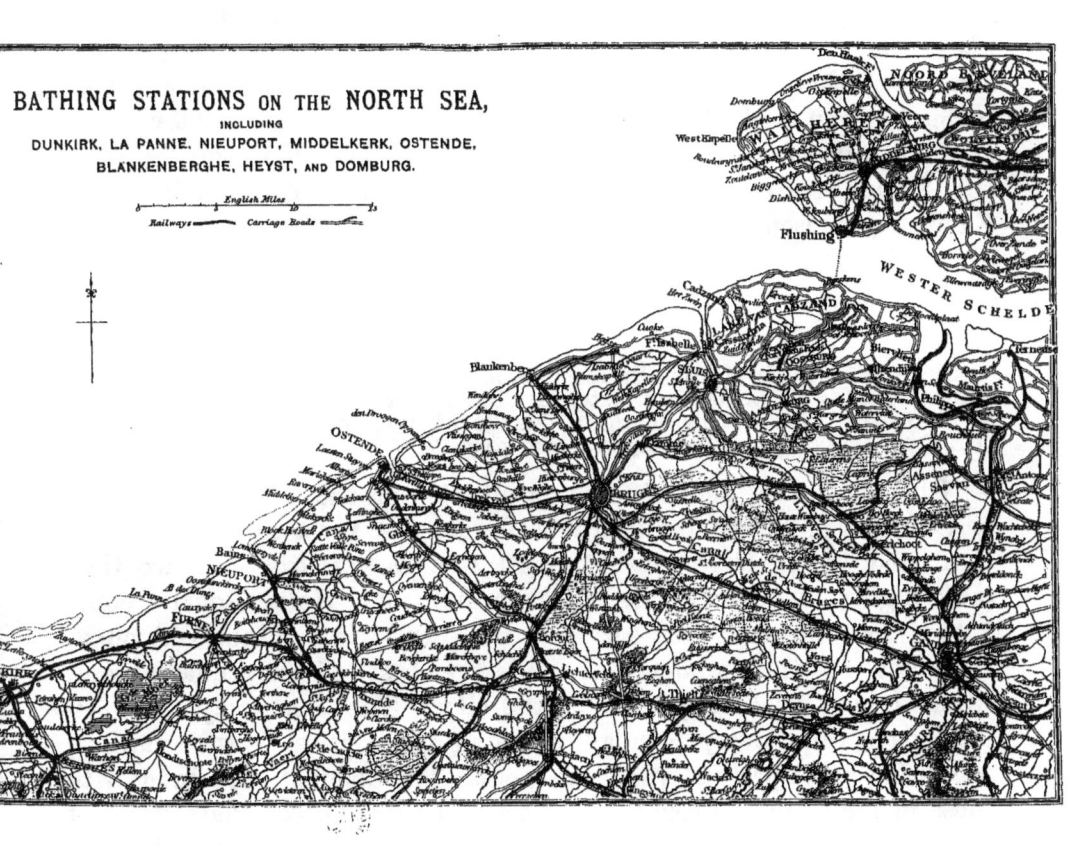

LA PANNE. GHENT. HOTELS.

Inns: at the entrance into the village are the Pelican and the Esperance. Pension in both 5½ frs. Much better situated, and a better house is the *G. H. Panne-Bains, pension 5½ to 6½ frs. A path through the garden leads across the sand dunes to the beach. Coach three times a week between Furnes and La Panne.

La Panne is a straggling village, nestling behind the sand eminences or dunes of the coast, which here are covered with more than the usual amount of verdure. A considerable fishing trade is carried on in this place; but as there is no harbour the boats lie out at anchor, or, in stormy weather, are hauled up on the beach. The beach is smooth and perfectly clean. Machines, with dress and two towels, cost 50 c.

Four miles from Adinkerke is the little village of Ghyvelde, with the French custom-house. The train, after passing the villages of Zuydcote, Roosendael, and Tente-Verte, arrives at Dunkerque, p. 26.

GHENT.

Ghent is 35½ m. N.W. from Brussels, 31 m. S.W. from Antwerp, 26 m. E. from Bruges, and 14½ m. farther from Ostende. Ghent is 26 m. S. from Terneuzen, and 65 m. N. from Charleroi by Sottegem, Grammont, and Enghien. Ghent is 68 m. N.E. from Dunkerque. See Map, p. 1 and page 154.

Ghent or Gand, pop. 122,000, is situated on the Schelde or Escaut and the Lys; whose ramifications divide the town into 26 islands, connected by 42 large and 46 small bridges. *Hotels:* the two that rank highest are the H. de la Poste and the *Hotel Royal (rooms 3 to 4 frs., dinner 4 frs., service 1 fr.), both in the **Place d'Armes**, the best of the promenades, and the best of the squares, and situated in a healthy quarter of the city. The band plays here on feast days, and every Sunday morning there is a flower market, consisting principally of plants in pots. The bouquets are inferior to those in the Grande Place of Brussels and those in the Place Verte of Antwerp. The best restaurants and cafés are also in this " Place." At No. 1, the site now occupied by the Café des Arcades, stood the house in which the brothers Eyck lived, and where they painted their famous picture. Opposite the Hotel Royal is a cab-stand, and in the immediate neighbourhood the theatre, the post and telegraph offices, the Palais de Justice, and the University. *Other hotels:* at the east end of St. Nicolas, and within 200 yds. of the Marché aux Grains, is the Lion d'Or, a comfortable house. Rooms from 2½ frs., dinner 2 frs., coffee, bread and butter 1 fr. By the south side of the church is the H. Comte Egmont, a smaller house. In front of the church, in the Marché aux

Ghent. Railway Stations. St. Bavon.

Grains, is the Hotel Vienne, a large and a good house, most conveniently situated for taking advantage of the trams. In the Rue du Miroir, the H. du Miroir, dinner 1½ frs.

The **Brussels railway station**, or the Station de l'Etat, is at the south side of the town, near the zoological gardens. In front of the arrival side are a cab-stand and the hotels Belle Vue, Cour d'Autriche, Pomme d'Or, Le Duc. A little way up the street to the right is the H. Grande Cour Royale, a plain, quiet house. From the departure side start the trams for the Marché aux Grains, which those carrying only handbags may take advantage of, fare 3 sous.

North from the Brussels railway station is the **Antwerp station** near the docks, the Grande Béguinage, and the ruins of the abbey of St. Bavon. In front are a cab-stand and the Hotels Leopold II. and the Cour Royale. From the corner starts a tram for the Marché aux Grains, but change at St. Jacques. Cab-fares, close cabs—the course 1 fr.; the first hour 1½ fr.; the others 1 fr. Open cabs ½ fr. more. The men carry their tariffs.

Principal sights—The Cathedral, with the picture of the Adoration of the Lamb, p. 156. The Belfry, p. 160. The exterior of the Hotel de Ville, p. 161. Van Dyck's picture in the church of St. Michael, p. 163. The Marche du Vendredi, p. 165. The Grande Béguinage, p. 167.

26 m. N. from Ghent by rail is Terneuzen, whence steamers to Flushing or Vlissingen, on the other side of the river. The great Ghent canal enters the sea near Terneus or Terneuzen.

Cathedral of St. Bavon, originally the church of St. Jean. The crypt below the choir dates from the 9th cent., but enlarged and repaired in 1228. Hubert Van Eyck (1426) and his sister Margaret were buried in it, but there is now no trace of their tombs. The choir was built in 1274, the nave and transepts in 1533, and the great square tower, 297 ft. high, in 1534. A series of 446 steps lead up to the terrace, whence there is an extensive view. Fee for from 1 to 4, 2 frs.; more than 4 ½ fr. each. Fee to visit the pictures in the church 1 fr. each, but less for a party. The beadles will be found in the sacristy; the door is in the north transept. Others offer their services, but they are of no use, as they cannot open the closed pictures. Within the left-hand entrance door, below the tower, is the font at which Charles V. was baptized. The globular basin alone is ancient. He was born on the 24th February 1500, in the new palace of the Counts of Flanders, of which no vestiges remain. The church shuts at 12 and opens again at 2. When shut knock loudly at entrance below the tower.

The Interior of the church is imposing. The nave is 390 ft. from W. to E., and the transept 150 ft. from N. to S., and the roof 100 ft. high. The windows, of which a few contain good glass, have quatrefoil and

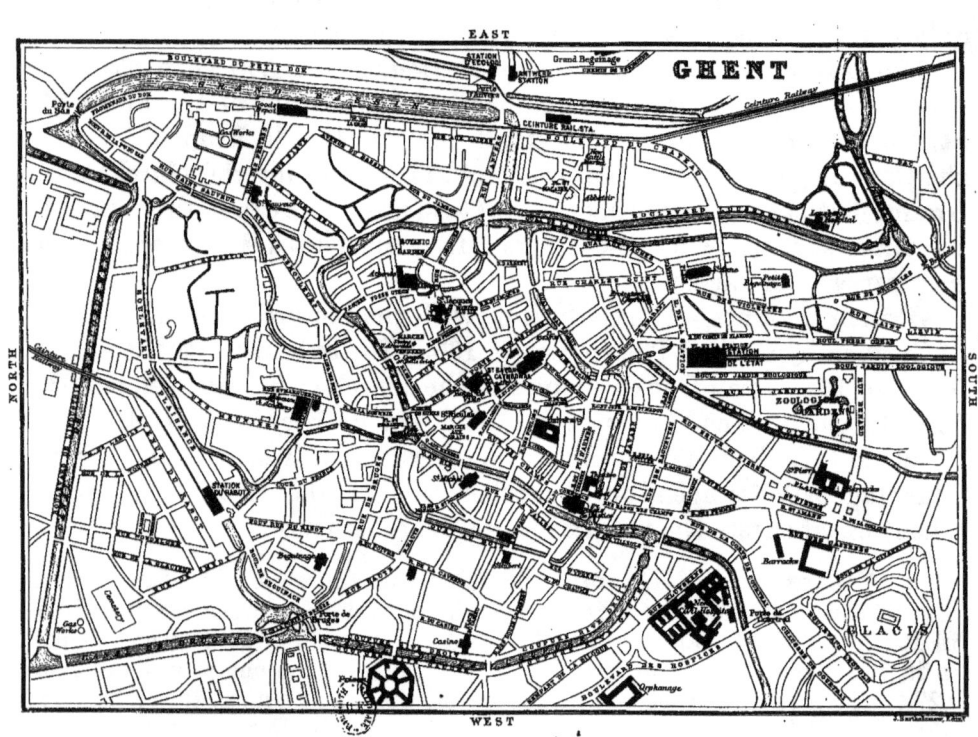

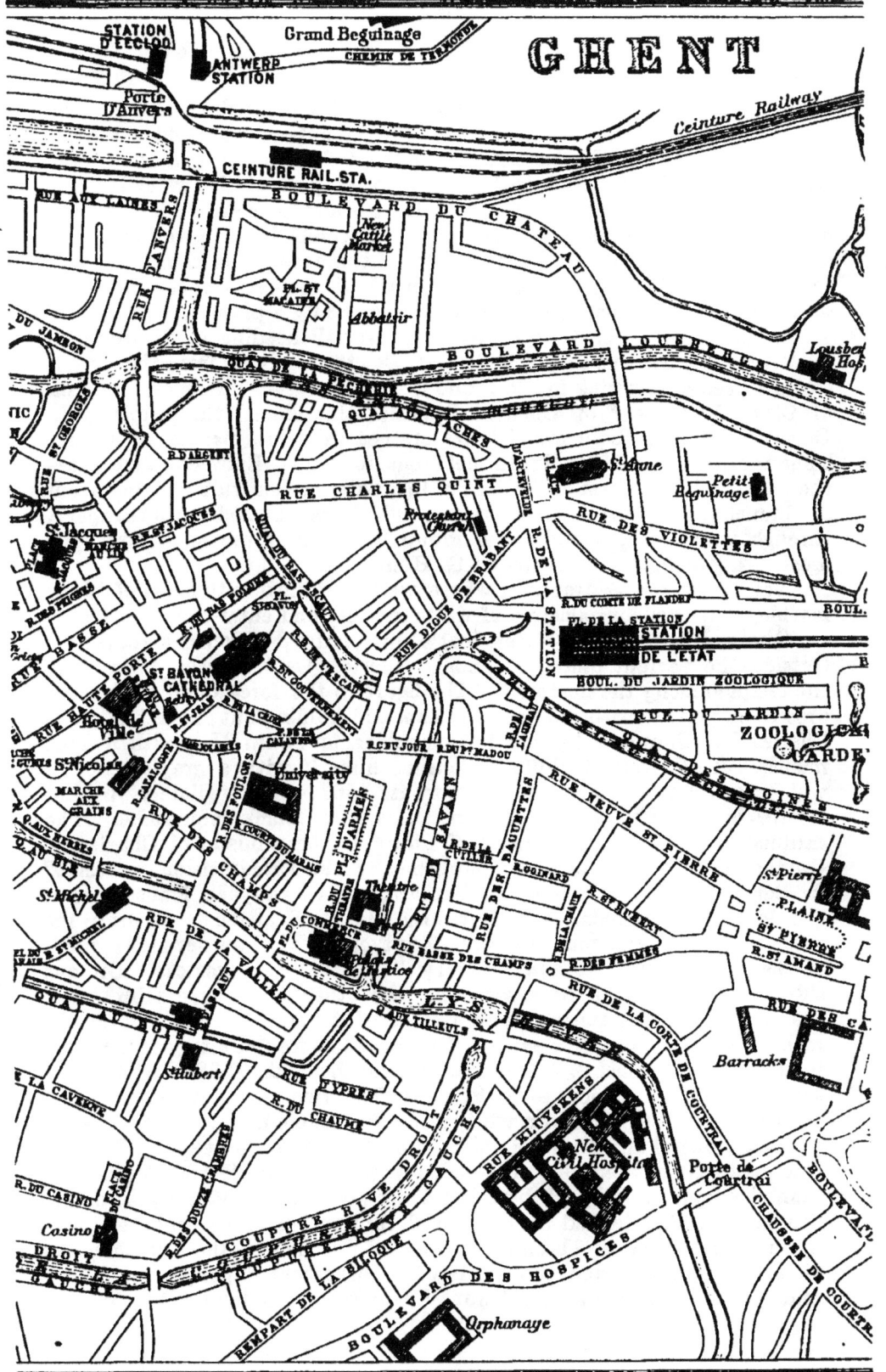

South Aisle.   Choir.   Pourbus.

heart-shaped tracery. From 26 plain piers rise pointed arches, having painted over them the escutcheons of the knights of the Golden Fleece, who were present at the last chapter of the order held here in 1559, presided over by Philip II. of Spain. The lower part of the walls is lined with a gray marble, relieved by a strip of white marble. All the best pictures are in the choir, and although a complete list is given below, it is unnecessary to visit those in the aisles of the nave. We commence the round by the chapels, S. aisle, right hand of main entrance. Reredos means altarpiece, sometimes a statue, but generally a picture.

South Aisle.—1. Reredos by G. Crayer. Beheading of St. John.—2. Reredos by Paelinck (d. 1839), "St. Coletta receiving from the magistrates a deed authorising her to found a convent."—3. Reredos, Baptism of Christ by Cauwer of Ghent. Opposite this chapel the pulpit by L. Delvaux. At the base are life-size statues in white marble of Father Time regarding the book Truth held out to him. Between them rises the pedestal in the form of the tree of life, with golden fruit hanging from its branches above the sound-board, which is covered with drapery, through which peep cupids, one group being busy raising a large gilt cross.—4. On wall Maccabæus by G. Honthorst.

Now cross the S. transept, whose walls are lined with slabs of black marble, supported by pilasters of white marble, and enter the

Choir, First Chapel—Reredos, Triptych by F. Pourbus (covered). Outside, the Saviour and the donor. Interior, Centre Piece, "Jesus in the temple among the doctors." The figure in the foreground to the left, dressed in yellow, with red hose and cap, and holding out his left hand, is Charles V. Standing by his left shoulder is Philip II., with a blue mantle. To the left of Philip is Pourbus himself with a grayish cap, on which is inscribed Franciscus Pourbus, 1567. Immediately behind Charles is the Duke of Alva, with black hair and black moustache. The cardinal in the red robe in front of Philip is the minister of Charles V. On the inner wings are the "Baptism and the Circumcision of Jesus." 2. Reredos, "Martyrdom of St. Barbara," by G. Crayer; Mausoleum of the brothers Goethals.—3. Reredos, The 4 Evangelists writing the account of the sacrament. On wall, Triptych, by G. Van der Meire, pupil of the Van Eycks, "Mount Calvary;" Three high crosses. On one side are 2 priests on horseback, on the other Mary in a faint. On the wings, "Moses raising the brazen serpent" and "Moses striking the rock."—4. Reredos, by Heuvelt, "Woman taken in adultery." Opposite tomb of G. Janssens, d. 1576, and Vander Lent, d. 1588, the first and second bishops of Ghent.—5. Reredos, The two stages of Lazarus and the rich man, the wings of a triptych by M. Coxcie in chapel 14, N. side.

6th Chapel in Choir, S. side, at the head of steps. Reredos, The justly famous painting on wood, representing the "Adoration of the Lamb," commenced by Hubert and finished by John Van Eyck, on the 6th May 1432, intended as a pictorial illustration of the sublime passage in Revelation v. 11 and 12; when John beheld the ten thousand times ten thousand and thousands of thousands of angels, living beings and elders round about the throne "saying with a loud voice, Worthy

Adoration of the Lamb.

is the Lamb that was slain to receive power and riches and wisdom and strength and honour and glory and blessing." It is a large picture with 2 pairs of shutters on each side; which close over it. All the paintings on these shutters are copies by Coxcie; 6 of the originals being in the Picture Gallery of Berlin, bought for £1640, and the remaining 2, representing Adam and Eve, in the Picture Gallery of Brussels. The large pictures on the four panels are original and although painted 450 years ago the colours are as fresh as if newly put on.

Exterior.—Among other pictures are an Annunciation and portraits of the donors Jodocus and his wife.

Interior.—When the 8 shutters are unfolded a large centre piece is displayed, with over it, 3 paintings on panels.

The Panels.—On the centre panel God is represented seated on a damask throne, with a tiara on his head, and attired in an ample scarlet robe trimmed with gold lace set with precious stones. In his left hand he holds a sceptre of gold, while the right is uplifted in the manner of the pope when he pronounces a blessing. The glowing flesh-like colour of the face is admirable, but the expression meaningless. At his feet lies a richly-jewelled crown, emblematic of martyrdom. On the panel right of God, sits Mary reading a book, which she holds in her hands, and is just turning over a leaf. She is dressed in a light blue robe trimmed with a narrow border of gold lace set with gems. On her head she wears a large and slightly gaudy crown, from under which fall profuse locks of fair hair. The expression of her face is simple and natural. On the panel left of God, sits John the Baptist with rather a woe-begone expression, and a profusion of hair about his face. On his knees is a large open illuminated Bible. Above a brown dress he wears a green mantle, clasped below his beard by a brooch with a large yellow gem.

Centre Piece.—Below these three panels is the chief picture, 7 ft. 8½ in. long, by 4 ft. 6½ in. broad. In the centre on a square red damask box, covered on the top and on the two ends with a white cloth, stands the **Lamb** in a stiff position, from W. to E., the tail being to the east and his head to the west, but turned round to the spectators. From his breast streams a jet of blood into a golden chalice standing before him on the box or altar. On the ground, at each side, kneel 6 angels with folded wings, in heavy blue and green clothing. In front, 2 angels in white, and with peacock-like wings, are waving censers. Before the Lamb, and in the foreground, on a greensward covered with lilies, is the "Fountain of life" in an octagonal basin.

To the right of the fountain stands a great assemblage of ecclesiastical dignitaries. In front are the 12 apostles with bare feet mostly kneeling, clad in gay violet-coloured gowns. Behind them are popes, cardinals, priests, and monks, arrayed in rich sacerdotal garments. On the left is a group of kings and princes in various costumes, and here, as in the other group, the foremost are kneeling, the rest standing.

From the N.W., through an opening of a thicket of trees and large flowering shrubs, advances a stately procession of popes, cardinals, monks, and pilgrims, while from the N.E., through a slight depression of the

GHENT. CATHEDRAL. CHOIR.

ground, march a throng of maidens with palms in their hands, headed by St. Barbara and St. Agnes carrying her lamb.

In the background are seen the spires of the New Jerusalem, and in the distance green hills receding in pleasing lines under a blue horizon.

Up in the sky, over the Lamb, is the Holy Ghost, with outspread wings.

Shutters.—On the shutter by the side of St. John is St. Cecilia in a black brocade dress playing upon an organ, accompanied by 4 angels with harps. On the next shutter stands Eve, less nude than she appears in the original. On the two corresponding shutters below are a great company of hermits, with staves and rosaries. Mary Magdalene and another female hermit behind them are marching round a wooded bank interspersed with palms and orange-trees. On the next shutter is a procession of pilgrims, headed by the tall figure of St. Christopher, with a great scarlet mantle thrown over his otherwise naked body.

Left hand shutters.—On the left shutter next Mary is a party of singing choristers. Next is the portrait of Adam. Below, on both shutters, is a company of crusaders on horseback, the 3 foremost carrying banners. On the last panel is Hubert van Eyck himself, riding on a white horse, and dressed in a blue mantle, fringed with light gray fur. His hair and his cap are brown. The third rider from him, in a black cap and mantle, and with a long coral necklace over it, is his brother John, with his face turned to the spectator.

The first sight of this picture is disappointing, caused chiefly by the odd appearance of the Lamb on the box, and the solid-looking angels around it. But when time and leisure have been given to study the more than 300 figures in varied attitudes, and finished with surprising skill and the most scrupulous minuteness, the spectator will admit the conclusion that "there is not to be found in the whole Flemish school a picture in which human figures are grouped, designed, and painted with so much perfection as in this, of the mystic Lamb.—Crowe and Cavalcasselle "On the Early Flemish Painters."

7th Chapel.—7. Reredos (covered), the body of Christ resting on the knees of Mary by G. Honthorst. Opposite, a very beautiful "Crucifixion," by Crayer.—8. Two beautiful mausoleums of bishops in white marble. To the right, mausoleum by Verschaffelt, of Anthony Van der Noot (d. 1770), represented on his knees in flowing robes before the Virgin, seated on a cloud, who holds the Child towards him. A drapery of veined marble is thrown over the black marble sarcophagus. On the left, mausoleum by Helderenberg of P. E. Vander Noot, who in a reclining posture is being directed by an angel to look up to a group, lifesize, representing the scourging of our Lord. Reredos by N. Roose. The Virgin surrounded by angels.—9. Chapel of the Virgin, behind high altar. Reredos by N. Roose, "The Virgin worshipped by the female saints of the Bible." In the corner, "The betrothal of the Child Jesus to St. Catherine," also by Roose.—10. In this chapel are two of the most skilful pictures in colour, drawing and conception, in Belgium, by Rubens and his master Otto van Venius. The picture to the left

GHENT.   NORTH AISLE.   SANCTUARY.   BELFRY.

is by Rubens, and in two parts. The upper portion represents St. Bavon, the patron saint of Ghent, having sold all he had, distributing to the poor. Two elegantly-dressed ladies look on in admiration. Above is St. Bavon, ascending the steps of the monastery, where a company of bishops and priests stand ready to receive him. St. Bavon, when distributing his goods, has gray hair and a gray beard; but when about to enter the monastery both are auburn. Opposite is "Christ raising Lazarus," by Otto Venius, a picture full of charming faces. Front wall, mausoleum of Bishop Damont, d. 1609. Here descend some steps.

11. Reredos by G. Zegers, Martyrdom of St. Lieven. Opposite, Death of St. Roch, by Picque.—12. Reredos, "Martyrdom of St. Catherine." Opposite this chapel, against the screen of the sanctuary, is the large mausoleum of Bishop Voucke, d. 1778. Two life-size female figures stand by the sarcophagus in dark gray marble. His portrait in mosaic, slightly injured, is above.—13. Reredos, "Ste. Marguerite," by Franck.—14, or first chapel of choir, N. side. "The 7 acts of charity," by Coxcie. The centre of the triptych of which the 2 wings are in the 5th chapel of the choir, S. side. Now cross the N. transept and walk down to the first chapel of the N. aisle, near the entrance door with the font at which Charles V. was baptized.

North Aisle.—1. Reredos, A Descent from the Cross, a *chef-d'œuvre* of T. Rombouts, the colouring wants harmony. Opposite is a Dead Christ by A. Janssens.—2. Reredos by Van Huffel, "St. Lambert when a chorister, bringing to the altar in his surplice a lapful of live charcoal with which to light the incense." The bishop and those around are astonished his dress does not catch fire.—3. Chapel covered with mural paintings. Reredos, "St. Macharius attacked by the plague" by Crayer.—4. Reredos, "An Ascension of the Virgin," by Crayer. Next it is the N. aisle.

The Sanctuary.—At the entrance are two chapels of painted and gilt wood-work, and two marble statues by Poucke—one represents "Paul at Melita shaking off the viper," the other, "Peter preaching." On reredos of high altar is a marble statue of "St. Bavon on clouds," by Verbrüggen. Before it stand four large copper candlesticks, which belonged to Charles I. of England, whose arms they bear, as well as those of the Antonius Trust, seventh Bishop of Ghent, who presented them to the church. This bishop's mausoleum is the second to the left of the altar. It was executed by Jerome Duquesnoy, who in a fit of jealousy poisoned his more famous brother Jean. He himself was burned alive in 1654, for a crime committed while engaged with this monument. On the right side of the altar is the mausoleum of Bishop C. Maes, d. 1608.

Between the cathedral and the Hotel de Ville is the **Belfry**, a square tower surmounted by a pinnacled spire, 375 ft. high, commenced in 1183, and continued till 1339. In 1855 it was repaired and the iron spire, painted like stone, added. The gilt dragon, 10 ft. long, on the top, was brought in 1204 from the church of St. Sophia in Constantinople, by the crusader, Count Baldwin VIII. It is ascended by 297 small steps the length of the first room, where the 8 men stand when they toll the large bell. 71 steps more lead up to the first gallery, and 31 more to the

Hotel de Ville—St. Nicolas.

chamber of the 4 large bells. The greatest or tocsin bell is in the middle. It was recast in 1659. On it is an inscription stating that its name is "Roland." When rung rapidly, there is fire; when slowly, a storm. The Austrians in 1789 fired a small cannon ball at the belfry, which pierced the side of this bell to the right, under the iron stair. From this 33 iron steps lead up to the room of the cylinder and the other mechanism of the chimes. 22 more lead up to the room of the playing apparatus, where there is a chime performance at 11.30 A.M., every Sunday, Monday, Wednesday, and Friday. Visitors go no higher. From the balcony is an extensive bird's-eye view, which the keeper explains. From this a ladder of 20 steps leads to the chamber, where the 40 bells which compose the chimes hang. The concierge lives in the first story of the tower. Fees, for 1, 1 fr.; for from 2 to 5, 2 frs. On the ground floor is the town prison.

Near the belfry is the **Hotel de Ville,** of which the richly-ornamented florid Gothic façade was built in 1482, and the other with rows of Doric, Ionic, and Corinthian columns in 1600. On the 18th of January 1794 the Duke of York gave a grand fête at the Hotel de Ville, to celebrate the birthday of his mother, the Queen of England. On the 14th July 1803 Napoleon, accompanied by his spouse Josephine and surrounded by his Generals with the prefect of the city, made a solemn entry into Ghent, at 6 o'clock in the evening, passing under a triumphal arch, on which were portrayed the great victories of the hero. The following day, the First Consul and his staff were entertained at the Hotel de Ville with a most sumptuous fête. In the grand hall, ornamented with laurels and military trophies, were exhibited the various manufactures of the city.

Near the belfry in the "Marché aux Grains" is the most ancient church in Ghent, the church of **St. Nicolas,** founded in 1051; of which, however, the oldest parts date only from the 13th cent., and the rest from 15th and 16th cents. From the centre rises a massive square tower, and two turrets at the W. end. In the interior there is nothing of great interest: the sculpture, painting, and architecture, are all mediocre. Commencing at the right hand of main entrance, we have, high up on the wall, next the organ, a Descent from the Cross, by Crayer. On the wall of the first chapel a "Pieta," by Rombouts, and on the reredos, The fall of the Angels, by Roose.—2. Reredos by Maes, a bright little picture representing Mary with the children Jesus and John.—3. On wall, a Crucifixion by Quellin.—4. On wall, Mary putting the child Jesus on the knees of St. Jerome, by J. Janssens. Cross now the S. transept to the **choir.** First chapel nothing particular. 2. Reredos, The good Samaritan, Roose. 3. Reredos, Mary showing the child Jesus to a saint. This window and some of the others in the choir have very good painted glass, executed chiefly in 1851.—4. Reredos a Trinity: opposite on wall a good Madonna.

The other chapels of the choir have some very fair pictures. The reredos of the high altar is Roose's best picture in the church. It represents a procession of ecclesiastics come to invite St. Nicolas to become a bishop. He seems surprised at the honour.

Now return to main entrance, and commence with the first chapel on the left or *north aisle.* Reredos, "John and Mary at the foot of the

Cross." On the pier opposite, between this chapel and the second, is a small picture representing the lady of the house distributing money, and her servant bread to the poor. Below an inscription in Flemish states that Olivier Minjau and his wife are buried here, after having had a family of 21 sons and 10 daughters. When Charles V. visited Ghent in 1526, he was so pleased at seeing Olivier standing at the head of his 21 sons, that he gave him a pension. Four years afterwards the whole family died of the plague.—3. Reredos, "St. Anthony preaching, surrounded by angels and men," Steyaert.

Between St. Nicolas and the Place d'Armes is the **University**, built in 1819. The façade consists of a colonnade of 8 tall Corinthian columns below a plain pediment, bearing on the frieze the simple inscription "Auspice Gulielmo Imo. acad. conditore, S.P.Q.G., 1821." The entrance gate is in imitation of the Baptistery at Florence, with the arms of the university sculptured on the entablature. The vestibule or court is supported by 4 columns and 8 pilasters of the Corinthian order, and covered by a cupola 86 feet high. Round this court is an arcade; above which runs a gallery with doors into the class-rooms. A few steps above the first court is the inner court, painted in fresco, and supported by handsome marble columns, and forming as it were a vestibule to the great hall, capable of containing an audience of 1700. The number of students averages 400. This and the university of Liège are supported by Government. Adjoining is a no less useful institution, the **School of Arts and Manufactures**.

Near the church of St. Nicolas is **St. Michel**, built between 1445 and 1480. The tower, built in 1515, was to have been crowned with a spire 400 ft. high, of which a model is seen in second chapel right hand.

S. aisle. First chapel right hand of main entrance. Reredos, "The Scourging of Christ;" and opposite, "The Incredulity of Thomas."— 2. Reredos, "Conversion of St. Hubert," by Bockhorst; model of spire that was to have been erected on the tower.—3. Over pediment of altar. "The Maries lamenting the death of Christ," by Heuvel. In front of this chapel is the pulpit, by Frank 1840, exquisitely carved and ornamented. At the pedestal, in white marble, is our Lord below a fig-tree giving sight to a blind man. The stair railing is one mass of beautiful carving on dark brown mahogany representing trellised vines. The tribune is square, adorned with delicately-cut reliefs in snowy white marble set into mahogany panels, which serve as choice frames.—4. Reredos, "Flight into Egypt," by Heuvel.

South Transept.—Two large pictures in front, covered, excepting on Sundays. The "Annunciation" is by A. Lens; the figure of the Virgin is very beautiful. The "Ascension," by François, whose best paintings are in the Palais de la Nation, Brussels. Opposite is "A cure effected through supplication to Mary," by Oost; not covered.

Choir.—First chapel, S. side. Reredos, "Souls delivered from Purgatory; others seen still in," by Cauwer.—2. Reredos, by Plaetsen, 1838. Louis IX. in a dying state, exhorted by a friar. He is on his knees, and has a scared and sad expression. On the wall, portrait of St. Francis,

CRUCIFIXION BY VAN DYCK.

by Ribera; dark, but beautiful.—3. Reredos by Crayer, "The Ascension of St. Catherine, the betrothed to Jesus Christ."—4. Reredos, by P. de Champaigne, a charming painting representing St. Gregory teaching the choristers to sing his own chant.—5. Reredos, by Mander, "Sts. Carlo, Borromeo and Sebastian."—6. Behind high altar reredos by Bockhorst, *The Old Testament,* represented by Moses and Aaron; and the *New Testament,* represented by St. John, St. Sebastian and the Pope.—7. Reredos by Maes, d. 1856, Holy Family.—8. Side wall, "Repentant David supplicating God's forgiveness;" a powerful picture by Bockhorst.— 9. Reredos by G. Zegers, "The scourging of our Lord."—10. Reredos by Thulden, "Martyrdom of St. Adrian."—12. Reredos by Crayer, "The Apostles and Mary on the day of Pentecost."

North Transept.—Two large pictures, both covered. One of them, the best picture in the church, is the famous **Crucifixion**, by Van Dyck, said to have been painted in 6 weeks. It was cleverly restored, having lost its colour. At the foot of the cross are John and the two Maries; while to the right, in the clouds, hover 5 little cupids. The fine horse is the same one on which he has drawn Charles V. in the gallery of Florence. By the side of it is rather a striking picture by Paelinck in 1811, representing the "Finding of the true Cross by the Empress Helena," whose figure, at the foot of the cross, is a portrait of the Empress Josephine.

Now walk down the N. aisle, and commence with the first chapel left hand of entrance. First chapel, left hand, Baptistery.—2. Reredos by Balen, an Ascension of Mary.—3. Reredos by Crayer, St. George in armour with Sts. Joseph and Bernard worshipping the Trinity, among whom is Mary.—4. Left wall, "The raising of Lazarus," by O. Venius.—5. Reredos, "An Annunciation." Then follow the N. transept, with the best picture in the church.

Behind the E. end or apse of St. Michael, on the opposite side of the Lys, at No. 16 Quai aux Herbes, is the house of the **Corporation of Watermen**, built in 1531; a good specimen of Gothic domestic architecture. The front is gabled with 5 stories above the ground floor; the first contains 6 handsome transomed windows, and the successive fewer, according to the breadth of the part of the gable. Over the elliptic archway of the door is a 3-masted ship in relief. To the watermen belonged the monopoly of piloting vessels through the canals of Ghent.

Continuous to the Marché aux Grains, in front of St. Nicolas, is the **Marché aux Legumes**, with a low obelisk in the centre. Occupying one entire side of this market is an ugly gabled building, the "Grande Boucherie," 77 yards long and 13 wide, in which the butchers have their shambles. Originally it belonged to the corporation of butchers, who, till the year 1794, were all descendants (Prince Kinderen) of Charles V. and the pretty daughter of a butcher. The entrance, most usually open through the day, is at the S. end, towards the Marché au Foin. At that end, in the interior on the wall, is a mural painting by N. Martins in 1445, "Mary worshipped by angels and saints."

On the other side of the Lys is the **Fishmarket**, entered by a large doorway, built in 1689 from the designs of Quellin, and surmounted by

GHENT. CASTLE OF THE COUNTS OF FLANDERS.

emblematical figures of the Scheld and the Lys, and a colossal statue of Neptune by Helderenberg. In 1539 the Gantois refused to pay an arbitrary contribution levied on them by Charles V. under pretence of supplies to carry on the war against France. This mark of disloyalty was highly resented by the emperor and his sister Mary, who thereupon beheaded publicly 14 of the ringleaders in the Fishmarket. The magistrates with 30 of the most distinguished inhabitants and the deacons of the trades equipped in black, their heads bare and their feet naked, with cords about their necks, were dragged to the market-place and after having been thus exposed to their fellow-citizens, were compelled to ask pardon on their knees for their disobedience. The famous bell Roland, for having on that occasion tolled treason with its tongue, was taken down from the belfry.

In a corner of the small square of Ste. Pharaide is still the turreted gateway which led into the castle of the Counts of Flanders, built in 868 by Baudouin of the Iron Arm, first Count of Flanders. They inhabited it till 1340, when they removed to the Prinzenhof, of which not a vestige remains. Between 1338 and 1340, Edward III. of England, with his family, resided in the castle. His Queen Philippa had here a son in 1340, who was called, from his birthplace, John of Gaunt.

The street in front, the R. de la Monnaie, and its continuation the R. Ste. Marguerite, lead to the church St. Augustin, and next it the Academie containing the Picture Gallery.

St. Augustin has on the reredos of the high altar an Adoration; on the reredos of the altar of the chapel to the right St. Nicolas celebrating mass, by Tolentino; and in chapel to the left, "Saints around Mary, whom an angel is crowning," G. Crayer.

A little beyond is the **Academie de Dessin**, with a Picture Gallery containing 150 paintings, chiefly of the Flemish school, such as Adrian Van Utrecht, Boel, Boyermans, Brueghel, Clays, Comein, Coxcie, Crayer, Dillens, Duchatel, Funck, Gallait, Jordaens, Keyser, Knyf, Koninck, Muller, Muyden, Neefs, Paelinck, Pourbus, Rombouts, Rubens, Verboeckhoven, and Wittcamp.

From the main entrance of St. Michel, walking up the Rue St. Michel and its continuation the Rue Haute, we approach, on the left hand, the Rue de la Caverne, with the church of the **Dominicans**, remarkable for its pulpit, font, altars, and confessionals, all being exactly in the same style, in carefully carved oak, surmounted by rich canopy-work and lofty elegant crocketed pinnacles. The finest execution is displayed on the pulpit and on the high altar, where a second pinnacle rises over the pinnacle of the tabernacle.

The first street right, the Rue Theresiennes, leads down to the Canal de la Coupure, with on one side the casino, and on the other the penitentiary. This prison or **Maison de Force**, with accommodation for 2600 delinquents, was commenced in 1772 and finished in 1825. In form it is octagonal, divided into 8 triangular departments, of which the apices terminate in an octagonal court. The men are employed in the manufacture of linen and other articles for the army. The women sew, knit, and weave. It has served as the model of many other penitentiaries.

St. Jacques.   Marché du Vendredi.   Mad-Meg.

The **Casino** is a large building, with ample accommodation for theatricals, balls and exhibitions. In front are tastefully planned gardens, with bowers, swards and coppices. The banks of the Coupure, planted with plane, elm and horse-chestnut trees, afford one of the most frequented public walks.

Towards the N. of the town is the venerable church of **St. Jacques**, founded in the 12th cent., and rebuilt in the 15th. In the interior, on the reredos of the chapel behind the pulpit, is the best picture of J. Maes-Canini, d. 1856, "The departure of Tobias." The pulpit itself is in excellent taste, with subdued decoration. At the pedestal is a beautiful white marble statue, life size, by Van Poucke, d. 1809, representing St. James preaching. On the chapel behind altar, right hand, is a high picture by Crayer, representing "Souls both in purgatory, and escaping and escaped from it." Over all is Mary interceding for them before Christ. On His left is another female figure, probably St. Catherine His betrothed. In the sanctuary on the left of high altar are the marble effigies of W. Bronchorst and wife, d. 1635 and 1636. Here also is a lofty tabernacle of various coloured marbles, erected at the expense of Luytens, d. 1709. The pyx with the host is kept in it. The painting on the reredos of the high altar represents the martyrdom of St. James. The horse is very good, but the hinder part is rather prominent.

Towards the N. side of St. Jacques, in a small church, is the **Bibliothèque de l'Université**, open from 9 till 3 and from 5 to 8. It contains above 100,000 volumes, 400 incunables, and 700 MSS. The church makes an admirable library hall.

Very near the Library, and entered from No. 21 Rue St. Georges, is the Botanic Garden, which, although occupying a very limited space, has a fair display of plants. It serves also as a park.

Nearly fronting St. Jacques is the **Marché du Vendredi**, the scene of all the great events in the history of Ghent. Here the Counts of Flanders were inaugurated with great pomp. Here in a civic broil between the corporations of the fullers and the brewers, headed by Jacob Van Artevelde, the fight became so bloodthirsty that 1500 citizens were left dead. Here also the Duke of Alva lighted the flames of the Inquisition, by which many thousands perished, and the best and most industrious of the citizens were driven to other lands.

In the centre is a statue of the famous Governor of Ghent, Jacob Van Artevelde, killed during an insurrection of the populace in August 1345. The house he inhabited, and where he was assassinated, stood on the site occupied by No. 9 in the Place de la Calandre. On the balcony is the following inscription:—"Ici périt victime d'une faction, le 17 juillet 1345, Jacques Van Artevelde, qui éleva les communes de Flandre à une haute prospérité." Jacques Van Artevelde was the friend and ally of Edward III. of England.

Taking the direction indicated by the right hand of the statue, we arrive at the famous cannon Mad-Meg, cast in the early part of the 15th cent., and employed at the siege of Audenarde in 1452. It is composed of welded grooved plates, bound together on the exterior by 60 massive

GHENT.   PETIT BEGUINAGE.   SAINT PIERRE.

hammered iron hoops. It is 15 ft. 9 in. long and 34½ in. in diameter at the muzzle, and in every way very similar to the Mons Meg of Edinburgh Castle. It bears the arms of Philip the Good.

Separated from the Place d'Armes by the **Theatre**, a large, handsome and commodious house, is the **Palais de Justice**, on the Lys, built in 1843. The great hall, called the Salle des Pas Perdus, from which doors open into the different courts, is 240 ft. long.

From the Place d'Armes, the Rue Digue de Brabant leads to the Station de l'Etat or the Brussels Station, passing by the Protestant Church, in which there is English service every Sunday. A little farther, by the Rue des Violettes, is the **Petit Beguinage**, resembling in its economy and regulations the Grand Beguinage, only a little more monastic. The number of sisters amounts to 375. None can be received here as a Beguine who does not speak Flemish, as all their church services are conducted in that language. Their church, in the middle of a wide lawn, is very handsome and comfortable. The statue of a priest holding a cross forms the pedestal of the pulpit. The houses are not uniform in height, though they may be in the number of rooms.

On an eminence S.E. from the Place d'Armes is the church of **St. Pierre**, destroyed by the Protestants in 1578, and rebuilt in 1629. It is in the Italian style, with a large cupola. In the interior there is nothing remarkable. The best of the pictures are,—1. Right hand of main entrance, a Nativity by N. Roose, a large and pleasing picture; the different faces are full of wonder and joy, even the Lamb's.—2. Behind pulpit, Triumph of faith and religion by E. Quellin.—3. In chapel, next to choir, is " Francisco Javier in India, surrounded by his converts," by N. Roose; below this picture are the grave and tombstone of Isabella, wife of Christian II. of Denmark, and sister of Charles V.—4. On pier, the "Angel delivering Peter from prison" by Abraham Janssens.—5. "Holy family, with cupids playing before the Child" by Avond.—7. Large landscape by A. Janssens, "The miraculous draught of fishes."—8. End chapel, right or south from altar, on side wall, 5 small pictures illustrative of the influence possessed by a miraculous image belonging to the church. Above them, destruction of the first church by the Protestants. The abbey buildings are still seen which then occupied the site of the present "Place." By the side of the chapel "The raising of Lazarus" by Zegers.

Now cross over to the corresponding chapel in the N. side.—9. On wall, right hand, Christ giving sight to the blind man by Zegers. Reredos, St. Benedict receiving the equerry of Totila, king of the Goths, by G. Crayer. On side wall, "Crucifixion," after Rubens.—10. Landscape, "Jesus giving sight to a blind man," Ryschot.—13. Against pier, by Heuvel, Mary with the Child seated on a throne, distributing rosaries to priests and nuns.—14. Triumphal procession of the Church; and—15. Victory of the Church over Schism by T. Thulden. On the ground lie exhausted and discomfited, Calvin, Luther, and the other reformers, among torn books and wild beasts, from which the winged figure of an old man rescues a female representing "Truth."

Between this church and the station are the Zoological Gardens. At

St. Bavon Abbey.   Grand Beguinage.

the N.W. corner of the Place St. Pierre is the **Cité Ouvière**, a quadrangle occupied by rows of low, one-storied, whitewashed brick houses, all rather dirty. A short way S.E. from St. Pierre is the Park, on the site of the fortress erected by the Dutch in 1822. On one side of the Park is the town hospital, and on the other the Ecole Normale, a large, handsome edifice. From the square of St. Pierre, the Rues Neuve St. Pierre and Agneau lead to the **Station de l'Etat**, the station for Brussels.

To visit the ruins of the **Abbaye de St. Bavon**, take the tram from the Marché aux Grains on its way to the Station d'Anvers, but alight at the Rue St. Macaire, with the church of that name. From the church, turn up the first street right, the Rue des Autrichiens, which walk down to the end, then turn to the right by the paling, where a bell-pull will be seen. If the concierge is not there, he will be found at the Estaminet (public-house) near the paling, at the foot of the Rue des Autrichiens. It was into this abbey, founded in 629, that St. Bavon entered, when he retired from the world, and to which he gave up his fortune. Nearly two sides of the cloister remain. On the right, in a square plot called the crypt, are two empty graves side by side, said to have been the tombs of St. Avon and St. Macaire, who both died here. Under the cloister is a statue of a tall knight in armour, said to represent the famous Eginhard, who, in the 9th century, built an addition to the abbey. The edifice, having been pillaged and destroyed by the Normans, was rebuilt in the 12th century, of which a great part was demolished by Charles V. to make room for the citadel. On the left hand of the cloister is an octagonal tower, the vaulted chamber in the ground floor of which is called the Chapel of St. Macaire, built in the early part of the 12th cent. A narrow stair leads up to the chamber above, covered with tessellated pavement. A few relics connected with the abbey are preserved here—such as skulls, bones, iron rings, sculptured heads, ornamental bricks, pottery, and old gun barrels. The ruins are on the south side of the present church of St. Macaire. Fee, ½ fr.

To go to the Grand Beguinage, take the tram from the Marché aux Grains in front of St. Nicolas, on its way to St. Jacques and the Antwerp Station. At St. Jacques change trams. From the terminus of the second tram, take the second street right, the Rue Oostacker, which leads to the principal entrance of the **Grand Beguinage**, founded in 1234 by the Countess of Flanders. It is a settlement of small nunneries enclosed by a brick wall, with a church in the large open space in the centre. Around the church and ramifying in tiny streets from it stand neat one-storied brick houses with dormer windows, each with a little garden fronted by a brick wall 7 feet high, with a door on which is the name of the patron saint of the occupants. On the ground floor are 4 rooms and 2 kitchens, and upstairs 4 bedrooms. The rent of each house is £16. But none of the sisters possess a whole house, the most having only a sitting-room and bedroom and their share of the kitchen, for which each pays £4. All repairs must be done at the expense of the occupants. The money is received by the lady superior, who from it pays the annual ground-rent due to the Count Arenberg, the city taxes, the expenses of the infirmary and of the church, and sundry casual items. Candidates are received into the sisterhood from the age of 18, and all must possess an income of at least £12. The most have little more, and are obliged to work diligently to maintain themselves. The principal occupations are sewing and lace-making, of which they manufacture and sell large quantities. The same discipline exists in all the different houses, be they poor or rich occupants. They rise at 5 in summer and 5.30 in winter, and go to bed at 9. Mass in the church from 6.30 to 7. There is nothing particular in their church services. Breakfast at 7. Coffee, milk, bread and butter. Dine at 12. Soup, vegetables, meat and a glass of beer (on Fridays no meat). Sup at 7. Cheese, bread and butter. They wear black gowns and white caps, and, in addition, throw a covering over their heads like a folded towel. Each house defrays its own expenses. No nun can go out on an errand without the permission of the lady superior. Any nun is at liberty to renounce the order when she pleases. At their death their property is sent to their heirs. Ladies, under certain conditions, are taken as boarders. Visitors in quest of lace, or further information, should apply to the lady secretary in the house of the lady superior, fronting the entrance into the church. It is the only large house, and the only one differing from the others. The settlement removed to this place in 1872 from their original site at the west end of the town. The number of sisters averages about 800, while there is less than half that number in the settlement near the Brussels station, called the Petit Beguinage. Both are quite independent of each other.

One of the principal amusements in Belgium, and especially in Ghent and in some other of the large towns, is archery. But they do not shoot at targets but at feathered knobs stuck on pins, standing on 3 or 4 cross bars of diminishing length at the top of a pole or perche 105 feet high. They have never to go far for the spent arrows, and very little ground is sufficient.

Thirty-five and a half miles east from Ghent is Brussels, and about half-way between these two towns is

ALOST, pop. 20,000. *Hotels:* Flandre; Poste; Arcades. This ancient town on the Dendre contains a curious Hotel de Ville of the 13th cent., with a belfry of the 15th. The church of St. Martin, still unfinished, possesses a picture by Rubens painted in 1631, representing St. Roch praying for plague-stricken people. In the "Place" is a statue by J. Geefs, of Diedrich Mœrtens, the earliest Belgian printer.

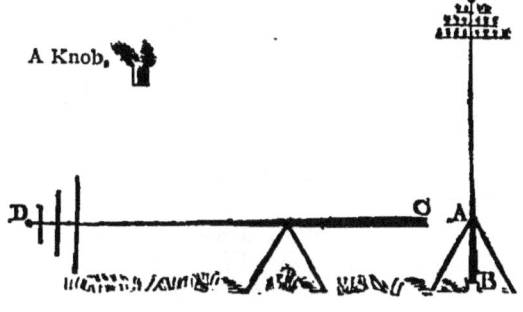

The end A B is thicker than the rest, and rests on a pivot. When all the knobs are shot off it is brought down like C D to be recharged.

BRUSSELS.

Principal Distances.—In consulting in Brussels the railway time-tables (*the Guide Officiel des Voyageurs*), be careful to observe from which station the desired train starts. Nord or simply N. indicates the Station du Nord; Midi or simply M., the Station du Midi; and Q. Leop. or simply Q. L., the station de Luxembourg, which is situated in the Quartier Leopold. Brussels makes excellent headquarters for visiting most of the important towns and places in Belgium. The railway fares are low, and the express trains have third-class carriages. It is 214 m. or 9 hours from Paris by Hal, Braine, Mons and Valenciennes; but only 193 m. or 8 hours 10 minutes by Hal, Braine, Mons, Feignies and Maubeuge. Brussels is 4 hours from Rotterdam by Antwerp, Roosendael, Zevenbergen and Dordrecht; 4 hours 38 minutes from Calais, by Lille, Tournai, Ath and Hal; $27\frac{1}{2}$ m. or 1 hour from Antwerp; $12\frac{1}{2}$ or 42 minutes from Malines; $61\frac{1}{2}$ m. or 2 hours from Liège; 18 m. or 33 minutes from Louvain; 136 m. or 6 hours from Luxembourg; $34\frac{1}{4}$ m. or 1 hour 14 minutes from Namur; $11\frac{1}{4}$ m. or 25 minutes from Braine l'Alleud, the station for the field of Waterloo. Brussels time is nine minutes before Paris time. See maps on pages 1 and 154.

Stations.—**Station du Nord**, at the N.E. part of the town, by the side of the Botanic Gardens. Station for Holland, Germany, Louvain, Malines, Antwerp, Bruges, Ghent and Ostend. Porters and cabs at the arrival side. Trams at the departure side. The best hotels here are in the square in front The * Four Nations, H. des * Boulevards and G. H. Gernay. In front of the departure side are the H. * Liegeois, Cologne and Angleterre. On the arrival side they are all of an inferior class, but the best are the Brabant, Comte de Flandre, Commerce, Mouscron.

Station du Midi at the S.W. end of the town. Porters, cabs and trams at the arrival side of the station. In the office in the front side tickets are taken for Waterloo, Namur, etc. Near it the best hotels are the Telegraph, Couronne, Paix. In the office on the S. side tickets are taken for Paris, Tournai, Lille and Mons. There the best hotels are the Calais and Europe.

In the high or E. end of the town is the **Luxembourg Station**. In the square in front is a statue of John Cockerill, see p. 240. Behind is the Musée Wiertz, see p. 194. The hotels at this station, all second class, are the Laboureur, Wavre, the Trois Arcades, Gembloux.

At the high end of the Rue de la Loi, where it joins the Boulevard Charlemagne, is a station, which communicates with all the other stations by the Chemin de Fer de Ceinture. It is near the Rond Point and the plain where the great exhibitions are held.

Hotels in the high town: Of the hotels, the largest, best, and most expensive is the Belle Vue, with an entrance from the Place Royale and from the Place des Palais, dinner 6 frs. The other first-class hotels in the high town are the Flandre and Europe, both in the Place Royale. In the Rue Royale are the H. de France and the H. Mengelle. In front of the Biblio-

BRUSSELS.   HOTELS AND RESTAURANTS.

thèque Royale is the Hotel et Taverne Anglais. In the Place du Trone, the G. H. Britannique. In the Rue de la Regence the H. Windsor. Dinner in the above, excepting the first, 5 frs. Rooms 3½ to 10 frs. H. Hollande R. de la Putterie, dinner 4 frs. H. Grand Miroir R. Montagne, dinner 3 frs. Hotel du Grand Café Rue des Eperonniers, dinner 3 frs.

In the low town the first-class houses are the H. de * Suede, dinner 5 frs.; good situation, with small garden. The Grand Hotel, a large house in the beautiful Boulevard Anspach, dinner 5 frs.; and near it at the Post-Office the H. Continental. The Grand Hotel has also a capital restaurant. In the Rue Neuve are the Univers, dinner 4 frs.; the H. Saxe, dinner 3½ frs.; the H. de l'Empereur, dinner 4 frs. The H. Wellington, in the Rue Neuve, near the church Finisterre, dinner 3 frs. In the Rue Fossé aux Loups, by the side of the opera, is the H. * de la Poste, dinner 3½ frs. In the Rue Fripiers (near the Bourse) the H. Grand Monarque, dinner 3 frs. By the side of the Bourse, in the Rue du Marché aux Poulets, the H. de la Campine, dinner 3 frs. * Hotel Frank Place des Martyrs, No. 13 good situation, rooms 2½ frs., service ½ fr. The H. Vienne Rue de la Fourche, dear considering its situation.

There are several houses which are comfortable and not so expensive as the above. In the Rue de la Fourche, *Hotel Cologne, rooms from 2 to 3 frs.; coffee, bread and butter, 1 fr.; dinner 2 frs.; pint wine 1 fr. The Pays Bas, near the old Palais de Justice. H. de la Porte Verte, near the Hotel de Ville. Hotel des Negociants, 40 B. de Hainaut. The * Hotel de Brabant, a quiet house, No. 18 Avenue du Midi, not far from the south station. Near it at No. 135 Rue du Midi, is the Hotel de Bordeaux a good and not expensive house. Taverne des Etrangers 36 R. Gretry, rooms from 1½ fr. H. Lion Blanc, Rue du Singe, dinner 2 frs.

There are some very cheap houses at the back of the Hotel de Ville, but not for ladies. A pint of very fair vin ordinaire costs from 1 to 1½ fr. in the second-class houses, but the same cost 2 frs. in the first class. In none of the hotels is the price of wine included. In some of the hotels, such as the Hotel de Saxe, the guests are charged more for their rooms when they dine out. The "porter," although he should do nothing, expects a trifle. In nearly all the second-class houses the service is ½ fr. per day, but many make no charge for lights. In the first-class houses the service is from 75 c. to 1 fr. per day. Rooms in the Splendide Hotel, 6 Rue Leopold, by the side of the opera-house, can be had for 30 frs. the month. Around it are numerous restaurants.

Excellent restaurants, cafés and brasseries (beer-houses), are all over the town, the best being naturally in the most frequented quarters, such as around the opera-house, in the Place Royale, in the neighbourhood of the Galeries St. Hubert, in the Rue Royale, in the neighbourhood of the Picture Gallery, and on the departure side of the Station du Nord.

Among the best are the Globe and Antoine in the Place Royale; Carter, Duvivier, and Fourdin in the Rue du Musée; Des Provenceaux, 40 Rue Royale; around the opera-house the Café Riche, Café Americain, Taverne Strasbourg, Perrin, and the Rocher de Cancale. The Maison Rohan, 41 Rue de la Fourche (near the opera), is among the cheapest.

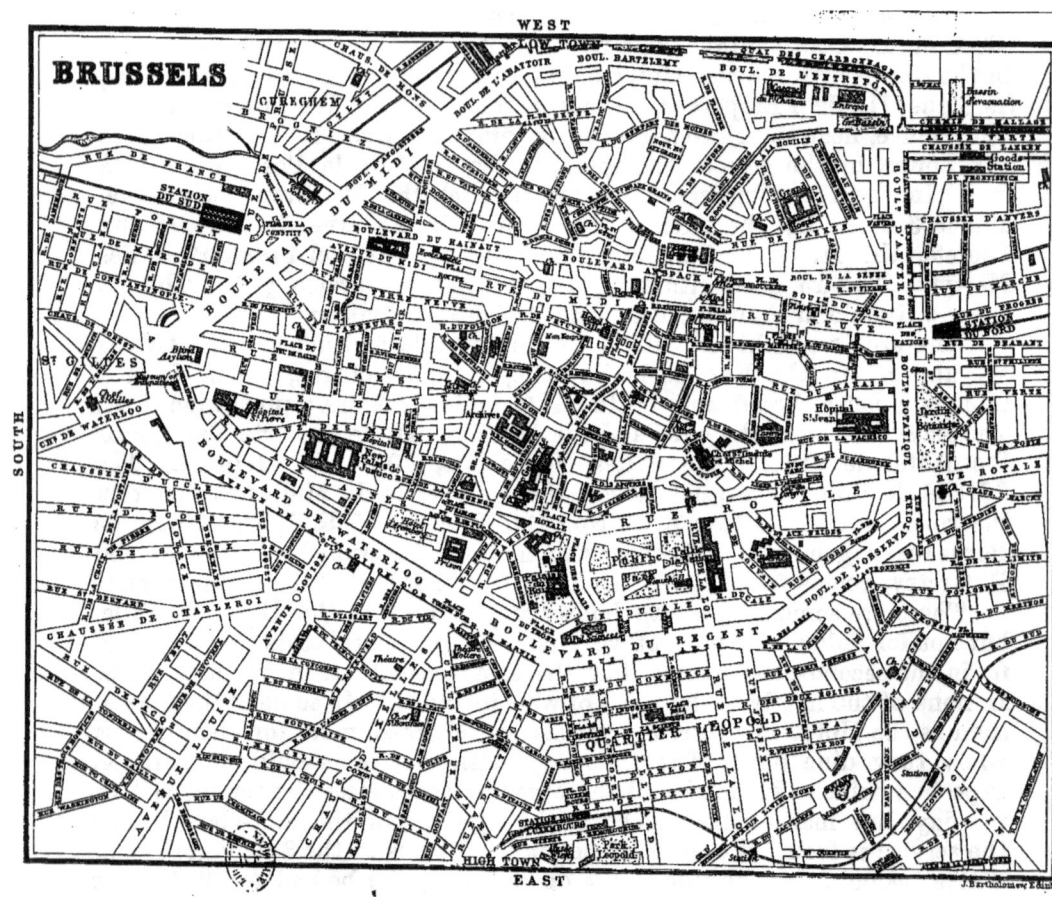

WEST

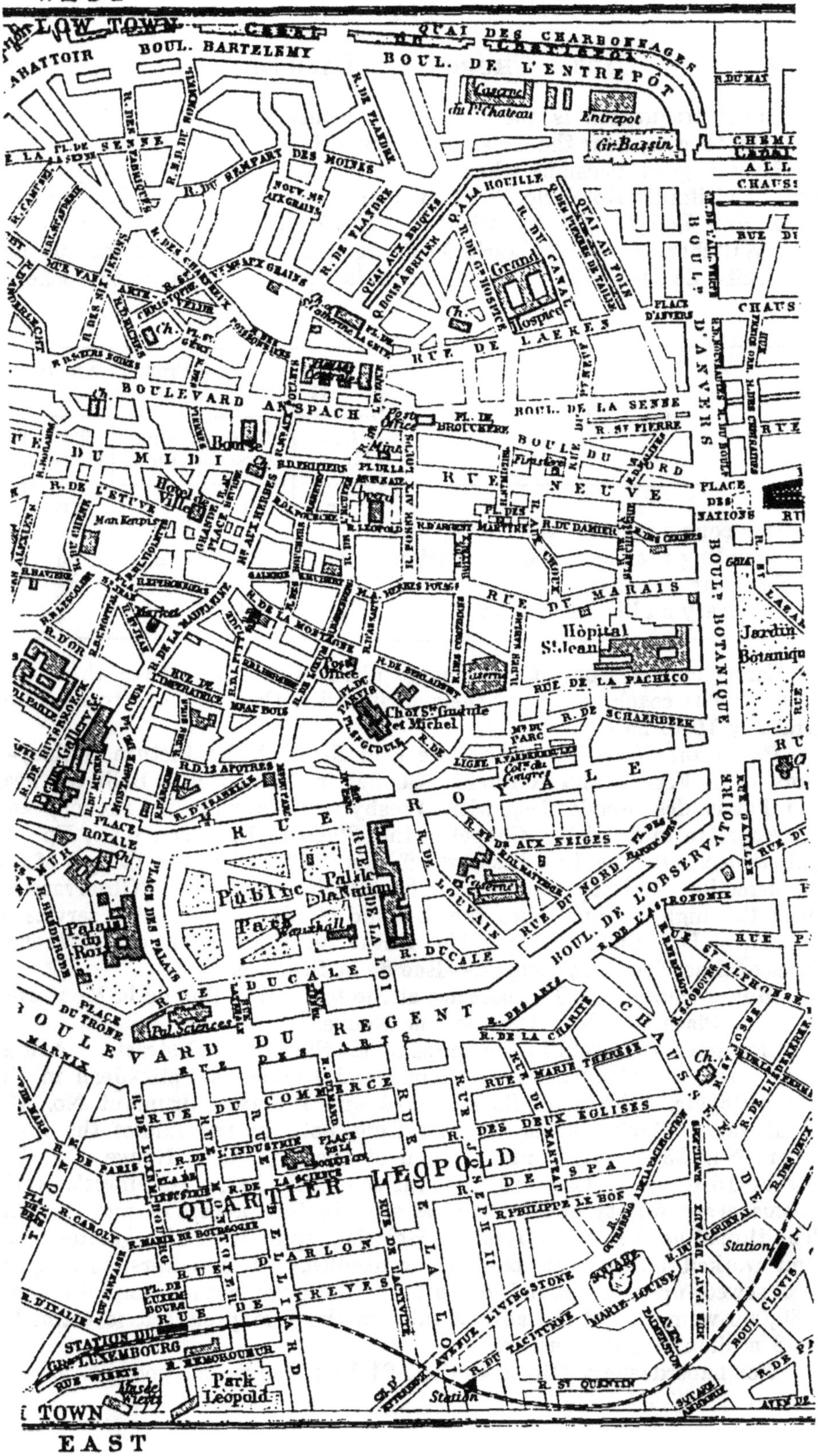
LOW TOWN
ABATTOIR
BOUL. BARTELEMY
QUAI DES CHARBONNAGES
BOUL. DE L'ENTREPÔT
Caserne du Pt. Chateau
Entrepot
Gr. Bassin
PL. DE SENNE
R. DU REMPART DES MOINES
R. DE FLANDRE
Q. A LA HOUILLE
QUAI AUX BRIQUES
QUAI AU BOIS A BRULER
R. DU CANAL
QUAI AU FOIN
Grand Hospice
PLACE D'ANVERS
BOULd D'ANVERS
RUE DE LAEKEN
Ch.
BOULEVARD ANSPACH
BOUL. DE LA SENNE
R. ST PIERRE
Post Office
PL. DE BROUCKERE
Bourse
Mint
BOUL DU NORD
RUE DU MIDI
Finistere
RUE NEUVE
PLACE DES NATIONS
Hotel de Ville
Opera
R. DE L'ETUVE
Man Kenpis
R. D'ARGENT
MARTYRS
R. DU DAMIER
Market
RUE DU MARAIS
R. DE LA MONTAGNE
Hôpital St. Jean
Jardin Botaniqu
BOULd BOTANIQUE
Post Office
RUE DE LA PACHECO
Chal St. Gudule et Michel
R. DE SCHAERBEEK
Col. du Congres
R. D. 12 APOTRES
R. D'ISABELLE
PLACE ROYALE
RUE ROYALE
R. DE LOUVAIN
Public Park
Palais de la Nation
Vauxhall
Caserne
RUE DU NORD
BOUL. DE L'OBSERVATOIRE
BOUL. DE L'ASTRONOMIE
RUE DE LA LOI
Palais du Roi
PLACE DES PALAIS
R. DUCALE
RUE DUCALE
PLACE DU TRONE
Pal. Sciences
BOULEVARD DU REGENT
R. DE LA CHARITE
RUE DES ARTS
RUE MARIE THERESE
RUE DU COMMERCE
RUE DES DEUX EGLISES
QUARTIER LEOPOLD
R. DE L'INDUSTRIE
R. DE LA SCIENCE
RUE DE SPA
RUE JOSEPH II
R. PHILIPPE LE BON
R. DE PARIS
R. CAROLY
R. MARIE DE BOURGOGNE
RUE D'ARLON
RUE DE TREVES
PL. DE LUXEMBOURG
SQUARE MARIE LOUISE
AVENUE LIVINGSTONE
R. DU TACITURNE
Station
BOUL. CLOVIS
STATION DU Gd. LUXEMBOURG
R. WIERTZ
Musée Wiertz
Park Leopold
R. ST QUENTIN
Station
TOWN

EAST

Cabs. Churches. Lace Shops.

The most frequented is the Restaurant Goldschmidt, 45 R. Ecuyer up from the theatre, near the Galeries St. Hubert.

Several good pensions where the charge is from 6 to 9 frs. per day. Culliford's Hotel No. 20 R. Bodenbroeck. S. Bernard No. 50 and Mme. Van Loo No. 22 R. Belliard. Hoffmann No. 51 R. Montoyer. Mrs. Wiltcher No. 25 R. Marie de Bourgogne. Brussels is famous for "Biscuits de Bruxelles," and "Pain à la grecque," sold in the bakers' shops.

CAB TARIFF.	From 6 A.M. to 11 P.M.		From 11 P.M. to 6 A.M.	
	One Horse.	Two Horses.	One Horse.	Two Horses.
	Fr.	Fr.	Fr.	Fr.
The course within the town, including the Luxembourg Station	1	$1\frac{1}{2}$	2	$2\frac{1}{2}$
Per hour	2	3	3	$3\frac{1}{2}$
For every additional $\frac{1}{2}$ hour	1	$1\frac{1}{2}$	$1\frac{1}{2}$	$1\frac{3}{4}$

Carriages not from stands charge about 1 fr. more than the above prices. The coachmen carry their tariffs with them. Each trunk 10 c. Gratuity 15 to 25 c.

Protestant Churches.—The State Church, next the Picture Gallery—worship in French and German. Chapel in No. 13 Rue Belliard, near the Palais des Academies, with Presbyterian service in French, and Episcopalian in English. Chapel in the Place de la Toison d'Or, Episcopal service. In the Rue Stassart off this "Place" is the Chapel of the Resurrection, Episcopal service. Chapelle No. 50 B. de l'Observatoire, near the high entrance into the Botanic Gardens, Methodist service in French and English. Chapel No. 1 Rue de Marnix (Place due Trone), Episcopal service. *Synagogue.*—Rue de la Regence.

Money-changers.—The best are at the top of the Rue de la Montagne, near the Place Royale and in the Rue Neuve.

Brussels lace is sold in the shops of all the principal streets. Among them are: the Compagnie des Indes and Doimeries-Petit-Jean in the Place Royale. Boval de Beck No. 74 and Duhayon-Brunfaut No. 109 R. Royale. Buchholtz et Cie. and Luig, both by the side of the opera. Baert No. 23 R. du Nord. Dudon et Cie. 120 Rue Neuve. J. Des Mares 15 R. de la Chancellerie, near the Cathedral. In Mares's workrooms every variety of lace may be seen in the process of manufacture. The thread used is made from the Hal flax, spun with the greatest care, and worked either with bobbins or needles. The flowers and figures are sewed upon a ground of tulle. The manufacture employs about 130,000 women, and the annual value of the lace produced is estimated at 8 million pounds sterling.

For haberdashery Hirsch et Cie., 21 Rue Neuve, is a good shop.

PLACE ROYALE.   GODFREY DE BOUILLON.   ST. JACQUES.

Brussels, the capital of Belgium, is situated on the Senne, a small tributary of the Schelde. With its suburbs it contains a population of 400,000. The low or old town occupies the N.W. part, and the high or modern the S.E., which is every day extending its limits over the high, healthy, sandy plains intersected by tramways. The park, the palaces, and the best streets, churches, and houses, are in the new town; the Bourse, the Hotel de Ville, and the two principal railway stations in the old town. On the top of the hill rising from the old or low town is the **Place Royale**, with an equestrian statue in bronze by Simonis in 1848 of Godfrey or rather Godefroid de Bouillon, born at Baisy about 1060, p. 215. He died in Palestine on the 17th of July 1100, and was buried in the church of the Holy Sepulchre. So impartial and temperate had been his rule, that Mahometans as well as Christians bewailed his loss. The statue represents the accomplished and brave crusader as he rode in 1097 through this same square, urging his countrymen to join him in his perilous enterprise.

Fronting the statue is the church of **St. Jacques sur Caudenberg** (cold mountain), built between 1776 and 1785. Under a colonnade of tall Corinthian columns is a statue by Olivier of Moses, and one by Janssens of David. On the wall are sculptures in relief representing the martyrdom of St. James. On the pediment, on a gold ground, is a fresco by Portaels in 1850, representing "Mary, the refuge of the mourners and the afflicted."

In the interior, at the entrance to the chancel, are two statues, by Godecharle, representing the Old and the New Testaments.

At the commencement of the Rue de la Regence is the Palais du Comte de Flandre. Immediately opposite it is the **Palais des Beaux Arts**, for the exhibition of modern paintings and sculptures. The entrance is by a handsome doorway under a portico of 4 large marble columns. The halls on the ground floor are devoted to sculpture, architecture and engraving. The great central hall, or rather court, is about 62 yds. long and 20 broad. Round this oblong square runs a wide and spacious gallery supported on 32 coupled reddish veined marble columns, and lighted from the flat glass roof over the court. In this gallery are hung the principal pictures, as also in the well-ventilated halls which ramify from it. 2 handsome staircases, each containing 51 broad veined marble steps, lead up to the picture department. Good cloak-rooms. Behind, and contiguous to the Palais, is the Bibliothèque Royale, which again adjoins the Museum and the Picture Gallery. A short distance S.W. by the Rue de la Regence is

BRUSSELS.   NOTRE DAME.   GRAND SABLON.   ARENBERG.

the church of **Notre Dame des Victoires**, founded in 1304, but rebuilt during the 15th and 16th cents., excepting the portal of the N. transept, which belongs to the 14th cent. On the N. or left side of the altar is the mortuary chapel of the Princes of Thurn and Taxis, lined with black marble, covered with statuettes and decorations in fine white marble. The sarcophagus is by Van Beveren, and the statuettes and ornaments by Cosyoss. The white marble statue of St. Ursula, over the altar, is by H. Duquesnoy, and the cupids by Grupello. On the right, or south side of the altar, is a similar chapel, built in 1690, containing the mausoleum of Count Garnier, secretary of the Duke of Parma. A little to the right of the chapel is a slab on the floor bearing, in large brass letters, the inscription, "Ici reposent les restes de J. B. Rousseau," a French poet, who died in exile, near Brussels, in 1741. The mural paintings on the choir are reproductions of those which formerly adorned it, executed in the 15th cent.

On the N. side of the church is the Place du Grand Sablon, having in the centre the fountain erected in 1751 with money bequeathed by Thomas Bruce, Earl of Aylesbury, in memory of his pleasant 40 years sojourn in Brussels.

On the S. side of the church is the pretty square, the Place du Petit Sablon, having at the high end the **Palais d'Arenberg** and in the centre the colossal bronze statues by Fraiken in 1568 of "Counts Egmont and Hoorn, as they walked to the scaffold." The palace, built in 1753 on the site of the residence of Count Egmont, contains a choice collection of 75 Dutch, 30 Flemish, 6 French, and a few German paintings. On the frames are the artists' names. Among the most remarkable are:— "Tobias restoring his father's sight" by Rembrandt or S. Koninck; "An old woman sitting by a table covered with gold pieces" by Gerard Dow; "Cupid" by Metsu; "Resting near the barn" by Paul Potter; "La Fête des Rois" by Jordaens; "The marriage at Cana" by Steen (bought for £840 at the sale of the Duchess de Berry's collection in 1837); G. Berckheyden, Inner court of the exchange at Amsterdam; Brouwer, The interior of a public-house; Jean van der Meer, Portrait of a girl; A. Van Ostade, Interior of a tavern, bought in 1838 for £520; Everingen, A waterfall; Gortzius Geldorp, Portrait of the theologian Corn. Jansenius; Teniers, Game of bowls; Van Craesbeck, A painter's studio; and several pictures by Rubens, Ruysdael, Jan Wouverman, and Van Eyck. Shown in the absence of the family from 10 to 4. Fee, 3 to 5 frs.

Nearly adjoining, in the Rue des Petits-Carmes, is the **Cellular**

BRUSSELS.   PRISON.   CUYLENBERG.   CONSERVATOIRE.

Prison called Les Petits-Carmes, erected in 1847 by the architect Dumont, in the English Pointed or Tudor style. It is fitted up with cells for solitary confinement. A Carmelite monastery formerly occupied this site. A little higher stood the house of Florent de Pallant, Count of Cuylenberg, where the meetings were held of the confederate nobles determined to resist the vexatious enactments of Philip II. Here they drew up and signed the petition which was presented on the 6th April 1566 to the regent Margaret of Parma, natural daughter of Charles V., praying her to abolish the edicts against religious liberty; and here, by Philip's order, the Counts Egmont and Hoorn were arrested and taken to the Grande Place, where they were beheaded.

The handsome building opposite the church of Notre Dame des Victoires is the Government school for music, or the **Conservatoire de Musique**, with a library and museum of musical instruments. The institution is under the direction of the Minister of the Interior, aided by a commission of 7 members nominated by the King, with the burgomaster of Brussels as honorary president. The instruction is gratuitous, and includes vocal and instrumental music, composition, and the Italian language. There are six bursaries of 250 frs. and ten of 125 frs. in connection with this institution. There is a similar establishment at **Liège.** Both vocal and instrumental music is much cultivated in Belgium. Next the Conservatoire is the Synagogue, built in 1878.

At the termination of this wide street, the Rue de la Regence, is the great and mighty edifice the **Palais de Justice**, 600 ft. long by 560 wide, the grandest building devoted to law, perhaps, in the world. The style is Græco-Roman, but almost Egyptian, only requiring the lions to be altered into sphinxes. This immense mound of masonry, ascending 270 ft. up to the skies, resembles on a misty day a tower of Babel. It cost upwards of 2 million pounds sterling.

The Park, Palaces, Wellington, Cathedral, and Bank.

Fronting the S. end of the Park is the **Royal Palace** with a frontage of 450 ft. In the centre is a portico consisting of 7 arches resting on 6 pillars, each from a single block. The interior is sumptuously furnished and contains some valuable paintings, of which the best are: A study of lions, by Rubens; Portraits of Duquesnoy and of Vos, the painter by Van Dyck, a small Rembrandt and a Hobbema. Among the modern painters are pictures by Ary Scheffer, Verboeckhoven, Keyser, and Gallait, one of whose finest works is the Temptation of St.

ROYAL PALACE.   RESIDENCE OF WELLINGTON.

Antony. Permission to visit the palace can be obtained during the absence of the royal family from the Maréchal du Palais, or from the Minister de la Maison du Roi.   Fee to concierge, 2 frs.

The present edifice which forms the palace was originally two separate buildings. The end with a colonnade of grooved Corinthian columns towards St. Jacques and the Place Royale was a mansion by itself, and in it, as far as I can ascertain, Wellington had his headquarters. If so, then it was here that he received, on the 15th of June at 11 A.M., the despatches from the Prince of Orange announcing the attack upon the outposts at Thuin and Lobbes, and here also it was where the prince himself arrived that same day from Binche at 3 P.M., and dined with the Duke. At 5 P.M. despatches arrived from Ziethen, which had been written at 10 A.M. After dinner the Duke, having completed his arrangements, went to the ball given by the Duchess of Richmond. Between 11 and 12, while conversing in a recess of a window with the Duke of Brunswick and one of his generals, an aide-de-camp handed him a despatch from Blücher, informing him that the French had taken Charleroi and were advancing on Quatre-Bras. He turned pale; but, soon recovering himself, ordered the troops to march at 2 A.M. instead of 4, as had been previously arranged.

About 4 o'clock in the morning of the 15th of June, Napoleon attacked the Prussian outposts in front of Charleroi, at Thuin and Lobbes, and was in possession of Charleroi by 11. The Prussians retired to a position between Ligny and St. Amand, nearly 20 m. from the outposts. At 3 o'clock in the afternoon, the 2d Prussian corps had taken position not far from Ligny and Blücher had established his headquarters at Sombreffe. The foremost division of the French left column was about 2 m. S. of Quatre-Bras at Frasnes. The centre column of the French army lay near Fleurus; the right column was near Châtelet, and the guard between Charleroi and Gilly.[1]

Nearly adjoining the Royal Palace is the Palais Ducal, or the **Palais des Academies**, the seat of the Royal Medical Academy, and also of Science, Literature, and Art. The former is divided into 6 sections, and has 36 titular and 18 assistant members, with 24 corresponding and an indefinite number of honorary members. Each of the sections has certain branches of medical science assigned to it. The Academy answers any questions that may be proposed to it by the Government

---

[1] See *Histoire du General Wellington*, par le Colonel Brialmont; and *War in France*, by Siborne.

Binche is 52 miles South from Brussels, see Map, page 212.

upon matters connected with public hygiene, and makes researches in all subjects connected with or tending to advance medical science.

The Royal Academy of Science is divided into 3 classes, for the sciences, literature, and the fine arts; the first two are each subdivided into 2 sections, and the last into branches, for painting, sculpture, engraving, architecture, and music. Each class is composed of 30 members, 50 foreign associates, and not more than 10 native correspondents; each class proposes annually certain subjects for essays, to which gold medals of the value of £24 are adjudged. In the "grande salle" upstairs (fee ½ fr.), under the gilt arches of the arcade are 12 cleverly executed mural paintings by Slingeneyer, representing the principal events in the political and social history of Belgium, from B.C. 54 to A.D. 1831:—

1. The ancient Belgians with their chief, Ambiorix, taking the oath to deliver their country from the Roman yoke in 54 B.C. 2. Clovis preparing to embrace Christianity before the battle of Tolbiac in 496. 3. Charlemagne publishing laws and regulations at a meeting at Heristal, 748-814. 4. Godefroid de Bouillon visiting the Holy Sepulchre after the storming of Jerusalem 1099. 5. Jacques Van Artevelde recommending the observance of neutrality in the war between England and France in 1337. 6. The institution of municipal corporations by Agneessens, the energetic defender of the country's rights against Austrian domination. 7. The foundation of the national dynasty in 1831. 8. Literature and learning; Albert and Isabella at a historical lecture by Justus Lipsius at Louvain. 9. Music, etc.; Willaert, Clement, Gretry, etc. 10. Ancient art; Philip, surnamed the Good, of Burgundy, visiting Jean and Marguerite Van Eyck. 11. Modern art; Rubens received by Van Dyck, Jordaens, Snyders, etc., on his return to his native country. 12. Natural science; Vesalius, the anatomist, attending Charles V. on the field of battle at Nancy.

Behind the Palais des Academies, by either the Rue Montoyer or the Rue Belliard, is the Musée Wiertz, see p. 193. Between the palaces is the **Park**, 492 yds. long and 350 in width, containing an area of 32 acres covered with fine trees, intersected by broad walks well lighted at night in summer, and ornamented with lakes, fountains, statues and large grass plots. Every afternoon the band plays. Chairs, 10 c. At the N.E. corner of the Park, fronting the Palais de la Nation, are the Park theatre and the Wauxhall Gardens, where in summer open-air concerts are given from 8 to 10 P.M.; ticket 1 fr. In the Rue de la Loi, facing the North side of the Park, is the

Palais de la Nation, built during 1779-1783 by Guimard. The sculptures and basso-relievos are by Godecharle. The vestibule, open to the public, is ornamented with colossal statues of Belgian person-

PLAN OF THE PICTURE GALLERY

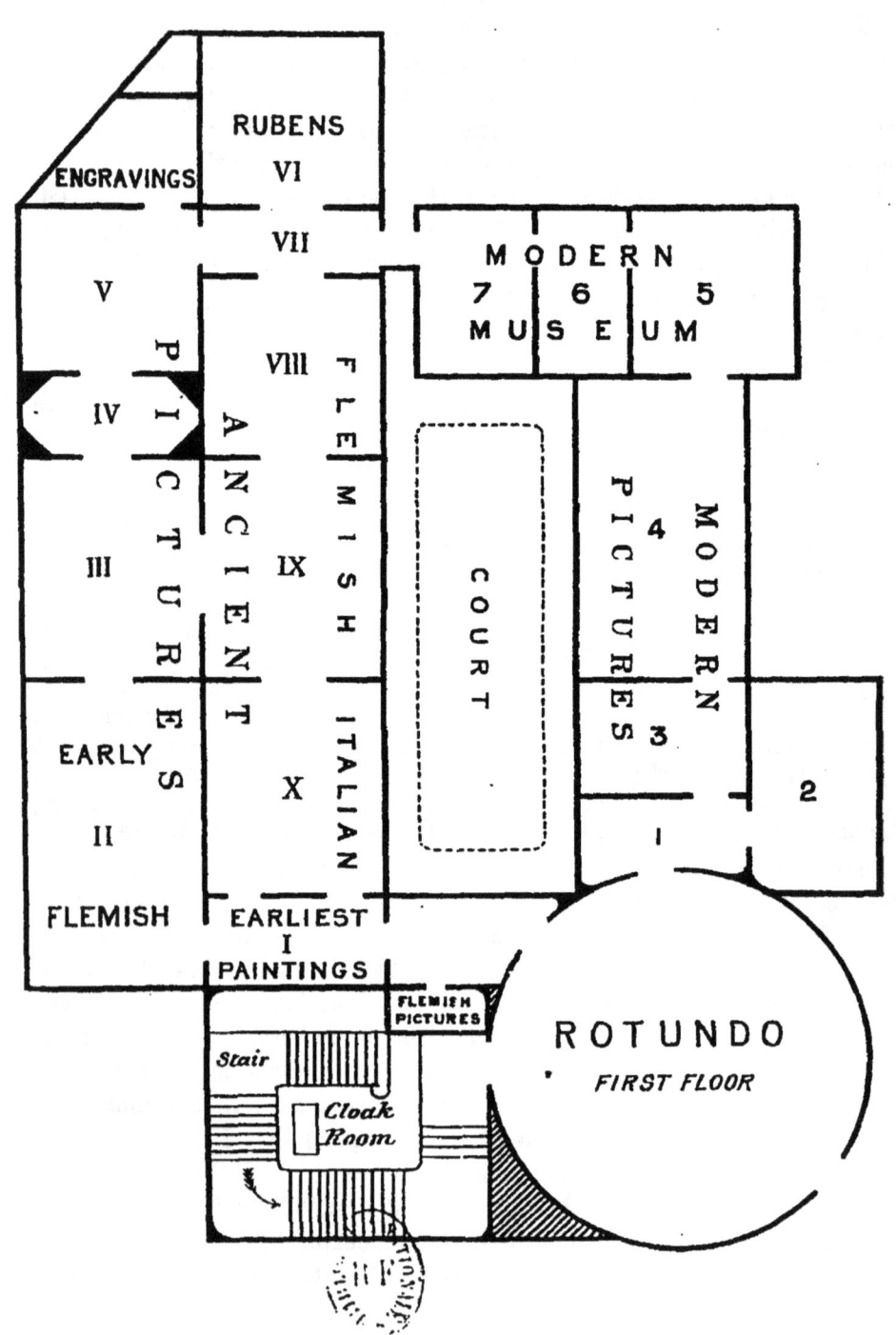

SENATE HOUSE.   HOUSE OF DEPUTIES.

ages, by Belgian sculptors. At the left end a broad staircase of Belgian marble leads up to the house of the senate, and at the other end a similar stair to the house of the deputies. Ascending the staircase leading up to the Senate-house, the first room visited is the reading-room, with portraits of Leopold I. and queen, and of the presidents of the Senate, by Keyser, Navez, Robert, and Lagye. From this we enter the great hall, of a semicircular form, with a richly gilt roof ornamented with the escutcheons of the 9 provinces. The walls are partly lined with massive sculptured mahogany panelling, which serves also as frames for the 15 full-length portraits painted by Gallait, on a gold ground, representing the counts, warriors, and legislators of Belgium. Over the president's chair is an allegorical painting, by Biefve, and on one side portraits of Leopold I. and queen, and on the other portraits of Leopold II. and his queen. In the smoking-room are some admirable portraits by Verboekhoven. In the president's room is a small but a good painting by Madou, "Villagers looking at a railway train."

The House of Deputies differs from the other only in the furnishing and fittings, which are much plainer. The statue over the Speaker's chair, representing Leopold I., is by G. Geefs. In the interesting picture by Starck, of Leopold II. taking the oath of the constitution (1865), are, in a front seat, Queen Victoria, with the Prince of Wales and the Princess Royal. In one of the committee rooms is the picture painted in 1817 by Odevaere, of the Prince of Orange wounded at the battle of Waterloo. And also by the same artist, in another room, Marie de Bourgogne, daughter of Charles le Téméraire, thrown from her horse while hunting; which caused her death. To visit the two houses a small gratuity is expected. They are shown by different doorkeepers. The sittings are from 2 till 5, and the session lasts from November to May or June. Deputies from the provinces receive £17 per month. To be qualified for a senator, a man must be 40 years of age, and pay in taxes at least £84:12s. Round the corner of the House of Deputies, at No. 22 Rue Ducale, is the Lucas Huys, a Flemish house, 16th cent., with a timber front.

On a small terrace, the Impasse du Parc, off the Rue Royale, at the Senate-house end of the palace, is a statue by G. Geefs to the memory of the Comte Belliard, d. 1832. Here are an English bank and one of the numerous dealers in laces. Farther west, and similarly situated, is the **Place du Congrès**, with the Colonne du Congrès erected in 1850-1859 to commemorate the first Congress (June 4, 1831) of the present constitution. Before it stand two fierce-looking lions by

BRUSSELS.   CATHEDRAL.   ENTRANCE.   SOUTH TRANSEPT.

Simonis. On the four short buttresses of the base are statues in bronze representing Religious Toleration, by Simonis; Liberty of Association, by Fraikin; Liberty in Education, and Liberty of the Press, by J. Geefs. At the base of the shaft is an allegorical relief by Simonis, and on the top, 154 ft. high, is a statue by G. Geefs, of Prince Leopold of Saxe-Coburg, their first king. It is ascended by a spiral staircase of 193 steps. The view is the best in Brussels. Gratuity to doorkeeper 25 c. Below are the covered markets, the Cathedral Sainte Gudule and the Banque Nationale.

The Cathedral, called St. Michel from the hill on which it stands, and Sainte Gudule from the relics it contains, was founded in the 11th cent. Having been destroyed by fire, it was again commenced in 1220, but not finished till 3 centuries later, indeed, it may be said, till the present century. It rises from a spacious platform approached on the west side by a flight of broad steps. The façade is flanked by two square towers 224 ft. high, connected by a mullioned pediment over a large and valuable stained-glass window representing "The Last Day" by Frans Floris in 1528, and restored in 1864. This window, a gift from Bishop Erard de la Marck of Liège, is remarkable for the number of figures it represents.

Entrance.—The doors at the ends of both transepts are open till 12. During worship enter quietly by the north transept and stand before the entrance to the Chapel of the Sacrament. Having seen the windows, slip out and go round the outside of the church to the south transept door, where take a look at the chapel of Notre Dame and its windows. The best time to visit the church is between 10 and 12, when it is free; unless in the case of some funeral or other extraordinary ceremony. From 12 to 2 the church is closed, and from 2 till 5 or 6 partially so. Enter then by south door. Fee at that time to visit the church 1 fr. or ½ fr. each when a party. As this money goes to the church, the beadle expects a trifle for himself besides. His services can be procured at any time; but when the church is open they are unnecessary.

South Transept.—Entering by the south transept, we have on the left wall a triptych by Coxcie in 1553, representing the Crucifixion. The large stained-glass window of the south transept is by Van Orley in 1538, and represents Louis of Hungary and his queen Mary, sister of Charles V., accompanied with their patron saints. Opening into the S. transept, but within the choir, is the Chapelle de **Notre Dame de Deliverance**, built in 1619, and lighted by 5 large stained-glass win-

CHOIR. NORTH TRANSEPT.

dows by Baer of Antwerp 1656, representing in superb colours, from designs by Thulden, incidents in the life of Mary. On them are also portraits of the donors, Ferdinand III. and Eleonora d. 1651, Archduke Leopold d. 1658, Archduke Albert with his spouse, d. 1663, Archduke Leopold-Guillaume, d. 1649, and Leopold I., d. 1705 ; which as portraits are worthless. Against the wall fronting the altar is the beautiful white marble monument by G. Geefs, to the memory of Count Frederick de Merode, killed in 1830 while fighting at the head of his volunteers at Berchem in 1830 against the Dutch. Above is an "Assumption" by Navez. At the east end of the chapel is the altar in black and white marble, by Voorspoel ; to the right is the mausoleum of Count Isenburg-Grenzau, d. 1664, and his spouse Ernestina, by Voorspoel ; and to the left that of Philippe d'Ennetières.

Choir.—High up at the east or apsidal end of the choir are 5 large stained-glass windows, executed in 1545. The first window represents, in a kneeling posture, accompanied with their patron saints, the Emperor Maximilian and Mary of Burgundy.—2. Philippe le Beau and Juana of Aragon.—3. Charles V. and Ferdinand his brother, sons of Philippe.—4. Philippe II. (son of Charles V.) with his queen Mary Tudor of England ; and 5. Philibert of Savoy and Margaret of Austria. Under each are their arms emblazoned on the glass. To the left or N. side of the high altar is the mausoleum of John II., Duke of Brabant, d. 1312, and of his wife, Margaret of York, daughter of Edward I., surmounted by a brass lion, cast in 1610, to replace the original one destroyed in the previous century. Opposite is the tomb of the Archduke Ernest, d. 1595, Governor-General of the Netherlands. At the back of the choir (13th cent.), behind the high altar, are seven stained-glass windows by Navez and Capronnier, of which the two best are in the small chapel, "de la Madeleine," immediately behind the high altar.

North Transept.—The best glass is in the north transept, and in the chapel off it, the "**Chapelle du Saint Sacrement,**" built expressly, between 1534-1539, to receive the three miraculous wafers [1] stolen by Jews

---

[1] In 1370 certain Jews who inhabited Brussels were accused of having stolen from the cathedral some consecrated wafers. On Good Friday they, out of rage and spite, stabbed them with their knives, when to their horror and dismay, blood spirted out of the dry pale-coloured substance. Through the information of a converted Jewess, they were recovered, and the guilty parties put to death and their property confiscated. The pricking of the wafers is said to have taken place in a synagogue ; whose site is now occupied by the expiatory Chapel St. Salazar built in 1436, recently restored and ornamented with appropriate mural paintings. It is near the university, in the Rue des Sols.

BRUSSELS.   CATHEDRAL.   SAINT SACRÉMENT.   NAVE.

in 1370. The principal events of the story are illustrated in subdued colouring on the 5 tall windows, on which also are represented the portraits of the donors in a kneeling posture. Before, however, commencing, observe the beautiful window at the end of the north transept, by Van Orley in 1538, representing Charles V. and his queen, with their patron saints. The triptych on the wall represents incidents in the life of Sainte Gudule, d. 712 at Hamme near Brussels, painted by Coxcie in 1592. First window, left hand at entrance to the chapel : John III. of Portugal and his wife Catherine, sister of Charles V. Above, Jonathan the Jew bribing Jeanne de Louvain to steal the wafers; painted by J. Haeck from designs by Coxcie.—2. Louis II. of Hungary and his wife Mary, sister of Charles V. Above, the Verification of the Wafers, also by J. Haeck.—3. François I. of France and his wife Eleonora, sister of Charles V. Above, by Van Orley, Jonathan the Jew being put to death.—4. Ferdinand I., brother of Charles V., and Anna his wife. Above, Catherine a converted Jewess receiving the wafers to take them to Cologne.—5. Over the altar, Charles V. and his queen Eleonora Louisa, painted by Haeck. Over the arch is a smaller window, representing the Adoration of the Sacred Wafer, admirably painted by Capronnier and Navez in 1848. The altar of the chapel "du Sacrément" is by Goyers, in 1849.

Nave.—The length of the nave and choir is 388 ft., and 164 ft. wide, bordered by circular piers, from which spring early pointed arches. The nave is lighted by two rows of large windows, of which those of the lower, 15 in number, were painted by Capronnier from 1860 to 1870, and were presented to the church by different families. From the nave the fine window by Franz Floris is seen to great advantage. On consoles, against the pillars, are statues of our Lord and the apostles, of which those of Paul, Thomas, Matthew, and Bartholomew, are by Jérome Duquesnoy, the brother of the famous sculptor. John, Andrew, and Thaddæus are by Fayd'herbe, d. 1694. The others are by Quellin. **The elaborate pulpit** was executed for the Jesuits by H. Verbruggen in 1699. After their suppression it was purchased by Maria Theresa, and presented to St. Gudule in 1776. It represents Adam and Eve, of the natural size, driven by the angel from Paradise. On the left Death is seen pursuing them; who likewise takes possession of the earth, represented by the hollow globe forming the tribune, resting on the branches of the tree of knowledge of good and evil. An enormous serpent coils its way up to the top of the sound-board, where it is crushed by the cross held by Mary and the child Jesus. The pulpit stair is by J. B. Vander Haeghen

BANK. ARCADE ST. HUBERT.

1780. The railing is a thick mass of carved foliage, and the balusters stumps of trees, on which disport animals and birds of various kinds, already showing symptoms of being affected with the consequence of the first transgression. In the corner, at the S. transept, is the beautiful monument in white marble of the Canon Triest, by E. Simonis, 1846.

(I have followed the above order in describing the cathedral, that the visitor may be enabled to see all the important parts without moving much to and fro.)

The handsome large building in the same square as the cathedral is the **National Bank**, constructed according to the plans of Beyaert and Janssens. The entrance and façade, by Houstront, are on the other side, fronting the Rue Berlainmont. This bank, instituted by charter granted in 1850, and renewed 1872, has branches in all the provincial capitals and several other towns, and is to Belgium what the Bank of England is to England. Its capital is £2,000,000, in shares of £40 each. It pays a dividend of 5 per cent upon the shares, and one-third at least of the profits exceeding 6 per cent goes to form a sinking fund. The administration consists of a governor nominated by the king, six directors, and a council of censors. The banking operations are superintended by a Government commissary; and a report upon its state is presented to the Government every month. The state funds are deposited in this bank. The Bank of Belgium, chartered in 1835, has also a capital of £2,000,000, but has not the official status of the Banque Nationale.

Grande Place, Hotel de Ville, Mannéken, Bourse, St. Nicolas, Halles Centrales.

Descending from the cathedral by either of the streets in front, we pass the entrances into the Arcade of St. Hubert, 698 ft. long, 59 high, and 26 wide, consisting of the Galerie de la Reine and the Galerie du Roi, built by J. P. Cluysenaar in 1847, who was also the architect of the arcade and the important covered market, a little farther up, entered from No. 35 of the Rue de la Madeleine by the Galerie Bortier, or from No. 12 of the Rue Duquesnoy. On the ground floor of this market are the shambles for the meat, fish, vegetables, and poultry, and in the upper gallery the game, fruit, and flower stalls. The busiest time is on Mondays, Wednesdays, and Thursdays, before 10 A.M.

The arcade of St. Hubert is much frequented as a promenade and for its excellent shops, cafés, and theatres; the Theatre des Fantaisies, the Theatre des Vaudevilles, and the Theatre des Galeries de St. Hubert.

Brussels. Grande Place. Corporation Houses.

Corporation Houses.—In the low town is the Grande Place, with the Hotel de Ville and the houses which belonged formerly to the city guilds. Standing with the back to the Hotel de Ville, we have on the left or north corner, in the Rue de la Tête d'Or, "Le Renard," the house of the silk-mercers and haberdashers. Panels with cupids in relief busy with silk extend across the front, under a massive balcony supported by caryatides and brackets. Next it is the house of the boatmen (bateliers), called also "la Maison Cornet," built in 1697. On the upper story is Neptune with his tritons, and over them, under the gable, two cannons, each guarded by a sailor. The adjoining house, No. 5 La Louve, belonged to the archers. Above centre window is a group representing the she-wolf suckling Romulus and Remus; hence the name. In second story four statues, and on the top a phœnix renewing its existence. Adjoining is No. 4 La Brouette, the house of the guild of carpenters, built in 1697. The first two stories rest on attached columns with gilt capitals, and the third on five caryatides partly gilt. Next it is No. 3 Le Sac, the house of the guild of printers and booksellers, built in 1697. The façade has three tiers of attached columns, the centre tier being twisted. Under the gable is a short, thick cylinder resembling a sack, on which are the names of Furst, Gutenberg, and Scheffer, and over it a medallion with their profiles.

At the other or right-hand corner of the Hotel de Ville is the Cygne, built by the *Butchers* in 1523, and rebuilt by them in 1695. A swan is over the door. The street at the corner of this house, the Rue de l'Hotel de Ville, and its continuation the Rue de l'Etuve, lead directly to the statuette fountain of the Mannéken, see page 185. Next the Cygne is the house of the *Brewers* (Brasseurs), surmounted by an equestrian statue by Jacquet, of Prince Charles of Lorraine, Governor of the Netherlands from 1741 to 1780. Between the two upper stories are three panels, with cupids making and drinking beer. Occupying the entire S.E. side of the "Place" is what was formerly the Hall of Weights and Measures. It is ornamented with busts, reliefs, and tall fluted pilasters. Next it, in the Rue de la Colline, is La Balance, with two negroes supporting a balcony. Under the soffit of the arch are two cupids, one with scales, the other with a trumpet. In the side fronting the Hotel de Ville are No. 25, the Taupe, belonging to the tailors' guild, with richly-gilt pilasters. Next it is No. 24, "The Pigeon," or painters' hall, with four lions' heads in relief on the wall. The most important of all the houses is the **Maison du Roi,** or Broodhuis, rebuilt 1882 according to the original plans. It was constructed in the 11th cent. to serve as a bread depot; but was afterwards occupied by the

Hotel de Ville.   Tower.

Government officials. Before this house were beheaded, by the order of the implacable bigot the Duke of Alva, many of the most noble in the land, including the Count of Egmont and the Count of Hornes or Hoorn, who spent their last night in this house. Next day, 5th June 1568, they were led to the scaffold by a planking extending from the balcony. The statues of the two counts by Fraiken 1864, which formerly stood here over the place where they were beheaded, now grace the square in front of the Palais d'Arenberg, formerly the residence of the Count Egmont. The Maison du Roi is a rectangular edifice, having on the ground floor 8 large Early Pointed mullioned transomed windows with narrow geometrical tracery. The doorway is in the centre, and corresponds with the windows. Above are two stories of 16 windows each, exactly half the size of the windows on the ground floor. In the centre of each row is a large window, corresponding in size and form with the doorway below. One side of the building is 9 and the other 7 windows deep.

The **Grande Place**, 355 feet long and 230 wide, was formerly a marsh, and was not known by its present name till 1380. One entire side is occupied by the **Hotel de Ville**, with a frontage of 195 feet and depth 162. The left wing, 15 feet longer than the other, was commenced in 1402 and finished in 1410. The short wing was commenced in 1444, and finished in the next century. On the 5th of March 1444 Charles le Téméraire, then a boy 10 years old, laid the foundation-stone of the tower, the finest structure of the kind in Belgium. It was finished in 1455, and is the work of Johann van Ruysbroeck, who bound himself by an oath to use none but the best materials in its construction. The basement of the edifice consists of six four-centred arches on one side of the tower, and of eleven on the other. Above the *six* arches rise two stories, each having eight plain square-headed transomed windows, and between each window a plain pinnacle, and over each a four-centred arch. Above the *eleven* arches on the other side of the tower are ten square-headed transomed windows, with statues ranged in canopied niches, both over and between them. Over them rises the second story, which is less ornamented, and is surmounted by an open rectangular balustrade. The **Tower** is square up to the fourth story, and the continuation octagonal in three diminishing stages, terminating in a crocketed pinnacle 344 feet high, and ascended by 407 steps. On the top is a statue 16½ feet high, by Van Kode in 1454, of St. Michael the patron saint of the town, waving his sword above the rebel angel whom he treads under his feet.

The doorway is set in square mouldings with pinnacled buttresses on

BRUSSELS. HOTEL DE VILLE. CORRIDORS. HALLS.

each side. The tympanum is sculptured and slightly recessed, and over it are rows of elaborately - sculptured niches, with statues. Within the court are two handsome fountains, designed by Agneessens. Just behind them, to the right, is the house of the concierge. Fee to visit the rooms 1 fr. ; and to ascend the tower 1 fr. The view is extensive, though many will prefer that from the Colonne du Congrès in the Rue Royale, a little way beyond the Park. It occupies a more elevated position, much is only 154 feet above the ground and ascended by 193 well-made steps, page 177.

Round two sides of the court runs a corridor, in which are two large and remarkable pictures, "The Last Moments of Evrard T'Serclaes," assassinated in 1388 while on the road between Brussels and Hals. Painted by Stallaert. In the adjoining corridor is "The Defeat of Attila on the Plains of Chalons in 451" by Coomans. In the corridor above this, in the first story, are portraits of former sovereigns of the Netherlands—"The baby Duc de Brabant, Godefroid III. at the Battle of Ransbeck" by V. H. Janssens; Charles VI. of Germany by Helmont; Prince Charles of Lorraine (by Stallaert), forty years Governor-General of the Netherlands during the reign of Maria Theresa, his sister-in-law. His statue, by Jehotte, 1846, is in the square in front of the Bibliotheque Royale. Next is the door opening into the passage leading to the "Cabinets du Bourgmestre," or Mayor, hung also with portraits —see below. On the other side of the door is a large equestrian statue of Maria Theresa, 1740 to 1780, by J. Milité. Her reign is still called "the good old time." Next is the portrait of her son Joseph II. of Austria, by Herreyns. Before he died, February 1796, he wrote for himself the epitaph, "Here lies Joseph II. unfortunate in all his undertakings." Charles II. of Spain, 1698, by J. Van Orley. On the right side of the narrow passage are six portraits of the Dukes of Brabant, by Grange—Phillipe le Bon, Charles V., Philip II., Albert and Isabella, Philip IV., and Charles II. At the end of this passage is the antechamber of the Mayor, having on panels under the ceiling 15 charming views, by Van Moer in 1873, of parts of Old Brussels which have been demolished. All this is public. For the rest the concierge is necessary. The door in this passage opens into the **Salle du Conseil**, adorned with mirrors in richly gilt frames, and hung with tapestry by Leyniers, from designs by Janssens, representing the "Abdication of Charles V.," which took place in 1555, in the palatial edifice of the Dukes of Brabant situated in the Park ; but accidentally burnt to the ground in 1731. In the foreground is Philip II. ; behind him Charles V. with Mary of Hungary. In the background is

EXCHANGE. ST. NICOLAS.

Alva, with a red cloak (see p. 192.) Then "The Coronation of Charles VI. at Aix-la-Chapelle," and "The Inauguration of Philippe le Bon of Burgundy." On a gilt silver salver are the two keys of the town, which were presented to Philip when he made his "joyeuse entrée" into Brussels. The painting on the ceiling, the *chef-d'œuvre* of Janssens (1664—d. 1739), represents the "Assembly of the Gods." Fame, with her trumpet, seems to have her head turned to the spectator at both ends of the room. Iris performs a similar feat, while Ceres changes her position. From the antechamber we are taken through the Burgomaster's room, with ceiling painted by Van Orley, representing "Genii uniting the escutcheons of Brussels, Antwerp, and Louvain," to the Salle Gothique, or the **Salle du Trone**, the largest hall in the house, 195 ft. long by 82 broad, used for festivals and great occasions. The walls are lined with sculptured panelling, enclosing full-length figures in modern tapestry. The next room is the **Salle des Mariages**, where the civil contract of marriage is executed before the Burgomaster. It is hung with Belgian 15th cent. tapestry, and Gobelins of the 17th. It was in this hall that the sentence of death was read to Counts Egmont and Hoorn.

Behind the Hotel de Ville, at the intersection of the Rue de l'Etuve with the Rue du Chene, is the odd statuette fountain called the "Mannékén pis," the "oldest citizen of Brussels," by the famous sculptor Duquesnoy, placed here in 1619. Although generally nude, he has a well-filled wardrobe and a valet to dress him on State occasions.

Between the Boulevard Anspach and the Rue du Midi is the **Exchange** (Bourse), designed by Suys. On the façade towards the Boulevard is a group representing Belgium in the midst of industry and commerce by J. Jaquet. The great hall, 141 feet long and 121 feet broad, is in the form of a cross. Twenty-eight columns in couples sustain the roof, terminating in a handsome dome 148 ft. above the floor, ornamented in the Renaissance style. Two wide marble staircases lead up to the galleries. It cost £160,000. Public admitted. Opposite the Bourse, but surrounded by houses, is the old church of **St. Nicolas**. On a pillar opposite the side door opening from the Rue des Fripiers is a charming little picture by Van Hoeck d. 1651, of Mary watching the child Jesus asleep. On the high altar is "Jesus and the woman of Samaria," by Van Helmont. On the side wall to the right of the altar a "Last Supper," by Herreyns. On one side of the altar, in the Chapel of the Virgin, is "David beseeching God to stay the plague," and on the other "Joshua fighting against the Amalekites," both by Janssens.

BRUSSELS. THE MARKET. PLACE DES MARTYRS.

A short way north from the Bourse, and by the side of the Boulevard Anspach, are the principal markets of Brussels, the

Halles Centrales, built of iron, and about 170 yards long by about 35 wide. One half is devoted to fish, with a piece at the end for the sales of the fish by auction as they arrive from the ports. The other half is divided into two parts, one an ordinary market for meat, poultry, fruit, and vegetables. The other half for auctions of these same articles. They are attended by immense crowds of all kinds of people. The person who has had an article knocked down to him receives a paper with the number of the lot and the price, which having paid at the "Caisse," he presents at the counter behind, and receives in exchange his purchase.

Near the markets is the new church of Ste. Catherine, by Poelaert, the architect of the new Palais de Justice and of the church at Laeken. Close to it, but surrounded with houses, is the old church of Ste. Catherine, 12th century.

Northwards is the church of the Béguinage, built in 1657 by Coeberger. It is 213 feet long and 82 feet broad, and profusely decorated. The carved stalls and other ornamented woodwork are from the old Benedictine abbey at Cortenberg. High up over the high altar is a statue of John the Baptist by Puyenbroeck. To the left is "Christ being wrapped in linen," by Otto Venius. To the right a "Nativity," by Van Loon. Over the altar of the chapel of Mary, a "St. Catherine," by Van Loon. The pulpit is well carved. At the pedestal a monk treads upon the prostrate body of a Mussulman, whose hand grasps the Koran, through which a serpent is gliding. The large building opposite is the Hospice for old men and the Professional Athenée, or college for learning trades. In the Boulevard Hainault is a panorama.

Church of Finistère, Place des Martyrs, House of Duchess of Richmond, Botanic Gardens, Hospice St. Jean, Observatory.

At the end of the Rue Neuve, towards the railway station, is the church of **Finistère.** In a long chapel to the right side of the entrance is a highly venerated image of the Virgin, brought from the church of **St. Macaire** in Aberdeen in 1625, and placed originally in the church of the Augustins, whence it was transferred to this church in 1814. The pulpit is by Duray, and the stalls by Vanderheyden.

Almost opposite this church, up the Rue St. Michel, in the centre of the **Place des Martyrs,** is the monument by G. Geefs, erected in 1838 to the memory of the 445 patriots who fell in

BOTANIC GARDENS. HOSPITAL.

the latter days of September 1830, fighting for independence against the Dutch. Their names are written in gold letters on black marble slabs placed on the wall within the underground arcade of 20 arches, round the four sides of the square. From the centre rises a pedestal, adorned with sculptured reliefs, and an angel in prayer at each corner. On the top stands a colossal white marble statue treading on a coil of broken chains, representing Liberated Belgium. It has just written on a tablet 23, 24, 25, 26 September. By its side reposes the Belgian Lion, now at peace.

The best as well as the most ornamented specimens of modern Belgian domestic architecture are seen in the Place Bouckère and in the Boulevard du Nord. Some are prize buildings. The B. du Nord is between the Place Bouckère and the Place des Nations, in which is situated the Station du Nord.

On the left side of the Place des Nations, standing with the face towards the Station, is the halting-place of the trams to and from Laeken, p. 198; while to the right, at the little wooden house in the Boulevard du Jardin Botanique, is the halting-place of the trams which make the round of the Boulevards. Below is the low gate into the Jardin Botanique; and opposite it, the entrance to the Rue des Cendres. At the house No. 7 of this street, with an end towards the Rue de la Blanchisserie, is the house in which the **Duchess of Richmond** gave her ball on the night of the 15th of June. It was then an isolated, handsome house, with a garden. The building is now occupied by the sisterhood of SS. Jean and Elisabeth.

Higher up the Boulevard is the **Hospital of St. Jean**, a most excellent institution, built in 1843, and capable of accommodating 600 patients. All are admitted and attended by the first physicians of Brussels. Those who can pay give for board and attendance 7 frs. per day.

Opposite are the Botanic Gardens, a pleasant resort in all seasons. They are open to the public the whole day; but the large hothouses only from 9 to 12 and from 1 to 4. The plants for study are arranged according to the natural system. In other parts of the garden they are grouped according to their use or their quality. The principal groups are the cereals, the vegetables, and the textile, poisonous and oil-producing plants. The high gate of the Gardens opens into the Rue Royal. To the right, in the B. Botanique, stood formerly the Porte de Schaerbeck. At No. 50 B. de l'Observatoire is the Methodist Chapel, bought from a preacher called Boucher; and a little farther up the same Boulevard is the Royal Observatory for astronomical and meteorological observations under the management of a director and three assistants.

BRUSSELS.   MANUSCRIPTS.

The Bibliothèque Royale and the Picture Gallery.

To the left of the equestrian statue of Godefroid de Bouillon, in a corner of the "Place," under 3 arches, is the entrance into the Rue du Musée, in which is situated the vast edifice of the **Bibliothèque Royale**, occupying three sides of a square. The north wing is the palace built by Prince Charles in 1744 for the Governors of the Netherlands; while the south wing and centre were built in 1829, just before the separation of Belgium from Holland. This important and well-arranged library contains 340,000 volumes, 22,250 MSS., 81,000 engravings, and 20,000 medals and coins, of which nearly 5000 relate to the history of Belgium from 1450 to the present time.

The reading-room is in the centre of the edifice, on the first floor, and is open from 10 to 4 to every one who desires to consult any of the works. The door opposite the reading-room opens into the Manuscript department, where the same regulations exist. The department of Engravings adjoins that of the Manuscripts; but the proper entrance is by the door lettered "Cabinet des Etampes," in the rotunda of the Picture Gallery, opposite the doors opening into the Ancient and Modern Paintings, page 190.

In the **Manuscript** department the earliest MSS. date from the 5th cent., but they are fragmentary. The earliest of the complete MSS. date from the 7th cent. Among the curiosities are a copy of Xenophon's "Cyropaedia," bought at Berne in 1833 at an auction. The "Cyropaedia," which belonged to Charles the Bold, and which was found on the field after the battle of Nancy, is in the library of Geneva. A Psalter in folio, written and illuminated in the 13th cent. at Peterburgh, which belonged to Charles V. of France. An illuminated folio, containing a collection of homilies, called from the first text "Blessed are the merciful," written in Brussels about 1476 for Charles the Bold and his wife Margaret of York, sister of Edward IV. It contains several portraits of her. The best is where she is seen kneeling in the cemetery before the church of St. Gudule. At the end is her signature, "Margarete de Yorke." A missal in folio which belonged to the Dukes of Burgundy and afterwards to Matthew Corvinus, King of Hungary, written and illuminated in Florence in 1483 by Attavante. The "Chronicles of Hainault," 3 volumes folio, with illustrated title-page representing Jacques de Guise presenting his book to Philip the Good. A charming view of Seville in water colours on parchment (16

ENGRAVINGS.   EGLISE DU MUSÉE.

inches by 11), by Gregorius Hofnagel of Antwerp, 1573. The *bijou* of the manuscripts is the Prayer Book, written and illustrated probably for the mother of the Emperor Charles V., by the same artists who illuminated the Breviarium Grimani in St. Marc's, Venice—the *chef-d'œuvre* of miniature painting. It dates from the beginning of the 16th cent. The page is about 4½ inches long by 3½ inches wide. This Livre d'Heures contains 56 exquisite miniatures—12 showing the agricultural operations of each month, 8 the Passion of our Lord, 1 Bathsheba in the bath, 1 Sts. Corne and Damien, 1 The Mass, and 29 historical subjects—all clearly and skilfully executed. The pages are on movable frames, attached to a stand, so that they can be easily examined. Near it are 2 genealogies of Charles V.

In the valuable collection of **Engravings** the greatest curiosities are: An engraving on wood dated 1418, 15¾ inches long by 10¼ wide, representing Mary and child, with St. Catherine, St. Barbe, St. Margaret, and St. Dorothea. It is the oldest dated woodcut known. The next in date is a St. Christopher, 1423, in the possession of Earl Spencer. Near it is one of the oldest known engravings on copper, representing the arms of Charles the Bold, dating between 1466 and 1467. The Legend of St. Anne, engraved in 1577 from the picture by Quentin Metsys, in the Picture Gallery. A small St. Gerome, B 115, by Durer. Over the chimneypiece is the largest engraving in the world, a "Last Supper," after Rubens, by P. Devaulx, 17th cent. It is 6 feet 9 inches long and 4 feet 6 inches wide. An exterior and an interior view of the first London Exchange, erected at the expense of Sir Thomas Gresham in 1569, after the plan of the Antwerp Exchange.

In front of the Bibliothèque Royale is a bronze statue of Prince Charles by Jehotte in 1846. Adjoining the south wing of the Bibliothèque is the Palais des Beaux Arts, with façade towards the Rue de la Regence. Contiguous to the north side are the Museum and Picture Gallery.

At the low end of the Rue du Musée, by the side of the archway leading into the museums, is the Protestant Church of the State, or the Eglise du Musée, formerly the chapel of the palace, of which the foundation-stone was laid by Prince Charles in 1760.

Under the archway, left hand, is the stair leading up to the Picture Gallery. In the left-hand corner of the court is the door opening into the museums.

The Picture Gallery is in two divisions, the Ancient and the Modern paintings. The first contains about 500 paintings, from the

BRUSSELS.   PICTURE GALLERY.   MUSÉE ANCIEN.

14th to the beginning of the 18th cent., in seven rooms, and one large hall the length of the five rooms. The earliest masters are in the first three rooms. It is a most charming and enjoyable gallery, where naturally the Flemish school predominates in all its naïve beauty and charm. The pictures, too, explain themselves by labels on the frames, so that the spectator is saved the annoyance of consulting a catalogue.

At the top of the stair are two doors; one is lettered "**Musée Ancien**," the other "**Musée Moderne**." Enter by the Musée Ancien door, and having passed through a hall hung with Flemish tapestry of the 17th cent., and ornamented with statues by William, Joseph, and Jean Geefs, C. A. Fraiken, A. Fassin, Braekeleer, Delvaux, E. Simonis, Jaquet, Barth, Sopers, and Frison, we enter a small room with pictures belonging to the early German and Flemish schools, but most of the names of the artists are not known. The principal pictures are C. Amberger 1500-1563, portrait B. Bruyn 16th cent., two portraits Lucas Cranach 1472-1553, full-length portraits of Adam and Eve, and portrait of Dr. Scheuring, Carlo Crivelli, a Madonna Hans Holbein 1495-1543, portrait of Sir Thomas More, Lord Chancellor of England.

The door to the left leads into the continuation of the ancient pictures, the door to the right to the great hall, containing the conclusion of the series, including the time of Rubens.

Enter Second Room. Almost entirely pictures of the early Flemish school. The principal artists are H. Bles 1480-1550, Temptation of St. Anthony; observe the owl, the sign of the painter. Lancelot Blondeel, 1495-1561, St. Peter, ornamented as his pictures generally are. P. Brueghel senr., d. 1569, Massacre of the Innocents. P. Brueghel jr., 1565-1637, "Fall of the Rebel Angels;" Bruyn. J. Van Coninxlo, born 1544, has several pictures. *__Hubert Van Eyck__ 1366-1426, Portraits of Adam and Eve, which originally formed two of the wings of the great picture in Ghent, the "Adoration of the Lamb," see p. 158. On the figure of Eve, Van Eyck "seems to have concentrated all his knowledge of perspective as applied to the human form and its anatomical development. Adam is equally remarkable for correctness of proportion and natural realism."—Crowe and Cavalcaselle, *Early Flemish Painters*. But it is a pity Van Eyck did not take a more handsome model for Eve, especially as Ghent, at that time at least, was famous for its beautiful women. On the outside of the shutter, painted also with extreme care, is a view of the house the brothers inhabited in Ghent. Observe also the towel and the basin. Van Eyck has also in this room an "Adoration of the Magi," in fresh glowing tints. J. Hemessen, 16th cent. Mabuse or Jean Gossaert, 1470-1532, Jesus in the house of Simon the Pharisee. Memling, d. 1495, Portraits of W. Moreel and of his wife, Barbara of Vlaenderbergh. *__Quentin Metsys__, 1509, triptych representing the story of St. Anne. In centre, Virgin and child; on the right shutter, "The Death of St. Anne;" on the left, the angel announcing to Jehoiakim the birth of the Virgin; on the exterior, the high priest refusing the offering of Jehoiakim because (it is said) he was only the reputed father of the

Picture Gallery—Rooms 3-6.

Virgin ; on the other wing, the high priest's offering to St. Anne after the birth of the Virgin. The picture hangs at the end of the second room. J. Mostaert, 1474-1555. B. Van Orley, 1490-1542, has five large paintings in this room, of which the best and the most truly Flemish is "Jesus tended by the Maries." M. Schoen, 1430-1492, Christ shown to the people. Dierick Stuerbout, a widow proving the innocence of her husband, who had been beheaded, by holding a hot iron bar in her hand. Susterman, 1506-1566, a Last Supper. Roder van der Weyden, 1400-1464, "Head of a weeping woman." Other eight pictures in this room are attributed to him.

Third Room. Brueghel senr., 1520-1569. Brueghel jr., 1564-1637. Clerck, 1570-1629. Coxcie, 1499-1592, Last Supper and Death of Mary, two large triptychs. F. Floris, 1520-1570. Heemskerk, 1498-1574. Jordaens, 1593-1678. Orley, "Guillaume de Norman." P. Snayers, 1593, after 1669, seven large battle-pieces. B. Spranger, 1548-1621.

Fourth, or the Octagonal Room. Arthois, 1613-1655. Berghem, 1623-1683. P. de Champaigne, born at Brussels in 1602, died at Paris in 1674 ; the best of his series of paintings in the room is "The child Jesus in the arms of Simeon." G. Crayer, 1580-1669, Ascension of St. Catherine, very large ; his best works in next room. P. Van Dyck, 1680-1752, Young Lady. Corn. de Heem, 1671, Flowers. Hondekoeter, 1636-1695. C. Poelenburg, 1586-1667, Landscape. A. Pynacker, 1621-1673. Van de Velde, 1839-1672, Fruit.

5. G. Backereel, b. about 1572. C. Bizet, 1633-1685, Tell stringing his bow to shoot the apple on his son's head. F. Bol, 1611-1681, Portraits of lady and gentleman. J. B. Champaigne, 1643-1681, Ascension of Mary. G. Crayer has in this room five large pictures, of which the best are: Christ on the knees of Mary, or a Pieta ; and an Ascension of St. Catherine and "The miraculous draught of fishes." Hughtenburgh, 1646-1733 ; J. B. Huysmans, 1654. P. Neefs, the elder, 1570-1651. P. P. Rubens, 1577-1640, Coronation of Mary. The room beyond, or end room, is hung with engravings. From the windows one good view of Brussels.

From Room 5 enter the large gallery, which separates the ancient from the modern paintings. At the end of this gallery in section 6, next to room 5, are large paintings by P. de Champaigne ; amongst the best is a Sts. Stephen and Ambrose. Crayer: portrait. A. Van Dyck : Sts. Francis and Anthony. Franck, 1581-1642 : Crœsus showing his treasures to Solon. C. Huysmans, 1648-1727, Landscape with animals. Jacques Jordaens, 1593-1678, St. Martin healing a lunatic—his *chef d'œuvre*—a spirited composition, in glowing colours, and Fecundity, an allegory. P. Meert, 1619-1669, Portraits of the presidents of the corporation of fishmongers. P. P. Rubens, 1577-1640, his large pictures occupy the greater part of the walls of this part of the hall. The most striking is the Martyrdom of St. Livinius : a man holding the cut-out tongue in pincers presents it to a hungry dog, while the operator with the knife between his lips, is looking sternly into the face of the dying man. Here, as almost in every other case, the Roman Catholic priests are made to suffer martyrdom in full canonicals. Also Christ warded off by Mary from destroying the world,

Continuation of Large Gallery.

while St. Francis intercedes for it; painted for the Franciscans of Ghent, and curious as showing how much more compassionate Mary is considered than Christ. Our Saviour on his way to Calvary. Otto Venius, 1558-1629, Betrothal of St. Catherine to the child Jesus. C. Vos, 1585-1651, The artist and family. In the small subdivision between this section and the next large section, is at one end a door to the ancient paintings, and opposite one to the modern.

Third section, or second large division. Flemish painters. F. Bol, 1611-1681, Saskia, Rembrandt's first wife. A. Both, born 1609, Landscape. Cuyp, 1605-1691, A stable; cow admirable. A. Van Dyck, 1599-1641, Crucifixion of St. Peter; grand picture. C. Heem, Fruit and flowers. Hobbema, born 1638, Haarlem wood. Jordaens, Triumph of Prince Henry of Nassau. P. Lint, 1609-1690, Portrait of himself. M. Musscher, d. 1705, Portrait of an engraver. N. Maes, 1632-1693, Old woman reading; very good. A. Van der Neer, 1619-1682. A. Ostade, 1610-1685, Woman winding yarn. Rembrandt, 1607-1669, Portrait; admirable. Rubens, Portraits of Cordes and wife; admirable. J. Ruysdael, 1625-1682, Landscape. There are no good specimens of the works of this, the greatest of Flemish landscape painters. J. Steen, 1626-1679, The gallant offer. G. Smeyers, 1635-1710, Death of St. Norbert. F. Snyders, 1579-1657, Game. D. Teniers jun., 1610-1690, The painter, his wife, and daughter, entering the village fair. In the background his chateau of the 3 towers, see page 216, his best here. P. Wouverman, 1623-1683, The riding lesson. J. Wynantz, 1641-1679, Landscape.

Fourth section or third large division. Flemish paintings, but as a whole inferior to the former division. N. Berghem, 1620-1683. Gerard Dou, 1613-1675. He himself sketching a Cupid by the light of a lamp. J. Fyt, 1609-1661. F. Hals, 1584-1666, Portrait of Heythuysen. Hals is one of the greatest Flemish portrait painters. His best works are at Haarlem. B. Helst, born 1613, An admirable portrait of himself. K. Jardin, 1625-1678, Returning to the stable. Keyser, 17th cent. G. Metsu, born 1630. A. Meulen, 1634-1690. A. Moro, born 1512, Duke of Alva. P. Neefs, Interior of Antwerp Cathedral; admirably painted. J. Van Oost jun., 1637-1713. F. Pourbus. Thulden. E. Witte, 1607-1692.

In the fifth section from the Rubens end of the hall, or the first section next the first room of the ancient paintings, are Italian and Spanish dictures by Bassano, 1558-1625. An. Caracci, Diana and Actæon. A. Sanchez Coello, 1559-1590, Jane of Austria, and Margaret of Parma, daughters of Charles V. Dasso Dassi, 1560, Jesus in the house of Simon the Pharisee. Ingres, 1780-1867. Claude Lorraine, Landscape. B. Manfredi, 1580-1617. C. Maratti, 1625-1713. Murillo, 1618-1682, Franciscan monk. Pannini, 1695-1768. Procaccini, 1548-1626, St. Sebastian. Guido Reni, 1525-1642. Velasquez, 1599-1660, Two children. Paolo Veronese, 1528-1588, several paintings. Tintoretto, 1512-1594. This section is the least interesting. Off the statue-gallery there is another hall with a few more Flemish paintings—C. Dusart, 1660-1704. G. Flinck, 1613-1660. M. Hondekoeter, 1636-1695. A.

Musée Moderne. Musée Wiertz.

Mignon, 1639-1679.   A. Mor, 1512-1581.   F. Moucheron, 1633-1686.
S. Ruysdael, d. 1670.   A. Sallaert, 1590.

Modern Paintings.

Now return to the Rotunda and enter by the door "Musée Moderne" the department of modern pictures, Room 1, All the pictures are labelled. To the right is room 2, hung with enormous pictures. The most important is the large painting by *E. de Bièfve in 1841, representing the Compromise or the drawing up of the petition on the 6th April 1566 in the house of Count Kuylenberg, to be presented to the Vice-Regent, Margaret of Parma, daughter of Charles V., praying her to abolish the inquisitorial courts. Count Egmont is sitting on a red velvet arm-chair, his cloak thrown over his left arm. Count Hoorn is signing the petition. Sitting in front of the table is Philip de Marnix, clad in armour. To the right of the spectator is William of Orange in blue, Martigny in white, and the Duke of Arenberg in light brown, behind the Prince of Orange. Under the colonnade to the left, the Count de Brederode is persuading others to add their names. Another large picture represents the battle of Worringen 1288. Siegfried, Archbishop of Cologne, stands before his captors, Duke John I. of Brabant and Count Adolph of Berg.

In **Third room**, good specimens of modern Belgian paintings.

The **Fourth** is the large hall; where the principal painting is by L. Gallait in 1841, representing The Abdication of Charles V. The Emperor, standing on a dais below a canopy, has his right hand on the head of his son Philip II., who is kneeling before him, while his left rests on the shoulder of the Prince of Orange, opposite whom stands Cardinal Granvella. To the left in an arm-chair is the sister of the Emperor, Mary of Hungary, dressed in white satin trimmed with ermine. B. G. Wappers, Charles I. on his way to the scaffold. Haas, Cattle. Lies, "The evils of war."

Fifth room, L. Gallait, "Art and Liberty." F. Stroobant, Guild houses in the Grande Place.—6. Small room with portraits of the Royal Family.—7. This room communicates with the large gallery of the ancient paintings. M. J. Van Bree and F. J. Navez have some good paintings here.

Museum of Natural History.—On the ground floor, in the court to the left, is the entrance to the Museum of Natural History. The department lettered "Ethnographie et Paléontologie des Cavernes de Belgique" is the most remarkable. At the entrance is an enormous skeleton of a young Mammoth found at Lierre, near Antwerp.

Fronting the R. de l'Imperatrice, to the left of the R. de la Madeleine, is the University, to which is attached a technological museum and a polytechnic school, where lectures are given on mining, metallurgy, practical chemistry, engineering and architecture. In front is a statue by Geefs of Verhaegens, d. 1862, one of its founders and most liberal of its patrons.

The **Musée Wiertz**, behind the Luxembourg station. Easily approached by the tram running from the right side of the statue of Godfrey in the Place Royale to the Rue Belliard. Request to be let down at the Rue du Remorqueur, which walk up to the first street left, the Rue Vauthier.

Wiertz Museum. St. Joseph. Rond Point.

At the top of the street is the Picture Gallery, formerly the residence and studio of Antoine Joseph Wiertz, a talented but eccentric artist, born at Dinant in 1806, d. 1865. Open from 10 to 4. Free. Round the great hall hang enormous paintings, mostly sensational—"The triumph of Christ," "Sects according to Christ," "Sects judged by Christ," "A scene in hell." In one corner on this side 2 delightful pictures, "The Concierges" and "La Confiance," and at the other corner, a lady presenting a rose. On the right hand wall "Un grand de la terre," "The Beacon of Golgotha," or the Erection of the Cross. On opposite side "Lutte (wrestle) Homerique," "The Greeks and Trojans disputing over the body of Patroclus." "The last cannon." In one corner at the inner end are small but curious pictures. 19. "Buried alive;" look through the hole. 34. "The devil's mirror;" look through both holes. 33. Two young girls, but one is a skeleton. 22. Suicide. 21. Hunger, madness, and crime; look through the hole.

There are besides other two rooms. In the first are drawings, and in a case some relics of the artist. In the other are small pictures, many unfinished. Among them are Laetitia, mother of Napoleon I., in her coffin. A head after decapitation. 108. Twenty sketches for a painting to represent the revolt in hell. 110. Eleven sketches for the painting which represents the Triumph of Christ. Most of the large pictures are labelled.

Next the Musée Wiertz is the Parc Leopold, formerly the Zoological Gardens. It is entered from the low end of the Rue Belliard, near the terminus of the tramway from the Place Royale. It is a very picturesque park with lakes, large forest trees, and wide sloping lawns. The large building on the eminence is to contain the Natural History Museum.

On the N. or left side of the Rue Belliard is, in the Place de la Société Civile, the church of St. Joseph, a spacious edifice in the Renaissance style, built in 1849 by Suys. The reredos of the high altar, representing a "Holy Family," is by Wiertz. On the pier to the left of the altar is a small picture, 15th cent., on a gold ground, representing Mary and Child, or as the inscription states, "Notre Dame du Perpetuel Secours. Image venerée à Rome." Round the walls are large paintings.

At the end of the Rue de la Loi (a long broad street, parallel to the Rue Belliard) are a railway station and a large square called the Rond Point. Beyond is a plain used for exhibitions and military exercises.

Notre-Dame de la Chapelle, Hospital St. Pierre, Porte d'Hal, Blind Asylum.

In the Rue Haute, a little way down from the Place Grand Sablon, see p. 173, is the church **Notre-Dame de la Chapelle**, founded by Godefroid I. in 1134. The choir alone belongs to the 12th cent.; the nave, which is more elegant, belongs to the 15th cent. The door generally open is in the south transept. Just within this door, on the

Notre Dame de la Chapelle.

south or right side of the choir, is the Chapelle de la Trinité, ornamented with 4 frescoes, by J. B. Van Eycken in 1850, who died 3 years afterwards. The fresco over the altar represents the Trinity. On the left wall is "Jesus inviting the weary and heavy laden to come to Him." To the right are portraits in a kneeling posture on a gold ground, representing the Infanta Isabel, d. 1633 (next altar); Queen Louise Marie d'Orleans, d. 1850; and the Duchess Juana de Brabant, d. 1406. On the ceiling are representations of the beatitudes. On the transept wall fronting the chapel is, also by Van Eycken, "The liberation from slavery by Christianity." Against the wall by the right side of the main or western entrance, are the mausoleum of E. Willaert by Tuerlinckx 1870, and next it the monument by Godecharle (his last work) to the memory of the painter Lens, d. March 1822. On the other side of the entrance is a monument by Tuerlinckx to the memory of the painter Sturm, d. 1844. The statues of the apostles and of Joseph and Mary on consoles against the pillars are by Duquesnoy and Faid'herbe. The "Via-Crucis" as the 14 pictures (round the nave) representing the sufferings of the last hours of our Lord are called, are by Eycken. Every Roman Catholic church is provided with a set; but they are very often carelessly painted or sculptured.

The reredos of the 5th chapel, right hand from chief entrance, is "Christ appearing to Mary" by Crayer. In the chapel behind the pulpit is the grave of the painter Peter Brueghel, d. 1569. Above the simple tombstone is one of his own pictures, "Christ giving the keys to Peter." The pulpit is by Plumiers. At the base is Elijah in a cave succoured by an angel.

On the N. transept is the "Healing of the child possessed of devils" by Van Eycken. In front is the Chapelle du Sacrement, built in 1654, on the left side of the choir. The monument on the column is by Van Gheel, to the memory of the Duc de Croy, d. 1624. On the other side an inscription recounts the virtues of the Belgian patriot Anneessens, beheaded in the Grande Place on the 19th of September 1719. Near the altar is the mausoleum by Plumier of the Spinola family—pure white marble statues on a jet-black marble basement. The 6 landscapes in this chapel are by Dartois and Achtschelling. The picture on the right side of the altar is by Crayer, representing Carlo Borromeo administering the sacrament to persons dying of the plague. On the left, by Van Thulden, "Intercession for souls in purgatory," of which the entrance is seen in the foreground. The high altar was constructed from designs by Rubens.

Museum in the Porte d'Hal.

S.W. from the church of La Chapelle by the busy street, the Rue Haute, is at No. 320 the large hospital of St. Pierre, and a little farther the Porte d'Hal, reached also from the Palais de Justice by the Rue aux Laines. The **Porte d'Hal**, built in 1381, is the last remnant of the old fortifications. During the reign of the Duke of Alva it was used as a prison; now it contains a Museum of **Armoury and of Mediæval Antiquities.** All the important articles are labelled and explained. Open from 10 to 4. In the garden outside are old cannons and mortars of various nations. In the interior on the ground floor are monumental inlaid tombstones, 14th to 16th cent., baptismal fonts, ancient mosaics, shafts and capitals of columns, and a model of the Bastille of Paris. Before ascending the spiral stair, enter the recess and look up.

In the **First Floor** is the collection of armour, ancient and modern. In front of door under glass case is the armour of Leopold I. of Belgium. At the end of the passage, the horse on which the Prince of Orange rode at Quatre Bras and Waterloo. Right hand of entrance in case, the helmet, gauntlets, and poignard of Charles V.

Second Floor, mediæval antiquities. Delicate and laborious carving in ivory and oak. Down the centre are 6 superbly-carved oak altar-pieces, and a very fine confessional. The first, left hand, represents the martyrdom of St. George in 7 exquisite groups, under a profusion of canopies: figures are from 13 to 18 in. high: date 1493. Next is a reredos from Luxembourg, with the passion and crucifixion of J. C. in quaint and expressive groups. God and the angels up in the corner have a curious simpering expression. Figures from 9 to 12 in. high, date 15th or beginning of 16th cent. 3. Genealogical tree of Jesse, and scenes from the life of J. C. in 7 groups of painted and gilded statuettes under canopies, date 16th cent., figures about 13 in. high. 4. Reredos, from Auderghem, 15th cent. J. C. between St. Anne and Mary: figures about 12 in. high. 5. Reredos, 16th cent., from Gestel, near Antwerp, 6 groups representing the birth and childhood of J. C., under rich canopy-work: figures 11 to 13 in. high. 6. Reredos 1530, from the abbey of Liessies, in magnificent transition Gothic, with 6 groups, representing the martyrdom of the Maccabees and of St. Ludgerus and St. Agnes. The figures, about 9 in. high, are admirably executed, and have over them a perfect forest of canopy-work. Then follow a pulpit and a confessional. To the left of entrance, under a large glass case, is some beautiful carved ivory—among others a reliquary, 12th cent., from the Abbey of Sayn, near

Porte d'Hal.   Bois de la Cambre.

Coblentz. An admirable miniature in relief of Juana Pernestan, with a garland of real rubies, emeralds, and pearls. In the smaller case behind are among others C. 48, ivory diptych, 8th cent., 12 in. long, 7 in. wide, the heel of the woman crushing the head of the serpent. On the other plate, 2 subjects, Elizabeth greeting Mary and the Coronation of Mary. C. 47. An ivory plate, 10th cent., 7 in. by 4¼, representing the birth and crucifixion of J. C., and the 4 Evangelists, one in each corner, writing the gospels. 7. The small but famous Diptychon Leodiense, representing the birth, crucifixion, descent from cross, and entombment of J. C., 6th cent.

Down the right side of the hall, 16th cent. tapestry, Sedan chair of Prince Charles of Lorraine. A door with lock and hinges on both sides, and opening at either, 17th cent. : the plan is simple. At the end of the room is the cradle of Charles V.

In the third story are seals, coins, specimens of marble, Venetian glass, mummies, and Egyptian, Greek, and Roman statuettes, vases, lamps, pottery, and jewellery. An easy way to get to the Porte d'Hal is by the Point Central - Uccle coach, starting every ½ hour from the corner near the Bourse, right hand. The coach passes the Porte. Near the Porte d'Hal, in the Boulevard Waterloo, is the Blind Asylum, a brick building, with a clock-tower, designed in 1858 by Cluysenaar. Near it is a "Home" for teachers and governesses without situations.

ENVIRONS OF BRUSSELS.

The **Bois de la Cambre**, 20 minutes southwards from the Park by either the tram that starts from the church of St. Marie at the north extremity of the Rue Royale, or the tram starting from the Godfrey statue in the Place Royale. Both drives are pleasant, and pass over much the same ground. The Bois de la Cambre is a delightful retreat consisting of 450 acres taken from the Forest of Soignies, intersected and surrounded by broad carriage-roads, from which ramify in every direction footpaths plunging into the dark recesses of the forest, or winding down grassy slopes to glades in the miniature valleys below. Down on the plain is a lake, with an island in the centre, where there is a good restaurant and boats for hire. A large ferry-boat or "bac" takes people to the island and back for two sous. In the wood there is also a good Laiterie, while in front of the entrance-gate are several restaurants, of which one is famous for "gauffres," a kind of dry pancake. Near the entrance to the Bois, below the left or west side of the Avenue Louise, is Ixelles. Trams every ten minutes to and from the Park.

Ixelles approached by the coach starting every $\frac{1}{4}$ hour from the Rue du Marché aux Poulets behind the Bourse, and ascending to the "Place" in High Ixelles by the Rues Madeleine and Montagne de la Cour, the Place Royale, and the Rue de Namur; or by tram starting from the top of the Rue Namur and running to the Place Ste. Croix of Low Ixelles by the Place de la Couronne, where there is a monument to Wiertz. From the Place in High Ixelles the street Chaussée d'Ixelles leads down to the Place Ste. Croix. At this "Place" are a park and two lakes. By the side of the higher of the two lakes are the buildings of the Abbaye de la Cambre, now a military college for officers, with about 100 pupils. The old church with its high-peaked roof is interesting. The steep road by the side of the college leads up to the Avenue Louise, which it joins within a short distance of the Bois de la Cambre.

Laeken by trams starting every 15 minutes from the Station du Sud, and halting on their way at the Station du Nord. At Laeken they stop at the bridge across the canal. The tram, which goes much farther up the town and stops in front of St. Mary's church, runs between Laeken and Anderlecht, $2\frac{1}{2}$ m. S. from Brussels. It passes through Brussels by the Rue Artevelde, and halts behind the Halles Centrales at the part called Le Point Central, nearly opposite the Bourse. Fare the whole way 60 c.

Laeken, formerly a separate village, is now a suburb of Brussels, connected all the way by houses and streets. One of the best of the restaurants is the Grande Grille, where the "plat du jour" costs 75 c.

The church of St. Mary at Laeken was built by Poelaert, the architect of the Palais de Justice. It is partly in the style of the 12th cent., in which stones in cubes are prominent. The façade is flanked by two open towers, while behind rises a structure, which in the distance resembles a glass-work chimney. Plain and ornamented gables, between attached and flying buttresses, crown the chapels and surround the edge of the roof of the choir. In the interior 32 whitewashed lofty piers, with pointed arches, support the roof. Behind the choir, and about 10 feet higher, is the royal burial-vault, containing in a crypt the tombs of Leopold I., d. 1865, and of his queen Marie Louise, daughter of Louis Philippe, d. 1850. The pulpit, organ-loft, stalls, and confessionals are handsome. Their towering slender pinnacles, terminating with sculptured finials, serve to counteract in some degree

Laeken. Palace. Racecourse.

the gaunt effect produced by the tallness of the piers. Behind is the old church, commenced in the 12th cent., now abandoned. The two churches look like two ships with their sterns toward each other.

The cemetery is overcrowded. Near the centre is the Galerie Funeraire, large underground vaults, divided into cells for coffins, like those in Genoa, Cadiz, and in other parts of the south of Europe. Although well ventilated, it is very questionable if this method of interment is advisable in a damp climate like that of Brussels.

From the church a wide handsome boulevard leads up to the principal entrance into the grounds of the royal palace. Beyond the private precincts is a large and beautiful park, a very favourite Sunday resort. On an eminence 19 feet high, fronting the entrance into the palace, is the monument to Leopold I., built by "La Belgique reconnaissante." It is in the form of a Gothic pinnacle, resembling the monument to Sir Walter Scott in Edinburgh. 51 steps lead up to the first gallery, and 33 more to the second. Both command delightful views of the park, palace, and Brussels. At the foot, in the centre, is a colossal white marble statue, by Geefs, of the King, looking towards the palace in which he died on the 16th December 1865.

The **Palace** was built in 1782 by the Austrian governor of the Netherlands, Archduke Albert of Saxe-Techen. The façade is composed of a peristyle of four Ionic columns, with a bas-relief by Godecharle, representing "Time presiding over the Hours and Seasons." Two pavilions form the wings. The rotunda, of blue granite, is decorated with sculpture, and the pavement with a mosaic of marble. Before the French evacuated Brussels in 1813, they sold the chateau to some of their confederates. It was at this chateau that Napoleon decided on the Russian war. The King resides in it for the summer and autumnal months. It may be visited in the absence of the Royal family. Beyond the palace the road divides into two, one branch going to the village and chateau of Grimbergen about 2 m. N.W., the other to the village of Meysse and chateau of Bouchout, the residence of the Princess Charlotte, widow of the Emperor Maximilian, shot at Mexico in 1867, as a usurper.

The Racecourse.—From Luxembourg station take train to Boitsfort station, 3¾ m. N.E. Boitsfort is a very pretty but a very straggling village, situated principally in a hollow on the north side of the railway. The racecourse is on the other side of the railway, in the canton of Uccle. It makes a very pleasant short excursion to take the train to Boitsfort, then walk down by the broad road to a sign-post, having

UCCLE. TERVUEREN. ANDERLECHT.

the racecourse on the left. To the left of the sign-post is Goenendael, 3¾ m. distant, and to the right is the eastern entrance into the Park de la Cambre, which walk through and take the tram for Brussels at the western gate.

Groenendael is the next station after Boitsfort, 5 miles from Brussels, picturesquely situated, with the remains of a celebrated priory.

Uccle, 3¼ m. S. from Brussels by the rail starting from the Station du Sud. A tram starts every half hour for Uccle from the left side of statue of Godfrey in the Place Royale, passing through the suburb of St. Gilles, 2 m. south. The facilities of transport afforded by the tramways is causing villas to spring up rapidly in the southern quarters, which are high, have a dry sandy soil, and are near the Bois de la Cambre. From near the right side of the Bourse, the Point Central, a coach starts every half hour for Uccle, or rather St. Gilles, where it meets the tram for Uccle. The coach halts both ways at the Porte d'Hal, with its museum, p. 196.

From the Hotel de la Verrerie a coach starts daily to Tervueren, 7½ m. S.E. from Brussels, passing at about halfway the prettily-situated village of Auderghem, with the ruins of the priory of Rouge-Cloitre. At Tervueren is a charming royal domain inhabited for a long time by the Princess Charlotte, widow of the Emperor Maximilian. The chateau was burned to the ground in March 1879. After the conflagration the pretty chateau of Bouchout, at the village of Meysse 3½ m. N. from Laeken, was fitted up for her. See page 199.

Tram to Anderlecht behind the Halles Centrales, running between Anderlecht and Laeken, and passing through Brussels by the Rue Artevelde, parallel to the Boulevard Anspach. **Anderlecht,** 2¼ m. S. from Brussels, is a large village with a church of the 15th cent. and crypt of the 12th, or perhaps earlier. Over the portal is a massive square tower, supported by round and square buttresses. The side chapels are gabled and supported by shallow receding buttresses. Right hand of door are small pictures illustrating the quaint history of St. Guidon, who figures again between a horse and a cow at the pedestal of the pulpit. The church contains also a picture by Crayer, and another by De Clerck. To the right of the altar is the tomb of Count Arnoul, d. 1505, and opposite a mausoleum in black marble, with the recumbent effigy of a knight, whose feet rest on a lion.

THE FIELD OF WATERLOO.

Start from Brussels by an early train from the Gare du Midi, with a ticket for Braine l'Alleud, 1 fr. 45 c., 1 fr. 10 c., 75 c. The tickets for Braine l'Alleud are sold in the office fronting the "Place." A cheap, interesting, and enjoyable trip. A coach for the field leaves every morning.

After passing 4 stations, the train reaches the station of Waterloo, 10 m. S. from Brussels, and ¾ m. W. from the village. At the station there are several cafés and restaurants. At the end of the station road where it enters the village, is to the left, within a small garden, the house where Wellington had his headquarters before the battle, and where he wrote his ever memorable despatch to the Earl of Bathurst, dated Waterloo, 19th June 1815. Up to 1880 there stood in the room the table at which he wrote it; while in the small room off were the stretcher on which the Marquis of Anglesea lay when his leg was amputated, and under a glass case the bones of the leg itself.

The Duke, in answer (Paris, August 17, 1815) to some questions from Sir Walter Scott for an account of the battle of Waterloo he was preparing, concludes his letter thus :—"These are answers to all your queries ; but remember, I recommend to you to leave the battle of Waterloo as it is." See Appendix, page 303. Here is, therefore, his own account, the best and most reliable of all, which he wrote in this humble little house the day after the battle :—

Waterloo, June 19th, 1815.

MY LORD—Bonaparte having collected the 1st, 2d, 3d, 4th, and 6th corps of the French army and the Imperial Guard, and nearly all the cavalry, on the Sambre, and between that river and the Meuse, between the 10th and 14th of the month, advanced on the 15th, and attacked the Prussian posts at Thuin and Lobbes, on the Sambre, at daylight in the morning.

I did not hear of these events till in the evening[1] of the 15th, and I immediately ordered the troops to prepare to march, and afterwards to march to their left, as soon as I had intelligence from other quarters to prove that the enemy's movement upon Charleroi was the real attack.

The enemy drove the Prussian posts from the Sambre on that day ; and General Zieten, who commanded the corps which had been at Charleroi, retired upon Fleurus; and Marshal Prince Blücher concentrated the Prussian army upon Sombreffe, holding the villages in front of his position of St.-Amand and Ligny.

The enemy continued his march along the road from Charleroi towards Brussels, and on the same evening, the 15th, attacked a brigade of the army of the Netherlands, under the Prince de Weimar, posted at Frasnes, and forced it back to the farmhouse, on the same road, called Les Quatre-Bras.

The Prince of Orange immediately reinforced this brigade with another of the same division, under General Preponcher, and, in the morning early, regained part of the ground which had been lost, so as to have the command of the communication leading from Nivelles and Brussels with Marshal Blücher's position.

In the meantime, I had directed the whole army to march upon Les Quatre-Bras ; and the 5th division, under Lieutenant-General Sir Thomas Picton, arrived at about half-past 2 in the day, followed by the corps of troops under the Duke of Brunswick, and afterwards by the contingent of Nassau.

---

[1] As the event alluded to happened during one of the longest days of the year, the Duke must have meant by the word "evening," some time after 7, or even some time during the ball, otherwise it is impossible to explain his tardiness in sending reinforcements to Quatre-Bras.

Wellington's Letter to Earl Bathurst.

Battle of Ligny. At this time the enemy commenced an attack upon Prince Blücher with his whole force, excepting the 1st and 2d corps, and a corps of cavalry under General Kellermann, with which he attacked our post at Les Quatre-Bras (page 212).

The Prussian army maintained their position with their usual gallantry and perseverance against a great disparity of numbers, as the 4th corps of the army under General Bulow had not joined them, and I was not able to assist them as I wished, as I was attacked myself, and the troops, the cavalry in particular, which had a long distance to march, had not arrived.

Battle of Quatre-Bras. We maintained our position also, and completely defeated and repulsed all the enemy's attempts to get possession of it. The enemy repeatedly attacked us with a large body of infantry and cavalry, supported by a numerous and powerful artillery. He made several charges with the cavalry upon our infantry, but all were repulsed in the steadiest manner.

In this affair His Royal Highness the Prince of Orange, the Duke of Brunswick, and Lieutenant-General Sir Thomas Picton and Majors-Generals Sir James Kempt and Sir Denis Pack, who were engaged from the commencement of the enemy's attack, highly distinguished themselves, as well as Lieutenant-General Charles Baron Alten, Major-General Sir Colin Halkett, Lieutenant-General Cooke, and Major-Generals Maitland and Byng, as they successively arrived. The troops of the 5th division, and those of the Brunswick corps, were long and severely engaged, and conducted themselves with the utmost gallantry. I must particularly mention the 28th, 42d, 79th, and 92d regiments, and the battalion of Hanoverians.

Our loss was great, as your lordship will perceive by the enclosed return; and I have particularly to regret his Serene Highness the Duke of Brunswick, who fell fighting gallantly at the head of his troops (page 213).

Although Marshal Blücher had maintained his position at Sombreffe, he still found himself much weakened by the severity of the contest in which he had been engaged, and as the 4th corps had not arrived, he determined to fall back and to concentrate his army upon **Wavre**; and he marched in the night, after the action was over (unknown to the French) (page 213).

This movement of the Marshal rendered necessary a corresponding one upon my part; and I retired from the farm of Quatre-Bras upon **Genappe**, and thence upon **Waterloo**, the next morning, the 17th, at 10 o'clock (page 214).

The enemy made no effort to pursue Marshal Blücher. On the contrary, a patrol which I sent to Sombreffe in the morning found all quiet, and the enemy's videttes fell back as the patrol advanced. Neither did he attempt to molest our march to the rear, although made in the middle of the day, excepting by following, with a large body of cavalry brought from his right, the cavalry under the Earl of Uxbridge.

This gave Lord Uxbridge an opportunity of charging them with the 1st Life Guards, upon their *débouché* from the village of Genappe; upon which occasion his lordship has declared himself to be well satisfied with that regiment.

Battle of Waterloo. The position which I took up in front of Waterloo crossed the high-roads from Charleroi and Nivelles, and had its right thrown back to a ravine near Merbe-Braine, which was occupied, and its left extended to a height above the hamlet Ter-la-Haye, which was likewise occupied. In front of the right centre, and near the Nivelles road, we occupied the house and gardens of Hougoumont, which covered the return of that flank; and in front of the left centre we occupied the farm of La Haye-Sainte. By our left we communicated with Marshal Prince Blücher at Wavre, through Ohain; and the Marshal had promised me that, in case we should be attacked, he would support me with one or more corps, as might be necessary (page 214).

The enemy collected his army, with the exception of the 3d corps, which had been sent to observe Marshal Blücher, on a range of heights in our front, in the course of the night of the 17th and yesterday morning; and at about 10 o'clock he commenced a furious attack upon our post at Hougoumont. I had occupied that post with a detachment from General Byng's brigade of guards, which was in position in its rear; and it was for some time under the command of Lieutenant-Colonel Macdonell, and afterwards of Colonel Home; and I am happy to add, that it was maintained throughout the day with the utmost gallantry by these brave troops, notwithstanding the repeated efforts of large bodies of the enemy to obtain possession of it (page 203).

Wellington's Letter to Earl Bathurst.

The attack upon the right of our centre was accompanied by a very heavy cannonade upon our whole line, which was destined to support the repeated attacks of cavalry and infantry, occasionally mixed, but sometimes separate, which were made upon it. In one of these the enemy carried the farm-house of **La Haye-Sainte**, as the detachment of the light battalion of the German legion, which occupied it, had expended all its ammunition, and the enemy occupied the only communication there was with them (page 207).

The enemy repeatedly charged our infantry with his cavalry, but these attacks were uniformly unsuccessful; and they afforded opportunities to our cavalry to charge, in one of which Lord Edward Somerset's brigade, consisting of the Life Guards, the Royal Horse Guards, and 1st Dragoon Guards, highly distinguished themselves, as did that of Major-General Sir William Ponsonby, having taken many prisoners and an eagle.

These attacks were repeated till about 7 in the evening, when the enemy made a desperate effort with cavalry and infantry, supported by the fire of artillery, to force our left centre, near the farm of La Haye-Sainte, which, after a severe contest, was defeated; and having observed that the troops retired from this attack in great confusion, and that the march of General Bulow's corps, by **Frischermont**, upon Plancenoit and **La Belle-Alliance** had begun to take effect, and as I could perceive the fire of his cannon, and as Marshal Prince Blücher had joined in person with a corps of his army to the left of our line by **Ohain**, I determined to attack the enemy, and immediately advanced the whole line of infantry, supported by the cavalry and artillery. The attack succeeded in every point; the enemy was forced from his positions on the heights, and fled in the utmost confusion, leaving behind him, as far as I could judge, a hundred and fifty pieces of cannon, with their ammunition, which fell into our hands (La Belle Alliance, p. 205).

I continued the pursuit till long after dark, and then discontinued it only on account of the fatigue of our troops, who had been engaged during 12 hours, and because I found myself on the same road with Marshal Blücher, who assured me of his intention to follow the enemy throughout the night. He has sent me word this morning that he had taken 60 pieces of cannon belonging to the Imperial Guard, and several carriages, baggage, etc., belonging to Bonaparte, in Genappe.

I propose to move this morning upon Nivelles, and not to discontinue my operations (page 215).

Your lordship will observe that such a desperate action could not be fought, and such advantages could not be gained, without great loss; and I am sorry to add that ours has been immense. In Lieutenant-General Sir Thomas Picton his Majesty has sustained the loss of an officer who has frequently distinguished himself in his service; and he fell gloriously leading his division to a charge with bayonets, by which one of the most serious attacks made by the enemy on our position was repulsed. The Earl of Uxbridge, after having successfully got through this arduous day, received a wound by almost the last shot fired, which will, I am afraid, deprive his Majesty for some time of his services.

His Royal Highness the Prince of Orange distinguished himself by his gallantry and conduct till he received a wound from a musket-ball through the shoulder, which obliged him to quit the field.

I should not do justice to my own feelings, or to Marshal Blücher and the Prussian army, if I did not attribute the successful result of this arduous day to the cordial and timely assistance I received from them. The operation of General Bulow upon the enemy's flank was a most decisive one; and even if I had not found myself in a situation to make the attack which produced the final result, it would have forced the enemy to retire if his attacks should have failed, and would have prevented him from taking advantage of them if they should unfortunately have succeeded.

Since writing the above, I have received a report that Major-General Sir William Ponsonby is killed; and in announcing this intelligence to your lordship, I have to add the expression of my grief for the fate of an officer who had already rendered very brilliant and important services, and was an ornament to his profession.

I send with this dispatch 2 eagles, taken by the troops in this action, which Major Percy will have the honour of laying at the feet of his Royal Highness. I beg leave to recommend him to your lordship's protection.

I have the honour to be, etc.

WELLINGTON.

Braine l'Alleud. Tour of Waterloo.

A little way up the street of the village of Waterloo, and to the right of the station road, is the parish church, with about 30 marble slabs to the memory of those who fell, and a bust of Wellington by Geefs. The sacristan lives in the shop opposite. Fee to open the door ½ fr. Waterloo is 1¾ m. N. from the village of Mont St. Jean. At the cross-roads of Mont St. Jean is the Hotel des Colonnes, a comfortable house, where it is said Victor Hugo finished his "Miserables." The Museum Hotel, at the foot of the Lion Mound, is about a mile beyond. It is not worth while stopping at the Waterloo station.

Braine l'Alleud.—11⅘ m. S. from Brussels by rail, 1¾ m. S. from Waterloo station, 11 m. N. from Nevelles, and 23 m. N. from Charleroi, is Braine l'Alleud station, a little above the town, pop. 6000. In the "Place" is the H. du Midi, and between it and the station, the H. de l'Etoile. The streets are clean, and some contain very nice houses. The parish church is a large brick edifice, displaying a certain degree of elegance in the interior, but only the half is finished.

Passengers who leave Brussels by the 10 or later trains will find the omnibus awaiting them from the Museum hotel. For those who are able and who desire to understand the nature of the field, it is better to walk to Hougoumont, about a mile from the station, and then across the fields to La Belle Alliance, in the centre of the French position. From this turn northwards to the Mound and Museum hotel, not forgetting to observe in passing, the farm-house of La Haye-Sainte, on the west side of the road. The Museum hotel is a clean and comfortable house, with moderate charges. It contains a good collection of books on Waterloo, and relics gathered from the field by Sergt.-Major Cotton, who fought at the battle. Guides are unnecessary (see Plan).

The Tour of the Field of Waterloo from Braine l'Alleud Station.—From the station, at the "Goods" end, take the Hougoumont road, then second road left, which joins the main road at a farmhouse. Cross the main road and walk up to Hougoumont. The entrance is round by the S.W. end. Fee ½ fr. each. Hougoumont is built in the same style as all the neighbouring farmers' or yeomen's houses, such as Papelotte, La Haye-Sainte, La Belle Alliance, and the large one at Maison du Roi—an oblong rectangle enclosed within a strong wall, round the sides of which are built the house, offices, granary, and stables. These buildings line only part of the walls, for the court is large and contains in the centre the dunghill. **Hougoumont** was of a superior class, and had a small chapel in the centre of the court. The crucifix which resisted the flames hangs still over the door. To the right of the entrance into the court of Hougoumont is the house which was inhabited by the gardener; it is all of the time of Waterloo, excepting the roof. The upper story has still a battered appearance. The offices to the left are also of the same period, excepting the large granary, which, with the exception of its buttressed stone wall, has been rebuilt. Nearly opposite, was the house or chateau which was burnt to the ground by a battery of howitzers ordered against it by Napoleon. The gate in the court wall opposite the northern end of the granary was the one burst

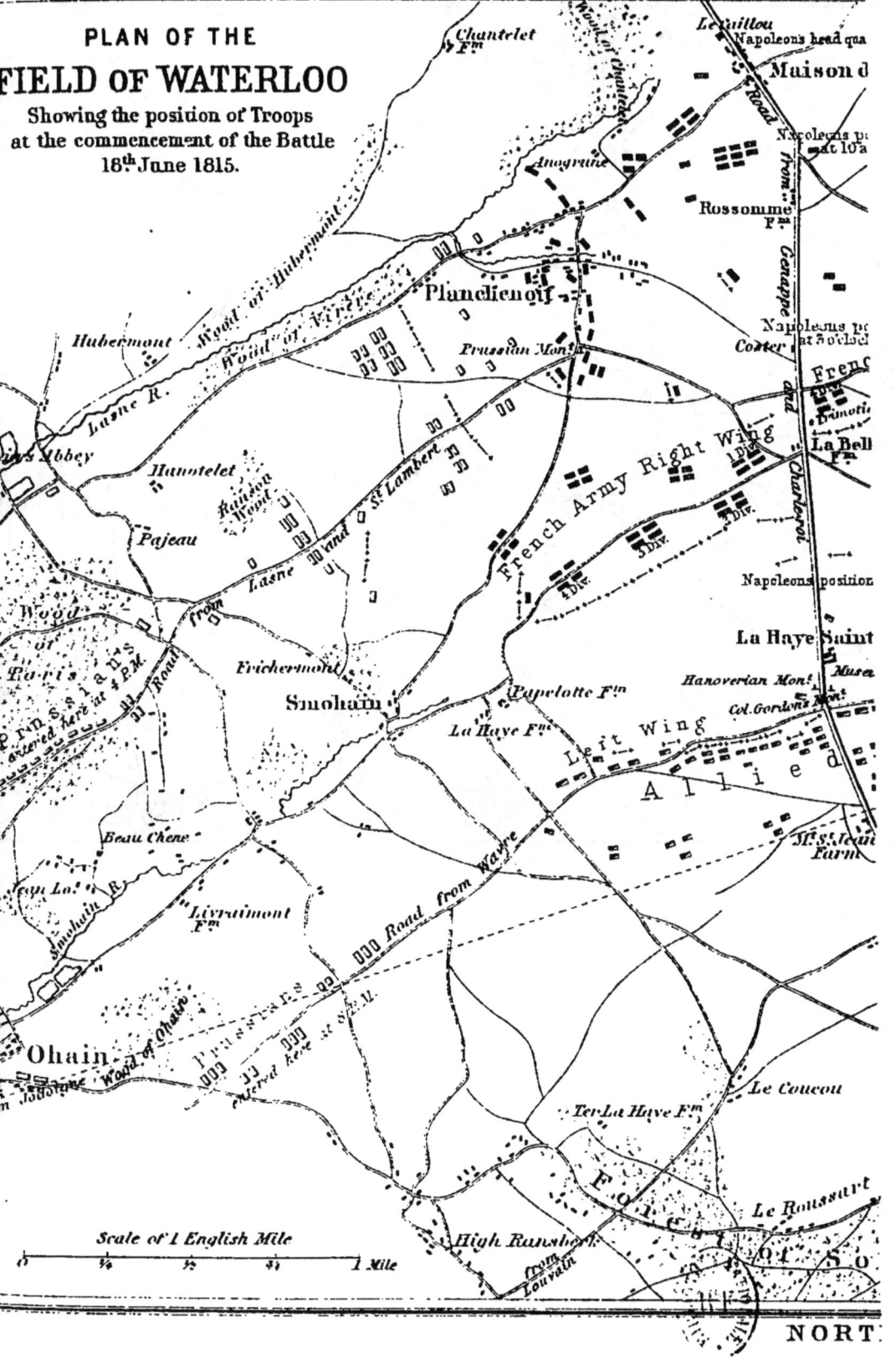

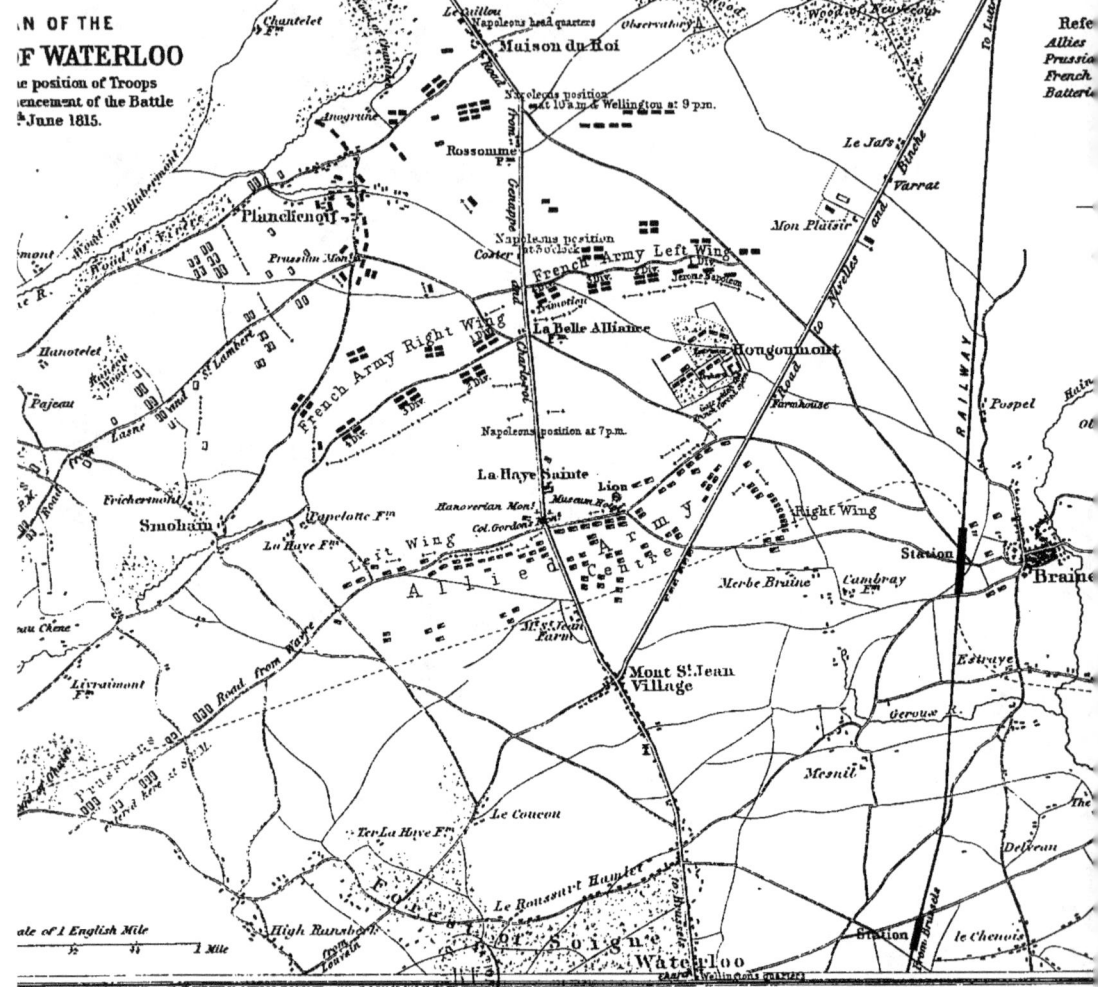

Hougoumont. La Belle Alliance.

open by the French, when a fearful struggle ensued between them and the Coldstream Guards, till at last Colonel Macdonnell, Captain Wyndham, Ensigns Gooch and Hervey, and Sergt. Graham, succeeded by main force and great exertion in again closing it in the face of the French bayonets. Afterwards a desperate assault was made against the back gate, the present main entrance, from which, however, the French were driven with great slaughter, as the position of the wall enabled the English to pour a murderous fire of bullets upon the assailants. Adjoining the S.E. side of the buildings is the orchard, protected on two of the outer sides by loopholed brick walls, but on the other, the N.E. side, merely by a hedge on an embankment. Around the orchard is the wood; which was defended by a Nassau battalion and a Hanoverian rifle company; while the orchard and the court were defended by brigades of the Guards under Colonel Macdonnell and Lord Saltoun. In the orchard, near the S.W. wall, are the graves of John Lucie Blackman, d. 18th June 1815, and Edward Cotton of the 7th Hussars, d. 24th June 1849. Some of the chestnuts and beeches are from the time of Waterloo. "The chateau, farm, walls, etc., were at the time of the battle of a substantial nature. The garden, or park, was enclosed, on the east and south sides, by a wall, in which our troops made loopholes. At the east wall, an embankment, and the scaffolds erected with some farming utensils, enabled the Coldstreams to throw such a fire upon the enemy's left flank when in the large orchard, that Colonel Hepburn, who commanded there, considered it (the east wall) as the strength of his position. The most interesting objects now at Hougoumont, for visitors to see, are the north gateway facing our position, by which the enemy entered, its burnt beams, the small barn where many of the wounded were burnt, the cannon-ball hole in the east gable of the building attached to the present farm-house, the perforated top part of the south gate, the battered front of the house and stables, the loopholed walls with the banked-up hedges and the hollow way. In the orchard is a tomb, beneath which lie the remains of Captain Blackman of the Coldstreams (brother to Sir George Harnage), who fell on that spot." Alongside is the grave of Sergt.-major Cotton, the writer of the above lines.

La Belle Alliance.—From the main entrance into the chateau of Hougoumont, the continuation of the path leads round by the orchard walls through the fields to the Genappe road, which it joins a little beyond the farm-house and "Estaminet" or beer-house of **La Belle Alliance.** Here it was where the two commanders met—Blücher on his way from Frichermont, and Wellington on his return from Maison du Roi. Over the door is the following inscription on a slab of white marble :—" Belle Alliance Rencontre Des Génereaux Wellington et Blucher Lors De La Memorable Bataille du xviii Juin mdcccxv." By the side of the house a finger-post indicates that it is 1¼ m. from Mont St. Jean, ¾ m. from Plancenoit, 1¾ m. from Braine l'Alleud, and 4¾ m. from Genappe. Wellington had pursued the French army to about 1¼ m. beyond this, to **Maison du Roi**, a little village on both sides of the road, with a church, an inn, some cottages, and some large farm-houses. A finger-post indicates that it is 2½ m. from Mont

Meeting of Wellington and Blücher.

St. Jean, ¾ m. from Plancenoit, $3\frac{1}{10}$ m. from Genappe, and 5¾ m. from Nivelles. Plancenoit is just behind Rossomme. About ¼ m. beyond, on the high part of the road, is the straggling little village of Caillou. Napoleon lodged on the 17th in the first house. It has a large garden, surrounded by a strong stone wall. Between the small farm-house of Rossomme and the village of Maison du Roi the road makes a bend, and cuts through a little hill. On this eminence Wellington halted with his advance of infantry and cavalry to allow room for the Prussians to pass. As they "passed us, for I had the honour and good fortune to be an actor in this scene, I heard their bands play 'God save the King,' which soul-stirring compliment we returned by hearty cheers. In the pursuit of the enemy from Rossomme to Genappe, the Prussian lance and sabre were busy in the work of death, and many a brave soldier who had escaped the bloody field fell that night beneath their cold deadly steel.

"The Duke, after clearing the high-road of the allied troops, in order to give full scope to the advancing Prussians, to whom he relinquished the further pursuit of the flying enemy, remained for some time with his advanced troops on the right of Rossomme in conversation with General Vivian, Colonel Colborne, and others; after which, promising to send the provisions up, his Grace turned his horse round and rode away. On returning leisurely towards Waterloo, about ten o'clock, at a short distance before reaching **La Belle Alliance**, he, aided by a clouded moon, descried a group of mounted officers making towards the Genappe high-road from the direction of **Frichermont**; the Duke turned off to meet them: it proved to be Blücher and his staff; they most heartily congratulated each other on the glorious result of the contest in which they had been so intensely engaged. The conference lasted about ten minutes, when the veteran Blücher, promising to leave his inveterate foe no rallying time on this side of the frontier, shook hands with his Grace and proceeded to Genappe. Our gallant chief now continued his way over the field to Waterloo. Before reaching La Haye-Sainte he was obliged to quit the high-road, on account of its being completely blocked up with guns and tumbrels, many of which were upset and lying topsy-turvy; whilst the frequent snort and start of the horses told but too clearly that the ground they trod was studded and strewed with the slain. His Grace, on regaining the high-road, was so affected by the cries of the wounded and moans of the dying as to shed tears, and on his way did not exchange a word with any of his suite, composed only of five persons."—Sergeant-Major Edward Cotton's *Voice from Waterloo*.

At 8.30 P.M., or perhaps later, Wellington's advance brigades had reached Rossomme, where the Duke had given orders that the main body of his army should halt, and that the pursuit should be continued by Blücher and his troops, which were comparatively fresh. On the elevated ground overlooking Maison du Roi, stood the Duke with his advance of both infantry and cavalry, as the Prussian regiments passed by, with their bands playing "God save the King," a compliment which was greeted on the part of the British by hearty and friendly cheers. Having ordered his advance guards to take up their bivouacs for the night, he returned

PRUSSIAN MONUMENT. FRICHERMONT.

from this distant part of the field and proceeded leisurely along the Charleroi road back towards Waterloo. On approaching **La Belle Alliance** he ordered the whole of his army to bivouac on the field of battle.

On reaching that point he met Blücher, when mutual congratulations took place between them on the splendid victory achieved. With the promise of vigorously following up the pursuit and of allowing the enemy no opportunity of rallying within a march of the field, Blücher took leave of Wellington, who then continued his way towards Waterloo, where he passed the night.—*War in France and Belgium in* 1815, by Captain W. Siborne. "A neuf heures du soir, Wellington et le vieux Blücher se rencontrèrent à **la Belle-Alliance**; où ils purent s'adresser de mutuelles felicitations."—*Histoire du General Wellington* par le Colonel Brialmont.

From the Belle-Alliance most tourists follow the high-road to La Haye-Sainte, the Lion Mound, and the Museum Hotel.

But to visit the Prussian position, it is necessary to walk across from La Belle Alliance to the **Prussian monument**, an iron obelisk erected by the King and the Fatherland, to the memory of the gallant heroes who fell in the desperate engagement, which lasted between 6.30 P.M. till past 8, when the Prussians, under their Prince William, drove the French from Plancenoit, the bulwark of their right flank. The fiercest part of the struggle was in and around the churchyard in the village below.

While a desperate conflict raged in front of the farm of Mt. St. Jean and around that of La Haye-Saint, Blücher was pressing onwards with unparalleled ardour through the forests behind **Frichermont**, but such were the difficulties of the passage, owing to the horrible state of the roads, that it was not till half-past four that Bulow, who led the advanced guard, was able to deploy from the woods. Long all their efforts were unavailing. The deep and miry roads between Wavre and St. Lambert had caused so many stoppages and breaks, that the column was stretched over miles. The guns often sank axle-deep; and such was the exhaustion of the horses that they were unable to drag them out. The men, wearied as they were, upon this were harnessed; and, as at the passage of the St. Bernard, their efforts were stimulated by the sounding of the charge—"We cannot get on!" they exclaimed. "But you *must* get on" was the loyal-hearted Blücher's reply. "I have pledged my word to Wellington, and you will not make me break it. Courage! my children!" Blücher's advanced column, headed by Bulow, sixteen thousand strong, appeared in the rear of the French right, and, marching in echelon, the centre in front, fell perpendicularly on their flank at Plancenoit.

From the Prussian monument be careful to take the proper road to **Smohain**, by the right wing of the French army. In the distance, to the S.E. is seen the spire of Hubermont, situated in the most picturesque part of the country, in the neighbourhood of the ruins of Aywier's abbey. Smohain has no church, and occupies a hollow at the foot of the wooded hill of Frichermont. The road up to Frichermont and thence to Aywier's abbey traverses the country the Prussians had to cross on their way to the battlefield.

Near Smohain is, on an eminence, the large farm-house of **Papelotte**, with a tower. It was occupied by the Nassauers, who were driven from the buildings by Durette's division, but regained their post on being reinforced. Below is the hamlet of Papelotte.

From Papelotte the road leads to the Mound, by the ground which

La Haye-Sainte. Lion-Mound. Genappe.

was occupied by the left wing and centre of the allied army, the scene of the fiercest and most terrible onslaughts.

On the Charleroi road, where it is intersected by the Wavre road, a finger-post indicates that it is $2\frac{1}{2}$ m. from Ohain, 2 m. from Braine l'Alleud, $\frac{3}{4}$ m. from St. Jean, and 5 m. from Genappe. Near the finger-post are the **Gordon** and **Hanoverian monuments**. Just beyond, on the other side of the road, is the farm-house of **La Haye-Sainte**, where the Hanoverians, amidst prodigies of valour, were slain almost to the last man.

"Donzelat's division speedily enveloped La Haye-Sainte, and pushed up the slope behind into the very centre of the British position. The 380 brave Hanoverians who garrisoned La Haye-Sainte long maintained their ground against the surging multitude. But their ammunition being at length exhausted, and all communication with the British line (of which that farm-house was the advanced post) cut off, the gates were forced open, and in the retreat, which had become unavoidable to the British line in their rear, great numbers fell, bravely combating to the last."—*Alison.*

Now visit the Lion Mound, 200 ft. high, ascended by 225 steps, and thrown up on the spot where the Prince of Orange was wounded.

From the Mound there is a capital view of the field, which the short tour just taken enables the traveller to understand. To facilitate consultation, the accompanying map is placed S. and N., consequently the W. is where the E. is generally in maps.

At the top of the Mound are importunate guides and vendors of photographs. At the foot of the Mound the Concierge tries to levy 25 c. and sometimes 50 c. on each person, to which, however, he has no right.

A coach leaves the Museum Hotel in time for the train.

$5\frac{1}{2}$ m. N.E. from Nivelles, and $11\frac{3}{4}$ m. S.W. from Wavre, is **Genappe**, pop. 2000, an unimportant town, with no good inns. The least bad is the H. des Voyageurs, $\frac{1}{2}$ m. from the station. It owes its interest to its connection with the battle of Waterloo. Genappe is $4\frac{1}{4}$ m. S. from La Belle Alliance, $1\frac{1}{4}$ more from the Mound, and $5\frac{1}{2}$ N.E. from Nivelles. The allied army passed through Genappe amidst torrents of rain on the afternoon of the 17th of June, having fought the previous day at Quatre-Bras, $3\frac{1}{2}$ m. S. After them came the two wings of the French army, one of them having fought at Quatre-Bras, and the other at Ligny.

On the evening of the 18th of June, the French army appeared as fugitives in the one long street of Genappe, which was so blocked with disbanded soldiers, generals without corps, officers without regiments, horses without riders, tumbrels, baggage, guns, and broken shells, that Napoleon himself had difficulty in moving along. When he rode off the field he did not stop to take refreshments till he reached Charleroi. The Prussians at Genappe obtained possession of all his baggage, and of his carriage, where, amongst many articles of curiosity, was found a proclamation intended to be made public at Brussels the next day. So confident had Napoleon been of victory, that his great fear on the evening before the battle was that the English would seek in the dark to elude his grasp. Accordingly, in the middle of the night he left his lodging at Caillou on

Napoleon's Fears.

foot, accompanied only by Marshal Bertrand, and passed through his line of Guards. The forest of Soignies in his front appeared one entire conflagration amidst the trees, from the multitude of bivouac fires of the English troops. There was no longer any doubt as to the presence of Wellington's whole army on the morrow. The most profound silence reigned over the two armies and between them. The Emperor advanced as far as the thick shrubbery which serves as an enclosure and a natural palisade to Hougoumont. It was then half-past two o'clock in the morning. While listening to the slightest noise, he heard the step of an enemy's column marching in the dark. He thought for a moment that Wellington was profiting by the night to raise his camp, and that this column was his rear-guard, ascending from the plain towards the forest, to escape before day the pursuit of the French. The rain, which fell in torrents, drowned the noise of these footsteps in the dark. Some officers whom he had sent farther forward to reconnoitre returned to tell him that nothing was stirring in the English army. At four o'clock his scouts brought him a peasant who had served as a guide to a brigade of Wellington's army, marching to its post on the extreme left. Two Belgian deserters who had just quitted their regiment repeated that nothing in the enemy's army indicated any intention to retreat.—Alphonse de Lamartine, *History of France during the Hundred Days.*

On the forenoon of the 18th a table and chair were placed on the eminence near the bend of the road, where Napoleon watched the battle.

The Position of the French Army.[1]

"As soon as the state of the weather on the 18th would permit, the French began to put themselves in order of battle, and the ground on which they drew up resembles very much, in its principal features, that which the Duke of Wellington had occupied. About 1600 or 1700 yards removed from the crest of the English position is a range of heights, which passes in a sort of semicircle from Frischermont on the east to a bend in the Braine l'Alleud road on the west, by which Hougoumont is overlapped. It is rather more elevated throughout than that on which the Anglo-Belgian army stood, and here and there it overlooks the latter position considerably; but in no part is it so elevated as to give a commanding view of what lay beyond the Duke's position, far less to offer facilities, by the fire of cannon, to impede the movements of his reserves. The two great roads from Charleroi to Nivelles passed through the French position, as they did through that of the allies. The Charleroi road, indeed, completely intersected Napoleon's line, just as it did that of the Duke of Wellington, while the chaussée from Nivelles, touching upon its extreme left, bore, though inclining eastward, through the centre of the English right, and would have led any columns that had succeeded in following it between Hougoumont and Merbe Braine. On this side of these downs, as well as on the other, the fields were open and in a state of cultivation. There was nothing to check the advance of troops, except the fire which

[1] See Greig's *Story of the Battle of Waterloo.*

The French Army at Waterloo.

might be directed upon them from the opposite ridge; and two country paths passing from the very centre of the position would have offered facilities for the movement of masses against both the right and the left of the English line if the intervening fields had not been open.

"The order of battle, as arranged by Napoleon, threw his army into two lines and a reserve. The first line consisted of infantry, flanked right and left by cavalry, and was composed of the 1st and 2d corps d'armée, commanded respectively by D'Erlon and Reille. The 1st corps was on the right. It extended from La Belle Alliance eastward in the direction of Frischermont, and was covered on its extreme right by Jacqueminot's cavalry division, which, facing Ohain, kept the château of Frischermont in possession, and threw out patrols so as to guard against the approaches of an enemy. The 2d stretched away in a curved line from the left of the same road, across the Nivelles chaussée, and had its flank protected, just beyond the latter, by Pire's cavalry. D'Erlon's corps comprehended four divisions, Reille's numbered but three. They were both drawn up in a double line of brigades—the first being in advance of the second by sixty yards only; and, strange to say for a French army, which seldom attacks except in column, every battalion was deployed. Five batteries, comprising eight guns in each, ranged themselves along the front of the right of this line, with a sixth, consisting of 12-pounders, in support, while six guns of horse-artillery took post on the right of Jacqueminot's cavalry. The left was strengthened by the presence of thirty-one pieces, besides six which stood upon the Nivelles road; and on either side of it, and in the direction of Braine l'Alleud, both infantry and artillery were detached.

"In point of mere numbers the strength of the opposing armies cannot be said to have differed very widely. But if the composition of the corps be taken into account, the preponderance on the side of the French was terrible. Napoleon's soldiers were all enthusiastically devoted to their leader. They were composed of one nation, had one system of tactics, knew their chiefs, were filled with military ardour, had been led to believe that they would find friends in the ranks that stood opposed to them, and counted on victory as certain. Wellington's army was made up of raw levies gathered from five or six separate sources. Even his British troops were not the men whom he had trained to fight and to conquer in the Peninsula; and as to the rest, they were all in a state of discipline which rendered it perilous, not to say impossible, to manœuvre with them under fire.

"At an early hour in the morning of the 19th, the allied troops got under arms. No movement in advance was however made; for the confusion in the rear had well-nigh equalled that which had prevailed among the broken masses of the enemy. Supplies were therefore slow of arriving; but they came at last, and after a hearty but rude meal the columns of march were formed. It was a wild, strange, and melancholy scene that spread itself out beneath the eyes of the victors. From the ridge above La Belle Alliance each regiment and brigade as it came up obtained a complete view of the whole field of battle. The sun, too, was shining brightly, and a clear blue sky overhung them there; but it hung likewise over the wreck of three great armies, and looked down upon terrible

VILLAGE OF QUATRE-BRAS.

things. Far and near, wherever the battle had raged, the corn was not only trodden down, but beaten into clay."

3½ m. S. from Genappe by the Charleroi road, causewayed all the way, is a hamlet of 5 or 6 large farm-houses, called **Quatre-Bras**, because at this point the road between Charleroi and Brussels intersects the road between Namur and Nivelles, thus making four arms. This was the scene of the battle of the 16th, between the French under Marshal Ney, and the British with the German and Belgian contingents, under the Duke of Wellington, who on this occasion narrowly escaped being taken prisoner.

The battle of Ligny, 10 m. N.E. from Charleroi, was fought on the same day, the 16th of June, between the Prussians under Blücher, and the French under Napoleon. During the night the Prussian army began to retreat towards Wavre, 16 m. N. by Tilly and St. Guibert. See p. 213.

SKETCH OF THE BATTLES OF LIGNY AND QUATRE-BRAS,

PRINCIPALLY FROM THE ACCOUNTS BY

Sir WALTER SCOTT and Sir ARCHIBALD ALISON.

Prince Blücher, with the Prussian army, occupied Charleroi, Namur, Givet, and Liège. The Duke of Wellington covered Brussels, where he had fixed his headquarters, communicating by his left with the right of the Prussians. See Map, page 212.

The Duke of Wellington's first corps, under the Prince of Orange, with two divisions of British, two of Hanoverians, and two of Belgians, occupied Enghien, Brain le Comte, and Nivelles, and served as a reserve to the Prussian division under Ziethen, which was at Charleroi. The second division, commanded by Lord Hill, included two British, two Hanoverian, and one Belgian division. It was cantoned at Hall, Oudenarde, and Grammont. The reserve, under Picton, consisted of the remaining two British divisions, with three of the Hanoverians, and was stationed at Brussels and Ghent. The Anglo-Belgic army was so disposed, therefore, as might enable the divisions to combine with each other, and with the Prussians, upon the earliest authentic intelligence of the enemy's being put in motion.

In the meantime, Napoleon in person advanced to Vervins on 12th June, with his Guard from Paris. The other divisions of his selected grand army had been assembled on the frontier, and the whole, consisting of five divisions of infantry and four of cavalry, were combined at Beaumont on the 14th of the same month, with a degree of secrecy and expedition which showed the usual genius of their commander. Napoleon reviewed the troops in person, reminded them that the day was the anniversary of the great victories of Marengo and Friedland, and called on them to remember that the enemies whom they had then defeated were the same which were now arrayed against them.

Upon the 15th June the French army was in motion in every direction. Their advanced guard of light troops swept the western bank of the Sambre clear of all the allied corps of observation. They then advanced upon Charleroi, which was defended by the Prussians under General

Preparations for the Battles of Ligny and Quatre-Bras.

Ziethen, who was compelled to retreat to Fleurus, and join the Prussian force which lay about Ligny.

Napoleon's numbers were unequal to sustain a conflict with the armies of Blücher and Wellington united, but by forcing his way so as to separate the one enemy from the other, he would gain the advantage of acting against either individually with the gross of his forces, while he could spare enough of detached troops to keep the other in check. To accomplish this masterly manœuvre, it was necessary to push onwards upon a part of the British advance, which occupied the position of Quatre-Bras, and the yet more advanced post of Frasnes 2 m. S. from Quatre Bras, 5½ m. S.E. from Nivelles, and 6¼ N.W. from Fleurus.

At 2 A.M. on the 16th of June Wellington commenced to move reinforcements on Quatre-Bras, where he himself arrived at an early hour, and immediately rode over to Blücher, with whom he had an interview at Bry, and concerted with him the plans for future operations.

Blücher with 80,000 men occupied the chain of gentle heights running from Bry to Sombreffe; in front of their line lay the villages of the Greater and Lesser St. Amand, as also that of Ligny, all of which were strongly occupied. From the extremity of his right, Blücher could communicate with the British at Quatre-Bras, upon which the Duke of Wellington was, as fast as distance would permit, concentrating his army. The fourth Prussian division, being that of Bulow, stationed between Liège and Hainault, was at too great a distance to be brought up, though every effort was made for the purpose. Blücher undertook, however, notwithstanding the absence of Bulow, to receive a battle in this position, trusting to the support of the English army, who, by a flank movement to the left, were to march to his assistance.

Napoleon had, in the meantime, settled his own plan of battle. He determined to leave Ney with a division of 45,000 men, with instructions to drive the English from Quatre-Bras ere their army was concentrated and reinforced, and thus prevent their co-operating with Blücher, while he himself, with the main body of his army, attacked the Prussian position at Ligny. Ney being thus on the French left wing at Frasnes and Quatre-Bras, and Buonaparte on the right at Ligny, a division under D'Erlon, amounting to 10,000 men, served as a centre of the army, and was placed in a position from which it might march either to support Ney or Napoleon, whichever might require assistance. As two battles thus took place on the 16th June, it is necessary to take distinct notice of both.

That of Ligny *was the principal action.* The French Emperor was unable to concentrate his forces, so as to commence the attack upon the Prussians, until three o'clock in the afternoon, at which hour it began with uncommon fury all along the Prussian line. After a continued attack of two hours, the French obtained possession of the village of St. Amand. The position of the Prussians was thus far defective, that the main part of their army being drawn up on the heights, and the remainder occupying villages which lay at their foot, the reinforcements despatched to the latter were necessarily exposed during their descent to the fire from the French artillery, placed on the meadows below. Notwithstanding this disad-

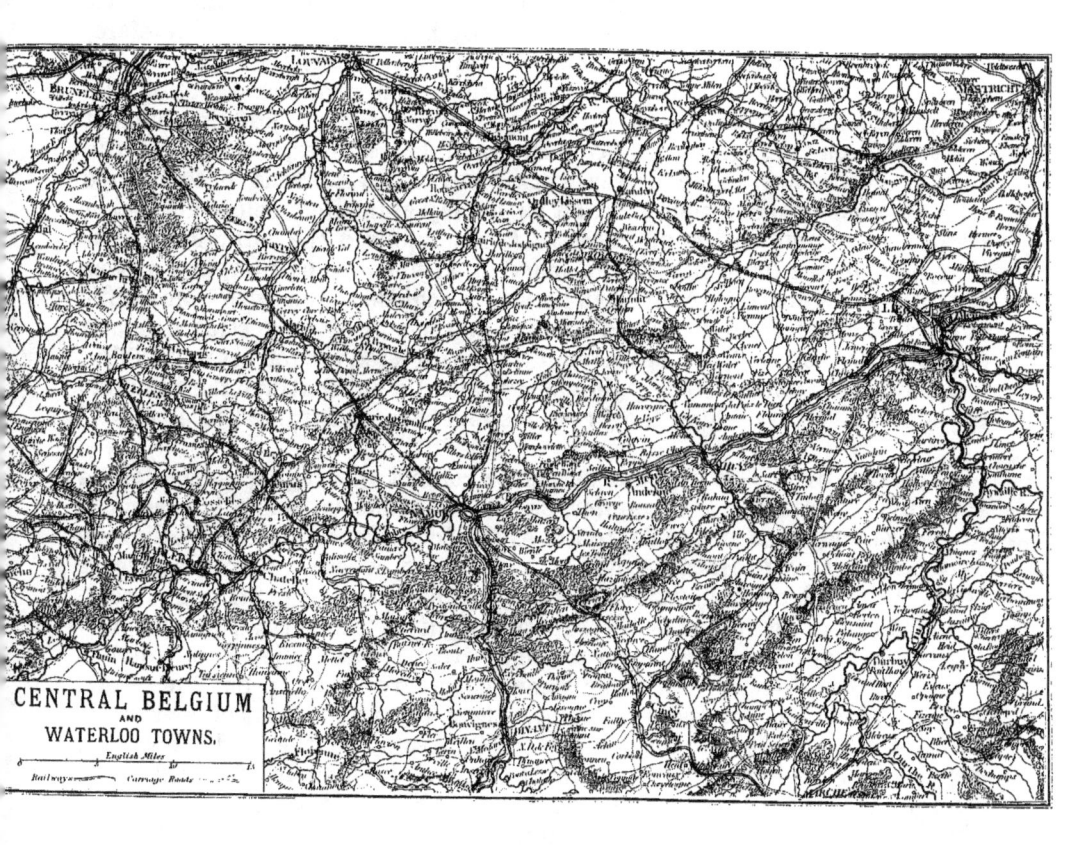

Battles of Ligny and Quatre-Bras.

vantage, by which the Prussians suffered much, Napoleon thought the issue of the contest so doubtful, that he sent for D'Erlon's division, which was stationed halfway betwixt Quatre-Bras and Ligny. In the meanwhile, observing that Blücher drew his reserves together on St. Amand, he changed his point of attack, and directed all his force against Ligny, of which, after a desperate resistance, he at length obtained possession. The French Guards, supported by their heavy cavalry, ascended the heights, and attacked the Prussian position in the rear of Ligny. The reserves of the Prussian infantry having been despatched to St. Amand, Blücher had no means of repelling this attack save by his cavalry. He, therefore, placing himself at their head, charged in the most determined manner, but was forced back in disorder. As the prince maréchal was directing the retreat his horse was struck down by a cannon shot, and he himself prostrated on the ground. The Prussian horse, overpowered by the French cuirassiers, were driven back, and the victorious French rode straight over the Prussian marshal as he lay entangled below his dying steed. A second charge of Prussian horse repulsed the cuirassiers; but they, too, in the dark passed the marshal without seeing him, and it was not till they were returning that he was recognised, and with some difficulty extricated from the dead animal, and mounted on a stray dragoon horse. When relieved, and again mounted, he directed the retreat upon Tilly, and achieved it unmolested by the enemy, who did not continue their pursuit beyond the heights which the Prussians had been constrained to abandon.

Quatre-Bras.—While this desperate conflict was raging on the left of the allied position, an encounter, on a less extensive scale, but equally desperate and more successful to the Allies, took place between Wellington and Ney at Quatre-Bras, a point of importance, where four roads diverge from it in different directions; so that the British general might communicate from his left with the Prussian right at St. Amand, besides having in his rear a causeway open for his retreat. The Allies were equal in number to the French, both being somewhat above 20,000; but the former had not above 28 guns, and no horse, except some squadrons of Brunswick hussars. The Belgians, indeed, had 2000 cavalry on the field; but they never could be brought to face the enemy, and, when led forward to the charge, fled with such precipitation in an early period of the action, that they swept the Duke of Wellington and his staff with them through Quatre-Bras, and were not again seen on the field.[1]

About three o'clock in the afternoon the main attack commenced, but was repulsed. The British infantry however, and particularly the 42d Highlanders, suffered severely from an unexpected charge of lancers, whose approach was hid from them by the character of the ground, intersected

[1] At the battle of Waterloo the brigade of Belgians of Preponcher's division gave way at the mere sight of the formidable mass of the French columns. Such was the indignation felt in the British ranks at their conduct, that they could with difficulty be prevented from giving them a volley as they hurried through to the rear. At another part of the battle the Marquis of Anglesea put himself at the head of Tripp's Belgian carabineers, but although that brave officer urged them forward with his accustomed gallantry, not a man would follow, and finally fled with such

Preparations for the Battle of Waterloo.

with hedges, and covered with heavy crops of rye. Two companies of the Highlanders were cut off, not having had time to form the square; the other succeeded in getting into order, and beating off the lancers. Ney then attempted a general charge of heavy cavalry; but they were received with such a galling fire from the British infantry, joined to a battery of two guns, that it could not be sustained. At nightfall Ney retreated to Frasnes, 2 m. S. from the field of battle; and Wellington's men, wearied alike with marching and fighting, lay on the ground on which they had fought at Quatre-Bras, surrounded by the dead and the dying. The British had maintained possession of the field with such obstinacy, because the Duke believed Blücher would be able to hold his ground at Ligny, and was consequently desirous the armies should retain the line of communication they had occupied in the morning.

Wavre.—But the Prussians, evacuating all the villages which they held in the neighbourhood of Ligny, had concentrated their forces to retreat upon the river Dyle, in the vicinity of Wavre. By this retrograde movement, they were placed 16 miles to the rear of their former position, and had united themselves to Bulow's division, which had not been engaged in the affair at Ligny. Blücher effected this retreat not only without pursuit by the French, but without their knowing for some time in what direction he had gone.

The English retire from Quatre-Bras.—About seven in the morning, the Duke having received intelligence of this retreat to Wavre, commenced a retreat on his part towards Waterloo, in order to recover his communication with the Prussians, and resume the execution of the plan of co-operation, which had been in some degree disconcerted by the sudden irruption of the French, and the loss of the battle of Ligny by the Prussians.

At three o'clock on the afternoon of the 17th, the British came on the field, and took up their bivouac for the night in the order of battle in which they were to fight the next day, on a chain of heights, extending from a ravine and village termed Merbe Braine, on the right, to a farm called La Haye on the left. All his arrangements having been effected early in the evening of the 17th, the Duke of Wellington rode across the country to Blücher to inform him personally that he had thus far effected the plan agreed on at Bry, and express his hope to be supported on the morrow by two Prussian divisions. The veteran replied that he would leave a single corps to hold Grouchy at bay as well as they could, and march himself with the rest of his army upon Waterloo; and Wellington immediately returned to his post. For the rest see page 202.

vehemence as well-nigh to sweep away two squadrons of the 3d Hussars of the King's German Legion. The 3d, however, soon recovered their order, and they, led by Anglesea, charged the cuirassiers with such vigour, that they broke through them. A regiment of Hanoverian cavalry, the Cumberland hussars 1000 strong, ordered up to the assistance of the 3d Hussars, having been received by a sharp fire on crossing the ridge, turned about and fled, never drawing bridle till they reached Brussels, where their unexpected entry created the utmost alarm.

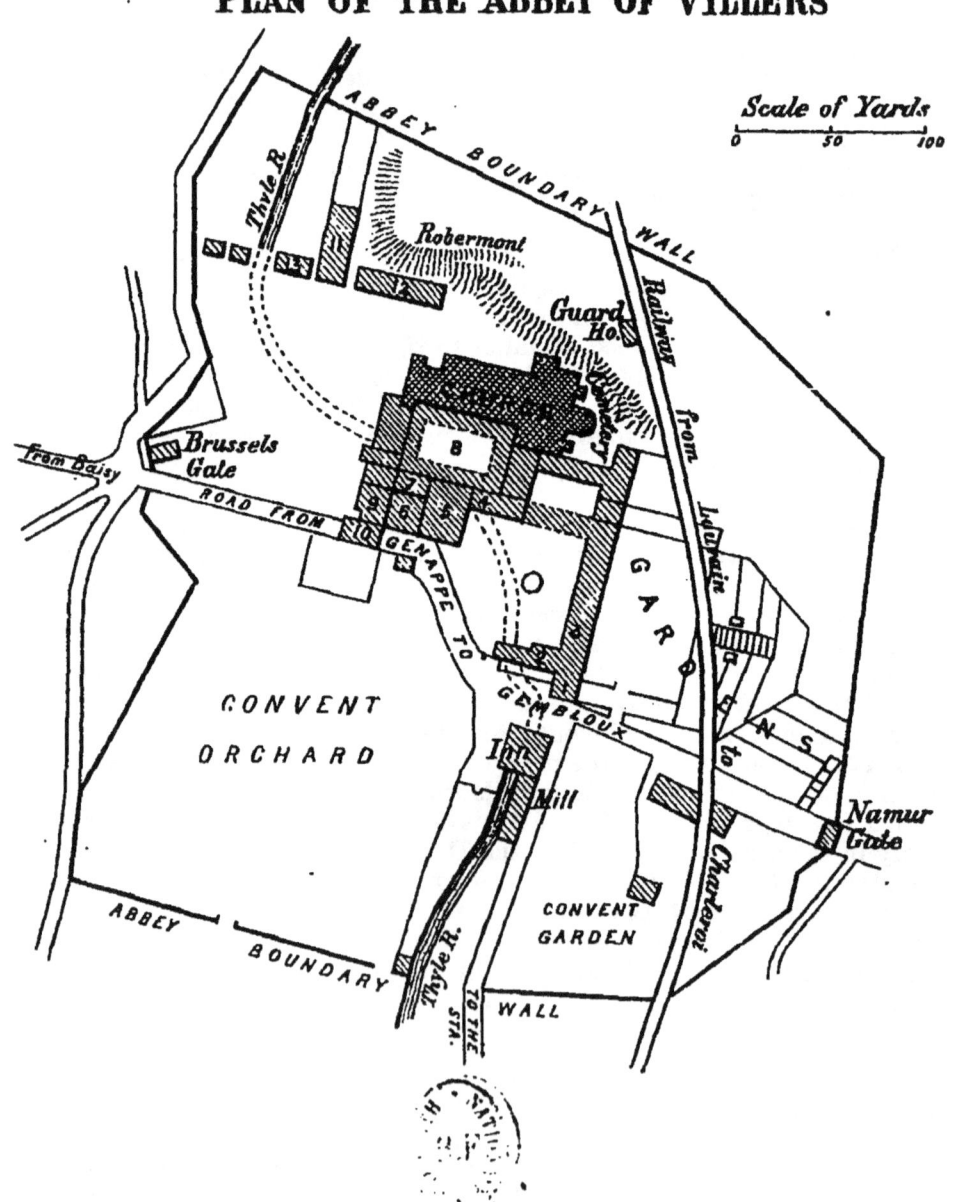

VILLERS L'ABBAYE,

22 m. S. from Brussels, by the train starting from the Luxembourg station. Change at Ottignies, p. 253. At some distance above the station is Villers la Ville, and immediately below Villers l'Abbaye. The first building on coming down from the station is what was formerly the old mill, now one of the best of modern mills. Next it is the Inn H. de l'Abbaye, comfortable bedroom 2 frs., including service. Breakfast of coffee, bread, and butter, 1 fr. Dinner from 2 to 3 frs., not including wine. Fee to enter abbey ½ fr. The mill, the abbey church and monastery are situated in a beautiful little valley, watered by the stream Thyle. The ruins are very extensive. The domestic buildings were constructed by the Abbot Hache in 1721, and were reduced to their present condition by a fire on the 12th July 1858. Among the public rooms were apartments for guests of distinction, a reception hall, a library, and a large saloon surmounted by a cupola. The windows looked on beautiful gardens arranged in terraces. The church, built in the 13th cent., was on the 25th July 1797 sold by auction to a tradesman of St. Omer called Terrade, who, to make the most of his bargain, dismantled the edifice and sold all he could—the lead, woodwork, and marbles. It is 336 ft. from W. to E., 105 wide, including the aisles, and 66 ft. high. The transepts are 165 ft. from N. to S. There are chapels only on the N. side. On the S. side is the cloister, of which two sides have disappeared. The side along by the refectory dates from the 13th cent., the other from the 17th. A niche to the right by the side of the church indicates the tomb of Gobert, the Lord of Aspremont, who, after returning from the crusades towards the middle of the 13th cent., entered this monastery.

In the interior of the church 18 columns and piers on each side support the arches of the nave and transepts, and 8 those of the choir. Above the triforium stage is the clerestory, a window corresponding to each arch below. On the hill Robermont, rising on the N. side of the church, the ruins of a small chapel mark the spot where St. Bernard, in 1147, planted his staff (bourdon), which grew into a great oak.

5½ m. S. from Villers by rail is **Ligny**, and 2½ m. farther **Fleurus**, 8 m. N. from Charleroi. On the road between Villers l'Abbaye and Genappe is the village of Baisy, partly in a low hollow and partly on an eminence—Godefroid de Bouillon was born in the low part in the 11th cent. The houses are mostly of brick, whitewashed, on stone foundations.

Nivelles.—On the line between Brussels and Charleroi 18½ m. S. from Brussels, 16¼ N. from Charleroi, 7 m. S. from Braine l'Alleud, and ¾ m. from Baulers junction, is **Nivelles**, pop. 10,000. *Inns:* In front of the Station du Nord (the more convenient of the 2 stations) is the H. Rusie. In the "Place" the Mouton Blanc and the Aigle Noir. A clean, quiet town on the Dodaine, which owes its origin to the convent founded in 645 by Ida, wife of Pepin of Landen, whose daughter, St. Gertrude, was the first abbess. Part of the exterior of the church founded in the 11th cent. has been rebuilt, while the whole of the interior has been repaired and modernised. Under the high altar is a crypt, said to be part of the original church built in the 7th cent., in which were deposited the remains of Pepin, brought from Landen. The interior contains a great many pictures. The two pulpits in the nave and group over the interior of the main entrance, representing the Conversion of St. Paul, are by Laurent Delvaux. One of the pulpits is a curious mixture of carved oak and sculptured white marble. At the base are life-size marble statues of our Lord and the woman of Samaria. From the side of the well rises a tree, whose trunk forms the pedestal of the tribune, while its white leaves and branches wave over the sound-board. Carefully-carved wreaths form the banister of the stair. Opposite the pulpit is the entrance into the cloister, of which part remains as it was originally, and part has been repaired. In the sacristy are preserved an ivory crucifix by Duquesnoy, a shrine or reliquary of the 12th, and another of the 13th cent., and a chalice of the 15th cent. On the southern turret a colossal gilt figure of a knight called Jean de Nivelles strikes the hours. It was from Nivelles on the 20th of June 1815, when about to enter France, that the Duke of Wellington issued his famous order to the army under his command, that France was to be "treated as a friendly country," "that nothing should be taken either by officers or soldiers, for which payment be not made," and that the commissaries were to be held responsible for whatever they obtained "from the inhabitants of France, in the same manner in which they would be esteemed accountable for purchases made for their own Government in the several dominions to which they belonged." See also page 42.

17½ m. S. from Brussels by Waterloo, and 40 m. N. from Namur by Charleroi and Tamines, is the important junction of Baulers.

Brussels to Antwerp.

27½ m. N., time 1 hour, Station du Nord of Brussels, and the Station de l'Est at Antwerp, by Schaerbeck, Vilvorde, Eppeghem, Malines, Contich, Vieux-Dieu, and Berchem. 6¼ m. N. from Brussels and 2¼ m. S. from Antwerp is **Vilvorde**, pop. 7000, on the Senne. *Inns:* the Couronne at the station, at the commencement of the road to Perck, 3 m. E. On the other side The Nacion and the Estaminet Belle Vue, where coaches can be had for Perck—there and back 5 frs. In the town there are several inns, one of the best is La Louve at the Grande Place near the Hotel de Ville 1870.

Vilvorde is a quiet Flemish town, with a few manufactories and two churches—Notre Dame, consisting principally of one large dome, surrounded by 6 small domes; and the parish church, a massive building, 13th cent., with a strong square tower. Near this church, at the foot of the avenue, is the chateau, a large ugly building, conspicuous from the railway, now the "Corps de discipline et de correction," a military prison, in which there are generally from 500 to 600 culprits.

Tyndale. Perck. Chateau de Steen.

William Tyndale, born at Nebly, Gloucestershire, about 1477, the author of the first translation of the Old and New Testament from the Hebrew and Greek, was, through the influence of the Anti-Reformation party in England, cast into prison here in 1535, and on the 6th of October of the following year led out to a small eminence near the prison, where he was first strangled and then burnt to ashes. The excellence of his version, the basis of all subsequent English Bibles, has never been called in question by candid and competent judges. The language is pure, appropriate and perspicuous; and is an astonishing monument of the indomitable zeal and erudition of this great and good man. His works, together with those of Fryth and Barnes, were collected into a large volume, and published in London in 1572.

3 m. E. from the station, by a road traversing a flat country, is the small village of **Perck**. Near the village, when having already passed the 1 kilometre stone, is to the left a small gabled two-storied tower rising over a low building. This tower formed a part of the chateau of the Drij Toren, which with the surrounding woods and fields belonged to David Teniers the younger. A view of the castle is seen in his "Village Fair" or "Kermes" in the large hall of the Picture Gallery of Brussels. It was in the small room of this remaining tower that Teniers painted so many of his pictures. In the chancel of the village church on the right or S. side of the altar is a beautiful painting by him, "St. Dominic kneeling before Mary." Against the N. wall, near the altar of the chapel of Mary, is the black marble slab to the memory of "Isabella de Freau Huysvrouwe Vanden Heer David Teniers," his second wife, buried here, and in this church Teniers himself. The sacristan lives in a small house to the left.

2 m. beyond Vilvorde is the station of **Eppeghem**. To the E. is the village of Elewit and the chateau de Steen, which belonged to Rubens. It is still in a pretty fair state of preservation. He and Teniers were not only near neighbours, but they lived on the most intimate terms with each other. Perck is directly S. from Elewit.

13 m. N. from Brussels, $14\frac{1}{2}$ S. from Antwerp, and $15\frac{1}{2}$ N.W. from Louvain, is **Malines**, pop. 41,000, on the Dyle. *Hotels:* at the station the Hotels Kempeneers, Nord, and the Couronne near the Post-office at the head of the street the Rue Egmont, leading into the town. In the town the best hotels are the H. Buda, in front of the principal entrance into the cathedral: near it the H. de la Coupe. In No. 88 Rue Notre Dame the G. H. Cigogne.

On arriving, do not walk down by the wide street in front of the

MALINES.   NOTRE DAME.   GRANDE PLACE.

station, but *by the wide street to the right,* the Rue Egmont, which continue to the last cross street before crossing the bridge. The street to the right, the Rue d'Hanswyk, leads merely to the church of Notre Dame d'Hanswyk 1678, and the park. This church consists chiefly of a dome, under which are large sculptures in relief, admirably executed by Fayd'herbe. The organ-loft is very handsome. The pictures under it are gifts to the miracle-working image, which acts principally in the cure of children.

The street to the left, the Rue Notre Dame, leads past the Hotel Cigogne to the church of **Notre Dame,** rebuilt in the 15th cent. The transepts were constructed in 1545, and the choir in 1646. In the chapel behind the high altar is one of the most powerful compositions of Rubens (covered), a triptych painted by him in his 41st year. In the centre is the "**Draught of Fishes,**" where amidst the life-like representation of posture and bearing in every member of the group, he has succeeded in blending nobility with gentleness in the Divine Master's countenance, who regards Peter full of kindness and compassion. On the left is the "Tribute Money," and on the right "Tobias extracting the gall from a fish to cure his father's eyes." On the back of the high altar, and fronting this chapel, is a large landscape by Huysmans, 1648-1727. In the large chapel to the left or N. of the high altar is a triptych by Coxcie, 1499-1592, the "Temptations of St. Antony." In the centre picture he is tried by female beauty. Against the wall is a relievo in stone, by Fayd'herbe, representing the erection of the cross—part of a "Via Crucis" (see p. 195). In the next chapel is "Christ being carried to the tomb," by an unknown artist. The reredos of the high altar representing the "Last Supper" is by J. E. Quellin, 1607-1678, but not one of his best works. On consoles against the pillars of the nave stand life-size statues of the apostles, 17th cent. Sacristan lives opposite main entrance, No. 58 Milsenstraat.

Now return to the main street the Rue Egmont and cross the bridge over the Dyle. To the right is the entrance into the Botanic Gardens, ½ fr. Continue walking down the main street till it reaches the **Grande Place,** nearly surrounded by gabled Flemish houses. In the centre is the statue of Margaret of Austria, by J. Tuerlinkx in 1849. She was the daughter of Maximilian I., and aunt of Charles V., for whom she acted as Regent of the Netherlands from 1506 till the year of her death in 1530. Under her benign rule the country enjoyed happiness and prosperity. Round the monument is a circle with Roman figures of the same dimensions as those on the faces of the two clocks on the tower. Behind the statue is the building called Les Halles, dating from 1340, but frequently repaired and altered. At the corner towards the right side of the statue is the commencement of a palace which Charles V., in 1530, intended for the high courts of law. Down this street are several interesting Flemish houses. Towards the left hand of the statue is an isolated gabled and turreted building, 15th cent., with transomed windows, formerly the Palais de Justice, now the Picture Gallery. Beyond is the Marché Balle de Fer, or aux Laines, with some curious houses. Among others, across the bridge left hand, is a house "au saumon," with a beautiful façade.

The great building in the Grande Place is the **Cathedral Saint Rombaut**, the metropolitan church of Belgium, a great imposing pile surrounded by decorated gabled chapels, between flying pinnacled buttresses. Over the main entrance rises 320 ft. a massive yet graceful unfinished tower, adorned with multitudes of canopied pinnacled niches and decorated buttresses. It contains a chime of 44 sweetly-sounding bells and a clock, of which each face is 49 ft. in diameter. The interior of the church is 306 ft. long by 89 high. The nave is of the 13th cent., and the rest of the church of the 14th and 15th. On the columns are statues of the apostles, 17th cent. The paintings on the large N. and S. transept windows represent respectively Pio IX. in St. Peter's, and the Archbishop of Malines in this church pronouncing the new dogma, that "Mary was conceived without sin." They are by Pluys, father and son, who likewise painted the windows of the choir.

In the S. Transept is the "**Crucifixion**" by Van Dyck, one of the finest of his works, painted by him in 1627. The distribution of the crosses is picturesque, and while the arrangement throws into the shade the harrowing struggles of the thieves, it brings out into strong relief the meek and resigned endurance of the Redeemer, which falls like a soft, radiant light from heaven between the two malefactors.

In Choir, S. side, first chapel is "St. Luke taking the portrait of Mary," by A. Janssens, 1567-1632. Second chapel, "The escutcheons of the governors of the Netherlands" and "Ascension," by Paelinck, 4. Altar and reredos of chased brass. On the reredos is an inlaid design by Minguay, representing the death of St. Engelbert, to whom the chapel is dedicated. In the next chapel, Mary's, is a still finer brass altar, gilt and adorned with small statuettes. The walls are covered with panels of inlaid brass. The large pictures in the choir representing scenes from the life of St. Rombaut, are chiefly by G. C. Herreyns, 1743-1827. In the N. transept beside the window, repre-

MALINES.   ST JEAN.   ADORATION OF THE MAGI.

senting Pope Pio IX., is an "Adoration of the shepherds," by Quellin.

In the N. aisle, first chapel, left hand of main entrance, is the mausoleum of Archbishop Meau, d. 1831, by Jehotte. In this chapel is also a Last Supper, by Wouters.

In the S. aisle, behind the pulpit, are 27 small pictures dating from the 14th cent., illustrating the life of St. Rombaut and the miracles wrought by his relics. His body is preserved in the shrine on the high altar. The elaborate pulpit by Boeckstuyns has at the pedestal a group representing the conversion of St. Paul. The attitude of the fallen horse struck back upon his haunches, and his fore-legs sinking under him, is wonderfully beautiful. The crucifixion and the figures by the side of the pulpit are most effective.

Leave St. Rombaut by the north transept, cross a bridge and turn to the right and enter the church of **St. Jean**. Here, over the high altar, is the celebrated triptych by Rubens, regarding which he used to say to his friends, "You should go to St. Jean of Malines if you wish to see my best pictures." And the great master in one sense was right, for they excel all the others in softness and delicacy of painting, in refinement and aptness of attitude, in strength and earnestness of expression, and in the elastic, life-like postures of every member in the different groups. In the centre is an "Adoration of the Magi," containing 21 figures. On the left wing is the Decapitation of John the Baptist, and on the back, "John baptizing Christ." On the right wing is the "Martyrdom" of John the evangelist, and on the back, "John on the island of Patmos." Below is a little Crucifixion, also by Rubens. In the chapel to the right of the high altar is "The Disciples at Emmaus," by Herreyns, and at the top of the black marble slab to the memory of Jacob Van Leyen, a *chef-d'œuvre* of Duquesnoy in white marble, representing St. Anne and her daughter Mary. The pulpit is, as usual, a masterpiece of carving. The group at the pedestal represents in an allegorical style the Good Shepherd, our Lord standing in the midst of his disciples, with sheep feeding beside them. It is by Verhaegen, by whom are also the organ-loft and case and the carved work round the two neighbouring columns. Outside, near the entrance, is a representation of Jesus on the Mount of Olives.

St. Jean closes at 10 and reopens at 4.30 P.M. Sacristan's house down that narrow lane in front of main entrance. Fee to uncover triptych ½ fr. The cathedral shuts at 12 and reopens at 2, but sometimes 2.30.

Direct communication between Malines and Terneuzen 2 hrs. 25 min.

TURNHOUT. HAL.

N.W., at the N. end of the Ghent and Schelde canal. *Inn:* Nederlandsch Logement. Steamer twice daily to Flushing 1½ hr. N. on the opposite or N. side of the Schelde. Rail also, 20 m. S.E. to Louvain.

From Malines the rail proceeds to Antwerp by Contich, from which a branch line extends 1½ hour N.E. to Turnhout by Lierre and Herenthals. Turnhout, pop. 17,000, on the frontier, has important cloth manufactories and leech-breeding establishments.

Beyond Contich is Vieux-Dieu, or Oude-God, among villas: and behind the fortifications, Berchem, within a mile of Antwerp.

Antwerp: arrive at the Station de l'Est. In front are numerous cabs. Those who come merely on a visit will find every 10 minutes, opposite the station, the tram, "Werf, Statie, Dryhoek," or in French, "Port, Gare, Trois Coins." Take it when running west, down the Boulevard, and ask to be let out at the cathedral; fare 15 c. or 3 sous. The Trois Coins, to the south of the station, is a beautiful suburb, with a park, long boulevards, and handsome dwellings. See page 266.

Brussels to Paris.
By HAL, BRAINE-LE-COMTE, JURBISE, MONS, and
TERGNIER JUNCTION.

BRUSSELS　　193 m. S.W., 7 hours 40 minutes by express.　　PARIS
MILES FROM　　　　　　See Map, p. 1.　　　　　　MILES TO

BRUSSELS. Start from the Station du Sud. After passing 193 four little stations, Forest, Ruysbroeck, Loth, and Buysingen, the train halts at **Hal**, 8¾ m. south from Brussels, pop. 8300, on the Senne and the canal of Charleroi. Tolerable restaurants at the station and in the town, but no good inns. In the centre of the town is the church of St. Martin, begun in the 14th and finished in the 15th cent. The interior is surrounded by 24 lofty pointed arches, over which rises a mullioned triforium, the part extending round the chancel being the most ornamented. The reredos of the high altar is of marble, admirably sculptured by Mone in 1533, and crowned by the figure of a pelican, a mediæval symbol of Christ. Over all, is the miracle-working small black image of the Virgin, which is said to have caught in the folds of its garments the 32½ cannon-balls, preserved behind a grating at the right hand of the main entrance. In the chapel behind it, is a very graceful brass baptismal font 10 ft. high, cast at Tournai in 1446 by Lefebvre. The pedestal rests on 8 small lions. The lid, which is pinnacled in three stages, and studded with statuettes and groups, is raised by means of a crane, likewise elaborately ornamented. Before

| BRUSSELS MILES FROM | BRAINE-LE-COMTE. MONS. | PARIS MILES TO |

the choir is suspended an enormous crucifix. Behind the left side of the altar are some quaintly-sculptured groups in stone.

Canal-boat building is an important industry in Hal.

18½ m. from Brussels is the important junction of Braine-le-Comte, pop. 6800. H. Charleroi. Town close to station. The flax of this neighbourhood is in high repute with the lace-makers. 3¾ m. further is Soignies station, close to the town, pop. 8000; with the abbey church of St. Vincent Maldegaire, said to have been founded as early as 650. It was rebuilt in the 12th cent.

30½ m. S.W. from Brussels, and 7 N.E. from Mons, is Jurbise. *Inn:* H. de la Gare, opposite station. Here change carriages for Valenciennes in France, or go round by Mons, the next station.

38 MONS (pronounce the s), pop. 26,000, on the Trouille and at 155 the junction of 4 important railways. In front of station is a monument to Leopold I., and among other hotels, the H. Tournai; Gare; Esperance. A little way up the main street is the H. France; and at the end of this street, in the Grand Place, next the Hotel de Ville, is the principal hotel in Mons, the *Couronne. On the opposite side is the hotel *Taverne Allemande. Fronting the station, in the higher part of the town, are the church of St. Waudru and the belfry.

Mons, the capital of the province of Hainault, is supposed to occupy the site of the Roman station, defended so bravely by Quintus Cicero, brother of the orator, against the attacks of the Eburones, the Nervii, and other Gallic tribes. It is situated in the centre of most productive coalfields, containing upwards of 450 pits from 400 to 530 yards deep, producing annually 12 million tons of coal.

The ancient ramparts, which encircled Mons, have been levelled and converted into a beautiful promenade, with five rows of poplars all the way round. The town consists of clean, wide, silent, roughly-paved streets, lined with commodious houses. The most important edifice is the church of **Sainte Waudru**, on the site of a chapel built in 653, dedicated to St. Peter. The first stone of the present building was laid in 1450, and continued till 1589. The façade is imperfect. Four ugly buttresses rise at each of the two corners, but the fine tower they are intended to aid in supporting is not yet begun, while the stair leading up to the entrance is in an unfinished state. With these exceptions, this beautiful church presents throughout great elegance and harmony, coupled with boldness. It is 355 ft. long and 116 wide. Thirty-two grooved stone piers in two rows surround the nave and chancel. From them rises to the keystones a profuse groining, which ramifies over the wide extent of roof, 80 ft. high. From the chancel (1502) project, in a semicircle, 15 three-sided chapels.

Above the piers round the entire church is a triforium with geometrical tracery, and over it a range of clerestory windows with flamboyant tracery, one over each arch of the nave and chancel. The 15 round the chancel and 4 in the transepts are filled with valuable 16th cent. glass. In the chapels of the nave, between the piers, are several reliefs in marble, executed in the 15th and 16th cents. The first chapel, right or south side of choir, has a richly-sculptured stone reredos surmounted by 3 elaborate canopies. In the next chapel are paintings (16th cent.) on 12 panels, representing scenes in the life of the monk St. Michael.

Above St. Waudru, on the highest part of Mons, is a park within the walls of the old chateau, to which belonged the belfry, with a set of chimes, built in 1662 by the Spaniards. It is a square tower in three stages, faced with pilasters and columns at the angles, and surmounted by a balloon-shaped spire rising from between 4 small turret-balloons. On this elevated spot Julius Cæsar, during his campaign against the Gauls, established a Castrum.

At the end of the street leading from the railway is the Grande Place, with the Hotel de Ville commenced in 1458. The handsome spire was built in 1718. On the front are 2 ranges of transomed canopied windows.

From Mons the train passes Cuesmes and Frameries, and halts at

47 QUEVY. Belgian custom-house and time. 146

49¼ FEIGNIES, pop. 2700. Hotel du Nord. French custom- 143¼ house and time, 9 min. behind the Belgian time. About 1 m. beyond Feignies is the first-class fortified town of Maubeuge, on the Sambre, pop. 15,000. *Hotels:* Nord; Grand Cerf; Commerce. The town possesses important manufactories of carriage-springs, files, weighing scales, and cutlery. The painter Jean Gossaert, surnamed Mabuse, was born at Maubeuge. He died in 1562. Maubeuge is 30 m. E. from Valenciennes. See pages 41 and 42.

From Maubeuge the train proceeds to Paris by Aulnoye, 134 m. from Paris, p. 41; Busigny, 113 m., p. 40; St. Quentin, 95 m., p. 37; Tergnier, 81 m., p. 36; Chauny, 77 m., p. 35; Noyon, 67 m., p. 32; Compiègne, 52¼ m., p. 31. Then after passing Creil Junction arrives at the Station du Nord, Paris. Cabs and omnibuses both with tariffs at station.

ATH. BELŒIL. TOURNAI.

Brussels to Lille.

67¾ m. S.W., whence Calais is from 2 hrs. to 4 hrs. according to the correspondence of the trains. This route passes Ath, Tournai, Courtrai, and Ypres.

BRUSSELS, from the Station du Midi. See Map, page 1. At Hal, p. 221, 8½ m. S.W. from Brussels, carriages have sometimes to be changed. 9½ m. beyond Hal is Enghien, pop. 4400. Hotel du Parc. Straight up from the station is the parish church, and the entrance into the park with a chateau of the Duke d'Arenberg.

15 m. farther W. or 33 m. from Brussels is **Ath**, pop. 8300, on the Dendre. *Hotels:* opposite station the Univers; in the town, the Cygne; Paon d'Or. Of the church of St. Julian, the principal entrance, choir and tower belong to the 14th cent., the rest is modern. The Hotel de Ville dates from 1600, and the Tour de Burbant from 1150.

7 m. S. from Ath, by branch line to Blaton, is Belœil, pop. 2900, on the patrimonial estate of the Princes de Ligne, to whom it has belonged since 1394. The chateau founded in 1164 is a vast square edifice, surrounded by a fosse. The park is intersected in all directions by hornbeam hedges, and the avenue in the forest is 2¼ m. long. The gardens, with 220 yards of hothouses, were designed by Le Notre. In the castle are several valuable collections—a library with rare manuscripts; a collection of firearms from the earliest times to the present day; the swords with which the Counts Egmont and Hoorn were beheaded; fragments of the true cross and of the crown of thorns; 125 portraits of the princes of the house of Ligne, and some admirable pictures by Holbein, Durer, L. da Vinci, Van Dyck, Salvator Rosa, and Velasquez. Admission generally granted in absence of family.

7½ m. W. from Ath is Leuze junction, and 12 m. farther or 53 m. from Brussels, and 14 m. E. from Lille, is **Tournai** or Doornick, pop. 31,000, traversed throughout its entire length by the Escaut canal, which divides the town into 2 nearly equal parts. *Hotels:* Imperatrice; Singe d'Or (less expensive); at the station, the Bellevue. The most ancient town in Belgium, the Civitas Nerviorum of Cæsar and the Tournacus of the 5th cent. In 448 it became the residence of Merovée, third king of the Franks, and was likewise occupied by his successor Childeric, who founded the cathedral and died in this town in 481. In 1295 it was fortified by Philip the Fair, and afterwards by Vauban, now converted into boulevards. Of its many sieges, the most famous is that in which it was heroically defended by Marie de Lalaing, Princess of Epinoy in 1581, against Alexander, Duke of Parma. On an eminence on the W. side of the canal, in a straight line from the station by the R. des Poteries, and its continuation the Rues Codiau

Tournai. Cathedral. St. Brice.

and Hôpital, is the **Cathedral of Notre Dame**, a very ancient structure (1030) of Romanesque and Ogival architecture, with fine pointed towers and a majestic interior, of which the choir is particularly admired. The nave, of which the arches are segmental, dates from the 11th cent.; the transepts, of which the arches are stilted, from the 12th cent.; and the choir, where we have the drop or obtuse-angled triangle arch, from the 13th cent. A beautiful rood loft, with sculptured white marble panels, separates the sanctuary from the transept. Over it is a group in bronze, representing St. Michael overcoming Satan. On the left side of the altar is an elaborately-wrought reliquary of St. Eleutherius, and on the other side is a similar reliquary of St. Peter the Martyr. Behind the high altar is a monument to the bishops of Tournai. The cupids are by Duquesnoy, and have more expression than even those at Louvain. In the first chapel, S. side of choir, is the picture of the "Rescue of the Souls from Purgatory," by Rubens. In the sacristy is an ivory crucifix by Duquesnoy, and 15th cent. tapestry representing scenes from the life of St. Eleutherius, bishop of Tournai in the 6th cent. Fee to see the cathedral, $\frac{1}{2}$ fr. each. Shut from 12 to 2. Doorkeeper lives opposite main entrance.

Adjoining the Cathedral, and in the Grande Place, is the **Belfry**, erected in 1190, rebuilt in 1391, restored in 1852, and ascended by 260 steps. Fee to doorkeeper 25 c., and to man on the top 25 c. Opposite is a monument to the Princess d'Epinoy. Near it is the church of **St. Quentin**, of which the end towards the square exhibits the Early Pointed style, but in the interior many of the arches and all the columns are Romanesque. The door, generally open, is at the N. side. From the Belfry, a short street, the Rue du Parc, leads to the Park, passing by the theatre. In the Park is the Hotel de Ville, with a small collection of paintings.

Almost opposite the cathedral, but on the right side of the river, is the church of *St. Brice*, with a large square tower built in the 12th cent. Under what is now the doorkeeper's house, No. 9 Rue Terrasse, was discovered, in 1653, the coffin of Childeric, king of the Franks, who died in 480. Among the curiosities found in the coffin were the gold bees which Napoleon wore on his robes on the occasion of his coronation. To ascend the tower apply to the doorkeeper. There are many other churches in Tournai, but they all bear the type of the Cathedral. A great many carpets are manufactured here, mostly in private houses. In commerce they are called Brussels carpets.

Courtrai. Picture Gallery. Notre-Dame.

20 m. N. from Tournai by Mouscron, or 23 m. N.E. from Lille, 54 m. W. from Brussels by Denderleeuw, Sottegem and Audenaerde, is

Courtrai, pop. 28,000, traversed by the river Lys. *Hotels:* at the station, the hotels Nord and du Midi. In the Grande Place, the Lion d'Or and the Damier. In the Marché aux Grains, the Postillon. On arriving, take the broad street, the Rue du Chemin de Fer, then second street right, which crosses the Grand Place to the church of St. Martin, founded in 652 by St. Elegius, the Apostle of Flanders. The present church, dating from the 15th cent., was restored and repaired after the fire of 1862, caused by lightning. Over the majestic portico rises a handsome Gothic tower. In the interior, the most striking object is the partially gilded stone tabernacle sculptured in 1385, standing by the left side of the altar. In the choir is a triptych by Ryckere 1587; the centre painting represents the Descent of the Holy Ghost, the wings, Baptism of Christ, and the creation of man.

Returning to the square, take the first street right, and then first left, where we have the Picture Gallery; entry 30 c. The great picture (No. 27) at the head of the room represents the Battle of the Spurs, when, in 1302, the Flemish weavers routed the flower of the French nobility under Count Artois. Fronting the door is No. 141 "Memling painting the Reliquary of St. Ursula" by Dobbelarre; next to it is No. 11 a landscape by Steinicke. At the other end of the room is No. 13 "The Interior of a Kitchen." The church beyond, or farther along this same street, is Notre Dame, founded in the 13th cent. In the chapel, exactly behind the high altar, is "**The Raising of the Cross**" by Van Dyck, an admirable picture; the expression of resignation in our Lord's face, and the posture of the workmen, are most remarkable.

On the right side of the church is the Chapelle Ste. Catherine, built in 1374, adorned with mural paintings of the 14th cent., representing the Last Day, and the Counts and Countesses of Flanders; recently restored by Van der Platz, who continued the series down to Francis II., Emperor of Austria, died 2d March 1835. The reliefs on the panels round the walls represent the 7 deadly sins. Near the church by the bank of the river is one of the old city gates.

Now return to the Grande Place, and visit the **Hotel de Ville**, 1528, recently restored, and the niches provided with statues. In the Salle Echevinale, on the ground floor, is a large sculptured chimney-piece, representing the escutcheons of Ghent and Bruges, and of the Knights of Courtrai, with statues of the Virgin, and of the Archduke Albert and his wife. Around the room are frescoes by Guffens and Swerts, 1875, illustrating scenes in the history of Flanders. Upstairs in the Council Chamber is a more beautiful chimney-piece, adorned with statuettes representing the virtues and vices, and reliefs representing their consequences. To the right are statues of Charles V. and of the Infanta Isabel; to the left Justice. The plans of the town on the wall were painted in 1641.

Opposite the Hotel de Ville is the Belfry built of brick, with four turrets.

The great industries of Courtrai are the manufacture of linen, and the making of Valenciennes lace, which is taught in the schools. The dealers supply the workers with the thread, needles, and parchment. The great market for it is the United States. An expert worker may earn by lace-making nearly a franc a day. Courtrai is also famous for its table-linen. A great deal of the finest flax, cultivated with the greatest care, is grown in the fertile plain around the town. The water of the Lys is said to be particularly suited for the bleaching of linen. The earliest cloth manufactories of Flanders were established at Courtrai in 1260. Courtrai was known in the time of the Romans under the name of Cortoriacum. In the 7th cent. it was a municipal city. On July 1302 was fought under its walls the battle between the Flemings and the French, in which the latter were defeated with immense loss, when about 800 gilt spurs of the killed and vanquished noblemen and knights were gathered on the field, and hung up as a trophy in the church of the convent of Groeniguen, now destroyed. On the right of the road, a little way out of the Porte de Gand, a small chapel indicates the site of the centre of the battlefield.

21 m. from Courtrai, 22½ m. from Lille by Comines and 19½ m. from Hazebrouck, is **Ypres**, pop. 1800, in a fertile plain on both sides of the Yperlée. *Hotels:* Tête d'Or, in the Rue de Lille; H. Chatellenie, in the Grande Place. Coach to Dixmude, 15 m. N. Fare 3 frs. In the 14th cent. Ypres had a population of 200,000, and employed 4000 looms. To these prosperous times belong the Halles, including the Hotel de Ville, a massive extensive edifice in the form of an irregular trapezium of two stories, covered with a high peaked roof, adorned with crockets on the apex.

The façade, 436 feet wide, is continued above the eaves in the shape of a battlemented balustrade, from the panels of which a linear decoration descends nearly the length of the windows. In the centre of the south side rises a square tower, with pinnacled turrets at each corner, similar to those at three of the corners of the edifice. On the south and west sides, between each of the windows of the upper story, are 68 coupled, life-size statues, representing the royal personages of Flanders, from Baldwin of the Iron Arm with his spouse who in 1200 laid the foundation of the building, to Charles V., with his spouse. Over the principal entrance is a Madonna, under a rich canopy. The entrance to the Hotel de Ville, the oldest part of the edifice, is in the side opposite the church of St. Martin. The Salle des Mariages is ornamented with frescoes by Guffens and Swerts, 1869, including portraits of the Flemish Counts from 1322 to 1476. In the hall is a handsome modern chimney-piece by Malfait. The reception-room is 165 ft. long by 100 wide, and is similarly ornamented. Fee for one, 1 fr., more than one ½ fr. each.

In the Petite Place is the Cathedral of **St. Martin**, an elegant Gothic edifice, commenced in the 13th cent., but never finished. The portal of the south transept, with a superb rose-window above it, forms the most beautiful entrance. From the principal or western entrance rises a great square tower, ascended by 368 steps, built in 1254 by Utenhove.

YPRES. JANSENIUS. DIAPER LINEN.

In the interior of the church the dark-blue stone of the arches and columns contrasts well with the rest of the building, which is rather overcrowded with statuary. The floor is laid with squares of black and white marble. The choir, dating from 1221, contains old frescoes restored in 1826, a winged picture painted in 1525, probably by P. Pourbus, representing the story of the "Fall of man and his redemption," and stalls skilfully carved by Urban Taillebert in 1598. On one of the white squares on the floor in front of the altar (of Carrara marble) is the number 1638, a figure in each corner, with in the centre a tiny cross, which is all that indicates the resting-place of Cornelius Jansenius, who died in that year bishop of Ypres, a victim to the plague. Although one of the most devoted champions of the Romish church, he left behind him a MS., on which he had laboured during the last twenty years of his life, and which was the means of damaging the Romish church nearly as much as the Reformation, and originated the controversy in which Pascal's "Provincial Letters" appeared. The church is closed between 12 and 4.30; when apply to the beadle, No. 27 Petite Place. Fee 1 fr.

Opposite Les Halles is a double-gabled 15th cent. building, containing on the ground-floor the Meat Market (Les Boucheries), and upstairs the Museum, with a few modern pictures and antiquities. ½ fr. Diaper linen is supposed to be derived from the expression d'Ypres linen. Linen, lace and thread are the chief manufactures. 22½ miles S. from Ypres by Comines is Lille (see under Lille).

Five miles west from Tournai is Blandain, Belgian custom-house and time. Five and a half miles farther west is Baisieux, French custom-house and time. The village, pop. 2000, is a mile from the station. 12 miles W. from Tournai, and 4½ W. from Lille, is Ascq, pop. 2400. Four m. S.E. is Bovines, where the Emp. Otto IV. was defeated in 1214 by Philip Augustus of France.

LILLE, 67¾ miles south-west from Brussels, page 23.

Brussels to Calais.

By Hal, Enghien, Ath, Leuze, Tournai, Lille, and Hazebrouck, 133 miles west.
Time, 4 hours 40 minutes.

BRUSSELS   See Map, page 1.   CALAIS
MILES FROM   MILES TO

BRUSSELS. Start from the Station du Sud. The first important station is Hal, 8¾ m. S. from Brussels, see p. 221. Then 33 m. S.W. from Brussels, or 23¾ m. W. from Hal, is Ath, p. 224. Station to visit Belœil, see p. 224.   133

52½ TOURNAI, see p. 224. 4½ m. from Tournai the train arrives 80½ at the Belgian frontier of Blandain, with Belgian custom-house and time. 3¼ miles beyond is Baisieux, the French frontier town, with French custom-house and time.

| BRUSSELS MILES FROM | SAVENTHEM.   LOUVAIN. | CALAIS MILES TO |

67 LILLE, see p. 23, half-way between Brussels and Calais. **66** From Lille the train, after passing Hazebrouck, 95 m. from Brussels, see p. 29, and St. Omer, 12 m. farther, see p. 22, arrives at Calais, 133 m. from Brussels.

Brussels to Luxembourg.

By Louvain, Tirlemont, Landen, Liège, Spa, Bovigny, and Mersch, 161 m. S.E., starting from the Station du Nord. The direct line to Luxembourg is by Ottignies, Gembloux, Namur, Marloie, St. Hubert, Neufchateau, and Arlon, 136 m. S.E.

| BRUSSELS MILES FROM | See Map on pages 1 and 212. | LUXEMBOURG MILES TO |

BRUSSELS. Start from the "Station du Nord;" the train **161** is to the left, a little back. This is the direct line for Cologne, as far as Pepinster, whence the Luxembourg train goes southward, and the Cologne train N.E. by Aix-la-Chapelle. The train, after passing the suburb of Schaerbeek, halts at Dieghem, 5 m. W., in a wooded valley and possessing a church with the "miracle"-working relics of St. Cornelius. 1¼ m. farther is Saventhem. In the church of this small village, on the wall of the S. aisle, is a picture painted by Van Dyck when staying here, representing "St. Martin giving half of his cloak to a naked beggar." He has just cut it in two with his sword. The house he occupied stood on the site of house No. 20, S.E. from chancel. Near it is a house with the date 1624. After Saventhem the train arrives at **Louvain**, 18¾ m. E. from Brussels, or 38 minutes by express. In the station, which is large and commodious, are the post and telegraph offices; *opposite is the starting-place of the tram, which runs to the Hotel de Ville,* and the church of St. Pierre; fare 2 sous. Also cabs. In the square in front of the station are a statue of Van der Weyer, born at Louvain in 1802, died in London 1874, and the *Hotels:* Industrie; Nouveau Monde; Nord; and Renaissance. In the centre of the town, near the promenade, the Hotel de Suede.

Louvain, pop. 35,000, a quiet but pleasant town on the Dyle, with walks, gardens, and villas, on the site of its former ramparts.

Stepping at the station into the tram-car, we arrive, by a handsome street, at the Hotel de Ville and the church of St. Pierre, the two principal sights. The **Hotel de Ville** is square, 100 ft. wide, and isolated on 3 sides. At the corners run up elegant attached octagonal turrets, terminating in pinnacles so profusely sculptured that they resemble the work seen on a Chinese ivory box. The edifice is 3 stories high, crowned by a lofty roof surrounded by an open balustrade. Each story contains 10 richly-canopied windows, while the space between them is entirely occupied by superbly decorated niches with skilfully sculptured statues, standing on corbels adorned with semi-detached, highly expressive, and frequently grotesque groups. The statues, numbering about 250, are about 4 ft. high, and represent citizens, nobles and kings, and, emblematically, the rights and privileges of the city. The building was commenced in 1448 and finished in 1463 by Mathieu de Layens, and restored in 1842 by Goyers. The interior has nothing remarkable. The best of the rooms are—the Salle de Mariage; the Salle de Conseil, with paintings by Verhaegen and Crayer; the Salle Gothique, where exhibitions are held; and the Salle de Musée.

Behind the Hotel de Ville is the University, in the building formerly occupied by the Cloth Market. The vestibule at the top of the double staircase is adorned with a large painting by Van Bree. The door in the left corner opens into the Salle des Promotions, and the door in the right corner into the Library, a magnificent hall both in size and construction, containing 80,000 vols. and 300 MSS.

Opposite the Hotel de Ville, and nearly surrounded by petty houses, is the venerable church of **St. Pierre**, built for the Count Lambert Balderic by Van Vorst, d. 1439. The tower, containing a set of sweet chiming bells, was originally 530 ft. high, but was thrown down by a hurricane in 1604. The interior of the church is 304 ft. long and 88 wide, and is lighted by 90 large windows with elegant flamboyant tracery. The best pictures are by Weyden and Stuerbout and the best sculpture by Papenhoven, who almost rivals Blasset.

The first chapel right from the richly carved main entrance door is the chapel of St. Charles. Reredos (covered) represents St. Charles dispensing the Sacrament to people dying of the plague. It is only a copy of a painting by Crayer. Also, statue of St. Charles by C. Geerts, 1855, and a quaint triptych, representing the martyrdom of St. Dorothea, by Baeren, 1594.—2. Chapelle du Christ Noir, a robed Crucifixion in dark wood, said once to have caught a thief.—3. Nothing particular.—4. Chapel of St. Sebastian, with picture representing his martyrdom. Old presses with curious hinges. Curious old Ecce Homo in stone statuettes. In front is the admirably carved **pulpit**, by Bergé, in 1742, representing on one side the Denial of Peter the Apostle, who is clutching his keys while regarding the cock crowing, and on the other the Conversion of St. Paul, a very fine group; the whole surmounted by waving palm leaves.—5. Chapelle du Sacré Cœur,

St. Pierre. Choir.

containing an ancient picture representing the carrying off of a cook for consecration, who, during the pontificate of Gregory V., was forced against his will to become a bishop, in consequence of the "miraculous" descent of a dove upon his head. The figures, nearly a hundred, are in good natural attitudes.

Between the nave and choir is a florid Gothic rood-loft, constructed in 1490 and repaired in 1833. It rests on 3 elliptic arches surmounted by statuettes in canopied niches. Over all rises a large Crucifixion, with John and Mary at the foot of the cross. In front is suspended a 12-branched candelabrum of wrought iron, by John Matsys or Massys, but too diminutive for the space about it.

Choir.—S. side, first chapel, after passing entrance to sacristy, St. Augustin, by Verhaegen.—2. Ecce Homo, G. Zegers, 1591-1651.—3. Nothing remarkable.—*4. Notre Dame des Sept Douleurs: and Triptych, by Stuerbout, died 1475. "The Martyrdom of St. Erasmus," the patron for the cure of colic; most skilfully drawn and painted, but painfully treated. On the wings, St. Jerome and St. Benedict.— 5. Chapel of the Trinity. Between the twisted columns of the altar is a "Trinity," by Crayer, and in the wall a sculptured representation in statuettes. Opposite the altar is a "Last Supper," a very fine and expressive painting by Stuerbout (covered.)—6. In this chapel used to be kept the triptych representing the Legend of St. Anne, by Quentin Metsys, now in the Picture Gallery of Brussels. It was sold for £8000. —7. Chapel of Ste. Marguerite. The reredos and the other 4 pictures are by Verhaegen, representing the life and martyrdom of Ste. Marguerite, 1225. The small door opens into a chamber where some relics of her are preserved.—8. Tomb of Henry, first Duke of Brabant, d. 1235. The tomb of his two wives is on the other side of the choir. The triptych (covered) is by **Vander Weyden, 1400-1464.** The centre is a "Descent from the Cross," and the two wings portraits of the donors.—9. The chapel of the Sacrament, on the left or N. side of the high altar. Observe here the beautiful *white marble balustrade* which serves for the communion table. The charming sculpture on the right-hand panel represents the Confession, on the centre one the Communion, and on the left one Baptism, each scene being personified by a pair of chubby cupids in pure white marble, sculptured by Papenhoven in 1709. Near the communion table, and to the left of the altar, is the Tabernacle, a six-sided Gothic stone pinnacle 50 ft. high, sculptured in 1433 with the delicacy of lace-work, by M. de Layens, the architect of the Hotel de Ville. "Jesu Deo-homini, sub specie

LOUVAIN.   SAINT GERTRUDE.   BEAUTIFUL STALLS.

panis hic realiter latenti."—10. Crucifixion, after Van Dyck. In the first chapel N. side of choir is the tomb of the two wives of the Duke of Brabant. In the N. transept is the monument to Xavier de Ram, d. 1854, sculptured with great refinement of taste. Above is an "Elevation of the Cross," by François. In the N. aisle, in the first chapel to the left of the main entrance, is a brazen baptismal font and iron crane, by John Massys. Fee to sacristan to uncover the pictures, 1 fr. Church shut from 12 to 2.

Leave St. Pierre by the main entrance and walk down the Rue de Malines to the church of St. Gertrude, right hand, easily recognised by its open crocketed spire. When shut apply to the doorkeeper, in the small house adjoining the main entrance. St. Gertrude, built in the 15th cent., has 52 stalls, carved by Mathias de Waydere, 16th cent., considered the finest in Belgium. They are, as usual, of oak. On the panels over the 28 stalls of the two higher rows are represented, in nearly detached groups, the life, death, and resurrection of our Lord, enclosed in a graceful framework of canopied niches. On the arms and partitions of the stalls are numerous miniature figures carved with great expression, ingenuity, and minuteness. The organ-loft on caryatides is very elegant. On both sides of the altar are marble mausoleums of bishops in a kneeling posture. The monument on the left is by Kerricx. In the chapel, right side of entrance, is the statue of St. Gertrude, with a mouse on her shepherd's crook. A little beyond is a triptych by Coxcie.

At the foot of the Rue de Malines are the remains of the Chateau de Cesar, built in the 11th cent., and famous for having been the place where Charles V. and his sisters were educated by Adrian Dedel, afterwards Pope Adrian VI. Edward III. of England, with his queen, passed the winter of 1485 in this castle. Ascend by the road to the left, the length of an archway on the right, which |pass through; the second large door, right hand, is the entrance; fee 4 sous. The interior, which is now a small farm, is visited on account of the excellent view of the town and neighbourhood had from the terrace.

Louvain is famous for its beer. One of the best places to take a glass of it is in that brasserie or beer-house opposite the Hotel de Ville. Good carved furniture, domestic and ecclesiastic, is also made in the town. Louvain has also an important bell foundry.

Thirty miles south-east from Brussels and 11¼ from Louvain is

Tirlemont, pop. 13,300. *Inns:* at station, the Nouveau Monde. In the principal "Place," the Flandre. The ancient walls, dismantled

TIRLEMONT. BOLLANDUS. TONGRES.

since 1804, form a circuit of nearly 6 miles, enclosing, besides the town, gardens and orchards on the site of the streets and houses that were destroyed by the conflagration of 1604. In the "Place" are the Hotel de Ville and the church of N. D. du Lac, founded in 1298, but nearly rebuilt in the 15th cent. The confessionals are adorned with sculptured angels and men, life size, in oak. Immediately within the entrance is an old curiously carved door, about 12 ft. high and 6 wide. Up the centre are three Maries, each representing an important attribute. The lowest is Mary the mother of our Lord, Mary nursing the child. The second Mary the anchor of our hope, Mary holding an anchor. The highest Mary our salvation, Mary giving us the flesh and the blood of her son in a chalice. The intervening spaces are filled up with cupids fluttering about the Maries.

Near Notre Dame is St. Germain, which, although founded in the 9th cent., is principally of the 12th cent. with parts still later. The choir is Transition. Both churches lack architectural ornament. The windows are great bays, glazed with panes of the size of roofing slates. In the south aisle is a robed crucifix, life size. Opposite is our Lord in the tomb guarded by two angels. To the left is a pietá. The pulpit is admirably designed and carved. Tirlemont is the native town of the learned Jesuit, John Bollandus, born August 13, 1596. He is celebrated as the first of that series of hagiographers, called after him Bollandists, who compiled the vast collection of the lives of Romish saints, known as the Acta Sanctorum, of which he completed five volumes. This immense work contains, with much that is useless and legendary, a valuable mine of facts in civil and ecclesiastical history.

From Tirlemont a branch line extends 62 miles east to Aix-la-Chapelle, by Neer-Linter, St. Trond, Tongres, Munsterbilsen, and Maestricht. Or, if preferred, from St. Trond go round by Hasselt, which, by distance, is a little farther, but by time generally shorter, see Map, p. 1. 12½ m. N.E. from Tirlemont is St. Trond, pop. 11,500. *Inn:* Commerce. Called after St. Trudon who wrought miracles and founded an abbey here. It contains the churches of N. Dame restored in 1858, and St. Martin in the Romanesque style. 15 m. east from St. Trond is Tongres, pop. 8000, on the Jaar. *Inn:* H. du Paon. Said to have been founded by Tongrus, its first king, 100 years before the foundation of Rome. It was the Roman Aduatica Tongri, the capital of Gallia Belgica, sacked by Attila, King of the Huns, in 455. Notre-Dame, the cathedral, was the first church dedicated to the Virgin on this side of the Alps, and was also considered the oldest. The earliest parts of the present edifice date only from the 13th cent. Near Tongres, in the estate of Betho, is a mineral spring mentioned by Pliny. For Hasselt, see under that name in the route from Antwerp to Aix-la-Chapelle, page 291.

Landen. Liège.

From Tirlemont by the valley and meadows of the Boschelle and the stations of Esemael and Neerwinden, where the French gained a victory over the allies in 1693, we come to the important junction station of **Landen**, 38 m. S.E. from Brussels, 24¼ N.W. from Liège, and 96¼ W. from Aix-la-Chapelle. Landen, pop. 800. *Inn:* Quatre Saisons. Now a poor village but once the residence of the Dukes of Brabant, among whom was Pepin, the first of the race, and the founder of the Carlovingian dynasty. He died here in 647, and was buried at the foot of the hill which still bears his name. The body was removed afterwards to Nivelles, for which see page 216.

After Landen the principal stations are **Waremme**, 47 m. S. from Brussels, and 15½ N.W. from Liège, near the intersection of the railway with the Roman road which extended from Tongres to Mons.

From Waremme the train enters the picturesque, fertile and great mining district of Liège, situated 62¼ m. S.E. from Brussels, 78 m. S.W. from Cologne, and 99 m. N. from Luxembourg.

Liège, pop. 122,000. Train arrives at the great station of Guillemins, which is also the station for Aix-la-Chapelle and Paris. Commodious refreshment-rooms. Behind, H. de Chemin de Fer. Trams from in front of the station run to different parts of the town. Also cabstand. Fares—In open 1 horse cabs, the course 1½ fr.; per hour, 2 frs. Course in 2 horse open cab 2 frs.; or per hour, 3 frs. Course in 1 horse closed cab 1 fr.; per hour, 1½ fr. Two horses, 1½ fr.; or per hour, 2 frs. Before starting on a long drive see the coachman's tariff.

Hotels.—The most expensive are the *Suede; Europe; Angleterre; Schiller—all around the theatre. The G. Hotel Charlemagne in the Place St. Lambert, and the Grand Cerf in the Rue de la Cathedrale.

Less expensive hotels.—The Deux Fontaines in the Place du Theatre. The H. Dinant and France near the church of St. Denis. The Flandre, Rue de la Regence. The H. Mohren next the cathedral. The H. Notger in the Place Notger. The H. Pommelette, Rue de Souverain Pont. The best cafés are in the Place St. Lambert.

Throughout the town are a great many gunsmiths—"fabricants d'armes à feu." These men are in reality however only the dealers, as the different parts of the firearms are made, adjusted, and put together by male and female artisans in their own houses. Temple Protestant in the Rue Hors Chateau. In all the principal streets are electric clocks.

Sights.—The exterior of the Palais de Justice. View from the Citadel Pierreuse. Cathedral. St. Jacques.

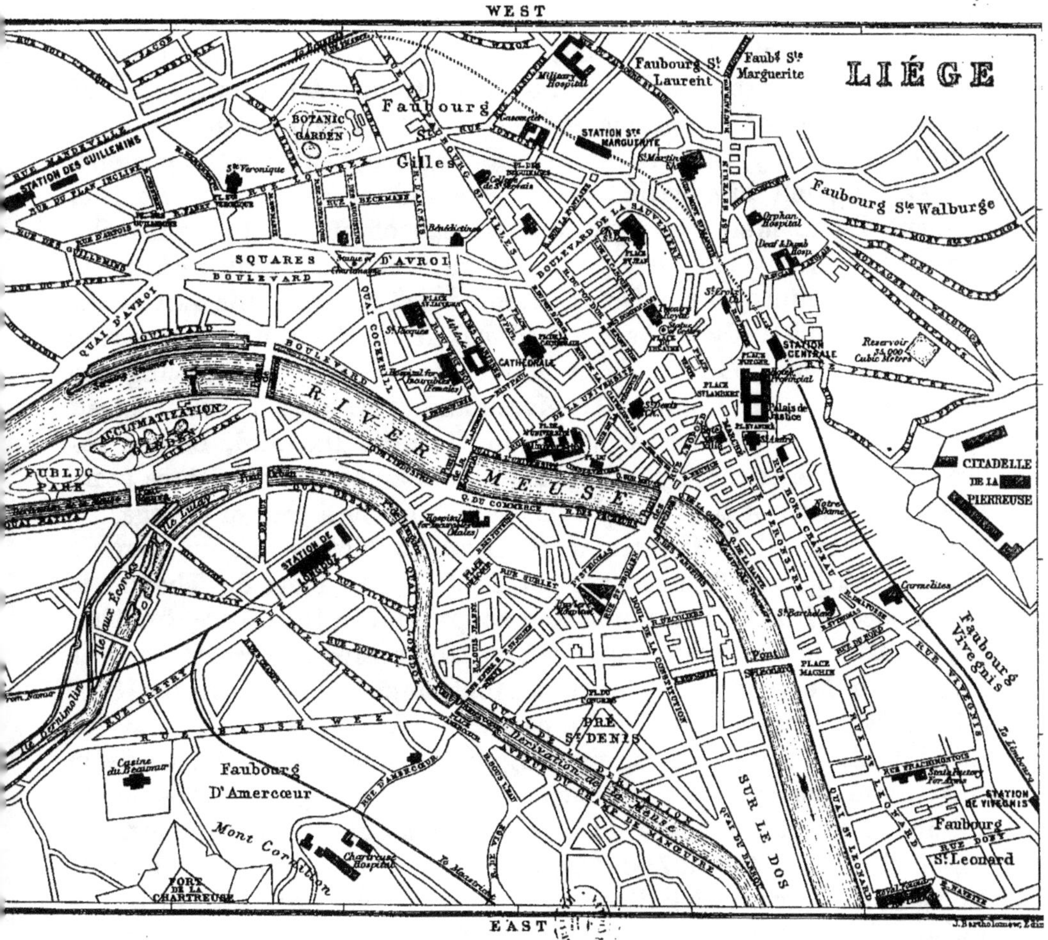
WEST
LIÉGE
Faubourg St Laurent
Faubg Ste Marguerite
Military Hospital
Faubourg St Gilles
BOTANIC GARDEN
STATION STE MARGUERITE
STATION DES GUILLEMINS
Faubourg Ste Walburge
Orphan Hospital
Deaf & Dumb Hosp.
SQUARES D'AVROI
BOULEVARD
QUAI D'AVROI
CATHEDRALE
STATION CENTRALE
Reservoir 24,000 Cubic Metres
PLACE ST LAMBERT
Palais de Justice
RIVER MEUSE
ACCLIMATIZATION GARDEN
PUBLIC PARK
CITADELLE DE LA PIERREUSE
Q. DU COMMERCE
STATION DE LONGDOZ
Notre Dame
Carmelites
Faubourg Vivegnis
St Barthelemi
PLACE MACHIN
Pont
PRÉ St DENIS
SUR LE DOS
RUE GRETRY
RUE MASSE WEZ
Casino du Beaumur
Faubourg D'Amercœur
Mont Cornillon
Chartreuse Hospital
To Maestricht
FORT DE LA CHARTREUSE
QUAI ST LEONARD
STATION DE VIVEGNIS
Faubourg St Leonard
To Limbourg
EAST
J. Bartholomew, Edin.

LIÈGE. LA MARCK. PALAIS DE JUSTICE.

Liège, the Birmingham of Belgium, was founded in the 6th cent. In 1482 William de la Marck, the Wild Boar of Ardennes, having entered into a conspiracy with the discontented citizens against their Bishop, Louis of Bourbon, marched to Liège at the head of troops composed chiefly of assassins, dressed in scarlet for a uniform, with a boar's head on the left sleeve. Upon this, the citizens who were engaged in the conspiracy came to their bishop, and offering to stand by him to the death, exhorted him to march out against these robbers. The bishop, therefore, put himself at the head of a few troops of his own, trusting to the assistance of the people of Liège. But as soon as they came in sight of the enemy, the citizens, as before agreed, fled from the bishop's banner, and left him with his own handful of adherents. At this moment De la Marck charged at the head of his banditti with the expected success. The bishop was brought before the profligate knight, who first cut him over the face, then murdered him with his own hand, and caused his body to be exposed naked in the square before the cathedral. This William de la Marck was of high birth, being the third son of John I., Count of La Marck and of Arenberg. But instead of having met his death as stated in Quentin Durward, he was beheaded at Maestricht, by order of Maximilian of Austria, three years after the murder of the bishop of Liège, in the 39th year of his age.

The "Places" du Theatre, de St Lambert, Notger and du Marché, all connected, form the best part of Liège. The Place du Theatre is surrounded with the best hotels and shops, and in the centre, fronting the theatre, is the statue, by Geefs, of the composer Gretry, born at Liège 11th February 1741, died at Montmorency near Paris in 1813. His heart is preserved under the pedestal. All the tram-cars traverse this "Place," while the car running to Longdoz, near the Fort de la Chartreuse (visited for the view), has its starting-point opposite the statue. Behind the Place du Theatre is the church of St. Jean, in which Bishop Notger (971-1008), the great church builder, is buried. In the next square, the Place St. Lambert, the great feature is the **Palais de Justice**, erected during 1508-1533 by Bishop Eberhard, a descendant of William de la Marck. The best of the façades of this vast building—which covers 3 acres—is the western, built in 1852, fronting the Place Notger with its little garden and grotto. To the left is the road up to the church of St. Martin (p. 238), and to the right, behind the "Station Centrale," the road up to the **Citadel Pierreuse**, whence there is the best view of the environs. Permits procured at the Bureau de Place, No. 32 Rue de la Regence.

LIÈGE. ST. BARTHÉLEMY. ST. DENIS.

The principal court of the Palais de Justice is surrounded by an arcade of 60 depressed four centred arches, resting on short banded bulging columns with heavy square foliaged capitals. Above each arch is a transomed window in 4 divisions, and over every alternate window on two of the sides of the parallelogram, crocketed pinnacled dormer windows united by an open balustrade. In the smaller court are the Musés Archeologique and Lapidaire. In the adjoining square, the Place du Marché, are the Hotel de Ville (1714-1718) and the Fontaine des Trois Graces by Delcour, 1696. Behind the houses is St. André, now the Exchange, with a great octagonal slated dome. A little way down the Rue Feronstrée is the church of St. Barthélemy, consecrated in 1015 but rebuilt. It contains in the first chapel left or north of high altar a circular brass *baptismal font, the work of Lambert Patras of Dinant, 1112. It is about 2 ft. deep, and 3¼ in diameter. Around the sides are groups in relief, engaged in the baptismal rite by sprinkling combined with immersion. One of the groups represent the baptism of our Lord. From the stone pedestal project 10 heads of horned cattle. At No. 65 Rue de Feronstrée is the Musée Communal, open on Sundays. It contains a few good pictures.

A little farther, opposite the Pont-Maghin, is the "Prison Cellulaire," surrounded by high crenellated walls. Then, on the same side, and fronting house No. 184, is the entrance to the Government manufactory of firearms. Farther down, but on the opposite side of the street, is the cannon foundry. All the above places can be easily visited by the car, which runs up and down the whole Rue Feronstrée. It can be picked up at the "Arret du Tramway," in the corner of the Place du Theatre, on its way down the B. de la Sauvenière, or in the Place de St. Lambert on its way to the Place du Marché.

The best of the streets is the Rue de la Cathedrale, which traverses the most important part of the town. About the centre is the church of St. Denis, and at the S.W. extremity, the cathedral and the church of St. Jacques; the two latter forming the principal sights in the town.

St. Denis, consecrated in 990 by Bishop Notger, was rebuilt during the 13th and 14th cents. The nave rests on two rows of Ionic columns. On the roof is the martyrdom of St. Denis. In the first chapel, north side, left of high altar, a *reredos in three stages, containing a multitude of figures in wood, partially gilt. The lowest stage represents scenes from the life of St. Denis. The other two the death and resurrection of our Lord. The chancel, which is small, is surrounded by 9 lancet windows with stained glass, separated from each other by the

CATHEDRAL. PULPIT.

thick shafts, whence springs the groining of the roof. The statues of Mary and St. Denis, at each side of the altar, are by Delcour.

In the Place de la Cathedrale is the **Cathedral of St. Paul**, founded in 967 by Bishop Heraclius, restored in the 13th cent., and left in its present form in 1528. It is in two stages, supported by double flying pinnacled buttresses. The windows have equilateral arches with trefoil and quatrefoil tracery. The interior is 276 ft. long by 112 wide, and 80 ft. high. The nave, finished in 1557, has on each side 8 plain round columns, from which spring pointed arches and triple vaulting shafts which ramify gracefully over the roof, ornamented with arabesques painted in 1579 and hung with gilt pendants.

Of the chapels the best are—First right, South Aisle, a Resurrection, by Ansiaux. 2d Chapel, white marble statuary by Delcour, 1696, representing "Our Lord in the Tomb, guarded by 2 angels." The bronze Christ over the N. portal is also by Delcour. 3d Chapel, Martyrdom of St. Lambert, by Tahan. Opposite is the pulpit, by W. Geefs, a magnificent combination of admirably-sculptured marble statuary, with charming and elaborate wood carving. Four of the statues represent Saints Peter, Paul, Lambert, and Hubert, while the fifth represents the woman treading on the head of the serpent. Behind the pulpit, at the foot of the stair, is Satan in chains, by J. Geefs. The sound-board is in delicate pinnacle-work, 57 ft. high, which is a little too lofty. The large and splendid window of the S. transept is radiant with most superb 16th cent. glass—that of the N. although modern (Capronnier) is beautiful. The sanctuary, shut off from the transepts by a massive brass railing, contains delicately-carved stalls, and is lighted by 5 windows with 16th cent. glass. In the chapel in the north aisle fronting the pulpit is an Ascension of Mary by Lairesse. In the next, a "Baptism" by Carlier 1600. Under it is the curious tombstone of Antony Gal, d. 1680. In the treasury are a silver gilt bust of St. Lambert, numerous costly sacerdotal vestments and a gold statuette of St. George and Dragon, with a kneeling figure of Charles the Bold presented by him in 1471 to the church in expiation for the cruelty of his troops to the wives and daughters of the citizens of Liège, when called in 1486 by the Bishop to suppress an insurrection in the town.

Attached to the cathedral are the cloisters, 16th cent., containing some large monumental slabs.

Near the cathedral is the church of St. Jacques, founded in 1016 by Bishop Balderic II., whose tomb is in the southern or the longer of

LIÈGE.   SAINT JACQUES.   CORPUS CHRISTI.

the two transepts. The present edifice, with the exception of the western façade and tower (1173), dates from the 16th cent. It stands free and unencumbered with houses, is a perfect specimen of the 3d period of Gothic architecture, and is entered through a long arched passage. The church is 270 ft. long by 100 wide, and 75 high. The arches of the windows are drop and segmental pointed, and their tracery trefoiled and entwined. An open balustrade runs round the top of the building. In the interior, plain piers support arches hung with a double fringe from impost to impost. In each spandrel is a linear decoration round a head in bold relief, representing a king or queen, a priest or prophet of Israel. In the choir such personages are represented by statues on consoles, chiefly by Delcour and Simon Cognoulle. The roof is most elaborately groined. The ribs are painted light brown, with bands of red, blue, and white; while the roof itself is painted in arabesque and studded with embossed ornaments. The 8 beautiful stained-glass windows of the choir date from the 16th cent. The organ-loft and case (17th cent.) and the stone sculpture in the choir are by A. Severin of Maestricht.

To go to the church of St. Martin, ascend the steps in the Place Notger, then turn to the left and walk up the Rues St. Pierre and St. Martin. The first church passed is Ste. Croix, 12th-14th cent., on slender columns, and lighted with modern glass. At the top of the street is **St. Martin**, founded in 962, burnt down in 1312, and rebuilt in 1542. From the tower is an extensive view. Fee 1 fr. A marble slab on the organ-loft records that in this church, in the year 1746, was celebrated the (Quintum Solemne Jubileum) 500th anniversary of Corpus Christi, a feast-day instituted in this church in 1246, on the faith of a vision seen by Juliana, abbess of the neighbouring convent of Cornillon. Pope Urban IV. in 1264 ordained its celebration in all the Roman Catholic churches. In the first chapel next the organ-loft are 14 reliefs by Delcour, in white marble, set in frames of beadwork surmounted by a scroll, illustrating incidents having connection with the communion. The roof of the choir is painted in arabesque. On the sides of the wall are four immense panels with reliefs in stucco, by Franck, representing the principal events in the life of St. Martin. The landscapes are by Juppin, d. 1729. The only good glass (16th cent.) is in the 5 lancet windows behind the richly gilt high altar.

From opposite the statue in the Place du Theatre, a tram-car runs to the old Casino near the Chartreuse citadel. On its way down the Rue de l'Université it passes the entrance into the Passage Lem-

SERAING. JEMEPPE.

monier, the Post and Telegraph offices, and the University, a large, plain building on the left hand. The different faculties are taught by 41 professors. It contains a library with 100,000 vols., 565 MSS., and 2600 medals. In the natural history department are fossils and bones of antediluvian animals, from the caves of Ombray, Limbourg, and Maestricht. After the university the tram crosses the Meuse by two bridges, and arrives at the station of **Longdoz**, the second station in importance, and the only station on the right side of the Meuse. A little beyond is the abandoned Casino Beaumur. There is still a good view from the hill behind the house. The fortifications are a little farther off, and are approached most easily by a cab; if open and with one horse, the fare is 2½ fr., two horses 3½ fr.; closed cabs ½ fr. cheaper. The view is generally taken from the Hospice de la Chartreuse. Gratuity 1 fr.

Excursion to Seraing.—If by rail start from the Longdoz Station, approached easily by the tram. If by boat, take the car that halts at the commencement of the Boulevard de la Sauvenière on its way to the Guillemins railway station; but alight at the **Statue of Charlemagne** by Jehotte, between the Boulevard d'Avroy and the Bassin du Commerce. The pedestal, which is of Caen stone, is ornamented with statues of Pepin of Landen, Pepin of Heristal, Charles Martel, Pepin le Bref, and Queen Bertha. From the statue proceed first right, and then left to the steamboat wharf. See Map, page 212, and Plan.

Seraing, by rail, is 5 m. up the Meuse, and about 7 by the boat. The sail is interesting. After the stations of Fragnie and Angleur the steamer passes a series of foundries and works of various kinds with tall chimneys, which continue all the rest of the way. The first important town is Ougrée, pop. 6000, on the right bank, but the left when going up the river. In the neighbourhood are the woods of Kimkempois, which here cover the banks of the Meuse and the Ourthe. On the other side is Tilleur, which stretches up the river to Jemeppe, pop. 5000. *Inn:* H. du Nord at the bridge. Jemeppe is opposite Seraing and connected by a suspension bridge. The steamer before arriving at Seraing passes a long winged building with 80 windows in the upper story, occupied by the Seraing work-people. A few yards higher is the former palace of the bishops of Liège, now the offices of the works. The large gate forms the principal entrance. The steamer having passed below the bridge, moors close to it. At the landing-place is a little waiting and refreshment room. The street, Rue Cockerill, in continuance with the bridge, leads to the Seraing railway station, arriving at Liège at the station de Longdoz, whence trams run to the Place St. Lambert. The Jemeppe station is on the other side of the river about 1 m. distant, behind the parish church. Passengers from Jemeppe arrive at the Guillemins station, whence tram to the Place du Theatre.

In the "Place" of Seraing, just above the bridge, is a statue to the

MAESTRICHT. PETERSBERG.

memory of John Cockerill, an Englishman, who founded this immense establishment in 1817, and had for his associate William I. of the Netherlands till the revolution of 1830, when, having purchased his royal partner's share, he became the sole proprietor. Now it belongs to a company. John Cockerill was born in 1790 and died in 1840.

The area occupied by the establishment measures 195 acres, and comprises within itself the elements necessary to construct a highly-finished locomotive or a steel ship from its own coal-pits and iron-mines.

On an average they employ throughout the year 10,000 workmen, spend in wages upwards of £400,000, and the average annual value of the produce is £800,000. They have 259 steam engines, with an aggregate of 6600 horse-power, and have manufactured above 60,000 steam engines and 600 iron steamboats. The Waterloo Lion was cast at Seraing. Visitors should bear in mind that the workmen dine between 12 and 1.

Liège to Maestricht.—From the Quai de Batte, steamers sail down the Meuse to Maestricht—distance 19 m., time $3\frac{1}{2}$ hours. By rail (Longdoz station) it is only 70 minutes. The steamer having passed the Mont de Pieté, on the left bank, and the cannon foundry with the citadel in the background, arrives at Jupille, $3\frac{1}{4}$ m. distant, pop. 3120, where Pepin died in 714. It was a favourite residence of his and of Charlemagne. 8 m. Argenteau, picturesquely situated at the foot of two wooded hills connected by a high bridge. They form the park of the Mercy-Argenteau castle. At Visé, 10 m. distant, pop. 2600, is the Belgian custom-house, and the most northern vineyards in Europe. At Eysden, $12\frac{1}{2}$ m., pop. 1300, is the Dutch custom-house. At Maestricht arrive at the quay Vrouwepoort. **Maastricht** or Maestricht, pop. 30,000, on both sides of the Maas or Meuse. At the railway station sovereigns are taken for 25 frs. There are two railway stations, both on the right bank of the Maas and near each other. *Hotels:* Levrier, in the Boschstraat. Opposite it the Aigle Noir. Near the Petersthor, the Hotel Manel in the Peterstraat. Guides to the caves of the Petersberg, including torches, 6 frs. or 3 Gulden; carriage there and back 9 frs.

In general the town is closely built, but it has two open spaces, the Great Market Place, in which is the Hotel de Ville, built in 1662, containing the Public Library, with 15,000 vols., and a Picture Gallery, with tapestry dating from 1704, representing scenes connected with the journey of the Israelites through the wilderness, and some good Flemish paintings. The other square is called the Vrijthof or Place d'Armes, in which William de la Marck, the Wild Boar of Ardennes, was beheaded in 1485. In this "Place" is the Cathedral, 12th cent., with carefully-carved pulpit and confessionals. The descent from the cross on the reredos is by Van Dyck. In the treasury are preserved the shrine or reliquary of St. Servatius, 12th cent., of gilt enamelled copper, set with precious stones, and some church plate and insignia, fee 1 fr. The great object of interest is the **Petersberg Sandstone Quarry** in rocks rising about 320 ft. above the river, and covering an area of 12 m. long by 7 wide, intersected in all directions by a labyrinth of most intricate subterranean galleries averaging 12 ft. wide, and from 10 to 50 high. To

Chaudfontaine. Pepinster.

reach it from the station cross the bridge, and having walked up to the top of the Rue du Pont or Burgstraat, turn to the left and walk to the Peterstraat, or Rue de St. Pierre, passing by the Church and Place de Notre Dame. At the end of the Peterstraat keep to the left till the road bordering the canal is reached. Continue this road for about 1 m. to a small house at the foot of a hill, on which stand the ruins of the castle of Lichtenberg. At this house procure a guide, if one has not been already got in the Rue St. Pierre. At the mouth of the cave there is a Casino, where refreshments can be had. The view here of the plain is pleasing. This stone, similar but inferior to the Caen stone, is sawn out in blocks. Near the part quarried by the Romans are the remains of a fossil tree.

Liège to Marloie.—From Liège a branch line extends 40 m. S. through a picturesque country to Marloie on the Ourthe, see p. 247.

$2\frac{1}{2}$ m. E. from Liège, but almost a suburb, is Chènée, pop. 4500, on the Vesdre, at its junction with the Ourthe. The town contains important foundries and zinc-works, the ores being procured from the neighbouring mines. From Chènée a branch goes round to Verviers by Beyne, Herve, and Chaineux. $2\frac{1}{2}$ m. farther, or 5 from Liège, is

Chaudfontaine, pop. 1000, on the Vesdre, $66\frac{1}{2}$ m. S.E. from Brussels, and 73 m. W. from Cologne. Immediately in front of the station is the Kursaal, within its own grounds, and a few yards farther, on the other side of the Vesdre, the *Hotel des Bains, with the bathing establishment adjoining, situated among wooded hills similar to those of Spa. The hotel is very comfortable, and charges per day from 7 to 9 frs.; this sum includes tea or coffee in the morning, a meat breakfast, and dinner. The bathing establishment is plain, but comfortable. The water is feebly mineralised, a pint containing only $1\frac{1}{2}$ grain of common salt, and rather less of the carbonate of lime. The temperature is 95° Fahr., and its principal action is on the skin, which it renders soft and pliant. A first-class bath with linen costs $1\frac{1}{2}$ fr., a second-class with linen 1 fr. Behind the hotel a road provided with seats winds up the hill through the woods, disclosing many pleasing views. Almost adjoining the bathhouse are small ironworks where spades and shovels are made; the canal or mill-race, which makes an island of the hotel and bath establishment, drives the wheels. Near Chaudfontaine, $2\frac{1}{2}$ m. E. by rail, is Le Troos, with its old turreted castle, used for a century as a cannon and gun-barrel manufactory.

Pepinster to Spa.

$74\frac{1}{2}$ m. S.E. from Brussels, 22 m. W. from Aix-la-Chapelle, and $7\frac{1}{2}$ m. N. from Spa, is Pepinster, where change carriages for Spa and

Theux. Franchimont. Remouchamps.

Luxembourg. At Pepinster station there is a poor inn. The village is a little below. 3½ m. S. from Pepinster is **Theux**, on the Hoegne. On the other side of the stream, on a hill laid out in pleasure grounds, are the ruins of the castle of Franchimont, destroyed in 1145, but rebuilt by the Cardinal Erard de la Marck, who died in 1538. Later it was used as a prison, and afterwards it was converted into a powder manufactory, of which the frequent explosions reduced it to its present condition. According to a legend, it was the property of a robber knight, who buried in it immense treasures, "amass'd through rapine and through wrong." Close to Theux, on each side of the road leading N.E. to Verviers, are quarries of red marble and mines of calamine or zinc. Coach from Spa to Theux and Franchimont and back, with 1 horse 10 frs., 2 horses 12 frs.

5 m. S. from Pepinster and 2½ m. W. from Spa is **La Reid Station**, nearly 2 m. E. from the village. The easiest way to visit Franchimont castle from Spa is to take the train to Reid Station, and then to walk on by the castle to Theux, 2 m. distant. Return by rail from Theux. 4½ m. W. from La Reid, or 9 m. from Spa, is the village of Remouchamps, pleasantly situated in the valley of the Amblève. *Inns:* Etrangers; Grotte. Between the two inns is the entrance to the cave; 2 frs. each; costume for ladies 1½ frs. It is of considerable dimensions, and not all on the same level, and, like other cavities in limestone rocks, contains both stalactites and stalagmites. On the opposite side of the river, on a wooded eminence, is the ancient chateau of Mont Jardin. Here, as elsewhere in limestone strata, there are not only parallel underground openings or caves, but also vertical clefts, called in some places puits, in others entonnoirs, down which streams and even rivers disappear, as happens with the Rhone at Belle Garde. The largest of these vertical clefts in this neighbourhood is the Entonnoir of Adseux, 4 m. N. by the villages of Becheval, Denié, and Rougethier. 4 m. W., or down the lovely valley of the Amblève by the village of Aywaille (*Inn:* H. de Luxembourg), are the hamlet of Amblève and the ruins of the castle of the Quatre Fils Aymon, sometime inhabited, also, by William de la Marck, the Wild Boar of the Ardennes, whose exploits are so vividly depicted in Quentin Durward.

The inns at Remouchamps and Aywaille make good headquarters. Carriage with 2 horses, from Spa to Remouchamps and back, 25 frs.

82 m. from Brussels is **Spa**, pop. 6200, one of the oldest and most charming of the watering-places, situated at the foot of the beautifully-wooded hills of the Heid-Fanard, Annette et Lubin and Montagnes Russes, which protect it from the N. and N.E. winds, and are furrowed in all directions with roads and paths provided with seats and pavilions at the best points for views. Long and broad avenues, bearing fanciful names, extend from the town into the wooded dells of

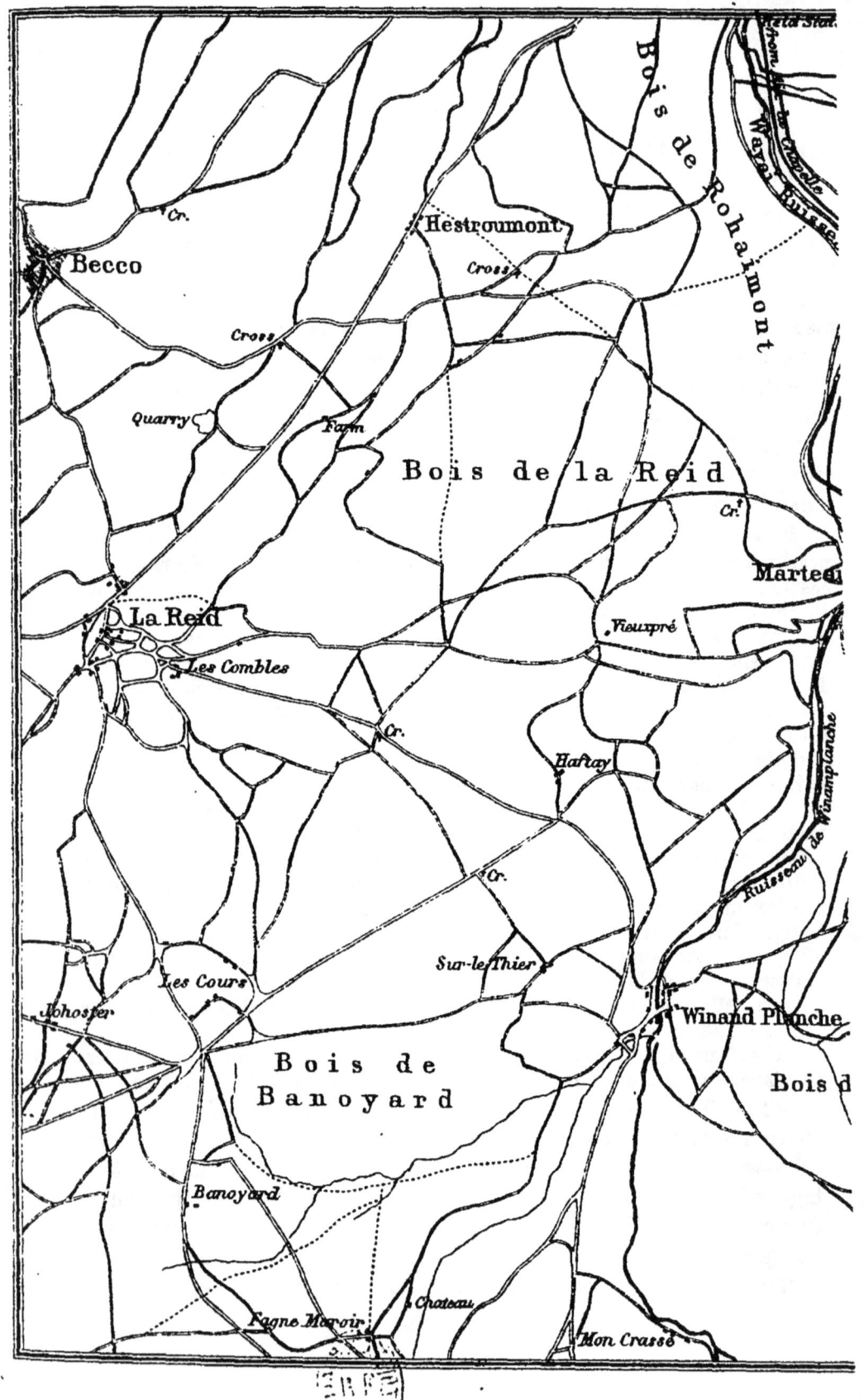

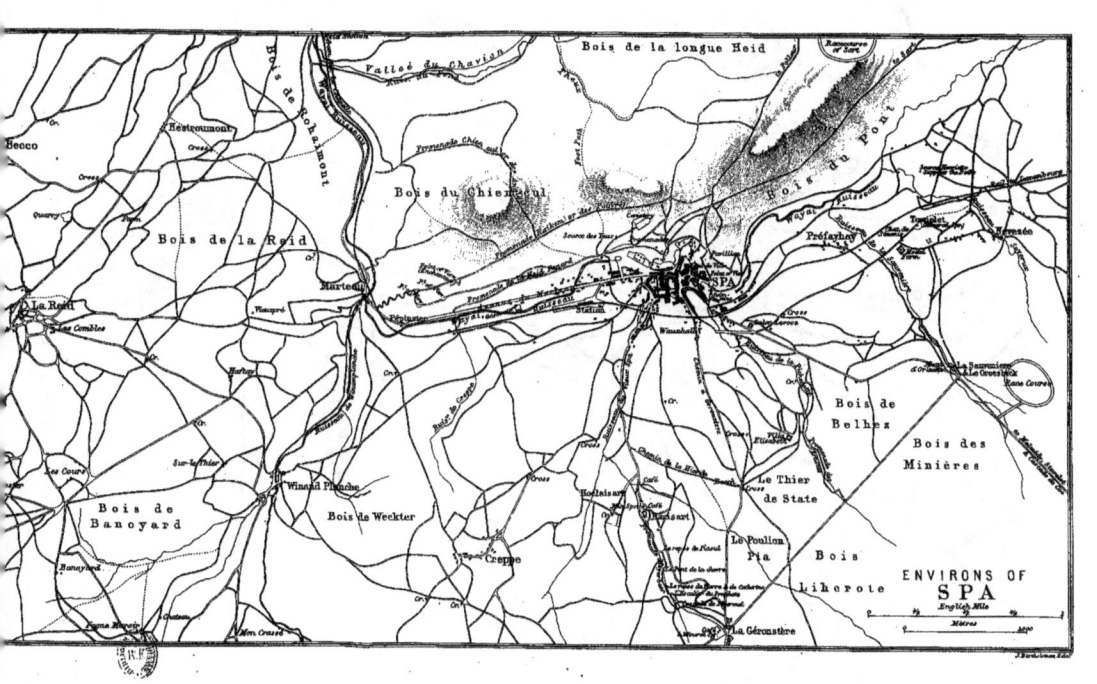

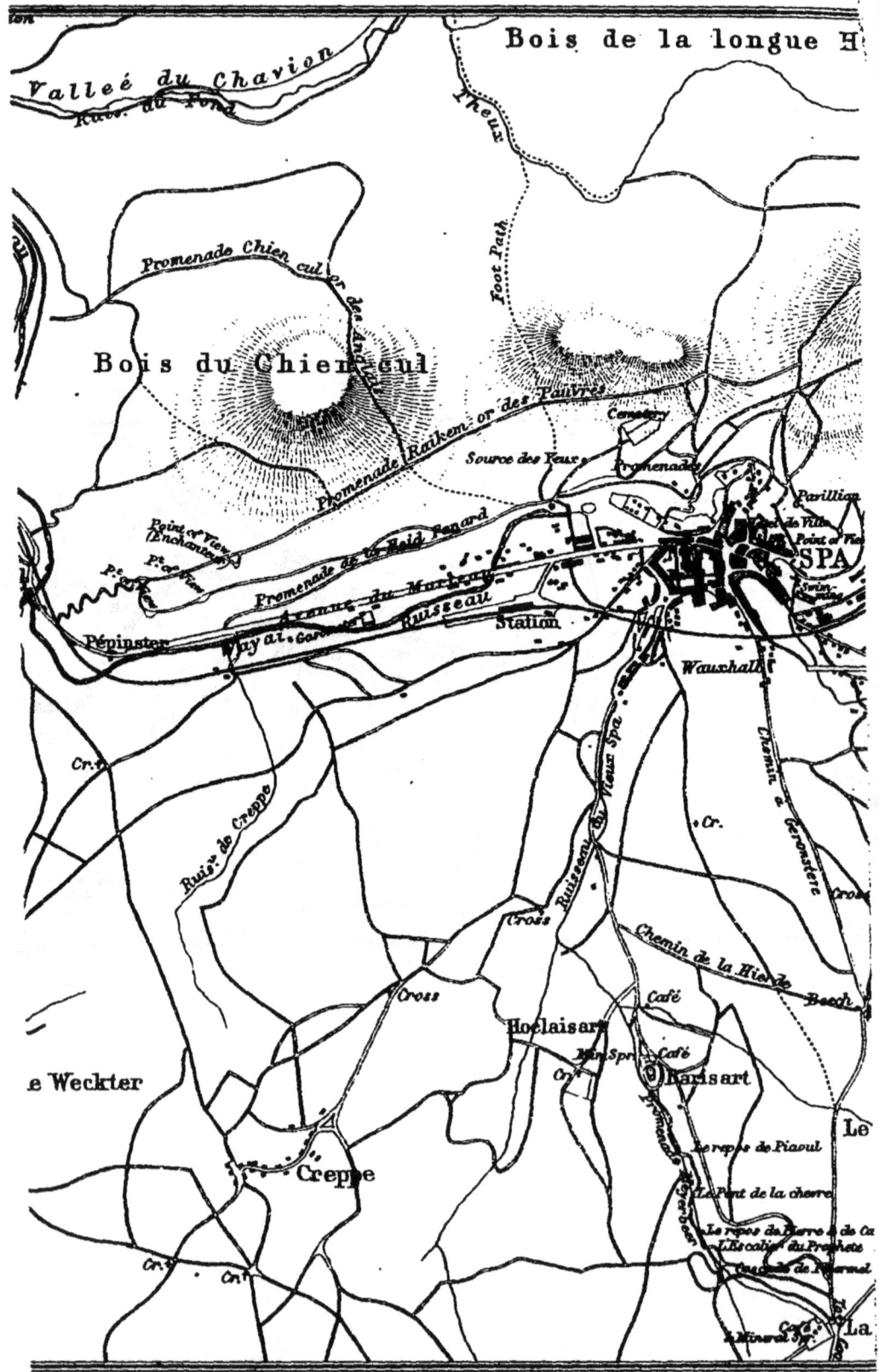

SPA. HOTELS. ELIXIR. CASINO.

these protecting hills, or stretch up to the mountains towards the S. and S.E., on which are situated all the springs excepting the 2 Pouhons.

Spa is largely supplied with hotels, well patronised only in August and September, which causes them to be rather dear. Furnished rooms can, however, be had at a more moderate price, to which dinners can be sent from any of the many restaurants.

Hotels: in the Place Pierre-le-Grand, around the spring Pouhon, the *Pays Bas; Etrangers; *Poste; *Palais-Royal; Lorraine; Nord; Deux Fontaines. Immediately above the Pouhon pavilion is the principal hotel in Spa, the *Flandre; near it, the H. des Iles Britanniques; higher up, in this same direction, are the hotels *York, Europe, and *Britannique, near the English church. In the street between the Pouhon and the Place-Royale are the Royal; Deux Fontaines; *Orange; Laeken; Quatre-Saisons; Portugal. In the Place Royale, opposite the Etablissement des Bains, the hotels *Limbourg; des *Bains. In the Avenue du Marteau, commencing at the Place Royale end and going towards the station, Angleterre, small with furnished apartments; the Belle-Vue, with windows looking into the Casino grounds; the Cologne; Midi, below the station. Near the Hotel de Ville is H. Versailles, a good third-class house. In the Avenue du Marteau are some very good furnished apartments. The price per day in the hotels of the first class is from 13 to 20 frs., which includes only 2 meals, and both without wine; in the second class 8 to 12, not including wine. The hotels with stars are first-class.

Up from the Hotel de Ville, on the wooded slopes of Mont Annette et Lubin, is the French Protestant church. In the Boulevard des Anglais is the Anglican church, a handsome edifice built in 1876, and "dedicated to the glory of the Undivided Trinity, and to the memory of SS. Peter and Paul."

The shops of Spa are full of a variety of articles made of varnished wood. The Elixir of Spa is a liqueur resembling the Chartreuse (near Grenoble), and, like it, distilled from the aromatic herbs which grow on the mountains; it costs 5 frs. the litre bottle. For walking excursions in the valley of the Amblève, a good map on a large scale is the "Carte topographique et minéralogique de Spa," 75 c.

On different sides of the Place Royale are the Casino and the Etablissement des Bains. The Casino is a large building in the midst of extensive grounds at the foot of Mont Annette and Lubin, up which pleasant shady roads lead to the top. Tickets for 8 days 9 frs.

The Bath establishment is a handsome edifice, built in 1868 of a

Spa. Baths. Pouhon. Tonnelet. Sauvenière.

light brown sandstone, at a cost of £80,000. On one side are the baths and waiting-rooms for gentlemen; on the other those for ladies. Yet here, as at Vichy, the drinking of the water is by far the more important. The baths are more especially necessary for those not in the habit of practising ablutions at home, nor of using the flesh-brush. The mineral water is heated by steam, which, they say, can raise the water to a very high temperature without decomposing the constituents and driving off the free carbonic acid gas.

The rocks to the N.W. of Spa are calcareous, but those to the S.E., in which are situated the springs, are schistose. The water is cold, limpid, agreeable to the taste, easily eliminated, and highly charged with free carbonic acid gas; it contains a little silica, chloride of sodium, and carbonates of soda and magnesia. In much larger quantities, the carbonate and protoxide of iron and the carbonate of lime. It is tonic and stimulant, and very efficacious in allaying or curing almost all chronic diseases of an anæmic character, and is recommended especially in those cases in which a course of steel drops would be deemed advisable. The most important spring is the **Pouhon**, in a large and handsome edifice in the centre of the Place Pierre-le-Grand. Although it contains a large quantity of the carbonate of iron, it has no great metallic taste, owing to the pungency caused by the very large proportion of free carbonic acid gas with which it is charged. Peter the Great partook of this spring for the cure of a kind of dropsy. A narrow lane descending from the "Place" leads to the Pouhon of Prince Condé, in a tastefully arranged artistic grotto. The water of this spring suits some stomachs better than the other. Both are 814 ft. above the level of the sea. Pleasant shaded roads lead up to the other springs, situated on the sides of wooded hills. They are all about 1½ m. from the town by their direct roads, excepting the Géronstère, which is 2 m. To the E. of Spa, by the road following the railway, is the spring Tonnelet, 250 ft. above the Pouhon. A few yards beyond, in a field, is the spring Marie-Henriette, whose water from a deep well runs 2 m. in a pipe to the bathing establishment.

Less than a mile S. from the Tonnelet, or about 1½ m. by the direct road from Spa, and 460 ft. above the Pouhon, are the springs **Sauvenière**, the most ancient of all, and the **Groesbeck**, especially recommended for its diuretic and resolvent properties. A monument erected by Louis Philippe commemorates the cure of his mother, the Duchess of Orleans, of a dangerous illness by the waters of the Sauvenière. 2 m. S. from Spa, and rather less from La Sauvenière, is the **Géronstère**,

GÉRONSTÈRE. BARISART. SOURCE DES YEUX.

situated also in a wood 425 ft. above the Pouhon. This spring was much frequented by Peter the Great, whose physician extols its virtues in a document still preserved at Spa. The continuation of the road southward leads to the waterfall of Coo, 7 m. dist., passing by Gleize.

From the Géronstère, a pretty road through the wood by the bank of a small stream called the promenade Meyerbeer leads down to the Barisart spring, 245 ft. below the Géronstère, and 180 ft. above the Pouhon.

One of the most frequented drives is round by these springs, called the "Tour des Fontaines;" time 2 hours; carriage with 1 horse 8 frs., with 2 horses 10 frs. As exercise is necessary to assist the efficacy of the waters, the walk to any of them is more beneficial and less monotonous than under the galleries or in the hall attached to the pump-room of the Pouhon.

Near the cemetery, on the way up to the promenade Raikem, is a spring, the Source des Yeux, recommended for sore eyes. The drive round by Raikem and back by the Avenue Marteau requires 1 hr.; with 1 horse 4 frs., with 2 horses 5 frs.

In the ravine of the Picherotte is the promenade Des Artistes, about ½ m. long. Meyerbeer preferred this ravine to all other places, and it was here that a large part of his opera "Robert-le-Diable" was composed. At this same place, in the summer of 1782, Gretry composed the air, "Si l'univers entier m'oublie," in the opera of "Richard Cour-de-Lion."

Spa to Luxembourg.

15½ m. S. from Spa by rail, or 97½ from Brussels, is **Stavelot**, pop. 4000, H. Orange. A busy manufacturing town on the Amblève, owing its origin to a famous Benedictine abbey founded in 651 by King Sigbert, on the advice of St. Remaclius, who was Bishop of Liège from 652 to 662. In the parish church is a costly shrine, probably of the 14th cent., containing relics of Remaclius. It is in the usual Noah Ark shape, made of embossed gilded copper adorned with jewels and statuettes in niches. Diligence twice daily to the prettily situated and curious Prussian town of Malmedy, 5 m. E., pop. 4000. *Inns:* Cheval Blanc; Etrangers. Famous for the manufacture of sole leather, tanned by the no less famous bark from the oaks of the Ardenne forest.

The rail now follows the Amblève to the next station, the village of Trois Ponts, 3¼ m. S.W. from Stavelot. From Trois-Ponts two roads, one on the right and the other on the left of the Amblève, lead

GOUVY. ETTELBRÜCK. ECHTERNACH.

to the cascade of Coo, 2½ m. northwards, in a mountainous and most picturesque neighbourhood. Near the waterfall are 2 comfortable *Inns:* the Grand Hotel and H. Baron, pension 7 to 9 frs.; carriage from Spa to the waterfall and back 25 frs.

After Trois-Ponts the train ascends the romantic ravine of the Salme to the Grand-Halleux, 21¾ m. from Spa. Other 3¾ m. beyond is the village of Vielsalm, with a nice clean *Inn:* the Bellevue, and a picturesque neighbourhood, with a fair share of game.

33 m. from Spa is **Gouvy**, the Belgian frontier town, and 6 m. farther is Trois-Vierges or Uflingen, the German custom-house station, and the commencement of the Luxembourg railway. The country now becomes picturesque and mountainous, and watered by numerous rivers and streams. The prettiest part is between Goebesmühle and Ettelbrück. Goebesmühle is a little village situated on the confluence of the Sure with the Wolz. **Ettelbrück** (H. Luxembourg) is on the Attert, a tributary of the Sure. From Ettelbrück a branch line extends eastwards to Trèves, following all the way the course of the Sure. Another branch extends westwards to the main line between Brussels and Luxembourg. On the branch to Trèves there are some pretty places to stop at, such as Diekirch—*Inn:* Des Ardennes—on the Sure. 6 m. N., up the valley of the Our, is the village of Vianden, pop. 1600, *Inn:* H. Luxembourg, with the picturesque and imposing ruins of a castle of the counts of Nassau on a rock above the river. 9 m. E. from Ettelbrück, and also on the Sure, is Echternach, pop. 4000, *Inn:* H. du Cerf. The abbey, founded in the 7th cent. by St. Willebrord, an Englishman, is now a barrack. The basilica St. Willebrord built in 1031 was restored in 1868. On Whit Tuesday a singular procession is held here, when young and old of both sexes commence to caper and dance singly. It originated from a public thanksgiving, made ages ago, for the disappearance of St. Vitus's dance from the inhabitants of the district.

From Ettelbrück the railway follows the course of the Alzette to Luxembourg. About half way, at the confluence of the Eischen and the Mamer with the Alzette, is **Mersch**. *Inn:* Petite Croix d'Or. Pleasant rambles up the valleys. Near the village of La Rochette, on the Erens, to the E. of Mersch, is one of the finest castles of the Prince d'Arenberg. 11 m. farther S. is Luxembourg, 161 m. from Brussels by this way; see p. 260, and for the above towns, Map, page 1.

The Valley of the Ourthe.

Liège to Marloie.

40½ m. south by rail, along the valley of the Ourthe. A very enjoyable excursion: but much of the scenery is lost to the travellers by rail by the deep cuttings and tunnels. Map, page 212.

LIÈGE, p. 234. Start from the Station des Guillemins. At Angleur the train enters the valley of the Ourthe, and after passing the Chateau Colonster, and the Chateau Ancre, arrives at **Tilff**. *Hotels:* Amirauté; Etrangers. A prettily-situated village, with, on the hill behind, a stalactite cavern, and higher up the chateau of Brialmont, founded in the 13th cent.

10 m. from Liège is **Esneux**. *Hotel:* Bellevue. A singularly situated village on and at the base of a lofty rocky promontory, round which the river sweeps in a sharp curve. Steep steps communicate between the low and the high town. 3 m. beyond Esneux the train passes Poulseur, and some slate and limestone quarries, and then crosses at Douflamme the Ourthe and the Aywaille or Amblève, and arrives at Comblain-au-Pont. Hotel et Pension Ninane in the village. At the station the Beau Rivage. Those wishing to explore the beauties of the Ambléve generally commence here.

20¼ m. is **Hamoir**. Hotel de la Station, close to the station. The best part of the valley is between this large village and the next station Bomal, also a large village, 4½ m. S. from Hamoir. Bomal, Hotel de la Station, is situated on the confluence of the Aisne with the Ourthe. From Bomal there is a very pleasant excursion of 4½ m. up the rocky and picturesque valley of the Aisne to Roche-à-Frène, where there is a comfortable inn, from which delightful rambles may be taken among grand and fantastic rock scenery. The return journey should be made to Barvaux by Mormont and Eveux. A short distance S. from Eveux is the prettily-situated village of Erezée, whence a coach from the post-office starts early in the morning for Melreux, 6 m. S.W., see below. **Barvaux**, on the east bank of the Ourthe. *Hotels:* Liège; Aigle Noir; both good and moderate. A pleasant road of a little more than two hours extends up the west bank of the river to Durbuy, pop. 500, *Inn* Montagne, a decayed picturesque village with a mediæval bridge, an old chapel, and a ruined tower, all that remains of its fortifications, destroyed by order of Louis XIV. By the right side of the river the distance between Durbuy and Barvaux is 2 miles.

32¼ m. from Liege is **Melreux**. *Inn:* H. des Voyageurs. Coach in the evening for Erezée, 6 m. N.E. Coach 3 times daily for La

Givet. Heer-Agimont. Hastière.

Roche, 11½ m. S. up the Ourthe by a very pretty road. *Inns:* Ardennes; Etrangers. From La Roche another coach starts for Houffalize, 20 m. E. *Inn:* H. des Ardennes. Beautifully situated on the Upper Ourthe, where there is capital fishing. Coach from post-office twice daily to Bastogne railway station, 10½ m. S.

38½ m. from Liège, and 2 from Marloie, is Marche, pop. 3000. *Inn:* Cloche d'Or, formerly a fortress, which stood on the march or limit between the Duchy of Luxembourg and the Bishopric of Liege. Lafayette was taken prisoner here by the Austrians in 1792.

From this the train goes to Marloie, on the line between Brussels and Luxembourg, page 254.

Givet to Namur.

68¼ m. N.E. through a picturesque country.

GIVET is 40 m. N. from Mezières, and 202 m. N.E. from Paris, by Meaux Epernay, Reims, and Rethel. See p. 55. Givet is 56 m. S. from Brussels by Doische, Belgian custom-house; Florennes, Charleroi, and Ottignies. Map, page 212.

Givet is a manufacturing town, ¾ m. from the station, on both sides of the Meuse, spanned by a bridge. *Inns:* Mont d'Or, and L'Ancre, both near each other. The part of the town on the left bank is called Grand-Givet, and on the right Petit-Givet. In Grand-Givet is the church of St. Hilaire, built by Vauban. Although otherwise plain, the aisles are wainscoted with carved cedar-wood 9 feet high, and the chancel 12 feet high. By the side of the church in the "Place" is a rather odd bust of E. N. Mehul, the composer, a native of Givet. From this, a short way up the left bank of the Meuse, a road diverges to the right, which leads to the top of Fort Charlemont, 705 feet above the river, commanding a good view, especially of the fortifications. To visit it permission must be procured from the commander, who resides in the town. Above Petit-Givet rises the Fort Mont d'Or, also first-class, but neither sufficiently isolated nor precipitous to command an extensive prospect. The parish church of Petit-Givet, Notre Dame, built in 1720, is 155 feet long, with a span of 42 feet of roof. Givet is famous for the manufacture of pencils of black lead, and of different coloured chalks. It manufactures white clay and other smoking pipes.

Givet is the French custom-house station. 2½ miles beyond is Heer-Agimont station. Belgian custom-house and time. 5½ miles farther is Hastière station. Junction here with line from Paris by Hirson, Laon, and Soissons 168½ m. S.W. Hastière, pop. 1200, about a

Dinant on the Meuse.

mile from the station, is prettily situated on the Meuse. It has a comfortable rural inn, much frequented by the people of the neighbouring towns, who come here to ramble in the woods that cover the hills and valleys. On the opposite side of the river is a church, founded in the 10th cent., reduced to its present condition by the French in 1794. Between Hastière and Huy is the finest part of the Meuse. Great limestone, marble, and sandstone cliffs, heaved up, and twisted into every conceivable form and angle, pierced and intersected by dikes which encroach upon the river, and force it to run through deep gloomy gullies. The more conspicuous rocks have received fanciful names answering in some degree to their general appearance.

177 miles from Paris, and $14\frac{1}{4}$ from Givet, is **Dinant**, pop. 6300, on both sides of the Meuse. The station is on the left bank. Opposite the station is the Hotel de la Poste, 8 to 10 fr. Adjoining are the second-class houses,—Europe, pension $4\frac{1}{2}$ to 5 frs., and Nord. Above the station is the College.

On the right side of the Meuse are: the church at the foot of the castle rock, and near it, at the commencement of the Grande Rue, the *Tête d'Or, pension $7\frac{1}{2}$ to 8 frs. Farther up the same street the Belle Vue pension, $6\frac{1}{2}$ frs. Then follow the post and telegraph offices, and the Casino. From the Casino there is a pleasant road up to the castle. When on the summit of the hill, keep on the path to the left till arriving at a house where beer is sold. Here cross over to the road which leads up to the gate. The castle may be also entered from the stairs commencing at the church, or by the path commencing from behind the Tête d'Or. The castle, in the form of the bow of a vessel, is about 450 feet above the Meuse. The staircase leading up to it from the church contains 408 steps. From the "Pointe de Vue," in the castle, there is a capital birdseye view of the town and valley, fee $\frac{1}{2}$ fr. At the foot of the cliff is the church, 13th cent., with tall gabled buttresses at each side of the portal, and between them an octagonal tower, crowned with a balloon-shaped spire 210 feet high, having at the top a prolongation for the bells.

Dinant is famous for Couques, a thin flat tough cake, containing a little honey. A better kind is also made, called Couques de Reims, which have a pleasanter taste, and are more easily masticated. Large and savoury crawfish, the best in France, are caught in the Meuse. From Dinant, from the Bureau des Postes, a coach runs to Ciney, 10 m. E., whence the caves of Rochefort and Han can be easily visited, p. 255.

The Tête d'Or and the Poste keep carriages for excursions in the neighbourhood, of which the best are to Waulsort, there and back, 10 frs. To Walzin, on the banks of the Lesse, which flows into the Meuse near the Roche à Bayard. To the royal park of Ardennes, 15 frs. To the cavern of Han, there and back, 25 frs.

Dinant to Namur.—From the bridge a steamer sails down the Meuse to Namur, time 3 hrs. Fare 1 fr. 70 c. By rail the distance is 16¾ m., time 1 hr. The steamer wharf is near the railway station. The banks of the river are certainly beautiful; but for most people, quite enough can be seen from the windows of the railway carriages. At different parts of the river are sluices, which retard the progress of the steamer and make the voyage rather tedious.

The first place the boat calls at is the ancient village of Bouvigne, pop. 950, at the foot of a hill on which are the ruins of the castle of Crèvecœur, destroyed by the French in 1554. A little farther down on right bank, opposite the 2d sluice, are the ruins of the Chateau Monay, and on the plateau higher up, the ruins of a fortress destroyed by the French in 1554. After this, the steamer calls in succession at Houx, Anhée, and Moulins, this last being a pretty village with a bridge across the river. From Moulins, 4 m. up the little valley of the Molignie, are the ruins of the castle of Montaigle, considered the most interesting remains of an ancient fortress in Belgium. Opposite Moulins is Yvoir, a steamer and railway station, with the H. des Touristes and large quarries. The steamer shortly after this, and just before reaching the next station, Rouillon, passes by the prominent "Roche aux Corneilles," thus named from the number of jackdaws that build their nests in the crevices. 6¼ m. by rail from Dinant is the large village of Godinne, both a railway and steamer station. Near the rock Frappe-Cul is the cave Chauveau; where bones of men and animals have been found. Now follow the railway but not steamboat stations of Lustin 8¾ m. from Dinant, Dave 12½ m. and Jambus 15½ m. Passing these, the steamer calls at the large village of Rivière, with 2 good inns and a bridge across the river. It then calls at Profondville, with quarries, inn and restaurant at landing place. Taillefer, with quarries. Fooz, opposite Dave. Wepion and La Plante, a pretty suburb of Namur. At Namur the steamboat wharf is about 1 mile from the railway station, and the nearest hotel, a second-class house the H. Richard-Portes. Cabs at the wharf.

Namur is 194 m. from Paris, 35 m. from Brussels, 115 m. from Cologne, 101 m. from Luxembourg, 37½ m. S.W. from Liège, 56 m. S.W. from Maestricht, and 31 m. N. from Givet. See page 253.

The Meuse. Huy.

Namur to Liège.
Map, page 212.

The rail between Namur and Huy runs through the luxuriant and picturesque valley of the Meuse, full of unexpected turns and sudden surprises, passing fantastically shaped rocks and pretty villages. 5½ m. from Namur is Marche-les-Dames, with iron mines and foundries, situated among trees, between cliffs and the river. Close to it is the chateau d'Arenberg, on the site of the abbey founded in 1101 by the noble ladies whose husbands had accompanied Godfrey de Bouillon to the Holy Land. 11 m. E. from Marche-les-Dames is the station for Andenne and Seilles, two manufacturing towns close to each other, with paper-mills, lime-kilns, potteries and metal-works.

19¼ m. E. from Namur, 214 m. from Paris, and 96 m. from Cologne, is **Huy**, pop. 12,000, on both sides of the Meuse, the more important part of the town being on the right or S. side; where are situated the Citadel, the Collegiate church of Notre Dame, the best shops, the Huy-Tilleul station, and the best hotel, the Aigle Noir (pension 6½ frs.), situated on the bank of the river at the commencement of the Promenade. On the other side are situated the principal railway station, and near it some hotels, of which the best is the Couronne, pension 5½ frs., and a little farther off, in the Rue Entre-Deux-Portes, is the Mouton Blanc, same price. Coach from station to **Hamoir** on the Ourthe, 17 m. S.E., page 247.

At the foot of the citadel, constructed in 1822, is the church of Notre Dame, commenced in 1311, but the greater part of the present edifice was built between 1523 and 1526. The square tower is 150 ft. high. Over the passage into the church from the street is a gateway (11th cent.) adorned with quaint figures in high relief. The interior of the church is of lofty proportions. It is 239 ft. long by 78 ft. wide, and 82 ft. high. The tall piers are of dark blue limestone. Behind the altar is a magnificent window filled with modern glass, of the same breadth as the choir and nearly of the same height. It is divided into three parts by two slim grooved shafts. At the corner of the choir is a handsome sculptured pulpit. The three colossal figures round the pedestal represent Faith, Hope, and Charity. Over the main entrance is a rose window, placed too low and set in a heavy frame of blue limestone. In the neighbourhood is the rather curious church of St. Mencold, called after a holy man, said to have been born in England. Down the promenade from the H. Aigle Noir, is the statue by Geefs,

HUY.   PETER THE HERMIT.   CINEY.   FLEMALLE.

of Joseph le Beau a native of Huy, one of the most zealous supporters of Leopold I. Beyond at the extremity of the promenade is the Chateau Godin, on the site of the once powerful abbey of Neufmoustier, founded by Pierre l'Hermite, who died here in 1115.

In a vault near the house is his mausoleum of white marble, with upon the top the recumbent figure of the "Apotre des Crusades," and round the sides, figures in bold relief, representing incidents in his life. Outside, in a prominent position, is an expressive statue of the preacher. Both mausoleum and statue were erected in 1857 by Charles Godin.

To get from Huy on to the main line, between Namur, Arlon, and Luxembourg, it is generally necessary to go a short way W. to Statte station; where change carriages for Ciney 27¼ m. S. Or leave Huy for Ciney by the Huy-Tilleul station. At Ciney change carriages for Jemelles, Arlon, or Luxembourg. **Ciney**, formerly the capital of Condroz, is a clean little town. At the station are the inns, the *H. du Commerce, pension 5 frs., and the Luxembourg. In the town the H. des Voyageurs, and the H. du Condroz, both comfortable, and both have their omnibuses at the station. The coach for Dinant, 10 m. W., starts from the H. du Condroz. Time, 2 hrs.; fare, 1 fr. 60 c.

From Huy the line follows the Meuse through a populous manufacturing district. The first town after the tunnel, 405 yards, is Ampain, pop. 2000; then Amay, pop. 3250. Romanesque church with 3 towers; Hermalle on the right bank with handsome chateau, 17th cent., and a little beyond important lead and zinc works; Engis between the railway and the Meuse, where in the surrounding limestone rocks numerous fossil bones have been discovered. At some distance from the N. bank of the river, at a depression between the hills, are the conspicuous white walls of the Castle of Aigremont, which in the 15th cent. was the stronghold of William de la Marck, the Wild Boar of the Ardennes. 2½ m. farther, or 11 m. from Huy, is **Flemalle-Haute**, pop. 2000. Passengers for the ironworks of Seraing, 3¼ m. N.E., change carriages here. A little beyond Flemalle-Haute, on a rock rising from the N. bank of the river, is the castle of Chokier. The line then passes Flemalle-Grande, pop. 2700, and the station for Jemeppe, pop. 4600, with coal-pits and manufactories. The station is 1 m. from the town, which is on the Meuse opposite Seraing, page 239.

From Jemeppe arrive at Les Guillemins station of Liège, p. 234.

Brussels to Luxembourg.

136 miles southwards by Ottignies, Namur, Ciney, Marloie, Poix (St. Hubert), Libramont, Neufchateau, and Arlon. See Map, pages 1 and 212.

BRUSSELS. Start from the Luxembourg station. This route passes through a great deal of picturesque scenery. The line, after

OTTIGNIES. TILLY. NAMUR.

passing the pleasant little towns of Watermael, Boitsfort, Groenendael, and La Hulpe, with their villas, gardens, and woods, arrives at **Ottignies**, 15 m. south from Brussels. Junction here with branch to Charleroi, 23½ m. south from Ottignies, or 38½ from Brussels, passing Villers-la-Ville 7 m. S. from Ottignies and 22 from Brussels, p. 215. Tilly 9¼ m. S., the birthplace of John Tzerclas, Count Tilly 1559, the opponent of Gustavus Adolphus; and Ligny 18 m. S. from Ottignies, or 33 m. S. from Brussels. Junction at Ottignies with branch to Louvain, 17½ m. N., passing Wavre 3¼ m. N. from Ottignies.

18 m. south from Brussels is the junction station and little town of Mont Saint Guibert in the midst of a pleasing hilly country. It was by St. Guibert that Blücher retreated to Wavre after his defeat at Ligny.

24¼ m. from Brussels is Gembloux, pop. 2400, with an agricultural college. Junction with line to Sombreffe 5 m. S.W., where Blücher had his head-quarters before the battle of Ligny. 2 miles farther is Ligny, and other 2½ m. Fleurus, see page 215 and Map, p. 212.

A few miles southwards from Gembloux the line having passed through some deep cuttings in blue limestone rocks, emerges into the beautiful valley of the Sambre at **Namur**, pop. 27,000, on the confluence of the Sambre and the Meuse, 35 m. south from Brussels and 101 m. north from Luxembourg. *Hotels:* opposite the station the *Flandre; *Nord Hollande; Couronne. In the centre of the town, near the theatre and the Place d'Armes are the *Harscamp, the principal hotel in Namur; the Monnaie and the Hollande. At No. 15 Place d'Armes is the "Etat Major de la Place," containing the "Bureau du Commandant," open from 9 to 12 and 2 to 4. Apply here for permission to visit the citadel. The post and telegraph offices are at one end of the station, and at the other a statue of Leopold by Geefs, erected in 1869 by the "grateful citizens." To visit Namur rapidly, descend the street, the Rue Godefroid, opposite the large central door of the station, then first left, the R. de Bruxelles, and then first right, the Rue de l'Ouvrage. At the end of the first narrow street right is the cathedral, and a little farther down the Rue de l'Ouvrage is the church of St. Loup. The church of St. Loup, erected by the Jesuits in 1621, has a handsome exterior and a richly-decorated interior. Twelve columns with banded, rose-coloured marble shafts and black marble capitals and pedestals, support the stone roofs of the nave and aisles, all sculptured by a monk who lay on his back on the scaffolding while he was performing his work, with glasses over his eyes to protect them from the dust which fell at every stroke. The carving is bold and effective. The chancel is of rose-coloured marble, with cornices and niches of black marble. The pulpit and confessionals are elegantly carved, especially those with the fluted spiral colonnettes. The **Cathedral** of brick faced with stone was built by a Milanese architect in 1751-1772. In form it resembles St. Paul's of London, on a small scale. The marble statues of Peter and Paul by the side of the high altar, and those in wood of Saints Ambrose, Gregory, Jerome, and Augustin, at the 4 corners of the transept below the dome, are by Delvaux. Against the back of the high altar is a black marble slab bearing an inscription in gilt letters, by Alexander Farnese, to the memory of his "amatissimo avunculo," John of Austria, the conqueror at Lepanto, who died in his camp near Namur in 1578. In the N. or left transept is the mausoleum in white marble by Parmentier of Ghent, of Bishop C. F. Pisani, d. 1826; and opposite, that of another ecclesiastic, who distinguished himself in the propagation of the dogma of the immaculate conception of Mary. Of the beautiful pulpit by Geerts in 1848, the most striking parts are the large sound-board, apparently too heavy for the angels that support it.

To the right of the cathedral, on leaving it, a street leads to the bridge, which is the way to take to visit the citadel. At the Rue du Pont, near the bridge over the Sambre, is the Archæological Museum, containing articles from the time before the invasion of Cæsar, when it was already an important place. The **citadel** of Namur, the Namucum of the 7th cent., is upon a hill on the tongue of land between the Sambre and the Meuse. The present edifice was built in 1794, and strengthened under the inspection of the Duke of Wellington, partly at the expense of Great Britain. Since then it has at various times received additional fortifications, but with the use of long-range guns, it has lost much of its importance, as it can now be commanded from various points. Namur produces excellent cutlery, and in the neighbourhood are rich mines of coal, iron, and marble. From Namur, by boat or rail, up the beautiful valley of the Meuse to Givet, 31 m. S.W., by Dinant, p. 250. The steamboat wharf is about a mile from the station, and the nearest hotel to the wharf is a second-class house, called the H. Richard.

56 m. S. from Brussels, and 19 m. S.E. from Namur, is Ciney, junction with line to Huy, 25 m. N. Ciney, pop. 2000. *Inn:* H. de Condruz. Coach to Dinant. For Ciney, see page 252.

10½ m. beyond Ciney, or 66½ m. from Brussels, is **Marloie**, a pleasant town on the Ourthe, with good fishing. Junction at Marloie,

JEMELLE. ROCHEFORT. TROU-DE-HAN.

with line to Liège, 40½ m. N., up the valley of the Ourthe. There are a great many lovely spots and picturesquely-situated villages on this river, which are much frequented by the people from Liège in summer. Two miles up the river is Marche, pop. 3000, see p. 248.

70¼ m. S.E. from Brussels is **Jemelle**, a small village with limestone quarries, at the confluence of the Wamme with the Lomme. Near the station is the cave of the Wamme, smaller and narrower than the more famous caves of Rochefort and Han. 2½ m. W. by branch line is the village of **Rochefort**, on an eminence above the Lomme, pop. 2500. *Hotels:* Biron, and Etoile; both good and moderate. Families are in the habit of staying here some time, as the country around is salubrious and picturesque. Board 7 frs. per day, including breakfast, hot lunch, dinner, and service; but neither wine nor beer. The draught beer is good and cheap. In the village are the remains of a castle of the 12th cent. Near the hotels is the entrance to a very large stalactite cave, visited without difficulty, and walked through in about 2 hours. 5 frs. each. When the party amounts to 20, 2½ frs. each. In the most remarkable parts magnesian lights are kindled. This cave, like all the other limestone caves in this neighbourhood, consists of a series of vast chambers, called Salles, connected by galleries or passages more or less narrow. The largest of the chambers is the Salle du Sabbat, nearly 500 ft. high, hung with beautiful stalactites. As the magnesian lights are not sufficient to give a correct idea of the area of this vault, a fire-balloon is sent up, which, as it ascends, has its light reflected from the countless glittering crystals.

Omnibus from hotel 3¾ m. W. to the village of Han-sur-Lesse and to the **Trou de Han**, 5 m. W. from Rochefort. Visitors enter the cave at the distant end from the village, near the spot where the Lesse plunges into its subterranean passage, and leave the cave where the river issues from it, about 1½ m. from the village of Han-sur-Lesse. *Inn:* H. Belle Vue. Fee, 5 frs. each. If cannon is fired ½ fr. each extra. Guides expect besides gratuity. From 2 to 2½ hrs. required to walk through the cavern, 1 m. long; consisting of galleries at different levels, either narrow like those in copper mines, or widening into the size of tunnels, leading at intervals into a suite of ten chambers averaging from 30 to 60 feet high, ornamented, generally scantily, with nearly opaque brown stalactites. The largest, the Salle du Dome, has no stalactites. The roof is 205 ft. above the Lesse, which traverses this chamber. Across the stream is a wooden bridge. Wine sold here to the company. From the Dome a series of ascending gal-

Poix.   Saint Hubert.

leries lead first into the Salle des Draperies, then into the Salle du Trone, above the roof of the Dome. From it the visitor descends to the cavern called the Salle d'Embarquement on the Lesse, where the visitors enter a boat and are rowed slowly out of the cave. It is here, when desired, that the noise is made with the cannon. A great deal of nonsense is written about the imposing grandeur of this cavern. Those who have never entered a large cave will find the one at Rochefort the most convenient and quite enough to satisfy their curiosity. All caves are very much alike, the large as well as the small, in the general darkness which prevails, and which it is not in the power of the fitful and feeble lights used to dispel.

Eastward from Han, on the other side of the river, is the village of Eprave, with another limestone cave. Guide from the village inn.

4 m. E. from Rochefort is the pretty village of La Roche. *Inns:* Ardennes; Etrangers; p. 247.

12 m. S. by rail from Jemelle, or 82½ m. from Brussels, is **Poix**, where omnibus awaits passengers for **St. Hubert**, 4¼ m. N.E., pop. 2500. *Inns:* H. du Chemin de Fer; H. Luxembourg. A tidy little town on an eminence, with a parish church, 12th cent., and a handsome abbey church, 16th cent., seen from a great distance. The façade, erected in 1700, presents a large flat surface, having on the top a sculpture in relief, representing the apparition of the stag to St. Hubert. On each side is a low tower covered with slate. The interior is spacious, light, and elegant. There are no chapels in the aisles of the nave. In the S. transept is the chapel of St. Hubert, and in the next, La Chapelle du Sacré Cœur, with some old Limoges enamels, 12th cent., representing the passion of our Lord. In the N. transept is the modern **mausoleum of St. Hubert**, by W. Geefs. The statue, in a reclining position, is of white marble, while round the sides are sculptured reliefs representing incidents in the life of the saint. The next chapel is the treasury, where the relics of St. Hubert are preserved. They consist of a large ivory hunting-horn, an ivory crosier, and an ivory comb, with which he combed his beard. The gates which shut off the choir from the nave are of wood, most elaborately carved. The sanctuary is surrounded with a marble screen. The altar is in two stages of lofty marble columns, held together by the force of gravity alone. The stalls were finished in 1738. Below the sanctuary is the crypt (12th or 13th cent.), with a tessellated pavement and short slender columns, from which spring heavy masses of groining.

Every vocation had, in the Middle Ages, its protecting saint. The

St. Hubert. Industrial School. Libramont.

chase, with its fortunes and its hazards, the business of so many, and the amusement of all, was placed under the direction of St. Hubert.

This silvan saint was the son of Bertrand, Duke of Aquitaine, and, while in the secular state, was a courtier of King Pepin. He was passionately fond of the chase, and used to neglect attendance on divine worship for this amusement. Once while engaged in this pastime a stag appeared before him, having a crucifix bound betwixt his horns, and a voice menaced him with eternal punishment if he did not repent of his sins. Shortly after, on the death of his wife Floribane, all his tastes for mundane enjoyments having ceased, he took orders and retired from the world. Pope Sergius appointed him Bishop of Tongern and in 708 he succeeded his friend and teacher, Bishop Lambert, to the see of Maestricht and Liège. He died in 727, and in 825 his remains, which are said not to have suffered decay, were removed to the Benedictine monastery of this place. From his zeal in destroying the remnants of idolatry in this part of Belgium he is called the Apostle of the Ardennes and Brabant. His descendants were supposed to possess the power of curing persons bitten by mad dogs.

Adjoining the church are the very handsome abbey buildings, now converted into a Government reformatory for boys who have committed petty crimes. The buildings have ample accommodation for 500; but there are generally only about 400, whose ages vary from 9 to 21 years. They are taught the trades of marble-cutting, smiths, joiners, shoemakers, and agriculturists. The greatest number choose the first two trades. Everything connected with the house is done by the boys themselves. They wash, sew, and mend the clothes, cook the victuals, bake the bread, and do the repairs about the buildings. Every other day they receive $\frac{1}{2}$ lb. of meat; on other days they receive soups, consisting either of pulse, or rice, or potatoes, mixed with American lard. Their bed, school, and working rooms are lofty and well aired. The beds are all boarded off from each other, and communicate with the common passage by a door of netted iron wire, locked during the night. The theoretical and practical teaching is ably conducted.

90 miles from Brussels is **Libramont**, junction with line to Bastogne 18 m. N.E. From Bastogne a coach runs to Wiltz, 14 m. E., whence another runs to Kautenbach, 7 m. farther, a village on the Luxembourg railway, at the confluence of the Wilz and Wolz.

Coach from Libramont to Bouillon, $21\frac{1}{4}$ m. S.W., passing at about half-way Bertrix, a dirty little village inhabited by wood-cutters and small farmers, on the railway between Arlon and Gedinne. It was by

Marbehan. Florenville. Carignan.

this road that the Prussians brought their prisoner Napoleon III. from Bouillon to Libramont, where they put him into the train for Germany on the 4th September 1870. Near Bertrix are important slate quarries. The road is uninteresting till within a few miles of Bouillon.

Bouillon, pop. 3400. *Inns:* H. de la Poste, where Napoleon III. and suite spent the afternoon and night of the 3d September 1870. Napoleon's bedchamber was room No. 1, immediately over the room to the right of main door, standing with face towards the house. On the other side of the bridge is the inn H. des Ardennes. Bouillon is situated at the foot of steep wooded hills on both sides of the Sémois, which nearly encircles it. Above the town, on a rock in the narrowest part of the bend, is the castle founded in the 7th cent., but built principally by Godefroy de Bouillon and Charles V. The fortifications occupy a considerable area, though in height they are somewhat stunted. From the top of the donjon tower, built in 852, there is a charming birdseye view of the little valley. Along the river sides are walks, of which the prettiest but dirtiest, extends round by the old walls garnished with pentagonal towers, which now enclose the barracks, but formerly an advanced post of the castle. A long avenue, shaded by elms, leads to the cemetery, in which a great many German soldiers were buried. Coach from Bouillon to Sedan, 12 m. W. For Sedan, page 65. 96 m. from Brussels is Longlier, station for Neufchateau 1 m. W. Coach from Neufchateau to Bouillon.

106 m. from Brussels is **Marbehan**. *Inn:* Cornet. Junction with line to Montmédy 26 m. S., by Virton, Lamorteau, Belgian time and custom-house, and Ecouviez, French time and custom-house. See page 68. 31 m. S.W. by rail from Marbehan, by Virton, is **Florenville**, pop. 3500. *Inns:* Commerce; Poste. Both good and comfortable; pension, 5½ frs. Excellent headquarters for visiting the neighbourhood. Carriages for drives 12 frs. per day. Coach between Florenville and Carignan 9 m. S.W., on the line between Sedan and Montmédy. Carignan is 185 m. from Paris and 77 from Metz, see p. 68. Florenville, 1½ m. from the station, is situated on an eminence rising from the plain watered by the Semois or Semoy, an affluent of the Meuse, of which an excellent view is obtained from behind the handsome modern parish church. Among the many pleasant excursions in the neighbourhood, the most interesting is to the abbey of Orval, founded in 1124, 5 m. south by a pretty road. The monastery, reduced to its present condition by the French in that fatal year for so many noble edifices, 1794, stands in a narrow secluded dell close to the French

ARLON. ATHUS. LUXEMBOURG.

frontier. It is built on terraces, enclosed by a substantial wall 20 ft. high. On one of the highest of the terraces is an interesting Romanesque chapel, while on a level with the conventual buildings is the church rebuilt in the 16th and 17th cents. The monks belonged to the Benedictine order, were famous locksmiths, and had important ironworks.

16 m. S. from Marbehan is **Virton**, pop. 2500. *Inns:* Croix d'Or and Cheval Blanc, both good. The environs are pleasant and picturesque. 119 m. from Brussels is

Arlon, the Roman Orolaunum Vicus, pop. 7500. *Hotels:* at the station the Luxembourg. In the town the Nord, Europe, both good. At the partition of the Grand Duchy of Luxembourg in 1831, two-thirds were assigned to Belgium, of which Arlon was made the capital. It occupies a healthful situation, on a plain 1245 ft. above the sea. Extensive view from the terrace of the church. ¡Roman antiquities found in the neighbourhood exhibited in the Hotel du Gouvernement. Arlon is $17\frac{1}{2}$ m. W. by rail from Luxembourg, and 103 m. N. by rail from Longuyon. At Athus, $9\frac{1}{4}$ m. S., is the Belgian custom-house, and at Longwy, 2 m. farther, the French custom-house. Athus is $6\frac{1}{2}$ hours from Nancy by Longwy, Conflans-Sarny and Frouard. For Longuyon and Longwy see page 68. The train after passing several minor stations arrives at

Luxembourg, 136 m. from Brussels, 950 ft. above the sea, pop. 16,000. *Hotels:* Cologne, Europe, Luxembourg, Ardennes. Their omnibuses await passengers. Luxembourg is situated on a small plateau nearly completely surrounded by lofty escarpments and dismantled forts, which add greatly to the natural picturesqueness of the position. The best view is from the parapet at the foot of the Rue de Beaumont, the first street to the right in going from the Hotel de Cologne up the Rue Porte Neuve towards the gardens. A similar view is had from the gardens to the right of the gate, or rather of the place where the gate used to be.

Below are the valley of the Petrusbach, and the Unterstadt, or Low Town, and opposite, high cliffs, crowned with dismantled forts.

To descend to this quarter, take the first street going downwards to the left of the Hotel de Cologne, the Grand Rue, or Grosz Strasse, and its continuations, the Rues Marché aux Herbes, Boucherie, Marché aux Poissons, and St. Michel, whence pass through the Porte de Trèves or Trier. At Luxembourg junction with line to Thionville or Diedenhofen, 23 m. S., from which Metz is 17 m. farther S. Thionville is 215 m. from Paris by Sedan, p. 65, Reims, and Epernay. Metz is 126 m. from Strassburg, see page 69.

Ygel Column. Trèves.

Luxembourg to Trier, 34 m. N.E. by rail, and thence by the Moselle to Coblence. Shortly after leaving Luxembourg the train enters at Oetringen the pretty valley of the Sire, an affluent of the Moselle. 24½ m. from Luxembourg, and 9½ from Trèves, the train enters Prussia at the village of Wasserbillig, on the Moselle at its junction with the Saur. 3 m. farther is the station and village of Ygel. Towards the end of the village to the left, is the **Ygel Column**, consisting of a square tapering reddish quadrangular pillar, 70 ft. high, 16 long, and 13 broad. It is covered with partially defaced sculptures in relief. On the top is a pediment, over which rises a peaked roof, terminating in a finial in the form of an eagle. This most remarkable structure is supposed to have been erected in the 2d century by Secundinus Aventinus, and is one of the most perfect Roman monuments north of the Alps.

5 m. from Trèves is **Cons**, a most important railway junction, but rather a small station. Junction with line to Saarbrucken, 47 m. S. **Trier**, or Trèves, pop. 24,000, on the Moselle. *Hotels:* Rothes Haus, in the Hauptmarkt. Before the entrance into the Rothes Haus, a short street, the Fleisch Strasse, leads directly to the Kornmarkt, in which are situated the Post-office and the Post Hotel. From the Hauptmarkt a short narrow street leads to the cathedral, and a long broad one in the opposite direction to the Porta Nigra. At the foot of the Brod Strasse, and opposite each other, are the Hotels de Trèves, de Venice or Venedig, and de Luxembourg. Their omnibuses await passengers at the railway station. Churches closed after 12 A.M.

Cab-stands in the Hauptmarkt and in the Kornmarkt. Fares—from any one point to another in the town, 60 pfennig for two persons, and for every other 25 pfennig more. By the hour, for 2 persons, 2½ marks. See the coachman's tariff.

Junction with line to Duren, 108 m. N. Duren is 15 m. west from Cologne. 87 m. S. from Trier, at the station of Enskirchen, a branch line of about 15 m. extends to Bonn.

The railway station is a little above the bridge, on the left bank of the Moselle. The greater part of this bridge was built by the Romans.

The steamboat wharf is a little below the bridge, on the right bank of the Moselle. In winter the steamers sail for Coblence at 7.30 A.M., and in summer at 6 A.M.; time 9 to 11 hours. Fare 8 marks. Coblence is reached in 8 hours from Trèves, by taking the rail by Saarbrucken. Passengers by the steamer wishing to break the journey must, before leaving the boat, request the purser to visé (bescheinigen)

TRÈVES. CATHEDRAL. LIEBFRAUENKIRCHE.

their ticket. Fare to ¦land by small boat, ½ mark, including luggage.

Trier, considered the oldest town in Germany, was in the time of Julius Cæsar a large and important city, the capital of the Treveri. At present it is remarkable for its Roman remains.

From the Hotel Rothes Haus across the Hauptmarkt, and then up a narrow street, the Stern Gasse, is the **DOM** or Cathedral, founded in the 4th century, but of the original church all that remains is a short massive granite column, lying near the main entrance.

The present edifice, built of alternate layers of stone and brick, is 362 ft. long, 160 wide, and 100 high. Strong piers, adorned with curious sculpture, support semicircular segmental four-centred and equilateral arches. Behind the high altar is preserved the great relic of the church, the coat without seam Jesus wore before his crucifixion, but it is shown only on great occasions. In the church of Argenteuil, near Paris, is a similar vesture. Under the organ-loft, surrounded by marble colonnettes, is the mausoleum of Archbishop Baldwin of Luxembourg, brother of the Emperor Henry IV. In the crypt under the church are more mausoleums, yet none of any remarkable beauty excepting that of Johann III. d. 1540. Adjoining is the **Liebfrauenkirche**, built in a circular form. It was commenced in 1227, and finished in 1244. On the richly-sculptured portal are represented scenes from the Old and New Testaments. The interior, 180 ft. long, 147 wide, and 124 high, rests on twelve round columns, with round gilded capitals, each bearing on the shaft a painting, 15th cent., in fresco, of an apostle, all of which are visible from the diamond-shaped piece of blue marble in the floor a few steps in advance of the entrance. Behind the pulpit is a painful-looking Entombment. Now go up the narrow street to the Pallast Platz, a very large square, of which one end is occupied by the palace barracks, or Caserne, and the **Basilica**, a great brick building, 235 ft. long and 104 high, now used as a Protestant place of worship. At the opposite end of the square are seen the very interesting ruins of a Roman palace and baths. To reach them it is necessary to leave this square by the narrow street to the right of the Basilica, the Jesuiten Strasse, and then first street to the left, the Weberbach Strasse, leading to the Weber Thor. Those, however, who desire to visit the Library and Museum (open every weekday from 10 to 12) should walk up the Jesuiten Strasse till they arrive at a large building on the left hand, comprehending the gymnasium, the library, and museum. Among the MSS. the most precious is

Trèves. Amphitheatre. Porta Nigra.

the Codex Aureus, containing the four Gospels written in gold letters on parchment, superbly bound, and adorned with precious stones and a large onyx cameo. This MS. was presented by Ada, sister of Charlemagne, to the Abbey of St. Maximin. To reach the **Roman Baths**, having passed by the Weber Thor, or gate, turn to the left, and keep the road alongside the wall, till having reached a small house beside a wooden railing. The doorkeeper lives here. Fee 50 pfennig each. These ruins were originally a Roman palace, built in the 1st century, of which the baths formed only a small part. From the top of the tower, ascended by 76 steps, there is a good view of the town.

The high road in front of this tower, leading in the direction towards the hill, conducts to the **Amphitheatre**, about ten minutes' walk distant, in an open space on the left of the road. The small diameter is 159 ft., and the large 210. It was capable of containing 30,000 spectators. Now return again to the Hauptmarkt, and walk up the Simeons Strasse to the **Porta Nigra**, a large gateway, erected probably about the beginning of the 4th cent. It has a frontage of 125 ft., is 29 ft. deep, and its highest part is 99 ft. The two gateways, composed of great blocks of sandstone, have semicircular arches, and are 23 ft. high. Over them are two stories, each having six windows, with stilted arches, separated by colonnettes with cushioned capitals. On each side rises a spacious tower, similarly constructed, of which one rises a story higher than the rest of the building. By the side of this tower a modern addition was built, which was used as a church. Beyond the Porta Nigra is the church of St. Paulin, with frescoes painted by Scheffer.

Trèves to Coblence.—From Trèves we can take the line to Duren, 108 m. N., or the line to Saarbrucken, 55 m. S., or take the steamboat to Coblence. The sail down the Moselle in the summer season, when fruit is plentiful, is preferred by some to the sail on the Rhine, as the Moselle is much narrower and more sinuous, but it has neither such important towns nor such romantic castles on its banks. The largest towns passed on the way down from Trèves are—Neumagen, pop. 2000, with the ruins of a castle; Pisport. *Inn:* Hayn, whose vineyards produce one of the best Moselle wines; Berncastel, pop. 2000, with a pier, at which the steamer halts. Above, on a hill, is a ruined castle built in 1036. Trarbach, pop. 2000, chiefly Protestants. *Inn:* Allmacher, near the pier. This is one of the cleanest and best towns on the Moselle. Zell, pop. 1800, with a pier, and near it the Rothes Haus inn. Alf, pop. 1500. *Hotels;* Post; Bellevue.

Trèves to Coblence.

This is the station to land at for the Baths of *Bertrich*, 6 miles distant. During the bathing season an omnibus awaits the passengers from the steamer. Bertrich lies in a hollow, protected from the north and east winds, and has, on account of the efficacy of its mineral waters, been increasing rapidly. Their temperature is 89° Fahrenheit, and in their composition are nearly similar to those of Carlsbad in Bohemia.

After Alf follow the ruins of the Marienburg, the largest on the Moselle. Cochem, pop. 2900, with an old castle. *Hotels:* Union; Kehrer, near the pier. Moselkern, station to alight at to visit the beautiful and admirably situated castle of Eltz, built in the 10th cent., on a cliff nearly 1000 feet above the sea-level. It is about 3 miles distant by the footpath up the Eltzer stream.

Coblence, on the confluence of the Rhine and Moselle, 56 m. from Cologne, and 81 from Frankfort. *Hotels:* on the Rhine, fronting the steamboat wharf, are the Belle Vue; Geant; Ancre. In the Clemensplatz, adjoining the theatre, the Hotel de Trèves. Between the railway station and the Moselle steamboat wharf is the Stadt Luttich, all first-class. Near the Rhenish station the Berliner Hof.

Post-office at the end of the street (the Schwanzenpfort Strasse), between the Parade Platz and Clemensplatz.

The Moselle steamboat wharf is immediately above the stone bridge over the Moselle.

Cab-fares.—The course, for 1 to 2 persons, 75 pf.; and for 3 to 4 persons, 1 mark; per hour, 2½ mark. 10 pf. for each portmanteau.

English Church service in the English Church in the Schloss.

To visit Ehrenbreitstein cross over to the right bank of the Rhine, then turn to the left and walk down the Hochstrasse to the first gate with drawbridge. Pass through and enter to the right the Commandant's house, where the names are taken and tickets delivered, 50 pf. each. On the top, at the Felsen Thor, visitors are received by a soldier, who conducts them over the fortress, fee 1 m. Then ascend. The road up is good, and never very steep, although it is 400 feet above the bed of the Rhine. Near the summit there is a well 380 feet deep.

Steamboat from Coblence to Mayence in 7½ hours, but from Mayence to Coblence 4¾ hours. See Black's *Holland and the Rhine*.

Charleroi.

Charleroi is 35 m. N. from Brussels, by Baulers; 164 m. N.E. from Paris; 142 W. from Cologne; 22½ m. W. from Namur. See Map, pages 1 and 212.

CHARLEROI, pop. 20,000, on the Sambre and the Pieton. Opposite the railway station is a large square with the hotels: the *Grand Hotel; Europe, plainer and cheaper, but good; Duc de Brabant. From this, a few yards up the main street, is the H. Beukelers, also a good house. A short way farther, to the right, is the most important square and market-place, the Place du Sud; whence the Rue du Pont and the Rue Charles II., lead up to the Boulevard Central of the high town, containing the Palais de Justice, the Temple Protestant, the most handsome houses, and at one end the Park.

From the station trams run to Gilly, about 3 m. N.E. from Charleroi, and about 2¼ m. N. from Châtelineau. Fare for the whole way 45 c. The tram, after running round the low town, ascends to the very highest part of the high town; whence it descends to Gilly. At the highest part is the station of the trains arriving from Brussels by Ottignies, Fleurus, and Lodelinsart, 37¼ m. by this way. This station is inconvenient. From the top of the hill there is a good birdseye view of the surrounding coal and iron mining country, with its dense population, both the tram and the railway passing through all the way a succession of towns and villages, where tall chimneys are the most conspicuous objects. Of this region the great industrial centre is Charleroi, with large manufactories of glass, iron, cutlery, cotton, and cloth. Several thousand persons are engaged in the nail trade alone, while the forges of Couillet furnish a third of the quantity of cast-iron produced in the kingdom. Upwards of 24,000 persons are employed in the coal-mines, and about 3,832,900 tons of coal are extracted annually. Around Charleroi are the towns of Roux, H. du Nord, close to the station; Marchiennes (H. de la Paix, close to the station); Chatelineau (*Hotels:* Commerce; Midi, close to the station); and Tamines (H. de la Station, close to the station), all similarly situated among great coalfields and iron-mines; and in all the industries are similar forges, foundries, and metal-works. Charleroi was founded in 1666 by the Marquis of Castel Rodrigo, on the site of the village of Charnoy, who, in compliment to his master Charles II. of Spain, changed the name to Charleroi.

5½ m. E. from Charleroi, and 40½ m. S. from Brussels, is **Tamines**, pop. 2100. *Inns:* H. de la Station; Midi, a busy mining village on the

The Sambre and Meuse from Charleroi to Charleville.

Sambre. 11 m. W. from Namur, and 2½ m. E. from Tamines, is the village of Jemeppe-sur-Sambre, with an important and extensive mirror manufactory, in the suppressed abbey of Ste. Marie d'Oignies.

From **Tamines line to Mettet**, 13 m. S. through a country abounding in marble and limestone, with a little coal. 2½ m. S. is Falisole, pop. 1600, on the Biesme, an affluent of the Sambre, with some coal-pits. 7 m. S. is **La Fosse** (pronounced Fausse), pop. 4000. *Inns*: at the station the H. de la Station. In the town the H. des Quatre-Bras. La Fosse, the principal town on this line, is about 10 min. walk from the station. The streets, though narrow and crooked, contain some very good houses. The parish church, St. Feuillen, has been rebuilt of brick, excepting the façade and the curious square tower over it, which date from the foundation of the church, 12th cent. In the sanctuary a series of large pictures illustrate the miracles and martyrdom of St. Feuillen, the patron saint of Fosse. At the W. end is an entombment, with 8 life-size figures. In the 7th cent. La Fosse formed part of the domains of Pepin of Landen. In 974 Bishop Nodger surrounded it with a wall. 11¼ m. S. is Saint Gérard, pop. 2000, on a low eminence, with limestone and marble quarries. It owes its origin to a chapel, built here by Pepin of Landen. In 928 St. Gérard added a monastery, of which he himself was the first prior. The remains of the buildings are occupied by a farm-house. Saint Gérard inhabited also Toul, see p. 82. 13 m. S. is **Mettet**, pronounced Mettey, pop. 2000. *Inn*: H. de la Station, close to the station. About 10 min. distant is the village, with some large farm-houses.

Charleroi to Charleville in France.—From Charleroi a very picturesque and interesting railway route leads 72 m. S. to Charleville, by the Sambre and the Meuse, the wooded banks of both rivers being studded with towns situated among coal and iron mines, and limestone, marble, and slate quarries. To go by this line it is necessary to ask for a ticket to Charleville by Vireux. On leaving Charleroi take one of the carriages nearest the engine, otherwise, it is necessary to change carriages, not trains, at Walcourt. 34¾ m. S. from Charleroi is Vierves, Belgian custom-house and time, and 5 m. farther is Vireux, on the Meuse, French custom-house. An important town with great forges, surrounded by wooded hills. On the opposite side of the Meuse, 5½ m. farther S. is Haybes.

186½ m. E. from Paris, and 48 m. S. from Charleroi, is **Fumay**, pop. 5000. H. de la Poste, almost surrounded by the Meuse, and picturesquely situated at the foot of wooded mountains. This little town has in its neighbourhood very important slate-quarries, of which the mine called the Moulin Ste. Anne produces annually 35 millions of slates. Among the many beautiful excursions are, to the Montagne, 1494 ft., and to the woods of the Haute-Manise, by the side of the river.

4½ m. farther, and also on the Meuse, is Revin, pop. 3500, with forges and tanneries. From the inn at the station, the Hotel de la Gare, start the omnibuses for Rocroi, pop. 2300. *Inns*: France; Commerce. A fortified town 7 m. W., on a plateau, 1290 ft. above the sea, good botanising ground. From Revin the train passes the cliffs called the Dames de la Meuse, and the villages of Laifour and Déville, and arrives at the

The Meuse. Binche. Baulers Junction.

station for Monthermé, 22½ m. from Virieux. The town is 1¼ m. from the station. A tram awaits passengers. **Monthermé**, pop. 2600, good country inn. Most picturesquely situated on the Meuse at the head of a valley, hemmed in by wooded hills from 1000 to 1500 ft. high. Forges and foundries. Near it is the abbey Val-Dieu, suppressed in 1794. Monthermé and Fumay are the two best stations for tourists in this valley.

A little farther S. is Braux, pop. 2500, with forges and ironworks. 6¼ m. S. from Monthermé station, and 4½ m. N. from Charleville, is Nouzon, on the Meuse, pop. 5500, with forges and nail manufactories. For Charleville, see p. 64, and Map, page 1.

Charleroi to Brussels, 35 m. N. by Marchiennes, Luttre, Nivelles, Baulers, Braine l'Alleud, and Waterloo, see Map, pages 1 and 212. 2½ m. W. from Charleroi is **Marchiennes**, in a country rich in coal and iron, and studded with foundries, glassworks, and manufactories. 5 m. farther west is Fontaine l'Evêque, with the ruins of the once famous abbey of Alne situated in a mountainous neighbourhood.

8¾ m. W. from Fontaine l'Evêque, or 17½ W. from Charleroi and 14¼ E. from Mons, is **Binche**, pop. 7500, on a tributary of the river Haine. The staple female industry here is the preparing and sewing flowers and patterns for the manufacturers of lace in Brussels.

From **Marchiennes** the train ascends northwards by Roux, Gosselle, and Luttre to **Nivelles**, 11¼ m. N. from Charleroi, and 23¾ S. from Brussels. For Nivelles see p. 215. 3 minutes beyond Nivelles is **Baulers** junction, where change for Genappe, 5 m. E., p. 208, and Wavre, 20¼ m. N.E. See Map, page 214.

4½ m. N. from Baulers and Nivelles is **Braine l'Alleud**, p. 204. 11¾ m. from Brussels, and 1¾ m. farther, is **Waterloo**, p. 201, 10 m. from **Brussels**, where the train arrives at the Station du Sud. Cabs, trams, and porters at arrival side of station.

ANTWERP.

Antwerp or **Anvers** (pronounce the s), pop. 175,000, a strongly fortified city, is 60 m. from the sea on the Schelde or Escaut, where the river is about 2200 feet broad, with a depth of from 30 to 40 feet at ebb tide, and a rise at spring tides of from 12 to 14 feet; and as this depth increases towards the sea, large vessels can come up to the wharves. The advantageous situation of Antwerp did not escape the penetrating eye of Napoleon, who spared no labour nor expense to render it the rival of London in commerce, and of Portsmouth as a military establishment. Excellent steamers sail between Antwerp, London, Leith, and Hull. From London Antwerp is 210 m. by the Thames. Time 17 to 19 hours, of which the sea passage is about 6. Rail from London (Liverpool Street) to Harwich, whence steamboat to Antwerp, 15 hours for the entire journey. Luggage examined on board before arriving at the

ANTWERP. INSTITUTIONS. SIGHTS.

quay. See the Continental Time-book of the Great Eastern Railway, 1d. They give through tickets to the principal towns on the Continent. Steamers daily from Queenborough to Flushing. Time 8½ hours. Flushing, by the river, is 62 m. from Antwerp, see p. 294.

Antwerp by rail is 27½ m. N. from Brussels, 31 m. from Ghent, 69 from Bruges, and 83½ from Ostende. It is 91 m. N.W. from Aix-la-Chapelle, and 100 m. W. from Gladbach, the last Belgian station, whence Düsseldorf on the Rhine is only 32 minutes farther.

The manufactures of Antwerp are various and considerable, the principal being lace, silk, linen, cotton, tapestry, galloon, twine, sugar, white lead, litmus, starch, printers' ink and malt liquors. The lapidaries of Antwerp are celebrated for their skill in diamond-cutting. The shipbuilding is considerable, and the timber used for that purpose is principally brought by water from the interior. Antwerp contains many educational and literary institutions. It has a Royal Athenæum, in which most of the usual branches of literature and science are taught, schools of navigation, medicine and surgery, a botanic garden, a public library and various scientific and literary societies. It has also a Royal Academy of the Fine Arts, which affords gratuitous instruction in painting, sculpture, architecture and engraving. At the competition which takes place in one of these arts annually, the laureate receives a pension of £100 for four years, to enable him to pursue his studies in Germany, France and Italy. The second prize is a gold medal of the value of £12. Among the distinguished men born at Antwerp are Quentin Metsys, Van Dyck, the two Teniers, Jordaens, Floris, Crayer, Zegers, Snyders and Edelinck the engraver. Here Rubens also, although not a native, received his education and resided. They form together the great masters of the Antwerp school of art.

Sights.—The principal sights are near each other, which having seen, a cab should be taken for the others if time is limited.

The **Cathedral** has all its pictures uncovered on Thursdays and Sundays from 9 till 12. For worship the church is closed between 12 and 4.30, when visitors are admitted on payment of a franc. The **Picture Gallery** is open from 9 to 4; admission free. **St. Jacques** is closed for worship between 12 and 4.30, when visitors are admitted on payment of a franc. At that time, as at the cathedral, the chapels are open, the pictures uncovered and visitors may walk freely about the church. The **Plantin-Moretus Museum**, unique of its kind, of especial interest to those connected with printing and engraving, is open from 10 to 4, free. Cheap drives may be taken about the city and suburbs in the trams.

ANTWERP.   HOTELS.   ENGLISH CHURCH.   CABS.

Hotels: in the Place Verte, of which the cathedral occupies one entire side, are the St. Antoine, the first and most expensive hotel; the Europe and the Flandre. In the Place Meir, the H. Grand Laboureur, and near it the English church. English private hotel, 24 Rue des Recollets, near the Picture Gallery. These may be considered the first-class houses of Antwerp.

Among the second-class houses, where the dinners cost 2 frs., breakfast 1 fr., rooms from 1½ to 3 frs., service ½ fr., the best are the **Commerce**, on the E. side of the Bourse, in the Rue de la Bourse; the Couronne, on the west side of the Bourse, in the Rue des Israelites; near it, in the Marché aux Œufs, the Cheval de Bronze; the Grand Mirroir between the Place Verte and the river; between the Place Verte and the Place Meir the H. de la Paix; in the Grande Place the H. du Nord; by the side of the cathedral, in the Rue des Moines, the Fleur d'Or.

Near the wharf of the London steamers, on the Quay Van Dyck, are the Hotels Rhin; Angleterre; and Danemarck. From the corner of this hotel starts the tram "Dryhoek, Statie, Werf," or "Port-Gare-Trois Coins," running every 10 minutes up to the station, 15 c., whence it runs south to the pretty suburb, with large avenues and handsome houses, called the Trois Coins. Those who wish to be near the Hull and Leith steamers should take the Hotel Phönix on the Quai Aldegonde.

In front of the station are the Hotels Pelican; Union. But the best is a first-class house, the H. Chemin de Fer, a little way back at No. 21 R. de la Station. In the Avenue Keyser are the Hotels Londres; Keyser; and Strasbourg. The best cafés and restaurants are in the Place Verte and the Place Meir. From the Quai Van Dyck a steamer crosses every ¼ hour to the Tête de Flandre.

The tram from the station running down the Avenue Keyser, halts in front of the Post-office in the Place Verte. On the opposite side of the "Place" is the Cathedral. The English church is in the Rue des Tanneurs, off the west end of the Place de Meir. The principal Protestant church (German) is north from the church of St. Jacques, by the Rue de la Princess, in an enclosure off the Rue de la Boutique.

Cabs.—For 1 or 2 persons, the course, 1 fr.; 3 to 4 persons, 1½ fr. Per hour 1½ fr., and each succeeding ½ hour 70 c. Luggage, 20 c. each. Before engaging request to see tariff.

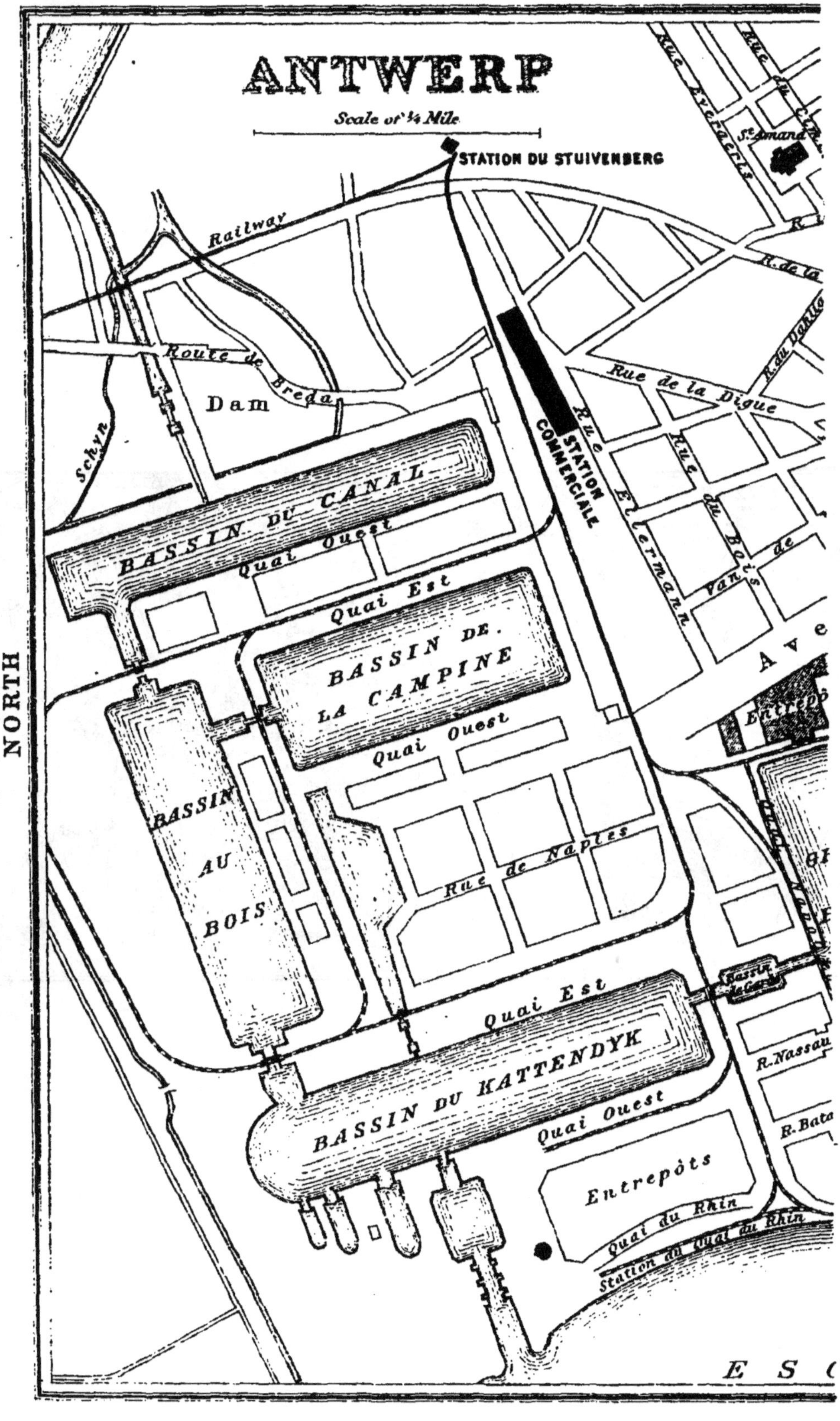

ANTWERP
Scale of ¼ Mile
STATION DU STUIVENBERG
Railway
Route de Breda
Dam
Schyn
BASSIN DU CANAL
Quai Ouest
Quai Est
BASSIN DE LA CAMPINE
Quai Ouest
STATION COMMERCIALE
Rue Ellermann
Rue de la Digue
Rue du Bois
BASSIN AU BOIS
Rue de Naples
Quai Est
BASSIN DU KATTENDYK
Quai Ouest
Entrepôts
Quai du Rhin
Quai du Rhin
Station du Quai du Rhin
Bassin de la Garde
R. Nassau
St. Amand
E S C
NORTH

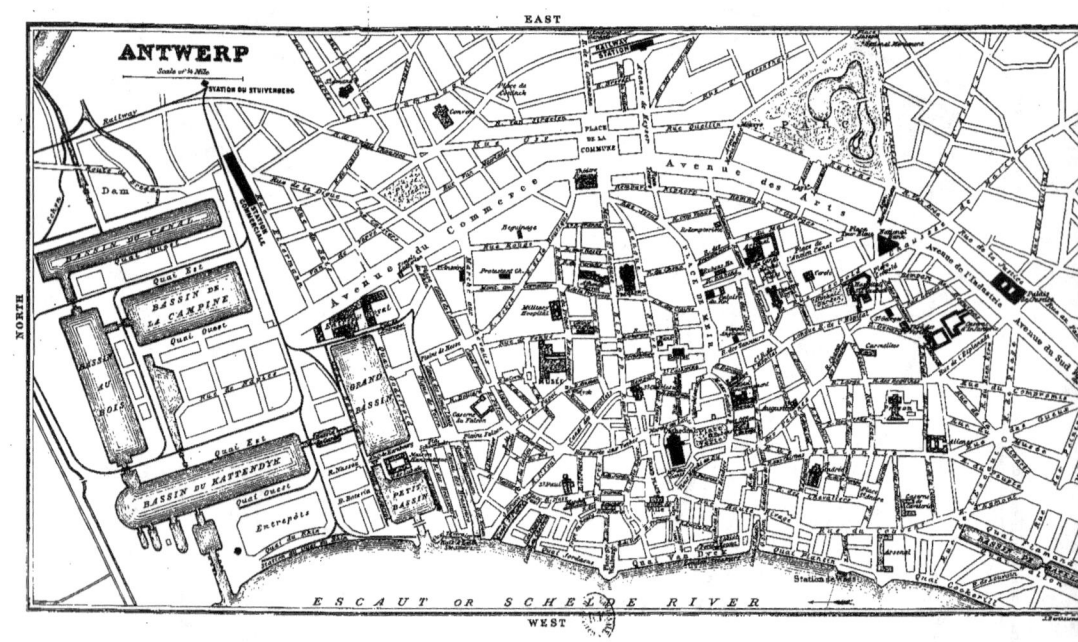

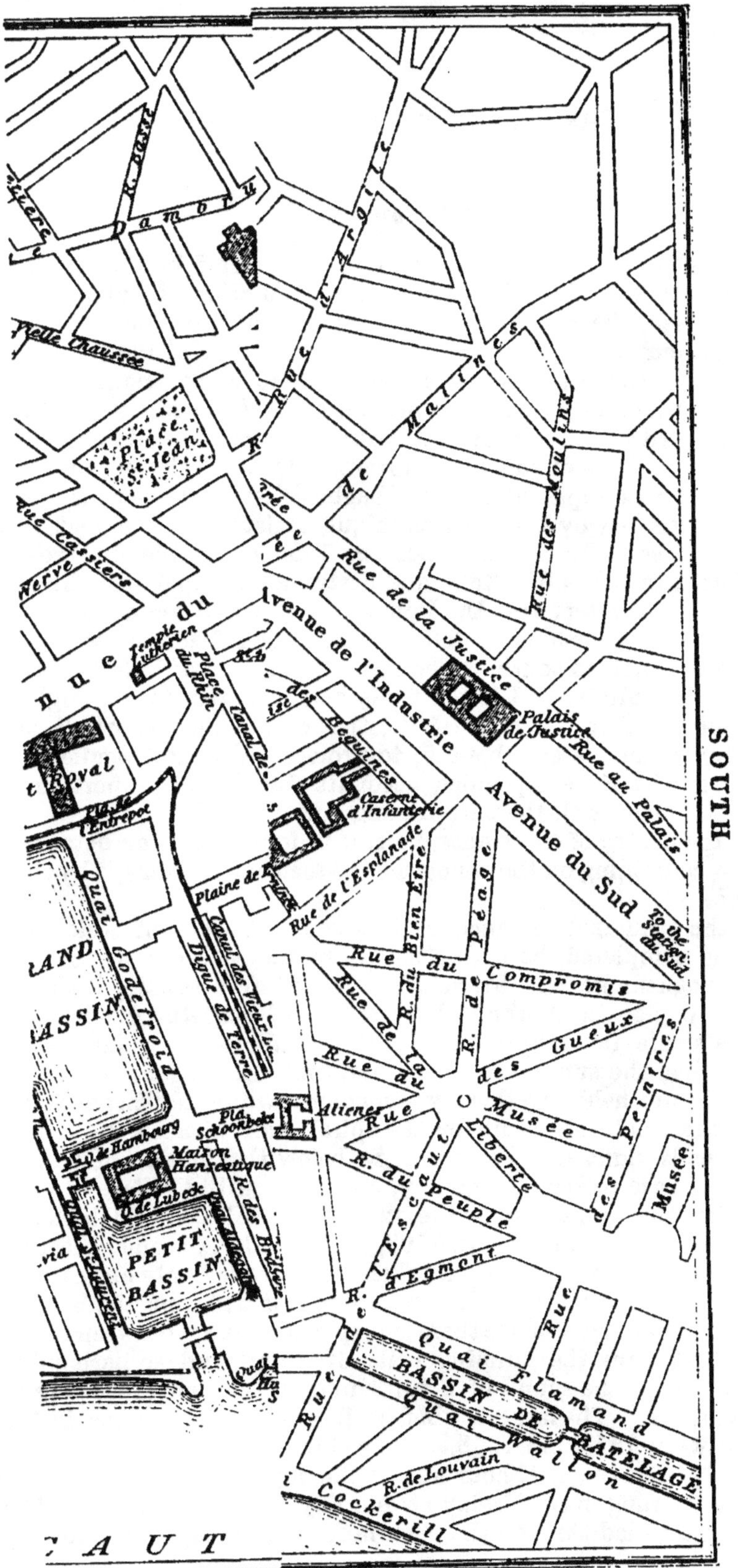

J. Bartholomew, Lith.

The Tower with its Chimes.

The Cathedral.

The first church that stood on this site was erected in 900, and rebuilt in 1124 on a larger scale. The wealth and population of Antwerp having rapidly increased, the canons resolved to erect an edifice on a more magnificent scale, and accordingly in 1352 the foundations of the present choir were laid. The earliest architect of whom there is any mention is Pierre Appelmans, who, in 1430, was the chief mason. After his death, in 1434, he was succeeded by his son Jean Appelmans, to whom is due a large part of the nave as well as of the north tower. He was followed by Everard, who, in 1475, was replaced by H. Waghemakere, who, at his death in 1502, was succeeded by his son Dominique, assisted by Rombout Keldermans of Malines. On the 6th October 1535 a terrible fire broke out, which reduced to ashes 57 altars, and destroyed the roof and the lantern tower. One year afterwards the injury was repaired under the direction of Dominique Waghemakere. The church is 384 feet from west to east, and 214 from north to south. The nave has on each side 3 aisles and 20 piers without capitals, is 170 ft. wide, and the roof 90 ft. high. The pavement of the nave was raised 4 ft., that of the choir nearly 7, and the ground around the towers about 5, to protect the church against the inundations of the Schelde, which accounts for the disproportion in the height of the piers with the surrounding parts.

From the centre of the transept rises, in four stages, an octagonal lantern tower, containing on the cupola an "Ascension of Mary," by C. Schut, 1592-1655.

Over the principal entrance are two square towers, of which only the northern is completed, both due chiefly to the younger Appelmans and the two Waghemakeres. From a base of 57 feet square, it rises like a full-grown poplar, in 9 diminishing stages of sculptured open mullion-work to a single tapering pinnacle 407 feet above the ground, especially beautiful when the sun is low in the horizon. In the more delicate parts, the mullions are held together by stanchions, while additional stability is given to the whole structure by the spiral stair within a mullioned case which ascends right up the centre, to below the finial. 383 steps lead up from the base to the first gallery, on a level with the face of the clock. Just under this gallery hang the 42 tolling bells, of which the largest, weighing 1600 lbs., was cast in 1507, and is called Carolus, because at its consecration Charles V. stood godfather. It is tolled only on feast days; 6 men are required to work it. 131 more steps, or 514 from the base, lead up to the second gallery, whence there is a splendid view. Between this gallery and the first hang the chiming bells, 40 in all, and so harmonious and concordant that the sound of a full chime in their chamber does not feel harsh to the ear. The largest, which strikes the hours, was cast in 1310, the others between 1655 and 1658. They chime at every quarter. The hour is struck both at the half hour and at the full hour. A great chime of $\frac{3}{4}$ of an hour is rung every Friday at mid-day. 84 more steps, or 598 steps from the base, lead through the open mullion-work up to the third gallery,

ANTWERP. CATHEDRAL. THE DESCENT FROM THE CROSS.

or the gallery round the tapering pinnacle, whence there is a magnificent view. 18 more steps, or 616 from the base, lead up to the top under the point of the finial. The steps are good all the way, and the view of Antwerp and of the country around for an immense distance grand.

Fee for one of a party 75 c., for the others of the same party 25 c. each. This admits only to the second gallery. To ascend to the top and to visit the bells and chimes, the party must give a trifle more.

At the foot of the tower is the famous canopied draw-well, by Quentin Metsys in 1490, and repaired in 1849. To the left of the main entrance is a copy of his tombstone, in the place formerly occupied by the original one now in the Picture Gallery, p. 274. He was by trade a blacksmith, and, according to the legend, falling in love with the daughter of a painter, was told that her hand should be given to no one who was not himself a painter. Impelled by devotion to the object of his admiration, he studied the art with such diligence and success, as induced the father to consent to the union.

Those who have little time should devote it all to the inspection of the three magnificent paintings by Rubens. The first, "The Descent from the Cross, is in the south transept; the second, the "Hoisting up of the Cross," is in the north transept, and the third, the "Ascension of Mary into Heaven," over the high altar. The first two are always covered, excepting on Thursdays, Sundays, and feast days, from 9 to 12. Between 12 and 4 the church is closed for worship. Admission then 1 fr. each, when all the pictures are uncovered. The doorkeeper is in the little house to the right of the entrance. No guide necessary. Entering the cathedral by the portal at the south transept, fronting the Place Verte, we have on the right hand the greatest masterpiece of Rubens, painted by him in 1612, when 35 years old. It is a picture consisting of three pieces, called a triptych. On the centre piece is the **Descent from the Cross**, and on the left wing the Child Jesus in the arms of Simeon, and on the right, the Meeting of Mary with Elizabeth. This wonderful composition, which arrests the attention of even the most untutored eye, is considered the masterpiece of Rubens. The linen sheet in which the emaciated body of the Redeemer is partially shrouded is only a degree more blanched than His pale form, and stained by only a few drops of blood from His lacerated hand. On the right wing, Mary in blue, before Simeon, is a portrait of the first wife of Rubens; while on the left wing, the girl with a basket on her head is a portrait of their daughter. On the outside of the wings is St. Christopher carrying the Child Jesus, guided by a hermit with a lantern. On same side is also St. Francis, by Murillo. Opposite, Last Supper, by O. Venius, 1558-1629, the master of Rubens.

Choir.

Marriage at Cana by M. de Vos, 1531-1603. The stained-glass window is modern, and represents saints from the Old and New Testaments.

Choir.—From the S. transept commence the round of the 12 chapels in the choir. The first is the Chapelle du Sacré-Cœur, with stained glass by Didron, 1872.—**2.** Tomb of John Moretus, partner and son-in-law of Plantin, d. 1610, and of his wife. Above, triptych by Rubens (covered). Centre piece, Resurrection of Christ; wings, John the Baptist and St. Catherine. Above triptych portrait of Moretus, by Heereyns. Opp., by Pepyn, 1687, St. Norbert worshipping a consecrated wafer. From this chapel there is an admirable view of Rubens's picture of the Ascension of Mary, over the high altar; but for effect, the best point is from the entrance into the sanctuary. The drapery and grouping and arrangement of her attendant angel cupids, suggest in a most vivid manner the idea of floating and fluttering in the air, although she herself seems less buoyant. Below stand in silent amazement and exultation the apostles and the two Maries she has just left.—**3.** Monument to Bishop Capello, d. 1676. On front wall diptych by Balen; Christ before Pilate, and an Adoration of the Magi. Over door, a Madonna, by F. Duquesnoy.—**4.** Tomb of Plantin, the famous Antwerp printer, p. 286, d. June 1589. Above, triptych by Backer (covered). Centre, Last Day; right wing, Plantin and his son and patron saint; left wing, his wife and daughters and their patron saint. Over triptych, portrait of Plantin, by Herreyns.—**5.** Monument to Verdussen, by J. Geefs, in alto-relievo, in white marble.—**6.** In a niche, "Christ in the tomb." Fronting this chapel, and at the back of the high altar, is a large picture representing the death of Mary, by A. Matthyssens. Immediately below, in wonderfully skilful imitation of relievo, are three panel drawings by Van Bree, representing the Annunciation, the Marriage, and the Meeting of Mary with Elizabeth. Below this are three alto-relievos on panels of white marble, by L. Willemsens, representing cupids making wine. On the mausoleum in front is the recumbent effigy of Isabelle de Bourbon, d. 1456, wife of Charles Le Téméraire.—**7.** Descent from the Cross, by De Heere. Entombment, by O. Venius. The Young Men of Nain, by Francken.—**8.** Copy of Christ à la Paille. Reredos of altar, a painting on wood, 15th cent., with 8 groups, the largest and the centre one being St. Michael. Below, 7 small panel paintings, with a Pietá in the centre.—**9.** Confessionals, by Verbruggen. Reredos of altar composed of 8 gilt groups in the style of the 15th cent. On left wing of altar, St. Joseph and Pio IX. On right wing, Philip IV. dedicating Belgium to St. Joseph. On left wall, triptych by De Vos the elder. Centre, Descent from the Cross; on wings, portraits of De Vos and wife. Opposite, triptych by A. Mytens the elder. The stained glass of the wheel window represents the genealogy of Christ, by Stalins and Janssens.—**10.** Crucifixion, life size, by Van der Neer. The cross is of the purest Parian black marble, and the body of white marble.—**11.** Contiguous to 10, a small chapel, with a Mary and Child, after Van Dyck.—**12.** Within these two chapels is a long chapel, having for the reredos a statue of St. Anthony with the Child Jesus, by A. Quellin. Three stained-

The Elevation of the Cross.

glass windows, 16th cent. One represents the conclusion of a commercial treaty between Philip I. of Castile and Henry VII. of England.

Enter the North Transept. On the eastern wall is the "Erection or Hoisting up of the Cross with Jesus nailed to it," by Rubens in 1610, and retouched by him in 1627, when he added the dog. Here all is excitement and bustle, excepting in the meek, benign, and placid countenance of the Redeemer, who partly reclines and partly hangs from the cross, which the surrounding half-naked men are making vigorous efforts to raise. In the distance, women from afar are seen gazing on them with wonder and mute astonishment. Mary and St. John stand apart—Mary apparently stunned with grief. On the other wing the most prominent figure is Longinus on a spirited gray steed, which seems unwilling to be a spectator of the sublime and awful scene.

Opposite is a triptych by F. Francken, d. 1642, representing "Christ disputing with the Doctors." The heads of the three men to the right, examining a passage in the Scriptures, are remarkably fine. Opposite them is Calvin with a skull-cap, to his left Erasmus, and behind them, Luther. On the wings are portraits of the Church fathers. The large stained-glass window, 1616, contains portraits of the Archduke Albert and of his wife Isabella. In the sanctuary are double rows of canopied stalls, and two lofty pinnacled thrones by W. Durlet, d. 1867, and C. Geerts of Louvain, d. 1855. The high altar, designed by Rubens, has for its reredos his painting of the Ascension of Mary, already referred to. Over it, in the tympanum, are represented in white marble the Trinity awaiting her entrance with a crown.

Nave.—First chapel W. from N. transept: The Virgin's chapel, with charming reliefs, by A. Quellin, in white marble, on the altar. After this follows a magnificent row of grand confessionals, with expressive life-size statues beautifully carved. On the left of the main entrance is a monument to the family of Queyrich. The statues by Scheemaeckers, of white against black marble, represent Death seizing a female figure.

S. aisle, or right hand of main entrance, Tomb of Ambrosius Capellus, 1676. The sound of the trumpets of the angels on the last day has awoke him from the sleep of death. In the S. aisle is a very large chapel, the Chapelle du Saint-Sacrement (the communion chapel), lined with 14 pictures representing the last hours of our Lord, called a via crucis, painted by Vinck and Hendrickx under the direction of Leys. The reredos, representing the disciples at Emmaus, is by G. Herreyns, d. 1827, and the beautifully sculptured white marble balustrade in front of the altar by Artus Quellin. Opposite is the pulpit by Michel van der Voort, covered by intertwining twigs and branches peopled by strange birds.

High Mass on Sundays and feast days at 10 A.M., accompanied with very fine music. Chair, 2 sous. The choir of this cathedral is one of the

Antwerp. Picture Gallery.

oldest and most celebrated in Europe. Already, in the 13th cent., it was well organised, and had a school for the instruction of the choristers. In 1435 it had 77 voices, and numbered among the instrumental performers some of the greatest musicians of the day, such as J. Okeghem, J. Obrecht, Cockx, and G. Turhout.

Fronting the S. entrance into the cathedral, in the centre of the Place Verte, is a bronze statue of Rubens, by W. Geefs, 13 ft. high, on a pedestal 20 ft. high, erected in 1840. Facing the statue is the post-office.

The **Musée** or **Picture Gallery** is open to the public from 9 to 4. All the pictures bear the artists' names on the frames, and the numbers they occupy in the catalogue. The small catalogue costs 1 fr., and saves a great deal of time; the large detailed catalogue costs 4 fr.

Within the vestibule is a large white marble bust of Rubens, by Pecher, 1877, on a bronze pedestal. Opposite, a statue of Van Bree, d. 1839, by Cuyper. Around are small busts of other Antwerp painters.

The 3 largest of the fresco paintings on the walls, by Keyser, 1872, contain 136 portraits of the painters of the Antwerp school. The smaller pictures represent scenes showing how highly their works were appreciated in foreign countries.

The collection contains nearly 700 paintings, in which all the members of the Antwerp school are admirably represented; they occupy 5 rooms, of which the second is the largest and most important. The next in importance is the last or fifth, containing the works of the early masters, of which one of the remarkable characteristics is the brightness of their colours, which, notwithstanding their great age, glow even still with a fresh brilliancy.

In the **1st Room** is the chair used by Rubens when president of the corporation of St. Luke; while his death is represented in a very large painting by Van Bree. Two of the most noble works by Rubens are in this room, No. **297** The Crucifixion of Christ with the malefactors, painted in 1620, and opposite it, **298** an Adoration of the Magi. In the Crucifixion, the centurion, with his hands on the nape of his horse's neck, is leaning forward gazing at the writhing thief, while one of the soldiers is piercing the side of Jesus, from which Mary Magdalene, with outstretched arms, is beseeching him to desist. The straight, lengthened appearance of the body of Christ indicates that he has been as patient under the acutest and severest physical pain as under the most intense mental agony. The soldier with the iron bar, in breaking the legs of the impenitent thief, has so tortured the unhappy man that, in the violence of his contortions, he has torn his left foot from the nail. The other malefactor is composed, and dies in peace, regarding the Saviour.

The Adoration of the Magi contains, amidst a gorgeous display of colouring, 16 human figures life size, mostly crowding eagerly round the manger to get a glimpse of the child Jesus. The gray-bearded king, with gold goblets in his hands, represents admirably the stiff constrained gait of an old man. The head of the ox in the corner is most charming; it also seems to stare in wonder, with its great unexpressive eyes. Next it is 221 Jordaens' (1593-1678) Adoration of the Shepherds. No. 48 by Braekeleer, 1792, a very large picture represents the sacking of Antwerp by the Spaniards. The largest, however, No. 282 represents the Pool of Bethesda by J. E. Quellin, 1634. No. 53 Elijah in the desert by G. Crayer; 372 and 374 Scenes from the martyrdom of St. George by Coxcie.

2d Room.—Among the many great works here are: in nearly the centre, the triptych, **245**, 246, 248 by Quentin Metsys in 1508. The centre piece, an Entombment, is a marvel of painting, drawing, and grouping, especially for the period when it was executed. The dead body of Christ, however, is that of a starved man; while his hair, smoothly parted, hangs down in corkscrew ringlets as if it had never been disturbed by the crown of thorns nor by the hustling and buffetings it had been so roughly subjected to during the many rude and terrible encounters of that eventful afternoon. Mary kneels over Christ in a semi-theatrical attitude, and neither the hue of her face nor its expression indicates profound grief, while St. John supports her with an air of indifference. The other female faces resemble each other, including those of Herodias and her daughter on the left wing. Herodias, who has as innocent and as beautiful a face as any, is made to show the depth of her depravity by playing in a frivolous way with the head of John the Baptist with the knife she has been eating with, while her daughter starts from the sight of it, although Herod, who is intensely ugly, tries to pacify her. Nicodemus on his knees, and Joseph of Arimathea standing, are supporting Jesus. The homely, manly countenances of both beam with kindness. On the other wing is the martyrdom of St. John the Evangelist in a caldron of seething oil. Below the picture is the tombstone of Quentin Metsys, which was originally by the left side of the entrance into the cathedral.

A little to the left, and on the same side, is **300** the same subject by Rubens, painted by him about the year 1617, and called "Christ à la Paille," because the body of Jesus is leaning against a sharp-edged

Christ à la Paille.

stone, on which is a sprinkling of straw. Blood is oozing out of the pinched nostrils, the head is thrown back on the left shoulder, the hair is tangled and dishevelled; while the collapsed and exhausted attitude of the body against the cold, rough stone, tells of the bitter, fatiguing affliction and harrowing scenes our ever blessed Redeemer has just passed through. Mary, ashy pale and looking up to Heaven, seems in the depth of her agony to wail for help, while Mary Magdalene, with her hands clasped, appears not to have realised as yet the full significance of the event. Nicodemus alone, perfectly self-possessed, has begun to shroud the body in the most gentle and loving way possible.

Nearly opposite is **401** painted in 1629 by Van Dyck at the dying request of his father, a **Christ on the Cross.** Although around all is of a dark cold gray, light is made to play on the fine form of Jesus, beautiful even in death. St. Catherine, with her eyes closed in grief, embraces his feet. St. Dominick on the other side looks upward. Picture No. 406 is the same subject on a much smaller scale.

On same side as 401 and 406 is, a little farther on, 299 by Rubens, St. Theresa interceding before Christ for souls in Purgatory. At the feet of Jesus are men and women being tormented in the flames, from which the compassionate Theresa on her knees supplicates Jesus to deliver them. An angel-cupid in expectation of her successful mediation has already seized the hand of Bernardin of Mendoza, founder of a Carmelite convent at Valladolid, to pull him out, as soon as Theresa obtains permission. The composition exhibits much freedom of pencil. Next it is 112 by Frans Floris or Vriendt in 1554, the "Expulsion of the Rebel Angels." A terribly confused medley of human forms with the heads of beasts, being thrust down into a pit by St. Michael and his angels. The humble-bee on the ham of the man in the right corner has been wrongly attributed to Metsys. It would not have done him much credit.

Here also is 403, and opposite to it **404**, the same subject as 300 and 245 the body of "Christ before being laid into the tomb," Van Dyck. 404 is the more beautiful of the two. Unfortunately the colouring is faded, and besides the blue of the sky has a bad effect against the blue of Mary's mantle. The placid countenance of Christ rests on her knee, while his body lies partly on an admirably-draped sheet. St. John is showing to 2 angels the wound of the nail in the left hand of their crucified Lord, at which one of them veils its face as too horrible to behold, while Mary, with outstretched arms, seems to exclaim, in an ecstasy of grief, "Behold what they have done to him!" Next it is

ANTWERP.   PICTURE GALLERY.   HALS.

293 a famous portrait by Van Dyck of his first wife Saskia Van Ulenburg. A little farther to the right, on this same side, is the triptych 307, by Rubens, "Our Saviour satisfying the incredulity of Thomas," calm, serious, and expressive. On the wings are the still more famous portraits of Nicolas Rockox, Burgomaster of Antwerp, and his wife. F. Hals, 1584-1666, one of the great portrait painters, has only one specimen, but that a very good one, in this collection, **188** a fisher boy. It is on this same side, but near Room 1. In this neighbourhood is 104 by De Vos, d. 1651, a famous portrait of Abraham Grapheus, a knavish keeper of the house of the Corporation or Academy of St. Luke, who is helping himself to one of the many precious objects of art which were presented to the association. At the other end, right side, are 305 "St. Francis taking the Communion," and 306 "St. Anne teaching her daughter Mary to read," both by Rubens. The latter is a favourite subject with sculptors and painters. Rubens, in this case, has made Mary too old. All the above are merely a few of the best paintings in this room—Room 2.

3d Room.—Rubens is represented in this room by 5 pictures, but none of them rank among his best. At the end of this room is an ancient and capital copy of the famous altar-piece by the brothers Van Eyck, consisting of 12 pictorial interpretations of the sublime passage in Revelation v. 12. See under Ghent Cathedral, page 156.

313 is Christ on the cross by Rubens.   265 St. Francis by Murillo.

4th Room.—Near door No. 60 by Van Lerius, 1823-1876, "Lady Godiva compelled by her husband to run naked through the streets of Coventry." Rubens has in this room one of his earliest works, No. **312** "A holy family," called the Virgin with the parrot. Mary seems to be tickling the neck of the child. On the left wall, H. Leys, 1815-1869, has a good picture, No. 237 Rubens at the fête given in his honour by the carbiniers of Antwerp. Near it, on the front wall, by De Vos, is St. Luke taking the portraits of Mary and child. 371 Triptych by M. Coxcie or Coxcyen, 1499-1592, martyrdom of St. Sebastian. Wings, by A. Framken, 1645-1618, martyrdom of St. Crispin and Crispinian, the missionary shoemakers. Wing 153 Sebastian healing Zoe, wife of Nicostrates. Among the landscapes is "Calm water," by Solomon Ruysdael in 1657, d. 1670. James Ruysdael, d. 1681, has also a landscape, No. 320.

5th and Last Room, containing some of the best works of the early masters. Projecting from the side of the door are 2 small diptychs, 8 inches by 4½ each, believed to be by C. Horebout. No. **530**

Early Flemish Painters.

is J. C. in a white robe, with a gold crown on his head, from which fall profuse clusters of ringlets on to his shoulders. In his left hand he holds an open book, and with his right gives his blessing. He stands against a crimson curtain, with a violet-coloured fringe, embroidered with gold. On the curtain are embroidered with gold A. W. and P. F., with the date 1499. By the side is **531** Portrait of the donor, a Cistercian abbot. On other side, Mary and child in scarlet mantle, lined with blue, standing in the nave of a large cathedral. On the jubé is a Crucifixion, and by the side of the cross are statues of herself and John. Next it, portrait of the donor, Christian de Hondt, 30th abbot of Les Dunes, near Bruges, elected in 1495. On the front wall is one of the most valuable pictures in the collection, No. **393** an altar-piece by Roger Van der Weiden, d. 1464, representing a Crucifixion in a cathedral. Mary is fainting in the arms of John. Behind, a priest before the altar is consecrating a wafer. On one wing is a baptism, and on the other a dying man is about to take a consecrated wafer. Close to it is **124** a small portrait of Frederick III. of Saxony by Albert Durer, 1471-1628. Then **411** a small Virgin Mary by J. Van Eyck, 1390-1440. Also by him, 410 an unfinished sketch, and 412 another "Mary." No. 182 Portrait, J. Gossaert or Maubeuge, d. 1532. He has 5 more small pictures, all Biblical excepting 184, Portrait, Margaret of Austria, Regent of the Netherlands under Charles V., a small portrait of a plain-looking face, a little to the right from Weyden's altar-piece. To the left of Weyden's altar-piece is **4** by A. Messina in 1475, "A Calvary." Jesus nailed to a cross and the malefactors to withered trees are vividly prominent against a bright sky, with a blue sea in the distance. Under glass, by Weyden, 396, an "Annunciation," 8 inches by 6; and also by him, 397, Philip the Good of Burgundy. 253 H. Memling, d. 1495, portrait of a canon of the order of St. Norbert. L. Cranach, 1472-1553, No. 42 Adam and Eve. 43 Charity. **241** Head of Christ, and **242**, of Mary, exquisitely painted in glowing colours by Metsys, d. 1530.

The other masters who have pictures in Room 5 are Bles (47), d. 1450. Clouet, 33 Francis II. d. 1572. Cuyp, 46 Cavaliers, d. 1691. Dunwege (123), d. 1520. A. Goubau, 1616-1698. F. Goubau, 1622-1678. Hans Holbein, 1498-1543, portrait of Erasmus 198 and 199 of a gentleman. Van der Meire, born 1427, triptych 383, diptych 388. Van Orley, 1488-1542, four pictures. Patinir, 1490-1524, a Madonna. Rembrandt 1608-1669. 293, 4 and 5 Portraits of lady, fisherman, and Jew. Wouverman 1620-1668, Nos. 500 and 501 Horsemen.

ANTWERP.   ST. JACQUES.   SOUTH AISLE.

East from the Cathedral, by either the Longue Rue Neuve, or the Rue Ripdorp, is the next edifice in importance, the church of St. Jacques. By referring to the plan, it will be observed that at about a third of the way the church of St. Charles is passed, from which the Picture Gallery or Musée is only a little northwards. If time be limited, it is better, after the Cathedral, to take the Picture Gallery, which, with the Cathedral, are unquestionably the two grand and principal sights in Antwerp. For St. Charles see page 281.

Saint Jacques, commenced in 1491, and finished in 1661, is full of beautiful marbles, sculpture, woodwork, and paintings, but the principal attraction is the Rubens chapel, where the great master is buried. Between 12 and 4.30 the church is closed for worship. During that time knock at the door of the S. transept, opening to the Longue Rue Neuve, pay each 1 fr. and walk in. Here, as in the Cathedral during that time, every chapel is open, every picture uncovered, and every part may be examined freely and comfortably.

South Aisle.—First pier, right hand of main or west entrance, we have a "Resurrection" by H. van Balen, d. 1632, and over it a portrait of himself and wife. Now, **first chapel, right**, Reredos of Altar—St. George and Dragon, by A. Van Dyck, opposite tombstone of Bogaerts, died 1851, with portrait by Keyser; below, wood statuette of St. Sebastian by A. Quellin. The beautiful reliefs in white marble are by Geefs and others, and form part of a Via Crucis, continued in the other chapels of the nave. The stained glass is 1870.—2. Reredos—Temptation of St. Anthony by M. de Vos, d. 1603. In small shrine, relics of St. Anthony. Monument to Van Ertborn, with a beautiful Mater Dolorosa by Guido Reni.—3. Reredos by E. Quellin, St. Roch, 1660, cured of the plague. Opposite monument to Bergeyck Moretus with Madonna. On centre wall, Shrine, with relics of St. Roch. Small 15th cent. paintings in this and two next chapels, illustrating the life of St. Anthony.—4. Reredos—Mary surrounded by Saints; and opposite, St. Cecilia, and Jesus Christ appearing to Mary Magdalene, by O. Venius.—5. Reredos—A Holy Family, in company with a more than usual number of female figures, painted by F. Floris, in a quaint but unvigorous style. Opposite Monument to N. Mertens, d. October 1586, and wife, February 1592, with portraits of both by Francken.—6. Reredos between spiral columns—Baptism of Christ, by M. Coxcie, d. 1592; Triptych by A. Francken le Vieux; Jesus on the Mount of Olives. Wings—Restoring to life daughter of Jairus, and Woman caught in Adultery; Martyrdom of St. James, by M. de Vos.

Now enter the **South Transept.** Up against the right-hand wall is a large alto-relievo cut out of a single stone, representing the Raising of the Cross, by Van der Voort, 1719. Over the portal is a triptych. The centre picture, "Christ casting out the money-changers," is by Honthorst, 1590-1656, and the wings, Interviews of J.C. with a nun, Crayer 1582-1669.

Rubens' Chapel and Tomb.

To the left or E. side of S. transept is the Chapelle du Saint-Sacrement, a long chapel extending into the aisle of the choir. The reredos of the altar, a "Last Supper," by O. Venius, is between two elegant spiral marble columns and statues of Peter and Paul, which, with the delicately sculptured white marble balustrade in front, are by P. Verbruggen. The other statues are by L. Willemssens and Kerricx, 17th cent. The best of the 3 stained-glass windows (1626) here represents Rudolph von Hapsburg on his knees offering a gift to the priest. The confessionals in this chapel and in the choir are by A. Quellin, Willemssens and Kerricx.

On the sanctuary screen opposite the Sacrament chapel are a Dead Christ by Goubau 1618; Mary and child surrounded with flowers by Heyden, d. 1712; and Christ with crown of thorns, M. de Vos, d. 1603. Then follows a Madonna in a somewhat novel style, by Verlinde, in 1870.

First chapel, with entrance from **choir**. Reredos, Trinity, by Balen. Opposite is a much better picture by A. Noort, d. 1641, Christ calling Peter to follow him.—2. Reredos, St. Yves, by Zegers. Opposite, on sanctuary screen, Mary and John bending over the body of Jesus, by C. Schut.—3. Reredos, by Zegers, "Christ appearing to Mary;" and next it by Voort, a group in white marble representing the Scourging of Christ. Triptych by Janssens, God and Christ crowning Mary in heaven; on the wings, a Nativity and an Adoration.

4. Chapel of Rubens, with the tomb of Rubens, born 1577 and died on the 30th of May 1640. In this same vault were also interred several members of his family. When opened a few years ago, it was found to contain the relics of 14 bodies, so mixed up with each other and with fragments of coffins that it was impossible to distinguish what had belonged to Rubens. On each side is a mausoleum of two different families connected with Rubens. The white marble reclining statues on them are by W. Geefs, in 1839 and 1850; the one on the left represents the Dying Christian, and the other Eternity. The reredos, painted by Rubens expressly for this chapel, represents Mary and child Jesus with saints, generally believed to be portraits of members of his family. Mary is said to represent Mlle. Lunden, whose portrait, called the "Chapeau de paille," was bought by Sir Robert Peel for 3500 guineas. At the opposite side is Rubens himself as St. George in full armour. Before him, and partly nude, is his second wife as Magdalene; to her left, and with light hair, is his first wife as Martha. Between her and the Virgin is his father as St. Jerome, wearing a red mantle; he is kneeling before the Child. In front, to the left of Mary, is his grandfather in the allegorical character of Time, with a gray beard. Over all stands the marble statue of Mary, by Faid'herbe, by whom are also the two cupids holding the crown.

ANTWERP. ST. JACQUES. NORTH AISLE.

In the space on the wall outside the Rubens chapel is a triptych by J. Rombouts the elder; centre, Marriage of St. Catherine with Jesus Christ, wings, monks.—5. Reredos, St. Charles beseeching Mary to stay the plague.—6. Reredos, Peter taking leave of Paul, by Lint, d. 1690. Opposite, Entombment, and Jesus Christ appearing to Mary, by A. Francken, d. 1648.—7. Reredos, Meeting of Mary with Elizabeth, by Wolfvoet, d. 1652, a pupil of Rubens. On wall, Disciples at Emmaus, by Moons, 1843. Both pictures very good.

Now follows the large Mary chapel, opening into the N. transept. Before entering, observe Trinity by Balen, d. 1632; against pier fronting transept portal, a Dead Christ, by C. Schut, d. 1655; by side of portal, Adoration of Magi, by Thyssens, d. 1679; over portal large triptych, centre, Christ among the doctors by J. Honthorst; wings by Zegers, an Annunciation and Adoration. The altar consists of 4 monolith spiral marble columns, entwined with wreaths of flowers and foliage, enclosing a Madonna and angels in white marble against black marble. The stained glass dates from 1641.

The high altar in the sanctury, designed by Rubens, consists of 6 monolith white marble spiral columns and 2 plain black marble columns, which support a tympanum in black marble, wherein are seated the Trinity surrounded by angels in white marble. Below, and immediately over the altar table, is a colossal statue, by A. Quellin, d. 1670, in white marble, of St. James, attired as a Roman Catholic bishop, with a long crosier.

Chapels on North side of nave. Commence at left hand of main entrance. First chapel, tomb and mausoleum of Don Francisco Marcos de Velasco, governor of the castle of Antwerp, born in Burgos and died at Antwerp, June 1693. All the background and shroud, which has a gilt fringe, are in faultless black marble, while the statues and insignia are in pure white marble. The marquis himself is in a reclining posture regarding the figure of death, showing him that his sand-glass has run out. An unclothed skeleton waits to carry him into his tomb.—2. Opposite altar, triptych by M. de Vos; centre, the Virgin entering the temple; on the wings, death of martyrs. Tomb of C. Lantschot, d. April 1656, with oval portrait by Van Dyck.—3. On the wall, continuation of the Via Crucis groups. Opposite altar, tomb and admirable portraits, by Ryckaert, of Joannes Doncker and wife, d. 1591. Reredos, triptych by Van Balen; centre, an Adoration; wings, an Annunciation and a Salutation.—4. Opposite altar triptych (covered) centre, Last Day; wings, portraits of Rockox, the donor, and his family. This picture was painted by Van Orley after his return from Italy, where he had studied art under Raphael. It is considered one of his best. He died in 1542. On the wall 3 more groups of the Via Crucis.—5. Reredos by M. de Vos, d. 1603; centre, the Trinity crowning Mary; below, a multitude of female figures. On wall, by P. Avont, d. 1652, Mary and Child in garden, with cupids and ladies.—6. Next to N. transept. On wall, St. Helena giving the cross on which Christ had been crucified to her son, the Emperor Constantine, by Coberger, d. 1635. Pulpit, by Willemssens, in 1671, pupil of A. Quellin, by whom are also some of the confessionals and statues.

St. Charles.   St. André.

Near the cathedral, and easily recognised by its neat square tower in two stages, crowned with a circular domed turret, is the church of St. Charles, built by the Jesuits in 1621 from plans by Rubens, destroyed by lightning in July 1718, and shortly after rebuilt in the same highly decorated style. In the interior the walls are lined to about the height of 10 ft. with wainscoting of oak, on which are carved in high relief, within ornamented medallions, scenes from the lives of Loyola and Francis Xavier. From the wainscoting project at intervals handsome confessionals, with statues life size of saints and angels. On the high altar are exposed alternately an Assumption, by C. Schut; a Crucifixion by Zegers; and an Invocation of Mary by M. G. Wappers. The organ-case, on the gallery opposite, is curiously shaped.

Of the whole church the most profusely ornamented part is Mary's chapel, to the right, containing some of the original marbles. The reredos, by Wappers, d. 1874, representing a "Presentation to the temple," is between pure white marble spiral columns covered with sculptured foliage, while in front is a delicately-chiselled balustrade of the same material. In the corresponding chapel, on the left side, the reredos is a relief in marble representing Saint Xavier kneeling before the Virgin.

St. André, St. Augustin, The Bourse, The House of Rubens, St. George, The National Bank, The Park, St. Joseph.

South from the Cathedral, and W. from St. Augustin, by the straight, narrow street the Rue de la Clef, is the church of **St. André**, built in 1529. On a pillar in S. aisle, tablet to the memory of Barbara Mowbray and Elizabeth Curll, ladies of honour to Mary Queen of Scots, who, after her execution, came to Antwerp, where they died, and were buried in this church. One of them received her last embrace. The portrait of the queen over the epitaph is by F. Pourbus. In chapel beyond, at the S. side of high altar, a "Last Supper" on the reredos by Franck. To the right, the child Jesus in his cradle and Jesus at Emmaus by E. Quellin. To the left, the raising of Lazarus, by Zegers.

The Chancel.—The high altar is an immense structure, supported by 8 veined marble columns, with statues and angels in white marble. The principal group represents what is called an assumption. Five persons having opened the coffin of the Virgin Mary, find to their astonishment nothing else in it but sweet-smelling flowers. Mary had ascended to heaven. On the wall right is "The guardian angel of youth" by Quellin, and on the other side, the crucifixion of St. Andrew by Otto Venius.

In the chapel at the E. end of N. aisle, the flight into Egypt by Gobaerts, and St. Anne instructing her daughter Mary by Zegers. The 14 large modern pictures which hang on the walls of the nave form a Via Crucis, before each of which a prayer is said during Lent.

The pulpit is a very large and complicate structure in carved oak, by

ANTWERP. ST. AUGUSTIN. BOURSE.

Van Geel and Van Hool, representing "Jesus Christ appearing to Peter after the miraculous draught of fishes"—here miraculous in kind as well as in quantity. The figures are life size, and skilfully and vigorously executed. Jesus, with a benign expression, stands on the shore. Peter, with his accustomed impetuosity, has leapt out of the boat and is hasting towards the Master. Andrew still sits quietly in the boat among the fish and the net, over which crawl a long lobster and a big crab. One great basket full of fish has already been sent ashore. The sound-board is covered with trees, drapery, and cupids.

Near St. André is the Musée Plantin-Moretus, page 286.

South from the Place Verte by the Rue Nationale and the Rue des Peignes is the church of **Saint Augustin**, built in 1615. Over the high altar is the painting by Rubens, representing the marriage of Christ with St. Catherine, who on her knees receives a ring from the child, whom Mary holds forward to her. Peter is looking over Mary's shoulder, and on the steps, left hand, is John the Baptist. The picture contains above 20 figures, all very much faded, but grouped with much animation. The best is the figure of St. Catherine, and especially the head. The naked figure between St. George and the Pope in the foreground seems unnecessarily prominent.

S. aisle, right hand of main entrance, by Cels, Meeting of "Mary with Elizabeth;" Simeon with the child Jesus, by Lens. On reredos of the chapel at the end of this aisle the martyrdom of St. Apollonia (a painful subject) by Jordaens. The gray horse biting his knee is admirable. Now return and cross over to the north aisle. Large picture by Van Bree representing the baptism of St. Augustin. At the end of this aisle, on the reredos over the altar, is "St. Augustin in a trance," the first historic picture painted by Van Dyck after his return from Italy.

To the right of the chapel of St. Apollonia is a large almost circular chapel, covered with frescoes, many on a gold ground, by Bellemans. The lowest row form a beautiful and expressive Via Crucis, while above are full-length portraits of bishops and pilgrims.

Directly E. from the Cathedral is the **Bourse**, rebuilt in 1872, after the fire of 1858, which destroyed the original structure erected by Waghemakere in 1531, and from which the London Exchange was copied (see the Collection of Engravings, page 189). It is situated at the meeting of four streets, which causes a constant traffic of foot-passengers through the great hall, 168 ft. long and 132 wide, roofed partly by glass and partly by timber, on which are emblazoned escutcheons and insignia of Belgium, Antwerp, and the provinces. Round the sides runs a spacious corridor, with two rows of short stone columns with sculptured shafts, 30 being in the outer row, and 38 in the inner. The latter support by bossed stone groining the brick roof, divided into neat concave sections. The outer row supports the arches on which the upper gallery rests, which is exactly half the width of the corridor below, to give room for the apartments of the telegraph and other offices, all on the first floor. On two of the sides of the upper gallery are

House of Rubens. St. George. Park.

handsome oriel projections, like balconies, which might serve as tribunes or pulpits. On the walls of the corridors are painted maps of the great commercial coasts in the world, those of Belgium and Holland being on the largest scale.

At No. 50 Place de Meir is the Royal Palace, built in 1755. At No. 52 stood the **House Rubens** built for himself in 1611, and in which he died on the 30th May 1640. All that remains of the original mansion is in the garden of house No. 7 Rue de Rubens, consisting of a profusely-decorated portico, by Fayd'herbe, which separated the court from the garden, and a pavilion or kind of summer-house at the end of the garden. The two yews were planted by him. Be careful not to enter by No 9.

The present house at No. 52 was almost entirely rebuilt in 1703, and restored in 1864. The exterior does not resemble in the least the original house. In the centre was a building with 5 tall round-headed windows on the ground floor, and above them a row of 5 short square windows. On one side was a low wing of 5 windows in the upper story, and on the other a similar wing with 7 windows. The most sumptuous sculpture was in the drawing-room, and on the side of the house fronting the garden, in which stand still the portico and the pavilion. See plate 102 in case up centre of Room 11, upper floor in the Plantin-Moretus Museum.

After the battle of Marston Moor the Duke of Newcastle came to Antwerp and rented this house from the widow of Rubens, in which he entertained Charles II. and several distinguished refugees.

On one side of the Place Leopold is the Hospital St. Elizabeth, and by the side of it a small botanic garden. To the west of the Hospital and the Place Leopold is the church of **St. George**, built in 1853, and easily recognised by the two pinnacled spires over the main entrance. The interior represents an arrangement repeatedly met with in Belgium. Long, tall, grooved columns, with narrow capitals, from which the groining springs, within a few feet of the roof; which is covered with arabesques partly gilt. The tracery in the windows is short. The walls of the nave are covered with most pleasing frescoes by Guffens and Sweerts, representing scenes in the teaching and life of our Lord. Each is accompanied with an explanation, or quotation from Scripture, in Flemish. Round the chancel are the apostles, painted on a gold ground. The woodwork would be considered remarkable in any country but Belgium. At the pedestal of the pulpit is St. George slaying the dragon.

Occupying the triangular space between the Place Leopold and the Avenue des Arts, is the large and handsome building, the National Bank. The base, or façade, is towards the avenue, the apex to the square, in front of the equestrian statue of Leopold I., by Geefs. Opposite, is the Avenue Marie Henriette, leading into the **Park**, designed by Keilig, who planned also the Bois de la Cambre of Brussels. A little farther north is the principal entrance to the park, embellished with a statue of the painter Leys, d. 1869. Still farther north is another entrance, embellished with a very handsome marble statue of Quentin Metsys or Matsys, d. 1530. The park is a very pleasant resort, and although small, contains a variety of pretty landscapes. Diminutive hills and valleys, intersected by broad

Loos Monument. Corporation Houses.

roads and covered with groves of fine old trees, amidst well-kept grassy slopes, border the banks of a lake, crossed at one part by a suspension-bridge, resting on high cliffs, partly artificial. The streets and houses of this quarter are spacious and handsome, and unlike those in the old town.

At the east end of the park is the church of St. Joseph, with 2 spires, all built of brick. The interior is painted in arabesque, and round the church is a Via Crucis in fresco. All the windows are filled with stained glass. In front is the handsome Monument de Loos, erected to commemorate the destruction of the walls built here by the Spaniards in 1545, and which were cleared away in 1859, during the Mayorship of de Loos. Around the base are 4 colossal allegorical statues, and on the top a large upright figure of Antwerpia.

At the southern end of the great avenues is the Palais de Justice, a handsome building with pavilions on the 4 corners and a tower over the façade. Beyond, where formerly stood the citadel, are more avenues, squares, and streets, and the new railway station for Ghent.

Hotel de Ville, Corporation Houses, Boucheries, St. Paul, Maison Hanseatique, Docks, Plantin-Moretus Museum, Porte de l'Escaut, Steen Museum.

Near the west end of the cathedral, towards the river, are the Grande Place and the **Hotel de Ville**, erected in 1560 by C. de Vriendt; better known by the appellation of Floris. It is a plain, three-story, four-sided building, of which the depth is rather less than half the width. The uniformity of the frontage (279 ft.) is partly relieved by making the centre project in the form of a square pavilion, with an obelisk on each side of the summit, where it terminates in two diminishing stages 125 ft. high. The principal hall is called the Salle de Leys, because covered by him from 1864-1869, with fresco paintings representing incidents in the history of Antwerp. There are also some handsome chimney-pieces. Admission after 12; apply to concierge. Fee 1 fr., for party 2 frs. In the second story is the public library, open from 10 to 5.

As in the Grande Place of Brussels, the different corporations had their houses in this square. Of them, the most prominent is at No. 15. La Vieille Arbalète, or the Hall of the Archers, a tall, narrow house, with a blackened front, on the north side of the Place, built in 1513 and recognised by a bow at each corner of the base of the gable. Higher up are two archers. The house consists of 6 stories of 5 windows each, excepting the two highest. Next it is the Hall of the Coopers, built in 1579, and repaired in 1628. It consists of 3 stories of 5 windows. But the two best houses are to the right, on the other or south side. No. 40, the Carpenters' house (1644), with a panelling in front in high relief, representing little carpenter cupids busy at their work. Next it is the Drapers' house (1644), with two rows of panelling, representing in relief the sale and purchase of cloth. In the narrow street, the Rue Bouchers

St. Paul.   Mount Calvary.   Pictures.

(off the N.W. corner of the Grande Place), is the old **Meat Market**, or Vieilles Boucheries, 1503, now a granary. It is a four-sided, two-storied building, of alternate layers of stone and brick, supported by buttresses and garnished with 5 tall pentagonal towers, in each of which is a spiral stone staircase. It is 20 yards wide and 50 deep. The lower windows are large, and traceried like those of a church, the upper are transomed.

A short way N. from the Cathedral, in front of the Marché au Betail is the Dominican church of **St. Paul**, built in 1571. Shut like all the others from 12 to 4.30. Admission then, ½ fr. The door most generally open is at the S. corner, giving access to a long passage. A door (never locked) on the right of this passage opens into the court of the cloister, crowded with statues, single and in groups, representing scenes from the last day of Our Lord. Against the S. transept of the church is built in four stages a **Mount Calvary,** composed of black slag and bits of sandstone, mixed with nodules and fossils of cetaceæ. In the lowest stage, or ground floor, is a Holy Sepulchre containing a statue representing the body of Jesus. To the left is a flaming representation of purgatory, full of agonising souls in that place of torment. On the second stage stands a pope pointing upwards to the cross. On the third a monk does the same. And on the fourth and highest is Christ on the cross, with Death vanquished at the foot of it in the shape of a broken skeleton. By the side stand Mary and John.

At the end of the long passage is the entrance into the church. The first picture left hand over the door is by Teniers le Vieux, and represents the "7 acts of charity." There are no chapels along the N. and S. aisles; but instead, a row of handsome and richly sculptured confessionals with life-size statues of monks and angels. At the end of the S. aisle in the S. transept, are 2 chapels, side by side. The reredos or altar-piece representing the body of Jesus tended by the Virgin, Mary Magdalene, and John, is by Crayer. The chancel beyond has very elegant carved oak stalls with graceful spiral columns. The table of the high altar is several feet above the level of the floor, and is of white marble. The reredos, "a Descent from the Cross," is between red marble columns, under a black marble pediment. Along the **North Aisle** is a series of 15 pictures, representing incidents from the life, death, and resurrection of Christ and Mary. It commences with an Annunciation by Balen, d. 1632, a Visitation by Francken, d. 1616, and a Nativity and Purification by M. de Vos, d. 1603. Then scenes from the life of Christ, of which the 2 best are Christ bearing the cross, an early painting by Van Dyck, d. 1641, and a Crucifixion by Jordaens, d. 1678. At the end of this aisle, in the N. transept is the celebrated picture by Rubens, the **Scourging** of Christ, uncovered on Sundays and feast days. The subtle concentration of light on the bleeding back of the Redeemer, revealing with all the exactness of nature the wounded flesh, is almost too true to be beautiful. The reredos of the altar represents Mary and Child giving rosaries to St. Dominic— copied from Caravaggio.

At the N.W. corner of plan in front of the Petit Bassin is the

Plantin the Printer.

Maison Hanseatique, "Domus Hansae Teutonicae," a vast ugly three-storied four-sided brick building, 266 ft. long and 214 ft. wide, of which the ground floor is occupied by ship chandlers' offices and public-houses, while the upper floor is used as granaries and store-rooms. It was constructed by the Hanseatic League in 1564 and called the Osterlingshuis; in 1863 it was made over to Government in consideration of certain navigation immunities. The Leith and Hull steamers moor in this neighbourhood, those from London and Harwich at the Quay Van Dyck. The entire area occupied by the quays and docks is 10,000 acres.

Museum Plantin-Moretus.

Although everything in this museum is carefully labelled and explained, a copy of the very excellent catalogue, price 1 fr., will be found very serviceable and even necessary.

A little to the S.W. of the Place Verte, in the Marché du Vendredi is the house of Christophe Plantin, born at Tours in 1514, married Jeanne Riviere in Caen in 1546, went to Antwerp in 1549, where he established himself as a bookbinder, but registered his name on the 21st March 1550 in the corporation of St. Luke as a printer, which he shortly afterwards again became, and by which he made a handsome fortune. He died in June 1589, and was buried in his own vault under the 4th chapel in the choir of the Cathedral. From 1554 he carried on the printing business with great ability, which after his death was as ably conducted by his son-in-law Jean Moretus and his descendants, till the year 1800, when it began to languish. Jean Moertorf, who latinised his name to Moretus, was born at Antwerp on the 22d May 1543, entered the employment of Plantin in 1557, married his daughter Martine in 1570, received the charge of the establishment in 1589, and died on the 22d Sept. 1610.

In 1800 the Moretuses having lost certain privileges, without which they were unable to compete with more active rivals with modern machinery, their business began to decline year after year down to the time of the last possessor, Edward J. H. Moretus, b. 1804, d. 1880, who in 1876 sold the house, plant, furniture and pictures to the city of Antwerp; which converted the antiquated establishment into a museum of great interest, not only to printers and engravers, but to all lovers of 16th cent. houses and furniture. Admission free. Open from 10 to 4.

Over the main door are the arms of Plantin, with his motto "Labore et Constantia," sculptured by Artus Quellin, d. 1668, for Balthasar Moretus.

MUSEUM. PORTRAITS. EARLY PUBLICATIONS.

Within the vestibule is a statue of Apollo by Godecharle in 1809. Enter first room, right hand. It is small, has a handsome chimney-piece, and the walls are hung with Flemish tapestry. Over the chimney-piece is a curious painting by A. Casteels, d. 1682, representing the Ommegang, as the semi-religious procession was called, which marched through the principal streets of the town on the Kermes day.

Room 2. Walls hung with dark green damask, and round them 13 half-size portraits, of which 4 are by Rubens. They represent members of the family, and their intimate friends and coadjutors. The most interesting are portrait by Rubens of Arias Montanus (1527-1596), the Oriental scholar sent by Philip II. to revise the proofs of the polyglot Bible, whilst passing through the press; portraits of Christophe and of his wife Jeanne Rivière, b. at Caen, d. 1596. Down the centre of the room are designs for the title-pages, frontispieces, vignettes, borders, and pictures of their publications by the greatest artists of the day, such as Rubens, who supplied the greatest number. M. de Vos, 1531-1603. Van den Broeck, d. 1601. Borcht, who worked for the establishment from 1565 to 1599, as a drawer and engraver on copper. Many too of the most beautiful capital letters were designed by him and engraved on wood. N. Horst, d. 1646. A. Van Noorst, 1557-1641. E. Quellin, who supplied many frontispieces. Werden, 1658. Corneille Schut, 1597-1655. G. Maes, 1649-1700. De Kock, d. 1735. Tassaert, 1757. Beugnet, 1764, Corn. J. d'Heur, 1707-1762 and Van Orley, 1758.

Enter now 3d Room. Round the walls 34 half-size portraits, of which 5 are by Rubens and others by Bosschaert, d. 1668; Van Uden, d. 1673; Leyssens, d. 1710; Reesbroeck, d. 1704; and Ykens, d. about 1662.

Down the centre of the room, in one side of the glass case, are 63 manuscripts from the 12th to the 15th cent. On the other are copies of the earliest works published by Plantin. They are all beautifully printed. The most remarkable are—64 Michel Bruto, "L'instruction d'une fille de noble maison," 8vo, 1555, the first book printed by Plantin with his name. 65 The fifth volume of the Polyglot Bible, folio, dated 1572. It is printed on vellum, contains the Hebrew and Greek text of the Xantes Pagnini, Bible, with translation in Latin. The whole Bible, 8 volumes, was printed from 1568 to 1573, of which 12 copies were on vellum. The greater number, 960 copies, were printed on the fine royal paper of Troyes, which were sold to the booksellers for £6 each, and to the public for £7. 66 Flores de Seneca, 8vo, 1555. 69 Nonnus, Dionysiaca, in Greek, 8vo, 1569. 67 P. Belon, Observations on remarkable things found in Greece, with woodcuts in the letterpress, 8vo, 1855. 73 Pentateuch, in Hebrew, 8vo, 1567. 74 Plantin, Dialogues Française, with preface in French verse, 8vo, 1567. 81 Clement Perret, Exercitatio Alphabetica, with copy lines engraved on copper, oblong folio. Round each page of the letterpress is a handsome border 2 inches deep. 86 Kalendarium Gregorianum, 32mo, 1585. 87 C. Clusius, Rariorum Stirpium Historia, with woodcuts, 8vo, 1566. 88 Hebrew and Latin Dictionary, 8vo, 1588. 89 M. de Lobel, Kruidboek (Botany), folio, 1580, illustrated with coloured plates. 90 Vesalius, Anatomy, folio, 1568, with

Shop. Readers', Type and Press Rooms.

plates. 91 L. Guicciardini, Description of the Netherlands, folio, 1582, with large plates. 92 The first Flemish dictionary, 4to, 1573. 93 Ortelius, Atlas of the World, folio, 1612, with coloured maps (J. Moretus). 97 Fr. Aguilonius, Treatise on Optics, folio, 1613, with plates, (J. and B. Moretus). The letterpress of all the books is clear, even when printed with woodcuts. The drawing and engraving of the illustrations, ornamental borders, and frontispieces, evince great care and taste, as was to be expected, when such men as Rubens, Teniers, Jordaens, Brueghel, etc., did not consider it beneath their dignity to employ their talents in this way.

Then follow a number of receipts and letters by the early members of the firm.

Leave Room 3 at the door in the corner, and enter the court, just under the beautiful staircase, constructed in 1621. The well is about the same date. The large vine which spreads its branches over the opposite side of the court is above 300 years old. Round the courts are busts of different members of the family by Artus Quellin and J. C. de Cock.

At the foot of staircase enter door which opens into the back shop, with furniture of 1635. The little shop has still books on its shelves and its small counter. To the left is the Salon à Tapisseries, hung with ancient Flemish tapestry in excellent preservation, with unfaded colours. Large handsome chimney-piece, and piano with two rows of keys at the end and one row in front, made in 1735 by J. J. Coenen, organist of the cathedral.

From this cross the court and enter by a small door into the room of the **Readers**, occupied by them for more than two centuries. The ornaments on the lintels of the door were sculptured by Paul Dirickx in 1638. Among the earliest readers were Pulman, an erudite philologist and commentator; Kiel, who entered the employment of Plantin in 1558, and who was eminently useful in preparing the Flemish dictionary. François Ravelingen entered Plantin's office in 1564 as a reader, at 40 florins for the first year, and 60 for the second. He was a great Greek and Oriental scholar, and was one of the principal assistants of Arias Montanus in revising the sheets of the Polyglot Bible. In June 1565 he married Marguerite, the eldest daughter of Plantin. The table at which they sat is still in this room, with all the other furniture, while round the walls are the portraits of some of them. Next is the **Office**, a very small room hung with gilt embossed leather, and having a large window protected with a strong railing. Next to it is the room of Justus Lipsius, with a large chimney-piece, and hung with Cordova leather. Over the door is a portrait of him, on which are the words "Ætatis 38 Ano° 1585," and his motto "Moribus antiquis." He was the intimate friend of Plantin and the instructor of his grandson Balthasar Moretus, the greatest and most famous member of the firm.

Enter Passage. On the walls are the woodcuts with the impressions of 26 ornamental alphabets by Borcht, E. Quellin, C. Perret, G. Ballain and others.

Now enter **Type-room**. In 1575 Plantin possessed 38,121 lbs. of type, divided into 73 different characters.

Adjoining is the **Press-room**, as it was used for three centuries,

Collection of Engraved Blocks and Copper-Plates.

from 1579 to 1865. In 1565 Plantin employed 7 presses, and in 1576, 22. Of the 7 presses at present in the room only the 2 at the end belonged to Plantin, the others belonged to his successors.

Now ascend the stair to the **Exhibitions**, commencing with first room left hand. Under glass cases collection of printed books from other offices from 1470. 2 The same continued, with specimens of faience and Delft ware. 3 Petite Bibliothèque. Under glass cases, family letters and documents. Among others from Arias Montanus and Justus Lipsius, 18th July 1576. 4 Collection of **Woodcuts** and their impressions. The oldest are being rapidly destroyed by the wood-worm. 5 Lobby, with a few engravings. 6 Continuation of woodcuts and their impressions. Those in this room are in better condition. The chimneypiece and door are by Paul Dirickx in 1622 and 1640. 7, or XIX in catalogue, Gallery of **Copper-plates** and impressions from them. Neither the rooms devoted to the exhibition of the woodcuts, nor those to the exhibition of the copper-plates, are sufficiently large to contain all that were used to illustrate the books published by the Plantin-Moretus. Among them are copper-plates engraved by R. Pauwels, 1635; T. Galle, 1609; C. Galle, 1631; C. Mallery, 1634; Passe, 1587; Borcht, 1602; Lauvray; L. van Leyden, 1521; Lauwers, 1653; J. Wiericx, 1622; J. Neeffs, 1638; J. Sadeler, 1579; P. Huys, 1562; and P. Jode, 1642. 8, or XX in catalogue, A sitting-room. Walls hung with gilt embossed leather. Chairs and table in oak. Japan vases on cabinet. Chimneypiece by Paul Dirickx in 1638. Portraits. 9 "Chambre des privileges." Under glass cases the documents from emperors and princes conceding to the family privileges and monopolies in the exercise of their trade. 10, or XXII in catalogue, Salle des Gravures d'après Rubens, Van Dyck, et Jordaens, all under glass, with the engraver's name.

Now up the steps to 11 or XXIII of catalogue **Salle des Graveurs Anversois**, containing characteristic specimens of the works of the most eminent members of this school. Among them are, besides those already mentioned: Corneille Metsijs, 1499-1560; P. Perret, b. 1555; P. Coeck, 1507-1550; the four Sadelers, Jean, b. 1550 the oldest, and Raphael, b. 1584 the youngest; P. Brueghel, b. 1520, d. 1569; Hans Bol, 1534-1593; the three brothers Wiericx, 1549-1624; Gheyn, b. 1565; Queborne, b. 1580; Bye, b. 1580; Barra, 1581-1620; Tulden, b. about 1607; T. Rombouts, 1597-1637; Uden, 1595-1672; Jacques Jordaens, 1593-1678, Cacus stealing the cows from Hercules. 44 P. P. Rubens, 1577-1640, St. Catherine. 45 G. Crayer, 1582-1669, the Resurrection of J. C. 50 C. Schut, 1591-1655. 51 David Teniers, 1582-1649. 53 David Teniers, son, 1610-1690. A. Van Dyck, 1599-1641, 62 portraits of F. Franck, Josse de Momper, Adam Van Noort, P. Brueghel, J. Brueghel, J. Sustermans, J. Wael and Erasmus. 72 Hub. Quellin, 1619-1687. 74 R. Eynhoudts, b. 1613. 75 G. Edelinck, 1640-1707. 87 E. Quellin, 1607-1678. 96 P. Pontius, 1603-1658. 99 L. Vorsterman, 1580-1640.

In case 28 is plate **102** by Jacques Harrewyn, born 1657, representing views *of the house and garden of Rubens as they were in the time*

House of Jacob Jordaens.

of the great master. 12 Le Petit Salon, with portrait of the last owner, Edouard Moretus-Plantin, d. 1880. In this room is a rare collection of engravings by Jerome Wiericx entitled, "het Loon der Tyranner," the tyrants' punishment. Off it is a small room with oak furniture, and by another door it communicates with a bedroom, of which the walls are hung with embossed leather. From this a stair leads up to the type-foundry, with its tools, furnaces, crucibles, and moulds. Typefounding was not carried on long, because it was found to be more profitable to buy the types than to make them.

Now descend to the Grand Bibliothèque, containing about 12,000 vols.

The next room contains specimens of most of the works printed and published by Plantin and his successors.

In the adjoining and last room are the archives from 1555 to 1864, including the ledgers, day-books, letter-books, account sales, receipts, inventories, catalogues, as well as numerous papers and documents relating to the family and the business.

Behind the Musée Plantin on the Quai Vandyck is an old gateway of Antwerp, the **Porte de l'Escaut,** designed by Rubens and adorned with colossal sculptures by A. Quellin. According to the inscription, it is dedicated to the "Magnus Philippus" or Philip IV. of Spain, grandson of Charles V., in whose reign Spain lost Portugal in 1640, and the Netherlands in 1648.

The house in which **Jacob Jordaens** lived and died, 1678, is at No. 43 Rue Haute. The front is completely changed, but not the court round by the back, entered by the large door, No. 4 Rue de Reynders. His studio was on the left side, his dwelling-house on the right. At No. 54 Rue Haute was the house of the corporation of the cabinetmakers. The R. Haute is close to the Museum. Any one can point out the way.

At the N. end of the Quai Van Dyck (see plan) is the fishmarket, with in the corner, the Chateau s'Heeren Steen, or simply Steen, both situated in the Burcht, the oldest part of Antwerp, dating from the 7th cent. In the Place Ste. Walburge stood a church dating from the introduction of Christianity to this part of the Netherlands in 660, by St. Amand, and dedicated to St. Peter and Paul. It was destroyed by the Normans in 835, but shortly after rebuilt, and by a bull of Pope Lucius III. placed under the protection of Ste. Walburge. Ste. Walburge was an English lady of royal descent, who came to Antwerp in 726, and spent her time principally in the church built by St. Amand. She died in 776 in Heidenheim in Bavaria, and was canonised in 870 by Pope Adrian II. The church was frequently rebuilt. On 8th May 1816 it was demolished. and the materials used in the construction of the quays. The **Chateau Steen** was built in 1200, but of the present building only the lower part and the pepper-box turret belong to that date; the rest was constructed by Charles V. in 1520. At first a palace, it became one of the prisons of the Inquisition. All their instruments of torture were still in the dungeons below up to 1794, when they were destroyed by the French. Now there are only a few rings and chains to which their victims were fastened. Till 1827 it became one of the town prisons, and in

LIERRE.   HASSELT.

1862 it was converted into a museum of antiquities, open from 10 to 4, free.

Behind the railway station is a very pleasant zoological garden. Admission 1 franc.

Antwerp to Aix-la-Chapelle.

91 m. S.E. by Aerschot, Diest, Hasselt, and Maestricht; see Map, p. 1. A direct line to Cologne and the Rhine. Cologne is $43\frac{1}{2}$ m. by rail from Aix-la-Chapelle.

$9\frac{1}{2}$ m. from Antwerp is **Lierre**, pop. 17,000. Junction with line to Gladbach $94\frac{1}{2}$ m. E., see p. 292. The best building in Lierre is the church of St. Gommarius, 1425-1557. The picture representing "the marriage of Mary" is by Memling. The 3 coloured windows at the end of the chancel were presented by the Emperor Maximilian. The train having passed several minor stations beyond Lierre, arrives at **Aerschot** on the Demer, 26 m. from Antwerp and 28 m. N.E. from Brussels by Louvain, pop. 5100. *Inn:* Ange. In the parish church, dating from 1336, is buried the wife of Quentin Metsys, who, it is said, presented in memory of her the chandelier now suspended in front of the beautiful rood-loft of the choir, but originally over her grave. The stalls, 15th cent., of the same date as the jubé, are carefully carved.

From Aerschot the train ascends the valley of the Demer to **Diest**, $37\frac{1}{4}$ m. from Antwerp, pop. 10,000. Junction with line to Tirlemont, $19\frac{1}{2}$ m. S. on the Louvain and Liège line, see p. 232; and with line to Moll, 22 m. N. on the railway between Antwerp and Gladbach. Brewing and distilling form the principal industries of Diest.

50 m. from Antwerp and 41 from Aix-la-Chapelle is **Hasselt**, pop. 12,000—*H.* Limburg—the chief town of Limburg, and as at Diest, junction with a line which connects the rail from Antwerp to Gladbach with the rail between Brussels and Liège. From Hasselt a branch line extends 25 m. N. to Maeseyck, on the Maas, the birthplace of the brother painters Hubert and John Van Eyck, to whose memory a monument was erected in 1864. Coach from Maeseyck, 4 m. E., to Susteren on the line between Venloo and Maestricht.

After Hasselt follow Beverst 56 m. and Munsterbilsen $58\frac{1}{2}$ m., from both of which ramifies the junction by Tongres with the Brussels and Liège line. Tongres or Tongeren, 10 m. S. from Beverst, is situated on the site of a fort built by Drusus, see page 233.

64 m. from Antwerp and 27 from Aix-la-Chapelle is Lanaeken, Belgian custom-house and time. $4\frac{1}{2}$ m. farther is Maestricht, Dutch custom-house and time, p. 240. The train then traverses the Dutch

LUNATIC ASYLUM.

territory of Luxembourg by the stations of Meersen, Fauquemont or Valkenburg, Wijlré, and Simpelveld, the Dutch custom-house of the S.E. frontier of Luxembourg, 82¾ from Antwerp and 8¼ from Aix. 91 m. from Antwerp is **Aix-la-Chapelle**.

Antwerp to Düsseldorf.

By Gladbach, 115 m. E. by that nearly straight railway on the top of Map, p. 1. Time by fast trains 4 hrs. 50 min.; first class, 18 frs. 10 c.

From Antwerp the train having passed Bouchout, Lierre, Nylen, and Bouwel, arrives at **Hérenthals**, pop. 5000, on the Campine canal, 21¼ m. from Antwerp. *Inn:* Ville de Lierre. Principal building, St. Waltrude, with carved reredos representing the "Martyrdom of St. Crispin," by Raephorst in 1470.

7¼ m. farther, or 28½ m. E. from Antwerp, is **Gheel**, pop. 11,000, *Hotel:* Agneau, the principal station of the colony of lunatics, averaging 1000, located here, and in the neighbouring villages on this wide dreary plain, whose peasantry have acquired a *spécialité* in the treatment of lunacy, which originated in the supposed miraculous curative power of the relics of St. Dymphna, an Irish princess and the patroness of lunatics, who suffered martyrdom on a spot near the church on the 30th May 600. The reredos of the high altar represents her ascent to heaven, while on the reliquary are represented scenes from her life. In former times the insane used to be exorcised in the cells round the church. The Government supports the pauper patients.

5½ m. farther E. is **Moll**, junction with Diest 22 m. S.; 48½ m. E. from Antwerp is **Neerpelt**, junction with Eindhoven 15¼ m. N. and with Hasselt 22 m. S.; 5½ m. farther is Hamont, Belgian custom-house station; 1¼ m. beyond is Budel, Dutch custom-house station.

75 m. E. from Antwerp is **Ruremonde** or **Roermond**, pop. 10,000, on the Roer, at its confluence with the Meuse. *Hotels:* Lion d'Or; Empereur. A manufacturing town, with the handsome church of **Notre Dame** built in the 13th cent. and recently restored by Cuypers.

84 m. E. from Antwerp and 31 m. W. from Düsseldorf is Vlodrop, Dutch custom-house station, and 1¼ m. beyond Dalheim, German custom-house station. 100 m. E. from Antwerp and 15 W. from Düsseldorf is the important manufacturing town and railway junction of **Gladbach-München**, pop. 33,000. 5½ m. farther E. is **Neuss**, pop. 13,000, *Inn:* Rheinischer Hof, 22½ m. N. by rail from Cologne. This town, founded B.C. 35 and fortified by Drusus, is frequently mentioned

DÜSSELDORF. KAISERSWERTH.

by Tacitus under the name of Novesium. The most interesting edifice is the Quirinuskirche, a basilica commenced in 1209, an excellent specimen of the transition from the Round to the Pointed style.

115 m. from Antwerp is **Düsseldorf**, pop. 81,000, on the confluence of the Düssel with the Rhine. *Hotels:* in the Allée Strasse, the *Breidenbacher Hof; opposite the Cologne and Minden railway station, the *Hotel d'Europe and the H. Stelzmann; in the Flinger Str., the *Kölnischer Hof. Episcopalian service held in the church in the Berger Strasse. Trams traverse the town in all directions. *Cabs:* the course for 1 or 2 persons 60 pf.; for every additional person 25 pf.

Düsseldorf is a pleasant town with straight streets and handsome buildings. It has considerable manufactories, but is known chiefly as one of the great German schools of painting, of which the seat is in the "Academy of Art" on the S. side of the winter harbour. There are several private collections, in which most of the pictures are for sale, such as the Galleries of Schutte, 42 Allée Strasse, and of Bismeyer and Kraus, 5 Elberfelder Strasse. A large art exhibition is in the great hall of the Friederich's Platz.

6 m. from Düsseldorf, on the right bank of the Rhine, is **Kaiserswerth**—*Inn:* Rheinischer Hof—containing the principal training school of the **Protestant Sisters of Charity**, founded by the benevolent pastor Fliedner in 1836. In the Roman Catholic church is an exquisitely executed reliquary, 12th cent., containing some of the bones of Suitbertus, an Irish missionary who came to this place in 710. From Düsseldorf to Rotterdam or Cologne by rail or steamer, see Black's *Holland and the Rhine.*

London viâ Queenborough, to Flushing.

From the Victoria station of the London, Chatham, and Dover Railway to Queenborough pier, 1½ hour. Steamer from Queenborough to Flushing wharf, 8½ hours; whence to Antwerp, by Roosendaal and Esschen, 4 hours south. Fare 29s. 7d. or 19s. 8d. From Flushing to Rotterdam, by Roosendaal and Dordrecht, 2¾ hours north. Fare 30s. or 20s. Through tickets given by the Company to Aix-la-Chapelle, 56s. or 39s. 9d. To Bonn, 57s. 7d. or 41s. To Cologne, 55s. 2d. or 39s. 2d. For details, see the " London, Chatham, and Dover Continental Timetables," 3d. A Dutch steamer leaves daily from the Flushing wharf for Terneuzen, on the other or south side of the Schelde; whence rail to Ghent. The Terneuzen pier is 2½ m. from the railway station. Ghent is 2 hours or 26 miles south from Terneuzen by rail, see p. 155. The Flushing wharf is provided with a customhouse, a money-changer's office, and a railway station with waiting and refreshment-rooms. The town railway station is ¾ mile farther inland, where the omnibus from the H. du Commerce awaits passengers. Travelling in Holland is

FLUSHING. MIDDELBURG.

more expensive and less comfortable than in Belgium. The Belgian railway fares are the lowest in Europe. It is a good plan to send on the heavy luggage, and to retain only what can be taken into the carriage.

Vlissingen (Flushing), Hotel du Commerce, pop. 12,000, is situated at the mouth of the Schelde, on the southern extremity of Walcheren, one of the 9 islands which compose the province of Zeeland. These low, flat islands, intersected by canals, are protected against the encroachments of the sea partly by a natural rampart of sandhills, and partly by about 350 miles of broad dykes, resembling railway embankments, but more solid. The greatest and most expensive of these dykes is at Westkapelle, at the westmost point of Walcheren. It is 4700 yards long and 30 feet above the ground. Besides excellent pasture, these islands produce large quantities of corn, beetroot, vegetables, willows, and apples in the more sheltered parts. Vlissengen is the native town of the greatest naval hero of the Dutch, Admiral de Ruyter, the son of a ropemaker, born 1607, died 1676. In 1667 he ascended the Thames, burned the English fleet, and set fire to the Tower of London. Near the harbour is a monument to his memory.

3¾ miles north from Vlissingen by rail or steamboat, is **Middelburg**, pop. 17,000. A good resting-place. *Hotels:* next the church with its pleasant-chiming bells, and in the semi-monastic Abbey square, is the Hotel Abdij. Next the Hotel de Ville, in the principal square, is the Hotel Nieuwe Doelen. In the street with the greatest traffic, the Lange Delft, the Hotel de Flandre. Just behind it is the abbey church. Their omnibuses await passengers at the station.

Middleburg is a curious and very Dutch town, with a large dock, the Prins Hendriks Dok, opened in 1876, and connected with Flushing by a broad canal and a railway. In the centre of the town is the principal market-place, or "Place," with the Hotel de Ville, of which the greater part was erected at the commencement of the 17th cent. Two sides are adorned with pointed transomed windows, with, on the front side and round each corner, statues of the counts and countesses of Flanders and Zeeland, under richly-canopied niches. From the centre, over the high-peaked roof, rises a handsome square tower with an octagonal termination 180 ft. high, built in 1513.

A large hall on the ground floor is occupied by the meat market. In the floor above are; the Court room, with a handsome carved oak screen before one of the doors; and the Museum of Antiquities, containing escutcheons, medals, tankards, carved furniture, and a quarto volume of the works of Jacob Cats, born 1577, died 1660. Among the

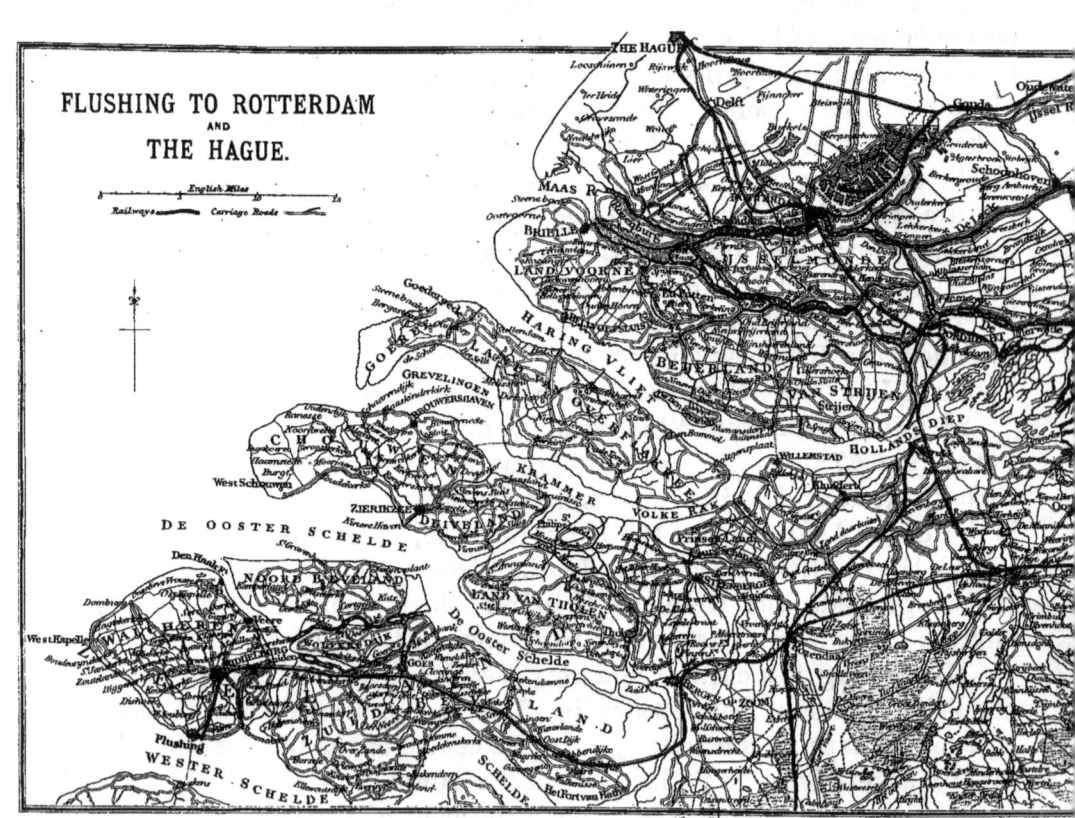

archives is a charter granted to Middelburg by William of Holland in 1253, said to be the oldest deed in the Dutch language.

From the Square is distinctly seen the spire of the Abbey church. Descend to it by the Lange Burg. When opposite the church a lane, the Lomberdstraat, leads to the Museum. A little farther down the Lange Burg is the butter-market, and to the right, under the low archway "Spour," the entrance into the Abbey square.

The Abbey church, founded in the 12th, but rebuilt in the 16th cent., has an octagonal tower surmounted by 3 balloon-shaped stages. It contains a very fine set of chiming bells, which in tone resemble those of Antwerp. Within the church are monuments to the memory of William of Holland, d. 1256, and to the two Evertsens, Dutch naval heroes, killed in 1666.

The **Museum**, open from 12 to 4, contains among other things in first room left hand ground floor, portraits of Admiral Ruyter by F. Bol, 1611-1681. William III., Prince of Orange and King of England, painted in 1676. John de Witt, born September 1625, d. 1672. Hans Holbein the elder, born 1502, d. 1554, and his wife. In the next room are a microscope, and the tubes of the first two telescopes invented by Zacharias Janssen and Hans Lippershey, spectacle-makers, in 1601; both natives of Middelburg. In this cabinet are also two of the first tobacco-pipes. To the right is the wheel of the rudder of the ship in which Admiral Ruyter sailed up the Thames. Above it is an old Dutch painting representing the Admiral's ship bombarding the Tower of London. In the same room is a portrait of Jacob Cats, the Dutch poet. In another room are sculptures from an old heathen temple found in the neighbourhood of Domburg, $9\frac{1}{2}$ m. W. on the coast, near the Westkapelle dyke. Domburg and all the neighbouring villages were swallowed up by the sea in 1808; when Middelburg narrowly escaped the same fate. They have all been rebuilt since. Upstairs are the library, a very interesting herbarium, a collection of medals and coins, and a few antiquities.

In summer an omnibus runs twice daily to **Domburg** (Bad. Hotel: Schutterhof Hotel) now becoming a favourite sea-bathing station.

After Middelburg the train passes the station of Arnemuiden and crosses to Zuid-Beveland, in which is situated **Goes**, $15\frac{1}{2}$ m. E. from Flushing, pop. 17,000. A short avenue from the station leads to the town, where the most prominent object is the Gothic church, 15th cent., with a lofty tower in the centre. On the continent, $38\frac{1}{2}$ m. N.E. from Flushing, is **Bergen-op-Zoom**, pop. 11,000. *Hotels:* close to the station,

ROOSENDAEL. ESSCHEN.

Hotel Damen; in the town, the Hof von Holland; the Prins von Luyk; their omnibuses await passengers. In the Hotel de Ville are portraits of the Margraves, and a handsome chimney-piece. In the church is a monument to Lord Edward Bruce, killed in 1613 in a duel with Sir Edward Sackville, afterwards Earl of Dorset.

46½ miles N.E. from Flushing, 36½ miles south from Rotterdam, and 23 miles north from Antwerp is **Roosendaal**, pop. 9000. Dutch custom-house station. Small refreshment-rooms. Just behind the station the Hotel Pays-Bas. Those going on to Antwerp or Brussels change carriages here. 5 miles south from Roosendaal, and 18½ north from Antwerp is **Esschen**, the Belgian custom-house station. 70 miles east from Flushing by Roosendaal and Esschen is **Antwerp**, and 27½ miles more, **Brussels**.

ROTTERDAM.

Rotterdam, pop. 151,000, on the Maas, at its confluence with the Rotte, 14 m. from the sea. *Hotels:* in the Westplein, near the wharf of the Harwich, Leith and Liverpool steamers, the **Lijgraff**, very pleasantly situated near the entrance to the park. A little farther up the Maas, in the Willems Plein, is the Hotel Victoria. A tram from this Plein or Square runs to the Bourse. Near the Victoria, in Wijde Nieuw-Steeg, is the Scotch church. Still higher up, at No. 40, Boompjes, near the wharf of the Hull, London and Rhine boats, is the **New Bath** Hotel; rather high charges, and inconveniently situated for the sights and railways. Nearly opposite are the public and railway bridges across the Maas. The viaduct of the railway bridge is of great service in enabling strangers to find their way through the intricate mixture of the canals and streets of Rotterdam, because from the Maas, or base of the equilateral triangle, on which the town is built, it passes straight up the centre to the apex, where are situated the Dutch Railway Station and the Zoological Gardens. About ⅓ of the way are the Central Railway Station, the Bourse, the Post and Telegraph Offices, and the Hotel de l'Europe very conveniently situated. Near the Europe, at No. 12 of the Groote Markt, is the Hotel **Guilljams**, amidst all that is characteristic of Rotterdam. In front is the continuous throng of purchasers of fruit, flowers and vegetables, among whom may be seen a few, becoming gradually fewer, women wearing the old Dutch head-dress, a curiously-shaped cap, more or less embroidered, large gold earrings, generally of skilful workmanship, and by the side of each eye a gold wire twisted into the shape of

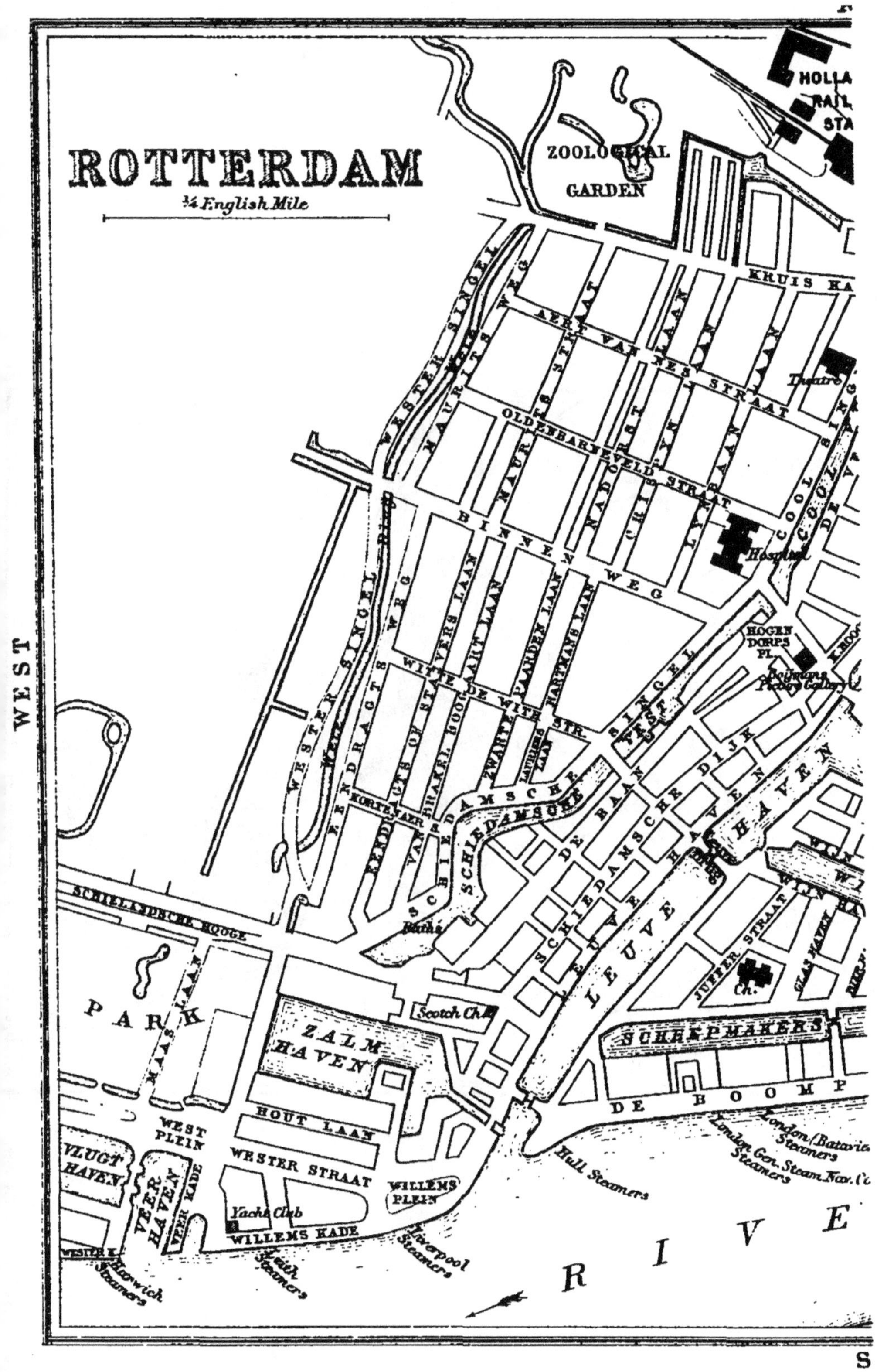
ROTTERDAM
¼ English Mile
WEST
ZOOLOGICAL GARDEN
HOLLA RAIL STA
KRUIS KA
AERT VAN NES STRAAT
Theatre
OLDENBARNEVELD STRAAT
BINNEN WEG
Hospital
WESTER SINGEL
MAURITS WEG
MAURITS STRAAT
NADORST
CHRISTYN
LYNBAAN
COOL SINGEL
COOL
HOGEN DORPS PL.
Boijmans Picture Gallery
WITTE DE WITH STR.
EENDRAGTS WEG
VAN STAVERS LAAN
BOOMGAART LAAN
PAARDEN LAAN
HARTMANS LAAN
ZWARTE
SCHIEDAMSCHE
KORTENAER
VAN BRAKEL
EENDRAGTS
SCHIEDAMSCHE DIJK
HAVEN
DE BAAN
SINGEL
LEUVE HAVEN
LEUVE
JUFFER STRAAT
Ch.
GLAS HAVEN
Baths
SCHIELANDSCHE HOOGE
PARK
MAAS LAAN
ZALM HAVEN
Scotch Ch.
SCHEEPMAKERS
DE BOOMP
HOUT LAAN
WEST PLEIN
WESTER STRAAT
WILLEMS PLEIN
Yacht Club
WILLEMS KADE
VLUGT HAVEN
VEER HAVEN
VEER KADE
WESTER K.
Harwich Steamers
Leith Steamers
Liverpool Steamers
Hull Steamers
London Gen. Steam Nav. Co
London (Batavia) Steamers
R I V E
S

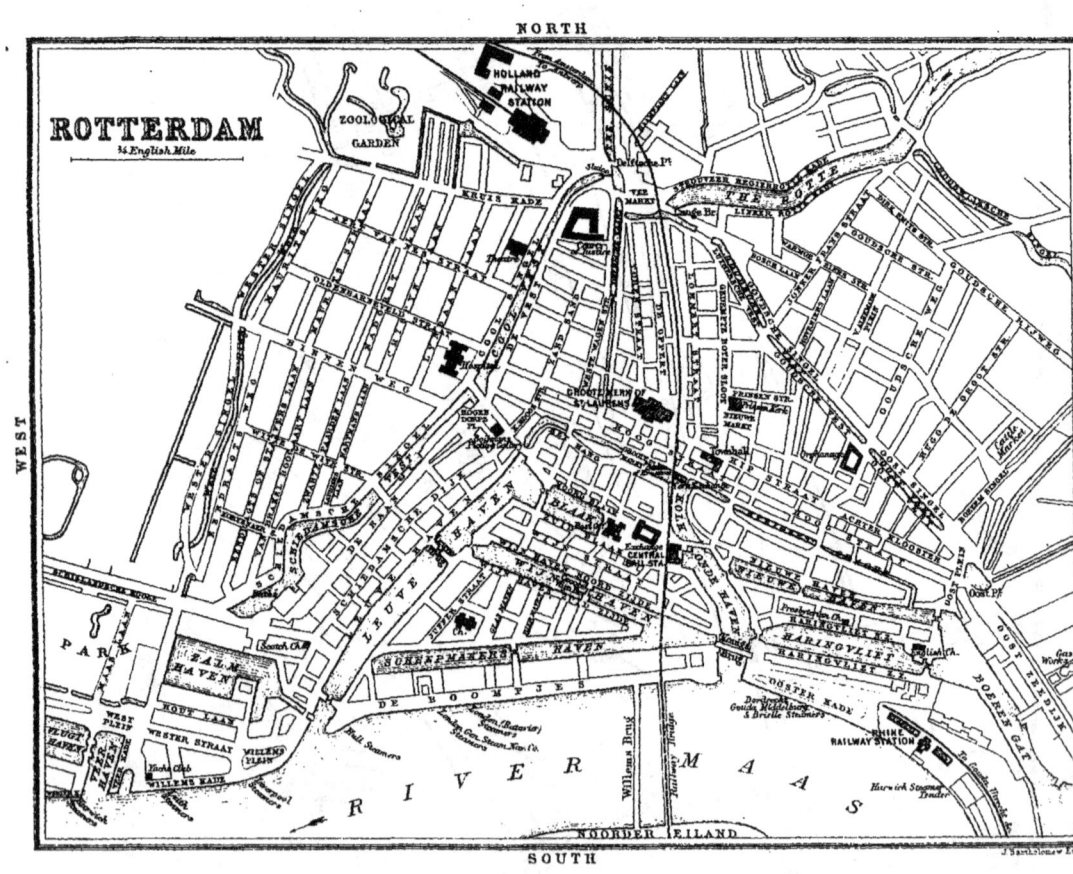

a filter, or in the form of a small square gold plate like a horse-blinder, or a beautiful piece of filigree-work in gold. The corresponding bonnet resembles in shape a small coal-scuttle, but the more advanced of the Dutch peasantry have discarded it for the latest French styles. On one side of this market is the brick house in which, on the occasion when the Spaniards butchered so many of the inhabitants, those within killed an ox, and making the blood stream out from below the doors, caused the assassins to think it was unnecessary to enter, as all the inmates must have been already slaughtered. Under the gable are the date 1594, and the words "In Duizend Vreezen," To the thousand sighs. Opposite, on the bridge, is the statue of Erasmus, and on the way towards the Groote Kerk, in the street called the Wijde Kerkstraat, is the house in which he was born on the 28th of October 1467. Between the 2 windows of the upper story is a statuette of him. The street descends to between the S. transept and the tower of the church.

At No. 13 Korte Hoogstraat is the **Grand Hotel** du Passage, a first-class house. Adjoining is the H. Pays-Bas. In the Hoogstraat, which extends by the S. side of the Groote Kerk, are at No. 327 the H. St. Lucas and the H. Hollande, good second-class houses. Not far from this, in the Hoofdsteeg, is the Hotel **Coomans**, a very large house, much frequented by commercial travellers.

At the W. corner of the quay, Haringvliet is a good Dutch house, the Hotel Verharren. At the other end of this quay is the Episcopalian Church, built of brick, and leaning slightly to one side. The Camper, Zwolle and Haarlem boats start from this quay. In Holland the hotels are dearer than in Belgium and France—that is, less value is given for the sum paid. In Belgium, but more universally in Holland, a general breakfast-table is spread from an early hour in the morning, with bread, rolls, rusks, cheese, and butter. Under the kettle is generally a small piece of incandescent peat.

Railway Stations.—For those going up the Rhine the station is the Rhine Railway Station on the Oosterkade (east quay), the continuation of De Boompjes. Passengers arriving by the Harwich boats are brought up to it from the Westerkade, by their tender. From the Oosterkade several steamers sail to different towns in Holland.

By the side of the railway viaduct, near the exchange, is the Bourse or Central Station, a supplementary station of Hollandsch-Spoorweg or Dutch railway. It is the station for Antwerp and Brussels, Haarlem, Alkmaar and Amsterdam, Flushing and Queenborough. The main station is at the N. end of the viaduct, near the Zoological Gardens.

Rotterdam. Trams. Cabs. Steamers.

Trams.—The Beursplein (Exchange Square) is also the starting-place of the trams. One runs to the Diergaarde (Zoological Gardens), and the Dutch Railway Station passing through the whole of the old town. In returning, be careful to take the tram for the Beursplein. Another tram runs in much the same direction to the Jonker-Frans-Straat and the Rotte, at the N.E. extremity of Rotterdam. At this part the Rotte is lined with breweries and distilleries and covered with timber brought down in rafts. Tram to Willem's Plein on Willemskade. Passengers staying in the Europe or the Guilljams Hotel, and having merely hand baggage, will find it a cheap way to get to the Hull, Liverpool, and Leith boats. The best tram runs to the Park, just beyond the farthest down quay, the Westerkade; where the Harwich and Cork boats are moored. It passes by the Museum-Boijman and through the new part of the town, consisting of handsome houses in gardens. The Park, very well laid out, has in the centre a statue to the popular poet Hendrik Tollens, d. 1856. From the quay at the end of the Park the small steamer or tender of the Harwich boat sails at stated hours up to the Niederlandische Rhein Eisenbahn. On the river side of the Park is a bathing establishment.

Cabs.—From the steamboats or railway stations with luggage 1 gulden. The course for 1 or 2 persons, 60 c. For 3 or 4, 70 c. The hour, 1 gulden 20 c.; and 1 gulden for each additional hour. Coachmen must produce tariff. *Omnibus* at stated hours starts from the front of Boymans Museum to **Schiedam**.

Sights.—The most conveniently situated hotels for the sights, trams, and railways are the Europe in the Beursplein and the Guilljams in the Groote Markt, which, with the statue of Erasmus, the house in which he was born, the Groote Kerk, the Hoogstraat, and the Picture Gallery, all near each other, form the principal sights.

Steamboats.—The trains of the Great Eastern Railway leave their station in Liverpool Street, London, for Harwich, 2 hours before the sailing of the steamer. The passage between Harwich and Rotterdam, or *vice versâ*, takes 12 hours. On the arrival of their boat at Westerkade (west quay), a small steamer takes the through passengers for the Rhine to the Dutch Rhenish station on the Oosterkade. Passengers with through tickets to other parts are conveyed by omnibus, either to the central station in the Beursplein, or to the Holland railway station at the north end of the town. No charge is made for conveying passengers holding through tickets between the Harwich steamer and the different stations. Luggage registered through from

LUGGAGE. TIME-TABLES.

England to places beyond Rotterdam will be conveyed from the steamer to the railway stations, without the intervention of the passenger and without charge. Passengers not holding through tickets will be charged 10 cents if they make use of the steamer, but from the landing-place on the Oosterkade must themselves take care of their luggage. All luggage, unless registered through to Germany *viâ* Emmerich or *viâ* Cleve or *viâ* Venlo, must be examined by the customs officers on board the Harwich steamer during the passage in the river before arrival at Rotterdam. Luggage from the Continent will be examined at Harwich in the custom-house room alongside the steamer, and passengers must personally attend to the examination of their luggage.

The registration of baggage saves the passenger all trouble and expense of landing and shipping the baggage, and conveying it between the train and boat; secures an allowance (25 kilos. or 56 lbs.) of baggage free of charge (except the registration fee); also the privilege of paying before departure the charge for the conveyance of excess baggage, according to a fixed through rate. *See the Continental Time-book of the Great Eastern Railway, price 1d.* The General Steam Navigation Company have a boat thrice weekly from St. Katherine's Steam Wharf, London, and from the Boompjes, Rotterdam. Time 22 hours. The Netherlands Steamboat Company once weekly from Brunswick Wharf, Blackwall. From both Hull and Leith there are steamers once weekly. The Leith steamers require 48 hours, the Hull steamers 30.

Time-Tables.—No one should travel in Holland without a copy of the "Officiele Reisgids voor Nederland," 15 cents, sold at all the stations and in most of the bookshops. The index of the places served by rail is at the commencement. V.M. means forenoon, N.M. afternoon. V = departs. A = arrives. Uitgang = way out. Engang = way in. En = and. Naar = to. Van = from or of. Kaarte = ticket. At the end of the book is the list of places, alphabetically arranged, served by the steamboats, trékschuits, and diligences. It is generally best to turn up the place to be visited. The place of departure (Plaats van vertrek) is on the second column; the kind of conveyance (Aard van het vervoer) on the 3d; the direction on the 4th; the destination (Bestemming) on the 5th; the distance (Afst. contraction of Afstand) on the 6th, the measure being the Stunde or Uurgaans, equal to $3\frac{1}{2}$ miles. On the railways the measure is the kilometre. Afvaart of afrid = place of sailing or departure on the 7th. Tijd van vertrek = time of leaving on the 8th. Duur der reis = duration of the journey on the 9th. Vrachtprijs = fare on the 10th. On the last column the list of the principal places passed.

ROTTERDAM.   ERASMUS.   GROOTE KERK.

Dutch Money.—The Dutch money is in gulden and cents. The gulden is worth 20d. English, consequently the 5-cent piece is equal to 1d. ; or 2 sous French, Belgian and Italian currency; or 8 pfennig Prussian currency. At the railway stations English and French coins are taken at the current rate of exchange. The general value allowed is for—

	Gulden.	Cents.
1 Sovereign	11	90
A 20-franc piece	9	40
A 10-franc piece	4	70
1 Shilling	—	58
1 Franc	—	46

The 10 and 25 cent pieces are made of white metal, and are worth respectively 2d. and 5d. The pieces under 5 cents are in copper.

Postage Stamps in Holland are called "post-zegels," and are sold at the post-office, and also at some of the shops, where they cost a cent more.

Rotterdam is a busy town, intersected by a multitude of canals, bordered with trees, and crammed with shining barges. At the west end is the Park, with pleasant shady walks, and in the neighbourhood handsome villas and streets with modern dwelling-houses. Of the sights, the most pleasant is, especially during the fruit season, the Groote Markt, whose stalls are loaded nearly the whole day. On one side is the brick house, already alluded to, and opposite, on the bridge, the bronze statue erected in 1662 to the memory of Gerrit Gerritsz, latinised into Desiderius Erasmus. He was born at No. 5 Wijde Kerkstraat, see above. At the foot of this street is the **Groote Kerk**, or church of St. Lawrence, an immense structure of brick, built in 1472, whose square tower, 297 feet high, ascended by 320 steps, offers one of the most extensive views in Holland of towns, windmills, meadows and canals. Sunday service begins at 9.30 ; in most other churches in Holland it begins at 10, and in all it lasts a trifle over 2 hours. During the sermon the money collectors go round with their bags on poles. Every one gives something. If the church be well attended it takes them nearly an hour, or nearly the whole time of the sermon. Hats may be worn till the commencement of the service. All the organs are powerful, and the congregation sing heartily to their lead, without the accompaniment of a choir. The effect is thrilling. This church and all the other great churches in Holland are on the same model. Vast plain cruciform buildings, with a puny spire at the point of intersection, and sometimes, as here, a square tower over the principal entrance. Only a part of the great churches is fitted up for service. The chancel

PICTURE GALLERY. SCHIEDAM.

of St. Lawrence, shut off by a handsome marble and brass screen, contains monumental tombs to Admirals de Witt, d. 1658, and Cortenaer, d. 1665, Contre-Admiral Brakel, d. 1690, and others, erected by the States-General, with epitaphs in Dutch and Latin verse. The organ here, as in most of the churches, is at the west end. It is 90 ft. high, has 90 stops and 6500 pipes, the largest being 36 ft. long and 17 inches in diameter. A private exhibition of the organ costs 10 gulden. The sacristan's house is at the S. transept. Fee to visit church when shut 25 cents, and tower 50 cents.

Now go to the Beursplein and take the tram (12 c.) to the Park. On returning, request to be allowed to alight (descendre) at Boijmans (Boymans) Museum, open from 10 to 4, tickets 25 c., and on Sundays 5 c. There are above 300 pictures almost all by Dutch painters, and as a large proportion is modern, this gallery gives a true idea of the state of art in Holland. The Schiedam omnibus starts from the southern corner. At the N.W. side of the museum is a statue by Jozef Geefs of G. K. Van Hogendorp, b. 1762, d. 1834, the Dutch apostle of free trade, and the founder of the land laws of the Netherlands. Return to the Bourse and take the tram to the Zoological Gardens and back. If time permit take the tram to the Jonker-Frans-Straat and the Rotte and back. Grinling Gibbons the famous wood-carver was born at Rotterdam; also James Crofts, Duke of Monmouth, son of Charles II. and Lucy Waters, in 1649.

$3\frac{1}{8}$ m. W. from Rotterdam, and 49 m. S. from Amsterdam, by the Beurs station, is **Schiedam** on both sides of the Schie, an affluent of the Maas, pop. 24,000. Schiedam makes a very pleasant change from the noise and bustle of Rotterdam. Everything is built of brick—the houses, mostly of one story; the windmills from 90 to 120 ft. in diameter, the churches, the distilleries, the walls and the pavement. From the station, walk down towards the town by the Roman Catholic church, after which several windmills are passed, rising like great towers in the middle of the road. Now take right hand, the Hoogstraat, parallel to the Schie, lined with distilleries chiefly on the High Street side. The best shop to buy gin is No. 92 Hoogstraat, on left hand. At the end of this street are the Stadhuis (1637), and the parish church, a large edifice. On the way back advantage may be taken of the Rotterdam omnibus, which starts from a little house at the railway end of the High Street. The drinking water is brought in small carts to the town. Gin is a malt spirit flavoured with the essential oil of the juniper, hence the name gin, a contraction of the Dutch word genever

DORDRECHT. HOLLANDSCHDIEP.

The wash and refuse of the grain are bought by the owners of the surrounding dairy farms. Schiedam has a nice little park and walks on the banks of the Schie. 2 m. W. from Schiedam is Vaardingen, on the embouchure of the Maas, the principal station of the Dutch herring and cod fishery.

Rotterdam to Antwerp and Brussels.

ROTTERDAM, start from the Beurs station, which is 1¼ m. nearer than the principal station, the Delftschepoort station. The train after crossing the Maas arrives at Dordrecht or Dort, 11¼ m. from the Beurs station and 12½ m. from the Delftschepoort station, on the Merwede, an arm of the Maas, pop. 26,000. *Hotels:* Bellevue ; Armes de Hollande, their omnibuses await passengers. Steamer to Rotterdam. The principal edifice in this, one of the oldest towns in Holland, is the Groote Kerk, with its conspicuous tower, commenced in 1339 and finished in the 16th cent. The church contains some delicately carved oak stalls, 1547, a sculptured marble pulpit, 1756, and among the numerous monuments, one over the tomb of the brave Lieutenant John Western, R.N., buried here in 1793, in the presence of the Duke of York. Near the church is a Picture Gallery, open from 9 to 4.

6½ m. farther is Willemsdorp on the N. side of the Hollandschdiep, and at the N. end of the great iron bridge which crosses this estuary. It is nearly 1 m. long and consists of 14 arches, each 110 yards span, and 15 ft. above the highest tides, resting on 13 stone piers, 10 ft. wide. It was commenced in 1868 and finished in 1871, and cost £475,000.

21½ m. or 20¼ from Rotterdam, and 3⅛ m. S. from Willemsdorp, is Zwaluwe, the station nearest the southern end of the bridge. The train next halts at Oudenbosch, 31 m. S. from Rotterdam, and 56 m. N. from Brussels, with a handsome church and large nurseries.

50¼ m. S. from Rotterdam and 36½ m. N. from Brussels is Roosendaal, with Dutch custom-house, 46½ m. N.E. from Flushing, see p. 295. 5¼ m. farther S., or 45¼ m. N. from Brussels, and 41¾ m. S. from Rotterdam is Esschen, with the Belgian custom-house and time. The train after having passed 4 minor stations arrives at Antwerp, 27½ m. N. from Brussels, and 59½ m. S. from Rotterdam. See p. 266. From this the train, having passed Malines and Vilvorde, arrives at the "Station du Nord" of Brussels.

Passengers going the reverse way, namely from Brussels or Antwerp to Rotterdam, will find it more convenient to take their ticket for the Bourse (Beurs) station in Rotterdam.

APPENDIX.

LETTERS FROM WELLINGTON TO SIR WALTER SCOTT.

To WALTER SCOTT, Esq.

"PARIS, *August 8th*, 1815.

"MY DEAR SIR,

"I have received your letter of the 2d, regarding the battle of Waterloo. The object which you propose to yourself is very difficult of attainment, and if really attained, is not a little invidious. The history of a battle is not unlike the history of a ball. Some individuals may recollect all the little events, of which the great result is the battle won or lost; but no individual can recollect the order in which, or the exact moment at which they occurred, which makes all the difference as to their value or importance.

"Then the faults or the misbehaviour of some gave occasion for the distinction of others, and perhaps were the cause of material losses; and you cannot write a true history of a battle without including the faults and misbehaviour of part at least of those engaged.

"Believe me that every man you see in a military uniform is not a hero; and that, although in the account given of a general action, such as that of Waterloo, many instances of individual heroism must be passed over unrelated, it is better for the general interests to leave those parts of the story untold, than to tell the whole truth.

"If, however, you should still think it right to turn your attention to this subject, I am most ready to give you every assistance and information in my power.

"Believe me, etc.,

"WELLINGTON."

(*Gurwood*, vol. xii. page 590.)

To THE SAME.

"PARIS, *August 17th*, 1815.

"MY DEAR SIR,

"I have received your letter of the 11th, and I regret much that I have not been able to prevail upon you to relinquish your plan.

"You may depend upon it, you will never make it a satisfactory work.

"I will get you the list of the French army, generals, etc.

APPENDIX. LETTERS FROM WELLINGTON TO SIR WALTER SCOTT.

"Just to show you how little reliance can be placed, even on what are supposed the best accounts of a battle, I mention that there are some circumstances mentioned in General Müffing's account which did not occur as he relates them.

"He was not on the field during the whole battle, particularly not during the latter part of it.

"The battle began, I believe, at eleven.

"It is impossible to say when each important occurrence took place, nor in what order. We were attacked first with infantry only; then, with cavalry only; lastly, and principally, with cavalry and infantry mixed.

"No houses were possessed by the enemy in Mont-St.-Jean, excepting the farm in front of the left of our centre,[1] on the road to Genappe, can be called one. This they got, I think, at about two o'clock, and got it from a circumstance which is to be attributed to the neglect of the officer commanding on the spot.

"The French cavalry were on the plateau in the centre between the two highroads for nearly three quarters of an hour, riding about among our squares of infantry, all firing having ceased on both sides. I moved our squares forward to the guns; and our cavalry, which had been detached by Lord Uxbridge to the flanks, was brought back to the centre. The French cavalry were then driven off. After that circumstance, repeated attacks were made along the whole front of the centre of the position, by cavalry and infantry, till seven at night. How many I cannot tell.

"When the enemy attacked Sir Thomas Picton I was there, and they got as far as the hedge on the cross-road, behind which the —— had been formed. The latter had run away, and our troops were on our side of the hedge. The French were driven off with immense loss. This was the first principal attack. At about two in the afternoon, as I have above said, they got possession of the farm-house on the highroad, which defended this part of the position; and they then took possession of a small mound on the left of the highroad going from Brussels, immediately opposite the gate of the farm; and they were never removed from thence till I commenced the attack in the evening: but they never advanced farther on that side.

"These are answers to all your queries, but remember, I recommend to you to leave the battle of Waterloo as it is.

"Believe me, etc.,

"WELLINGTON."

(*Gurwood*, vol. xii. 609-610.)

---

[1] La Haye-Sainte.

INDEX.

ANTWERP.

ABBEVILLE 10
—— to Crecy 10
—— to Eu 10
—— to St. Riquier 10

Achiet 20
Adinkerke 30, 154
Aerschot 291
Aigremont 97
—— Castle 252½

Aillvilliers 99
Aix-la-Chapelle 50

Albert 20
Alost 167
Altkirch 105
Alt-Münsterol 105

Amagne 63
Amanweiler 76
Ambleteuse 3
Amblève 242
Amiens 11
Ammerschweier 118

Ancy 79
Andelot 128
Anderlecht 200
Anizy 47
Anor 49

Antwerp 266
. Bank 283
. Bourse 282
. Cathedral 269
. Chateau Steen 290
. Corporation houses 284
. Hotel de Ville 284
. Hotels 268
. House of Jordaens 290

AUDERGHEM.

Antwerp, House of Rubens 283
. Institutions 267
. Loos Monument 284
. Maison Hanseatique 286
. Park 283
. Picture Gallery 273
. Plantin Museum 286
. Porte-Escaut 290
. St. Augustine 282
. St. André 281
. St. Charles 281
. St. George 283
. St. Jacques 278
. St. Joseph 284
. St. Paul 285
. St. Walburge 290
. Sights 267
. Statue, Leopold I. 283
. —— Leys 283
. —— Metsys 283
. —— Rubens 283
. Steamers 266
. Vieilles Boucheries 285
. Zoological Garden 291

Archery 168
Arcier 125

Ardres 2
Argenteau 240
Arlon 259
Armentières 23
Arras 18
Ars-sur-Moselle 79

Ath 224
Attigny 63
Attila 74

Audenarde 30
Auderghem 200

BATILLY.

Audun-le-Roman 69
Aulnoye 41
Auxonne 121
Avioth 68
Avize 58
Avricourt 85
Ay 59
Aywaille 242

BACCARAT 85
Bains 103
Baisieux 26, 228
Baisy 215

Balinghem 2
Ballon-Alsace 114, 116
Ballon-Gebweiler 115, 116
Ballon-Servance 114
Bapaume 20

Barbery 18
Bar-le-Duc 80
Bar-sur Seine 95
Barvaux 247
Basel 120
Bas-Evette 105

Baths, Aix-la-Chapelle 50
—— Bains 103
—— Bourbonne 97
—— Chaudfontaine 241
—— Contrexéville 98
—— Luxeuil 102
—— Martigny 99
—— Plombières 100
—— St. Amand 41
—— Rosheim 93
—— Spa 242
—— Sulz 93
—— Sulzbach 113
—— Vittel 98

Batilly 76

BRUGES.	BRUSSELS.	CHARLEVILLE.
Baume-les-Dames 125	Bruges, Les Halles (markets) 146	Brussels, Palais Justice 174
Bazancourt 63	. Mausoleums 142	. ―― Nation 176
Bazeilles 68	. Notre Dame 140	. ―― Royal 174
Beaurainville 9	. Palais de Justice 148	. Picture Gallery 190
	. Prinzenhof 150	. ―― Modern 193
Belfort 104	. Shrine Ursula 144	. ―― Wiertz 194
Bellegarde 129	. St. Anne 151	. Porte d'Hal 196
Beloeil 224	. St. Jacques 149	. Prison 174
Benfeld 116	. Saint Sang 148	. Protestant Churches 171
Beningen 77	. St. Walburge 151	. Railway Stations 169
Bennweier 118		. Sainte Gudule 178
Berck 9		. St. Jacques 172
Bergen-op-Zoom 296	Brussels 169	. St. Nicolas 185
Bergues 28	. Athenée 186	. St. Salazar 179
Bertrix 257	. Aylesbury 173	. *Statues*—Belliard 177
Besançon 121	. Bank 181	. ―― Charles 198
―― to Locle 124	. Bibliothèque 188	. ―― Cockerill 169
Bethune 18	. ―― Engravings 189	. ――Egmont and Hoorn 173
	. ―― Manuscripts 188	
	. Beguinage Church 186	. ―― Godfroid 172
Binche 266	. Blind Asylum 197	. ―― Mannéken 185
Bitsch 77	. Bois Cambre 197	. ―― Verhaegens 193
Bitschweiler 115	. Botanic Gardens 187	. ―― Wiertz 198
	. Bourse, 185	. Racecourse 199
	. Cabs, 171	. Uccle 200
Blainville 85	. Cathedral 178	. University 193
Blandain 26, 228	. Cluysenaar 181	. Wiertz 194
Blankenberghe 135	. Colonne Congrès 177	
Blesme 80	. Conservatoire Musique 174	
	. Environs 197	Bruyères 108
Boisleux 20	. Exchange 185	Burtscheid 53
Bollweiler 119	. Finistère Church 186	Bussang 114
Borcette 53	. Galerie Hubert 181	Busigny 40
Bossuet 56	. Governess Home 197	
Bouillon 258	. Halles-Centrales 186	CAFFIERS 2
Boulogne 3	. Hospice 186	Calais 1
―― landing arrangements 5	. Hospital St. Jean 187	―― to Brussels 22
Bourbonne-les-Bains 97	. ―― St. Pierre 196	―― to Paris 1
Bourbourg 27	. Hotel de Ville 183	Calvin 34
Bourg-en-Bresse 131	. Hotels 169	Cambrai 40
Bouvigne 250	. House Architecture 187	Campbell 7
Boyelles 20		
	. ―― Corporation 182	
	. ―― Cuylenberg 174	Carignan 68
Braine-l'Alleud 204	. ―― Deputies 177	Carvin 21
Braine-le-Comte 222	. ―― Egmont 173	Cassel 29
Breteuil 14	. ―― Lucas 177	Cateau-Cambresis 4
Bricon 95	. ―― Richmond 187	
Brienne 95	. ―― Senators 177	
Briey 76	. ―― Wellington 175	Cernay 115
	. Ixelles 198	Chalindrey 96
	. Lace 171	Chalis 43
Bruges 136	. Lacken 198	Chalons-sur-Marne 72
. Academie 150	. Maison du Roi 182	Champagne wine 58
. Beguinage 145	. Marché couvert 181	Champagnole 127
. Belfry 146	. Money-changers 171	Champlieu 33
. Cathedral 137	. N. D. Chapelle 194	Chantilly 15
. English Nuns 152	. ―― Victoires 173	
. Grande Place 146	. Palais Academies 175	
. Hospital St. Jean 143	. ―― Arenberg 173	Charleroi 264
. Hotel de Ville 147	. ―― Beaux Arts 172	Charles the Bold 84
. Jerusalem Church 152	. ―― Flandre 172	Charleville 64

DIEUZE.	FLUSHING	GIVET.
Chateau-Thierry 57	Dijon 121, 129	Folkestone to Boulogne 3
Châtelay 127	Dinant 249	Folleville 14
Chatillon Michaille 130	Dixmude 153	Fontoy 69
Chatillon-sur-Saone 97		Forbach 77
Chatillon-sur-Seine 95		Fougerolles 102
Chaudfontaine 241	Dole 121	
Chaulnes 40	Dolhain 50	
Chaumont 95	Domburg 296	Franchimont 242
Chauny 35	Domrémy 106	Froissart 41, 49
Chauvency 68	Donchery 65	Fröschweiler 78
Chelles 55	Donon 87, 111	Frouard 82
Chenée 241	Dordrecht 302	Fumay 265
Chevremont 105	Dormans 58	Furnes 154
Chilperic 1, 55	Douai 21	
Chimay 49	Doullens 9	
	Douzy 68	
	Dover to Calais	Gebweiler Lake 116
Ciney, 252, 254		—— Mount 116, 115
Circy 85		—— Town 116
Clairvaux-sur-Aube 95	Drei Achren 113	Geisberg 78
Clermont de l'Oise 14	Dunkerque 26	Geispolsheim 116
	Dun-sur-Meuse 76	Genappe 208
	Durbuy 247	Geneva 130
Coblence 263	Düsseldorf 293	Gérardmer 112
Coiffy 97		Gesoriacus 3
Colmar 118		Gewenheim 115
Cologne 54		Gheel 292
Comblain-au-Pont 247		
Comines 26	Ebersheim 116	
Commercy 81	Echternach 246	Ghent 155
Compiègne 31	Ecoust 20	. Abbaye St. Bavon 167
Conflans-Jarny 76	Ecouviez 68	. Academie 164
Cons 260	Egisheim 119	. Artévelde 165
Contrexéville 98	Elwit 217	. Beguinage-Grand 167
Coo 246	Enghien 224	. —— Petit 166
	Epernay 58	. Belfry 160
	Epinal 108	. Bibliothèque 165
Cornimont 111	Eppeghem 217	. Boucherie 163
Corny 79	Eprave 256	. Cité-Ouvrière 167
Coucy-le-Chateau 35		. Dominican Church 164
Courtrai 226		. Fishmarket 163
Crecy 11	Erménonville 43	. Gateway of Castle 164
Creil 15, 31	Esneux 247	. Hospital 167
Crépy 44	Esschen 296, 302	. Hotel de Ville 161
Crotay 10	Etaples 8	. House of the Eycks 155
Culoz 129	Ettelbrück 246	. —— Watermen 163
Cuperly 74	Eysden 240	. Mad Meg 165
		. Maison de Force 164
		. Marché aux Legumes 163
Dambach 116	Falkenstein 76	. —— du Vendrédi 165
Dammartin 43	Faymont 102	. Palais de Justice 166
Damme 152	Fegersheim 116	. St. Augustine 164
Dammerkirch 105	Feignies 42, 223	. St. Bavon 156
	Fenélon 40	. St. Jacques 165
	Ferté-Milon 44	. St. Michel 162
Delle 106	Ferté-sous-Jouarre 57	. St. Nicolas 161
Devant-les-Ponts 69	Feuillée-Dorothée 101	. St. Pierre 166
Diedenhofen 69		. University 162
Dieghem 229		. Zoological Gardens 166
Diekirch 246	Flemalle-Haute 252	
Dieulouard 78	Florenville 258	Ghyvelde 30
Dieuze 85	Flushing 294	Givet 248

JOUY.	LIVERDUN.	MONT ST. GUIBERT.
Göbesmuhle 240	Jovinus 62, 78	Longport 44
Godinne 250	Jupille 240	Longpré 11
Goes 296	Jurbise 222	Longueau 14, 21
Gorze 79	Jussey 99	Longuyon 68
Gouvy 246		Longwy 68
		Lons-le-Saunier 127
		Louis XI. 38
Gravelines 27	KAISERSLAUTERN 77	Louvain 229
Gray 121	Kaiserswerth 293	
Greiffenstein 87	Kautenbach 257	
Guines 2	Kaysersberg 118	Lunéville 85
Guise 38	Kestenholz 116	Lure 104
	King William's letter 66	Lüttenbach 113
	Kinzheim 117	Lutterbach 119
		Lutzelburg 86
		Luxembourg 259
HAGENAU 78		Luxeuil 102
Hal 221		
Ham 36	LABARRE 121	
Hamoir 247	La Bresse 111	
Han 255	La Cheppe 74	
Hasselt 291	Lady Hamilton 2	MAESTRICHT 240
Hastière 248	Laeken 198	Maeseyck 291
Hayingen 69	Lafontaine 57	Malines 217
Hazebrouck 29	La Fosse 265	Malmédy 245
		Malplaquet 42
		Marbach 78
Heidenmauer 94	Lagny 55	Marbehan 258
Herbesthal 50	Lake Blanc 113	Marche 248
Herenthals 292	Lake Fondromaix 114	Marche-les-Dames 251
Hericourt 126	Lake Longemer 112	Marchiennes 266
Hesdigneul 8	Lake Nantua 131	Marquise 3
Hesdin 9		Mariembourg 49
Heyst 136		Markirch 110-119
Hirson 49	Lake Noir 112	Marloie 254
	Lake Retournemer 112	Marquion 20
	Lake Sylant 131	Martigny-les-Bains 99
Hoh-Barr 86	Lake Vert 112	Masmünster 115
Hohenkönigsburg 117	Lamorteau 68	Maxcy, 106
Hohenlandsberg 114	Landen 234	Maxonchamp 114
Hollandschdiep 302	Langres 96	Maubeuge 42-223
Homburg-l'Evêque 70	Laon 47	
Houffalize 248	La Panne 30, 155	
Hüningen 120	La Reid 242	Meaux, 56
Huy 251	Laveline 108	Melreux, 247
	La Voulte 131	Mennelstein 94
		Mersch 246
		Metz, 69
	Leberau 110	Mettet 265
IGNEY-AVRICOURT 85	Le Sage 7	Mezières 64
Ingelmunster 30	Liancourt 15	
Is-sur-Tille 96	Libramont 257	
Ixelles 198		Middelburg 294
		Mirecourt 108
	Liège 234	Molsheim 87, 93, 110, 111
	—— to Maestricht 240	Momignies 49
	—— to Seraing 239	Money, Dutch 300
JANSENIUS 228	Lierre 291	—— German 51
Jeanne d'Arc 106, 60, 31		·Mons 222
Jemelle 255		Mt. Brezouard 110
Jemeppe-s-Sambre 265	Ligny 215	Mt. Donon 110
Jenner 8	—— Battle of 212	Mt. Hoheneck 112
Jessains 95	Lille 23, 229	Mt. Oderen 111
Jouy 79	Liverdun 82	Mont St. Guibert 253

PFIRT.

Montbeliard 125
Monthermé 266
Montmédy 68
Montreuil-sur-Mer 9
Morillon 127
Mouchard 127
Mourmelon 74
Mouzon 68, 76.
Mülhausen 119
Munster 113, 119
Mutzig 110

NAMUR 253, 250
Nancy 82
Nanteuil 43
Nantua 131
Napoleon III. 36, 66
Neuchatel 128
Neufchateau 107
Neuss 292
Niederbronn 77
Nieuport 153
Nivelles 215

Nogent-sur-Sein 94
Noveant 79
Noyelles-sur-Mer 10
Noyon 33
Nuits-sous-Ravières 95

OBER-EHNHEIM 94
Obernai 94
Oderen 111
Odilienberg 94
Oiry 58
Orval 258
Ostende 133
Ottignies 253
Ougrée 239
Ourscamps 33
Ourthe valley 247

PAGNY-SUR-MEUSE 81
Pagny-sur-Moselle 79
Panne—see La Panne
Pepinster 241
Perck 217
Peronne 38
Perte du Rhone 130
Petit-Croix 105

Pfalzburg 86
Pfirt 105

SAARGEMUND.

Picquigny 11
Pierrefonds 33
Pierrepont 69
Pinon 47
Plessis-Belleville 43
Plombières 100

Poix 256
Poligny 127
Pont-à-Mousson 78
Pontarlier 128
Pont-de-Roide 126
Porentruy 106
Port d'Atelier 99

Quatre-Bras 211
—— Battle of 213
Quevy 42, 223

RACINE 44
Rambervilliers 85
Rappoltsweiler 117
Reichshofen 77
Reims 59
Remouchamps 242
Rethel 63
Revin 265

Ribeauville 117
Ribemont 38
Rixheim 120
Rochefort 255
Rocroi 265
Rohrbach 77
Romilly 59, 94
Roosendaal 296, 302
Rosheim 93
Rothau 110
Rotterdam 296
Rousseau, J. J. 43

Rue 9
Rufach
Ruremonde 292

SAALES 110
Saaralben 77
Saarbrücken 77
—— to Mannheim by Kaiserslautern 77
Saarburg 86
Saargemund 77

STANISLAS.

Sail on Meuse 250
Sail on Moselle 262
Saint Dié 109
Saint Hubert 256
Saint Louis 120
Saint Omer 22
Saint Pilt 117
Saint Trond 233
Saint Valery 10

St Menehould 75
St Amand-les-Eaux 41
St Amarin 115
St Arnual 77
St Aubin 94
St Avold 76
St Gérard 265
St. Gobain 35
St. Hilaire-au-Temple 74
St. Hippolyte 126
St. Johann 77

St. Laurent 128
St. Leger 20
St. Louis 105
St. Marie 110, 119
St. Maurice 114
St. Odile 94
St. Pol-sur-Ternoise 9
St. Riquier 11

Salins 127
Saulxures 111
Saverne 86
Scherweiler 116
Schiedam 301
Schirmeck 110
Schlettstadt 117
Schlucht 112
Schneeberg 87

Sedan 65
Senlis 16
Sennheim 115
Sentheim 115
Seraing 239
Seyssel 129
Sillery 74
Sluys 152

Soignies 222
Soissons 44
Solre-le-Chateau 42
Sombreffe 253
Soultz-les-Bains 93
Source of Moselle 114
Spa 242
Spicheren 77
Stanislas 83, 85

TYNDALE.	WAREMME.	ZABERN.

Stavelot 245
Stenay 68, 76
Strassburg 87
Sulzbach 113
Sulz-Bad 93
Sulzeren 113
Sulzmatt 113, 119
Swiss Verrières 128

TAMINES 264
Tente-Verte 28, 30
Tergnier 36
Terneuzen 220
Tervueren 200

Thann 115
Theux 242
Thionville 69
Thomas-à-Becket 23, 27
Thourout 153
Tilff 247
Tilly 253
Tirlemont 232
Tongres 233
Toul 82
Tournai 224

Trèves 260
Trier 260
Troos 241
Trois-Epis 113
Trois-Ponts 245
Trou de Han 255
Troyes 95
Türkheim 113
Turnhout 221
Tyndale 217

URBÈS 114

VAGNEY 111
Vaivre 103
Valenciennes 41
Valmy 74
Varennes-en-Argonne 75
Vaucouleurs 106

Vendenheim 78, 87
Vendeuvre 95
Verdun, 75
Verton 9
Vertus 59
Verviers 49
Vervins 49
Vesoul 103

Vianden 246
Vielsalm 246
Villers-Coterets 44
Villers l'Abbaye 215
Vilvorde 216
Vireux 265
Virton 259
Visé 240
Vitry 97
Vitry-la-Ville 80
Vitry-le-François 80
Vittel 98
Vlissingen 294

WALCOURT 265
Wangenburg 87
Waremme 234

Wasselnheim 87
Wasselonne 87
Wasserbillig 260

Waterloo 201
—— Tour of Field 204
—— Train to 201
—— Wellington's account 201
—— Proclamation 42, 216
Watteau 41
Wavre 214

Weiler 115
Weissenburg 78
Wesserling 114
Wildenstein 114

Wimereux 3
Wimille 3
Winzenheim 114
Wissant 3
Worth 78

XERTIGNY 103

YGEL COLUMN 260
Ypres 227
Yvoir 250

ZABERN 86

THE END

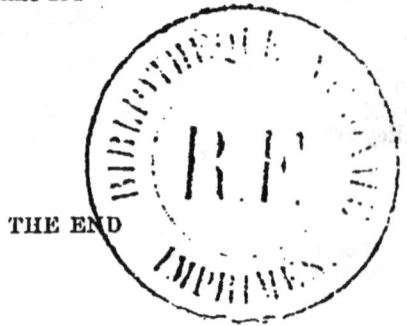

Printed by R. & R. CLARK, *Edinburgh.*

www.ingramcontent.com/pod-product-compliance
Lightning Source LLC
Chambersburg PA
CBHW070845170426
43202CB00012B/1952